Becoming
BEYONCÉ

J. Randy Taraborrelli is the bestselling author of fourteen books, including *Michael Jackson: The Magic and the Madness*, *Madonna: An Intimate Biography*, *The Secret Life of Marilyn Monroe*, *Elizabeth*, *Once Upon a Time: The Story of Princess Grace, Prince Rainier and Their Family*, *Call Her Miss Ross*, *Jackie, Ethel, Joan: Women of Camelot*, *The Hiltons: The True Story of an American Dynasty* and *Sinatra: The Man and the Myth*. He is also a CBS TV news analyst, and lives in Los Angeles.

D1151150

3 . .∠∪ ∪2689573 0

ALSO BY J. RANDY TARABORRELLI

After Camelot: A Personal History of the Kennedy Family—
1968 to the Present

Jackie, Ethel, Joan: Women of Camelot

Once Upon a Time: Behind the Fairy Tale of
Princess Grace and Prince Rainier

Elizabeth

The Secret Life of Marilyn Monroe

Michael Jackson: The Magic, the Madness, the Whole Story (1958–2009)

The Hiltons: The True Story of an American Dynasty

Sinatra: Behind the Legend

Becoming
BEYONCÉ

The Untold Story

J. RANDY TARABORRELLI

PAN BOOKS

First published 2015 by Grand Central Publishing

First published in the UK 2015 by Sidgwick & Jackson

This paperback edition first published in the UK 2016 by Pan Books
an imprint of Pan Macmillan
20 New Wharf Road, London N1 9RR
Associated companies throughout the world
www.panmacmillan.com

ISBN 978-1-4472-8635-6

Visit **www.panmacmillan.com** to read more about all our books
and to buy them. You will also find features, author interviews and
news of any author events, and you can sign up for e-newsletters
so that you're always first to hear about our new releases.

For my niece Jessica . . .
and dreamers everywhere

CONTENTS

PART SEVEN: *Run The World*

Becoming
BEYONCÉ

When you're famous, no one looks at you as human anymore. You become property of the public. There's nothing real about it. You can't put your finger on who I am. I can't put my finger on who I am. I am complicated. I grew up with a lot of conflict and dramas. I've been through a lot.

—Beyoncé Giselle Knowles-Carter, December 2014

Author's Note

"Beyoncé."

The name, once thought of as unusual, is now a universally recognized signifier for talent, beauty, and determination. It also calls to mind the very definition of celebrity in our culture today. In fact, there are but a handful of famous people known by a one-word appellation, and many are pop music icons whose imprint on our society is as indelible as it is undeniable. Think Cher. Madonna. Bono. Prince. And, of course, Jay Z. Once upon a time, though, the iconic personality known simply as "Beyoncé" was just a wide-eyed little girl with big dreams and an abundance of ambition and talent. This is the story of how that girl—Beyoncé Giselle Knowles—became one of the wealthiest, most significant power players in show business, a recording artist who has to date won twenty Grammy Awards and sold 60 million records as the lead singer of Destiny's Child and more than 100 million more as a solo artist.

She once described herself as "just a country girl from Houston." What does it take, then, for someone from humble beginnings to become one of the most powerful artists in the world? After all, not just anyone can step into the spotlight and become ... Beyoncé. It takes more than just talent.

Through the years she's been carefully packaged, marketed, groomed, and promoted, spending most of her life, from childhood through her teenage years and into womanhood, nurturing and projecting a very precise image of herself to the public. Her fascination with image is nothing new. It's as old as show business itself. Her critics have charged her with being a manufactured product, as if anything less could ever be successful in a competitive entertainment industry—as if she doesn't have the talent necessary to back up her marketing campaign. In truth, she manages her career on the one hand, and her personal life on the other, with a calculating, decisive will. What the public will know and what will be off-limits is really just classic public relations strategy and, to a certain extent, marketing. They call it "branding" these days. Some are good at it and some are great. Certainly Beyoncé falls into the latter category.

While Beyoncé is engaging in interviews, she is not known for her candor. Many a reporter has been frustrated trying to extract just a hint of something personal from her. That wasn't always the case. When I interviewed Destiny's Child back in 1999, all four girls—at that time, Beyoncé,

Kelly Rowland, LaTavia Roberson, and LeToya Luckett—were forthcoming. Back then, they had more limited lives; there wasn't much for them to conceal. Since that time, Beyoncé the woman and "Beyoncé" the brand have become more calibrated to suit an ongoing marketing plan: Since 2002, she has rarely, if ever, discussed her personal life in much detail. It was actually a good decision. By doing so, she forced the public to evaluate her not by her private life but by her work: her art.

This mandate would make writing the first ever in-depth biography about her difficult. There was no road map to follow, no other valid research to help construct a reliable narrative about her life. However, as happens with books of this nature, one interview with a very good source generated another with someone else well placed ... and another and another ... until, finally, not only did the timeline begin to emerge, but so did the story you'll read in the following pages.

I found that there's much more to the story of Beyoncé than talent and branding, and a lot of it has to do with the influence of outspoken, independent females who surrounded her in her formative years, assertive women with names like Deborah Laday, Denise Seals, and Andretta Tillman—powerful, matriarchal figureheads who inspired Beyoncé to greatness. You will meet these formidable women in these pages for the first time. Along with Beyoncé's mother, Tina Knowles, they helped motivate Beyoncé to become the dominant force of nature she is today.

You will be surprised by many elements of this book, not the least of which is the extreme sacrifice Beyoncé's parents, Mathew and Tina, made to help their daughter's dreams come true. At one point they couldn't even pay their tab at Blockbuster video rental. Yet they continued pouring money into their daughter's career.

In the end, though, this is the story of the long road traveled by a talent show contestant, pageant winner, and girl group singer as she evolved into the vocalist, actress, pop star, businesswoman, wife and mother she is today. More than that, it is also the story of a darker side that is unfortunately often the price of great success. The path to converting Beyoncé the woman into "Beyoncé" the brand was, for many people in her life—her father, her mother, her sister, her managers, and her singing partners—as treacherous as it was profitable. She too would experience as much pain and heartache as she did glory on the long, twisting road to becoming ... *Beyoncé*.

J. Randy Taraborrelli
Summer 2015

Prologue: A New Dawning

October 2, 2009—New York City

It was to be just another monumental day in an already much-rewarded, greatly privileged life. At least that was what Beyoncé Knowles probably figured as she prepared to accept *Billboard*'s 2009 prestigious Woman of the Year award. Professionally, she'd already had a most incredible year with the success of her album, *I Am . . . Sasha Fierce*. It had debuted at number one on the *Billboard* charts, selling almost a million and a half units in just the first six weeks. It would go on to win a record-setting six Grammy Awards and sell more than three million copies. One standout song from the album, the danceable "Single Ladies (Put a Ring on It)," would become not only one of Beyoncé's most identifiable hits, but a feminist anthem as well. It too had peaked at number one on *Billboard*'s chart, becoming one of the bestselling singles of all time, with more than six million copies sold.

Such unprecedented success was nothing new to Beyoncé. At just twenty-eight, she'd been at the top of her game for the last twelve years, ever since the release of Destiny Child's first hit, "No, No, No," in 1997. That was followed by a string of hits, such as "Say My Name," "Independent Women," and "Bootylicious," which led to solo success for her with the albums *Dangerously in Love* and *B'Day* in 2003 and 2006, respectively. Award-winning songs from those albums, such as "Crazy in Love," "Déjà Vu," and "Irreplaceable," remain to this day memorable touchstones of her career.

At the Pierre Hotel, Beyoncé would find herself posing on a red carpet in front of a backdrop emblazoned with the distinctive *Billboard* logo as flashbulbs popped all around her. Wearing a simple but elegant knee-length sea-foam-green skirt with a ruffled, scooped top, she looked every bit the fashion icon. Large diamond hoop earrings framed her lovely face, her straight light brown hair cascading to her shoulders, parted to the left. She smoothed her skirt, patted her hair, and then walked the red carpet with total assurance and regal bearing, just as she always did when in the public eye. As she posed for the cameras, her dazzling smile lit up her face with a rare beauty all her own.

Later, Beyoncé would stand onstage at a podium in the Pierre ballroom before two microphones while gripping her prized award. After graciously acknowledging the standing ovation from a formally dressed audience of industry heavyweights, she began her prepared talk. Though she'd given dozens of these sorts of speeches over the years, they were still not something that she, a naturally bashful person, enjoyed. Standing in front of an audience as herself, not her "Sasha Fierce" stage persona, remained difficult. Doing so felt too revealing, too invasive—and never more so than on this afternoon. In fact, she could barely get through it.

"I can't believe all of the things I've been blessed to do this year, and I know it would not be possible without my family," she said. She appeared to be visibly choked up, as if overcome by a wave of bittersweet nostalgia. Shifting her gaze to her mother and father, Mathew and Tina Knowles, who were sitting at a nearby table, she continued, "My parents are here. I've worked with my family since the beginning of Destiny's Child. Actually, I was nine years old," she said. Then, with her glance settling on her mother, she continued, "I am the luckiest young woman in the world to have my parents. And to have that connection and that genuine love, and people to tell me when I'm wrong and people that always support me and love me unconditionally. I am so, so lucky," she concluded, now looking at both parents, "to have you guys in my life."

In the days that followed, Beyoncé's heartfelt words would be broadcast around the world. But as is often the case in show business, private events unfolding behind the scenes would paint a very different picture than the public image of family solidarity Beyoncé attempted to convey with her speech. The truth is that the family to which she so graciously gestured that day was fissured by suspicion: By then, Beyoncé was in the midst of having her father, Mathew, audited, with subsequent press reports referencing unconfirmed allegations he had stolen a great deal of money from her. This was a stunning turn of events. Her longtime manager, Mathew was in many ways responsible for her success. They had been an incomparable team. He loved her deeply, and she felt the same about him. At the same time, Beyoncé was her father's daughter in many ways, not the least in her uncompromising determination not to let anyone, regardless of who they might be, take advantage of her.

The bad situation was to get much worse. On the same day as the *Billboard* Women in Music function, Mathew was served with a paternity lawsuit by a woman in Los Angeles named AlexSandra "Alex" Wright.

The only people who really understand what goes on in a marriage are those in the marriage themselves. Everything else is just conjecture and interpretation. The parameters to which Mathew and Tina had agreed to stay married aren't clear, nor what led him to fall for another woman, but fall for Alex he did. It would be untrue to say that Mathew had been living a double life. After all, if it's not a secret, is it truly a double life? A private life, yes, but not a double life. Apparently Tina and everyone else in the immediate family knew all about Alex. Her pregnancy, though, was a complete surprise, at first revealed to no one but Alex's immediate family. But on the day of Beyoncé's *Billboard* honor it would become known to the entire world. This stunning revelation would prove a game-changer for the Knowleses, one that would force a crucible upon them the likes of which they'd never before experienced.

The truth is that change had been a long time coming. Over the years, the Knowleses had seen each other through many challenges, fortifying themselves against internal divisions for the sake of the image and the success they were all protecting. The challenge for them had always been to perform "the Knowles family" as a united, dynamic success story for the public in order to nourish the "Beyoncé" myth, while at the same time navigating the rocky terrain of their private world. Everyone knew that Beyoncé's talent had always been the family's founding principle, its hope and grace, the fulcrum around which they all came together. Father Mathew famously managed Beyoncé; mother Tina designed her wardrobe; sister Solange was inspired by her success. But there was so much more going on behind the scenes, the constant unfolding of family drama, not unlike that of many families in the public eye, but private just the same.

Now, in 2009, it was time to let the truth stand and take a leap of faith. Without ever planning to do so, each Knowles family member would bear witness to the transformation of his or her life, the sun already beginning to shine on a new dawn. In so many ways, it had been not only their successes but their secrets that had imprisoned them. Now they would each finally be set free . . . with Beyoncé leading the way.

PART ONE

Tina & Mathew

Tina

$\mathcal{P}$retty is as pretty does," Agnez DeRouen Beyincé used to tell her daughter, Tina. "You are a very pretty girl. But that's not enough. You have to be pretty inside."

"Yes, Momma," the teenage Tina would say, rolling her eyes. That quaint adage had been pounded into her head for so many years, she was a little tired of hearing it. But somehow Tina Beyincé knew she'd end up telling her own daughter the exact same thing one day...and that her daughter would then repeat it to a child of hers. "Beauty on the outside fades," Tina would later observe. "That was my mother's message, but just one of many."

In Tina's mind, family has always been about the small traditions. It's often the seemingly most trivial of moments that matter most—those intimate conversations parents have with their children that form not only who they are as role models but who they all are as a family. Tina says that her mother was such a special person, she always wanted to emulate her and do whatever she advised. "I've always hoped my daughters would feel the same way about me," she said.

Family would always be of the utmost importance to Tina. Many of the decisions she would make in her lifetime would be predicated on how they would affect her relationships with her husband and her children, and theirs with one another. "Going all the way back, we Beyincés have been very close," she once said. "It's just who we are, who we'll always be."

In tracing the maternal side of Beyoncé's family history, one learns that the parents of her mother, Tina, were both French-speaking Creoles of predominantly French, African, Spanish, and Native American descent. Tina's father, Lumis Albert Beyincé (also spelled Buyincé and Boyance), was born in 1910 in Abbeville, Louisiana, the son of Alexandre and Marie Oliver Boyance. Not much is known about the light-skinned, handsome, and athletically built Lumis, who passed away in August 1982. In interviews, Tina rarely mentions him, focusing on memories of her mother. (In contrast, Mathew Knowles rarely speaks of his mother, remembering instead his father.) Relatives say that Lumis was an excellent student as a youngster, popular in his neighborhood, outgoing and gregarious. Fluent in French, he worked as a longshoreman. As a result of a mine explosion, he was deaf in one ear.

Tina's mother, Agnez DeRouen (or Deréon), was born in 1909 in Delcambre, Vermilion Parish, Louisiana, a town near the city of Abbeville. (She would die on July 4, 1980.) Daughter of Eugene-Gustave "Eugenie" and Odelia Broussard DeRouen, the pretty, light-skinned Agnez was raised in Police Jury Ward 2 in Delcambre, a middle-class neighborhood. A census taken in 1920 when she was eleven has her race listed as "mulatto." It also suggests that she was unable to read or write and notes that, as well as her parents, there were seven siblings living at home ranging from the ages of a year and a half to twenty-four. Tina has said that her mother and father were "poor but upwardly mobile."

Agnez DeRouen met Lumis Beyincé when they were fifteen and sixteen, respectively. By this time, Lumis was a studious-looking young man, given to wearing sharp pinstripe suits and well-knotted ties when he wasn't working at the docks, which wasn't often. Though he was a hardworking laborer, people in his neighborhood who didn't know him well viewed him as being professorial. "With his hair slicked back and with his spectacles and formal weekend attire, he always stood out," said one of his relatives. "People who didn't know him thought he was a teacher. As well as being big and strong, he was smart and well-spoken."

Agnez and Lumis settled in Galveston, where they raised their three daughters, Selena, Florence, and Celestine Ann (Tina), and four sons, Marvin, Larry, Roland, and Lumis Jr. Tina was the youngest; she was born on January 4, 1954. "I got the sneaking suspicion, since they were forty-four, that I might not have been planned," Tina once quipped.

"Growing up in Galveston was amazing," Tina said in a 2011 oral history for the Living Archives at the University of Houston, "because it's a small island, so a lot of activities revolved around the beach. My mom's house was open to all children, all the kids in the neighborhood, and we had a ball."

Though they were very popular in the neighborhood, Agnez and Lumis made it clear to their offspring that the needs of their nuclear family should never be overlooked or ignored. For instance, Agnez made sure they all had dinner together every night. It was required that the siblings, especially when they were teenagers, converge over a meal at the requisite hour, for that was the opportunity to check in with one another and cherish their connection. Also, relatives on both sides of the family were often at the

Beyincés' home, a large and sometimes unwieldy group present for all holidays, birthdays, and other important celebrations. Agnez and Lumis both agreed that all of those in their bloodline were worth nurturing; nobody was left out. You didn't walk away, not from family. It would be a philosophy Tina would take with her as a wife and mother and one that would enrich the lives of her own offspring.

As a young woman, Agnez was a highly sought-after, self-taught seamstress with many wealthy clients who paid for her unique designs that creatively featured appliqués, embroidery, and smocking. Some viewed the designs, with all of their beads and jeweled buttons, as gaudy. However, examining them all these years later, it seems clear that her creations were purposely theatrical and certainly not meant for daily wear. In other words, Agnez had show business in her blood. A supremely imaginative woman, she considered her work a means of escapism, a fantasy. It's one of the reasons she was so popular. Her customers loved her flair.

"My mom didn't have much money but she had a lot of style," Tina recalled. "She also upholstered furniture, she did wallpaper, she painted and did everything to redecorate the house. She could do just about anything. I learned a lot from her. Even today I love to redecorate, I love to remodel houses and design things, not only for clothing but for the home as well." Tina believes that if her mother had been "born in another time or place," she might have become quite famous.

In a keynote speech she gave in October 2014 for the Texas Women's Empowerment Foundation's Eighth Annual Women & Money Leadership Luncheon, Tina joked, "All four of my siblings and myself attended Holy Rosary Catholic Prison." Then, with a chuckle, she added, "I mean... *school.*" After the laughter subsided, she said, "I joke about that because if any of you attended Catholic school back in the fifties and sixties—and I see hands—you know exactly what I'm talking about."

Holy Rosary Catholic Church was Texas's first African-American Catholic school and church. Organized in 1889 by its first resident pastor, Father Phillip Keller, it moved to its present site on Avenue N between 30th and 31st Streets. "The nuns, for one thing, they picked on us a lot," Tina continued. "I didn't understand it. The nuns were very hard on me, saying, 'You know, you really don't belong here. If you only knew, you'd be very grateful to be here. You've got a rebellious spirit. We need to take down that spirit and control it.' It was always these things to kind of put me in my place."

As a youngster, Tina couldn't fathom the reason her parents were so solicitous of these angry and abusive nuns, and why they demanded the same of her and her siblings. "My mom did the altar boys' uniforms and she worked for the nuns," Tina recalled. "My dad chauffeured the nuns around, my brother cleaned the schoolyard. And I often wondered why we were indentured servants to the church.

"What I found out later is that my parents were actually bartering for us to go [to the school]." With tears in her eyes, she continued, "I get choked up about it because it was such a sacrifice for them to work and humble themselves just so that we could get an education. That's why the nuns were saying the things they were saying, because we were the poor kids there, and they felt like we didn't fit in.

"The thing I take away from that is that I became a warrior at five. I refused to let [the nuns] take my spirit. I decided then that I would never let anyone decide for me who I am or what I was. I had to fight for myself."

And she did. Tina would always be tough-minded and assertive, a woman who to outsiders sometimes seemed defensive, as if she wanted to be sure she wasn't taken advantage of. No shrinking violet, as a teenager she sometimes displayed a fiery temperament with the boys she dated. As she got older, she became a no-nonsense personality, someone who never suffered fools gladly. Not only had the nuns toughened her up, but she took after her mother, who was also a pragmatic, outspoken woman.

Despite whatever happened to Tina at school, church was still very important in the lives of all the Beyincés. "This was as much a meeting place for those of us who lived in the neighborhood as it was hallowed ground," recalled Bea Thomas, who remembers Tina sitting on the church's steps after service and "being very social with the other parishioners. She held court, or at least that's my memory of her as a teenager. People gravitated to her. In my mind's eye, I still have an image of her sitting on those steps with a crowd of people around her. She was entertaining, was animated, and always had a good story to tell. She was popular, someone who stood out not only because of her great beauty but her big personality. She was also very stylish. She liked to wear an enormous Afro wig—it was huge. She always had on the best clothes. All of that said, you knew not to cross Tina. She had a little temper on her. She was definitely a firecracker."

As she got older and began to date, Tina and her sisters were imparted the same wisdom from their mother. "She used to say, 'Never give yourself one hundred percent to any man. Always keep something for yourself,'" recalled one of Tina's relatives.

During an era when very often the best a woman could hope for was to snare a good man, marry him, and raise his children no matter the circumstances, Agnez was quite the feminist. She never wanted to live a restricted life. She wanted her own career, her own friends. She was devoted to the notion of family, as are most Creoles, but when it came to her husband she had a very specific agenda. "No man needs to know everything about you," she used to tell her daughters. She had other axioms as well: "No man needs that much control." "Don't give away your power." "Live your own life." "Find something to do that is your own." These kinds of sentiments, especially during Agnez's time, were practically revolutionary. Who knows what it was in her childhood, what she may have witnessed in the marriage of her own mother, that had led her to these ideas. But she held fast to them and passed them on to her daughters.

Tina, whose nickname was always "Tenie B.," took her mother's advice that she should find a career for herself, and an early ambition was to become a singer. After she left Catholic school in the sixth grade and went on to a public junior high in Galveston, she became a member of a performing trio act called the Veltones. She and her mother designed the costumes for the group; a photo shows two of the girls in miniskirts—one rose-colored, the other cream—and the third in a pantsuit that merged both colors. Tina says one of her fondest memories of her mom has to do with their designing such costumes together for her group, "and us rehearsing and her giving her input on that. It would come full circle because I'd be able to pass those things on to my daughter." Of the Veltones, she added, "We were known as much for our costumes as for our talent. Just singing in this group and practicing and doing the outfits and all of that prepared me for what I would do later."

Mathew Knowles recalled, "At one of the showcases, the group got to the finals and people in the record industry were coming to see them. Typical story: The night before, one of the girls' mothers told her she couldn't be in the act anymore. So they ended up not going. Who knows what would have happened?" From there, Tina became the lead vocalist in a cover band. That didn't last long, though; a career in show business just wasn't in the cards for her.

"Even though Galveston is such a small town in Texas, you're only limited by the expectations you put on yourself," Tina would say, "but as a child, I didn't have a lot of role models of people who were fashion designers or the music business or any kind of business other than the local industry of hotels and the large medical center there. But I always had a great love for fashion. I made all of my clothes growing up. My nephew, Johnny, who was also a designer and a seamstress, we made all of our clothes for school and we were the best dressed in school. I dressed all of my friends for the proms."

Tina graduated from Ball High School in 1972. "I admire people who know exactly what they want to do when they get out of school," she's said. " 'I want to be a doctor.' 'I want to be a lawyer.' 'I want to go to college.' 'I want to be a nurse,' or whatever. I didn't know what I wanted to be. I just knew that I wanted to get out of Galveston and do something that related to beauty, something that would make women feel good about themselves."

Though Tina would not get a degree, she would take some courses at a Los Angeles community college. Then she would work at World Wide Health Studios, a fitness gym, for three years. After that, she moved to Denver. "I did a little modeling," she remembered. "I learned how to walk in heels. All of these experiences were tools that I didn't know I was collecting, which I would use later. That's how God works," she continued. "Sometimes you don't understand it, but He is giving you things that you can take out of your toolbox and use later in life."

Mathew

*I*n 1964, twelve-year-old Mathew Knowles sat on a dusty old sofa in the middle of the cluttered living room of the small Gadsden, Alabama, home he shared with his parents and siblings. It was more like a clapboard shack than a dwelling for a family. Or, as Mathew would later recall, "Our house looked like Sanford and Son's. We had old cars, lumber, copper, refrigerators, batteries. It was a disaster zone." While he pretended to be watching the small black-and-white television, Mathew listened to his parents as they argued in the kitchen. "I'm sorry, but we can't live on thirty dollars a week," Lue Helen Knowles said.

"What are you talking about?" her husband, Matthew, responded. "Last week I brought home fifty dollars."

"Well, it's not enough. We got six kids to feed!"

"Get off my back, will you?" Matthew demanded of his wife. "I'm doing the best I can."

With that, Lue Helen stormed out of the kitchen, through the living room past her son, and then into the bedroom. She slammed the door. She had a hot temper and it was often on display, especially when it came to her husband's income. Matthew chuckled as he walked into the living room and sat next to his boy in front of the television. "Times are tough," he told him, "but you know what I got that all the money in the world can't buy?"

Young Mathew may have thought his father was about to pass on some wisdom along the lines of "Money can't buy happiness," but that's not where his father was headed in this brief chat. "What's that, Pop?" the teen asked.

"A-1 credit," Matthew said proudly. "You're a black man," he continued. "You want to get ahead in this world as a black man? Then pay your bills on time. I got no money, but I got A-1 credit, and if I have to use it, which I ain't, at least I got it. You understand, boy?"

Mathew nodded.

"Now, let me go see if I can calm your mother down," the older Matthew said as he rose from the couch. "A-1 credit," he repeated. "Remember that, boy."

Of course, Mathew would never forget it. He would grow up to become a raconteur of the first order, and this was a story he'd tell many times over. It was a light moment in an otherwise bleak childhood, a very painful period in his life. If it's true that everyone's childhood plays itself out repeatedly into adulthood, it would seem that Mathew's influenced many of his personal choices.

Mathew Knowles (spelled with one t) was born to Matthew and Lue Helen Knowles on January 9, 1952, one of seven children. The family lived in the small city of Gadsden, about fifty-five miles northeast of Birmingham.

Mathew's father, Matthew Q. Knowles (born on April 4, 1927, and died on December 30, 1996), was a large man who stood well over six feet tall and weighed almost three hundred pounds. His wife and mother to his children, Lue Helen—who would die in September 1977—was a pretty and stately woman who attended Lincoln High school with Coretta Scott King. An industrious woman, she worked as a maid for a white family during the day, earning three dollars a day, while at night and on weekends she sold handmade quilts. She would also can peaches, string beans, and other fruits and vegetables and sell them for a small profit, anything to help the family get by.

Just as his wife, Tina's, biggest inspiration was her mother, Agnez, the greatest influence in Mathew's life was his father, Matthew, known to his friends as "Big Boy," or sometimes "Big Mack." He was employed as a produce truck driver for Stamps & Co., a wholesale fruit and vegetable company. Matthew was renowned in the city as someone who could lift hundred-pound sacks of potatoes and toss them onto a truck with ease, and the other employees at Stamps & Co. always sought to be partnered with him because he made their work so much easier. "If you were partnered with Big Boy," said one of the former employees years later, "you knew you were going to have an easy day. He was like a machine. He could do the work of three men."

An enterprising man, Matthew convinced Stamps & Co. to allow him to use their truck in his spare time. During that time, as Mathew recalled it, "he'd tear down houses and then use the truck to haul copper, metal, the refrigerator, batteries, car parts, whatever . . . and sell it all for money." Mathew's half-Cherokee maternal grandfather, David Hogue, was also a go-getter; he owned a three-hundred-acre farm that he leased to a local paper mill. "My people didn't have a lot of education," Mathew has said, "but they had drive and ambition, a strong work ethic, and a business savvy which I recognized at an early age and began to emulate."

Matthew Knowles became noted in Gadsden, however, not for his work at Stamps & Co. but for his spare-time endeavors as a volunteer fireman. In December 1972, the *Gadsden Times*'s George Butler wrote a profile of Knowles ("Big Boy's Always There") and his dedication to being a volunteer fireman. At the time, Knowles—who was forty-six and lived with his family at 502 Pioneer Street in East Gadsden—had been volunteering with the fire department for more than twenty years.

"When you have to drag lines around lines that are charged with water, they get hard to handle," fire chief James R. Speer told Butler. "But when Big Boy gets hold of them, the lines start moving." He noted that it often took two firemen to handle high-pressure hoses, but that Knowles had been known to do so by himself on several occasions. The writer noted his participation in one major fire in the neighborhood "involving three homes in the Negro section." All of the residents had been rescued except for one man too drunk to make sense of the situation. Without concern for himself, Knowles rushed into the burning building and carried the man to safety on his shoulders "like a sack of flour."

Knowles was known to stay up all night battling fires for free, and then showing up first thing in the morning at his day job. His work ethic was one about which his friends and family marveled, and it was a character trait he would pass down to his children. "I didn't realize when I was a kid how poor we were," Mathew told the radio host Tony Cox in 2006. "My father made between thirty dollars and fifty dollars a week. And the reason why I know that so vividly is my mom used to constantly give him a hard time for that." Mathew may not have been conscious of his family's poverty when he was younger, because it was all that he knew. It was not an easy life, though, and he would most certainly bear the scars of his youth.

"Mathew told me they had to use an outhouse," AlexSandra Wright, who would have a romantic relationship with Mathew in 2008 recalled, "so that tells you how poor they were. He often talked about his childhood with great sadness. This is a man who wanted more from life than what he had as a kid, and I think he was somehow defined by the stigma of extreme and absolute poverty."

Unlike the Beyincés, the Knowleses didn't have a very close bond. Eating dinner together to check in with one another was not something they did very often—it wouldn't have occurred to them. Mathew and his siblings were self-sufficient, some of them fairly close to one another, others not so much. They were also largely independent of their parents, none of them seeming particularly attached to them. Of course, it's imprudent to try to summarize complex relationships that span many decades. Most certainly there had to have been times along the way when some of the Knowleses were bonded to one another, but to say that they were a closely knit family would be overstating it. There were relatives Mathew didn't even know, on both sides of the family. Unlike the Beyincés, they didn't make much of an effort to connect. However, they were satisfied with that status quo. It was all they knew.

Mathew started his education in the small Catholic school St. Martin de Porres in Gadsden. Darryl Dunn went to the same school and recalled, "We went to St. Martin's from the first grade to eighth together. We were actually altar boys together. Yes, Mathew was an altar boy!"

When he was eight, Mathew went into business—selling candy. "I knew from this young age that I wanted to be a businessman," he recalled. "I would buy a dollar's worth of candy and then sell it to others for three dollars. Then I would convince the store owner to give me a discount since I was a regular buyer, and repeat the cycle. At the time, I had no idea what I was doing, only that it was working for me."

Knowles then became one of the first African-American students to enroll in Litchfield Junior High School. "On my first day, a traumatic experience for me was standing up and reading and being laughed at by the white kids because I made a mistake," he recalled. "This was the eighth grade. It was a traumatic experience that forced me to always want to learn more. So as a kid I was always inquisitive and always reading. I wanted to know what I was saying, and speak with confidence."

Mathew was later also one of the first African Americans to attend Gadsden City High School. It was there in sports that he distinguished himself. "It was the challenges, working together to overcome those challenges, the teamwork and trust, believing in each other," he recalled. "Sports was a very exciting time in my life."

"Mathew wasn't a real good basketball player," recalled Darryl Dunn, who went on to become a Gadsden High Basketball Hall of Famer. "Some guys are natural athletes, but not Mathew. He practiced a lot, though, was determined to play, and eventually he got real good. He was always a very focused individual." (Knowles still enjoys playing basketball, though, like many weekend warriors, he has had his fair share of sports-related injuries; he has undergone at least five surgeries as a result of playing. He also suffers from rather serious knee problems.)

"He was also popular with the ladies in school," Dunn recalled, laughing. "He was just this tall, lanky, good-looking drink of water. His nickname was 'Pool Stick' because he was so slim—though not the best pool player in the world! Always had a mischievous look in his eyes. I thought he might one day be a singer because he had a pretty decent voice."

"In high school, I had these three friends and we had this boy band," Mathew recalled. "I went to a Catholic school early on, and I was in the choir there, so, you know, I enjoy singing. But my girls—Beyoncé and Solange—they tell me not to sing. 'Don't sing, Daddy. *Please*, don't sing!'"

Of course, because of the climate of the era, both Darryl and Mathew saw their share of ugly racism. There was racial division in movie theaters in the city, for instance, with blacks relegated to the balcony seats, separate bathrooms and water fountains, and a side door from which to enter and exit. Like many cities in the South in the 1950s and '60s, Gadsden suffered from extreme bitterness between the races. As riots and protest marches became the norm, federal courts made integration in the school system mandatory. The National Guard was recruited to make sure it was a peaceful process. "You don't experience this kind of thing without taking some scars from it with you through life," said Darryl Dunn. "Black youngsters were begrudgingly welcomed into the city's formerly all-white high school, Gadsden High. And when I say begrudgingly, I mean *begrudgingly*."

"My father was part of the first generation of black men that attended an all-white school," Beyoncé confirmed in February 2015, "and he has grown up with a lot of trauma from those experiences. I feel that, now, I can sing for his pain," she said, "and I can sing for my grandparents' pain as well," she added, noting that her paternal grandparents marched with Dr. Martin Luther King Jr.

"I remember that when I got accepted into the Hall of Fame they had a little club for teenagers. I was never allowed to go in there, even though I was one of the best team players," Darryl Dunn remembered. "The whites didn't want us mixing with their kids, and then the black kids in other schools didn't like us because not only were we in this formerly white school, we were beating them at basketball. So, even in the best of circumstances, there was severe and very, very hurtful racism. Mat would say, 'It is what it is. But that doesn't mean I can accept it, and I swear to God, I never will.' It made him angry. We both had this sort of rage.

"Mathew was a product of this ugly world. If there are people who have viewed him as being ruthless in business, it's because they don't know where he came from. In our time, Negroes were hardened by what we went through in our youth. You can't separate it out and say, 'Okay, that was then and now is now.' No. Now is then. And then is now."

As the number two scorer on the team—with Darryl Dunn the number one—Mathew was able to secure a basketball scholarship. He attended the University of Tennessee at Chattanooga, being one of the first African Americans to enroll there. He then continued his education at Fisk University, an elite black university in Nashville. This scholastic transition presented a bit of a culture shock for him because, as he explained to Jamie Foster Brown in an interview for *Sister 2 Sister* magazine, "At Fisk, when I went in 1972, one of the most unpopular things was to be an athlete. You weren't cool because you were a basketball or football player, you were cool if you were *smart*. And if you had smarts and had swagger, then you were really cool." Mathew would graduate from Fisk in 1970 with degrees in both economics and business administration.

Mathew—now tall (well over six feet), lean, and exceedingly handsome—moved to Houston in 1976 at the age of nineteen. "I couldn't wait to get the hell out of Gadsden and I never looked back," he said.

In 1976 and 1977, Knowles would work a variety of jobs, from selling insurance for Metropolitan Life to postage meters for Pitney Bowes to telephone equipment for Southern Bell. Around 1978, he went to work for Xerox Corporation selling copiers and duplicators, then in 1980 for the company's Xerox Medical Systems division. He was eventually promoted to their so-called elite division, where he sold medical systems, most notably breast cancer detection and ultrasound technology. By 1981, he was driving a Jaguar XJ6 and earning a six-figure income, quite unheard of for a black salesman in Texas in the 1980s.

What most people who did business with Mathew came to know about him was that he was obsessive about his work. Doggedly determined to distinguish himself, he never let up on himself or on the people with whom he worked. He was tough on everybody, but certainly toughest on himself. "He was a pit bull," recalled one coworker. "This is a man who would call fifty times an hour to get something he needed from you. He wasn't the kind of person to whom you could say, 'I'll get back to you in fifteen minutes.' Not Mathew. He would be back on the phone in five minutes asking again for whatever he needed, and he would be on you like white on rice until he got it. On one hand, you had to have great admiration for him. On the other, you wanted to tell him to take a pill and relax. He was determined, to put it mildly."

Engaged

*M*athew Knowles met Tina Beyincé in Houston in 1978. By this time, she was working as a secretary for a credit card company, while he was at his job at Xerox Corporation.

Tina was a knockout, her shoulder-length, wavy dark hair highlighted with flashy red streaks. She wasn't a skinny girl by any means; she was curvaceous. Her skin, the color of dark copper, was flawless, her lipstick usually bright cherry red—a color she still favors to this day. She had gone to a Saturday evening party with a man who happened to be a friend of Mathew's. She and Mathew made eye contact throughout the night, with Tina wondering all the while when the handsome, tall, and athletic-looking stranger might make his move. Finally, Mathew walked over to her to make small talk. They clicked. Soon Mathew, a man of great charm and self-assurance, was asking her to have lunch with him the following Monday. She agreed to meet him at noon at her job. "What struck me about her? Woo! She was damn good-looking," he recalled many years later. "But she also seemed like a good person in heart and spirit."

That night, Mathew went home and, using his little General Electric "shoebox" recorder, taped himself saying her last name, "Beyincé," before he could forget how to pronounce it. Then on Monday, at the appointed hour of noon, he showed up at the MasterCard office in downtown Houston looking for Tina. However, he was told by the receptionist that no one by that unusual last name worked there. "Are you sure?" he asked, completely bewildered. "It's Tina Beyonah, or Beince, or…" Finally he told the receptionist that he was MasterCard's local Xerox representative and asked her to go inside to check their copiers for efficiency. Actually he was just looking for an opportunity to take a look around himself and see if he could find Tina. After a thorough search of the premises, Tina was nowhere to be found. Mathew left, feeling rejected. Obviously she had steered him to the wrong place in an effort to ditch him.

An entire year passed.

One day, Mathew was walking down the street at about 9:30 in the morning and saw Tina in a coffee shop. Though he recognized her immediately, he walked right by her. He had his pride, after all. But then, a few hours later, by sheer coincidence he saw her again at the popular Foley's department store in downtown Houston with some of her girlfriends. Though they made brief eye contact, he decided to ignore her—or at least act as if he was ignoring her. "Then, at 3:00, downtown Houston, I'm standing at a stoplight," he recalled, "and there she is again! She's on one side of the road and I'm on the other. We're looking at each other…" While crossing the street, they had no choice but to acknowledge each other. When they met halfway, Mathew asked to have a word with her.

"You're that pretty chick who *said* she worked at MasterCard," Mathew told Tina. "I made a date with you, but you don't work there at all. Why'd you blow me off like that?"

Tina had to laugh. "*Fool!* First of all, can we please get out of the middle of the road?" she asked. They walked to a curb.

"So, why'd you tell me you worked at MasterCard?" Mathew asked again. "You could have just said you weren't interested."

"*Fool!*" she repeated. "I told you *Visa*. Not MasterCard. You went to the wrong place!"

That was the beginning of what felt at the time like a head-over-heels romance. It wasn't long before the couple was engaged. At the time, Mathew told family members he was looking for a partner as much as he was a wife. He wanted someone who would stand by his side as he conquered the world, and Tina Beyincé definitely seemed to fit the bill.

"Mathew had been raised to be productive," recalled one of Tina's relatives, "and this is something Tina found compelling about him. He was anything but lazy. She felt she would have a good life with him, that he would be able to provide for her. Besides that, the passion she shared with him was strong."

What Mathew took note of about Tina very early in the relationship was that she could stand up to him if need be. If he was late for a date, he heard about it. If he said something she regarded as insulting, he would be taken to task. He was intrigued by her forceful personality and appreciated that she had a backbone, that she would gladly put him in his place.

He also noticed that she was guarded. Maybe it was because Tina seemed to sense something about Mathew early on that made her go deep into self-protection mode. She was rarely completely vulnerable with him, always reserving a big part of herself. It wasn't just what her mother had taught her about life and love, either. It was as if she had some sort of women's intuition about Mathew specifically. "She somehow knew she needed to protect her heart," said one of her relatives in looking back at this time.

Despite any misgivings Tina may have had about Mathew, their engagement was officially announced in the *Galveston Daily News* in the summer of 1978. While most couples would likely announce their impending nuptials with a happy photo posed together, Tina's notice was accompanied by a lovely picture of her alone, looking like the most celebrated of movie stars—head tilted, a pensive look in her eyes, full glamour makeup, and a luxurious flowing mane of hair cascading to one shoulder. The couple would be wed on January 5, 1980, at Holy Rosary Catholic Church in Galveston.

Trapped

Like all couples, Mathew and Tina entered into their marriage full of optimistic hopes and dreams. However, from the start it was as if the union was fraught with grim omens.

The warning signs started shortly before the marriage took place. "I was so excited about my dad walking me down the aisle," Tina recalled. "But the day before the wedding he had a heart attack." Of course this put a cloud over the proceedings, but the ceremony went on. However, the bad luck would continue. "The next day we were supposed to go on our honeymoon, but we missed the flight," Tina continued. "So I called to see how my father was, and they said, 'Oh, your dad is in intensive care. He had a massive heart attack!'"

The couple immediately abandoned plans for leaving on the next flight for their honeymoon and instead rushed to Galveston. "My dad was really bad," Tina said, "I decided to stay at the hospital. Mathew went back to the house because his parents were in town. And then he called me crying that his grandfather had died! So it was like, 'Okay, what's going on here?'"

By Wednesday Tina's father was stable enough for her to attend Mathew's grandfather's funeral. "I went to the funeral on Thursday, and then when I got back on Friday, my *mom* was in intensive care," Tina added, still in disbelief so many years later about this unfortunate chain of events. "It was a tough time," she concluded, an understatement if ever there was one.

Along with all of the immediate familial turmoil came the question of the newlyweds' finances. Mathew's job at that time wasn't paying much; Tina felt she should contribute. "No," he insisted. "You don't have to work. You should go and take care of your parents."

"I treasure that to this day," Tina recalled of Mathew's gesture, "because within six months my mom passed away."

After her mother's death, Tina didn't immediately reenter the workforce, a decision she would later greatly regret. Instead she enrolled in beauty school. Then she got pregnant.

"After I got pregnant, my marriage just got really bad," Tina recalled in October 2014. She didn't elaborate on the nature of the problems she was experiencing with Mathew, but certainly later on his infidelity would become an issue. Tina did spend a lot of time wondering about Mathew's devotion, especially in the first year of their marriage. He seemed always to be restless and unhappy, as if searching for validation. He was never satisfied, and somehow to her it felt connected to his disadvantaged youth, to being thought of as "less than" back in Gadsden. Whatever his personal demons, they began to influence his marriage early on, and there wasn't much Tina or anyone else could do about it. It was as if she had come into the picture too late. Mathew was already who he was going to be, and now she would just have to find a way to deal with him as best she could.

It was upsetting, but from all available evidence, Tina suppressed her acute sadness and did what she could to go on with and manage her life. This was an unusual turn of events for her. Before Mathew, she had a fiery temper and could be explosive when pushed, the kind of woman who would not put up with much from a man. Something happened to her, though, when Mathew came along. Who knows what psychology in her would be triggered by her abiding love for him, but after Mathew she would never be quite the same. The way she concealed her unhappiness and maybe even her anger at this time in her life would become a template for the way she would handle her issues with Mathew in the future. It was also a behavior that appears to have been passed on to her daughter Beyoncé, who would one day seemingly deal with conflict in her life in much the same manner.

Within a year of their wedding, Tina already thought of leaving Mathew, but says she felt utterly trapped. First, she didn't have any money of her own. More urgent, though, was that she was out of the job market, a decision she now regretted. Plus, the premium she placed on the notion of family trumped all desire to leave the marriage. There was something about Mathew that drew her to him and made her think he might still be the answer to her deep longing for family. "I think she felt she could possibly fix him," said one of her friends from that time in her life. "I know for certain that she loved him with all her heart and wanted his children. At the end of the day, that was the real problem, wasn't it? It wasn't just her being out of the job market, it wasn't just her not having money, it was as simple and as complicated as her loving him and wanting desperately to bear his children."

A pressing question for Tina was how she had allowed herself to get into such a quandary. Somehow it had come to pass that she now relied for safety and security on a man. Though this was typical for many women of her generation, it most certainly wasn't what she had had in mind for her life. Just the same, within the span of only a couple of years she'd found herself dependent on someone she'd had serious doubts about from almost the very beginning. Considering how many times her mother had warned her about such romantic entrapment, this was a rude awakening. Tina wasn't just frustrated by this turn of events, she was angry about it—angry at Mathew, angry at herself, and angry at the circumstances of her life as they had unfolded.

"Things got very rocky and my marriage became *very* tumultuous," Tina recalled. "I was having all of these problems and I thought, '*What have I done?*' I'd been out of the job market for four years [actually, at this point it was two] and my self-esteem was low. I was, like, 'What do I do now?'"

With just three months left of beauty school before graduating, Tina sensed that her education could be her saving grace. "I knew I had to do something," she said, "so I got very focused about school." After she graduated, "I built a little salon at my house and I did hair," she recalled.

Tina may have hoped the arrival of a new baby would help her through what she later called "the adversity of a bad marriage." However, if it didn't, at least she now had her own business. In other words, she was preparing for a life that didn't include Mathew—unlikely as it still seemed to her—if it were to come to that. As she became more focused on business, she saw that she actually did have the acumen for it. Nothing was going to ruin her, she decided early on—not even Mathew Knowles.

Headliners

*B*eyoncé Giselle Knowles was born on September 4, 1981, at the Park Plaza Hospital, a relatively new medical center in Houston's Museum District. Tina and Mathew agreed that she would pick the baby's first name, he her middle name. Beyoncé, of course, is derived from Tina's maiden name, Beyincé. Because only one of her brothers had a son, Tina had feared that her family name would die out. "I said, 'Oh, God, we'll run out of Beyincés,'" she told the journalist Touré for *Rolling Stone*—thus her idea of naming her daughter in a variant of Beyincé. Her father, Lumis Beyincé, didn't much like the idea, though. "My family was not happy," Tina confirmed. "My dad said, 'She's gonna be really mad at you, because that's a last name.' And I'm like, 'It's not a last name to anybody but you guys!'"

"She was a beautiful baby," Mathew Knowles recalled of the infant Beyoncé. "I can't describe the excitement I felt as a father, holding her for the first time. Everywhere I'd go, I would take Beyoncé with me. It was kind of an automatic duo."

Though she was overwhelmed with joy at becoming a mother, it would seem that the most important thing in Tina's mind, at this juncture anyway, was her freedom. After taking out a small-business loan, she was able to finance the opening of her own beauty salon. It would be tough going at first and would take all of her focus, time, and energy, but she knew she had to strike while the iron was hot. Therefore, when Beyoncé was about two months old, Tina says she took her to live with her paternal grandmother. She recalled, "I said, 'Listen, you gotta keep her because I need to open a business.'" At that same time, she remembered thinking, "I will never be in this position again. I will never be totally dependent on someone. I will never give up myself."

There seems to be something missing from Tina's story, though. She specifically leaves Mathew out of the equation, begging the question: Why would she take baby Beyoncé to his mother's if he was home and available to help out? Some say that what was really going in the Knowles household was that Mathew either left Tina at this time or she asked him to leave.

"She felt she couldn't raise the baby on her own and also focus on starting a business, and that *this* is why she took Beyoncé to her mother-in-law's," says one source. Though we really don't know what happened, the theory would make sense. One of Tina's relatives explains further. "It's no surprise that there would be confusion," she says, "because Tina is not always forthcoming about these things, and why should she be? I don't know if she asked Mathew to leave or if he left by his own accord. But whatever happened, it motivated her even more and pushed her forward to give everything she had to the starting of her own business, which is how her baby ended up staying at her mother-in-law's for six months. This was a woman who was not going to stop until she was self-sufficient."

Whatever the circumstances, in 1985, Tina opened her own hairstylist operation called Headliners Hair Salon on Montrose Avenue in Houston. Her business, which was geared toward black hairstyles, started slowly and would be unsteady for a number of years before it began to thrive, which it would do for long afterward. At first the staff consisted of just Tina, her niece, and another employee. However, Tina worked hard and saw her clientele grow steadily. She would eventually move the business to Bissonet Street, near Rice University.

"She was more than a hairstylist, she was a therapist," Beyoncé would observe many years later. "A lady could come into that salon with problems, express herself to my mom, get a complete makeover…and then walk out feeling like a new woman."

When Beyoncé was just a tyke, Tina would let her sweep up the hair from the floor and spend time with the customers. (Beyoncé would save the money Tina paid her from tips and use it to buy a season pass to Six Flags, where she loved riding the roller coasters.) In 2013, she would say that her takeaway from those many hours interacting with the women at Headliners was that "we're all going through our problems, we all have the same insecurities and we need each other. I have been around the world, I've seen so many things," she concluded, "but there's nothing like a conversation with a woman who understands you. I grow so much from those conversations. I *need* my sisters."

Headliners salon gave Tina the opportunity she so craved to learn, grow, and become independent of Mathew. As well as a venue for her to make an independent living, Tina's place of business was "a labor of love," she says. "I loved making women feel good and it was an opportunity to do it and do it in a big way. The adversity of me having this bad marriage caused me to do something about my situation."

When Tina retrieved her baby from her mother-in-law, Mathew apparently returned to her as well. Was she now happy? That's difficult to say. She was still angry at him for whatever had occurred, that much seemed clear to her friends and family. But still she took him back. If her marriage worked out, fine. If not, at least she now had options.

Childhood Days

*B*eyoncé Knowles was about six years old when she came home from school one afternoon and proudly announced to her mother that her first-grade teacher had taught her a new song. "Really?" Tina Knowles asked.

"Okay," she said, drying her hands with a dishtowel. "I'd like to hear it, then." She sat down at the kitchen table and listened as Beyoncé sang a nursery rhyme. Beyoncé didn't just sing it, though. She acted it out; she performed it. Whereas most kids her age might have sung the little song with their eyes cast bashfully downward, not Beyoncé. She made direct eye contact with her mom and delivered the rhyming tune with total authority. "I sat there thinking, 'My goodness, this is really ... *something,*'" Tina would recall many years later. "It was a moment I don't think I'll ever forget." She wasn't the only one struck by it. "I'll never forget that feeling," Beyoncé would recall as an adult. "I loved performing for my mother in that second. It was a rush." There weren't a lot of other happy memories attached to her school years, which is another reason why this one seems so significant.

Beyoncé has said that her school years—grades one through eight, before she was homeschooled and tutored from about the ninth grade onward—were problematic, that she was targeted because of her light skin and hair.

"Sometimes in the black community, it's the lighter girls who are picked on," Tina Knowles confirmed. "Of course, the opposite is often true as well, sadly—the darker girls are also picked on. It's a shame, but it's a fact of life. Beyoncé would often come home crying that the other girls were making fun of her. 'I wish I was darker,' she would say. I wanted her to embrace who she was. 'Don't wish to be anything other than what you are,' I would tell her. I know it's easy for adults to say such things, but harder for little girls to understand."

It has never been easy to pigeonhole Beyoncé into a specific racial category. Questions about her race and heritage have been raised ever since she became famous. In fact, according to Google's own statistics, Beyoncé's ethnicity remains a subject of fascination, with more than two thousand users per month typing into its search engine the question "Is Beyoncé black?" and another two hundred wondering, "Is Beyoncé full black?" Over two hundred more pose the question "Is Beyoncé white?" Like most African Americans of mixed descent, Beyoncé self-identifies as black. In truth, she epitomizes the notion of America as being a "melting pot" of cultures, with a father, Mathew, of African-American extraction and a mother, Tina, of French Creole ancestry.

Her unusual, exotic-sounding name was also a reason for some children to single her out. "I hated my name when I was a kid," Beyoncé has said. "It was just something else for them to use against me."

Then there was the matter of her ears. "My head was smaller and I looked like I had big Dumbo ears," she would recall. "I still do not wear my ears out [from behind her hair]. That's also why I wear big earrings, because they camouflage your ears."

In short, she didn't fit in, or at least that's how the other kids in school made Beyoncé feel. The result of schoolyard taunting was that she became incredibly shy and withdrawn, so much so that some of the students viewed her as snobbish or maybe even egotistical. "I couldn't win," she recalled. "I was bashful because the kids picked on me. And I was then picked on because I was bashful."

"I would go to pick her up at school and she'd just be pushing the swing by herself with no one on it," Tina recalled. "I once asked this little girl in the school playground, 'Why don't you like Beyoncé?' and she got very flip with me and said, 'I just *don't like* her!' I thought, 'Oh my Lord! What am I going to do about this?'"

After watching and listening to Beyoncé singing around the house, Tina started to think that perhaps she had some talent and that maybe it could somehow be used to help her out of her bashful nature. "I began to notice that she was a little more extroverted when she was singing," said Tina. "So when she was about seven I signed her up for dance classes at a local studio to bring her out of her shell. I also wanted her to make new friends and meet people other than the mean kids at school. It was in those dance classes that she started to get just a bit of self-esteem," Tina concluded. "Then one of the dance instructors arranged for Beyoncé to be included in a community show performance, and that's when things really started coming together."

"For that first performance, both my mom and dad came," Beyoncé recalled. "It was the first time I had ever walked onstage in front of an audience. I looked into the crowd and saw teachers, classmates, and parents fanning themselves with the paper programs and trying to get comfortable on yellow plastic chairs. Then I opened my mouth and started to sing. My parents were shocked. I can still see the looks on their faces. I'm not sure where I found the courage," she recalled of this defining moment. "All I know is that I felt at home on that stage, more so than anywhere else. I saw my parents stand up and clap after I sang. I knew they were very proud of me.

"From that moment on, I decided that all the world would be a stage— chairs, tables, the kitchen countertop," Beyoncé recalled, laughing. "I made my own stages. That's how I expressed myself—through music. I only felt comfortable when I was singing or dancing. My personality would totally change. It's still true today. Normally, I keep to myself, and you wouldn't even know if I was in the same room. But when I'm in performance mode, I become a totally different person."

After Beyoncé won that first talent contest, Tina decided to enroll her in local beauty pageants. She wasn't interested in seeing her daughter model pretty clothes on a runway (in makeup that would probably be considered inappropriate for a tyke) as much as she wanted her to have a venue in which she could sing. While Beyoncé enjoyed the talent part of these shows, she detested the beauty segments. "Getting all dolled up was not for me at that age," she recalled. "I was too self-conscious and didn't feel like I was as pretty as the other girls." On the plus side, though, the contests taught her the value of healthy competition, "and also how to learn from everyone else on the show," she said, "kids who were better than me. I became a sponge."

It was at around this time that Mathew began to share Tina's enthusiasm for Beyoncé's budding talent. He wasn't sure what to make of it yet, but if performing was something she enjoyed, he wanted to encourage it. He began talking to her more about it, wanting to know her specific thoughts and feelings. He liked what he heard. It wasn't so much the performing aspect of it as the fact that she *wanted* something, that something *mattered* to her. Anytime a kid of Mathew Knowles's was going to be directed and focused about anything, whatever it was, Mathew was going to approve. "I'm going to help her," he told Tina. "If only to encourage her to do more pageants. I think it's good for her. I'm one hundred percent behind it."

Tina was happy about Mathew's enthusiasm, though maybe also just a little wary of it. She knew that once Mathew became invested in something, he didn't give half an effort to it. He went all the way. "He can be a little—sometimes *a lot*—obsessive," is how she once put it. She was just thinking hobby where Beyoncé's pageants were concerned, and she didn't want Mathew to have bigger ideas. Still, she liked seeing his support of their daughter and definitely wanted it to continue. She would monitor it, though—in her own way.

In 1988, when Beyoncé was seven, she won in the "Baby Junior" category of the Sammy Awards—an homage to the great entertainer Sammy Davis Jr.—at a local recreational center. A year later, in the fall of 1989, she returned to the Sammy Awards, not as a contestant but as a guest performer. Wearing a white blouse and a sequined blue dress with white leggings, her curled black hair falling to her shoulders, she sang "Home" from the 1975 Broadway musical *The Wiz*. It was a good—if also maybe just a tad overwrought—performance. At its end, she managed ten little spins, and then, flashing a big and dazzling smile, a graceful curtsey.

It's easy to put a glossy cast on the unfolding of these early years, if only because Beyoncé was so precocious a child, and also one so obviously eager to please. Looking back on it now, it was obviously the dawning of something very big and exciting for her and her family. She wasn't being forced into these pageants, either. Once she got started, there would have been no way for her parents to talk her out of participating in them—not that they would have tried to do so. Still, though, she would apparently spend many years dealing with unresolved feelings where this time in her life is concerned.

It's not unusual that people who become famous at an early age feel a loss of their childhood in the process; it's the most common complaint of child stars. Unlike Michael Jackson, for instance, who became famous at about the age of ten, Beyoncé would not become truly well known until she was sixteen. Definitely, though, when it came to her early years of performing in pageants and talent shows—those years of putting herself forth for harsh judgment and heavy scrutiny—she would later look back and feel a certain amount of discontentment. Was she talented enough? It was a question constantly drummed into her head just by virtue of the competitive venue in which she found herself. More to the core of a young girl's soul, though, was always the pointed question: Was she pretty enough?

In her 2013 video for her song "Pretty Hurts," Beyoncé's message concerns the pitfalls of pursuing unrealistic notions of physical perfection as dictated by the media, and the destructive nature of such a hopeless quest. In the video she portrays a contender at a pageant, calling herself "Miss Third Ward." She frames her message with the story of beauty contestants furiously grooming and preening in preparation for a big competition. "I basically starved," she recalled in speaking of her inspiration for the video. "I neglected all of the people that I loved. I conformed to what everybody else thought I should be . . . and [then] I have this trophy. What does it all mean?" she asked. "The trophy [in the video] represents all of the sacrifices I made as a kid. All of the time that I lost, being on the road and in the studios as a child, and I just want to *blow that shit up!*"

In fact, in the video an infuriated Beyoncé is actually shown destroying the trophies, breaking them into pieces in a violent rage. "I have a lot of these awards...I worked my ass off," she later explained. "I worked harder than probably everybody I know to get those things."

The "Pretty Hurts" video was Beyoncé Knowles at age thirty-two, a woman finally grappling with deep-seated confusion and obviously even a certain amount of rage about her hardworking childhood. But as a little girl, she was just on autopilot. On some level, maybe she was angry back then, even if she didn't yet recognize it, or even understand it. Or maybe she somehow knew how to suppress it. It would seem, though, that at least based on what she would later say as an adult, the anger was there just the same.

"People Don't Need to Know"

*A*t a very young age, Beyoncé Knowles began to understand that one way to keep her privacy was to compartmentalize her life. Of course, today she's an expert at it. Certainly the way she controls what she allows to be known about her is an important part of her business model. In fact, most of her public doesn't know very much about her personal life at all, except what she has decided to spoon-feed them. "She makes it clear that there's a difference between business and personal, and she keeps those two things sacred," is how Kwasi Fordjour, the creative coordinator at Beyoncé's Parkwood Entertainment company, succinctly put it in 2014. In the end, it's a clever way of guaranteeing that her public focuses on her artistry and is not unduly distracted by any details of her personal life. "They see the talent, and that's all they see," Fordjour concluded.

When she was a child, the children who ridiculed Beyoncé at school knew virtually nothing about her many pageant wins. "I didn't dare tell anyone because the last thing I wanted was more attention," she recalled. "Plus, I knew they'd make fun of me: 'Who does she think she is, a beauty queen?' That would have been my absolute nightmare."

"I didn't know a thing about her having done anything like that until many years later when she became famous," said Chester Maddox, who attended school with Beyoncé. "I'm not sure I would have believed it anyway," he added. "Not our little Beyoncé. I remember her as having no self-confidence whatsoever. So, no, I wouldn't have believed she was fearless enough to be entering and then winning beauty or talent contests. No way."

Beyoncé also didn't tell the girls at the pageants and shows anything about her life outside of that particular venue. "I distinctly remember trying to engage her about her school," Denise Watkins, who competed with Beyoncé in many talent shows, recalled. "We were little kids yet she didn't want me to know where she went to school. I thought, 'Well, that's a bit odd.' My mother said, 'What's with that little girl and all her secrets?' When I later found out she was a singer, I wasn't surprised. My feeling was that I knew only a small part of her life and that the rest of it was known by others. I also felt that they didn't know the small part I knew. To keep all of this straight at eight years of age, I don't know how she managed it."

Taking it a step further, her classmates in school didn't know anything about her home life. "It was like I had two different lives," she would observe to Australian television personality Liam Bartlett in 2007. "I've been that way all of my life."

"What I most remember of Beyoncé as a kid wasn't the bullying, it was the mystery of her," recalled Jerome Whitley, who attended the fourth grade with her. "I would ask about her mother or her father, and she would get very quiet. Other kids always talked about their parents. Not Beyoncé.

"I remember when her mother would come and pick her up from school. Whereas the other kids' parents would show up in their beat-up old cars, Beyoncé's mom would make a big splash. Here would come this Hollywood-looking woman with big sunglasses in a shiny new convertible, her long hair blowing in the breeze. 'Come on, now, Beyoncé,' she would say. 'We got things to do.' I actually thought Beyoncé's mom was some kind of celebrity, and that *this* was why Beyoncé didn't want to speak about her. I was sure of it, in fact. I remember going home at night and flipping through all the channels on the television looking for this stunning woman I later learned was Tina Knowles."

A Real Find

*O*h my God, Deborah," exclaimed Denise Seals. "Did you hear the way that little girl sang? I can't believe a child can sing like that!"

Denise Seals and her close friend Deborah Laday were driving in Denise's car after having just left the Evelyn Rubenstein Jewish Community Center, where an eight-year-old girl had knocked their socks off. As they drove down South Braeswood Boulevard through Houston, they couldn't contain their enthusiasm. In fact, Deborah said she was so excited she was "fixin' to cry. That girl is *a real find*, Denise!" she exclaimed.

Denise nodded enthusiastically. "*Finally*, we found somebody who can really sing," she said. "How many girls have we seen? A hundred?"

"*Two* hundred," Deborah exclaimed.

"But it was worth it just to find this one," Denise added. "What was her name again?"

Deborah thought it over. "Was it Bernice?" she asked, unsure. No, she didn't think that was it. "Belinda?" "Bernadette?" "Benita?" They simply could not remember. Deborah said she would call the dance studio in the morning and ask. "It's a name I've never heard before," she said, "with such an incredible voice. Imagine what we could do with that kind of talent!"

For the last three months, Denise and Deborah had been searching for pretty young girls with singing or dancing ability. It was actually Denise who first had the idea of forming a musical revue that would feature at its center a girls' group. "At the time, the group En Vogue was big, and I wanted to do something like that but with much younger girls," she recalled. "My prior experience was that I had a background in music and had sung backup for several artists in the Houston area. I met Deborah through a mutual friend, and she too had the same desire. So we partnered up."

Deborah Laday, a professional bookkeeper, had also competed in beauty pageants along the way, so she understood the business. The two women were ideal counterparts, both big dreamers who were quite serious about their joint venture from the start, so much so that the first thing they did was form D&D Management, using the first initials of their names. They then rented office space from which to conduct business. Though it was all pie-in-the-sky stuff, they were determined to give it their all.

"I had seen MC Hammer in concert and he had a revue, a group of singers, dancers, and rappers—and that's sort of what we wanted to do," Deborah Laday recalled. "First, we wanted to form the girls' group part of the act, which would really be the foundation of the revue. To that end, we took out advertisements in the *[Houston] Chronicle*, saying we were looking for talent. Denise also knew quite a few choir directors in local churches, so she also put the word out to them."

The two women were in search of young girls between the ages of eight and twelve who not only could sing and dance but also had charisma and personality. Once word about their endeavor got out in the area, the floodgates opened. "We saw maybe a hundred girls right off the bat," Denise recalled, "every parent in the Houston area who thought his or her kid could sing."

One day, a local dance instructor telephoned Deborah Laday to tell her that she'd been working with an eight-year-old named Beyoncé Knowles. She said she'd heard about the talent search and that this girl was so talented, she needed to be seen and heard to be believed. She told Deborah that Beyoncé would be singing at the Evelyn Rubenstein Jewish Community Center. "If you go, you will not be sorry," she said. Of course, Deborah and Denise felt they had no choice but to attend.

During the talent show, as soon as Beyoncé opened her mouth to sing her signature song, "Home," the two women looked at one another with surprise. She sounded like a youngster who'd already had a great deal of professional experience. Her tone was clear, as was her enunciation. She also had a certain undeniable presence. She was confident, not at all shy. The way she connected with the audience, especially her eye contact with those seated in the front row, was fascinating.

After Beyoncé finished her performance, Deborah and Denise went in search of her parents. They found Mathew and Tina completely surrounded by smiling, enthusiastic people, all of whom seemed to be singing Beyoncé's praises. A beaming Tina held the hand of three-year-old Solange as she graciously accepted these compliments from strangers. Towering at her side was Mathew, seeming proud. Deborah and Denise made their way through the crowd. "Your daughter!" Deborah exclaimed once she was standing before the Knowleses. "Oh my God! She's so *good*." She told the Knowleses that she and Denise were attempting to form a girls' group, and that they would love for Beyoncé to be their first acquisition. When Mathew wondered what sort of group the ladies were thinking of, they said they envisioned something along the lines of En Vogue or the Supremes, but much younger. As for what they planned to name the act, Deborah explained, "We were thinking that maybe it's the girls' time to shine in this business. So," she said, "we're thinking . . . Girls Tyme—that would be T-y-m-e."

As if on cue, little Beyoncé ran up to her parents. She was wearing a white blouse with a light blue dress that featured a crisscross pattern, her hair adorned with blue-and-white silk ribbons. "These ladies say they're starting a girls' group," Mathew told his daughter as she looked up at him with adoring eyes. "They want you to be in it! So, what do you think of that?" The little girl smiled broadly. "Pleased to meet you," she said, extending her hand to Deborah and then to Denise with no prompting at all from her folks. "I'd love to be in a group. Would that be okay, Mommy?" she asked. "We can talk about it, Beyoncé," Tina said, nodding. Studying Beyoncé's face, Deborah suddenly realized that she was already familiar with her; Beyoncé and Deborah's daughter, Millicent, had previously competed against one another in local beauty pageants. When prompted, Beyoncé remembered Millicent. "She's so pretty. You know her too, Mommy," she said. Tina smiled vaguely, as if trying to remember.

"I wanna be in a group too," Solange piped up, pouting.

"You'll get your chance, little girl," Mathew said, scooping her up into his arms. "When you're too big for me to do this," he said, lifting her over his head as she squealed with delight, "then maybe you'll be ready to be in a group."

Phone numbers were exchanged all around.

In about a week's time, there was another round of auditions, this one including Beyoncé. "That's when I met her for the first time," LaTavia Roberson, who would sing with Beyoncé in Girls Tyme and then Destiny's Child, recalls. "There were lines and lines of girls, all of us sitting together waiting to sing, dance, rap, and do whatever we could do to convince these ladies [Deborah and Denise] to work with us." It took some time, but eventually Laday and Seals found the talent they felt they needed for their homespun revue, which, as it would happen, would comprise three acts:

There was "M-1"—Millicent LaDay, Deborah's eight-year-old daughter, who acted as a "hype-master," the girl charged with revving up the crowd and keeping it on its feet.

Then there was Girls Tyme, the girls' act featuring Beyoncé Knowles, eight; Staci LaToisen, ten; and Jennifer Young, eleven. This was the singing group that was to be at the center of the revue.

There was also Destiny, the hip-hop dance troupe consisting of LaTavia Roberson and Chris Lewis, both nine-year-olds. When Deborah and Denise decided to add two more dancers to Destiny, they auditioned and then accepted LaTavia's cousins Nicki Taylor, eleven, and her sister Nina, eight.

It was Denise Seals who would train the girls vocally. Though they had singing ability, they were obviously still just children who didn't yet know how to control their voices. They also didn't know how to sing harmony.

So Denise trained them to listen carefully to each other as they sang so that they could learn to stay on pitch. "Beyoncé picked it all up so fast, it was a little startling," she recalled—and it should be acknowledged here that Denise would have been Beyoncé's first vocal coach. "Of the girls in her group, I would have to say that she was most advanced," she added. "She was a quick study, not afraid to ask questions, and—good Lord!—the questions!" she exclaimed. "Nothing got by her. At the age of eight, she wanted to know all there was to know about singing. I remember walking into rehearsal one day and there she was giving the other girls their parts as if *she* was the vocal coach. 'You sing this part,' she was saying to one of them. 'Then you sing this part,' she said to another. 'If y'all do it right, it'll be harmony. But if y'all do it wrong, it'll be *terrible*.' I laughed to myself and thought, 'Okay, so *that's* how it's gonna be with this one, is it?' "

Now that managers Laday and Seals had the personnel of their three acts confirmed, it was time to begin trying to book the revue around town. The way they'd planned and rehearsed the show, the girls would bound onto the stage with a prerecorded announcement, complete with bombastic fanfare music, proclaiming, *"Ladies and gentlemen, you are about to experience the ultimate masterpiece: M-1, Destiny, and Girls Tyme!"*

In June 1990, the revue would make its debut at Hobart Taylor Hall at Prairie View A&M University in Prairie View, Texas, during a variety program of local up-and-coming talent. That more than two thousand people showed up to see a gaggle of little girls who were virtually unknown speaks to how successful the enterprising women of D&D Management were in getting the word out about their new charges. "What made the revue so special was that there was no one star," said Deborah Laday. "That was our vision, to feature all of the girls in one way or the other. We wanted to build their self esteem as much as we did their careers. That was so important to Denise and me. There would be no one star. They were all stars."

"I was nine the first time we performed," Beyoncé has said. (Actually, she was eight.) "I realized then how much I loved being in a group, because I was always so nervous. So to have those girls with me before the stage, during the stage, and after the stage—and we could talk about all of it—was very exciting for me."

It wasn't long before the revue began to play even larger venues such as the AstroWorld amusement park in Houston. "When we played Astro-World, my gosh, we thought, 'Okay, now *for sure* we've made the big time,'" Nina Taylor recalled. "I remember Beyoncé saying, 'AstroWorld! It don't get much bigger than *AstroWorld*! Just think about it: We can do our show and then go on the Cyclone ride, over and over and over again!'"

"It all fell together quickly," said LaTavia Roberson. "I think it was, like ... '*What*? We're actually going onstage already? That fast?' Then, when we got out there, it was as if we had no choice but to show the audience what we had to offer. We'd see the smiles and hear the applause and look at each other as if to say, 'Wow ... maybe we actually *can* do this thing!' It was a baptism by fire, now that I look back on it. We just went out there and made it happen. It was either that or fail, and none of us wanted to fail."

One of Deborah Laday's earliest memories of Beyoncé has to do with what happened when Deborah and Denise scheduled two last-minute performances during a time when the Knowleses were going to be out of town for the weekend. The shows, held in a local park, were hosted by the shoe company Reebok. Beyoncé couldn't make the first one because she hadn't yet returned from the family's vacation. So Staci LaToisen sang her part in the show.

When she heard that the Knowleses had returned, Deborah telephoned Tina to tell her about the second show. "Oh, but Beyoncé is so tired from the drive," Tina said, "I don't know if she can make it." That was no problem, Deborah told her. She said that Staci would simply sing Beyoncé's part again. Deborah recalled, "I then heard Tina say, 'Don't worry, honey, Staci is going to sing your part like she did for the first show.' At that point, Beyoncé came on the line and, with this little eight-year-old voice, said, 'Can you pick me up, Miss Deborah? 'Cause I want to sing my own part.' I said, 'But your mommy thinks maybe you're too tired, Beyoncé.' She came back with, 'But I ain't too tired to sing *my* part, Miss Deborah! So please come get me, okay?'"

Family First

I actually think women *can* have it all," Tina was telling Deborah and Denise. Tina had just gotten back from a vacation in the Bahamas with Mathew and the girls, so she was therefore darker than usual and looking even more exotic, her hair in an elaborate French twist. She said that her mother had always held fast to the philosophy that there were no limits to what a woman could do, and that in this regard she was most definitely ahead of her time. When she was younger, Tina said, she thought it was a tall and maybe even impossible order. As a grown woman, however, she no longer felt that way. Now she believed it could be done. "And," she concluded, "I'm trying to do it every day."

The three women were casually enjoying take-out deli sandwiches in the D&D Management offices during a break in the girls' rehearsal. In talking to the business partners, Tina came to realize that she had a good deal in common with them.

First of all, of course, both Deborah and Denise were women of color, both about the same age as Tina.

Denise, divorced, was raising a son, Chad, thirteen. After having worked for sixteen years for Houston Lighting and Power, she'd just been laid off and had received a nice severance package, much of which was now being used to help finance the all-girls revue. Deborah, who was married, had the one daughter, Millicent. Because she was an accountant for the county by trade, her primary responsibility with D&D Management was to keep the books. As a Brownie troop leader and a former pageant contestant herself, she was also familiar with the local venues available for talent shows. Therefore, she sometimes handled the bookings. Moreover, she knew people from regional record labels whom she'd often bring in to see the girls' showcases, all in the hope of perhaps securing a contract.

Deborah and Denise were fascinating counterparts. Deborah was impulsive, blunt, and to the point; she spoke her mind. By contrast, Denise was more careful, measured, and reserved; she was strategic in her thinking. Tina realized early on that both were commanding, independent women who, like herself, had made up their minds that they weren't going to just devote themselves to their spouses and children at the exclusion of their own pursuits. Maybe it was no coincidence that they'd chosen to form and then mold an all-girls revue; after all, they wanted nothing more than to help young women view themselves in a strong and empowered way. There was nothing wrong with staying at home and raising a family, they agreed. However, there was also nothing wrong with wanting more.

"Sometimes it's a madhouse, though, isn't it?" Denise asked Tina. "Trying to keep home and office straight?"

Tina threw her head back and laughed. "Yes," she said, "but I'm a list-maker, and that helps me cut through all the unnecessary bullshit." Tina's language would always be colorful, and she would never apologize for it, either. She added that for her it was all about organization and prioritization, that there was simply no other way. She said that if she left it up to Mathew, the family would probably live in complete and utter chaos. He was more cavalier about the scheduling of his day, Tina said, whereas she was more structured. Her business, she concluded, "ran like clockwork." But still, she allowed, Mathew was a very good provider. "We're actually an amazing team," she concluded.

Within a few years after Beyoncé's birth, Mathew and Tina were financially secure enough to purchase a large, impressive-looking four-bedroom, three-and-a-half-bathroom home with a two-car garage at 3346 Parkwood Drive in Houston's Third Ward. It was an upper-middle-class, mostly integrated neighborhood. "Me and Beyoncé grew up in an area called Third Ward Texas," Solange Knowles once confirmed for a VH1 documentary about Destiny's Child. "There were all of these African-American families, most of them doctors and judges."

At work, Mathew remained competitive and successful. A framed correspondence from Xerox was proudly displayed on the family's fireplace mantel, congratulating him for winning the Salesman of the Year award in 1986 as a result of "being 100 percent or better in each performance category, and generating over $2 million in revenue. You have unquestionably earned the coveted Sales Representative of the Year for the third time in the last four years," it proclaimed. It concluded, "Your sustained excellence in achievement has set an example for everyone associated with Xerox Medical Systems."

As Mathew stayed busy with his burgeoning career, Tina remained at the helm of her hairstyling business, Headliners. Though her husband was pretty much a loner, Tina enjoyed a wide circle of friends. A member of the congregation of St. John's United Methodist Church, she was involved in all sorts of activities there. She was anything but a stay-at-home mom. "In fact, they had a lady who cleaned their house for them," Nicki Taylor recalled, "and I remember as a kid thinking, 'Wow, that's really something.' You didn't see a lot of that in our world at that time. I think Tina made a decision early on that she was not going to be remembered as the wife of a man who did something great with his life. She wanted to do something great too."

Despite their great ambition, though, Tina, Deborah, and Denise agreed that no matter what activities unfolded for them outside of their roles as wives and mothers, nothing was worth sacrificing their domestic lives for.

If her family suffered because of D&D Management, Deborah said, then D&D Management would just have to go. Denise wholeheartedly agreed. Tina said she felt the same about Headliners. "It's ironic," she opined, "that as much as we want to have it all as today's black women, it always goes back to the same family values we've all held for generations. We'd give it all up, every last bit of it, for family, wouldn't we?"

"Family first," Deborah said, raising her soft drink bottle.

"Yes," Tina and Denise agreed, smiling. They clinked Deborah's bottle with their own. "Family first."

Andretta

*W*ithout a doubt, one of the most important figures in the professional career of Beyoncé Knowles was a woman whose great contribution has gone largely unrecognized: Andretta Brown Tillman. Born on March 31, 1958, the eighth of twelve children to Jimmy and Effie Lee Brown in the small town of Whitehouse, Texas, Andretta was an attractive and stylish petite black woman. With her engaging personality and uncanny work ethic, she was popular and well known in her community. Only a few close friends of hers, such as her most trusted confidant, Brian Kenneth Moore—known as Kenny—knew the truth about her. "Sometimes it took every bit of strength she could muster just to get through the day," reflected Moore. "She'd been through a lot and suffered some personal and unspeakable tragedies in her personal life."

Andretta married Dwight Ray Tillman on December 3, 1977, in Whitehouse, at just nineteen. Dwight was twenty-two. Joyous at the thought of their entire lives ahead of them, they happily settled into a small house in Houston, where Dwight would teach at Booker T. Washington High School. Andretta had wanted to work in television as a news anchor, but this was to become a dream deferred when she became pregnant. Her first son, Armon Roshaud, was born in 1980, and then in 1982 came Christopher Raynard. Meanwhile, thanks to Dwight's steady income as well as Andretta's from the Houston Lighting and Power Company, the family was soon able to move into a larger, two-story home in affluent Cypress. In

1984, the Tillman family was completed with the happy arrival of a baby girl they named Shawna Marie.

Though Dwight was a mathematics teacher, he also fancied himself an up-and-coming musical entrepreneur in the fashion of the legendary Berry Gordy Jr. Actually, the manner by which Gordy had built his iconic Motown empire in the late 1950s and into the 1960s had inspired African Americans all over the world. As the civil rights movement influenced the scope of what black people thought possible in their lives and in those of their children, Gordy instituted a sort of automobile assembly-line strategy in Detroit as a model for his own self-mobilized venture, Motown Record Corporation. His artists—such as Diana Ross and the Supremes, the Temptations, the Miracles, and Stevie Wonder—were groomed by mandatory classes in music, choreography, etiquette, and fashion. This was the way Dwight envisioned his own music empire one day, and he shared that dream with Andretta.

In August 1986, Dwight, now thirty-one, decided the time was right to devote himself fully to his ambitions as a talent manager and possibly record producer. Therefore, he left his teaching position. By October, he'd already made several contacts and had his sights set on several bands in Tyler, Texas. He was fully ready to embark on this next phase of his and Andretta's life together. Of course, Andretta stood firmly behind him, anxious to support him in any way possible. It was not meant to be, though. On October 26, 1986, the Tillman family was involved in a horrendous automobile accident in Tyler. The vehicle in which they'd been traveling was hit on the driver's side by a drunk motorist, "spinning the car completely around," as Andretta's brother, Lornanda—known as To-to—would recall it, "and smashing it like a sardine can."

"I heard that the boys, Armon and Chris, were thrown from the car," added Andretta's best friend, Pat Felton, "though they may have been pulled from the wreckage by a passerby. Dwight was not so lucky; he was killed instantly behind the wheel. Ann happened to have had Shawna on her lap; the infant was smashed into her chest. Though paramedics revived Shawna, she died at the scene."

To-to was at his sister's side at her hospital bed when the doctors gave Andretta the terrible news that her husband and baby daughter had been killed. "There's no way to express the devastation," he said. "How do you put that kind of pain into words. There's no way..."

"Ann was hurt so badly, she could barely attend the funerals because of her injuries," continued Pat Felton. She blamed herself for the accident, because she was the one who had wanted to go to Tyler for the holiday, not Dwight. I used to tell her, 'Ann, God just takes people. You can't be held responsible. Nobody is in control.'"

As if fate hadn't already dealt Andretta Tillman enough hardship, within two years of this tragedy she was diagnosed with lupus erythematosus, the autoimmune disease that affects skin, joints, organs, and blood vessels. There was no cure. "This was really a cruel twist," recalled her nephew Belfrey Brown (his father and Andretta were siblings). "How much more could she take? She was only twenty-eight. But she knew she had to go on for her boys. She wasn't going to let it get to her. Her first reaction to the diagnosis was, 'Screw this! I don't want to know nothin' about no lupus.' Really, that's how she looked at it; she wouldn't accept it in her life. Still, she would suffer for years to come, especially when she was under stress— that's when she would have the worst lupus crises. It was bad all around, but my aunt had a kind of courage I don't think I've ever seen in anyone else."

The void in Andretta's life left by Dwight's death was so great that she didn't know quite what to do with herself. She just knew that she didn't want to spend the rest of her life grieving over her late husband while obsessing over her illness. One day, almost as if in some sort of predestined way, she received a telephone call from a friend with whom she attended the Yale Street Baptist Church—Denise Seals. Andretta was aware that Denise had formed a management company with her close friend Deborah Laday, called D&D Management. Denise told her that she had a revue she and Deborah were managing in the Houston area. The acts in it were unpolished, she explained, but there was still something compelling about them. She wondered if perhaps Andretta might be willing to invest in the talent, or maybe even help manage them.

In fact, Andretta—who was still employed by Houston Lighting and Power—knew precious little about show business. Her son Armon recalled, "She knew my dad had wanted to change the world like Berry Gordy, and she started thinking that maybe his dream could, or should, now become hers. She thought, 'Well, look, I have the resources, I have the time, and I have my husband's dream...Maybe I should try to do something with all of it.' That was very much like my mom, ready to take on the world. So she bought a book called *Music Industry 101* and she studied it night and day learning what she could, as fast as she could. That's basically all she had: this doggone book, my dad's dream, some ambition...and a whole lot of hope."

Andretta immediately became interested in a group her brother To-to had started called Tayste, four excellent singers and dancers in the tradition of the male groups popular at that time, such as Boyz II Men. The group also consisted of Harlon Bell, known by his middle name, Keith, who was eighteen and fresh out of high school in Tyler, as well as his brother, Mitchell, and their cousin Alaric Jordan. They ranged in age from eighteen to twenty-two. To-to, who had recently obtained an honorable discharge from the Air Force, convinced Andretta to put a little of her money behind Tayste just to see what might happen. "It was as if all of these coincidences were coming together in a divine way to sort of push my sister into show business," he recalled.

"She had gotten about half a million dollars from Dwight's life insurance policy," Pat Felton recalled, "and about another $40,000 from a different settlement relating to the accident. This was a lot of money. While she was weighing Denise's offer, she started to think that maybe something good could happen as a result of something very bad. She thought Dwight would be happy if she used the money for something he might have wanted. Therefore, she started Tillman Management with the goal of managing singing groups in the Houston area. It was a natural fit. First of all, she was brilliant. She was articulate. She was always well dressed and looked great. I believed she could go very far in show business as a manager."

"You have to see these girls, Ann," Keith Bell told Andretta one morning over breakfast. "I just checked them out at the Sharpstown Mall [in Houston]. They are so good I've decided to work with them, teach them some routines."

"But how good can they be?" Andretta asked. "They're just kids, right?"

"That's what makes them so incredible," Keith explained. "And they have this girl named Beyoncé. She's wild, Ann. You won't believe it when you see her."

"How old is she?"

"I don't know. Eight or nine?"

"Oh my God," Andretta exclaimed. "Eight or nine? I don't know, Keith. That is really young."

It was the summer of 1990, and Keith Bell was trying to sell Andretta Tillman on the all-girls revue Denise Seals had previously mentioned to her. "I was already the choreographer for Tayste," recalled Bell. "Then, when Denise and Deborah started D&D Management, I became their in-house choreographer. So I was just this young and determined kid dancer anxious to help them make things happen."

"I think they need money, Ann," Keith said. "Maybe you could back them or something? Would you at least meet with them?"

"Well, okay, I'll meet with them," Andretta said, with no small amount of hesitation. "But I can't promise anything. I'll call Denise and set up a meeting."

A few days later, Andretta did as promised: She called Denise, who arranged a meeting with Deborah at the D&D Management office. When Denise finally introduced Andretta to Deborah, the chemistry between the two women was instantaneous. Andretta, with her dazzling smile and dancing brown eyes, made an immediate impression. In fact, the three women seemed a great team from the very beginning. They were about the same age, each in their early thirties, each an independent, formidable African-American woman with a desire to do something unusual with her life—to be in the show business management game.

After Andretta agreed to invest, Deborah said that what mattered most to her was that the three of them worked together as a team. She suggested that they always have each other's backs, because "who knows what we'll be up against out there? This is a dirty business," she concluded, "but as a team I know we can do it if we just stick together. Agreed, ladies?"

The three women shook hands; they had a deal.

Ninth Birthday

*I*t was Tuesday night, September 4, 1990, in Dallas.

"But what do you mean, I can't see Beyoncé?" Tina Knowles was asking. "*Of course* I can see my child."

"I'm sorry, but there's no way," responded a very distracted Deborah Laday. Deborah had a lot on her mind while backstage at a community center. As she busily fielded questions from stagehands about sound and lighting cues, anxious little girls tugged on her skirt and wondered about the songs they were about to sing. Meanwhile, parents, like Tina, were demanding to see their daughters to wish them luck before their performance. Still, despite all of the chaos, Deborah managed to comport herself with calm authority. "Look, Beyoncé is fixin' to perform," she told Tina. "Plus, I'm trying to keep this area back here clear!"

"But this is her *birthday*. She's nine today!" Tina exclaimed. Though

Tina was now thirty-six years old, she looked far younger, maybe in her early twenties. Her light brown skin still had a youthful, luminescent quality. Her hair was curly and chestnut-colored, now styled in a short, jazzy bob. Her makeup was expertly done, her favorite shade of red lipstick framing a full and dazzling smile, light blue eye shadow above green eyes. According to photos taken that evening, she was wearing a white blouse, sleeves cut at elbow length, with white silk pants and a large gold metallic belt cinching her waist. Long, dangly earrings matched her belt. Clutching her hand was four-year-old Solange, now a cute little tyke in pigtails. Tina would recall this evening with vivid clarity in a sworn deposition and subsequent affidavit she would give twelve years later, in 2002.

"Tina, you don't get it," Deborah said, an edge to her tone. "The moments before a big show are *crucial.*" She added that Beyoncé needed to focus and couldn't risk any distractions. She suggested that Tina wait until after the show to see her. "I hope that's okay," Deborah said apologetically. As she rushed off, she said that she hated to be so short, but that she had a job to do and she needed to get back to it

Tina wasn't used to being told no. In fact, she could probably count on one hand the times she'd accepted it as an answer. She seemed to have met her match in Deborah, though, and she didn't much like it. Although they'd started off on a nice footing, Tina would take a dim view of Deborah after this day, and once Tina Knowles had her mind made up about someone, it was difficult to move her from that viewpoint. Now silently seething, she stood in the hallway leading to the dressing room where the girls could be heard noisily changing into their costumes. Meanwhile, ticket holders began to stream into the five-hundred-seat auditorium. They'd come to see the free show hosted by Deborah and Denise, their so-called ultimate masterpiece: M-1, Destiny, and Girls Tyme.

As Tina stood in the hallway debating whether to heed Deborah's advice or just go ahead and find her daughter, she heard a voice behind her. "How can I help you?" It was Andretta Tillman. After making her acquaintance, Tina explained to Andretta the problem at hand. With a warm smile, Andretta said she absolutely agreed with her. "A mother *should* be able to see her child on such an important day," she said. She then suggested that Tina follow her; she would take her back to see her little girl.

Tina followed Andretta behind a curtain and down a long hallway, holding Solange's hand the entire way. "The kids are in there," Andretta told her when they finally reached a room at the end of the hall. "Obviously,"

Tina said with a chuckle. One could plainly hear gales of laughter on the other side of the door.

After Andretta opened the door, Tina and Solange walked in and quickly surveyed the room in search of Beyoncé. They found her sitting alone in front of a mirror gazing at her reflection. Her dark brown hair, parted in the middle, fell into long pigtails with russet-brown silk ribbons on both sides of her head. Wearing gold lamé pants and a white blouse, she was an adorable, very small girl with light skin and perfect features. As soon as she saw their image reflected in the mirror, she whirled around. "Mommy! Solange!" she exclaimed as she jumped to her feet. After she ran to her mother and sister, they all embraced in a group hug. "We just wanted to come back and wish you a happy birthday, Beyoncé," Tina said, kneeling down to the child's level. "And good luck!" She bussed her on the forehead. When Solange asked if she was nervous, Beyoncé shook her head and simply answered, "Nope."

"Then you just go out there and knock 'em dead," Tina said. She told her that they would be watching from seats in the front row, which Mathew was presently saving for them. "Okay, Mommy," Beyoncé said with a big smile.

After just a few more moments, Tina and Solange said their goodbyes, told Beyoncé how much they loved her, and then left her with her little friends in the dressing room. Keith Bell then gathered all of the girls and began working with them on last-minute changes to one of their many dance routines.

With Andretta at her side, Tina walked back down the hallway on her way out of the backstage area. "Are you a mom, Ann?" Tina asked as she reached for Solange's hand. Andretta said she was the mother of two young boys, Armon and Chris. This pleased Tina. She said she hoped Andretta would join the management team, "because we could always use another mother's touch. Deborah and Denise are mothers, too, you know?"

"Well, there can never be enough mothers, I guess," Andretta said, laughing.

"Ain't that the truth!" Tina exclaimed. She then entwined her arm around Andretta's as the two walked into the crowded auditorium. Already it was as if they were good friends.

Crossroads

*T*hree days passed. Now it was Friday afternoon, September 7, 1990.

The show Tuesday night had gone very well. Tina and Mathew knew that Beyoncé had done her best, and in fact, they believed her to be the only one onstage who truly had any talent. Her voice was quite a wonder, as were her performing skills. Now the Knowleses were sitting with a group of other parents on the curb under a blazing hot sun in front of a small office building. Everyone looked disgruntled. "Ain't this something?" Tina asked. "We drove all the way out here, and for what?" Mathew forced a smile and regarded his wife thoughtfully. "Well, you know, these things happen," was all he could say.

This afternoon, Mathew was wearing a black gabardine suit that hung on him with precision; clearly it had been tailored by one of the best clothiers in Houston. A starched white shirt and pearl-gray silk tie finished the look. His large-framed glasses gave him a professorial look. He had taken time away from work to meet Tina.

After the show the other night, the parents of the performers had all congregated backstage and, in a quick meeting, agreed that Deborah Laday and Denise Seals needed help. They wanted to discuss their children's future with the two managers and then take a vote to decide how to proceed. All agreed that Deborah and Denise had worked hard for the last six months. However, they feared that maybe the women didn't have the financial resources to take the girls to the next level of success.

One might have thought the parents would have given Deborah and Denise a bit more latitude since it had only been six months since they began working with the girls. Were these kids to become stars overnight? However, the parents' impatience was tied to the urgency many of them felt about seeing their children become famous. The Knowleses were the exceptions. Mathew had a good job and was making excellent money for the times. Tina had Headliners, and though business was spotty, she was still able to turn a good profit. The Knowleses lived in a fashionable home and had two very nice luxury vehicles. They didn't need Beyoncé to become successful in order for them to sustain their good life. However, the other parents had different stories and if their daughters' talent was to be a possible solution to their fiscal problems, there was no time to waste.

Therefore, they made an appointment with the managers, and then took the drive to the bucolic suburb of Greater Greenspoint where Deborah and Denise had their D&D Management office space and rehearsal studio.

The parents were used to this trek to Greater Greenspoint, which could be anywhere from thirty to forty-five minutes each way. After all, every night, after their daughters finished some of their homework, they would drop them off at this very location, usually at about 6:00 p.m. The girls would then practice with Keith Bell until about 9:00—taking frequent homework breaks—and then the parents would have to retrieve them.

On this day, the parents assembled at the appointed hour in the middle of the afternoon while their children were still in school. They waited outside for the entire group to assemble—eight parents in all. When everyone was present, the contingent walked across a wide courtyard to the office complex in which D&D Management was housed. But at their destination, much to their dismay, they found something they did not expect: a padlock on the door and an eviction notice! "Everyone was pretty frustrated at that point," Tina Knowles would later recall. "That's the last thing we expected. I remember standing at that door, looking at that padlock, and thinking, 'Oh no! You have *got* to be kidding me.'"*

"We can't even tell Beyoncé about this goddamn thing," Mathew said, according to Tina's memory.

"Why?" Tina asked.

"Because I don't want to discourage her," he said. He then explained that he felt they should keep anything from her that would make her not want to give her all to the endeavor. She was a very determined little girl and he wanted to keep it that way.

It was certainly true that even at the age of nine, Beyoncé was laser-focused on one goal: She wanted to sing. For instance, Deborah and Denise had recently aligned themselves with Pro-Line and Soft & Beautiful products, leading hair care lines for women and girls of color. After looking at pictures of all the girls, the company wanted to audition LaTavia for national commercials and print advertising campaigns. Rather than single out her own daughter, LaTavia's mother, Cheryl Mitchell, felt that

---

* Though Tina Knowles, under oath on March 22, 2002, provided the account as outlined, Deborah Laday and Denise Seals insist that they were never threatened with eviction from their office space. Neither Laday or Seals have any memory of a time when their office was padlocked.

all of the group members should audition. "So we all piled into a fifteen-passenger van and went to Dallas to meet with the Pro-Line executives," LaTavia recalled. All of the girls were excited about auditioning, except for Beyoncé. "It's just not what I want to do," she said. There was no mistaking that she wasn't a little girl who just wanted to be in show business and would settle for any venue. She wanted to be a singer, and that was it. (Incidentally, LaTavia was hired for the job and became the face of Pro-Line for young girls for the next ten years.)

On this hot, summer afternoon, judging from the grim expressions on the faces of the other couples—all of them sitting on the curb, lined up in single file—similar conversations about the children's futures were taking place.

"But did you hear how hoarse her voice was this morning at breakfast?" Tina asked. Mathew nodded. Tina said that when she asked Beyoncé about the hoarseness, she told her that she had to sing all of the girls' parts while teaching them.

"Yeah, but sacrifice is the name of this game," Mathew said. According to Tina's later testimony, he then asked her about the woman she'd met at the recent show in Dallas—Andretta Tillman. He wondered if she was "on the up-and-up." Tina said she "seemed nice" but that she wasn't sure what to make of her, at least not yet. As they continued to talk, Mathew mentioned that he wasn't "crazy" about Deborah Laday, noting that every time he had a conversation with her, he liked her just a little bit less. Tina agreed, saying that she liked Denise more. "But who down here in the South knows how to manage singing groups anyway?" Mathew asked. "Shit! We're in Houston. This sure ain't Hollywood."

Years later Tina would recall, "The next day, we all took a vote and decided that Andretta definitely should come in as a manager. We weren't sure she would accept the job, though. Then one day soon after she called me and said that, yes, she was going to be co-managing the girls with Deborah and Denise. She said she had a producer and a songwriter and that she was going to pay for some studio time. This was exciting. I was happy, as was Mathew. We definitely started to feel a lot better about things for Beyoncé."

Fine-Tuning

*W*hile the concept Deborah and Denise had for their "Ultimate Masterpiece" revue was a solid and entertaining one, it was also a little unwieldy. There was a "hype-master," there were dancers, and there were singers. Some were good, some not so good. When she finally saw it, Andretta thought the package needed to be pared down and fine-tuned. "The dancing is great, but there are just too many moving parts," was how she put it. "Too many girls doing too many things, and some not very well." Since she was now the primary investor, she had latitude to do whatever she felt was best. That's where Alonzo Jackson came into the picture.

Alonzo, whom everyone knew as Lonnie, was a young, ambitious, and immensely talented writer and producer from East Oakland, California, whom Deborah had earlier met at Ultimate Sound recording studios in Houston. He describes himself as having been "twenty-one years old and hungry as hell, having only been in Houston for a short time. Creative and eager to be heard, I was producing local talent at Ultimate Sound and also acting as an engineer there. Anybody who had ears to sit down and listen to my ideas, to what I believed in, I was willing to talk to. Andretta was one of those people. Deborah and I had just started talking about things when she brought in Andretta, and then Andretta became the main contact."

To also work with the team, Lonnie recruited Anthony Moore, whom everyone called Tony Mo., a talented young songwriter who was raised in Missouri City and also worked at Ultimate Sound. "We ended up being good friends and great collaborators," Lonnie said of Tony Mo. "We fed off each other, me doing the music, him doing the lyrics. It was a good marriage."

Andretta's idea was to pare down the three separate acts in Deborah and Denise's revue into one very strong vocal and dancing group. It would be up to Lonnie then to take a look at all of the youngsters and decide which could stay and which had to go. Then new girls would be auditioned to replace the ones who didn't make the cut.

Lonnie immediately decided he wasn't interested in working with Millicent Laday, Deborah's daughter, known as M-1, the act's DJ. Thus she was the first to go. Deborah understood; it was a business decision, and she would see what she could do with her daughter on her own. In fact, Milli-cent would continue her career as "M-1, Tha [sic] Lyrical Mistress."

From the group called Destiny, Lonnie released Chris Lewis. However, he decided to keep dancers Nicki and Nina Taylor and their cousin, rapper LaTavia Roberson. "I liked LaTavia a lot," he recalled. "She had this great, big personality and attitude. I was a fan of that kid's right away."

From the group Girls Tyme, Lonnie let Staci LaToisen and Jennifer Young go. That left only Beyoncé. "I then needed to find two girls to sing with Beyoncé," Lonnie recalled. "The vision Andretta and I shared was to create a group around Beyoncé that had the old-school harmonies of a rhythm-and-blues sister act from Chicago called the Emotions and the con-temporary edge of two other girl groups popular in the late 1980s and early 1990s—En Vogue and SWV."

To that end, Lonnie and Andretta added Kelendria Rowland, known as Kelly. At ten, Kelly was bashful and unsure of herself, but her tone was clear as a bell. Though they felt she sounded like a young Whitney Houston, they never intended for her to sing lead. Rather, she would be a backing singer. "I had some doubts about Kelly, if you want to know the truth," Lon-nie said. "But there was just something about her. I felt like I wanted to give her a chance, a shot, you know?"

They also added Ashley Davis, eleven. The complete opposite of Kelly in personality, Ashley was outgoing and precocious. She had a strong voice and little trouble using it. Lonnie knew he had found someone special in her, a second lead singer with Beyoncé. "Ashley was a real discovery," he recalled. "There was a grown-up quality about her that intrigued me. She had a surprising amount of power in her voice. When I heard her sing, I knew right away I wanted her to be included in the act."

Ashley was an interesting counterpoint to Beyoncé. Whereas Beyoncé sounded like a young girl who could sing, Ashley sounded like a seasoned adult. She actually had more range than Beyoncé. In some ways, she rep-resented what Beyoncé would morph into with time. When the two girls traded leads in early rehearsals, the way they played off one another seemed natural and effortless. "I think they were a good team," LaTavia Roberson recalled. "They had a great blend. There was something about the two of them that inspired the rest of us. In a sense, they were both so good they made the rest of us want to work even harder."

And so it happened that by the fall of 1990, Andretta Tillman and Lon-nie Jackson finally had their girls' group—three singers, Beyoncé, Kelly, and Ashley; one rapper, LaTavia; and two dancers, Nicki and Nina. Lonnie and Andretta liked the idea of the name Girls Tyme, so it was decided to keep it. Thus the six girls became the new, streamlined, and easier-to-digest version of Girls Tyme. "It was a good, viable package," Lonnie Jackson recalled. "I felt that with Andretta managing, me producing, and Tony Mo. writing, we could really take this group right to the top."

"A Family We Get to Choose"

*H*ow does one ever get over the loss of a child? Andretta Tillman had been asking herself that question ever since her infant daughter, Shawna, was taken from her by a drunk driver. With her husband, Dwight, also gone, she was forced to think of her family in smaller terms—now it was just her and her boys, Armon and Chris. "We were everything to my mother," Armon would later recall. "Family mattered to her so much, and we had our own little unit. We were fractured. We were damaged. But thanks to my mother, what was left of us still felt bound together."

"Still, there was a hole in her heart; she missed Dwight and Shawna," Andretta's other son, Chris, recalled. Though there wasn't anything Andretta could do to completely fill the void left by Dwight, she tried to compensate for the loss of Shawna by taking on the youngsters in Girls Tyme as surrogate daughters. Chris remembered, "She began to love each of those girls as if they were her own. Actually, it was when Girls Tyme started practicing at our house that we started to feel like maybe our family wasn't so ruined, like maybe there was some hope for the future."

"As I came to know Ann, it was apparent to me that Girls Tyme filled the emptiness in her heart left by Shauna," recalled Kenny Moore. "These little girls filled her house and her heart. Every day she was with them, the more time she spent with them, the more she loved them. Her life soon began to revolve around this newfound love affair with not one little girl, but six of them. There were actually times that Ann would call Shauna's name instead of one of the girls' names and have to quickly correct herself. 'Shawna...oh my Lord, I mean...*Beyoncé*, you missed a step!' In spirit, I came to believe that each girl represented some aspect of Shawna.

Andretta loved and supported them as if it was Shawna she was loving and supporting."

Girls Tyme would spend as much time as possible in rehearsals at Andretta's home now, instead of at D&D Management. Deborah and Denise were still involved, but they became much less prominent once Andretta began taking over. Most, if not all, of the girls' business started filtering through Andretta's company, Tillman Management. Not only did the group quickly become attached to the ambitious but maternal woman they now called "Miss Ann," but their parents also started to trust her. They marveled at the way their daughters blossomed under her careful tutelage. "Not taking anything away from Beyoncé, because she's obviously an amazing performer," Kenny Moore observed, "but the fact is that she was not born to be a star. Nobody is *born* to be a star. She was *taught* to be a star by Andretta. She was just receptive to the teaching. If you want to keep it real, that's keeping it real."

"Chris and I were just little boys at the time, but I remember we had a second level on our house that we could stand up on and look down into the living room," recalled Armon Tillman. "We used to watch the girls perform, and my mom was always right on top of them, telling them what to do, how to act, keeping their spirits up, even giving them a sense of self-worth. 'Beyoncé, it's too much, pull back,' she would always be heard saying. Or, 'Kelly, you need to give more. You're not putting yourself out there enough.' In terms of discipline, my mom was old-school. It was the same with me and my brother as it was for the girls—just a very severe look was all you needed from my mom to know that you needed to get right."

"I remember that it was the same routine every day," Beyoncé recalled. "We would get home from school and then race over to rehearsal at Miss Ann's. Some days we wouldn't even go home first, we'd just go straight to practice. We loved it so much, we couldn't get enough of it. That first year, we did a lot of shows. So it was just practice, practice, *practice*. Someone told me in school that practice makes perfect, and I remember thinking by the beginning of 1991, 'Well, we must be pretty darn perfect by now, 'cause we sure have practiced enough!'"

"We had this big guy in our group named A. J. Alarich, who was maybe three hundred pounds," recalled Keith Bell of Tayste. "What a singer this guy was! He had such incredible range. When he would do something really cool, Beyoncé would put her little nine-year-old hands on her hips, give him a sassy look, and say, '*I hate you!*' That's the sound *I* want! Now how'd you get that sound?' It was all in fun, but we all knew she really wanted his range and was still too young to develop it. '*Dang!*' she would say to A.J., 'that's what I *love*. That's how I want to sound. I sure hope I don't have to gain three hundred pounds to sound that way, though!'"

Despite the unpredictable nature of their lives in those days, the Tillman sons still felt not only secure but also somehow attached to something that seemed vitally important. Indeed, the fulfillment of their mother's dreams had become the family's new mandate. "This is our lives now, boys," Andretta told them. They couldn't do anything about what had happened in the past, she said, because it had all been God's divine plan. They couldn't even question it, she told them. It was actually one of the rare times Andretta even referred to the accident that had so completely transformed their lives. It simply wasn't something she felt comfortable discussing, even with her own sons.

"It's not fair what happened to us," Chris said.

"Life's not fair," Andretta told him. "But look at us now," she added, "and look at all of the people we have surrounding us who love us: the girls... their parents. If you think about it, we have a whole new family," she concluded, "a family we get to choose."

Buckin' and Poppin'

*G*irls Tyme—Beyoncé, Kelly, LaTavia, Ashley, Nicki, and Nina—quickly formed an overnight sisterhood. There was no jealousy between them; they didn't seem to care who sang lead and who didn't, as long as they were singing together. "Singing with your best friends, there's nothing better when you're a little kid," Beyoncé once recalled. "Every day felt like summer vacation."

Recalled Nina Taylor, "We were always teasing each other like sisters. I remember we used to tease Beyoncé because she didn't like boys. She was only nine or ten. I don't know what it was like for her at school, but after our shows the boys liked her a lot. But she was like, 'Oh, gross! Get them away from me!'"

At this time, 1991, Beyoncé was completing the fourth grade at Parker Elementary, an academy specifically designed for students interested in and excelling in music. There were some problems at the school, though. For instance, Mathew and Tina knew that the choral director there, Cindy Pack, was annoyed with Beyoncé for not committing to the school's choir. After joining, Beyoncé had lost interest in it. She was too individual a performer to be in a choir anyway. Once, she had a small solo at a choral presentation, but didn't show up for it. Mathew and Tina didn't know about it, or they most certainly would have made sure she was present. Beyoncé wanted to sing, if not by herself, with one or two others, but definitely not in a chorus where she couldn't be heard. She was very clear about it. Another teacher, Miss Preston, complained to Tina that Beyoncé was not doing her homework. Tina explained that the problem was that Beyoncé didn't have time for homework; she was always practicing or performing.

While Mathew and Tina wanted Beyoncé to have a good education, it wasn't at the expense of her singing. In that respect the teachers at Parker were becoming a bit of a hassle. Finally Tina just told Cindy Pack that Beyoncé would not be returning for the fifth grade. They'd find another school with less structure.

In the fifth through seventh grades, Beyoncé would attend two private Catholic schools—St. Mary of the Purification in Houston and St. James the Apostle in nearby Spring. (She would also attend the High School for the Performing and Visual Arts for a very short time.) The eighth and some of the ninth grade would find Beyoncé attending Welch Middle School, a public school. Then she would drop out and be tutored or homeschooled. She was happy about that turn of events, never feeling that she ever really "belonged" to a student body.

"Beyoncé was just so shy," LaTavia Roberson said. "She had to really know you before she let you in. But once you were friends with her, you knew you could trust her. You could say, 'Beyoncé, I need to talk to you about something,' and you knew it was going to stay between the two of you. She wouldn't tell the other girls if you asked her not to. She was very family-oriented and wanted us to always be together. She didn't have any other friends, actually. It was just us girls. We would ask, 'What about the kids in school, are you friends with them too?' And she would say, 'Nope. I don't know any of them.'"

The Knowleses had an apartment over the garage, overlooking their backyard, that was sometimes used as a guesthouse. The girls would often have slumber parties there, feeling so grown up in their own little home. Nina recalled, "Mathew would say, 'Y'all stay in the apartment. Don't y'all come into the main house and wake everyone up, hear?' In the middle of the night, we would play Truth or Dare. Beyoncé would say, 'I *dare* you to go into the main house and get some ice.' And we would all be, like, 'No *way*! Mathew will kill us!'

Meanwhile, fun times aside, there was always business at hand. Almost immediately, Ashley became more of a focal point of the group, to the exclusion of Beyoncé. It wasn't a conscious decision on Andretta's or Lonnie's part. When Andretta booked the girls to sing at places like the Sharpstown or Greenspoint malls, Ashley was just so good, she *had* to be more featured. Beyoncé didn't seem to mind, but even if she had it wouldn't have altered the decision. Andretta and Lonnie felt sure they knew what they were doing, and the children certainly weren't going to be dictating anything to them. However, the challenge Ashley presented was that even though she was an exceptional vocalist, she didn't have much stage presence. Maybe that's why producer Lonnie Jackson couldn't help but secretly gravitate toward Beyoncé.

"Even though she wasn't singing lead, Beyoncé was—wow!—from the beginning she was just so soulful," Lonnie recalled. "She wasn't as polished as Ashley. But she had passion, and it somehow didn't seem natural for a little kid to have that kind of passion. You watched her and thought, 'This little girl has got something special, something memorable.' You felt about her the same way you felt about Michael Jackson when you first saw him perform on television.

"In fact, I spent many afternoons with Beyoncé watching Michael Jackson videos as part of her development," Lonnie added. "She would study those videos like schoolwork, extracting movements and ideas that she wanted to incorporate into Girls Tyme. I also talked to her about music history because I wanted her to know where Michael and Prince had come from, how they were influenced by people like Jackie Wilson and James Brown. I wanted her to understand how Diana Ross came to be, what influences shaped her. I wanted her to know that she was part of a bigger context, that if she was going to be in this business, she should understand who came before her. She was curious about all of it, just wanting to learn as much as she could. Looking back, I think I had it in the back of my mind that this girl was going to end up being the focus, that we were just waiting for her to grow up a little."

"What's goin' on with that girl in front next to Ashley?" Kenny Moore asked one day during rehearsal. By this time, Andretta had brought Kenny into the fold to help her manage Girls Tyme. Kenny, a former singer in the military with a group called Black Satin, had great instincts when it came to show business. Like everyone else on the team, he had no real experience. However, what he did have was drive, ambition, and very good taste. He was also upbeat and positive, always with a smile and an encouraging word. His relationship with Andretta was so close, some people actually thought they were siblings. He would always go the extra mile for the woman he lovingly called "'Dretta."

"Oh, that's Bey," Andretta said of Beyoncé, according to Kenny's memory. "She's somethin' else, that one."

"I'll say," Kenny agreed, "but, 'Dretta, why's she buckin' so damn hard?" he asked, tickled at the sight. "She's really goin' to town with those dance moves."

"She's enthusiastic, all right," Andretta observed. "But that's just Bey. Offstage she's shy, but once onstage, she's a different girl."

"But all that buckin' and poppin' she's doing is pulling focus from Ashley," Kenny observed. "It also makes the other girls look like they're not working as hard."

Andretta had to agree. "That Beyoncé," she concluded, "she's one little fast-tail girl, all right."

If she wasn't "buckin' so damn hard," a very young Beyoncé could be found sitting alone, pensively writing song lyrics. "We used to have this exercise where we'd put the girls in a room and have them put pen to paper and try to write their own songs," recalled Tony Mo. "One by one, each girl would give up and leave the room. I'd finally come into the room and Beyoncé would be the only one left. 'I'm done,' she'd say. 'Well, cool, let me hear it,' I'd tell her. And damn it if she hadn't written a pretty decent song!"

"You would listen to her lyrics and think, 'Not bad. Not bad at all,'" Belfrey Brown recalled. "On the one hand you would think, 'Isn't it cute the way that little girl is so serious about her music?' But then on the other you would think, 'Hold up! That little girl *sure is serious about her music.*'"

When she wasn't writing, she was still studying Andretta's other act, Tayste, as they rehearsed. To-to, Andretta's brother, who was a member of the group, recalled, "So, we'd be rehearsing, right? And this little kid, Beyoncé Knowles, would be sitting and watching and taking notes. And I was like, 'What's up with that?' Then, when I would hear her rehearse with Girls Tyme, sure enough, she had my licks down pat, I mean, perfect. I told the guys, 'Man, that little kid over there, that one on the end, she's stealing from us! I ain't kiddin' either.' We'd ask her, 'Beyoncé, why are you here when we're practicing? Go find your girls.' And she would look at me innocently and say, 'But I'm just watchin'. I ain't doin' nothin'.' But, oh yeah," he concluded, chuckling, "she was doin' something, all right."

First Recording Session

*A*t the beginning of 1991, Andretta Tillman and Lonnie Jackson arranged for Girls Tyme to go into the recording studio for the first time and cut some songs. This of course was a big deal; everyone was excited. The intention was to record a tune called "Sunshine," which, as produced by Lonnie, would go on to become the group's signature song. "That was actually a very good song," Beyoncé would recall years later, calling it "our 'Heal the World' type song." The recording would be made at Digital Services Recording Studio in Houston, a major establishment, not some small mom-and-pop operation. In years to come, Destiny's Child would either record or mix many of their best songs there.

Mathew and Tina accompanied Beyoncé, who was still nine, to the session, with Solange, of course, in tow.

By this time, Solange, who was barely four, had pretty much decided that she too wanted to be a singer and songwriter. She carried with her a notebook in which she jotted down poems whenever they came to her. Mathew was more encouraging of her aspirations than Tina was. "I know Beyoncé's got talent, but you should see what Solange can do," he told Kenny Moore one day. "She's a star too." The next day, Mathew brought Solange to rehearsal. During a break, he pushed her into the middle of the room. "Go on and sing that song you were singing at home," he told her. Though she was extremely bashful, the youngster closed her eyes and sang. "See," Mathew said proudly, "I told you! Better get her now while she's hot." Kenny Moore recalled, "I thought to myself, yeah, well, Mathew you'd better just keep ridin' the horse you're already on, okay?" After Solange's impromptu audition, Tina asked Mathew to wait a little longer before working with her. She had already started to have concerns about how fast things were moving for Beyoncé, and if it were up to her, Solange would focus on some other aspiration—*any* other aspiration.

During the recording session, Mathew, Tina, Solange, and the other girls' family members all watched on one side of a glass booth as their daughters worked out the harmonic arrangements of the songs on the other. Lonnie and Tony Mo. coached them every step along the way. Lonnie was a perfectionist, eager to make sure everything was just right. Tony Mo. was more patient with the girls, carefully explaining his ideas behind the songs and doing whatever he could to get the girls excited about and then invested in the material. Of course, Andretta was present too, as were Deborah Laday and Denise Seals.

"What I found intriguing right away was that even though she had a cold or an allergy that day, somehow she rose above it," recalled Tony Mo. of Beyoncé. "Most kids are whiny when they're sick. Not her—she forced herself to sing even when she could barely talk."

Actually, throughout her life, Beyoncé has suffered from severe sinus problems. Armon Tillman recalls, "Okay, this is gross kid stuff, but it's true. Her nose was stuffed up all the time. It was an ongoing problem. She would lay a sheet of paper down on the floor and then stand over it. Then she'd put pressure on one nostril with her index finger and blow out. And the snot would just go flying. She'd do the same with the other nostril. We'd all say, 'Beyoncé, that is just *nasty*,' and she'd laugh and said, '*I know!* But if y'all want me to sing, this is what I gotta do! Turn y'all backs if you don't wanna see it.'"

"Sometimes, before she would practice, she would lay on the couch with her head hanging off it," recalled Nina Taylor, "and she would put her thumb on the roof of her mouth and just wait for her sinuses to drain. Miss Ann would say, 'Come on, Beyoncé! We gotta get to work,' and she would say, 'Y'all get started. If my sinuses are messed up, so's my voice!' I remember so many times she would be laying on the couch with one hand in her mouth, and the other snapping us on cue as we sang and danced. She'd be draining and spitting and counting, all at the same time, at the age of about nine. ("My nose runs a lot," Beyoncé, as an adult, has said, "and when you're singing, you can't blow it. So, there have been moments"—she laughed—"when I've had the occasional bubble." As it happened, Beyoncé would record her popular 2013 song "XO" while sick with a sinus infection. She liked the rawness and imperfection of her performance, though, which is why she decided not to redo it. The vocal she recorded while ill was ultimately the one released to the public.)

What's probably most compelling about the final product of "Sunshine" is the contrast between Ashley's and Beyoncé's voices. In this feel-good midtempo song, Ashley immediately commandeers the recording with her opening lines. When Beyoncé finally comes in for her middle lead, hers is clearly a different sound; it's not nearly as developed as Ashley's. However, what Beyoncé lacks in style, she makes up for in conviction. The girls also recorded an upbeat new jack swing number song called "Say It Ain't So," lyrics by Tony Mo. and music by Lonnie Jackson.

This environment was a whole new world for Girls Tyme as they were exposed not only to the recording process but to elements of the music business they'd never before known. "I used to smoke a lot of weed back in those days," Tony Mo. recalled. "I would go outside to write, smoke a little, write a little, and Beyoncé would come out and find me and innocently ask, 'So, whatchu' doin' out here, Tony?' I would quickly hide the joint and, searching the sky, I'd casually lie, 'Oh, I'm just out here talkin' to the birds, Bey.' Though she was just a little kid, she was on to me. From that point on, whenever anyone couldn't find me, Beyoncé would say, 'Oh, Tony's probably just outside talkin' to them birds again.'"

"All of this is pretty damn great," Mathew Knowles said to Lonnie and Tony Mo. when the recording session was finally completed. He seemed a little starstruck by the proceedings. "This is very professional, top-of-the line stuff, isn't it?" he asked as the producer and songwriter began to pack up the tapes.

"Only the best for these kids," Lonnie said.

Mathew then asked the men what they thought of Beyoncé. They both agreed that she was coming along nicely, but hastened to point out that *all* of the girls were making progress. Though Mathew said he couldn't argue with that conclusion, he added that he felt Beyoncé was "just a little more special" than Ashley.

"Yeah, but Ashley has an incredible maturity to her sound," Andretta observed as she approached the fellows. She quickly added that she enjoyed the way the two girls worked together, and then complimented Lonnie and Tony Mo. on the concept.

Mathew didn't look very convinced. "She's all right," he said of Ashley, "but Beyoncé, now *she's* got something Ashley doesn't have. I mean, am I nuts, or what?"

"Not nuts," Andretta said with a tolerant smile, "but maybe a little biased."

With a smile of his own, Mathew agreed that Andretta was probably right. Besides, he said, he trusted that she and her team knew what they were doing. "I'm just a parent carrying my kids' stuff around from one place to the next," he offered. However, he couldn't help but add that, in his opinion anyway, Beyoncé should probably get a little more play. It was just a suggestion, he said. As he walked away from them, Lonnie, Tony Mo., and Andretta looked at one other with raised eyebrows. "That was sort of interesting, huh?" Tony Mo. observed.

"Yeah," Lonnie said. "Very interesting. What do you think that was about?"

Andretta seemed a little troubled. "I think we need to watch out for Mathew Knowles, that's what I think," she finally concluded. "I definitely got my eye on Beyoncé's daddy. Trust."

California Bound

One evening in the summer of 1991, Beyoncé Knowles came home from rehearsal at Andretta's with a big announcement. As she sat at the dinner table with Mathew, Tina, and Solange, she exclaimed, "Guess what? We're going to California."

Tina looked at her daughter with surprise. "Says who?" she asked.

"Says Miss Ann," Beyoncé responded.

After dinner, Mathew telephoned Andretta to find out what she had in mind. Andretta said that her late husband had once told her about a West Coast talent gathering called the Gavin Convention, also known as the Gavin Seminar for Media Professionals. Calling upon an important contact of hers in California, Teresa LaBarbera Whites, who worked as an A&R scout for Sony (artist and repertoire is the division of a record company that signs new talent and assists acts already on the label), Andretta was able to book a coveted slot for Girls Tyme at the convention, which was coming up in July. This gig promised to expose them to a wide range of record company executives. There would also be an array of performers from a cross-section of musical genres, including LL Cool J representing hip-hop. Andretta explained that she was going to pay not only for the children's airfares and accommodations, but also for the parents'. Mathew couldn't help but be not only intrigued but impressed.

The next evening, Andretta invited all of the parents to attend rehearsal at her home, after which she explained the details about the trip. They had about five weeks to get ready for the show, she said. They would need to perform three songs. "Are you girls game?" she asked, looking at the group. With wide eyes and big smiles, they all nodded enthusiastically.

As the date neared, the girls rehearsed their songs day and night. "By this time, we were performing at my mother's shop, Headliners, every other day for the customers there," Beyoncé recalled. "Looking back on it, you have to feel badly for those poor women. My mother would say, 'Okay now, here's Girls Tyme, so enjoy, y'all. And it didn't matter whether they liked us or not, they were obligated to applaud. It was good for our egos but maybe not so good for the customers," she concluded, laughing.

"You would be amazed at how much we learned by performing in Miss Tina's shop," LaTavia Roberson adds. "They would sit there with their arms folded across their chest as if to say, 'Okay, little girls. Let me see what you got.' You really had to show them something. But looking back on it now, I don't think Miss Tina would have had us out there singing if she didn't think we could deliver. She was very protective of us and would've hated to see us criticized by anyone, especially at that age. We always delivered, though. Then, after we sang, everyone would compliment us as Miss Tina handed us brooms and made us sweep hair from the floor."

"At this same time, we started this program we called 'Boot Camp,'" Tony Mo. recalled. "It was mostly Lonnie's idea. He worked the girls hard every day, even having them sing while jogging so they wouldn't get winded while dancing and singing onstage. We prepared hard for this convention."

The weekend before the show, Andretta took the youngsters to have their hair styled at Headliners and their nails done. At a local clothing store, she purchased sparkly white tuxedo jackets with shoulder pads and silk blouses and bow ties for the girls to wear onstage, along with stretch pants and matching patent leather Mary Jane shoes. It was a good look for them, a Motown-infused, Jackson 5 kind of image. By hand, Andretta and Tina then added sequins and purple appliqué to the outfits so that they would pop under the spotlights. The two women spent hours on the couch at Tina's home, sipping coffee and laughing while working on what they called "the girls' uniforms."

"Then Miss Tina took us to the Galleria," the preeminent shopping mall in Houston, recalled LaTavia Roberson. "She'd seen these glow-in-the-dark boots and thought they'd be cool for us to wear if we booked another showcase while we were in California. 'You never know what can happen,' she told us, 'and you have to be ready with a change of clothes.' A change of clothes! Well, *that* had never even occurred to us!"

"When we got to the shoe store, the boots were way out of our budget," Nina Taylor continued. "'Oh, come on, now,' Miss Tina said, pleading with the clerk. 'You just *have* to give us a discount. The girls are going to perform in California!' But he wasn't budging. Finally, Miss Tina said, 'Okay. Well, what if the girls perform right here and now? I promise you they'll bring a huge crowd into this store, and that'll be good business for you!' And we were like, 'Miss Tina, we're in the middle of a mall! And we have no music! And you want us to perform?' But before we could even protest, Beyoncé just fell right in line with her mother's idea and said, 'One, two, three, *hit it, girls!*' and we all started performing out little song, 'Sunshine.' And, sure enough, we drew a nice crowd *and* got a sweet discount on those glow-in-the-dark boots!"

The next day, Mathew, Tina, and Beyoncé awoke at the crack of dawn to prepare for their trip. Mathew had to take a couple days off from work, and Tina away from the shop—they would leave Solange with a relative—but it was worth it just to see firsthand how things would turn out for Beyoncé at the convention. Of course, the flight to the West Coast was memorable. "It was everyone's first time on a plane," Beyoncé once recalled. "I remember looking out the window of the jet as we took off and thinking, 'Wow. Okay, now. Will you just look at this!'"

Before the show, Mathew gave Beyoncé a little pep talk. "The only thing you can do out there is give it your best, and leave the rest to the audience," he told her in front of some of the other parents. As it would happen, Mathew would unknowingly author the template for similar talks of encouragement the other parents would give their daughters. Soon other adult voices were heard echoing the exact same phrase: "The only thing you can do out there is give it your best, and leave the rest to the audience." When Mathew heard Ashley's mother, Carolyn, parrot his advice to her daughter, he could only chuckle.

"But what if I get scared and forget my words?" Beyoncé asked Mathew.

"First of all, you won't get scared," he said. "But if you do, you just look out to the front row and you'll see me there, and when you see me, you won't be scared anymore. Okay?"

She nodded.

"And if you forget the words..." he began.

She leaned in, paying very close attention. Forgetting her lyrics was a big concern of hers. Even as an adult it would be a great worry.

"If you forget the words, just act like you're home writing a song," he told her, "and just make up any old words. The audience, they don't know the difference."

Beyoncé laughed. "You so crazy," she exclaimed. She then hugged him tightly.

At the Gavin Convention, Girls Tyme was to entertain on a bare stage with just a riser upon which would sit the instruments that would be used by the other bands. The girls would perform live with background instrumentals on tape as recorded earlier and produced by Lonnie Jackson. In their slick white-and-purple stage wear, the group looked very professional and polished, not at all like amateurs. The three in front—Beyoncé, Ashley, and Kelly—wore head mikes. Ashley looked to be about four inches taller than Beyoncé, maybe more. Beyoncé was short and round, built pretty much like many nine-year-olds. Kelly, thin and wiry, appeared to be very nervous.

During a musical break in the song "Boy, I Want You," Beyoncé stepped forward and beckoned the audience to "wave your hands in the air, wave your hands like you just don't care." Then the three girls up front sang an interesting, jazz-inspired harmonic riff that sounded almost exactly like the bridge in the 2001 Destiny Child's hit "Bootylicious." In retrospect, it seems obvious that Beyoncé was inspired by "Boy, I Want You" when she wrote that particular Destiny's Child hit. At the end, in a music break, each girl went to the front of the stage to be encouraged by her group members in a dance-off ("Go, Ashley! Go, Ashley! Go, Beyoncé! Go, Beyoncé!"). Finally, LaTavia stepped forward with a little rap that included the names of some of those on their creative team: "I like Lonnie / Lonnie's cute / 'specially when he wears / his tailored suit."

The group was a real crowd-pleaser; the audience was on its feet as soon as they finished their final number. "We would like to thank Andretta Tillman," Beyoncé said, to which Ashley added, "and Lonnie Jackson and Tony Mo., too." As the girls bowed and accepted their standing ovation,

Mathew stepped forward from the audience in a smartly tailored suit and handed each a red rose.

A Star Is Born

A few days after everyone returned from the Gavin Convention, there was another parents' meeting at Andretta's. The showcase had been so successful, Andretta told everyone, that an executive from the Plant Studios in Sausalito, California, by the name of Arne Frager had contacted her to offer to record the girls. The Plant Studios—formerly known as the Record Plant—was one of the most famous studios in the country. Stevie Wonder, Fleetwood Mac, Prince, Sly Stone, and pretty much every major recording artist had at one time or another recorded there. The girls jumped up and down and squealed as they always did when they got good news. Meanwhile, the parents stood on the sidelines, shaking hands, slapping each other on the backs, and hugging each other.

Andretta then outlined the plan: In two weeks, the contingent would leave for California. However, she explained that since they were now on such a tight budget, she couldn't afford to spring for tickets for everyone. This time, Ashley and Beyoncé—"the co–lead singers," as she put it—would be the only ones traveling, along with herself, Kenny Moore, Lonnie Jackson, and Tony Mo. Of course, this news didn't make the four remaining girls and their parents very happy, but it wasn't negotiable. Arne Frager was cofinancing the trip with Andretta, and their limited budget precluded travel by all.

Beyoncé and Ashley actually got along quite well. There was no jealousy between them. They were just little girls who wanted nothing more than to sing and were grateful for the opportunity to do so. When they shared a lead, they could be found in a corner, commiserating with furrowed brows as they reviewed their parts and offered each other helpful tips. They quickly starting making plans for their little adventure, excited about what they might experience in California.

Also at this time, Arne and Lonnie formed a production company called A&A Music, which was established to produce the music of Girls Tyme. Tony Mo. signed a deal that tied him to A&A Music as a songwriter. Andretta also had the group sign a more official contract with her Tillman

Management/Girls Tyme Entertainment. Deborah Laday and Denise Seals still had a side deal with Andretta, so that agreement had to be revised as well. In about two weeks, the paperwork for all of the deals was finalized… just in time for the trip to California.

On October 9, 1991, Andretta and Kenny found themselves at the Houston Intercontinental Airport with Beyoncé and Ashley and their parents, Mathew and Tina and Carolyn and Nolan. (Lonnie and Tony Mo. had caught an earlier flight.) It was difficult for the parents to say goodbye. After all, this was the first time they'd allowed the girls to travel without them. "The first of many times, I'll bet," Carolyn Davis said sadly. "I want her to make it," she told Tina of Ashley, "but right now, I don't think I can let her go."

Tina felt the same way. "They're just so damn little," she said, embracing Beyoncé. "My God! They're only ten!"

As Mathew rushed off to buy going-away flowers, Tina pulled Beyoncé aside and suddenly became very emotional. "She couldn't keep her composure," Kenny recalled, taken aback at how quickly she became overwrought.

"I just think they're too *young* for this," Tina said. "They're just babies!"

"What are you talking about, Tina?" Carolyn asked, surprised. "No they're *not*," she added. "They're fine, Tina. The girls are *just fine*! They *want* this!"

Beyoncé and Ashley looked from one adult to the other with wide eyes, not saying a word—maybe even a little frightened that their trip might suddenly be canceled.

"Tina, let me promise you something," Kenny finally said. He reached out and took both her hands into his own. "As long as I have anything to say about it, I promise that I will never let anything happen to Beyoncé."

Tina looked at Kenny with hopeful eyes. "Really?"

"Yeah, really," he said. "I promise, Tina."

"Okay," Tina said. "I'm trusting you, Kenny. You'd better not let me down. I'm serious." The way she looked at him, he knew she meant business.

"I won't."

Dabbing at her eyes, Tina started to calm down just as Mathew was returning with flowers for the girls. He immediately noticed that his wife was distressed. "What goin' on?" he asked, concerned. "Oh, nothing," Tina said, trying to compose herself. "Everything's okay." Mathew pulled her aside and held her in his arms for a moment, trying to relieve her sadness. "It's okay," he told her. "Beyoncé wants this, Tina. She and I talked about it.

She really does." Beyoncé nodded her head vigorously. "It's okay, Momma," she said, joining her parents in a group hug. "I'll be home soon," she added. "Don't worry."

Finally, the parents said goodbye to their children, telling them how much they loved them and would miss them. Then the girls and their chaperones were off to the West Coast.

During the flight to San Francisco, Ashley sat next to Andretta and Beyoncé and Kenny Moore sat across the aisle, all four in first class. Kenny recalls Beyoncé peppering him with questions during the entire flight. "She talked pretty much nonstop, excited about what hotel we'd be staying in, what the studio might be like. She was very chatty, giddy with excitement," he recalled. "I wanted to sleep, but there was no hope of that ever happening," he recalled, laughing. "At one point, she asked me to take a picture of her in the plane. She wanted it for her scrapbook. From that time on, I always called her 'my Bey,' because after those hours together, I felt we had a special kind of friendship.

"When we finally landed, she and Ashley were blown away by the fact that Andretta had a white stretch limousine waiting for us. 'I sure could get used to *this*,' Ashley said. We were then driven to the Claremont Hotel, which, as a five-star hotel, was impressive. Both girls' eyes were wide open."

The next day, October 10, Ashley and Beyoncé rerecorded "Sunshine" at the Plant Studios with Arne Frager at the recording console as engineer (with his colleague Scot Skidmore) and Lonnie Jackson producing. Arne, a white guy who with his long gray hair looked like a hippie, had a terrific sense of humor and a way of making the girls feel comfortable.

A second round of recording sessions in Sausalito would prove the venue for what can only be described as a defining moment in the career of Beyoncé Knowles. It happened during the recording of a song Tony Mo. wrote for the girls called "Blue Velvet." The song boasted a tricky melody involving fast, syncopated phrasing that ran so counter to the musical norm even a seasoned vocalist might have trouble with it. "I was proud of it because it was so different," Tony Mo. would recall. "I wanted to write a song that was so sassy and quick with the tongue, you'd listen to it and ask, 'What did she just say?' because it was just that fast! I knew it wouldn't be easy to record, though, especially for a young girl."

He was right. The song was almost impossible for Ashley Davis to get through in the recording studio. Producers Lonnie Jackson and Arne

Frager continued to slave away with her, hoping for the best, and even Tony Mo. added his two cents to help out, but it was slow going and tedious. "She was definitely struggling with it," Tony Mo. recalled. "I thought maybe we'd have to just abandon the song."

Meanwhile, as Ashley and the creative team tried to harness Tony Mo.'s beast of a song, Beyoncé sat on the other side of the glass booth next to Kenny Moore and behind Andretta Tillman, waiting for Ashley to finish. She was fidgety and impatient, Kenny recalled, "as if to say, 'Hurry up and get it done so we can just move on . . . *dang!*'"

"Beyoncé, what the heck is *wrong* with you?" Kenny finally asked. "Settle down, now, girl."

She rolled her eyes, tilted her head back, and stared blankly at the ceiling.

"Do you think you can sing that song better?" Kenny asked.

"Yes, Mr. Kenny," she answered, suddenly perking up. "I sure do. Heck yeah, I do."

He studied her for a moment and realized she was serious. From her expression and conviction, he could tell she truly believed she could nail "Blue Velvet" if just given the opportunity.

"Andretta," Kenny finally said, tapping her on the shoulder. "Let's put Beyoncé in there," he told her when she turned around. "Let Beyoncé try."

"Hell no," Andretta responded. "Ashley's just fine. Give her more time. She'll get it."

"But Beyoncé can do it right quick," Kenny said. "Let her try, at least." He noted that they had a lot of songs left to record. It made no sense to sit there all day long while Ashley worked on the one tune. Beyoncé had sung leads every now and then, why not now?

"Oh, *goddamn!*" Andretta exclaimed. She was annoyed at the interruption, especially as she was trying so hard to concentrate on Ashley's work. "Okay, *fine*," she decided. She turned to Lonnie and Arne and told them that she was sending Beyoncé in to sing "Blue Velvet." Ashley was out.

"*Oh, hell no*," Lonnie exclaimed, echoing Andretta's first reaction. He said that he'd been working with Ashley for more than an hour and he intended to finish with her. Andretta reminded him that she was paying for the session, "so, please, let's try it with Beyoncé. If she can't do it, fine," she said. "We'll just send Ashley back in."

They made the switch: Ashley was out, Beyoncé in.

Once Beyoncé got into the studio, it was quickly obvious to all that she knew exactly what to do with the complicated arrangement. "Her phrasing, her articulation, her sense of rhythm, all of it was . . . bananas!" recalled the song's writer, Tony Mo. In about fifteen minutes, Beyoncé had recorded "Blue Velvet," not only to everyone's satisfaction, but to their astonishment. It was as if in those few moments a star had been born.

"Goddamn! Now will you just listen to that little girl sing?" Arne said with a satisfied smile as he played back the tape.

Lonnie nodded his head as he rocked back and forth in his chair to the music. "She's good, all right," he observed, not really surprised. After all, he had always had a secret fascination with Beyoncé's talent. "Technically, Ashley still had the better instrument," he recalled. "But what she didn't have was Beyoncé's *execution*. We decided right then and there we had to explore her sound. We had no choice."

"It was like listening to a young, female Michael Jackson," Kenny Moore recalled. "It was one of those amazing moments where you just had to stop and take it all in and say, 'Wow! What the hell just happened here?'"

As the adults played back the song, Beyoncé stood in the corner with her eyes closed, as if deeply concentrating on her performance. "I think maybe I can do it better," she finally offered. "I don't like the bridge." The bridge! Already, she was using obscure musical terms. She wanted to make it better, perfect it, or, at the very least, try it another way. She was told that what she'd already done was good enough—that actually it was amazing.

"Beyoncé then did another song I wrote called '632-5792,'" recalled Tony Mo. "It was *dope* what she did with that tune."

"We were definitely getting pumped about Beyoncé after '632-5792,'" confirmed Lonnie. "As a producer, I quickly started to enjoy her. I saw that I could get technical with her and she could keep up. I would say, 'Beyoncé, I need your timing to be a little different,' or 'I need you to create a *character* with this song. I need a vibe.' Sometimes I would want more of a whisper in her voice, other times I would want more power. She could adapt and totally accommodate whatever I needed."

"Then I would try her in the background—and she was amazing there too. I could layer her voice, and before you knew it, she was doing the lead, she was doing the background, and the whole record was just her. As a producer, how can you not be completely blown away by that?"

Kenny looked over at Ashley, who now seemed just a little stricken. "Oh, Lord, this is killing me," Kenny finally muttered to himself after Beyoncé finished yet another one of her songs. Motioning to Ashley, he leaned over and whispered to Andretta, "I think we're scarring this kid for life."

"But this was *your* big idea, Kenny," Andretta reminded him.

"Yeah, I know, but let's think about what we're doing here," he observed, still looking at Ashley. "The kid's only ten, 'Dretta. Come on, now. This isn't right."

Andretta had to agree. "Okay, that's it for today," she suddenly announced. She said they would all reconvene tomorrow in the same studio. As everyone began to close shop for the day, they couldn't ignore that nothing short of a seismic shift had occurred in the careers of Girls Tyme and their handlers. From this point onward, nothing would be quite the same for any of them—certainly not for Ashley Davis, and especially not for Beyoncé Knowles.

Parents' Reaction

*A*ndretta Tillman knew she would have a difficult time explaining to Carolyn Davis why Beyoncé's voice was now on songs that had originally been sung by Ashley. Everyone knew that Carolyn was Ashley's biggest champion and that she was determined to see her become a major recording artist. The fact of the matter was that Ashley *did* have an immense talent, so it wasn't as if Carolyn was delusional. Thus Andretta sensed that there would be problems when the parents finally gathered in her living room to listen to the songs the girls had recorded in Sausalito.

Complicating things was that even before the girls and their creative team left Sausalito, word started filtering through the record industry about Beyoncé. "As we were wrapping things up there," Kenny Moore recalled, "the songs already started going out to various record industry executives for consideration. Before we even left town, things were popping off. The one name that kept coming back was: Beyoncé ... Beyoncé ... *Beyoncé*."

Arne Frager confirms that it was clear from the initial reaction he'd gotten that his contacts in the industry wanted to hear more from Beyoncé, perhaps not to the exclusion of Ashley but certainly in tandem with her. It was also decided to fly LaTavia Roberson out to Sausalito to have her rap on some of the songs thus far recorded. She too was someone who seemed to be generating great interest, especially since she had a national television commercial for Pro-Line. "Record companies started wondering about me and Beyoncé as a duo," LaTavia recalled. "I think they wanted us to be sort of a female version of Kriss Kross (a popular rap duo of the 1990s). When LaTavia showed up, Arne thought it would be interesting to shoot a video with her and Beyoncé just fooling around and shopping. He then added LaTavia to some of the songs. "In the end, we stayed a little longer in Sausalito than expected until we had a full album's worth of songs, and I felt they were very good songs, too," he recalled.

Upon the girls' return to Houston, they learned that Arne had submitted the songs they'd thus far recorded to Prince, a recording artist with whom he had worked in the past. "He would call me two weeks later and say, 'I love this stuff!'" Arne recalled. "He said, 'These girls are incredible and I want to sign them to Paisley Park,' his label. So that was the first nibble. I was hopeful."

As usual, Andretta had all of the parents to her home for a meeting during which the new songs were played for everyone. One by one, the tracks were played, and, one by one, it seemed that Beyoncé was the featured singer. LaTavia was also heard more than ever before. Ashley, though, was relegated to just a few small parts here and there. As the tunes played, Mathew and Tina nodded and smiled to one another, seeming pleased. Though Beyoncé had told them that she had sung more than usual, this was a real surprise for them—as it was for Carolyn Davis and her husband, Nolan. The Davises seemed to grow increasingly unhappy with each passing recording. By the time they got to the fourth song, they were staring straight ahead, not making eye contact with anyone in the room.

After all of the songs were played, everyone broke out into big applause and began to congratulate the girls on a job very well done. The youngsters were also elated, jumping up and down and squealing with delight, as they always did in victorious moments. Beyoncé and Ashley seemed to make an effort to not betray any indecision about what had occurred in the recording studio. However, it did seem that there was now some tension between them. When Beyoncé walked over to Ashley to say something to her, the little girl seemed to walk away from her. Beyoncé later caught up to her and said that she had some thoughts about the recordings, a way to maybe improve on their vocals. She wasn't quite satisfied, which would be a normal state of being for her in years to come when it came to her art.

However, Ashley didn't seem interested in hearing any suggestions from Beyoncé—not at this moment, anyway.

Meanwhile, a disgruntled Carolyn pulled Andretta aside. "You all should have *told* me," she told Andretta. "If I had known *this* was going to happen…" She didn't finish her thought, but though she didn't make a scene, she was clearly agitated. "I'm not sure how I feel about any of this," she told Andretta quietly so as not to have Ashley overhear her. "I need to discuss it with Nolan."

Andretta promised that Ashley would continue to be a featured vocalist, but also explained that "a few changes have to be made" in order for the group to be more viable as a commercial property for a record label. "We'll straighten it out," she said. "We all love Ashley."

Carolyn said she would have to think things over. "You have to know that this is quite a shock," she said. Then, after finding her hat and coat, she told Nolan and Ashley that it was time for them to take their leave. The Davises didn't say goodbye to anyone; they just got out of there as quickly as possible.

"There's sure a lot of interest in Beyoncé out on the West Coast," Andretta told Mathew and Tina after Carolyn was gone.

"People are really loving her," Kenny Moore added, according to his memory.

"Well, for a long time now, people have been saying she's sort of special," Tina said with a proud smile. She turned to Mathew for confirmation, but he didn't say anything. From his expression, it was as if he was studying the moment, perhaps waiting to see what else Andretta and Kenny had to offer.

"So we're going to feature her more," Andretta said of Beyoncé.

With his arms folded across his chest, Mathew nodded a few times.

"Well, we know you'll do whatever you think is best," Tina told Andretta and Kenny.

"I've actually been thinking for a while that Beyoncé was the standout," Mathew suddenly offered. "I even told Lonnie and Tony Mo. that I thought Beyoncé was more special than Ashley."

"*Shhhh*, Mat," Tina said, looking around to see if anyone was listening. "Keep your voice down."

"Hey, I'm not saying anything that everyone here doesn't already know," Mathew said, not lowering his voice, and in fact maybe even raising it just a little.

Mathew Makes His Move

$\mathcal{W}$hy, oh *why*, did Andretta ever have to tell Mathew that Beyoncé was the standout in the group?" That would be the question Deborah Laday would ask many years after the fact in 2014. "I remember telling Ann, 'You've made a big mistake here. That man did *not* need that information.'"

Almost six months had passed, with tensions still building behind the scenes. As Beyoncé became more featured in the group, Ashley was pushed more into the background. Mathew and Tina continued to watch with great interest from the sidelines, as did the disgruntled Carolyn and Nolan Davis.

In August 1992, Andretta had a serious bout with her lupus that landed her in the hospital for about a week. No sooner had she been released than she got a telephone call from Mathew wanting to meet with her. She agreed to see him, reluctantly, because she wasn't well. When they got together at her home, Mathew was direct and to the point. "It's pretty clear to me now that Beyoncé is becoming the star of this group," he observed, according to what Andretta later recalled. "Would you agree with that?"

Andretta didn't want to go that far. She would allow that Beyoncé was talented, but certainly not the *star* of the group. Mathew reminded her that she and Kenny had, months earlier, said Beyoncé was the group's star attraction. Again, Andretta refused to concede as much, as if her instincts had told her that she shouldn't encourage Mathew in this regard. "What we *said* was that people in California had been interested in her," she stated. "That's what we *said*."

"That's true," Mathew said. "But, look, my whole thing is this," he continued. "I want more of a hand in how this thing plays out for my daughter. I want to co-manage the group."

"*And there it is*," Andretta later recalled thinking to herself. She'd had her eye on Mathew for some time, wondering what he had in mind. Finally it was revealed: He wanted to co-manage Girls Tyme with her. When she asked him what he knew about managing a singing group, he explained that because he had a corporate background he felt he could contribute a great deal. After the two went round and round about it, Andretta cut the meeting short. "Okay, let me think about it," she said.

"Sure," Mathew told Andretta. "If you don't agree, I can totally understand it," he said, trying not to be boorish. He hastened to add, at least according to Andretta, that if they couldn't come to terms, "I'll be pulling Beyoncé from the group so I can manage her on my own."

Now Andretta didn't know what to think. It felt like Mathew had just issued an ultimatum; certainly, pulling Beyoncé from the act would affect everything. She asked to take some time to consider her options.

The next day, Andretta asked for a meeting with Tina at the Knowles home. When she arrived, Tina and Cholotte—Nicki and Nina's mom—were happily chatting while sewing new outfits for the girls. After she excused herself, Tina went into the kitchen with Andretta. Immediately, Andretta wanted to know how Tina felt about Mathew's proposal. Tina was quite clear. Her position was that if her daughter was going to continue to be involved in the group, things had to be run properly. If it was to be a family hobby—as she and Mathew had first envisioned it—that was fine and good and, as such, deserved the appropriate amount of attention and investment. Clearly, though, this venture had become much more than just a family hobby.

"I agree with my husband," Tina finally said, "that the way to get this thing really right is for him to co-manage." She pointed out that because of his work, Mathew had the communication skills to talk to promoters and possible investors. "You don't know him," she told Andretta, "but I can tell you that once he makes his mind up, there is no stopping him." She said that he believed wholly in himself and refused to compromise. Tina's mind was all but made up, and she could not be swayed: Mathew should definitely be allowed to co-manage the group. It was best not only for Beyoncé, she said, it was best for her entire family, all of this as per Tina's memory in a later sworn deposition.

Andretta left Tina's home feeling conflicted. Once back at her desk, she called Kenny Moore. "Mat is coming in at the last minute when there's real interest in the group," she told him, "and after all the money I spent to get them this far and all the legwork I put into this thing, now he wants a fifty-fifty split! Or he says he's taking Beyoncé out of the group. Can you believe this shit?"

"Damn, that's cold, 'Dretta," Kenny said, according to his memory. "You think he really means it?"

"Yeah, I do," Andretta exclaimed. "I think he'll do it, too."

"Everyone was up in arms about it pretty quickly," Kenny Moore recalled. "On one hand, I remember thinking, 'Okay, well, look, he's the girl's father and he has every right to want to look after her interests.' But on the other, I was thinking ... '*Oh, hell no! That ain't gonna happen.*'"

In the days to come, Andretta even discussed with her creative team the option of moving forward without Beyoncé. After all, Ashley was such a strong vocalist, did they really need Beyoncé?

"Hell yeah, we need her," Lonnie Jackson said, "if only because people in the record industry have been talking about her now for six months. What are we supposed to do, go back to everyone and say, 'You remember that kid you liked so much with the funny name? Well ... um ... she's not here anymore. Sorry about that. But we do have Ashley.'"

After finally conferring with her brother, To-to—who was opposed to the idea—Andretta reluctantly agreed to grant Mathew's request. Or, as she told Deborah Laday and Denise Seals, "We have no choice but to go along in order to get along. We can't let Mathew pull Beyoncé from the group. That would ruin everything we have worked for. So ... he has to be the co-manager."

Thus Mathew and Andretta made their co-management deal; he would get half of a management commission (usually about 10 to 15 percent) of all money and all deals, and Andretta would get the other half. Of Andretta's 50 percent, her partner Kenny Moore would take 10 percent. Andretta and Kenny's was a deal made between very good friends who were just trying to come up with a way to continue to work with a young Beyoncé Knowles. "We weighed all of the options, and we felt that, in the end, Beyoncé was going to be a big enough star that this gamble would eventually pay off," Kenny Moore recalled.

The ever-enterprising Andretta also made a side deal with Deborah and Denise, which most people didn't know about at the time and some don't even today. Both would remain silent partners of Tillman's in whatever happened with the girls.

It wasn't the money, though, that was at issue with this new arrangement as much as it was the power of the position. Now Mathew would have an equal say in all decisions. Because he was Beyoncé's father, the idea of such control gave everyone pause.

Andretta didn't tell her team and the parents about the finalization of the deal, not yet anyway. She could be secretive, even with her own colleagues. Kenny knew about it, of course, but no one else. Andretta continued to procrastinate about the announcement for a few days, until finally

Mathew did what he would do many more times in the weeks, months, and years to come: He took matters into his own hands.

A Fateful Meeting

On a hot summer night in July 1992, Andretta Tillman and Denise Seals pulled up in Denise's car in front of Mathew and Tina Knowles's home at 3346 Parkwood Drive. The first thing they noticed was what looked like a security guard standing in front of the entrance. "What the hell?" Denise asked. The two women sat in the car, stunned. "Is this to keep Deborah out of the meeting?" Andretta wondered. Denise didn't know for sure, but it certainly seemed that way. Earlier, Mathew had been very specific that he didn't want Deborah Laday to attend this particular parents' meeting. It was actually unusual to have such gatherings at the Knowleses. Usually they were held at Andretta's. This meeting was different, though, or so Mathew had explained to Denise. He specifically said that he wanted her and Andretta to be present, but not Deborah.

Mathew had been at loggerheads with Deborah for several months. In fact, anytime Deborah had any exposure to Mathew, it didn't go well. "I'm just gonna have to kill him," she had jokingly told Andretta. When Andretta asked why, Deborah said that Mathew had been questioning her and Denise's contribution to Girls Tyme in light of Andretta's participation. She said that Mathew had also continued to threaten to pull Beyoncé from the group, "and then let the chips fall where they may"—Deborah's words, not Mathew's. At one point, Deborah said that Mathew, no doubt equally exasperated by her, even mentioned facetiously that he was in possession of a gun. Deborah said she told him, "Oh yeah? Well, I've got a *bigger* gun!" She concluded to Andretta that life was too short for such drama. Andretta suggested that Deborah let her handle Mathew. However, Deborah didn't think Mathew could be "handled," she said, "and the shame of it is that Beyoncé is very good, though I don't think she is worth all this!"

Now, days later, Denise was sitting in front of Mathew's house with Andretta, watching a security guard as he paced back and forth in front of the front door. They weren't sure what to think. "*Giiiiiirl*," Denise said, drawing out the word, "this is ridiculous." Andretta had to agree. "We are just working women," Denise went on, "single mothers trying to make something happen for our children." She said she couldn't believe that Mathew would have a guard stationed in front of his house as if to protect his family from criminals. "Like we're gonna start a riot or something?" she asked. At that, they dissolved into gales of laughter.

After the two made their way to the front entrance, the guard sized them up and then opened the door for them. In the entryway, they found Tina. She greeted them both with smiles and hugs, made a sharp right into the living room, and then took a seat. Denise and Andretta followed.

Sitting in the parlor, Denise and Andretta found Beyoncé's, Ashley's, LaTavia's, and Nicki and Nina's moms: Tina, Carolyn, Cheryl, and Cholotte. Kelly's mother, Doris, wasn't present since she now lived in Atlanta. "Most of these moms had been calling me for a week complaining about Mathew possibly taking over and maybe pushing Beyoncé in front, especially Carolyn," recalled Denise Seals, "and now they were all present. I knew this was going to be a very interesting meeting."

Smiling broadly, Mathew walked into the room and greeted all of the women warmly. He was as good-looking as ever. In fact, he seemed to get better with age, with his strong jawline and wide-set eyes behind large, studious-looking glasses. A clean-cut, well-trimmed Afro framed his angular face. Some of the women in the room seemed dazzled by him. All charisma and personality, he was usually hard to resist when he wanted to please, and tonight he definitely wanted to do just that. "I want you to know that I'm now going to be taking a bigger hand in things," he began. "Ann and I agreed that I'm going to now be co-managing the group." Denise looked at Andretta for a reaction, but Andretta just stared straight ahead. She hadn't said one word to Denise about finalizing any sort of co-managing arrangement with Mathew.

"I have a lot of ideas," Mathew continued, "and I promise that I will do the best job I can for you and for all of our daughters." Then he added, "It's not going to be just Beyoncé, either. It's going to be Beyoncé *and* Ashley in the lead." Carolyn smiled at him and nodded. "I will now give each of you two minutes to say whatever you want to say about me working with Ann. So, which of you would like to go first?"

Denise stood up and faced Mathew. If any of the women were impressed with him, she had already decided to do her best to disabuse them of that notion. Dressed well in her finely tailored skirt and blouse, she presented herself with just as much style and panache as Mathew. It was usually

Deborah who was the outspoken one, and Denise the more strategic. But in Deborah's absence, Denise would now have to speak for both of them.

"First of all, I told him it was going to take me longer than just two minutes to say what I had to say," Denise would recall. "And I said, 'So, if you're going to kick me out of your house you may as well do it now.' Mathew shrugged and extended his hands at me, beckoning me to continue. My first question to him was, 'How will you coming in as co-manager affect me and Deborah?' He answered that he would love for me to stay on the team as his *assistant*. But not Deborah. In fact, he said he didn't want Deborah to have anything to do with his daughter. I was shocked. I told him that Deborah hadn't done anything to Beyoncé other than help her try to achieve her goals. 'Don't forget,' I told him, 'we discovered Beyoncé at the Jewish Community Center. We're the ones who brought her into Girls Tyme!' Then, directing my attention to the mothers, I asked if any of them ever felt that either I or Deborah had mistreated their daughters. All of the women looked at Mathew and then back at me with blank faces and didn't say a word."

Now Denise was getting frustrated. "Y'all have been calling me for days, upset because you think this man is taking over, and now y'all have nothing to say?" she asked the moms. Still no reaction. Then, looking at Mathew, she said, "How dare you tell me I can work for you as your assistant. Deborah and I *discovered* Beyoncé, so you can just kiss my ass if you think I'm going to be working for you!"

"Excuse me," Mathew said, struggling to keep his cool. "But *Tina and I* discovered Beyoncé. She is *our* daughter." Plus, he added that Beyoncé didn't like Deborah. He said that he and Tina, as her parents, had every right to make the decision about to whom she was exposed. "So don't get it twisted, Denise," he warned.

"Deborah and I have a *contract* with Beyoncé," Denise shot back. "Don't *you* get *that* twisted, Mathew." Then, once again addressing the other women, she continued, "This man has you thinking there can be no group without Beyoncé. But I am telling you that this is not the case. You have to have enough faith in your child's ability to know she can stand on her own *without* Beyoncé Knowles!" Still nothing. "Look, I don't want to see Beyoncé go either, but if she leaves," Denise added, "that does *not* mean the end of Girls Tyme. Ashley is a very good singer!"

"But I *just said*, it's going to be Beyoncé *and* Ashley in the lead," Mathew interjected, his temper rising. "Why are you being so hostile, Denise?"

"You say that now, but we all know where this thing is headed," Denise responded. "We all know what you have in mind for your daughter at the expense of the other girls." She looked at Andretta for help, but Andretta just lowered her eyes. Exasperated, Denise turned to the other women and said she was going to poll them one by one to ask if they were in agreement that Mathew should now be the group's co-manager. She asked each woman for a simple yes or no. They all answered yes—even Carolyn. Denise didn't even bother asking Tina. "Well, hell, then, there isn't anything else for me to say, then, is there?" she asked, discouraged.

"Guess not," Mathew said, rising from his chair as he glared at Denise. Bristling, she went back to her seat.

"I just want to be clear," Mathew began, again taking charge. He said that if any of the other women present had any problem with anything that was going on, they should feel free to express themselves. No one said a word. He further explained that he had big plans for Girls Tyme, citing more upcoming recording sessions and concerts and a bigger budget for wardrobe. However, he allowed, it was important that they continued to communicate, "because this ain't no war," he said, looking directly at Denise. "This is for our daughters. If we're fightin' anyone, it's got to be anyone who wants to keep us out of the record business, not each other."

"As the women began to file out of the room, I pulled Tina aside," Denise recalled. "Because we had always gotten along, I felt I could reason with her. 'Are you in agreement with what Mathew is doing?' I asked. Tina didn't say anything. She just glared at me. I had gone against her husband in a public forum, and she clearly did not appreciate it."

After an uncomfortable beat, Denise said, "Fine. Your silence speaks for itself, Tina." Then she turned and walked out the door with a silent Andretta by her side. On the way back to her home, Andretta remained very quiet, as if she didn't wish to discuss the meeting.

Beyoncé's Hurt Feelings

*I*n the days after the contentious parents' meeting at her home, Beyoncé seemed not only distracted but uninterested in going to rehearsal at Andretta's. Usually she was the first to show up. Now she was missing practice. She was only ten, so who knows what childhood problem she might have been dealing with? When she was unhappy about something, she would usually retire to her room and not be seen for a couple of days. Mathew and Tina gave her the space to do so, even sacrificing schoolwork if necessary. They knew she was a brooder, that even as a child she needed time to sort through confusing feelings. She had a lot on her plate for a youngster, and no doubt felt a great sense of duty where Girls Tyme was concerned, especially after the revelatory Sausalito sessions. She must have felt it was her responsibility not only to sing well but also to make sure the other girls had their vocal parts down. "She's such a deep thinker for a little girl," was how Tina put it at the time. Complicating matters, Beyoncé didn't have the normal recreational outlets of other girls her age. It wasn't as if she could just go out and play with her friends to distract herself. Her only friends were the other singers in Girls Tyme, and although she had fun with them, it was still work. Sometimes Kelly and Solange would go into Beyoncé's room to see if she wanted to talk and would find her lying on her bed intently studying publicity photos of Girls Tyme. It was as if the group was her entire life.

Some people who knew her at that time feel that Beyoncé may have overheard the heated conversation that had taken place at the meeting in the Knowleses' living room. It was entirely possible. When a person walked into the Knowleses' home on Parkwood, the first thing he would see was the staircase that led to the second floor. If he made a sharp left, he would find himself in the living room. A sharp right would take him to the family room. From either vantage point, it would be impossible to see anyone sitting on the staircase. Many years later, Beyoncé would say that she and Kelly would sometimes sit on those stairs and listen in on conversations being had by adults in either room. Had Beyoncé overheard the argument about whether Mathew should become its co-manager or whether or not the group could continue without her?

If so, one can't help but wonder about the long-term effects that hearing such an argument about her would have on a child. After all, Beyoncé had never asked to be the center of attention. If the trend had turned toward making her the lead singer of the group, it wasn't by her own design. It hadn't been Mathew's idea to feature Beyoncé either, though he did touch upon the idea from time to time.

Two weeks after that difficult meeting. Tina invited Andretta and her boys, Armon and Chris, to the house to talk things over. Tina enjoyed preparing her specialty gumbo whenever the Tillmans came over for dinner, which was just about every Sunday.

"When we got together at the Knowleses, it was fun, not business," Armon Tillman recalled. "It was family. My mom and Tina were good friends, and my mom had a rapport with Mathew, even though sometimes it didn't seem that way. She was unhappy about the co-management deal, for sure, but she definitely accepted it. It wasn't like they were always fighting. They went off to the den to talk business while Tina and us kids stayed in the living room and played games.

"After my mom and Mathew were finished with business, Mathew and I went out to his basketball court to play one-on-one. Man, was he ever competitive! Usually older guys will give a kid a break, you know? Not Mathew Knowles. He played hard and he played to win, even if he was playing against me, a ninth grader. In months to come, we would have a lot of talks while playing ball. He was just so interesting. You had to hand it to him, because he was a black man living the American dream making good money and raising his family in this big ol' house. He told me so many stories that inspired me about his growing up, the challenges he faced as a black man in the South, the way he had dealt with racism. He made me feel I could achieve anything in my life. My father died when I was about six, so, with Mathew, I sort of hung on to every word. Besides all of that, we also had a lot of fun in his house, too.

"At one point, Beyoncé thought Chris had done something to her—I can't remember what it was—and she came racing down the steps from the second floor. 'You punk!' she screamed at my brother. 'I hate you!' All of us—Tina, Mathew, me, Chris, Kelly, and my mom—were looking at her like, 'What in the world is wrong with this girl?' And then, before anyone could stop her, she ran right up to Chris, who was just standing there with his hands in his pockets, and kicked him right in the nuts! The poor kid fell right to his knees like a sack of potatoes. 'Beyoncé! Why did you do that?' Tina screamed out. After we sorted it all out, Beyoncé realized that Chris hadn't in fact done what she thought he'd done. 'Then you need to apologize to Chris,' Tina said, and of course, Beyoncé did just that. As an adult, Chris would laugh about the fact that he once got kicked in the nuts by Beyoncé at her momma's house."

"Beyoncé's gonna be a star one day," Mathew said, pulling her up on his lap.

"All of the girls in Girls Tyme are stars," Andretta hastened to add.

"I'm not so sure about that," Mathew responded. When Andretta continued to insist that all of the girls were special, Mathew shrugged. "If you say so," he told her, not caring to discuss it any further. At that point, Beyoncé jumped off her dad's lap and, seeming uncomfortable with the conversation, left the room quickly, saying she wanted to go and play with the other kids.

After a couple of days, Mathew and Tina managed to straighten things out with Beyoncé. She was back at rehearsal. "Whatever was going on just made her stronger," said one person who knew her well at the time. "It motivated her. Her parents propped her up, got her through it, and then she just plowed forward. She was that kind of girl. I don't know how, at the age of ten, she got it in her head to take adversity and use it as motivation. She just loved singing too much to let anyone stop her from doing it. Whatever the case, one thing was sure: There was just no stopping this kid. I remember her telling me, 'People can say what they want about me, I'm still gonna sing.'"

For his part, Mathew was unrepentant about the way the meeting had gone. After all, he already had a very well-paying job, one at which he excelled. He certainly didn't need to spend his spare time co-managing his daughter's little singing group. He did it because he wanted to help Beyoncé make her dreams come true. If the parents and creative team took issue with him, that wasn't his concern. He wasn't out to make friends, he was out to make his kid a star—because he knew that it was what she wanted. "If she had told me she wanted to be a doctor, I would have said, 'Fine,' and I would have figured out a way to buy her a hospital," he once concluded. "I knew what my job was as a parent, and that was to support my girl's dream."

Mathew Taking Over?

$\mathcal{N}$ow, I'm not even sure it was such a good idea to go to that darn talent show at the Jewish Community Center," Deborah Laday said after she heard about the contentious meeting at Mathew's to which she had not been invited. She didn't mean it, of course. It's just that the day she and Denise Seals discovered Beyoncé was remembered by both as having been so momentous, it was difficult to believe how much things had deteriorated. Here the partners were at a definite crossroads, and all because of their big discovery—Beyoncé.

It was at this point that Deborah decided to bow out. "All I can say is that if I had stayed one second longer, I would have gone down in history as the gal who shot Beyoncé's daddy," she recalled. "Mathew was destroying my and Denise's original vision, which was that there should be no one featured star in the group. We wanted all of the girls to shine. He and I had a fight about it. I had a little temper on me at the time and told him to go to hell. Then, I was done. I told Denise and Ann both, 'Ya'll do ya'll's thing. Good luck with him. I'm gone.' It was as if I could look into the future and see a whole world of trouble I didn't want in my life. So, whatever little part I had in Beyoncé's early career, I'm happy to have done," she concluded. "I'm very proud of her. But her father? No. Sorry. Not for me."

After Deborah was gone, the official announcement was made by Andretta and Mathew. "Miss Ann called us all together for a meeting at Mathew's house," recalled Nina Taylor. "We all sat around the big dining room table, wondering what this was about. 'From now on, Mathew is going to be helping out as my co-manager,' Miss Ann said. And we looked at him and he was smiling, and our whole thing as little kids was, 'Great. Cool. The more help, the better. He's with us all the time anyway, so why not?' In the back of my mind, though, I have to admit, I was also thinking, 'Hmmm...I wonder what *this* is gonna mean?'"

"I remember Mathew saying something like, 'Ya'll need to make the best of this situation now, because I don't know how much longer ya'll will be together,' recalled Nina's sister, Nicki. "One of you might leave for a solo career. Who knows? That's what happens with groups. One girl becomes the star and she leaves, and that's the end of that." I thought, "Oh no! We all kind of looked at each other with big eyes, not sure what he meant."

The first order of business for Mathew was to relocate group rehearsals to his home. Most of the girls lived closer to the Knowleses' spacious two-story home on Houston's south side than to Andretta's on the north side, LaTavia and Kelly being the exceptions. Mathew had already discussed it with LaTavia's mother, Cheryl, and she agreed to get LaTavia to the Knowleses' on time for practice every day. However, Andretta argued that getting Kelly there meant that she would have to drive her, which promised to be a daily inconvenience. Sometimes Nicki and Nina's mom, Cholotte, would pick up Kelly and take her, but it was always a hassle seeing to it that she was present for practices.

Andretta's concern was obvious: Moving the whole operation to Mathew's house when it had always been at hers felt like a power play on his part. The fact remained, though, that the majority of those involved with rehearsals did live closer to Mathew. Therefore, in the end he would prevail—rehearsals were moved to his home, into the family room to the right of the entryway. It was carpeted and had recessed lighting, which seemed to make it the perfect place to practice. A large leather couch took up one entire wall, and there were sliding glass doors that led out to a patio. There was plenty of room for all six girls to rehearse, usually in their stocking feet.

Outside, in the backyard, Mathew would soon build a large wooden deck that would be used as a makeshift stage. "My dad got a Casio [sound machine] and little mikes and we would go in the backyard and practice all day," Beyoncé once recalled. Kelly added, "I didn't want to go outside and play. I wanted to go outside and pick up a microphone."

"Okay. Question," Mathew would say after the girls would finish a song. "What are we singing about? What is this song about?" He actually was very good with the girls, trying his best to get them to connect with the songs they were performing.

At his home, Mathew also continued with the girls' artistic development. "I came up with this idea we called a boot camp," he explained many years later. (He seemed to have forgotten that, at least from all available evidence, this concept was actually Lonnie Jackson and Tony Mo.'s.) Mathew continued, "We did choreography and vocal lessons and team building and we jogged for physical fitness. That's what we did all day."

History would bear out that it had been a pretty good idea to have the girls rehearse at the Knowles home. In fact, they seemed to thrive there, even if Mathew pushed them hard. "The girls could never have relaxing or downtime," recalled Beyoncé's cousin Ronald Thomas. "They were kids, but Mathew would talk to them like they were in their twenties. We were always teasing him. I would call him 'Joe Jackson'"—the patriarch of the Jackson family, who notoriously ruled over his sons with an iron fist and transformed them into the Jackson 5.

Very often, Mathew would pull Beyoncé aside to have a few private words with her. He had specific ideas as to how she should deliver a song, how she should move onstage—even how she should handle a microphone.

It was as if he had years of show business experience. Actually, he was just a student of Motown, of watching old videos, of studying the Supremes and the Temptations. He had very good instincts, though. "You never know when it's going to happen for you," he would tell her, "so you have to be ready, just in case it's now or even tomorrow." Beyoncé listened to everything her dad had to offer and soaked it up like a sponge.

What to Do About Kelly?

*A*fter Mathew Knowles had the Girls Tyme rehearsals relocated to his home, he set his sights on how to handle the matter of Kelly Rowland and the trouble she had getting there. Some viewed his efforts as problem-solving, while others felt he was just looking for more ways to be controlling.

Kelly's story was a sad one. Her biological father was not a part of her life. "Honestly, what I remember best about him is the fact that he was never there," she once said of her father, Christopher Lovett. "I'll never know why he didn't stay around. I had so many questions about my dad that I wanted to ask my mom—like, for starters, Mama, why did he leave?—but I didn't."

The story passed down over the years is that Christopher was an alcoholic and physically abusive to his wife, Doris, Kelly's mother. They say that this was why Doris and Kelly had fled to Houston back when Kelly was about six. With every story having two sides, Christopher's version of events is somewhat different.

When Kelly was a small child, Christopher Lovett says he had a good job at Lockheed Aircraft Company in Atlanta, first as a flight line assembly worker and then as an inspector. Though he was making decent money, the hours were long. He says he barely had time to spend with Doris (who was his second wife) and Kelly. The fact that Doris was also working long hours at her own job made their lives even more stressful. He insists, however, that he was not an alcoholic, and he also says he was never abusive to his wife. Because of their money woes, he recounts, they were evicted from their home in Decatur. That's when they decided to split up.

Christopher says Doris took Kelly and moved in with an aunt. Still, husband and wife rendezvoused every week at a Holiday Inn where

Christopher would have a chance to visit with Kelly. One day, he says, he went to the Holiday Inn at the appointed time, but Doris and Kelly didn't show. Worried, he says he started asking around. Soon he learned that Doris had moved to Houston with Kelly. According to Christopher, he didn't know—at least not until he was interviewed for this book—that Doris had been working as a live-in domestic for a family in Decatur, and that when the family relocated to Houston they took her and Kelly with them.

In Houston, Doris only continued working for the family for a short time before losing her job. She and Kelly then moved in with Yvonne Boyd, the sister of LaTavia's mother, Cheryl. Yvonne says that Doris and Kelly "never mentioned Christopher Lovett at all." Meanwhile, Kelly ended up singing in Girls Tyme.

Sometime in the summer of 1992, Doris announced that she was moving back to Atlanta. She was just trying to do what she could to make a living to support herself and her child. Would this mean that Kelly would have to leave the act? Of course it would. How would she be able to attend rehearsals if she was living in Georgia? It was Andretta who came up with an alternative idea: have eleven-year-old Kelly move in with her and the boys. After all, Kelly had become like a daughter to her anyway. Still, this was a big change for everyone.

The other girls all liked Doris very much. On weekends she would whip up hot dogs and Tater Tots for them, listen to their adolescent problems, and give them all great advice. She was someone they'd begun to depend on, a woman whose work ethic they all admired. So when she left for Atlanta they were all quite sad. Kelly moved in with Andretta.

After a couple of months of Andretta driving Kelly back and forth from rehearsals at the Knowleses' home, Mathew finally asked, "Doesn't it just make more sense for Kelly to move in with me and Tina? Beyoncé and Kelly are so close, I know Beyoncé would love it." Andretta felt this was pushing it and wondered what Mathew was up to now. No, she decided. She had already promised Doris that she would be the one to care for her daughter. Mathew had won the co-management battle, but the Kelly Rowland battle would be hers.

Weeks later, though, Andretta walked in on her son Armon—who was in the ninth grade—on the couch making out with Nina Taylor, one of the two sister dancers in Girls Tyme. This bothered her. Considering that her boys were obviously growing up, she decided to reconsider her position where Kelly was concerned. So she made the tough decision to allow Kelly to move into the Knowles household—and it would be there that Kelly would remain for the rest of her youth, raised by Mathew and Tina.

As far as Tina was concerned, Kelly was a welcome addition to her family. The connection she had with her was instantaneous, as if somehow divinely guided. Kelly seemed like a third daughter. "You will always be a member of this family," Tina told Kelly. She meant it, too. "I owe Tina and Mathew Knowles everything," Kelly would say in years to come. "I don't think words can express how much."

Many years later, in February of 2001, Christopher Lovett and his wife, Gracie, would drive all the way from Atlanta to Houston to see Destiny's Child perform at the Astrodome. After the show, he tried to go backstage to greet his daughter, whom he hadn't seen in almost fifteen years. However, someone on the security team refused him access; his name wasn't on "the list." He recalled, "That was a bad night for me. My wife and I drove eight hundred miles back to Atlanta without saying one word to each other. We were just quiet. We couldn't believe it had happened."

To this day, Lovett has not been able to reconnect with Kelly. He says that when he hears in the media that she is in the Atlanta area, he often goes to the city's most popular mall, Lenox Square, and takes a seat on the upper level at the entrance of Bloomingdale's thinking he might get lucky and spot her either coming or going from the high-end department store. "It's never happened, though," he concluded, sadly. "To this day, it's never happened."

Star Search

*I*n the fall of 1992, Arne Frager secured a booking for Girls Tyme on the television talent program *Star Search*. This was a major deal, national exposure on a show that was a precursor to *American Idol*. (Britney Spears and Christina Aguilera would both get their first big breaks on *Star Search*.)

The *Star Search* taping was scheduled for November 3, 1992, in Orlando, Florida. The show would be broadcast the following February. As planned, Girls Tyme would perform one number on the broadcast, as would another competing act. Voters would weigh in, and a winner between the two acts would be revealed. It was a gamble. If Girls Tyme won, the victory would go a long way toward securing a record deal for them. However, if they lost, they'd likely be tagged as "that group who blew it on *Star Search*." Thus song choice was key, and this was where there would be some disagreement.

Andretta, Kenny, and Tony Mo. wanted the group to sing "Boyfriend," on which Beyoncé and Ashley shared the lead. However, Lonnie and Arne felt the girls should go along with the present consensus to showcase Beyoncé. The song they had in mind, "That's the Way It Is in My City," was Beyoncé's all the way through, with just a very brief rap by LaTavia at the beginning and another by Ashley at the end. Mathew sided with Lonnie and Arne in using the song that featured his daughter—no surprise there. Though Andretta, Kenny, and Tony Mo. still disagreed, the decision was made to go with the Beyoncé number.

Right before it was time to leave for Florida, Andretta had to go back into the hospital to battle a secondary illness to her lupus condition, Raynaud's disease. In the process, she had to have two fingers and a toe amputated. While in the hospital, she learned that Mathew had made a business trip to Los Angeles and had connected with one of her chief contacts, Teresa LaBarbera Whites at Columbia/Sony. To her, it felt like another power play, even though in all fairness, Mathew, as the group's co-manager, was probably entitled to do such business. "It just added stress to an already stressful situation," said Andretta's best friend, Pat Felton. "She didn't want anyone to feel sorry for her, plus she didn't want it to be perceived by Mathew that she couldn't do her job. Through it all, she continued to go to work at Houston Lighting and Power; they would end up having to have a special kind of prosthetic with plastic fingers made for her so she could type. She also continued to devote all of her free time away from her job to Girls Tyme, especially to the *Star Search* rehearsals. This was a lot on the plate of a woman who was very sick."

Andretta still had her sense of humor, though. Since she'd had her middle finger removed, she told Kenny Moore in the hospital that if he ever saw her put a piece of white surgical tape on her nose during a meeting it would be their secret code for "Fuck Mathew Knowles." The two shared a good laugh.

There was no way Andretta could go on the trip to Orlando, so the departing contingent would consist of Lonnie, Mathew, and the mothers of Beyoncé, LaTavia, and Ashley: Tina, Cheryl, and Carolyn.

"You know how they separate the coach cabin from first class with a curtain?" asked Nicki Taylor. "Well, we all sat in the first rows behind that curtain, in coach. We were making so much noise, Mathew kept standing up, turning around, and saying, 'Y'all need to be quiet. First class is gonna think we're having some kind of riot back here!' We laughed. 'We *are* having a riot,' Beyoncé said. Lonnie egged us on; he was just a big kid himself. We had a good time on that plane ride down to Florida."

Backstage before their *Star Search* appearance, the girls met with one of the show's producers, who explained that if they won the contest they would get $100,000. Of course, that announcement elicited its fair share of girlish shrieks and squeals. Even if they lost, the producer further explained, they would still receive a $250 stipend to cover their expenses. Considering that the six girls, three mothers, and Mathew and Lonnie made it a group of eleven flying from Houston to Florida and then needing to say in a hotel for two nights, $250 wasn't going to stretch very far. "Can I ask a question?" Beyoncé said, raising her hand. All eyes turned to her. "Now, let me get this straight. Is that $250 for *each* of us? Or is that $250 for the whole group?" When told it was a sum for the entire contingent, Beyoncé and the girls shrieked with delight. Indeed, there was pretty much nothing you could tell them that would dampen their enthusiasm. "What they don't know," Mathew said, "is that they have to give me *all* $250 for expenses." Again, everyone laughed and cheered. "*Dang*, Daddy!" Beyoncé exclaimed. "That just ain't right!"

On the day of the show, Girls Tyme watched from the wings as the show's reigning champs, a white rock group called Skeleton Crew, performed their high-octane number to great applause. Mathew went over to Beyoncé and knelt down in front of her to check in and ask how she was doing. He'd wanted to feature her, but hadn't considered the pressure it would put on her. It suddenly hit Mathew that it really was a lot to ask. He may even have felt a little guilty. However, it was too late to do anything about it. He took her by the shoulders. "What do I always tell you?" he asked her.

"Do your best and let the audience do the rest," she answered.

He smiled. She had taken his advice and turned it into a little rhyme. He brought her in for a big hug.

As the girls waited on the darkened stage for their cue, they said a private prayer, including Andretta in it. Ed McMahon, the host of the show, then introduced them as "a young group from Houston. Welcome

Beyoncé, LaTavia [which he pronounced as La*Tivia*], Nina, Nicki, Kelly, and Ashley, the hip-hop, rapping Girls Tyme."

When the lights went up, the girls made their way upstage in their little jackets and short pants outfits—Kelly and LaTavia in bright purple, Beyoncé and Ashley in lime green, and Nina and Nicki in white—all six with high-top sneakers. LaTavia started the performance with her rapping skills ("Yeah, GT [Girls Tyme] in the house with a brand-new slam..."), her big personality and great stage presence on full display. From that point, Beyoncé took over, singing and moving across the stage like an entertainer with triple her experience. Ashley only had, at best, maybe five seconds of spotlight time, rapping—not even doing what she did best, which was of course singing.

In the end, unfortunately, it was just a fair performance. Lacking a strong melodic line, the song really had been the wrong choice. Though Beyoncé did her best with it, the background harmonies were at times off key. The dancing was proficient, but for the most part the group looked like it needed more work. However, Beyoncé's stage presence was not lost on anyone. She was all over the stage, dominating the performance and clearly the true star of the night. She was not only talented, she seemed hungry for the spotlight and eager to please her audience, as if born to do so.

Despite whatever Beyoncé had brought to the proceedings, the judges gave Skeleton Crew four stars and the challengers, Girls Tyme, three. In other words, the girls lost the competition. They stood poised onstage as they got the news, forcing smiles but with dazed looks on their little faces. Once they were backstage, the waterworks began to flow. "As soon as we were behind that curtain, we started bawling and crying and boo-hooing," recalled Beyoncé. "It was so devastating. The moms were all saying, 'Oh, don't worry, baby, those guys were so much older than you! They have so much more experience.' But we didn't care. We had never lost anything! We were always winners back in Houston, so this was a rude awakening."

Of course, Mathew was upset by the defeat. He called Andretta and, according to what she later told Kenny Moore, he wondered if racism was the reason. It's doubtful that skin color had anything to do with the defeat (and his comments were made in the heat of the moment so he may not have really felt that way once he got over the disappointment). Lonnie and Arne blamed the loss on the fact that Girls Tyme was up against a band of rockers who were in their midthirties. That's possible. It didn't make much sense to have a group of prepubescent girls compete in a sing-off against an adult rock-and-roll band. But actually, song choice was the most likely culprit. The new jack swing, hip-hop tune Girls Tyme performed seemed completely wrong for the program.

As part of the promotion for her eponymous 2013 album, Beyoncé recorded a series of interviews to be released on YouTube in which she described her inspiration for some of the songs. In one of them, she showed clips of Girls Tyme's performance on *Star Search* in talking about the video for her composition of "Flawless." She explained, "When I was in the studio threading the songs together [for the album], I thought of this performance, which was a really defining moment in my life as a child. You know, I was only nine years old. [She was actually eleven.] At that time you don't realize that you could work actually super hard and give everything you have . . . and lose. When I put Ed McMahon introducing us as 'the hip-hop, rapping Girls Tyme,' it clicked something in my mind."

She also used the *Star Search* clip in the video for "Flawless," a feminist tune in which she questions society's restrictive nature concerning young women and their life choices. "We teach girls to shrink themselves," she sings. "My daddy taught me how to love my haters." And the angry refrain of the song? "Bow down, bitches."

After the performance on *Star Search*, Mathew says he walked over to Ed McMahon, the host of the show, and asked what he would recommend for the girls. "I've seen a lot of crying kids on this stage," McMahon reportedly told Knowles. "And I can tell you that the ones who make it in the end are the ones who don't quit. They go back and woodshed and reinvent themselves, and then they're stronger for the loss, not weaker." Mathew has said that McMahon's words made a lot of sense to him. In fact, he has said that this conversation was a defining moment in his life and gave him clarity on how to proceed.

The Blame Game

*T*he morning after the *Star Search* performance, the moms planned to take the girls to Disney World. They had told them they'd only be allowed to go if they won the contest, but actually that was just to motivate them. The mothers always intended to treat them, *especially* if they lost.

Hopefully, the kids would forget their troubles for at least one day before flying back to Houston.

First, though, there would be a group meeting in Lonnie Jackson's room. He'd gotten a videotape of the girls' performance and wanted to show it to them so that they could analyze what might have gone wrong. The meeting took a dark turn, however, when Lonnie decided that it was Kelly who was the group's true weak link. "Look at you here," he told her, singling her out. "*Wrong*, Kelly! After all this time, you still haven't learned to sing and dance at the same time, have you?" Kelly immediately burst into tears. Lonnie played the performance again, and then again. "Look at *that*," he charged, pointing to her image on the screen. A couple of the other girls started to cry. "I'm just trying to help, ya'll," Lonnie said, frustrated. "You should know that by now."

Eventually, Mathew joined the meeting, took a look around, and realized that things were going off the rails. "The problem is, *all* of y'all made mistakes," he said, not making the situation any better. He wasn't particularly happy about all of the crying going on, either, saying that the girls needed to be tougher than that. When he looked at Beyoncé specifically, she seemed to stuff her feelings, taking a deep breath and forcing herself with all her might not to cry. The other girls, though, didn't have quite the same skill.

"Before we knew it, most of us were sobbing," Nina said. "Lonnie had drilled into Kelly so that was bad enough. But then Mathew added his two cents, and that made it worse. All of us were so upset, we didn't know what to say or do. Beyoncé went over to Kelly and kept saying over and over to her, 'It's okay. It's okay. It's okay.' Finally, Miss Tina walked into the room with Miss Cheryl and Miss Carolyn to find a whole bunch of little girls having nervous breakdowns."

"What is wrong in here?" Tina asked.

"*Kelly* is what is wrong in here," Mathew said. "Lonnie thinks she's why we lost. He and I aren't sure she should be allowed to go with us to Disney World, Tina." By this time, Kelly was facedown in a pillow.

"What is wrong with you?" Tina demanded to know. "I will not have you talk to that child like this. *She is eleven years old, Mathew!*"

"But she made so many…"

Tina said she didn't care how many mistakes Kelly made, she was still just a little girl. She had worked as hard as the others and she most certainly was going to Disney World with them. "My God," she exclaimed. "This is not the end of the world! These are children!"

As Cheryl and Carolyn watched, both seeming very upset, Tina gathered the girls around her on the bed and began to talk softly to them. Beyoncé seemed rattled, but definitely not one to cry. It was as if one look from her father was all it took for her to force down any feelings of upset. "We just have to keep going and not stop until we are winners," she said, sounding more like Mathew with each passing day. She admitted that it had been far from a perfect performance and said that she could kick herself for not being better. Of course she was upset. After all, rarely had she lost a beauty pageant or a talent contest prior to joining the group. She reminded her friends that the reason they practiced so much was so that something like this would never happen. It had all gone "very, very wrong," she said, "and I don't know what the heck happened, but it can't happen again. I should have done better." She was hard on herself, when actually she had been the best thing about the show.

None of what Beyoncé was now saying was what Tina wanted to convey in that moment. She hushed her daughter and said, "I don't care about any of that right now." Wiping away the girls' tears, she added that she also didn't care if they ever won another talent contest. "The important thing is that we are all family here," she concluded, "and that's what matters. Family."

It took about a half hour, but Tina was eventually able to calm the girls. "Miss Tina's right. Let's just go and have a good time," Lonnie finally decided, now also eager to defuse the situation. He felt badly, realizing that he'd probably overreacted. "We'll figure it out later," he promised. "Let's just go have some fun."

"I admit it, I was pretty hard on Kelly," Lonnie Jackson would recall years later. "In my defense—if there is one—it was hard to keep perspective when we all had so much riding on this thing.

"So we took the girls to Disney World and we blew lots of spit wads and did all the crazy, fun stuff we always did," he continued. "We just put it behind us as best we could. Kelly eventually warmed up, too."

At one point, Lonnie shot a spitball up into the air and directed it so that it fell on the head of an elderly woman waiting in line for the "It's a Small World" ride. Dismayed, she searched the sky in vain to see where it had come from. Kelly burst into laughter. "You so crazy," she told Lonnie. So young, yet so resilient.

"The thing about Kelly is that even as a kid she knew this was a business, that it was not all fun and games and that it required a certain kind of rare tenacity," Lonnie recalled. "Most kids could never have survived what she survived just in terms of the battering her self-esteem might have taken if she wasn't such a strong child. So, my hat is always off to Kelly Rowland. She learned her lessons the hard way."

Life-Changing Decision

I think I need to start devoting all my time to Beyoncé and the girls," Mathew told Tina one evening soon after the *Star Search* defeat. The two of them were at a party at Pappasito's Cantina, a Tex-Mex restaurant in the Houston Hilton, with a few good friends and business associates. He said he had a feeling that if he put his mind to it, he could really make something big of the girls. Working part-time for the group wasn't going to cut it, though, he now felt. "Maybe I should leave my job," he mused.

By this time, Mathew had already departed from Xerox Medical Systems after the division he'd worked for there closed. He then spent a brief time at Philips Medical Systems North America, Inc., where he sold MRI and CT scanners. By 1992, he was working for Picker International, a global leader in the manufacturer and design of advanced medical imaging systems.

A year earlier, Mathew made a major sale for Picker to MD Anderson Cancer Center for a new and revolutionary CT scanner. It was the first sale Picker had ever gotten at MD Anderson—worth $4 million. But then, because of a distribution agreement gone bad, the company lost the sale. Mathew was bitterly disappointed; he had fought hard to establish Picker as a major force in an area where General Electric was dominant. "My manager and I saw total disagreements after that happened," he said. Mathew was anxious to leave Picker, and now he felt he had good reason.

After word spread about the *Star Search* defeat, things began to crumble for the girls—and this was before the show was even broadcast! "Word of the defeat got around and took the wind out of everybody's sails," Arne Frager recalled. "In the end, I couldn't secure a record deal for them. It was a shame."

Given these circumstances, Mathew more than ever didn't believe that

Andretta and her creative team were up to the task of managing Girls Tyme. He now felt an even more pressing need to look out for his daughter's interests. Given his personality and temperament, it made sense. After all, Mathew was a man who made things happen in his life, and now Girls Tyme was a big part of that life. Naturally he would feel compelled to apply to the endeavor of co-managing the group the same skill set he had deployed to make himself a star salesman—and that included his "all in" philosophy. It had always been virtually impossible for him to do anything halfway. It was actually a wonder he had lasted even a few months as a part-time co-manager.

After he made his declaration that he wanted to devote "all" of his time to "Beyoncé and the girls," Tina just stared at him over her coffee. According to the witnesses to this conversation, she didn't necessarily look happy. It would never have occurred to her, a more practical person than her husband, that he should quit his job. "Just my income, then, from the shop?" she asked. She was worried. "Is this what will be best for our family?" She seemed uncertain.

"Personally, I think you would be crazy to quit your job," one of their friends offered. "In this economy, Mat?" he added. "No way. Better keep that job, my brother."

Mathew nodded in agreement. He said that he believed his father would probably offer the same advice. "But Beyoncé wants this thing so badly," he said. "How am I not going to help her get it? That's my responsibility as her father, isn't it?" he asked. "Besides," he concluded, "sometimes you have to take a chance, especially for the people you love."

"Well, I don't know," Tina said, mulling it over. She took a tablespoon of vanilla ice cream from her dessert and dropped it into her coffee as she often did instead of using creamer. "Maybe we should back away from this thing for a while, let her be a normal kid for a bit. If she wants to pick it up later, then...okay."

Mathew shook his head. "Try telling her that," he said. He reminded Tina that he and Beyoncé often talked about her hopes and dreams, and she had repeatedly told him she wanted a career in show business more than anything else.

Tina agreed and admitted that she'd had similar conversations with Beyoncé. "We could maybe give it a year," she offered, stirring the coffee. She added that she would work extra hours at the shop, "and we'll just see what happens." She was trying to be supportive, but it was obvious that she had reservations. On this particular evening at Pappasito's, her expressive green eyes seemed full of despair.

"I love you," Mathew told his wife as he put his arm around her. Then, with a warm smile, he added, "I'm just sitting here right now thinking about how lucky I am." In response, Tina gave him a side glance and returned to her coffee.

"I'm not proud, nor am I ashamed of this stuff," Mathew would later admit relating to this time in his life, "but my wife, Tina, and I had some real problems with our marriage. I was having some affairs at the time. I went to a treatment facility in 1992 and they didn't have a real definition for my marital infidelities. But if you did a little alcohol or drugs, it was all lumped together as substance-abuse-related."

Considering that it's always of value to try to understand a person's challenges rather than just judge them, it's worth looking at what may have been a personal struggle Mathew and Tina had in common. Mathew has said he believes that at the root of his issues in 1992 was his driving ambition to make Girls Tyme a success. "I had this vision, and when it doesn't happen right away and your friends are saying, 'What is *wrong* with this guy?' that's bringing on some personal issues. That's pretty difficult," he observed. He seems to be alluding to problems with self-esteem, which, given his impoverished childhood, would not be surprising.

Tina has suggested similar personal challenges. "The amazing thing is that when you look at someone else you look at them and you say, 'Oh, they are attractive and they have a lot of good stuff going on and they have no right to have no self-esteem," she has said, "they have no right to feel sorry for themselves." Considering her own background, the way she was ridiculed by the nuns in her school when she was just a child, Tina's lack of self-esteem would also not be surprising. Certainly it would come as no surprise if the issue became even more magnified because of her husband's unfaithfulness. In recalling the darkest days of the Knowleses' troubled marriage, some in the couple's circle can't help but be reminded of a sentiment Tina expressed quite often: "Men need to be loved. Women need to be wanted."

Maybe Mathew and Tina were actually battling the same issue, but with different consequences. His low self-esteem, perhaps, was responsible for his unfaithful behavior, while hers was to blame for her acceptance of it in their marriage.

Marital problems aside, at the end of 1992, Mathew took the plunge and quit his high-paying job to devote himself full-time to Girls Tyme. "Mathew leaving his corporate job was very scary for me," Tina would admit many years later. "I don't know many people who would give up a job making the kind of money he made. I thought he had gone a little nuts. I was like, 'What are we gonna do?' I had a large salon and it was generating good money, but we were accustomed to two incomes. All of a sudden we had to totally alter our lifestyle."

By the end of 1992, Mathew would now have all the time in the world to devote to Beyoncé's career. He was willing to put in the work, too, to learn what would be necessary in order to manage an artist. Back in the early days, when Andretta decided to get into show business, she studied a book called *Music Industry 101*. She didn't have any experience and it was that book she relied on for direction. Mathew Knowles took it a step further; he enrolled in Houston Community College and signed up for three courses in show business–related management.

Tina Smooths Things with Andretta

*T*ime to eat," Tina Knowles said as she carried a large platter of gumbo from the kitchen to the dining room table. It was just another Sunday at the Knowleses', and as usual, the Tillmans were guests for dinner. Seated around the table were Mathew, Beyoncé, Kelly, and Solange, as well as Andretta and her boys, Armon and Chris.

Earlier in the day, Mathew had told Andretta that he'd decided to quit his job and focus on the girls. Of course, she wasn't exactly thrilled by the news. "She thought it was a terrible idea," said Armon Tillman. "She could see that he was going to be a much bigger problem in her life if he didn't have a job, if all of his attention was on Girls Tyme. She was civil about it, though. Given his earlier threat of pulling Beyoncé from the group, what could she do?"

As Beyoncé passed a warm basket of crusty French bread to Chris, Armon took one of the rolls and playfully tossed it at Solange.

"Hey! Don't do that," Tina scolded him. The families had the kind of relationship where the adults were free to chastise any child, regardless of to whom he or she belonged. "It's a sin to throw bread," Tina said, "so stop that, Armon!"

"That's right," Andretta said, smacking her boy on the arm. "Tina's right. Throwing bread is a sin!"

"Why is that?" he asked.

"It don't matter why," Mathew said, already tired of the discussion. "It just *is*, boy. Now hush up."

Tina disappeared for a moment and then returned with potato salad and a green bean casserole. When Andretta expressed amazement at how much food she had prepared, Tina explained that she very much enjoyed cooking. In fact, she said she'd been trying to teach Solange and Beyoncé. Solange seemed interested, but Tina was beginning to think that Beyoncé would never be able to handle herself in the kitchen. "I don't need to cook," Beyoncé said, "not as long as I have my momma," she added, beaming at Tina.

"Beyoncé is gonna hire a chef when she's a star," Mathew added, "so she'll have that covered."

"I don't want you to be upset about this thing with Mat," Tina told Andretta about an hour later, as the two were washing dishes in the kitchen. "He just wants to be more involved, is all," she said.

"But it feels like y'all think I don't know what I'm doing," Andretta said. She seemed sad and weak. "You know how much I love those girls," she added. She then mentioned that after Girls Tyme performed at the recent televised Miss Black U.S.A Metroplex Pageant, they were thrilled to learn that the popular group Boyz II Men wanted to meet them backstage. "That shows that we're making real progress, when Boyz II Men wants to meet the girls," she said, as if defending her role as manager.

In a deposition she would give many years later, Tina would say that her heart went out to Andretta. She testified that she told her she wished there were some way for Andretta to fully understand how much she and Mathew appreciated everything she'd done for Beyoncé and the girls. Being a parent, too, though, Tina felt Andretta should also understand that the Knowleses had no choice: They *had* to become further involved, for Beyoncé's sake.

Tina would also later admit that Andretta's illness had served to put her own life into perspective. Though she and Mathew certainly had their share of problems, at least they had their good health and also that of their children, and that was everything. "Do you want to pray?" Tina asked Andretta as she dried her hands with a dishtowel. Andretta nodded. The two women then sat at the kitchen table, joined hands, and prayed together.

PART TWO

One Step Forward, Two Steps Back

Ashley Leaves Girls Tyme

*I*n February 1993, after Girls Tyme's *Star Search* defeat was finally broadcast, Andretta called a meeting at her home to outline future plans. Since Mathew had recently signed his co-manager contract with Girls Tyme, his position was official, and as a result, there were a few ideas on the table for discussion.

As always, the girls and their parents arrived noisily, everyone greeting one another and seeming happy to once again be in one another's company. While the adults, including Andretta's creative team, settled in the living room, the girls went into another room to watch television.

Carolyn Davis had more than a few concerns, and she let them be known immediately. Never shy, she'd always been outspoken and determined to protect her daughter's interests. Where *Star Search* was concerned, she said she felt the girls should have performed a number that featured Ashley on lead, primarily because they knew those songs so much better than the one they had ended up performing. She was also very unhappy about the scene in the hotel room the day after the performance, when the girls were heavily critiqued by Mathew and Lonnie. "I'm sorry, but no one talks to my child like that," she said. "How dare you? That is not acceptable." It didn't take long for the conversation to become heated. Soon, Carolyn and Mathew were exchanging barbs, with Carolyn accusing him of "working my last nerve." Andretta did what she usually did in these situations, which was to try to calm down the parents. However, it quickly became apparent that no business was to be discussed on this day. There was just too much tension in the air.

After about fifteen minutes of sniping with Mathew, Carolyn called for Ashley, who came running out of the room followed by the other girls. All of them were smiling, giggling, and poking fun at one another; they had no idea there was trouble.

"Get your coat, Ashley, we're leaving," Carolyn said.

"But…"

"*Ashley Támar*, get your coat!" she repeated loudly. Ashley did what she was told. After she hugged all of the girls goodbye, the Davises quickly departed.

"Carolyn, Nolan, and I left together—or I should say we stormed out, because I was in complete agreement with them," recalled Tony Mo. According to him, as Nolan drove, a disgruntled Carolyn said she felt Mathew was all but blinded by his determination to make Beyoncé a star. "We all knew that Ashley wasn't a rapper and that the five seconds or so of rapping she did at the end of the song on *Star Search* didn't represent her well," Tony Mo. continued. "Carolyn was clear that if Mathew, as co-manager, had made the decision to have Ashley rap instead of sing just so that Beyoncé could be the one to shine, then she definitely didn't want her daughter to be in the group anymore. I had to agree with her. Beyoncé was incredibly talented. We all knew it. After all, we all—especially me and Lonnie—nurtured it. But Ashley was talented, too. It wasn't fair."

Carolyn turned and explained to her confused daughter that she would have to leave Girls Tyme and sing on her own from then on. "It's going to be okay, I know it is," she said.

"What happened?" Beyoncé wanted to know, back at Andretta's. "Why is everyone so mad? Did we do something wrong?" By this time, Mathew had gone into the kitchen to cool off. Beyoncé was standing in the living room with Nicki, Nina, LaTavia, and Kelly at her side.

"No one's mad," Tina said. She didn't really want to discuss it. She just asked the girls to gather their things so they could all leave.

"But Mrs. Davis sounded awful mad to me," Nicki said. "Is everything okay?"

"What did I just tell you, Beyoncé?" Tina said, ignoring Nicki. "It's time to go."

"Wait a minute," Beyoncé said, holding her ground. "*This is our group!* We deserve to know what the heck is going on."

"Yeah, this ain't right," Nina agreed.

Such a mutiny was rare. Usually the girls didn't question the adults' role in their young lives. Like most children, they just accepted that the grown-ups knew what they were doing and wouldn't steer them wrong. How else could it be? Were they to just manage themselves? Things were changing, though, now that the girls were becoming old enough to question their parents' decisions. Beyoncé in particular was becoming much more headstrong, especially where Mathew was concerned. At rehearsals, for instance, Mathew and Nicki would often butt heads. "It's not supposed to be that way, it's *this* way," Mathew would tell her. Nicki would stand up to him and hold her ground. Then, inevitably, Beyoncé would side with Nicki.

"No, Daddy, Nicki is right. You're wrong," she would tell him, and she would think nothing of doing so, either. Actually, contradicting her father had become par for the course with Beyoncé these days. Though still completely devoted to one another, father and daughter had begun to disagree on the creative side of things. Not surprisingly, nothing annoyed Mathew more than when Beyoncé sassed him. "I *know* you ain't talking back to me up in here, Beyoncé," he'd always tell her. She'd just shrug her shoulders as if to say, "Yeah, well…whatever." As she matured, she was becoming a very willful and outspoken girl.

Now the four little singers stood before Tina, their little arms defiantly crossed in front of them. "I thought we were gonna practice a new song," Kelly said.

"Now, how y'all gonna practice a new song when Ashley's not even here?" Tina asked. "Come on, Beyoncé and Kelly, please do as you're told. *I mean it.*"

Chagrined, Beyoncé and Kelly said goodbye to their friends, hugging each one tightly and vowing that they would all see each other tomorrow after school. The two then walked out of the house, trailing behind Tina and looking miserable. Soon after, Mathew came out of the kitchen and followed them.

An Important Lesson

*W*hat? No! *But that ain't right!*" Beyoncé exclaimed the next day when told of Ashley's departure from Girls Tyme. The rest of the team was also present at rehearsal when Andretta broke the news to the girls. "She didn't even tell us she was leaving," Beyoncé protested. "How come she didn't tell us?"

"That's just the way it worked out," Andretta said.

"Well, I'm calling her," Beyoncé said. When she said she wanted to hear the news directly from Ashley, Andretta wasn't sure how to proceed. She suggested that Beyoncé should take up the matter with Mathew.

Though she understood that Beyoncé was upset about Ashley, Andretta had her own challenges in that regard. What she'd gone through with the deaths of her husband and child had changed her in many profound ways, not the least of which was that she was adverse to losing people in her life. She didn't like to say goodbye. She definitely didn't want to see Ashley leave the act, and the only way she could live with it was to offer the girl a solo management deal. It was her way of keeping Ashley around. Mathew had to sign off on it, too, which he did. For whatever reason, though—and there are likely many of them—Ashley would not blossom under this new arrangement. "It's just something you deal with and move on," her father, Nolan Davis, would in years to come say of this time in his daughter's career.

"I *will* ask my dad," Beyoncé said before storming from the room, followed by Kelly and LaTavia. "You bet I will," she hollered out from the other room.

When Beyoncé spoke to Mathew, he laid it on the line for her. Carolyn Davis had other ideas for Ashley and had pulled her from the group, plain and simple. It was not his decision. Beyoncé wanted more details, but Mathew didn't give them. He said he was handling everything and that she shouldn't be concerned. When she said she wanted to speak to Ashley, Mathew told her not to do so, at least not at that moment. He said he wanted everyone to have a chance to calm down. As much as it bothered her, Andretta supported Mathew's idea for a clean break. In the end, Beyoncé didn't call Ashley.

It would seem that Beyoncé and her friends were in the midst of learning an important lesson about show business: There's little room in it for sentiment. True, the girls had worked together for years, enjoyed their victories, and suffered through their defeats as if they were true blood relations. However, when it came to Girls Tyme, a friend—or a "sister"—was only one for as long as she fell in line with managerial decisions. If she fell out of favor, she could easily exit the group without warning. This was a business, not a family, even if Tina had attempted to paint it that way. If there was any emotion attached to losing Ashley as a friend, it would have to be buried, and stay that way. This was the first time Beyoncé would bear witness to such a stark reality, but it wouldn't be the last.

"We never even *saw* Ashley again," said Nina Taylor. "She was just gone, as if she'd fallen off the face of the earth. All of those years together . . . over. Just like that. *Done*."

"Anytime one of us said we were going to call Ashley, either Miss Ann or Mathew told us not to," Nicki Taylor recalled. "'Ashley is doing her thing and you're doing your thing,' they said. Eventually, we stopped asking about her. We even stopped talking about her amongst ourselves. We somehow got it that we could not look back, that we had to keep moving forward. I remember Beyoncé saying something like, 'My dad says we have to focus on the present, not the past.' And that's what we did. As kids, you listen to what your elders say, at least we did. We felt that what Mathew and Miss Ann said was law."

After she left Girls Tyme, Ashley continued working with Tony Mo. and recorded at least another forty songs with him. In 2004, she would audition again for *Star Search*, and would again be defeated. However, she would soon begin working with Prince, and in 2006 would successfully tour with him, using her middle and last names—Támar Davis—to promote his album *3121*. On that record, she and Prince would cowrite and record a duet, "Beautiful, Loved and Blessed," which would go on to be nominated for a Grammy. She'd also record a couple of very good solo albums, and also act in several Tyler Perry productions. Most recently, she toured with *Motown the Musical*, playing several different characters, including the starring role of Diana Ross.

In Girls Tyme, a pretty twelve-year-old named LeToya Nicole Luckett, who happened to be a classmate of Beyoncé's, quickly replaced Ashley Davis. Andretta's assistant, Sha Sha Daniels, selected her photo out of a binder of pictures and résumés given to her to thumb through by her boss. "She sure has some big hair, that one," Andretta said when Sha Sha showed her the girl she'd chosen. "I'll bet the other girls will pick on her for that." Sha Sha laughed. "We can press it out, no problem," she said. "She's so cute. I think she'll work out great."

Born on March 11, 1981, in Houston, LeToya was the oldest of two children. She grew up singing in her local church, performing her first solo at the age of five. Mathew may have thought he had his hands full with Ashley's mom, Carolyn, but he would find LeToya's mother, Pamela, to be just as formidable. She was her daughter's biggest advocate and, as would soon be revealed, also had very specific ideas about the way she wanted LeToya's career to unfold.

"When LeToya came into the group, we sort of tried to forget that Ashley had ever been a part of us," concluded Nina Taylor. "But in the backs of our minds, we were thinking, 'Oh my gosh, if it could happen to her...'"

Desperate Times

$\mathcal{E}$ven though Mathew and Tina Knowles have talked publicly about the struggle of subsidizing Beyoncé's career when she was young, they've been very careful never to let it appear that while they were doing so they were in dire financial straits. In fact, they've often spoke of not being "like the Jacksons," the famous and talented family from Gary, Indiana, who faced great poverty and were, as a result of hard work and no shortage of good luck, able to leverage the success of five of their sons into financial salvation. Or as Mathew told reporter Jamie Foster Brown, "Tina and I were not sitting around saying, 'Wow, I hope our kids become successful so they can change our lives.'" Beyoncé has concurred that a Jacksons-like saga was never the Knowleses' story (except for that both fathers—Knowles and Jackson—made sacrifices for their children). "It wasn't about me being in show business for the money," she has said. Of course, the Knowleses *had* been living a good life in the 1980s when Mathew was working steadily. However, it would appear that the family was having at least some financial pressures before Mathew even quit his job at the end of 1992, since public records show a federal tax lien filed against them as early as March 1, 1990, for $11,419.

Every family in the public eye has to make a choice in terms of how much of their private lives they wish to reveal and what will ultimately service the image they are hoping to project. Beyoncé's image has always been wholesome, fresh, and somehow upwardly mobile—certainly not troubled, not gritty, not steeped in adversity. Considering the Jackson family once again, though the Jackson 5 were a scrubbed-clean Motown confection, the family and their record company never tried to hide its gritty urban roots. The family's dire financial situation was a big part of its success story. After all, "rags to riches" always works. It's the oldest trick in the book.

The Knowleses made their own decision when it came to their family's history and how it would inform the way the public viewed "Beyoncé" the brand. They would turn away from their struggle, bury it in the past, and refer to it only occasionally, and even then downplay it significantly. While part of the reason they persisted in this stance has to do with show business image-making, some of it can also be chalked up to plain old southern pride and decorum. In their view, why should anyone know anything more than what the Knowleses had chosen to reveal about their personal finances? However, fully understanding the gravity of their financial situation in the 1990s certainly doesn't diminish them. Quite the contrary, it only serves to more fully illuminate the scope of the extreme sacrifice both Mathew and Tina felt obligated to make for a daughter who would one day become world famous.

Besides pride, a bigger reason for their choices has to do with the building of "Beyoncé" as a show business brand. It has to do with how a carefully constructed mythology about her family's background might serve Beyoncé Knowles's public image. Unlike the Jacksons, the Knowleses never wanted to be perceived as lower-class or impoverished. It was as if their strategy when Beyoncé became famous was to wipe the slate clean and start over again in their messaging to the public. In terms of public relations, they wanted to be frozen in time as the upper-middle-class family they'd been in the 1980s before their lives took such a dramatic turn for the worse.

The truth was that the early 1990s were full of financial adversity for the Knowleses. By 1992, Tina's business, Headliners, had begun to suffer as a result of a poor economy. Because Mathew was no longer bringing in a steady paycheck, the pressure to maintain the family's standard of living became much more difficult to manage after he quit his job.

During a 2002 deposition in a legal case having to do with their finances, Tina would be forced to address this challenging time in her and her husband's lives. "Do you recall that a federal lien was applied on your taxes for every year—'92, '93, '94, and '95—because you were unable to pay your federal taxes?" attorney Benjamin Hall would ask her. "These were liens put against us, yes," Tina confirmed. "But this is not saying that we didn't pay our taxes. Discrepancies were found in the returns and they came back and did audits and put liens. That's different from not paying your taxes. And yes, I think we were negligent," she would concede. "I think we were young and supporting other things other than taking care of our own stuff. Such as Destiny's Child. Spending all our money on Destiny's Child." (Of course, she was referring to the groups that came before the one that would ultimately be named Destiny's Child in 1997.) "That's what I will admit to," Tina concluded, suggesting that there were other aspects of her past that she would just as soon conceal, and this was in a private deposition under oath, not a press interview for public consumption.

Tina in particular had a serious tax problem having to do with Headliners, which actually caused the Knowleses to have to file for bankruptcy in 1993. It was a decision they didn't take lightly, especially given the way Mathew's father had raised his son to put a premium on what he called "A-1 credit." The Knowleses' tax attorney, David Peake, had also warned them that their home at 3346 Parkwood Drive was in jeopardy. "We were advised by an attorney that the only way we could save our house was to file for this bankruptcy," Tina confirmed. "We had gotten behind in our house notes."

Beyoncé and Solange loved the home on Parkwood, as did Mathew. As much as Tina was attached to it, she was more practical about it than was her husband. She felt it could be sold and everyone would just have to adjust to new surroundings and move on. However, Mathew—maybe out of pride or maybe because he just didn't want to uproot the family—wished to hang on to the property for as long as possible. Thus the bankruptcy filing of 1993.

The problem was that after the Knowleses restructured their debt with their bankruptcy filing of 1993, they were still unable to make the payments they'd agreed to with their creditors. Thus the 1993 bankruptcy was dismissed. Tina explained that this occurred because one of her employees, who paid the bills, had neglected to do so for a couple of months, "and so we did then have to reinstate the bankruptcy in January 1994, but it wasn't because we were destitute. It was at the lawyer's advice having to do with taxes and reorganizing everything." All of this financial stress must have put even more pressure on Mathew and Tina's marriage.

A proud man, Mathew never wanted Tina or anyone else to think that he couldn't take care of his family. Of course, he had always been a hard worker—he'd had jobs since he was a teenager—so obviously it wasn't that he didn't want to work. If anything, his work had always been his life. It was just that now he wanted to work on one thing and one thing only: Beyoncé's career. Helping to realize his daughter's dreams gave him a real sense of purpose in life. "You have to believe in *something*," he used to say, "and this is what I believe in. I believe in my daughters, not just Beyoncé but Solange and Kelly, too."

Beyoncé, Solange, and Kelly seemed, at least from outward appearances, to be blissfully unaware of Mathew and Tina's financial struggles. Of course, there was no reason for the girls to know anything about any of it at their age—Beyoncé and Kelly were both twelve, and Solange was seven. When they were little girls, Tina would dress them in the cutest little outfits she could make by hand, curl their hair, and spend a lot of time making them feel beautiful and giving them a sense of self-worth, even reminding them of her mother's old adage, "Pretty is as pretty does." She'd shield Beyoncé and Solange from trouble and dote on them as would any good mother, and she treated Kelly the same way. Even though the Knowleses had so many money issues, they still made sure that Kelly was taken care of and treated as if she were their biological daughter.

The girls were Tina's life. In some ways, it was as if she had created a whole new and safe world around them, one that didn't necessarily include Mathew. It could be said that both Mathew and Tina had absorbed themselves into the girls' lives—especially Beyoncé's—the way troubled couples do when they find that the only thing they have in common are the children.

Though Tina felt there should be certain practical limitations as to how much money they should devote to Beyoncé's aspirations, even she would have to admit that they almost always exceeded what would have been a reasonable amount of time and money to spend on any dream. "Whether there was money available or not, it was spent on the girls," Tina would later testify, referring to the singing group. "That was the problem, I guess. If my utility bill was $2,000 because I had six girls over all the time, and my grocery bill was high because I was feeding them every day of the week, I'm not going to complain about it. That was the choice I made. I'm just going to make it work. So we made it work. We had to make it work for the girls and for our family."

Dissension in the Ranks

After Girls Tyme's *Star Search* defeat was broadcast in February 1993, Andretta and Mathew decided to change the group's name in an effort to distance the group from the loss. After much deliberation, Girls Tyme became Somethin' Fresh.

At around this time, a producer named Daryl Simmons—CEO of his own Silent Partner Productions—had begun to express interest in the group. Simmons had been in very successful business with L.A. Reid and Babyface, two important and talented producers who headed up their own production company, called LaFace. They'd had a great deal of success with artists such as Toni Braxton and TLC. Silent Partner Productions was Sim-mons's new solo endeavor—the name being a nod to the fact that many people in the industry viewed him as a "silent partner" of the much more highly visible L.A. Reid and Babyface—and he was vigorously scouting for new talent to produce.

"I was working on [R&B artist] Monica's first album and I got a call from someone who had seen Somethin' Fresh performing in Houston," Daryl Simmons recalled. "'Hey, these girls are really good down here,' I was told. 'You should come and check them out.' I said, 'Fine, but have them send me a tape first.' A few days later, I got a VHS tape in the mail from Mathew Knowles. When I viewed it, I thought, 'Wow, this group *is* pretty good.' I decided to take a flight from Atlanta to Houston [on April 23, 1993] to see them. After we met in the lobby of my hotel, the girls came up to my room. Once there, they sang the Michael Jackson song 'I Wanna to Be Where You Are' and their own song, 'Sunshine.' I fell in love with them right away, especially with Beyoncé. This little kid got all up in my face and sang so hard and had all of these neck movements and facial expressions, I was like, 'This girl is *crazy* good!' So I asked them if they wanted to come down to Atlanta to work with me. They knew about TLC, they knew about Toni Braxton…so, yeah, they were excited about my invitation."

The girls also knew the drill by now: They would sign with Daryl's production company, Silent Partner, and record songs under its auspices. Then, using those recordings as bait, Simmons would attempt to secure a record deal for them—just as Frager and Jackson had attempted to do before him. Hopefully, Simmons would be more successful. Lonnie Jackson would remain in the picture working behind the scenes with the girls, still as one of Andretta's trusted advisers.

The deal with Silent Partner Productions was signed and executed on June 11, 1993. However, as often happens in the record business, once the agreement was finalized, Somethin' Fresh had to wait until songs were selected for them to record. In the meantime, a problem came to light when Pamela Luckett—mother of new member LeToya—wanted her daugh-ter to be free to consider other opportunities, such as acting. She asked that LeToya continue to work with her theatrical agent, especially if she wasn't going to be singing lead. Pamela also said she wasn't happy with the management contract LeToya presently had in place with Mathew and Andretta. She wanted her attorney to once again review it.

Though Pamela was immediately viewed as a troublemaker, she was really yet another strong, forthright woman in Mathew's midst willing to go up against him if necessary. Maybe making things all the more annoying for Mathew was that she had a background in accounting. So she was definitely one to question finances.

Beyoncé liked LeToya. However, since she didn't know her very well, she had little patience for her or for her mother. One thing was certain: She believed that now was not the time for quibbling. She may have been only eleven—about to turn twelve in September—but she still believed that any dissension among the girls could prove detrimental to their future with Silent Partner Productions. The question immediately on her mind was: How is this going to affect the new deal?

Those who knew her at the time believe that to Beyoncé, the singing group had always been serious business. She'd learned when Ashley Davis left the group that the act was nothing more than a means to an end, a vehicle for all of them to make their dreams come true and to be successful in show business. It seemed that she now understood that the girls in the group were business partners, not just friends.

She called a group meeting to discuss the problem that had been presented by Pamela and LeToya. "Are we really going to just sit here and let everything we've worked for disappear just because of LeToya and her momma?" she asked Kelly and LaTavia, this according to her later testimony. The two girls didn't even know how to answer the question. Yes? No? Maybe? They were eleven, what did they know? They certainly didn't have Beyoncé's innate judgment about these things, or her uncanny understanding of them. They were just little kids singing in a girls' group.

Fine. If her friends couldn't make the decision, Beyoncé would be the one to do so: LeToya had to go, and immediately, "before we start recording, so we don't have to go back and put the new girl on all the records." One can't help but marvel at her prescience. It's as if she was born to be a career strategist, as if the idea of "branding" was second nature to her—and that nothing was going to get in her way on the road to stardom.

After the meeting, Beyoncé told Mathew that LeToya should be released. Fully ready to cut ties with anyone who didn't fall in line with group policies, she had Mathew's full support. He asked Beyoncé if she would sign a letter expelling LeToya. She said she would, and not only that, but she would make sure that the other girls did so as well. Mathew wasted no time. On October 4, 1993, he sent off a letter to LeToya's attorney, Warren

Fitzgerald, informing him that he and Andretta had decided to terminate their agreement with LeToya. Fitzgerald returned with a letter saying that LeToya had a contract, and that he believed it to be enforceable. "It's not enforceable if the girls want her out," Mathew wrote in a quick note back to the attorney. "What are you going to do, Warren? Force a bunch of eleven-year-olds to sing together if they don't want to? Beyoncé says the girls want LeToya out!"

In a subsequent letter, Mathew reminded the lawyer that he and Andretta had been down a bad road previously, with Ashley Davis acting independently of the group's interests, and that they didn't intend to make the same mistake with her replacement, LeToya. Moreover, he mentioned that he and Andretta had gone out of pocket for $7,000 for vocal lessons, and that much of that money was spent on LeToya "because of her vocal ability in relation to the other members of the group and her lack of concentration and confidence." He added that he would also not allow the Lucketts to renegotiate the management contract. "Next will they want to renegotiate their contract with Daryl Simmons?" he asked. He closed by saying that "at this time the decision of Andretta Tellman [sic] and Mathew Knowles is to terminate our agreement with LeToya Luckett and recommend to the members of Somethin' Fresh and Daryl Simmons of Silent Partner Productions a suitable replacement."

This was hardball. It didn't take long for Pamela Luckett to see it that way too. Very reluctantly, she backed down, and her daughter, LeToya, remained in the group.

Lyndall

*I*n the late winter of 1993, when Beyoncé Knowles was twelve, she met a boy who would go on to become an important fixture in her life for almost the next ten years. Lyndall Locke was about to turn fourteen when he began attending the nondenominational Abundant Life Center (also known as the Abundant Life Cathedral) in Houston. Kelly Rowland, who was twelve, was a member of the church's youth congregation. Lyndall Locke recalled, "One day Kelly brought a friend with her, this beautiful girl with dookie braids [large braids that were very popular in the early 1990s, often mistaken for dreadlocks]. She was wearing red-and-black Air Jordan basketball shoes—we used to call them 'jays'—with starched black slacks with a nice sharp crease on both legs. And she had on a bright red blouse. She was so cute, I couldn't take my eyes off her. Finally, Kelly introduced us. I said, 'Hi, I'm Lyndall.' She extended her hand and said, 'Hi, Lyndall. I'm Beyoncé. And I don't remember anything after that—I think I blacked out,' he recalled with a laugh.

"Later that night, I called Kelly to get Beyoncé's number," he continued. "A girl answered who I thought was Kelly, and I said, 'I know this may sound weird, but I'm hoping you can give me Beyoncé's phone number. She's so cute.' And the voice on the other end said, "This *is* Beyoncé.' Busted! How was I supposed to know they lived together? So, Beyoncé and I talked for hours that night, just kid stuff. 'I like you' and 'I like you too.' We talked about school. She told me she had this rabbit that she was totally obsessed with; when she said she was cuddling with it as she was talking to me, I remember feeling jealous of that damn rabbit! So, yeah, I guess you could say I fell hard right away, or as hard as a fourteen-year-old can fall, anyway. I hung up and thought, 'Okay, she's my girlfriend. Done!'"

Young Lyndall Eugene Locke's charisma and sense of humor were evident to all. He was a real charmer with a bright smile, dark dancing eyes, and a cocoa-colored complexion. The second child born to Lydia and Stephen Michael Locke on December 3, 1979, he has an older sister, Laura. Stephen and Lydia split up when Lyndall was three.

"I was raised by a single mother," Lyndall recalled. "As a kid, I didn't really have a relationship with my father. My mom worked two or three jobs to support us—whatever she had to do, she did. She always made it seem easy. Every now and then I would hear her crying in her bedroom, so I know it was tough on her. I think the reason I was this upbeat, positive kid was because I wanted to see my mom smile. I also think that's why Beyoncé gravitated to me. I saw right away that she was all about work, a very serious girl who needed someone in her life she could clown with. Someone who was light and easy. I think I was just what the doctor ordered."

At the time, Beyoncé was attending Welch Middle School, which was in Lyndall's neighborhood. Lyndall was in high school unusually for his age. However, he had started kindergarten a year earlier than most children, and because he was an honors student, was promoted an extra grade. "I would jump on my bike as soon as I got home from school and race over to Beyoncé's school," he recalled. "Then I'd wait until school let out, and there she'd be waiting for me with that knockout smile. We'd just stand there making eyes at one another and wait for her mother to pick her up.

"The first time I saw Tina was when she pulled up driving a drop-top [convertible] red car," Lyndall recalled. "She had Solange in the car. This vehicle was beautiful. I was, like, '*Whoa*, Beyoncé! What's goin' on in *your* family?'

"Tina was gorgeous. She pulled up to the curb and hollered out, 'Come on, now, Beyoncé. Get in the car. We're late.' I walked over to the car with Beyoncé and introduced myself to Tina. 'Hi! I'm Lyndall.' Tina said, 'Yes, I've heard all about you. Now come on, Beyoncé, get in the car. We're late!' And off they went in their luxury drop-top with Beyoncé waving goodbye to me, her braids blowing in the breeze. I thought to myself, 'Now that's a family that's successful, that's a family that has money... that's a family that's going places.'"

In Atlanta: The Dolls

*B*eyoncé didn't have much of a chance to get to know Lyndall Locke before she found herself in Atlanta rehearsing with Kelly, LaTavia, LeToya, Nicki, and Nina for an important event. Daryl Simmons had decided that the best way to interest record company executives in the group was to feature them in a showcase. Therefore, a performance would be held in the spring of 1994 at a famous rehearsal facility in Atlanta called Crossover Entertainment.

One afternoon, the girls were at Daryl's home in Atlanta, upstairs in one of the bedrooms being fitted into the new wardrobe he had purchased for them—black sequined tank tops and short studded jeans—when they heard the doorbell ring. "Girls, there's someone at the front door for you," hollered out Daryl. "Who would want to see *us*?" Beyoncé asked. "We're never gonna find out up here," LaTavia answered.

Then, as young girls often do, they all burst into squeals and shrieks as they bounded down the staircase and to the front door, falling all over one another. "Every day there was some new unexpected girlish thrill," Nina Taylor would later recall. "You just never knew what was going to happen."

Beyoncé was the first to the door. She swung it open and found a young, cute sixteen-year-old black kid standing before her, wearing an expensive leather jacket with large sunglasses. "Who the heck are *you*?" she asked. The youngster took in the six pretty girls in front of him, scrunched up his face, and said, "Now *that's* what I'm *talkin'* 'bout!" At that very moment, a full-figured African-American woman emerged from behind him and smacked him on the back of his head. "Boy!" she exclaimed. "What did I tell you, Usher? Behave, now!"

Fourteen years later, in 2008, Beyoncé would duet with Usher on the song "Love In This Club Part II" for his album *Here I Stand*. By that time both would be major, award-winning recording stars. Back in 1994, though, they couldn't have imagined the kind of success awaiting them. In the spring of that year, Usher Raymond III was the latest acquisition of LaFace Records. He had in common with Somethin' Fresh that he too had competed on *Star Search*. Unlike the girls, though, he had won. He was spotted on the program by an A&R person of LaFace, who recommended that L.A. Reid audition him. Reid signed the youngster to a deal. His first self-titled LaFace album—produced by Sean "P. Diddy" Combs—was about to be released in a few months. This kid was about to break big, but for now he was just a troublemaking sixteen-year-old flirt hanging out at Daryl Simmons's home.

"From that day on, Usher was always somewhere around us," recalled Nina Taylor. "My God! All of us had a crush on him. He was so cute, and what a little devil!"

The girls would go on long walks with Usher, the six of them dutifully following him around as if he were a teenage Pied Piper. "He'd show us Atlanta by foot since none of us were driving yet," Nicki Taylor recalled. "It was as if he could do the entire city by foot. At the end of the day, we'd be just so exhausted. But that boy, he had energy to spare. One night he had his heart set on playing Truth or Dare."

"Miss Tina was having a meeting with Daryl in one of the rooms on the ground level of the house," Nina remembered. "Meanwhile, Usher took us down a flight of stairs to the basement level where, at the end of the stairs, was the media room where you could watch movies or listen to music. It was to be Truth or Dare with one boy and six girls, so you know where this was headed. He dared my sister, Nicki, to kiss him on one cheek. Then LaTavia had to kiss him on the other." Things got so noisy they feared Tina would be checking in on them.

"Quick, put this movie in the video player," Usher suggested. He handed Beyoncé a cassette. It was the psychological thriller *The Crying Game*. Beyoncé took a look at the box and read the tagline aloud: "Some secrets should never be revealed." She shook her head and said, "This is just gonna make things worse!" Still, she popped the movie into the player as the girls quickly arranged themselves at a safe distance from Usher. They began watching the movie, acting as if they were completely absorbed in it. Seconds later, Tina burst into the room. "What is going on down here?" she demanded to know.

"Nothin', Mama," Beyoncé said innocently. "We're just watching a movie, that's all."

Tina looked around at all of the guilty faces in the room and said, "Y'all better behave down here, that's all I have to say." She then marched back upstairs.

"We all flopped on the floor, dying with laughter," Nina said. "Then Usher said, 'I better stop this movie, because there's a part coming up that you girls *do not* want to see.' And he popped the tape out of the box."

The girls couldn't spend as much time flirting with Usher as they might have liked, because the rehearsal schedule for the showcase was a grueling one. "Twelve-hour days," LaTavia Roberson recalled, "sometimes more. It was a matter of taking each song and going over every little part of it again and again—harmonies, dancing, stage patter. When Mathew came down to Atlanta, that amped things up, for sure. He was really on us, but a lot was riding on this thing."

At one point during a particularly tough day, Beyoncé walked to a corner to be alone and, once there, burst into tears. The other girls gathered around her, wondering what was wrong. The stress of trying to be perfect building with each passing day finally took its release with her tears. "It's not that I'm not happy," she said. "I don't even know what's wrong," she said. She was too young to identify that she was simply exhausted. "Ladies, we have to get back to work," Mathew said as he approached the huddle. "But Beyoncé's all upset," Nicki told him. Mathew came closer and examined his daughter, who clearly was out of sorts. He asked the others to give him a moment with her. Father and daughter then spent a few minutes talking to each other, Mathew kneeling before her with his hand on Beyoncé's slim shoulder. Finally, when it seemed as if she'd been boosted and was ready to get back to work, he led her by the hand back to the stage. "Okay, no more breaks," he told the girls. "When you're stars, there's not gonna be time for tears. There's only gonna be time for work."

"By this time—spring of 1994—Sha Sha Daniels and I were dating," recalled Andretta Tillman's nephew Belfrey Brown. "Ann came to me and told me that the girls needed money for the Atlanta gig, that there were certain expenses she was responsible for. She asked me for a few thousand dollars. I was nervous about giving it to her because of the way I was making my living at the time. I was selling drugs. Andretta didn't approve, but she also didn't want to ask Mathew for help, not that he would have had the money anyway," Brown recalled. "So I gave her the money and she used it for miscellaneous expenses.

"Actually, I had gotten used to bailing them all out," he recalled. "Once, Tina, Mathew, and Andretta went to the West Coast with the girls, I think it was for an audition at Motown. When they got to Los Angeles, they were asked to stay a few days longer, but didn't have the money to do so. Ann called me, panicked. 'How much do y'all need?' I asked her. And I heard Tina in the background holler out, 'Tell him to send us $750. More, if he has it. We're in big trouble out here.' So Sha Sha and I went down to the Western Union the next morning and I wired them $750. If I could help out, I definitely wanted to do that for them." There is no suggestion Tina or Mathew knew where Belfrey's money had come from.

The girls got along well with Belfrey, always knowing he was there to help in a pinch. He was in the inner circle, which meant he was as vulnerable to childhood pranking as anyone else trusted by the adults to watch over the kids. For example, one day, Belfrey took four of the girls—Beyoncé, Kelly, LaTavia, LeToya—as well as the Tillman boys—Armon and Chris—to the Greenspoint Mall in Houston. Once there, the six youngsters ran off to the arcade while he roamed the mall on his own. Eventually, he struck up a conversation with a pretty young woman. The two then went to the food court to get to know one another. "As we sat at a table, I started flirting with this girl, trying all of my best moves," Belfrey recalled, "when all of a sudden, the kids came out of nowhere talking about, 'Daddy! What are you doin' with that girl?' And Beyoncé said, 'We're sick and tired of you doing this every time we go out, Daddy! We're gonna tell Mama on you. Always picking up ladies in the mall! Ooooh, you're gonna be in so much trouble with Mama!' The girl I was trying to score with stood right up and said, 'You told me you were single and didn't have any kids! What a liar!' And she stormed right out of there. Beyoncé started laughing her fool head off, and then everyone else joined in. So, yeah, we always managed to have fun, even if there was this dark cloud hanging over our heads because of my aunt's terrible illness."

Because she was too sick to fly, Andretta—along with Armon and Chris—had to be driven down to Atlanta by Cholotte Taylor in her little Toyota Corolla. The small contingent stopped at the home of Andretta's sister's at the halfway mark so that Andretta could rest. She usually had to be on oxygen by this time; she often had a tank with her. Not only were many of her fingers by this time amputated, but she could barely walk because her legs were so swollen. Cholotte Taylor recalled, "Ann said, 'I will deal with this pain every day I have to, and I'm going to show up every day I can and live my life and have my career, and I don't care *what* it takes, I'm going to Atlanta to be with the girls.'"

When Andretta got down to Atlanta, she noticed a distinct difference in the girls' behavior toward her. Something was off; they weren't as welcoming as she had expected. Though she felt sure that they were acting on Mathew's cue, she had Sha Sha Daniels—who'd joined the Houston contingent—conduct her own investigation.

"Beyoncé told me straight out that Mathew had told them he was managing them now, and that Andretta was just going to be helping out a little here and there," recalled Sha Sha Daniels. "That was most certainly not the way Andretta was looking at things." When Sha Sha reported back to Andretta what Beyoncé had said, Andretta could barely control her fury. She immediately went to Mathew and demanded an explanation. "This isn't the time or place for this," he told her, unhappy about being confronted. He then pulled Andretta aside and the two had an animated discussion in a corner. In the end, they could come to no resolution.

"After she cooled off, she started thinking, 'Okay, well, maybe it's not so bad,'" recalled Sha Sha Daniels. "'Maybe Mathew is just trying to handle group business. He is the co-manager, after all. Maybe he's not withholding anything.' But then we started to look for our table at the showcase, and that's when it really hit us that things were bad."

Andretta noticed Beyoncé, LeToya, LaTavia, Kelly, Nicki, and Nina standing in a corner and giggling. "She heard one of them say, 'It looks like she got more fingers cut off,'" Kenny Moore recalled. Andretta had told him this later, adding that she'd felt the girls' giggling had been directed at her. "That really broke Ann," he said. "They were young and ignorant and she knew that, but still, they were like daughters to her. Sometimes it was easy to forget that they were just kids, they always acted so adult."

Things were about to get worse.

"On each table was a centerpiece, and within it were small Barbie dolls, each one painted a mocha brown," recalled Sha Sha. "Finally, we learned from someone that the reason for the Barbie doll centerpieces was that Mathew and Daryl Simmons had changed the name of the group from Somethin' Fresh to the Dolls. To do this without consulting Ann? We couldn't believe it until, sure enough, we heard the announcer say, 'Ladies and gentlemen—the Dolls!' Andretta and I just sat there in complete shock and disbelief. Ann started to cry. I said, 'Ann, don't cry. Don't let these people see you cry!' She said, 'I can't help it. Mathew's stabbed me in the back!' "

Actually, Daryl Simmons takes full credit for changing the group's name to the Dolls. He insists that there was no conspiracy with Mathew to do so. "They looked like little dolls, they were so cute," he says. "So I changed the name. Simple as that." Also for the record, Simmons says he doesn't remember Andretta as even having been in Atlanta! This suggests that she'd been so marginalized by this time, she was all but invisible even to those directly involved with the group. "I certainly never intended to offend her," he says, "I just didn't realize she had a proprietary interest in what was going on. My dealings had been with Mathew, not with Andretta. She wasn't even a factor. I just knew she was very sick, that's what I knew."

The showcase was a great success, even if it did get off to a shaky start. The Dolls' opening act, a twelve-year-old from Indianapolis named Keke Wyatt, "freaked out over something," Daryl recalled, "and refused to go on." Daryl had actually been considering adding KeKe to the Dolls, but not after this night. In fact, he was so disappointed in her, he dropped her as an artist. It did serve to remind, though, that it wasn't always easy for youngsters the Dolls' age to get up on a stage and be judged by adults. (KeKe Wyatt went on to a successful recording career and, in 2014, starred in "The R&B Divas of Atlanta" reality show with LaTavia Roberson.)

"After we realized that KeKe was not going to deliver, Beyoncé and the girls came through as expected and just blew everyone away," recalled Daryl Simmons. "I spent a nice sum on this event. I invited all the record company people from labels everywhere. We had costumes and lighting. I went the whole nine [yards] for the girls, and they definitely impressed."

After the performance, Beyoncé, Kelly, LaTavia, LeToya, Nicki, and

Nina gathered around Andretta and Sha Sha. "Oooh, Aunt Sha Sha, I have such a crush on that boy right over there," Beyoncé said, motioning to young Usher who was standing in a corner winking at her. He was wearing a white t-shirt with a big red heart on it, the logo for the film *Poetic Justice*; he appeared on the soundtrack with his song "Call Me a Mack." Sha Sha told Beyoncé to just go over and talk to him. "Oh no! He's so fine, he makes me nervous," Beyoncé whispered with a giggle. "He's gonna be at the barbecue tomorrow at Daryl's. Maybe I can talk to him then."

By this time, Andretta seemed very unhappy, staring into space. "Is everything okay, Miss Ann?" Beyoncé asked. "I'm worried about you," she said. "We all are."

"I'm fine, baby," Andretta told the girls as she drew an anxious breath. "Y'all were great. I'm very proud of y'all."

"Do you really think we were good?" LaTavia asked.

"I do," Andretta exclaimed.

"You know, we were just as surprised as you by the new name," Beyoncé said, maybe now realizing how upsetting it was to Andretta. She said that Mathew had told her that these things happen and that there wasn't much the girls could do about it other than to just go along with it. Andretta said this wasn't always true. "Sometimes you can speak up," she told Beyoncé. "In fact, sometimes you *must* speak up." She told her that Beyoncé shouldn't let the men in her life force her into making important decisions. "Your group's name? That's important," she said. "As a woman, you have to be strong, Bey."

Beyoncé's gaze turned quizzical. "But my dad said—"

"I know what your dad said," Andretta told her, cutting her off. "And I'm not saying Mathew is wrong. I'm just saying that sometimes young women have to stand up for ourselves." She urged them to please not allow the men in their lives to make important decisions for them.

"Yes, ma'am," Beyoncé said. "I understand."

"That's true, baby girl," Mathew said as he approached. He then took his daughter by the hand. "I want that for you, too," he said. "You *should* be strong." With that, he led his daughter away from Andretta. As she walked off hand in hand with her father, Beyoncé turned and looked over her shoulder at their debilitated "Miss Ann" still in her chair, with the others girls standing around her. There wasn't much Beyoncé could do in that moment other than what she did: She waved goodbye.

The day after the Atlanta showcase, everyone on the creative team, the parents, and the girls attended a big barbecue at the home of Daryl Simmons. As expected, Usher was present, but he and his mother took their leave before Beyoncé mustered up the courage to talk to him. "Star crossed lovers, I guess," Sha Sha Daniels observed with a smile. Later during the festivities, out of the blue Beyoncé asked Sha Sha, "Do I have to compete against TLC?" TLC was a very popular girls' group at the time, comprised of two singers, Tionne "T-Boz" Watkins and Rozonda "Chilli" Thomas along with rapper Lisa "Left Eye" Lopes. Simmons had worked with them at LaFace to terrific success. Beyoncé continued, "Because I don't think I can compete against them. They're so good." Sha Sha said, "You just be you, don't you worry about what other people are doing."

This wasn't the first time the two had had this kind of conversation. About a month earlier, Beyoncé had been at Andretta's home and was watching television with Sha Sha. Tyra Banks, the gorgeous supermodel, was being interviewed. At twenty, she had just returned to America from France, where she'd appeared in fifteen runway shows for famous designers such as Ralph Lauren, Yves Saint Laurent, and Oscar de la Renta. On the broadcast, she was telling the reporter that she'd just started her own company called Ty Girlz. Beyoncé's ears perked up when Tyra further explained that she had hired her mother as her manager and her father as financial adviser. "Aunt Sha Sha, do I have to compete against her?" Beyoncé suddenly asked.

"Against Tyra Banks?"

"Yeah, against her," Beyoncé said.

"I told her, 'Of course not, Beyoncé, she's not even in your age range," Sha Sha Daniels recalled years later. "Beyoncé said, 'But she's so beautiful. I can't possibly compete against that.' I told her Tyra was a model whereas she was a singer. But besides that, I told her, she didn't have to compete with anybody. 'You're gonna be a big star,' I told her. I told her I was sure of it, and that she should stop comparing herself to others."

In Atlanta, when the subject of competition came up again, Sha Sha thought she had satisfied Beyoncé. But apparently the youngster wasn't ready to let it go, yet. Ten minutes later, Beyoncé walked up to Daryl Simmons and asked him the exact same question: "Do you think I have to compete against TLC?" she asked after he complimented her showcase performance.

Daryl looked down at her, smiled, and said, "No, Bey. You have your own thing going on, so don't worry about it."

Sha Sha overheard the conversation and pulled Beyoncé aside. "Now, didn't I just tell you that you don't have to compete against TLC?" she whispered at her. Beyoncé looked sheepish. "I know. But I just needed to be sure," she explained.

Rejections—and Then a Deal!

 *A*fter the lavish showcase sponsored by Daryl Simmons for the Dolls in Atlanta, he expected the phone to ring off the hook with lucrative offers from record companies. That didn't happen. "Not one person called," he remembered. "When I finally did get feedback, it was critical about the girls' image. The way I had showcased them, they were very sexy. They had low-cut pants, tops that tied at their bare midriffs with their belly buttons showing. Tina had whipped their hair. They were *fine*, at least in my eyes. But people said, 'They're too grown.' 'They're too sexy.' 'They're too young to be up there doing what they're doing.' Nobody liked it. I was like, 'For real? Damn, *really*?' I couldn't understand it. The girls were hurt when I told them. They were crushed, actually."

Undaunted, Simmons was more determined than ever to place the Dolls with a major record label. "But why can't we sign with LaFace?" Beyoncé wanted to know. That made the most sense since not only had Simmons cut his teeth with LaFace, but he still had a strong alliance with the company's owners, L.A. Reid and Kenneth "Babyface" Edmonds. At this same time, though, Reid's estranged wife, Peri "Pebbles" Reid—the mastermind behind TLC—had just started her own company, Savvy Records. Since Reid and Pebbles were also battling it out at this time in divorce court, Simmons loathed having to choose sides between two good friends.

As it happened, Daryl might not have been able to sign the girls to LaFace anyway. Since Edmonds hadn't been able to make the Atlanta showcase, Daryl flew to Los Angeles with videotape in hand. He found Edmonds backstage at *The Arsenio Hall Show*, on which he was about to perform. Daryl popped the video tape into a VCR, sat back, and waited for Kenny's praise . . . which was not forthcoming. "I don't get it," Babyface said as he watched the girls perform. "I'm just not feelin' it."

"Really?" Daryl asked. "But that girl in front, Beyoncé. She's phenomenal."

"I guess she's all right," Babyface said.

"But, *damn!*" Simmons exclaimed. "That girl can sing so well."

"She's okay," Babyface said, clearly unimpressed.

"I was crushed, because I really wanted his approval," Simmons recalled. "That was my partner. We'd been best friends for thirty years!"

Edmonds's lack of interest was a sign of things to come. Clive Davis at Arista felt the same way, saying he wasn't sure if Beyoncé was a child, a teenager, or a young woman. Then, probably because he couldn't get a handle on her, he focused his critique on the songs, telling Daryl they weren't his "A songs." Meanwhile, Sean "P. Diddy" Combs, who had his own label, Bad Boy Records, felt the girls weren't "hip-hop enough." He said that the lead singer was pretty good and that he was fascinated by her name. However, in the end he passed, saying Beyoncé wasn't "edgy" enough and that she and her group needed "more flava" before he would ever be interested. Since they were getting passes from all quarters, Beyoncé began pushing harder than ever for a deal with LaFace. "I just don't understand why we're not going over there," she said, "considering Daryl's ties, and all." By this time, Daryl didn't even have the heart to tell her about Babyface's apathy.

One executive who was interested in the girls, though, was Sylvia Rhone, chairman and CEO of Elektra Records. The *Los Angeles Times* hadn't dubbed her "the most powerful woman in the record business" for no good reason. When she wanted to move, she moved fast. Daryl Simmons recalled, "Sylvia flew down to Atlanta for a private showcase at my studio to meet the girls. Because I was still nervous about the critique that they were too adult and sexy, I conformed a little for Sylvia. I went out and got the girls some jeans, leather jackets, and Timberlands [boots] to make them appear as young as they really were. When they performed for her, Sylvia loved them. She thought Beyoncé was going to be *major*. That's what sealed the deal, the fact that she loved Beyoncé. So, at around the end of 1994, I signed the girls to a joint venture/production deal with Elektra Records.

"Sylvia gave us a very good contract, money to operate, record songs, pay producers, and keep the ball rolling in Atlanta," Simmons continued. "It was my first deal on my own, and I was very happy with it, as was Mathew. The girls were excited too, as you can imagine."

It certainly now seemed as if all of the hard work on everyone's part was about to pay off. Beyoncé and Kelly were back in Houston at school when they got the news. "They called our names over the loudspeakers," Beyoncé recalled. " '*Kelly Rowland and Beyoncé Knowles, come to the office!*' And I thought, 'Oh my God, what did I do?' We went to the office and my dad was there and he said, 'Y'all got y'all's record deal! Y'all are gonna move to Atlanta for a while and we're gonna get y'all tutors!' " She said she and Kelly were so stunned, all they could do was stand in place and then… scream.

To celebrate the milestone, Mathew and Tina Knowles hosted a "signing party" at their home. Though very few people knew it, the Knowleses were still struggling with their finances, so news of this deal could not have happened at a better time. "There was a lot of excitement about Elektra," Belfrey Brown recalled. "It was just the shot in the arm everyone needed."

"Thank you for joining our family for this celebration," Tina announced to all of the guests, "and thank you all for being a part of us." As idealistic as ever, she said that all of them, the girls and the creative team and their relations, were part of the Knowleses' extended family. She made sure to go to each person and spend time with them—Daryl, Andretta, Armon, Chris, Kenny, Belfrey, Sha Sha, Tony Mo.—all of them seemed to matter to her. For his part, Mathew was, as always, focused on Beyoncé. "The pressure is on now more than ever," he told her in front of witnesses. "You have to be better than ever now, little girl. Do you understand that?"

"But I'm already tryin' real hard, Daddy," she said.

Mathew nodded. "I know you are," he told her. "I'm just sayin' you can't slack off now that we got a deal. In fact, you have to work *even harder.*"

"I will," she said. "I promise."

"*Show Business Is a Lot of Things…*"

*A*s you know, we are really on our way now," Andretta Tillman enthused. The Dolls were in her home, sitting around the dining room table during another of their group meetings. It was the summer of 1994. "The details of the record deal with Elektra are almost finalized," Andretta continued. At that, Beyoncé, Kelly, LaTavia, LeToya, Nina, and Nicki began to scream and clap their hands, giving each other high-fives. Andretta continued,

"I'm afraid I have some bad news, though." The girls' smiling faces turned serious. "It turns out the label wants a four-girl group," Andretta said. "They don't want any dancers or rappers," she added, looking at Nina, Nicki, and LaTavia, all three of whose mouths dropped open. "This means two of you won't be in the group anymore. They want Beyoncé. They want Kelly. They want LeToya. And one more. Nina, Nicki, and LaTavia," she concluded, "will have to audition for that fourth spot."

The six girls were quiet for a long moment. Kelly was the first to speak. "But Miss Ann," she said, "this is *our* group. They can't break us up, can they?" Beyoncé answered for Andretta. "They can do whatever they want," she said. "That's the way it works, Kelly," she added. She knew the drill by now, how the game was played.

"Beyoncé is right," Andretta said. "As much as I love you girls, there's not much I can do about this."

True to her nature, Andretta was against the idea of dropping any of the girls from the act. She'd already warned Cholotte, Nicki and Nina's mother, that her daughters were on the chopping block. She said that Mathew hadn't even wanted the sisters to be a part of the "Star Search" performance, but that she had insisted upon it. Now, she felt there was nothing more she could do. "It's bigger than Mathew," she said, "now, it's the label's call, though I think Mathew instigated it."

"Oh my God," Kelly exclaimed. "This ain't fair, Miss Ann."

Beyoncé didn't comment, but one might imagine that she was likely thinking, "Dang, Kelly! Get with it!"

Andretta stood up on shaky legs. "Show business is a lot of things," she said as she walked out of the room, "but fair isn't one of them."

"We were in shock," Nicki Taylor recalled, "but still, we knew that one of us was still going to be in the group. We just didn't know which one. LaTavia wasn't really a singer, she was a rapper. Nicki and I weren't singers either, we were dancers. The fact that we had to compete against one another as singers for that coveted fourth spot was upsetting since we were also cousins. But it was what it was.

"For the next week, Nicki, LaTavia, and I worked with a vocal coach day and night," added Nina Taylor. "Then, finally, we each auditioned for Mathew and Andretta and the vocal teacher. My mother later told me that the coach fought hard for me. Though he thought I had the most range, Mathew and Andretta really wanted LaTavia. Mathew had been against me and Nicki for a while, though. Anyway, since it was two against one, LaTavia got the one remaining spot in the group."

"I was elated," LaTavia Roberson said, "but the fact that my cousins were on their way out, well...that was devastating after all the work they put into the group."

Of course, Nina and Nicki had been with the act from the very beginning, having been recruited by Deborah Laday and Denise Seals in 1990. Therefore, this really was a bitter pill to swallow. "When we got over our disappointment, we were happy for the other girls," Nina Taylor recalled. "We figured we'd all still be friends, you know? Sisters. Miss Ann even said, 'You never know, we'll probably need dancers at some point anyway. Rather than hire girls, we'll just use you two.' So we didn't feel like we were out, necessarily. We felt, at the very least, we would all still be friends. But...it didn't work out quite that way."

In fact, the night Nicki and Nina left the meeting at Andretta's home— the one where it was announced that LaTavia had been chosen for the group—would pretty much mark the end of their friendship with Beyoncé, Kelly, and LeToya. It would also put at least a temporary crimp in their relationship with their cousin, LaTavia. "We called every day," Nina recalled. "We left so many messages, we lost track. 'Why aren't y'all calling us back?' Nothing. We kept going over to the house and they weren't there. It was like they had vanished. Finally, Miss Ann told us they had gone down to Atlanta to begin recording for Elektra. But without even saying goodbye? I was twelve. Nicki was fifteen. Can you imagine how we took this? After being with those girls every day for five years, day and night? We had just performed as a group for our Taylor family reunion in Louisiana, so the girls were a real part of our family as far as we were concerned."

"I just remember sitting in my room crying," Nicki Taylor recalled, "and one night, I got out a pen and paper and wrote Beyoncé a letter, something along the lines of, 'If y'all could just see the tears running down my face.' And since I actually *was* crying when I wrote it, one of my tears fell on the paper and made a wet spot. I wrote, 'Here's where it's wet because of my tears.' I was just a little girl, very dramatic and heartbroken. The letter got to Beyoncé. I know because Mathew called my mom." According to Nicki, Mathew expressed unhappiness that the letter had made Beyoncé cry.

If Beyoncé actually did cry upon receiving Nicki's letter, maybe it touched something deep within her, that part of her that was still just a child. One thing it apparently didn't do, though, was make her respond.

A Knowles family portrait taken in December 1990: Beyoncé, 9; Mathew, 37; Solange 4; and Tina Knowles, 35. By this time, Beyoncé was already winning first-place trophies in talent shows and beauty pageants. (*Paul S. Howell/© Houston Chronicle. Used with permission.*)

Beyoncé, age 10. (*© The Tillman Estate. Used by permission.*)

An early photo session of some of the many girls who auditioned for Beyoncé's first group, Girls Tyme:
(Bottom tier, l-r): unidentified girl; LaTavia Roberson; Angie Beyincé (Beyoncé's cousin); Nicki Taylor.
(Middle tier, l-r): (unidentified girl); Ashley Davis; Millicent Laday; (unidentified girl).
(Top tier, l-r): Beyoncé Knowles; Denise Seals; (unidentified girl); Cheryl Roberson, LaTavia's mom; Deborah Laday; Carolyn Davis, Ashley's mom. (© *Deborah Jackson Laday. Used by Permission.*)

Very early Girls Tyme photo in Houston (left to right): Staci LaToisen; LaTavia Roberson; (unidentified girl); Nina Taylor; (unidentified girl); Nicki Taylor; Millicent Laday; Beyoncé Knowles (in background). (© *LaTavia Roberson. Used by Permission.*)

Girls Tyme (from top middle clockwise): Kelly Rowland, Beyoncé Knowles, LaTavia Roberson, Nicki Taylor, Nina Taylor, and Ashley Davis. (*Howard Castleberry/* © *Houston Chronicle. Used With Permission.*)

Andretta Tillman was Beyoncé's and Girl Tyme's first official manager. Gone largely unacknowledged, she was the woman most responsible for the girls' early success. (© *The Tillman Estate. Used by Permission.*)

Denise Seals and Deborah Laday are the two women who discovered Beyoncé and managed her and her group before Andretta Tillman. (*Photo of Deborah Laday,* © *Deborah Laday. Used by Permission/Photo of Denise Seals* © *Denise Seals. Used by Permission.*)

There was interest in making Beyoncé and LaTavia—both ten years old—a duo act. Here they are in the fall of 1991 on their way from Houston to Sausalito, California, to film the video for their song, "S.Y.T." (© *LaTavia Roberson. Used by Permission.*)

Somethin' Fresh

…and then, in 1993, they were known as Somethin' Fresh. (l-r) LaTavia, Nicki, Nina, Beyoncé, LeToya, and Kelly. (© *The Tillman Estate. Used by Permission.*)

The girls are growing up. This photo was autographed by the four of them for "Ms. Ann"—Andretta Tillman. (© *The Tillman Estate. Used by Permission.*)

By 1995, the girls were a quartet known simply as Destiny. (l-r) Kelly Rowland, Beyoncé Knowles, LaTavia Roberson, and LeToya Luckett (© *The Tillman Estate. Used by Permission.*)

Beyoncé, Kelly, and LaTavia relax in Jamaica after performing two shows there with the reggae artist, Beenie Man. (© *LaTavia Roberson. Used by Permission.*)

Kelly, LeToya, Beyoncé, and LaTavia during a shoot for *17* magazine. (© *LaTavia Roberson. Used by Permission.*)

Mathew Knowles, Kim Burse (Mathew's A&R Director), producer, D'Wayne Wiggins, and Andretta Tillman pose in the Columbia/Sony headquarters in New York just after the girls signed their record company contracts. The photo behind them bears the group's name, Destiny, before it was changed to Destiny's Child. (© *The Tillman Estate. Used by Permission*)

In 1997, Beyoncé, 16, and her boyfriend Lyndall Locke, 18, attended his senior prom at Lee High School in Houston. The happy-go-lucky Lyndall was a breath of fresh air to the always-working Beyoncé. The two were together, on and off, for almost ten years. (© *Lydia Locke. Used by Permission.*)

Beyoncé presented Lyndall with a chocolate cake on his nineteenth birthday, December 3, 1998. Also in the photo: Lyndall's cousin, Dallas Gillespie, and sister, Laura (seated); Kelly Rowland (in cap, next to Beyoncé) and Beyoncé's cousin, Angie Beyince (to Beyoncé's left). (© *Lydia Locke. Used by Permission.*)

Teen cut-ups, Lyndall and Beyoncé. (© *Lydia Locke. Used by Permission.*)

In 1997, Destiny was renamed Destiny's Child. Here, the girls pose in front of the Sony building in Manhattan just before performing at an intimate showcase for record company executives. (l-r) Beyoncé, LeToya, LaTavia, and Kelly. (© *LaTavia Roberson. Used by Permission.*)

Beyoncé's aspiration to be a star was one thing Mathew and Tina Knowles had in common in an otherwise often-troubled marriage. They made many sacrifices to see to it that their daughter's dream came true. (*Photo by Jim Smeal/WireImage*)

But who knows? Maybe Mathew wouldn't allow it, feeling it would only upset his daughter further.

After that phone call from Mathew, Cholotte Taylor says she sat her daughters down and told them, "You need to stop. If it's for you, it's for you. But if not, God has another plan." She recalled, "I figured God wanted them to go to school and get their degrees, and that maybe that's what this was really all about. So I started pushing them in that direction. The way I raised them, they always knew they were going to do something great with their lives, singing group or not. But, oh my! They sure did miss their friends.

"None of the mothers called me, either. It felt like, 'Okay, that's it. See you no more.' When Ashley left, at least that was her mother's choice. But this was not my choice. My daughters were just dropped."

Mathew would no doubt have sat down with Beyoncé, Kelly, LaTavia, and LeToya and told them to focus on the job at hand and not to worry about their former group members. They couldn't afford to let anything stop this fast-moving train, not after all they'd been through. There was no time for tears. It was pretty much the same thing the girls—including Nina and Nicki—were told when Ashley Davis left the group. "It happened to her, and now it happened to us," Nina Taylor observed.

In the years to come, Nina and Nicki Taylor would leave show business, go on to college, and became schoolteachers. They would marry, have children, and live happy, contented lives. In a strange and sad coincidence, Nina would also suffer from lupus, the same disease Andretta battled. Nina went under the care of Andretta's doctor; she is presently in remission.

"The fact that, to this day, none of us talk to Beyoncé still bothers us," said Nina Taylor, also speaking for her sister. "For years, I kept thinking, was it really a sisterhood? Or was it just business? Because if it was just business, then I should have conducted myself in a different way. But as a little girl, you give your heart. You don't know any better. You give everything you have, everything you *are*, and you just never think you'll get hurt. Until one day … you do."

First Date

$\mathcal{T}$he Dolls—now just Beyoncé, Kelly, LaTavia, and LeToya—spent most of 1994 in Atlanta recording. Since all were just fourteen, they were chaperoned by LaTavia's mom, Cheryl, as well as by one of Daryl Simmons's assistants. Simmons also arranged for them to have home tutors so that they could remain on top of their studies. While the girls certainly missed their family members in Houston, they felt that their dreams were coming true in Atlanta and that it was well worth the sacrifice. Kelly would use her time there to reconnect with her mother, Doris.

At the end of 1994, Beyoncé Knowles returned home for the holidays, which also gave her the opportunity to see Lyndall Locke again after more than a year of long-distance "dating"—which meant plenty of telephone conversations. By now, Tina and Mathew felt they should get to know Lyndall better. "I finally had a chance to meet the parents," he recalls. "I went to the house for dinner. That's when I got to know Tina and Big Mac, which is what I started calling Mathew.

"Let me tell you, Big Mac don't play," recalled Lyndall. "I was scared as shit meeting him. Of course, he gave me the third degree: 'What are you about?' 'What kind of student are you?' 'Who are your parents?' But we liked each other right away. He was very protective of his daughter, and since I didn't have a father at home, I was intrigued by their close relationship. To see a dad be so involved in his kid's life was very interesting to me. Tina? Beautiful. I'd never met a woman that elegant before; she made a huge impression on me. She was someone who got right to the point, was very direct—no bullshit from Tina Knowles. She was a straight shooter."

Once Lyndall came into her life, Beyoncé wanted to spend as much time as possible with him—except when she was rehearsing or recording, which (as he was beginning to understand) was always to be a priority. When they were together, his sense of humor was something she came to really appreciate. There was simply no way to be in a room with him for more than five minutes without laughing. Because she was always so serious, Lyndall was a great distraction. Plus, he was sincere. He had a good heart, and she could sense it.

Especially where Lyndall was concerned, Beyoncé kept her career very much apart from her personal life. Lyndall recalled, "I didn't even know she was a singer! Someone mentioned it to me and I asked her about it, and she was vague and said something about playing the piano. ["I played piano for like a second but then stopped," Beyoncé explained in 2015. She does still play, though, as she does on her 2015 video, "Die With You."] We talked on the phone almost every night while she was in Atlanta and she never mentioned problems with LaTavia, Nina, Nicki…or whoever. I would really have to pull it out of her if she was having an issue in the group. She had her girls to talk to about that type of thing. With me, we had a whole other life."

One night, after bringing Beyoncé to Lyndall's home for a Friday night TV date, Tina had a conversation with Lyndall's mother, Lydia, while sitting in the Lockes' dining room. Over a cup of piping hot coffee, Tina talked about her daughter. "Tina said she found it amazing that for such a small child, Beyoncé had so much focus," Lydia recalled. "I told her that I wished Lyndall had some of that kind of focus. He was all over the map, that one! She liked Lyndall's energy, though. In fact, she said she wanted Beyoncé to have a little more fun. She sometimes found herself worried by how hard she drove on herself. 'I want her to have a more normal childhood,' she said. 'She has the advantage of youth, and when that's gone, you can't get it back. But,' she concluded, 'something tells me that boat has already sailed.'"

Childhood sweethearts Beyoncé and Lyndall didn't share their first kiss until they'd been together for a little more than a year and a half, in December 1994. Lyndall had just turned fifteen. Beyoncé was thirteen. The occasion was a concert by the R&B artist Brian McKnight, whose platinum-selling eponymous debut album had been released two years earlier. It was the first concert Lyndall had ever attended; Beyoncé saw her first concert when she was just six years old, Michael Jackson at the Summit in Houston, back in April 1988. Lyndall's mother, Lydia—who paid a couple hundred dollars for good seats for the McKnight show—had agreed to take the youngsters to the concert venue, the Arena Theatre in Houston.

"I was to chauffeur them to the show, and Tina was to pick them up after," Lydia Locke recalled. "This was really their first big date. I told Lyndall, 'Boy, you need to dress up for this big night.' So he put on a suit with a crisp white shirt, a nice tie—the whole nine yards. Then, when we got to Beyoncé's, she was dressed very casually in a little maroon pantsuit. I thought, 'Oh no. I clearly must have misread this thing.' Lyndall looked at me as if to say, 'Mom! I'm overdressed and it's your fault!' Tina got out her camera and had the kids pose for pictures. "We must have taken a hundred photos," said Lydia Locke. "We were so proud and excited. Beyoncé was just as sweet as she could be, a little southern belle. She and Lyndall were the cutest couple."

"Once we got to the auditorium, before the show started, I accidentally dropped our popcorn," Lyndall recalled. "Beyoncé and I both bent down to get it. When we did, our heads bumped. We looked at each other, and that's when it happened—the first kiss. I had never before felt anything like that in my entire . . . fifteen years," he recalled. "I'd been waiting for that kiss for a year! It was one of the most awesome kisses ever, and if she tells you any different, she'd be *totally* lying," he concluded, laughing.

Disappointment

$\mathcal{A}$t the beginning, my relationship with Mathew Knowles was cool," Daryl Simmons recalled. "My impression of him—and I still think it's an accurate one—is that he was hardworking, passionate, and determined. He respected me and I respected him. It was all good. Until one day . . . it wasn't."

Daryl had always believed it beneficial to hold what he called "morale meetings" with his recording artists. Not only did he view them as a good way for his acts to express any concerns or problems they may have had, but he also looked at the meetings as an opportunity to boost their spirits. His first "morale meeting" with the Dolls in Atlanta went well. Gathering them after a recording session, he said, "Girls, you know what? Everyone thinks that as soon as you have a record deal, you're going to have an album right away. But there's a process. And it's usually 'hurry up and wait.'"

"What's that mean?" Beyoncé wanted to know.

"It means we can rush our work and hand over the music to Elektra only to then have them sit on it and wait until they're good and ready to release it." With that being the case, he concluded, the best thing they could do was to just take their time and do the best job possible.

"That makes sense," Kelly said, nodding. The girls all agreed.

Beyoncé then wanted to know what would happen if the label didn't like the music once it was finished. Would it then drop the artist? Daryl said yes, under those circumstances the artist would likely be cut from the roster. When she said that this didn't seem fair, Daryl quipped, "Welcome to the record industry."

The producer and his charges then talked for another thirty minutes about the music business, the girls soaking up every bit of knowledge they could from him. The meeting ended with a group hug. Subsequent morale meetings went just as well. Somehow, though, Mathew, back in Houston, found out about Daryl's meetings with the girls, which was fine since they weren't meant to be kept secret. According to Daryl, Mathew was upset. He telephoned Simmons and let him have it. "Listen, don't you *ever* have meetings with my girls without me being there," he said, according to Simmons's memory. "Do you hear me? That is *not cool*, brother. That is not cool at all."

"*Whoa, Mat!*" Daryl exclaimed. "It's no big deal. It's just me keeping the girls' morale up."

Mathew said he was making plans to go to Atlanta immediately to discuss the matter in person. He drove seven hours from Houston and, by the time he got to his destination, was angrier than ever. "And he went off," Daryl recalled. "I mean, *he went off!* 'These are *my* girls,' he shouted at me. 'Don't you *ever* have no meeting without me being present.' I told him I was responsible for making their record, and in that capacity, *of course* I could have meetings with them. 'We're not talking business,' I said. 'These are just morale meetings!' Mathew wasn't having it, though. 'I handle their morale, not you,' he told me. 'This is my damn group, not yours!'"

Later that day, Mathew apparently told Tina what had happened with Daryl. Privately, Mathew's position was that he knew and understood Daryl as a producer and respected his views about the recording of music. However, he had no idea what his views were in regard to the record industry in general or, really, about anything else. His girls were of an impressionable age, and he didn't want Daryl or anyone else influencing them without his being able to first vet the process. It actually made sense. But there was probably a better way to handle the situation other than to just blow up about it. Mathew was never one to hold back, though; he could be passionate, blunt, and to the point, and that was just something people who did business with him had to understand. "At least with Mathew Knowles you always knew where you stood," Daryl Simmons would say about him.

Tina was unhappy about the way Mathew had handled things with Daryl. From the way Mathew described things it sounded to her like he had harmed the relationship. This was no time to cause trouble, not when the family was in so much financial turmoil. Soon Tina was on the telephone with Daryl, trying to smooth things over.

"She told me she was so sorry that Mathew went off on me," Daryl recalled. "'Mat respects you, Daryl,' she told me. 'He admires what you've done with your career. In a lot of ways, he wants to *be* like you.' I appreciated that but told her that the way I saw it, it just wasn't going to work with me and Mathew. I told her that if he would go off on me for something as minor as group meetings, what can I expect down the road from him?"

Tina finally hung up, but not before again apologizing profusely and expressing her hope that the two men might work things out.

At the beginning of 1995, the songs for Elektra were finally finished. Over the years, some people have suggested that they weren't of the quality that Sylvia Rhone at Elektra had hoped for when she signed the act. This is Mathew's memory of the situation. But according to Daryl, Rhone also had issues with Mathew. "Once the music was done," Simmons recalled, "true to the nature of the record industry, things didn't move as quickly as everyone would have liked. That's the way it goes. Hurry up and wait, just like I told the girls.

"But then Mathew started calling the record company every day, pushing Sylvia, asking, 'How come nothing's going on?' He was impatient. Of course, that was understandable. After all, he had put everything into this venture and he wanted it to work. But I think he was a little naïve when it came to dealing with people in the record business because, in my opinion anyway, you can't push. People don't respond well to that, especially if you have no track record of hits."

Certainly Sylvia told Daryl she was finding the phone calls a bit much. Whatever the reason—lack of interest from the record industry or Mathew's persistence—Elektra dropped a bombshell.

"Long story short, Sylvia Rhone decided not to release the girls' recordings," Simmons concluded. "In other words, she canceled the deal with Elektra. Finished. Over. Done."

It was up to Mathew to tell the girls that Elektra had elected not to go forward with them. He gathered them in the living room of their Atlanta accommodations to deliver the sad news. He told them it was a tough business and that it had just gotten a little tougher for all of them. "Elektra has decided to drop us from the label." The girls were confused. Did this mean their music wasn't going to be coming out at all? Mathew confirmed as much. He explained it by saying the label wanted "to go in another direction." That was all Beyoncé needed to hear to find some hope in the situation. "We can do that," she said eagerly. "We can go in any direction they want. All they have to do is tell us what they want, and we can give it to them."

"No, Bey," Mathew said sadly. "I'm afraid not. That door is closed." (To date, these Elektra recordings have *still* never been heard by the public.)

Making a bad situation in her life just a little worse was that at this same time, Beyoncé found out that Lyndall Locke—who was back in Houston—was having a sexual relationship with another girl. Lyndall, who was fifteen at the time, with his hormones raging, had lost his virginity to a girl from church. Maybe it wasn't surprising that he would want to see other girls, with Beyoncé gone so much of the time. Lyndall couldn't lie about what he'd done, and Beyoncé told him there was no way they would be together now.

Whatever sadness or anger Beyoncé was feeling about Lyndall's behavior would have to be pushed aside, at least for now while she was coming to terms with the loss of the record deal. When the girls said they wanted to talk to Daryl about it, Mathew decided to allow it. Beyoncé, LaTavia, Kelly, and LeToya then showed up at Daryl Simmons's studio, all four clearly upset. "We feel like we let you down," Beyoncé said.

"Beyoncé, it's not like that, at all," Daryl told her. "It's just that me and your dad are not gonna work out. He sees things going one way, and I see them going another way."

"But we've worked so *hard*," Beyoncé said.

"Look," Daryl began, "don't worry. You girls will get a record deal, I promise you. You deserve one and you will get signed."

"They were really a mess, all of them," Simmons said, "and, man, I felt so terrible. These kids were so puzzled by the whole thing. It was just business. But try explaining that to a bunch of eager and also exhausted fourteen-year-old girls. I thought, Wow, for their whole lives, it must seem like adults have been screwing with them. All of the decisions made for them over the years have been made by grown-ups with a vested interest in the outcome, and they've just had to deal with it. They haven't had much say in any of it. Looking at them before me, I could actually see the way it had worn them down."

Daryl was emotionally drained too. After the Dolls left his studio, he turned to his producer, Thom "TK" Kidd, and said, "Man! That was tough." The two then sat and stared into space for a long time, trying to collect themselves. "God forbid those kids ever make any money," Daryl finally said, breaking the silence. "Because, dude, if those kids ever make any money, it's not going to go smoothly."

Financial and Marital Woes

$\mathcal{T}$hough Mathew and Tina tried to shield Beyoncé, Solange, and Kelly from their ever-worsening financial situation, by the time the Elektra deal fell through the girls understood that serious trouble was in the offing. Everyone had been counting on Elektra to save the day, and now that it was obviously not going to happen, Mathew and Tina were out of options—especially since earlier, on March 30, 1995, another tax lien had been assessed against them for $38,845.30.

Tina would soon be forced to give a deposition in a lawsuit relating to their finances during which attorney Benjamin Hall would produce checks written against her 1995 business account and that had been returned for "insufficient funds." Not just one or two, either. He produced *eleven* of them and laid them out on the conference table before her, almost as if to mock her. It had to have been embarrassing. "Well, if someone gives you a bad check it causes your checks to bounce," Tina explained, trying to keep her composure.

"Assuming you don't have an operating balance in excess of that amount of money," the lawyer said, stating the obvious.

"*Assuming*," Tina snapped back.

Andretta Tillman was also having more than her fair share of bad luck. Back in June 1994, she'd been forced to file for bankruptcy. "She had gone through all her money," explained her brother To-to Brown. "She put all of it into the girls. We couldn't believe it. All that money from the accident settlement and insurance—gone!"

"I was there when her car was repossessed," recalled Pat Felton. "I remember telling her that she shouldn't spend money on new photos of the girls if she couldn't pay her car note. 'But we are so close,' she would tell me, 'I can feel success right around the corner.' She had invested so much into this dream, I felt that maybe she could no longer see things practically.

She was even selling off her furniture so that she could buy the girls new dresses.

"I went with her to the bankruptcy court and saw all the paperwork, and pretty much all of it had to do with the singing group. After her house was foreclosed on, she, Armon, and Chris moved into a smaller one. But only those in her inner circle knew all of these details. She was pretty private."

While Andretta didn't share her money challenges with the Knowleses, they didn't share theirs with her either. Even though they were all in the same sort of trouble, it was as if they had too much pride to admit it to each other. Just three days after Andretta's filing, Mathew and Tina refiled their own bankruptcy claim for a third time as they continued to sort out their debts.

"Did Ann know you were having all of these problems?" Benjamin Hall would ask Tina.

"She didn't know our financial situation at all because we were steadily putting out money every single day," Tina explained. "The girls continued to stay at our house and we continued to feed them every single day. The bankruptcy did not affect our ability to support them."

In the fall of 1995, Tina finally made the difficult decision to split up the family. It seemed there were still problems in her marriage. As much as she may have been concerned about appearances, Tina was also practical. There was no way to save the house, she decided. Thus the best strategy was to separate from Mathew, sell the house, and see what the future held. She knew what had to be done, and, as tough as she knew it would be on everyone, she decided to screw up all her courage and get on with it. She found a small town house for herself and the girls—Beyoncé, Solange, and Kelly. Wherever Mathew landed was up to him.

Big Changes

*I*t was a fall day in 1995. Beyoncé and Kelly, fourteen, and Solange, nine, were sitting on the top of three brick steps at the end of a cement walkway in front of the family's two-story home at 3346 Parkwood Drive. "Girls, you just can't sit there," Tina said as she approached them. "Come on, now, you have to move! Belfrey needs to get through here."

As if on cue, Belfrey Brown pulled up in a beat-up pickup truck with two close friends. "Thanks so much for coming," Tina said as she approached the young men. "This won't take long," she said, her manner officious. "It's just a bunch of boxes in the living room. Now, here's the address to the town house," she said, reaching into her pocket and pulling out a slip of paper. She handed it to Belfrey.

"Is everything okay, Tina?" Belfrey asked.

"Everything is just fine," Tina answered brusquely. "I'm just doing what I always do, Belfrey. I am taking care of my family. Thank you for your help," she said, kissing him quickly on the cheek.

"She was tense," Belfrey recalled, "and I knew she was in pain, but she wasn't going to show it, no way." Tina had called Andretta very late the night before to ask if she knew anyone who could help her move out of the house she shared with Mathew. Andretta suggested her nephew, Belfrey. "Of course, we had all heard that Tina and Mat were splitting up," he recalled. "We also heard a rumor that the house had been foreclosed on. [That was actually not the case; the house was being sold.] So, when Tina called and asked for help, I wasn't surprised."

"What about all of your furniture?" asked Belfrey.

"The furniture stays," Tina said. "There's plenty in the town house."

Belfrey and his friends entered the house to find stacked boxes on a wrought-iron-and-wood staircase in the entryway. As he looked around, the first thing that crossed his vision was a collection of what appeared to be expensive African art in the living room to his left. It was obvious that the house had been decorated during better times; the furnishings were exquisite.

Most everyone knew that Tina would end up in a town house somewhere, but Mathew's whereabouts would remain more of a mystery. "At first he stayed with my sister," Andretta's brother, To-to, recalled. "He didn't have any place to go, and Andretta was the kind of person who, no matter how she felt about you, she wasn't going to have you sleepin' in the street. He stayed with her for a short time. Then I think he got an apartment."

This breakdown of the family weighed heavy on Tina's mind and heart. She never imagined herself in a situation where she would be raising two children on her own—three, counting Kelly. With the marital bond she shared with Mathew now broken, her great concern was for the welfare of the girls. "'I will never give up,' she told me," recalled one of her good friends at this time. "'I will fight through the pain,' she said, 'and I will do it for Beyoncé. I will do it for Solange. And I will do it for Kelly.'"

Since money was so tight, Tina worked harder than ever at Headliners. "My mama worked until she had calluses on her fingers and swollen feet," Beyoncé said in 2011, "then she would find time to redecorate houses for her friends, and also make everyone's prom and wedding dresses. She took me and Solange to our dance classes and recitals, cooked us delicious meals, and brought us to church. On Sunday, it was family day. She worked hard and never stopped."

"I have always said that Beyoncé got her work ethic not from her father," observed Pat Felton, "but from her mother."

Still, despite Tina's strong work ethic, there were times when she couldn't make ends meet and was forced to put her pride aside. "Tina began calling Andretta more and more asking for money," recalled Sha Sha Daniels. "This is when we knew things were desperate, because for Tina Knowles to ask for help? She had to really need it.

"Beyoncé never talked to me about these problems," Sha Sha recalled. "I think in some ways, she shut down. She became much more shy, much less open. She would frown a lot. 'Girl, if you don't turn that frown upside down, it's gonna freeze like that,' I would tell her. Solange was smaller, but somehow she seemed more in touch with her feelings. She would talk about things, but not Beyoncé."

"I was too young to realize what was going on," Beyoncé would later remember. "It worried me, and I didn't understand what happened until I got older. Back then, all I knew for sure was that my mom and I were moving from a big house to a small house, and we went from having two cars to one car."

In December 1995, the house the Knowleses had so loved at 3346 Parkwood Drive was sold for $165,000, "way less than what we could've gotten if we'd had time to sell it right," Tina would conclude sadly.

"We went from living in a four-bedroom house with this beautiful living space," Solange Knowles recalled, "into a two-bedroom apartment..."

"...and that's when my mother told me she and my father had gotten a separation," Beyoncé continued. "To make things worse, it was around Christmas, when families are supposed to be together. It was such a painful time that I erased a lot of those memories from my head. Basically, I didn't know where my dad was, my mom was depressed, and we didn't have much money. Kelly and I had to share a very small room, and my sister shared a room with my mom."

"This was a dark time for the girls, but especially for Beyoncé," said one of her relatives. "The way she felt about her dad? Seeing him walk out the door like that was hard, and coming on top of losing Lyndall and then the record deal—it was too much." This relative says that Beyoncé "spent a lot of time alone in her room," which was par for the course for her. When upset and confused, she would almost always isolate herself. "When she got into a mood like that, it was hard to reach her," said the source. "The sensitivity that made her such a budding artist could work against her when times got rough. She could become very, very depressed. When this happened, Tina knew to just leave her alone."

Despite this upset in their lives, or maybe because of it, Tina continued to hold fast to her religious convictions. She didn't talk much about her spirituality, but it was a constant in her life. She made certain it was also a strong influence on the lives of her daughters and Kelly. One day during this time, when Beyoncé seemed particularly upset about what was going on, Tina sat her down with her and sang the old gospel hymn "Take My Hand, Precious Lord." She explained that it had been Dr. Martin Luther King's favorite spiritual and that Mahalia Jackson's version of it was the best-known and most respected. With her eyes closed and her hands facing her daughter, palms up in supplication, she then sang the hymn, almost as if in a trance, completely overtaken by the message. "Hold my hand, lest I fall," she sang, "take my hand, precious Lord, lead me home." It was a moment Beyoncé would never forget. "It was like she was a vessel," she would recall in February 2015, "with God using her body to speak and to heal." (In 2015, Beyoncé would perform a stirring, memorable rendition of this same song during the 57th Annual Grammy Awards presentation.)

If anything, the soulful connection between Tina and her girls was all the more strengthened during this time that Mathew was gone from them. It was as if Tina, more than ever, became the family's moral compass; Beyoncé depended on her for guidance, as she still does today. If there was a problem, they knew they had the tools to handle it within their own domain; there was no reason to share it with the world.

"Beyoncé was Daddy's little girl until Tina took the kids and moved into the town house," added Kenny Moore. "Then, from that time on, as far as I could tell, she was Mommy's little girl. It was 'me and Mommy against the world.' She became very protective of her mother, and also of Solange and Kelly. The women now presented a solid front. When they moved into the apartment, we started to see Beyoncé, in particular, become a whole lot less forthcoming about what was going on."

By the end of 1995, the family had been torn apart in large measure because of financial pressures. Of course, Mathew's personal issues also had great bearing on what had happened to his family. Though he was working on those problems in therapy, their roots were deep, and who knew how long it would take for him to reconcile any of it? Where business was concerned, though, he had a fuller grasp of what needed to happen.

According to what Tina would testify, "Mathew was becoming more and more disgruntled. He and I had conversations about Ann not being able to do her part because of her illness and financial situation. Mathew was contributing more to the group by this time. There were people who didn't even know Ann was still involved! Mathew told Ann he wanted to restructure the deal again where he would now end up with more money because he really was doing more work. My concern was hurting Ann's feelings. I remember, I was doing Ann's hair, which I did all the time," said Tina, "and we discussed it."

It was a day that also stood out to Bonnie Lee, who was one of Andretta's oldest friends. Many years earlier, when Bonnie moved to Houston from Trinidad, she opened a daycare business, and Andretta's boys, Chris and Armon, and infant daughter, Shawna, were the first children she looked after. She and Andretta had been good friends ever since.

"There was going to be a function at Ann's that night, and she wanted to get her hair done for it," Bonnie recalled. "Tina was going straight to the party from her beauty shop. Ann and I arrived early and waited for Tina. Ann said Tina was a good soul, that she and Mathew had separated. 'Tina is trying to keep it quiet,' Ann told me, 'so please don't mention it.'"

Ann also told Bonnie that she appreciated the fact that Tina went out of her way to make sure she felt good about herself despite her illness. Finally, Tina showed up looking regal in a full-length sable coat—in the middle of the day! The family may have been having money problems, but one would never know it by looking at Tina. "My goodness, it took my breath away, she was so beautiful," Bonnie would recall. "How's Kokie?" Tina asked Bonnie, referring to Bonnie's daughter, who was the same age as Beyoncé. "Tell her to come over and hang out with Beyoncé and the girls. I sure would love for Beyoncé to have at least one friend who's not try-ing to be the next Diana Ross," she said, chuckling.

As Tina cut and styled Andretta's hair, the two women had a serious business conversation. According to what Tina would recall, she told Andretta how much she loved her and that even though "business is busi-ness," as her friend she wanted to be sure that Andretta was amenable to a new arrangement that would give Mathew more money. Andretta said she felt badly that, physically, she couldn't do more. Tina urged her to not feel that way, especially since she had already done so much.

"Well, I'm not going to oppose anything that helps the girls," Andretta finally said. "If Mathew wants more money, I guess I have to accept that." It didn't seem as if she really meant it, though. However, she was so weak and tired, she was clearly losing her fighting spirit.

"We love you, Ann," Tina said.

"I know," she said halfheartedly.

After this conversation a new partnership between Andretta, Kenny Moore, and Mathew Knowles would be formed, called Music World Enter-tainment, a venture that would see Mathew now getting the lion's share of the profits.

Destiny

*I*n order to legally use the group's new name, the Dolls, the moniker had to be trademarked. Therefore, research was necessary in order to make sure the name wasn't being used by another act. Then legal papers would need to be filed to protect it. When Daryl Simmons did his investigation, he found that there was actually more than one group using the name, and that they were all fighting about it among themselves. He didn't want his act to be caught in the middle of all that contention. Thus the girls' name would have to be changed once again.

At this point, Daryl wanted to change the group's name to simply... *Beyoncé*. It was an interesting idea. Back in the 1970s, Patti LaBelle and the Bluebelles had changed their name to LaBelle. Carlos Santana's group was called Santana, Eddie Van Halen's band, Van Halen. Despite the fact that for the last few years he had obviously wanted to push Beyoncé forward,

Mathew had to disagree with Daryl. He said, "Oh, *hell no!* I can't do that. Those girls would kill each other if I did that." Simmons had to agree, "though I still thought it was an awesome name for a group."

Ultimately, the act's name was changed to Destiny.

Of course, this wasn't exactly an original idea. After all, Destiny had been the name of one of the three acts in Deborah Laday and Denise Seals's all-girls revue. As managed by Laday and Seals, the acts were M-1 (Millicent Laday), Destiny (the dancers), and Girls Tyme (the singers, of whom Beyoncé was one). Beyoncé lore has it, though, that Tina Knowles came up with the name Destiny to replace that of the Dolls. Tina says that it was inspired by a verse in the Bible, in Isaiah, chapter 65, verses 11–12:

> But as for you who forsake the Lord and forget my holy mountain, who spread a table for fortune and fill bowls of mixed wine for Destiny, I will destine you for the sword, and you will all bend down for the slaughter.

While it does seems a little odd that Tina would have picked out a name for her daughter's group based on such a foreboding Bible passage, that's her story and she's always stuck to it. She says that she happened to turn to that passage in the Bible, and that when she did, a photo of the girls (which she'd been using as a page marker) fell into her lap. She looked at the page and her eye went right to the word "Destiny"—and that, she says, is how she came up with the name.

In all fairness to Tina, it had been about five years since the Laday/Seals revue. So it's possible she forgot that the name Destiny had already been associated with her daughter's career, especially since Beyoncé wasn't actually a member of that particular group of dancers.

Columbia/Sony

*I*t was at about this time, 1995, that Lonnie Jackson's childhood friend D'Wayne Wiggins—the founding member of the popular R&B group Tony! Toni! Toné!—had his date with Destiny. Wiggins's own group was about to peak with its final studio album, *House of Music*, after a viable career that had begun back in 1988. The act had an astounding fourteen *Billboard*-charting R&B singles, including five number ones, and three Top Ten pop singles. They'd also been awarded one gold album, two platinum albums, and one double platinum album. With the act's success now on the wane (they would disband in two years' time), Wiggins—who was thirty-two in 1995—was determined to rebrand himself as a record producer.

D'Wayne had seen Destiny perform years earlier when they were still Girls Tyme, but had lost track of them. "Some years later, I happened to be at Lonnie's house and saw a picture of the girls on the wall," he recalled. "I asked Lonnie, 'Hey! Whatever happened to that group? They were *dope!*' He said, 'They're with Daryl Simmons now.' I told him I always thought they were special. A couple weeks later, Lonnie called and said, 'Hey, remember those girls you were asking about? They're having a problem with their deal at Elektra, something big happened … the whole damn thing fell apart. So Daryl is no longer working with them. I think their management wants to talk to you.'"

D'Wayne made contact with Mathew Knowles soon after, and Mathew sent him a tape of some of the girls' recordings. After one listen, he called Mathew. "Brother, these are no little girls," D'Wayne told him. "You must have sent me the wrong tape. I know what little girls sound like, and they sure don't sound like this!"

Mathew had to laugh. "But that's them!" he exclaimed. "I swear to God!"

"It all happened pretty fast after that," D'Wayne Wiggins recalled. "I just really wanted to work with them. I knew they'd been having a hard time and that they were very dismayed by the loss of the Elektra deal. I also suspected they were hungry. And Beyoncé, I mean, I wanted to get her into the studio as quickly as possible. So, yeah, I hammered out a production deal with Mathew and Andretta right away.

"Then, I got to know the Knowles family," he recalled. "I learned that if you're in the inner circle, they will open up to you about their struggles, and they had a lot of them, too. Otherwise, no, they're not givin' up no information. That's Mafia-style right there," he said, laughing. "It was such a dope family clique, I mean, they were unbelievably close. If they let you in, you felt for sure they trusted you. I felt cool about being let in, too."

In the spring of 1995, Mathew and Andretta's (and Kenny Moore's) Music World entered into a deal with Wiggins's production company, Grass Roots Entertainment, which was officed in his West Oakland, California, recording studio, House of Music. Just as with the other production deals in which the girls had been involved (with Arne Farger, Lonnie Jackson, and Daryl Simmons), D'Wayne Wiggins would produce songs for them, and then use those recordings to try to secure a deal with a record label. So Beyoncé, Kelly, LaTavia, and LeToya would now have to temporarily move to Oakland to record at House of Music. "I put them up in a six-bedroom house," Wiggins recalled. "It was a grinding schedule, but they were happy to once again be in the studio after what had happened down in Atlanta. Of course, they were privately tutored in Oakland, as they had been in Atlanta.

"My dealings with Andretta were usually on the telephone because she was so sick," D'Wayne recalled. "My dealings with Mathew were in person. I thought they were a pretty good team in the sense that they were always keeping each other checked. It was actually to the advantage of the girls that they had managers who maybe didn't trust each other very much. It kept everyone honest. Andretta would say to me, 'Watch out for Mathew. If he does anything sneaky, let me know.' I'd hang up and, ten minutes later, Mathew would say the exact same thing to me about her—'If she does anything sneaky, let me know.'"

Eventually, some of the songs recorded by Destiny in Oakland would end up on the desk of Teresa LaBarbera Whites at Columbia/Sony Records. This turn of events would prove to be a pivotal and defining moment in Beyoncé's life, and thus it would be prudent to credit the right person for the submission. But there's a great deal of disagreement about it. Mathew's friends and family say he sent the songs to Teresa. However, Andretta insists it was she who did so. LaBarbera Whites says it was Mathew, though, and probably she should have the final word on the matter. It's definitely true, though, that Teresa had been Andretta's contact long before she was Mathew's. "Andretta and Teresa were tied to the hip way before Mathew came into the picture," is how Kenny Moore put it.

Teresa says she had first seen the girls years earlier when she was working as a regional talent scout for Columbia/Sony, and this would have been back when Andretta was managing the girls by herself. "Beyoncé and Kelly were nine when I met them," she recalls. However, as a talent scout, she had very little persuasive power over the label, though she believed the group was worth signing. She says Mathew contacted her once the group had recorded songs for Grass Roots and sent her a selection on tape. By this time she was on the A&R staff at Columbia/Sony and empowered to make signing decisions.

After receiving the tape, Teresa went to Houston at Mathew's behest and attended a special showcase he set up for her there. The girls performed for her, but midway through their first song, Mathew stopped them. He had warned them not to go swimming the night before, telling them that it might affect their voices for the all-important showcase. "It's a very important day," he told them, "and you can't blow this. You're gonna be all stopped up," he said, meaning they would be congested, especially Beyoncé. The youngsters didn't listen to Mathew; they went swimming anyway.

The next day, the audition did not go well. "In the middle of the audition, I stopped and told them, 'I don't really care if Teresa is here. You see the price you're paying for going swimming the other day? This is *exactly* what I was talking about. You guys decided to go swimming, and now you're not sounding good.'"

Mathew was miffed. Beyoncé, in particular, was mortified. She knew she had let her father down, and in her mind, nothing was more debilitating. "Me? I thought they sounded great," Teresa said, laughing, "so I didn't know what was going on."

Mathew told the girls to get offstage and blow their noses, then return and sing the song again. It was easier said than done. Pulling themselves together took all of their resolve. "This means everything," Beyoncé told her friends. "We can't mess up!" This time, when they went back onstage, they were very good. Teresa was impressed.

After the audition, Teresa began to pressure the Columbia/Sony executives in New York into signing Destiny to a recording contract. To that end, another audition was conducted, this time for the suits in Manhattan. Mathew and Andretta were both at this one. "We had to perform in a conference room in the Columbia Records office in the Sony building," Beyoncé has recalled. "It was a tiny room with couches all around it. There were a bunch of men and women of all different races sitting so close that we could put our arms out and touch them if we wanted to. It was that small and informal. It felt too intimate, being that close. Having to make eye contact was very scary, but we knew that this might be our last chance."

PART THREE

Destiny's Child

Signing with Columbia/Sony

$\mathcal{A}$s Andretta and Mathew had long before figured out, the record industry often moves at a snail's pace. After they were finally given a commitment by Columbia/Sony, months passed with no formal paperwork. There was some hesitation from Columbia/Sony having to do with the Elektra deal gone bad. A great many questions were being asked about that arrangement, such as exactly how the money advanced by Elektra had been spent. The new label just wanted to be sure it was making a sound invest-ment. The girls were teenagers, though, so even they were as annoyed as the adults by the delay.

In order to give the record label a little more push, partners Knowles and Tillman decided to continue shopping for another deal, even if only to use it as leverage. As it happened, Polydor was keen on the idea of sign-ing Destiny, especially considering D'Wayne Wiggins's success there with Tony! Toni! Toné! Before anyone knew it, Polydor was actually drawing up contracts. After so much difficulty, Beyoncé's group suddenly had *two* pending record deals. It was almost more than she and the others could comprehend. "Very typical of the record business," Wiggins recalled. "I told the girls that you just can't predict this crazy industry. If they didn't believe me, they sure did now."

On October 15, 1995, with the paperwork under way at Polydor, Andretta telephoned Teresa LaBarbera Whites at Columbia/Sony to tell her that they'd decided to sign with another label. She was bluffing, hop-ing to get a rise out of Teresa. It worked. "Oh no you don't!" exclaimed LaBarbera Whites. "No way! We are flying all of you to New York tomorrow to finalize the deal with us!"

D'Wayne Wiggins happened to be in Washington at that time, at the Million Man March. The next day, he took a plane from there to New York to sit down with the Columbia/Sony executives. During their meeting with him, the label finalized a deal for Destiny that was much better than the one Polydor had offered. Now, just that fast—and so typical of the fickle record industry—Polydor was out and Columbia/Sony was in.

"One day I got a call from Columbia," recalled Daryl Simmons, who hadn't seen the group in many months, not since the deal with Elektra fell apart. "It was Teresa LaBarbera Whites. She says, 'I have the girls here with me.' I heard them all screaming out hello in the background. 'We're getting ready to sign them,' she told me. I said, 'Great! They're amazing.' And she said, 'Well, I know that when they were with you there were some issues. Is there anything we need to know?' I said, 'Look, the girls are great. I love 'em. They deserve a record deal. Mathew and I didn't see eye-to-eye, but it certainly had nothing to do with Beyoncé and them.' She said, 'Okay, great. I just wanted to get your thoughts, because I'm pretty sure we're going to sign them.' I was happy for the girls, I genuinely was."

For a short period, the group was simply known at Columbia as Destiny. But, again, there was a problem with the name. From 1978 to 1981, Polydor had a group under contract called Alton McClain and Destiny. The trio of young women had one big hit for the label in 1979 called "It Must Be Love," and then issued a few albums. Their back catalog at Polydor was still viable. Therefore, as Destiny's contracts were being finalized, some label executives thought there might be confusion about the name. Beyoncé lore has it that it was Mathew's idea to add the word "Child," thereby making it Destiny's Child. So at least according to this version of events, Tina came up with the first half of the name, and Mathew with the second.

"Guess what? We've got a new name," Beyoncé said, calling D'Wayne Wiggins on the telephone one morning.

"What is it?"

"Destiny's *Child*," she answered.

"Um … cool. But I was sorta thinking, the *Naturelles*," he told her, kidding. ("I was always gonna try to go Motown with it," he later explained.)

"*For real?*" Beyoncé asked, laughing. She said that she felt Destiny's Child had "a certain ring to it." She also noted that it was a phrase found in the Bible. "We love it," she exclaimed.

Destiny's Child signed with Columbia/Sony for seven albums. According to a deal memo (with Beyoncé's last name misspelled as "Knolls"), the budget for the first album was to be $85,000—not much in the record business. If the label were to continue with the group—and it had the option not to do so—the next album's budget could be anywhere between $350,000 and $700,000. The third was between $375,000 and $750,000, and the scale continued to rise until the seventh album, the budget of which could be as high as $950,000. The group would be allowed "consultation" on their album jacket design, but not "approval." The term's commencement date was to be December 5, 1995 (and, in fact, that would be the day the girls would sign their deal). The advance from the label was $400,000, which the group's recordings would have to earn back before anyone—they or their managers—saw any more money. It's not known how much of this actually ended up in the Knowleses' pockets, but it was most certainly enough to allow them some breathing room from bill collectors.

It was also at about this time that Mathew and Andretta struck a new partnership deal, one that concerned the group's royalties: Mathew would receive 15 percent, and Andretta just 5 percent. In exchange, Mathew said he would be responsible for 100 percent of the expenses, which is probably why Andretta agreed to a split that so favored him. "To be honest, Ann was just real tired by this time," said Pat Felton. "I mean, she was sick, tired, broke . . . and even though there was obviously some joy attached to the fact that the girls *finally* had a record deal, it was bittersweet. A lot of water had gone under the bridge. I know she *wanted* to be happy. I'm not sure that she was able to be completely thrilled, though. Also, I think she had pretty much had it with Mathew by this time."

Beyoncé's memory of the moment when she and her friends first realized they had recording contracts with Columbia/Sony is vivid. After church, the Knowleses always ate at Luby's cafeteria. Mathew decided to try to trick Beyoncé, Kelly, LaTavia, and LeToya by putting their contracts in Luby's company envelopes and presenting them to the girls one afternoon at Headliners. "I've got a little present for you girls," he said, smiling. He handed each girl an envelope.

"What's this? A gift certificate to Luby's?" Beyoncé asked.

"Could be," Mathew said with a smile. "Open it."

When the young ladies opened their envelopes, they found their recording contracts. "What *is* this?" Beyoncé asked, looking down at the paper. Then it dawned on her; the Sony letterhead was a dead giveaway. She was the first to scream with delight. She reached out to her father and pulled him into her arms, crying. "Is it true, Daddy?" she asked, as the other girls jumped up and down and squealed all around her. With tears in his eyes, Mathew told her that indeed it was true, that they'd finally reached this milestone and that they'd done it together as a team. "You deserve this, little girl," he told her as he hugged her tightly. Considering all of the personal and professional pressures of recent years, it must have felt to Mathew that he had somehow pulled off a miracle. After spending time with her dad, Beyoncé pulled away from him and joined her singing partners in their jubilation.

"The ladies with their heads under the dryers looked at us like we were crazy, because they couldn't hear what all the screaming and yelling was about," Beyoncé later recalled. "We ran all around the shop, jumping up and down, holding our contracts in the air for the customers to see. It was a beautiful day at Headliners, that's for sure."

Ice Cream Summit

Chocolate, vanilla, or strawberry?" Mathew would ask.

Those were the usual choices. Even though Mathew wasn't living with Beyoncé, he still spent much of his time at the town house visiting her, Solange, and Kelly. Often he and Beyoncé would find themselves sitting in the kitchen, just the two of them—like old times at the Parkwood house. Father and daughter would then take the time to re-connect.

"All three flavors, please," would usually be Beyoncé's answer to Mathew's question. He would scoop the ice cream into a bowl for his daughter and then spray whipped cream over it. After doing the same for himself, he would sit at the table across from her, just the two of them, which somehow always seemed just right. For Mathew, it wasn't like talking to a kid. Beyoncé had always been surprisingly grown up. There were moments, of course, when her youth was apparent, but for the most part, and *especially* when it came to Destiny's Child, she was wise beyond her years.

On this day at the end of February 1996, there was a lot going on. First, of course, was the excitement of the new record deal. Now that it was official that the group would be signed to Columbia/Sony, Beyoncé would say that her head was swimming with song ideas she was anxious to develop; she kept a notepad on her nightstand to jot down lyrics as they came to her, sometimes even in dreams. On this day, however, there were also other matters to consider, problems posed by LeToya Luckett and her mother, Pamela, and, to a lesser extent, by LaTavia Roberson.

Surprisingly, only half of Destiny's Child was immediately eager to sign their new deal with Columbia/Sony and ancillary management contracts with Mathew and Andretta. LaTavia wasn't so sure about it. In fact, she later said she felt that "it was ridiculous for us to have to sign contracts right then and there." She wanted time to take the documents home, maybe review them with an attorney.

LeToya was also a holdout. She recalled, "The [recording] contracts were laid out in front of us, everybody's excited, ready to sign, and then [Mathew] pulled out his management agreement and said, '*This* has to be signed before you sign *that*.'"

Just as had earlier occurred when the group signed with Silent Partner Productions (which led to their unsuccessful tenure at Elektra), LeToya's mom, Pamela, wasn't going to just go along with the program. She wanted to talk over her daughter's contract with a lawyer. "And why is that so unreasonable?" she asked at the time. "Any parent would do the same for her daughter." She remembers, "It became a really bad situation. The girls were looking at it like, 'Wow, LeToya is stopping our deal here!' Then, of course, [LeToya's] looking at me at that age saying, 'What are you *doing*, Mom?'"

This afternoon, the question before Mathew and Beyoncé was, "What are we going to do about LeToya and her momma?" About three years had passed since an eleven-year-old Beyoncé made the no-nonsense decision that LeToya should leave the group rather than risk ruining things for them all. LeToya ended up staying, but it was clear to everyone that she'd come very close to being dismissed. Now things were different; the girls were older and had their own points of view. It wasn't just little Beyoncé with her surprisingly pragmatic solutions to problems.

Mathew and Beyoncé knew that LaTavia and LeToya had become close in recent years. So there was probably no way LaTavia would go along with any program that would see LeToya pushed out of the group. On the other hand, they also knew that Kelly would be fine with seeing LeToya go. Kelly had already said she couldn't believe there was any hesitation at all about the contracts. She thought there should "only be gratitude, plain and simple." So in any major dispute, it would likely be two against two—Beyoncé and Kelly versus LaTavia and LeToya.

On this afternoon in their kitchen, according to what Beyoncé would later testify, she told Mathew that she'd spent the last few years "wondering when the other shoe would drop with LeToya and her mom." She liked LeToya well enough; they were friends. However, when it came to business, Beyoncé had always been able to look at things with clear-eyed unsentimentality. She said, "It feels like every time there is a victory for us, LeToya and her momma have something to say about it."

The bigger problem at this time was that Pamela felt that Mathew's ideas for how to maintain group morale were too extreme. In fact, she viewed a letter Mathew sent her a week earlier as "an ultimatum." It outlined specifically what he expected of LeToya if she were to remain in Destiny's Child. Pamela by now realized that Mathew was always going to be one for complete commitment, but she felt he was going too far. In the letter, Mathew said he would now require LeToya (and LaTavia too) not only to live under his roof, but also to eat the exact same foods as the other girls and work out at the same gym together.

"I just don't see what the problem is with that," Beyoncé reasoned. "They're here all the time anyway, aren't they? They eat all our food anyway, don't they? We go to the same gym, don't we? So what is the problem?"

Pamela disagreed. She said that Mathew's dictates were "unreasonable and somewhat ridiculous." She noted that she believed her fifteen-year-old daughter should be able to spend as much time with her brother and her parents as possible, and that this was not an unreasonable expectation. "The girls of this group are and have been homeschooled at your address for some time, five days a week," she wrote in a letter a few days earlier, on February 27. She noted that they already spent their Saturdays together and also went to church together on Sundays.

Maybe it wasn't the specifics of the demands that bothered Pamela as much as the tone of Mathew's letter. Pamela was never one to be lorded over by Mathew, not without a good fight anyway. "LeToya and I are devastated by your ultimatum for such unwarranted requests," she wrote. She sent copies of her correspondence to Teresa LaBarbera Whites at Columbia/Sony, as well as to D'Wayne Wiggins at Grass Roots. It was the copy to LaBarbera Whites at Columbia, though, that most concerned both Mathew and Beyoncé. They felt she was causing trouble for them at the label already, and they weren't happy about it.

On this day, over their ice cream, father and daughter were in total agreement: LeToya had to go, and before any recordings were released by Destiny's Child on their new label and the public became acquainted with her. At this point, she was anonymous enough to be easily swapped out, just like Ashley, the girl she had replaced a few years earlier. "It's inevitable," Beyoncé said, "so we should just get it over with."

Also at play was the concern that maybe LeToya was becoming a bad influence over LaTavia. There was no other reason they could think of as to why LaTavia—who had known Beyoncé since the age of eight—would suddenly now be taking LeToya's side against Mathew. Beyoncé may have had her issues with her dad from time to time, but she was eternally grateful to him for getting her this far in her career. More important, as she put it at around the time, "I am *proud* to be Mathew Knowles's daughter." So it was difficult for her to see LeToya's point of view. As far as the group went, though, Beyoncé didn't want to see LaTavia leave it too. After all, she'd been with the act since before Andretta! If LeToya had to be sacrificed for LaTavia, then so be it.

In the end, father and daughter made up their minds that they would try one more time to work things out with the Lucketts. However, if there was any more resistance, LeToya would have to go and LaTavia would just have to understand. When told of this decision, Tina was in total agreement with it. "From the time LeToya got in the group there was always drama, always jealousy, always madness," she would say.

In the days to come, there was a lot of back-and-forth between Mathew's attorney, Angela Phea, and the Lucketts. Eventually mother and daughter backed down. Phea then demanded that they not only verbally apologize to all of the group members, their parents and to Mathew and Andretta, but that they send a *written* apology to Teresa LaBarbera Whites for ever having questioned Mathew's and Andretta's management decisions. They also had to promise to never again have any communication with anyone from the record label. Also, Pam was asked to promise that, in the future, she would have "no input in <u>any</u> decisions." All of this was hardball, but what else could Pamela Luckett do but play? Her daughter wanted nothing more than to continue with the group, no matter the cost. "Anytime a contract came up, Mathew kicked me out of the group because I wouldn't sign just anything," LeToya would later say. "It was like a bad relationship. He would kick me out and then call me back a few days later saying, 'I need you, I need you, I need you.' He needs prayer. He needs a hug."

Tina's Request

*E*arlier, on September 4, 1996, the day Beyoncé turned fifteen, she and her ex-boyfriend, Lyndall Locke, reconciled. At the time, Lyndall was about to turn seventeen. "A friend came over to my house one night and said he was going to Beyoncé's birthday party," recalled Lyndall. "I knew that under the circumstances of how we broke up, I probably shouldn't go. I hadn't seen or talked to her in a year and a half. I went anyway. I was walking up a flight of stairs, and when I got to the top, there she was." As Lyndall recalled it, their eyes locked in an intense gaze that neither one was able to break.

"In that moment, Beyoncé was still the most beautiful girl I had ever seen," he remembered. "I asked LaTavia to get me her new telephone number, which she did. We started talking. By November, we were back together. I was older, she was older, and somehow it felt better, or maybe deeper. Funny thing, she never sang to me. Especially after we got together, I would say, 'Come on, girl! Sing something!' And she was so bashful, there was no way she was ever going to do that."

When Beyoncé told Tina she had gotten back together with Lyndall, Tina wasn't surprised. "That's how it is when you're a teenager," she told one relative. She said she wasn't going to discourage a reconciliation, that Beyoncé had to make her own mistakes in life and that "maybe this will be good for her. Who knows?" Tina actually liked Lyndall and was disappointed in him when he betrayed Beyoncé. However, she understood he was young and impetuous; she was willing to give him another chance. "The main message I got from Mathew and Tina was, 'Can you deal with our daughter and all the work she has to do with her career, and not distract her?'" recalled Lyndall. "I was good with that."

After Lyndall and Beyoncé were reunited, Tina pulled him aside to have a serious conversation. "Will you do me a favor," she asked, "and please, just wait until she's eighteen?"

Lyndall wasn't quite sure how to respond. Tina's meaning was obvious; she didn't need to spell it out for him. "It's my responsibility to make sure you don't do anything stupid," she said. She was candid and concerned. "I'm not leaving here until we have a deal," she told him.

"Okay, sure," Lyndall agreed, clearing his throat. "We have a deal."

"Thank you," Tina said. "I love you both," she added. "Now I'll leave so you two can talk about me behind my back," she concluded with a smile.

Recording the First Hit

*W*hen a young writer/producer named Rob Fusari walked into Sugar Bar, the intimate new nightclub on 72nd Street in Manhattan owned by former Motown staffers Nickolas Ashford and Valerie Simpson, he could feel the energy in the room. The place was absolutely teeming with Columbia/Sony executives as well as radio station disc jockeys, reporters from print and television media, and all sorts of other industry types. It was a Thursday night and, as was the custom at Sugar Bar, a new group was about to be showcased, an act who hadn't yet released any songs to the public but about whom the buzz was already strong. Rob's friend Vince Herbert had earlier promised that the two would produce one of Rob's songs for this group, so this was Rob's opportunity to meet them. After the two men rendezvoused, they made their way backstage. There they found the four young ladies of Destiny's Child in a small, cramped dressing room surrounded by well-wishers and fans. Somehow, they already had fans!

"I walked in and said to myself, 'Holy shit! I've just stepped into another era!'" Fusari recalled. "I was thinking, 'Okay, this is the Supremes, right? Except there are four of them and they are super young.' They were also beautiful in their sexy little sequined outfits. People were fussing over them, catering to them. A woman was teasing out their hair, someone else was tugging and pulling at their costumes. One of them, the lead singer, I figured, was giving instructions to the other three, saying things like, 'Don't forget to hit that note or the harmony will be ruined.' All the while, they were being very pleasant to one another and to everyone in the room, but also focused. There was a level of concentration, a seriousness, like I had never seen before from girls their age. When Vince introduced me, we said a quick hello and then left to find our seats. But already I was impressed."

A short while later, Beyoncé, Kelly, LaTavia, and LeToya made their way onto the small stage for their two numbers. Nickolas Ashford later recalled, "If you can make it at the Sugar Bar, you can make it anywhere, because it's a tough crowd of intelligent, mature listeners who have heard a lot." Suffice it to say, Destiny's Child did just fine.

"The girls kill it," Rob Fusari recalled. "The crowd goes crazy. I'm hearing Beyoncé sing for the first time, and she's incredible. I'm hearing the girls harmonize, and they're tight. I'm watching them move across the stage as a unit, and they're precise. I can tell they've worked hard on their presentation, that they aren't an act that has just been thrown together. 'Oh, boy!' I'm saying to myself. 'I want to work with them *so bad*! I hope Vince isn't bullshitting me.'

"Afterward, there's a buzz in the air. That's when you know an act is going to blow up. That's when you know it's not a fluke, that it's history in the making. I felt that same buzz again much later, the first time I saw Lady Gaga perform. It's just this thing that happens in a room when everyone is on the same page about the greatness they'd just experienced. In the record business, there's nothing more exciting."

Rob Fusari—who is now known by his stage name 8Bit—would go on to work with many iconic performers, including Britney Spears, Whitney Houston, Will Smith, and Lady Gaga (with whom he would have a romantic relationship; in 2010, Beyoncé would record a duet with Lady Gaga, "Telephone"). But his first act—in fact, the very first time he ever found himself in a recording studio—would be Destiny's Child with a song he wrote called "No, No, No."

Fusari was born and raised in Livingston, New Jersey. As a classically trained pianist, he first began writing songs while studying at William Paterson University. He wanted to write and possibly produce music, though he didn't know how to go about breaking into the business. Instead, he got a job in the corporate world. Bored and frustrated, he made a deal with his mother: If she would just allow him to live in her Manhattan home for just one year, he would devote all of his attention to music. If after a year he hadn't succeeded, he would abandon the dream and get "a real job." She agreed. He set up a small recording studio in the basement and went to work writing and producing his own material, playing keyboards, guitars, and drums. After a year, though, he still hadn't found a way to truly connect with the music world. But then, just as he was about to give it all up, he wrote "No, No, No."

"I was heavily influenced by R&B," he recalled, "and R. Kelly had produced a song called 'Stroke You Up' for a duo of girls called Changing Faces. That song inspired me to start writing 'No, No, No,' on one of my synthesizers. It had a very interesting vibe, I thought. I laid down a vocal I had written, the first verse and the hook, and I thought, 'Okay, well maybe I have something here.'"

A couple weeks later, 8Bit's buddy Vince Herbert came into town and wanted to meet up with him. Vince had produced most of the memorable songs on Aaliyah's groundbreaking *One in a Million* album. When he asked his friend what he was up to, 8Bit said, "I've got this song called 'No, No, No.' Let me play it for you."

"When I played it," 8Bit recalled, "I could see Vince light up; his whole face, his whole aura changed. That's when I knew I had something."

Vince then said he was getting ready to work with a new girl group at Columbia/Sony. " 'Can I take this song back to them?' " he asked. "Since I couldn't get arrested in the record industry," 8Bit recalled, "I said, 'Sure. Why not?' So he took the tape and left. I figured nothing was going to happen. I didn't think much more about it."

A couple hours later, Vince Herbert called 8Bit to tell him that he'd played the song for Teresa LaBarbera Whites at Columbia/Sony and that she had agreed to allow him and 8Bit to produce it for Destiny's Child. Not only that, Vince said, but it was going to be the girls' very first single release! Now Fusari was skeptical. How could Vince be sure it was going to be the first single? It turned out that Vince had been so confident that "No, No, No" was a hit, he told LaBarbera Whites that if she didn't agree to release it as Destiny Child's debut single, he was going to give it to Brandy, another artist he was working with at the time. LaBarbera Whites agreed. Likely, though, she just wanted to get Destiny's Child in the recording studio with the song, see how it went, and then deal with a release strategy later. After all, the girls hadn't even heard the tune yet, and neither had Mathew Knowles. So how could she make any real promises about it? It's likely she was bluffing as much as perhaps Vince was.

A couple days later, Vince Herbert took 8Bit down to Chung King Studios in Manhattan—famous as the studio where Run-D.M.C, the Beastie Boys, and LL Cool J recorded some of their classic hits. It would be here that DC [as some in the industry had already started calling Destiny's Child] would record "No, No, No." 8Bit had already recorded the instrumental track for the song, with a sexy melody and a fat, dark bass line, in his mom's basement; it took eighteen hours. So he couldn't imagine what else would be left for him to do at Chung King. Much to his surprise, he soon learned that he would be coproducing the girls' vocals with his friend Vince.

"I had never even been in a recording studio before," 8Bit exclaimed. "So I was freaking out. I was like, '*Woah! This is too much!*' Then Beyoncé and the girls walked in and I got a good look at them and I thought, 'Okay. Now, how the hell old *are* these girls? Fifteen? Sixteen?' Despite their youth, though, I could see right off that they were all business. No small talk, no nothin'... just Beyoncé saying, 'Hello, everyone, let's get to work.'"

Beyoncé was the first in the recording booth, ready to lay down the lead vocal to "No, No, No." She listened to 8Bit's demo all the way through, where he sang the song against the prerecorded backing track. Then she listened to it again, this time studying it carefully and taking notes about the lyrics on a legal pad. At one point, she observed, "This chorus, 'You be saying no when it's really yes,' is so interesting because that's usually what a *guy* would be saying to a *girl*, not the other way around. I like the message it sends to girls that they can be aggressive and clear about what they want. It's hot, it's sexy," she added, getting really charged up about it, "so let me just get in there and *cut this dang song!*"

Though 8Bit had no experience producing an artist's vocals, Beyoncé clearly had a lot of experience singing them. She finished all the verses in less than an hour, quick and easy. Certainly those many years at the knees of Lonnie Jackson, Tony Mo., and all of the others who had groomed her as a child were now paying off big-time, especially in terms of discipline and control. As it happens, "No, No, No" features one of her more conservative vocal performances. Absent are the kinds of vocal histrionics that—at least to a generation of young pop/R&B and hip-hop vocalists— would define singing with "soul." Rather, it's a simple, completely elegant performance.

"From the start, Beyoncé was...well...let's just say I knew it was going to be hard to break through her shell," 8Bit continued. "She wasn't standoffish or arrogant as much as she was just in her own little world. During the session when she'd take a break and come out of the booth, I would try to engage her. I quickly realized, though, that it wasn't going to be easy. She's not someone who's going to easily befriend you.

"I figured maybe the distance between us was because I was this white kid in his early twenties trying to break into an urban market," he recalled. "Funny thing, though, was that even though I would work with her many more times in the coming years, that first time I met her pretty much characterized every other time. It was always as if we'd just met. Even after we had a couple of hits together, it was never like, 'Come on over and give me a hug and tell me what's up.'

"Kelly is just the opposite," he continued. "She treats people like they are old friends, like, 'I have known you forever, let's go have coffee.' But Beyoncé is more aloof."

There are actually two versions of 8Bit's "No, No, No"—"No, No, No (Part 1)," which is the mellow groove the girls recorded with 8Bit and Vincent Herbert at Chung King, and "No, No, No (Part 2)," the remix that transforms the original track's slow tempo into a beat-heavy hip-hop sound. On this one, Beyoncé sings the lyrics in rapid-fire style. The track is interspersed with a rap by its producer, Wyclef Jean, leader and producer of the multiplatinum superstar act the Fugees. ("They went from a dream to the young Supremes.")

The more upbeat Wyclef Jean version of the song is the result of a silly moment from Beyoncé. Because the group was over budget with the album, when they went into the studio with Jean for the remix of "No, No, No," they had to do it in a hurry. With Wyclef at the control board and Beyoncé in the studio, she was taking her time, being very precise with her work, as usual. Frustrated, Jean said, "Come on, girl, we have to hurry this thing up." Joking, she began to sing the song in triple time, all the while using the syncopated style she had learned from her original writer, Anthony Moore—Tony Mo. "Wait. Hold up! I like that," Wyclef said. "Let's cut it like that." It took exactly fifty-seven minutes for her to record what was to be known as "No, No, No (Part 2)."

As for DC's cohesiveness in the studio, 8Bit says he didn't see much of it. "It wasn't a buddy-buddy 'you're my girls' kind of thing," he recalled. "They seemed like two separate units, Beyoncé and Kelly on one side and LeToya and LaTavia on the other. Beyoncé, even at fifteen, was someone you felt was very distinctive and unusual. And I mean no disrespect to the others, especially not to Kelly, who is a powerhouse vocalist on her own. [8Bit would produce three songs on Kelly's first solo album, *Simply Deep.*] But I do remember thinking there was no way Beyoncé was going to be in this group for very long."

Recording the First Album

*F*ew artists could ask for a better shot at making a first album than the opportunities afforded Destiny's Child with their debut. Thanks to the persistence and determination of Mathew and Andretta, the girls were able to work with some of the hottest producers and musicians of the period.

Among them were the aforementioned 8Bit along with Vincent Herbert and Wyclef Jean, as well as Jermaine Dupri and Tim & Bob (songwriters/ musicians Tim Kelly and Bob Robinson, who cut their production teeth on TLC and Boyz II Men). Also working on the album was Benjamin Wright, a veteran arranger/conductor whose résumé included soul legends such as the Temptations, Gladys Knight and the Pips, Aretha Franklin, and Barry White. Additionally, there was, of course, D'Wayne Wiggins, who had so brilliantly shepherded the girls' deal with Columbia/Sony through his production company, Grass Roots.

One of the immediate disagreements D'Wayne had with Mathew Knowles over the first DC album concerned the lead vocals on the songs he was producing. Wiggins wanted to make sure all four girls were showcased. However, Mathew, not surprisingly, was much more interested in positioning Beyoncé as the focal point. "I grew up listening to En Vogue and the Pointer Sisters," Wiggins recalled. "So as far as I was concerned, if it was a group then everyone got to shine, not just one person. But Mathew wasn't down with that. He was okay with the group when it came to harmony, but when it came to actual lead singing, he wanted that to be Beyoncé.

"I remember giving LaTavia a little part on a song, and then Kelly, and then LeToya. That's when Mathew and I hit a wall. From then on, we butted heads over the issue of lead singing because I campaigned hard for the other girls. For Mathew, though, it wasn't just his kid singing the songs, it was a matter of branding. For instance, back in the day, when you heard the Supremes you heard Diana Ross singing lead and that was the group's brand. There was no mistaking that sound, her voice. You heard it on the radio and you thought, 'Boom! That's the Supremes.' He told me that this is what he was after with Destiny's Child, an identifiable, branded sound."

An ironic point of contention between Beyoncé and Mathew was that she sided with D'Wayne when it came to divvying out lead vocals. It was as if she was so secure in her ability, she didn't need to commandeer every single lead. One day, D'Wayne had her recording the lead vocal to a song while Kelly, LaTavia, and LeToya watched solemnly from the other side of the glass, all three sitting with him and the engineer. "Why am I singing all of this stuff when the other girls can sing some of it too?" Beyoncé asked from inside the recording booth.

"Well, Mathew has a thing he's trying to do," D'Wayne said.

"Good Lord! Mathew ain't here now, is he?" Beyoncé asked, taking off her headphones. "One of the other girls can sing this part," she decided. "Like Kelly. Kelly can sing this just fine."

"Heck, yeah," Kelly said eagerly as she bolted from her chair. "Let me get in on there and do *my* thing!"

After Kelly went into the recording booth with Beyoncé, the two girls worked on the composition of the song together. Coaching her friend every step along the way, Beyoncé practically produced the session. When Kelly finally had her chance to shine, she sounded just fine. However, it didn't escape anyone in the studio that Beyoncé had a style of her own, and it was one that couldn't be matched. In the end, Beyoncé's vocal was the one that would be released.

"It was *ridiculous*, the way Beyoncé could sing," D'Wayne Wiggins exclaimed. I used to call her 'Beulah.' I'd say, 'Let's run that song down again, Beulah.' The first time I called her that she was a little put off and asked why I gave her that nickname. I said, 'Because you're just this little-assed girl, but you got the voice of a big-assed woman.' In fact, you got a voice that sounds like it should be coming out of a big ol' woman named Beulah. She loved that and the nickname stuck. Beulah!"

Many years later, in 2014, D'Wayne Wiggins would happen upon Mathew Knowles at The Essence Awards. "Aren't you glad I made the decisions I made back then when it came to Beyoncé singing all them leads?" Mathew asked D'Wayne with a smile. "I was right, wasn't I?"

D'Wayne Wiggins had to laugh. "Dude! I'm sure glad you did that shit," he said, vigorously shaking Mathew's hand. "*Thank you!* You were right. And we all made a whole lot of money because of it!"

"No Woman Deserves This"

$\mathcal{B}$y January 1997, most of the songs Destiny's Child planned to include on their first album were finally finished. There was a great deal of satisfaction about them, too. They sounded terrific, and it seemed to everyone that the girls were well on their way to stardom. There were other tunes they were still working on, though. In all they would record more than forty songs, and then whittle down the selection to a prized thirteen. The album was scheduled for release in February 1998, which sure seemed a long way off. Despite all of the anticipation, for the first half of 1997, Andretta Tillman's illness was really all that was on the minds of everyone who cared about her.

By April, Andretta was in and out of a wheelchair. Chemotherapy had turned her skin a sickly, darker color. Her hair was thinning. Tina Knowles still did what she could to style it, but it was becoming very difficult. Tina would go to Andretta's home to work on her since Andretta could no longer make it to Headliners. One day, she found Andretta in such a debilitated state, she felt certain she should be in the hospital. However, Andretta refused to go. She still believed she would recover. In fact, she refused even to have a will drawn up—she was that determined to get better. "But she looked like a little old lady who had just been whittled down to nothing," Pat Felton recalled sadly.

"In the end, Mathew's gonna get all the credit for the girls, you know that, don't you?" Andretta asked Tony Mo. "I'm going to be completely erased from history as if I never even existed on the planet." He told her he suspected that was true. "This is my legacy and it's going to be just gone," she sadly added.

"She was very upset about it," Tony Mo. recalled, "but comes a time, you know, when you're fighting for your life and there's not much you can do about a lot of things."

One weekend, Beyoncé and Kelly stayed with Andretta to try to help her out. They were just fifteen, but the girls wanted to do what they could for their "Miss Ann." It was very difficult. Even with the help of Andretta's boys, Armon and Chris, and her housekeeper, Janet, it was still too much for Beyoncé and Kelly to handle. Crying, Beyoncé told her mother that she and Kelly had tried to cheer Andretta up by singing to her, but that it didn't work. She said that Andretta was so weak, she didn't even leave her bed.

The next weekend Beyoncé and Kelly wanted to return to Andretta's, hoping they could help out in little ways, even if that just meant staying to pray with her. No, Tina decided. She felt that the last time had been too traumatic for the girls and she didn't want to put them through it again. She said they could spend time there after school, but that they should come home and sleep in their own beds. Reluctantly, the girls agreed.

"I remember going over to Tina's for lunch one day, and the whole household felt muted," recalled one friend of hers." Usually the Knowles home was a bustling, busy place with a lot of excitement. But not on this day. "'It gets to you,' Tina told me. 'Just knowing it's going on in the background every single, solitary day, it gets to you. Ann is such a good person. No woman deserves this.'"

Tina said she also felt badly that the girls had worked so hard to get to the point where they had a record label deal, only to now not be able to completely enjoy their victory. The weight of Andretta's illness was such a burden, it wore everyone down. Tina wanted to shield the girls from the despair, but she knew there was no way to do it. "This is a horrible reality of life that I think the girls need to understand," she told her friend. She said she couldn't protect the girls from it even if she wanted to, "because they are over to Ann's all the time."

The stress of Andretta's illness was really getting to Beyoncé. One day, Tina suggested that she call Lyndall Locke and have him take her somewhere just to relieve her anxiety. However, Beyoncé had her mind made up about Lyndall, especially when it came to Andretta's sickness—she didn't want to share it with him. She had long ago established very strict boundaries where Lyndall was concerned; his purpose in her life was for good times, nothing more. Actually, she was underestimating him. As lighthearted as he was, he did have a serious side.

One afternoon while Beyoncé was visiting with Armon and Christopher at the Tillman home, Andretta and Pat Felton got into a heated but whispered argument. "Don't you tell my kids *nothin'* about my health, do you hear me?" Andretta told Pat, trying to keep her voice low. "Not even with your last breath should you *ever* tell my kids anything about my health," she insisted.

Andretta's angst stemmed from a recent conversation Pat had had with Armon during which she told him that his mother's condition was very serious. Armon refused to believe it. "He's sixteen and he needs to know what's going on," Pat argued. "He has *enough* information," Andretta said. She said that she'd told Armon that she was diabetic, and that was all he needed to know.

The two friends agreed to disagree, said that they loved one another, and put the issue to rest. Within a week Andretta would tell Pat that she had finally confessed the truth to Armon. "I am very, very sick," she told her son through her tears as he tried to help her up the stairs. The teen was torn up inside; seeing his mother suffer was almost more than he could bear.

Unbelievably enough, at around this same time, Pat Felton was also diagnosed with lupus. She'd never even heard of the disease before, and now, after spending so much time nursing her best friend through it, she had it herself. "It seemed so cruel and unfair," Pat recalled. "But I knew my job was to help Ann, not feel sorry for myself. Now that I too needed treatment, I started looking for the best doctors for the two of us. It was as if lupus was the only thing going on in our lives."

5-16-97

*I*t was May 16, 1997. "Oh my, Ann! You look a lot better," Tina Knowles was telling Andretta Tillman.

"I actually *feel* better," Andretta said with a weak smile. She was in the intensive care unit of Park Plaza Hospital in Houston. She had been admitted the day before, so ill that Pat Felton could barely get her there, with Armon's help. Pat had read Bible passages with her that first night, and then went home to allow Andretta to get some rest. But then Andretta had a terrible time, suffering a heart attack and kidney failure both in that one evening. However, on this early Friday morning, she seemed much better.

Standing in the doorway watching Andretta and Tina was Pat. She'd shown up along with Cholotte Taylor (the mother of Nicki and Nina, the two dancers who had once been a part of Girls Tyme) to spend the day with Andretta as she underwent a battery of tests. According to Pat, the two women found their friend sitting upright in bed signing documents. After she finished, Andretta handed the documents back to Tina, who inserted them into a manila envelope. "You really do look so much better to me," Tina told her. "I'll check on you later, Ann," she said. "God bless you." She held Andretta's hand for a few moments before taking her leave, nodding at Pat and Cholotte as she departed.

"Ann, what in the world were you doing?" Pat asked as she approached her.

"Oh, Tina just had some papers for me to sign," Andretta said, according to Pat's memory of the conversation.

"But you are in *intensive care*," Pat exclaimed. "Are you okay to sign documents?"

"Oh, it was nothing," Andretta said. "Just some papers having to do with Destiny's Child."

"It was obvious to me that they were legal documents," Pat Felton said many years later. "I didn't know if Ann had called Tina, or how Tina ended up being there with these papers. It concerned me, though. I just didn't think Ann was up to signing anything important."

As part of her deposition for a later court case, Tina would deny that this happened and give a different version of events.

About an hour later, Andretta was being rolled down the hall on a gurney and then into an elevator, headed for an ultrasound and X-rays. "I think your boys should be here," Pat told her as she held her hand.

"No," Andretta said. "I don't want them seeing me like this."

As the necessary tests were being conducted, Pat and Cholotte waited in a small room and chatted with nurses. Suddenly a set of double doors swung wide open and out came Andretta's gurney, surrounded by a medical team. As they rushed down the hallway, a doctor gave Andretta, who was unconscious, chest compressions.

"What's going on?" Pat screamed.

"We have to get her back up to intensive care," said a nurse. "It's a Code Blue," she exclaimed.

"No, no, wait!" Pat said. As the team stopped rolling the gurney, Pat rushed to her friend's side. "Ann! *Ann!*" she screamed. There was no response. Andretta's body was still, her eyes closed. Panicked, Pat slapped her friend hard across the face. "*Ann!*" Suddenly Andretta bolted upright on the gurney, stiff as a board, her head tilted back. She made panicked eye contact with Pat and then took a deep, loud gulp of air. She then stared at the medical team surrounding her, all of them frozen in place, seemingly startled by her visage as her eyes focused on them like lasers. Then, just as suddenly as she'd come to, she closed her eyes again and collapsed onto the gurney.

"Come on! *Let's move it,*" a doctor said as the team began to shove the gurney into an elevator. "We have to get this patient upstairs."

After the medical team finally got Andretta back to intensive care, Pat and Cholotte gathered in an outside waiting room with Andretta's mother, Effie Lee Brown. Through a glass window, the three frightened women watched helplessly as the medics worked feverishly on their loved one. Though they couldn't actually see Andretta because she was hidden by those trying to save her, they could certainly hear her. "I can't breathe," Andretta screamed out in agony. "*I can't breathe!*"

Vigil

*B*eyoncé couldn't believe it when Tina told her that Andretta had died. Of course, she had long before realized that her mentor was very near death. Still, she somehow imagined that Andretta would pull through. Now, however, she had to face the harsh reality that it was not to be. "Maybe she's in a better place," she tried to reason. "How much does one person have to suffer? It just isn't fair."

By the time the Knowleses and Kelly got to Andretta's the next day, her home was filled with grieving friends and family members. LaTavia and her mother, Cheryl, were already present, as were LeToya and her mom, Pam. "Everybody was there," Kenny Moore, Andretta's good friend and business partner, recalled. "All the girls, all their parents, and everyone who ever knew Andretta. Andretta's mom, Effie, was there. There was a hug fest all the way from the front lawn and driveway to the inside of the house. People were standing around, crying. I went in to check on Armon and Chris. They were in a daze. I was hugging everybody, trying not to cry. I hugged Mathew, I hugged Tina, and some of the others. I hugged Beyoncé."

"Everyone was very upset and emotional," recalled Andretta's brother To-to. "And in his own way, I guess Mathew was, but some of his actions made us question it. His whole thing was that he was looking for any management papers and agreements between him and my sister. He was pushing hard for them, until finally my brother [Larrell] told him, 'No! You can't have them. We'll get back to you later about them.' Mathew said, 'Okay,' and then he took off." (Pat Felton says that some of the documents Mathew was looking for were under Andretta's bed.) Mathew gave a conflicting version of events in later testimony.

The wake a couple days later was, as expected, exceedingly sad. Everyone Andretta had touched over the years was present and grieving, including some who'd not been in the picture for some time. Pat Felton was inconsolable, as were Cholotte Taylor and Cheryl Mitchell. Tina looked as if she was deeply in prayer. Armon and Chris did their best to hold it together, but of course it was difficult. Now they would have to be uprooted and move to Tyler, where they would live with their uncle Keith.

The first people Kenny Moore saw when he arrived at the funeral home were the girls—Beyoncé, Kelly, LaTavia, and LeToya. Before they went inside, Kenny hugged each one. Beyoncé held on for a long time. After she broke away, Kenny looked at her and said two simple words: "*Finish it.*" She shook her head in the affirmative. "Yes, sir," she said, wiping away a tear. "We don't stop."

"She and I always had a special communication," Kenny recalled, "and she knew what I meant: Finish this goddamn thing. Be the greatest group in the world. Be the biggest star there is. Whatever you do, please don't let Andretta's death be in vain."

"Beyoncé cried her heart out, as did all the girls," Kenny remembered. "I started to really get it that they were just innocents in all of the games-playing that had been going on, that it was really the adults the whole time, arguing and fighting over shit. The girls were just pawns. They'd been manipulated into thinking one thing, then another, then another. I remember how upset Ann had been in Atlanta. But the girls' emotion told me how they really felt about her."

Andretta would be buried the next day, in Tyler. "Destiny's Child was supposed to sing at the funeral, but they didn't show up," recalled Armon Tillman. "Their names were in the program. We had been one big happy family, but I started thinking when they didn't show that maybe things would be changing now that my mom was gone." During the service, "No, No, No" was played in lieu of the girls singing. It's not known why they didn't show up and sing, if that had indeed been the intention.

Kenny says he had an unfortunate disagreement with Mathew at one of the services over some of the girls' Columbia/Sony masters. Apparently they had been in Andretta's possession before she died. "After that argument, which took place at probably the most inappropriate place—'Dretta's service—I was done with Mathew Knowles," says Kenny Moore. "I would make sure he'd get the masters as promised, but as far as having him in my life . . . no." (It should be noted here that Mathew seems to have no memory of this altercation. In a deposition he would give on January 29, 2002, when asked if he knew Kenny Moore, he would respond with a succinct, "No.")

Indeed, in the weeks after the Tillman services, Kenny began to distance himself from just about everyone connected with Destiny's Child. "The wake, that was the last time I ever saw Mathew, Tina, Beyoncé, Kelly . . . any of them," he said. "My last memory of Beyoncé is of her crying as they were carrying Ann's casket out of the church. After those services, Mathew took over. Those of us who loved her and worked with Andretta had to accept that things would now be changing. Now Mathew would be the one holding the keys to the kingdom. With that being the case, all I knew for sure was that I wanted the hell out of the kingdom. Therefore I chose my own destiny; I walked away from all of it and never looked back. It was painful, but necessary."

"Everything changed when my mom died," Armon Tillman confirmed. "It was, like, that's it...time to move on. Chris and I moved out of the city to live with our uncle, so no more Sunday dinners at the Knowleses. No more hanging out with the girls. No more basketball games with Mathew. But, worse yet, no phone calls from any of them to see how we were doing. Nothing. It felt as if they just went on with their lives and forgot all about us. It was sudden, too, not a gradual fadeout, just—boom! Over. Done. We would call and leave messages, but no one would return our calls. As a fourteen-year-old kid, you're just left to think, was any of it real? Or was the whole thing just one great big show?"*

Their Time Has Come

*A*fter the services for Andretta Tillman, Beyoncé was troubled by questions about her mentor. She didn't fully understand the troubled history between Andretta and her father, and she felt she was now old enough to have a more complete grasp of it. She called upon someone she trusted implicitly, her producer Lonnie Jackson. "Tell me everything," she said. "I need to know."

"Your father is a good man," Lonnie told her. "But, yes, he and Andretta had their problems."

"I told her the truth," Lonnie would later recall. "I tried to explain what happened and I tried to be as fair about it as I could. I felt that if she trusted me enough to ask, I owed her the truth. I told her that Mathew always had her best interests at heart, that he loved her and that whatever he did, he did for her. But I was clear that she also owed a great and incredible debt to Andretta. I would never want her to think otherwise, because the

---

* Mathew later testified that after Andretta's death he had tried in vain to contact Armon and Chris to see how they were doing.

truth is the truth. I told her that none of it would have happened if not for Ann."

"Deborah Laday and Denise Seals started it," he told her, "and then Miss Ann, me, and Tony Mo. picked it up and rehearsed you girls every day, coaching you, recording you, and doing everything we could think of to help make your dreams come true. And all of that was way before your dad."

Beyoncé was grateful to Lonnie and said she knew she could count on him "to keep it real with me." She said she loved him, and he told her he felt the same way about her. In the end, she decided that her father's actions had always been in her best interest. After all, he was her greatest champion. She couldn't very well expect everyone to agree with him all the time. She just had to have faith in him and realize that his relationship with Andretta was his own—and maybe none of her business anyway.

By the end of June, there wasn't any more time for serious reflection, because Destiny's Child's career was about to blow up. Doubtless, Beyoncé could have used more time to grieve, but it was just not possible. The girls were about to become incredibly busy, which would actually provide a much-needed distraction.

On July 1, 1997, the first Destiny's Child song was released. Called "Killing Time" and written by D'Wayne Wiggins and Taura Stinson, it was issued on the soundtrack to *Men in Black* on Columbia/Sony. It was ironic that "Killing Time" would be the act's first release, because the dramatic, yearning ballad with its sweeping string arrangement expresses a venerable musicality that's not typical of a young vocal group. At its elegant center are the earnest vocals of a young and ambitious Beyoncé Knowles as she eagerly develops her style and approach with every note.

Taura Stinson, who would go on to marry Lonnie Jackson, recalled, "D'Wayne had a studio in Richmond, California, which is where we recorded the song and where I first met the girls. Before I got there, D'Wayne said, 'This one girl, Beyoncé, looks so much like you, you won't believe it. [In fact, Taura and Beyoncé looked so much alike, Mathew eventually began to refer to Taura as "my third daughter."] He said all of the girls were so cute, and so country. When I finally met her, the first thing Beyoncé said to me was, 'I *love* "Killing Time." I can't wait to get into it.' She was so interested and invested. She had a couple different ways she wanted to end the song, so we tried them all out, and, honestly, one was as good as the other. I was really impressed with her skill level, especially given her age. I also remember her sitting behind the console in the studio giving the others their parts to sing. She was very . . . motivating, I guess is the word."

At the time, Randy Jackson (who has more recently become famous as a judge on *American Idol*) was the A&R director at Columbia/Sony. He and Lonnie Jackson were friends, both hailing from the Bay Area. During a meeting with Randy, Lonnie played him "Killing Time." "Brother, I'm gonna do you a favor," Randy said. "I'm gonna put this song on the soundtrack to *Men in Black*."

Lonnie scoffed at the notion. "Man, please, I'm begging you, do not put my song on some cheap-ass movie soundtrack."

Of course, no one could have predicted the kind of phenomenal success *Men in Black*, which starred Will Smith and Tommy Lee Jones, would have, except maybe Randy Jackson. "You're gonna thank me for this later," he told Lonnie with a laugh.

"Okay, dude, whatever," Lonnie said.

Taura had a similar conversation with Mathew. "He called me and said, 'You owe me, *big-time*,' " Taura recalled with a laugh. "I asked him why. He said, 'Because I just got your song on the soundtrack of what is going to be the biggest franchise in the history of the world.' I was amazed. I was just getting started! We all were!"

The first Destiny's Child song would actually be in stellar company on this soundtrack, an album that included songs by the movie's star, Will Smith, as well as Alicia Keys, Snoop Dogg, and singer/songwriter and actor Ginuwine. With Beyoncé on lead, this simmering ballad with soaring orchestration showed off not only her great ability but also the group's harmonic strength. Though still just a youngster, Beyoncé seemed to completely connect with the lyrical storyline of unrequited love.

Because the film quickly shot to the top at the box office, the soundtrack album was an immediate and unqualified success, spending two weeks at number one on the *Billboard* Top 200. It would go on to sell triple platinum—three million copies in the United States. (Except for the title song by Will Smith, none of the songs on the album was actually in the movie.) "Man, you can't tell me there aren't angels out there watching over us," D'Wayne Wiggins told Randy Jackson, who always believed the album would be a hit. "True dat," Randy said, laughing. "True dat."

"This soundtrack was the perfect venue for a Destiny's Child debut song," says Wiggins. "The fact that I cowrote and also produced 'Killing Time' made this premiere even more special for me. It really was the beginning for Destiny's Child, and I was proud to be on the ground floor of something we knew would be great."

Though "Killing Time" was not released as a single, it set the stage perfectly for the first Columbia/Sony single, the aforementioned "No, No, No" by 8Bit and Vince Herbert, which was finally released on November 11, 1997.

Beyoncé has recalled the first time she heard "No, No, No" on the radio. She and Kelly were in the new Ford Explorer that Tina had just bought. They'd left rehearsal and were picking up Solange at school. "I had just pulled up to the school when our song came on the radio," Beyoncé recalled. "We turned the volume up as loud as it could go and started running around the car singing along. The bell had just rung and my sister was walking out of class with her friends. When she got closer to the car, she heard the song playing and she dropped her bag and books and started running around the car too. It was really so cool."

"No, No, No" reached number three on *Billboard*'s Hot 100 chart. It went to number one on the R&B chart, and was also a hit all over Europe. "This was unbelievable to us," Beyoncé said. "To find that after all that hard work, it just happens sort of overnight. We thought we'd have to put out a bunch of songs before we had a hit. We never imagined it would be the first one."

After hurdling all sorts of personal and professional roadblocks, Destiny's Child released its debut album on February 17, 1998. It would very quickly soar to number four on the *Billboard* 200 album pop chart, where it would spend an astounding twenty-six weeks. Eventually it would go on to sell one million copies in the United States alone and three million copies worldwide. It would also earn Destiny's Child its first high-profile award, the Best R&B/Soul Album of the Year at the Soul Train Lady of Soul Awards.

Fittingly, "My Time Has Come" closes out the album. It could be argued even today that this song—produced and cowritten by veteran jazz/pop entertainer Sylvia Bennett, and lovingly dedicated to Andretta Tillman—is the best, most complete musical arrangement to which Beyoncé has ever laid her voice. On one hand, this big, expansive pop ballad sounds out of place among all of the R&B and hip-hop compositions on the album. However, the song's powerful sentiment of arriving at a great moment was more than appropriate. Beyoncé sings it with a fortitude and conviction that reflects her gratitude, and that of the other girls, to their "Miss Ann" for all she'd done and for everything she'd sacrificed to get them to this point in their careers.

On a night before her death that Andretta Tillman and Kenny Moore celebrated the girls' new recordings over a homemade meal of pork chops and rice, Kenny says Andretta couldn't stop playing "My Time Has Come." She had no idea it would be dedicated to her; she simply loved the song and marveled at Beyoncé's powerful and soulful delivery. "This one song pretty much says it all about what we've been through as a family," she told Kenny with tears in her eyes. It wasn't easy. It wasn't always fun, either. However, Andretta was sure it had been worth it. "Now, their time has finally come," she said of her beloved protégées. "Maybe that time has come for all of us," she concluded. "God willing."

Success

*T*he new year of 1998 was off to a good start for the Knowles family, which came as a great relief considering how bad 1997 had been. According to their 1997 tax filing, the Knowleses' annual income was about $32,000, down from the year before when they reported around $50,000. Happily, when the family looked toward 1998 with the new record deal in mind, they felt they'd finally get a reprieve from financial stress. Indeed, their income tax return for 1998 would show an almost triple increase from the previous year, with more than $85,000 in income. They still had a lot of cleaning up to do with their finances, though. Their savings account would be seized by the government to pay for back taxes, a "Seizure of Savings Account Notice" filed in March 1998. Certainly, if any two people ever paid their dues, Mathew and Tina Knowles did. For most of the 1990s, they dealt with one financial calamity after another during their long odyssey to eventual fame and fortune, and they did so with their dignity intact and without most people in their lives knowing anything about it.

With these intense financial pressures now easing up, Mathew and Tina also had a chance to sort out at least some of the problems in their marriage. Throughout their separation, the couple was constantly seen together, so much so that most people—other than their closest friends and some business associates—didn't even know they had parted. In particular, Tina didn't explain much, choosing instead to keep the secrets of her marriage sacred. Perhaps the closest she got to opening up was when she told one relative, "This separation is bad for our family. It's bad for the kids. Somehow, I must find a way to put this family back together."

Mathew and Tina did reunite and, despite their financial problems, they ended 1997 by purchasing a new family home at 8207 Braes Meadow Drive on December 5 for a little less than $100,000. (For reasons unknown, only Tina's name is on the deed of sale.) It was actually just as large (with five bedrooms) as the former residence on Parkwood. The ranch-style structure in a good, integrated neighborhood was a lateral move for the family.

Were Mathew and Tina happier now that they were together again? Most people who knew them at this time say that there seemed to be little change in the cool temperature between them. The girls were much happier, though, and maybe that would have to be enough. Indeed, Beyoncé, Solange, and Kelly were overjoyed to have Mathew back—though as DC's manager he had never exactly been hard to find—and they seemed to love the new home as much as the former residence. By habit, they usually stayed close to home.

"In my family, I was always off with my friends doing stupid stuff like any other kid," Lyndall Locke recalls. "My sister was always gone, my mother was always somewhere, busy. But there was no such thing going on at the Knowles household. For them it was, 'Let's go get some Popeyes fried chicken and come back and eat it and we'll all watch TV together and maybe have a talent show or do some arts and crafts.' We practically never left the house to hang out. But still, I loved going to the house on Braes Meadow because just being there was out of this world—you always felt that family love. Beyoncé had no friends outside of the house, other than the girls in her group," he continued. "She would say she didn't need friends. She had Mathew, Tina, Solange, Kelly, LaTavia, LeToya, Solange . . . and me. And that was about it."

One night, Mathew came home to Braes Meadow with Popeyes fried chicken for everyone and a bottle of champagne for him and Tina. He popped the cork, and as the young people ate their chicken, he and Tina toasted their newfound success. Tina remarked that she really couldn't imagine how they had done it, though she was thankful to God that they had gotten through it. Mathew had to agree. The two clinked glasses and celebrated their hard-earned victory.

This same year, Lyndall was excited to ask Beyoncé to be his date at his

Lee High School senior prom. Tina encouraged her to go, feeling that it would take her mind off her lingering sadness about Andretta. When she was working, Beyoncé was fine because she was distracted. However, on her off time she was definitely still grieving. "It was as if she had a hole in her heart that she just wasn't able to fill," is how one person who knew her at this time put it.

Beyoncé said yes to the prom and was glad she did. "It was the only prom I ever went to," she would later say. "I didn't know anybody but Lyndall. I didn't have any classmates, because by this time I was being tutored and homeschooled, so I never had that experience. I guess I sort of lived it vicariously through my boyfriend."

"It was a great night," Lyndall recalled. His mom had rented him a brand-new red Mustang convertible for the night to impress his date. The two dined at the classy Brownstone restaurant in Houston. "I pretty much had the most beautiful date at the prom," Lyndall recalled.

Beyoncé would in years to come re-create the concept of a prom date in her video for "Best Thing I Never Had," during which her character is rejected at the dance. Of course, that never happened. "And the jerk playing me had a flattop, and I ain't never had no flattop," Lyndall laughed. "I was so much *cooler* than the guy playing me in the video!"

Lyndall—No Direction?

*J*ust as there were two versions of the song released to the public, there were two videos for Destiny's Child's "No, No, No." One was in a concert setting for the more sedate "Part 1," and the other was in a nightclub for Wyclef's more dance-oriented "Part 2." What strikes the viewer about both is that the girls are uncommonly beautiful in them and seem mature beyond their ages, especially in the "Part 1" video.

In the concert video, after the young ladies are introduced in a trendy lounge setting, they take the stage before a small audience and sing the song. Although they are in their midteens—Beyoncé and LaTavia were fifteen, LeToya and Kelly sixteen—they are definitely not going for a teenage image. Flawlessly applied heavy makeup makes them appear years older. Their pouty, dark red lips and bedroom eyes are showcased in suggestive close-ups. Their costumes are clingy and revealing. The undeniable goal is to project adult sensuality. As the girls perform for an intimate crowd, their suggestive moves might be viewed by some as inappropriate given that they are underage.

"When I saw the first video for 'No! No! No!' I thought, *'What the hell?'*" recalled Daryl Simmons. "The biggest criticism of the girls when they were with me was that they were too adult, too sexy. But then I saw this video and they were way hotter and way sexier than they ever were with me. My friends in the business were asking me, 'Man! Have you seen this girl, Beyoncé? Damn!' When I would say, 'Dude, she's only, like, fifteen,' they would be shocked. They thought she was at least twenty-three or twenty-four."

"That sexy video was the beginning of a lot of confusion for me," Lyndall Locke recalled. "In the beginning, I was with the most beautiful girl I had ever seen. And then all of a sudden with the 'No, No, No' video, it was like, 'Uh-oh. Now I'm with this real famous chick who is totally hot, and everybody on the planet knows it.'

"I had always been this kid who was happy and self-confident," he continued. "However, when Beyoncé started blowing up, I started to not feel comfortable in my own skin. People who knew me would come up to me and say, 'Hey man! *That's* your girlfriend?' And I would say, 'Yeah, I wish.' That was my response to everyone: 'Yeah, *I* wish.' I started to think if I told people she was my girl, they wouldn't believe it, and I didn't want to have to prove it. She was becoming rich and famous, and I was just the same kid from Houston, no money, no direction...no nothin'. It started to mess with my head."

It was starting to affect Beyoncé, too. For instance, it seemed that she was beginning not to enjoy the attention she was getting as a result of the "No, No, No" videos. She'd tried to keep it a secret for as long as possible, especially from the other kids in the neighborhood. "We had a song that was about to go on the radio," she told Welsh interviewer Steve Jones, "we had shot our music video. I was in eighth grade. And I didn't tell a soul. Not one person. One day they just looked up and I was on television."

Jeff Harvey, a good friend of Lydia Locke's and a sort of paternal figure to Lyndall (who refers to him as his "Uncle Jeff"), recalled that Lyndall would often bring Beyoncé to his large home in Katy, twenty-five miles west of Houston. "I can remember her always saying, 'Uncle Jeff, please don't tell anyone I'm here,'" he remembered. "I would tell her, 'Beyoncé, no one knows who you are. You're not famous yet, but okay, I won't tell anyone.' She would then go upstairs to the bedroom and stay there while the living room was full of people, especially if Lyndall was having a big swim party. My impression was that she wasn't comfortable with getting recognized, with being singled out. I think she was shy."

"It's definitely an adjustment," Beyoncé conceded to Lyndall. "I don't know what to do with it. It's very confusing." On this day, to Lyndall's eyes, she was somehow already different. She wore a folded pink silk scarf around her forehead, her blondish hair exploding into an enormous mass of curls behind it. Wearing large hoop earrings with pink lipstick and matching eye shadow, she was still the old Beyoncé, but somehow now glossed up to near perfection.

"You're becoming a whole new kind of person," he told her. "Aren't you scared?"

"I am," she answered honestly.

"I just wish we could have a normal life," he told her.

"Well, we don't have a normal life," she said, matter-of-factly. "We have *this* life." Locked in on him and looking deeply into his eyes, she told him that she'd been preparing for success since the age of eight when she was discovered by Deborah Laday and Denise Seals. Then she added, "Maybe you should start thinking about what *you* want to do with *your* life, Lynnie." She looked at him with such intensity, it was clear that she really meant what she was saying; she wanted him to start making some adult decisions about his future, indeed their future.

Lyndall winced. He wanted to respond with authority, but he didn't know what to say. Not everyone was as directed and as focused as Beyoncé. He certainly wasn't—not at this time in his life, anyway. With her scrutiny on him so fixed and probing, he was at a loss. He felt cornered. "I might want to be . . . I don't know . . . a chef, maybe," he said, stammering.

"Okay. That's interesting," Beyoncé said, taking it all in and nodding thoughtfully. "Well," she began, "maybe you can be a personal chef for *me*, then." Everyone knew that she couldn't cook, she said, so *someone* would have to do it for her. "It might as well be you. Right?" she asked.

None of this was sitting right with Lyndall. Still, Beyoncé continued reasoning that if he were to become her personal chef they could spend more time together. "So, when do you think you'll go?" she finally asked. "To school, I mean. Soon, right?"

"Yeah, soon, I guess," he answered.

"Great," she said, melting into his arms. "Soon, then."

First Impressions

*D*estiny's Child hit the road in the spring of 1998 on their first major tour, as an opening act for Boyz II Men. Their premier date was April 28 in Memphis, Tennessee, at the Pyramid Arena; Dru Hill and K-Ci & JoJo were also on the show. It was to be a grueling itinerary; the girls would definitely miss home. At one point, Beyoncé telephoned Tina back in Houston to complain about the hotel food. That was all Tina needed to hear. That night, she prepared a big pot of gumbo and froze it. At the airport, she somehow managed to distract the guards at the security checkpoint from seeing the pot as it went down the conveyer belt and through the X-ray. Finally, she met the girls at their stop and, as she recalled, "we heated up that gumbo and had a good ol' time."

There were also dozens of press interviews while on the road, which also took extensive planning and forethought. "Don't tell anyone how old you are," Mathew had told Beyoncé before she left on her very first promotional tour with Destiny's Child, in 1997. He always displayed an almost uncanny intuition about public relations. "I don't want you to be child stars," he told the girls. "Some child stars grow up and have no future. Or the public won't *let* them grow up. No one needs to know your age." This was not difficult for the girls to do. With their total self-assurance onstage while wearing revealing costumes with polished makeup and adult hairstyles, they looked anywhere from sixteen to maybe twenty-six.

"I can't teach you how to sing, but I will tell you that when you enter the room, your interview has begun," their new publicist at the label, Yvette Noel-Schure, told Destiny's Child. "Everything is on the record, what you say, what you did, if you were slumping in your chair—so don't slump in your chair, because that's going to be part of the description in the interview."

"I saw a very meticulous fourteen-year-old girl," Noel-Schure would later recall of meeting Beyoncé. [Actually, Beyoncé was probably fifteen, maybe sixteen, when they met]. "To be so in-the-know at *that* age—I remember coming back to Sony and saying, 'This is my project. I'm gonna have the time of my life with these girls.'"

Noel-Schure added, "This is what I'm always gonna remember about Beyoncé: She takes you in. She looks you straight in your eyes when she's talking to you. I said [to myself], 'That is the trait of an honest person'—if you can look someone in the eye, a total stranger. In those days she was, 'Yes, ma'am, yes, ma'am,' to me, but she looked me right straight in the eye, did not blink, it seemed. I saw that boldness in her. To this day, when you talk to her, it's the same thing. I always say, 'Wow! You still do that.'" (Noel-Schure is still Beyoncé's publicist all these years later.)

Reggie Wells, the Emmy-winning makeup artist whose biggest claim to fame is his work with Oprah Winfrey, recalled, "Beyoncé was very interested in my life and what I had done with Oprah, with Whitney [Houston], and the others I'd worked for over the years. The first thing she said to me was, 'My mother told me all about you, and I'm so impressed. I'm honored to be *touched* by you.' That was powerful for someone just sixteen, very respectful.

"What I noticed about her right away was that she made her own statement, which was: 'Look at me. Give me your attention. Because I'm giving you something you've never seen before.' All four girls were unique, and my job was to make each stand out in her own way. But Beyoncé was the one with the most imagination. You might go in thinking about her colors one way, but she would have an entirely different view, a look you may not even have thought of. You could not sit down and tell her what was going to work. *She* would tell *you*, and she would be right."

Shortly after the first album's release, Beyoncé, Kelly, LaTavia, and LeToya enjoyed a celebratory dinner with friends and relatives, probably fifteen in all, at their favorite soul food restaurant, This Is It, in Houston. They ate oxtails, smothered pork chops, candied yams, fried chicken, and more food than their diets normally allowed. Beyoncé said she wanted "as much macaroni and cheese as possible."

"If Mathew finds out about all this food ruining our figures he's gonna kill us," LaTavia warned her friends. In fact, all four were more intimidated by Mathew now than ever before. With the stakes so raised, he was even tougher on them in rehearsals. Because Lonnie Jackson had been such a strict figure in their lives, they certainly knew how to bear up under pressure. However, Mathew took being a taskmaster to a whole new level. "He was a drill sergeant" is how LaTavia would put it.

"Oh absolutely, he was hard on them," said Sony's Chad Elliott. "But he was focused on the big picture, and his approach was to be successful by any means necessary."

Much of Mathew's attention was, of course, on Beyoncé. There were days when she felt she could do nothing right. She took it more in stride than the other girls, though, as if she well knew her father. Though he sometimes hurt her feelings, she rarely let him know it or see it.

In the end, the girls couldn't help but credit Mathew with their success, even though they had to sometimes question his methods. "Where was your mind tonight?" he demanded to know of Kelly after a recent show in Atlanta. "I watched you mess up *twelve* dance steps!" Now, a few weeks later as the girls celebrated their success, Kelly was able to be philosophical about it. "He's the only father I ever had," she said, "so I feel blessed. But, *doggone it!* He could be nicer! I mean ... *dang, Mathew!*"

"Honey, please! I been sayin' that for years," Beyoncé deadpanned, rolling her eyes.

Tina, Stylist

*I*t was at around the end of 1998 that Tina Knowles began working for Destiny's Child as the group's stylist. She had always been a self-sufficient woman with her own business. In fact, she had credited the fact that she was able to remain in her challenging marriage to her sense of individuality—she had more in her life than just her marriage. It could be said, then, that this sense of independence was once again tested in 1998. On December 22 of that year, Mathew would go into rehab therapy for a second time. "In 1998, when I was treated a second time, they had a more defined definition [of his condition] of sex addiction," he confirmed. "But sex addiction has such a broad range. My treatment was regarding my continued extramarital affairs."

As Mathew struggled with his demons, Tina did what she could to support him. However, in the end, she realized that it was really his battle to fight and, hopefully, to win. She found her greatest personal refuge in her own work with Destiny's Child.

At first, Tina was just doing the girls' hair. However, on a trip to Cancún for an MTV special, their luggage was lost in transit, including their wardrobe. In an effort to help the girls out of a bad situation, Tina decided to try to pull something together for them to wear onstage. "I went to a little village and found some camouflage at a flea market," she recalled, "and then I borrowed some camouflage pants from Wyclef Jean. In the end, the clothes for the girls came out so cute! Afterward, Wyclef came over and asked them, 'Yo, who styled y'all?' Beyoncé said, 'My mom!' and he said, 'Well, you should do it all the time.'" At first Tina protested and explained that she was just filling in. "But after that, I started styling full-time," she recalled. "At first I just wanted to be out with the kids so I could help protect them . . . but it wound up being a whole career for me."

Tina had been frustrated anyway by some of the clothing the girls were asked to wear, such as the revealing costumes in the "No, No, No" video. In her mind, not only did the wardrobe seem inappropriate for young girls, but a lot of it was in shades of gray and black, which made no sense to her. "I figured they would have years to wear all black," she said. "They were young," she reasoned, "and should wear bright colors."

"When the girls first started, we looked at tapes of Motown all the time," recalled Tina, "and if you look at the artists from Motown, such as the Supremes or the Jackson 5, you were excited to see what they had on, what they were wearing. You know, Michael Jackson had the fringe, the Jackson 5 had the big apple hats, Diana Ross and the Supremes had the beautiful gowns. It was all so memorable and bigger than life. If you were sitting forty rows back, you could see the sparkle and the dazzle.

"Mathew wanted to re-create Motown," she continued. "He was always a big fan of Motown's, and so we would watch tapes of those acts. Imaging was very important to Destiny's Child. The record label, on the other hand, kept saying we needed to put the girls in jeans and T-shirts. That's what Britney Spears was wearing and that's what they thought the girls should be looking like too. But we didn't want that."

Destiny's Child always had great input with their appearance. They would tell Tina what they preferred and didn't like, and were quite vocal about it. For instance, Kelly had an extremely small waist and enjoyed wearing midriff tops. Beyoncé had great legs and was always eager to show them off. The girls would cut out photographs of women in designs they enjoyed, and Tina would tape them on "inspiration boards" so that they could all agree on concepts.

"I remember we were on tour somewhere in New York, maybe Buffalo,"

Kim Wood Sandusky, who would soon become the girls' vocal coach, recalled. "We had to get new shoes for the girls. We got the shoes in but they weren't flashy enough. I walked into the dressing room and Tina was in there working on them with her niece, Angie, and assistant, Ty, the three of them very meticulously adding little jewels and sparkles to the shoes. 'Look, I'm not very crafty, Tina,' I said, 'but let me help you.' She laughed, handed me a glue gun, some sequins, and a high-heel and said, 'Here! See what you can do!' I sat there on the floor in the middle of the dressing room with beads, scissors, thread, needles—all of us in a circle working feverishly on these shoes. We were on a real tight timetable. I remember thinking, 'Oh, man! They're going to ask me to leave this little party, because I'm not nearly as fast as they are!' But they didn't, and we got it done! The girls wore the shoes that same night."

Tina would go on to spend many years designing clothes for Destiny's Child, and later Beyoncé. Most of the outfits worked very well and are definitely of a time and place, though a few even she would admit to perhaps being not the greatest of stage wear ever donned by a pop act.

Today, the ever-enterprising Tina Knowles has expanded her brand into a number of clothing lines, including House of Deréon (for more expensive clothing, sold in better department stores), Deréon (a younger, more lifestyle brand), and Miss Tina (stylish but affordable clothes for the more mature woman). She most recently curated a collection of twenty-four designs from Caché, everything from trendy leather dresses to elegant ball gowns with crop tops, her favorites. "I'm mostly looking for things that will be flattering to every woman," she says of choosing items for the collection. "Picking things that I know will work on many body types and many age groups."

Prepping for the Second Album

We didn't even know if there was going to be a second Destiny's Child album," Tina Knowles would once recall in a deposition. "I remember talking to the product manager at Columbia, who said the first album did okay but wasn't as big as they hoped. It just did all right. [Actually, the album continued to sell long after its release.] So whether there would be another album remained to be seen. Our deal with Columbia called for seven albums, but only if the label exercised its option after each one. So, yes, we were stressing out a lot over whether or not to expect a second album. You can imagine how happy the household was when Mathew came home one day and said, 'Yeah, they want it. It's time to start working on album number two.' Beyoncé and Kelly were jumping up and down and crying, and so was I!"

Unlike Destiny Child's debut album, where Beyoncé is credited with cowriting one song, during *The Writing's on the Wall*, she would find herself working with a cadre of go-to writers and producers of the day, including Rodney "Darkchild" Jerkins, Kevin "She'kspere" Briggs, Kandi Burruss, Missy Elliott, Daryl Simmons, and D'Wayne Wiggins. In all, Beyoncé cowrote eleven of the album's fifteen tracks; she is credited as a producer or coproducer on seven of them. "At this point, Beyoncé was really emerging as a songwriter," recalled her publicist, Yvette Noel-Schure. "You can't just sit on that. It was time for her to get those juices flowing, to start writing."

In preparation for the group's second opus, the girls sat down with pads and pens and made copious notes about what they liked about their debut recording, and what they weren't quite as happy about. "Beyoncé told me that there were elements of the first album she thought were maybe too mature," Daryl Simmons said. "She told me, 'Shoot! We're just teenagers. We want to have more fun than that.' So there was definitely a concentrated effort to create an album that was younger in its appeal than the debut."

Some of this second album would be recorded at SugarHill Recording Studios in Houston, one of the world's oldest (along with Abbey Road Studios in London) and, arguably, most famous studios in the world. Record producer and engineer Dan Workman is the president and CEO of the operation; he and his partner, Rodney Meyers, purchased the studio in 1996. Workman had been producing music since 1988, when he cut his teeth working with ZZ Top. By 1998, when he met Beyoncé, he was in his midforties.

"My wife, Christi, was working as studio manager," Dan Workman recalled, "and she came to me one day and said, 'Do you know a guy named Mathew Knowles?' I answered, 'Nope, never heard of him.' She goes, 'Well, he's on the phone and wants to book time for his daughter.' This was very common, you know, dads wanting to book studio time for their kids' little bands, or whatever. She said, 'He's insistent and he can't believe we've never heard of his girl's band.' I said, 'Well, what's its name?' And she said,

'Destiny's Child.' 'Never heard of 'em.' She said they were signed to Columbia, Wyclef Jean had produced their first hit, and the label was going to be paying for the sessions. Well, all of that piqued my interest. Anytime it's not the dad who's paying for the sessions out of his own pocket, that's good news. So I said, 'Great, let's bring her in.'

"A few days later, Mathew showed up at the studio with Beyoncé," Dan Workman recalled. "I actually thought the whole group was coming in, but no, it was just Beyoncé. Mathew was scoping out the studio, and she was behind him, taking it all in. Both were very intense. You could tell that for them this was serious business.

"He'd brought along some tracks she'd been working on, I spooled them, he left, and she went into the booth and started singing," Dan Workman continued. "Within five minutes, I realized, 'Okay, this is not just some teenager trying to be a singer. This is a real vocalist.' You could tell she knew her way around a studio. The way she intuitively used the microphone and asked for feedback showed a level of professionalism far beyond her years. She was even using terminology that was opaque to me. She'd say, 'Okay, cool. Let's start at the B section' [the 'bridge' or 'middle eight' of a song].' She also started schooling me on R&B music production, telling me how to double and triple different runs, copy and layer her vocals to make her one voice sound like a group of singers, all standard stuff in R&B, but I was this old rock-and-roll punk white guy who had never done soul music. While it felt a little weird having this teenager drive the session, she was so good I was blown away by the whole thing.

"At the end of the day, Mathew came to pick her up," Workman concluded. "'Man, we had a great time,' I told him. 'She's charming, easy to work with. We had a real rapport. Hope to see you guys back here one day.' You could tell he was happy to hear these compliments. The next thing I knew, he booked a week of studio time with the talented producer She'kspere."

The Writing's on the Wall

She'kspere (whose real name is Kevin Briggs) was best known for just having produced TLC's big hit "No Scrubs," very much the kind of feminist song for which Destiny's Child was becoming known. He, along with his wife at the time, Kandi Burruss (from the female group Xscape and who had also collaborated with She'kspere on "No Scrubs"), would join forces on productions of new songs for the second Destiny's Child album, which would be called *The Writing's on the Wall*.

Much of *The Writing's on the Wall* was written on the spot, while DC was in the studio recording it. Often the process was as impromptu as Beyoncé reaching into a stash of CDs of instrumental tracks that had been submitted by various producers and giving several of them a listen. She'd then decide which ones to complete by adding to them a vocal melody and lyric right there on the spot, sometimes with the help of the other girls. Then the group would instantly record what they'd come up with. It was a strange way of making records (and an even stranger way of writing songs). In a normal scenario, the song would already be written, its lyrics handed to the artist in the recording booth. Then, as the artist sang over the prerecorded track, a producer would oversee the endeavor. This standard process happened sometimes too, but for the most part Beyoncé and Destiny's Child charted their own course in the studio.

"The way these girls worked was totally unique to me," Dan Workman said. "They would come, take off their coats, kick off their shoes, make themselves at home in the studio, and write songs right there on the spot, just eating Cheetos and coming up with lines. Beyoncé would have most of it outlined, then one girl would add a word, and another would add a phrase and on and on…" It should be noted that it doesn't take much to get a songwriting credit in popular music these days. If one of the group members added so much as a single word—*voilà!*—she would get a songwriting credit…and royalties forever more.

"Kandi Burruss was very influential in this process," said Dan Workman. "She and Beyoncé worked well together. They had a way of grabbing hooks out of thin air, or turning phrases and finding rhymes. Kandi was She'kspere's secret weapon. She was like the heavyweight in the room, and Beyoncé was soaking up every bit of knowledge from her." (Today, Kandi Burruss is a regular on "The Real Housewives of Atlanta" television program.) "But there was often no actual recording going on," Workman continued, "just these sort of workshop dates.

"At one point, I told Mathew, 'I don't even know how to bill you for these strange sessions! Basically, we're just housing a bunch of kids and then ordering in lunch for them. Sometimes they actually record something.' He laughed and said, 'Well, figure it out, because that's their process, and it works for them.'"

A telling moment occurred during the writing process for the song "Bills, Bills, Bills," one that Dan Workman says he'll never forget. All of the girls had their pencils and pads out and were trying to come up with a line. However, everyone was drawing a blank. Suddenly, something came to Workman, just a little phrase. "How about..." he began, and then he blurted out his idea. "The room went dead," he recalled. "It was as if I had farted in church. There had been all of this excitement for the song and then, suddenly, within seconds, the girls just quit working on it. Finally, Beyoncé said, 'Okay, ladies, let's move on to something else now, shall we?' I was hurt." It could be that he had simply interrupted their flow, but after thinking about it, Dan theorized that the girls knew, even back then, that giving him a songwriting credit meant giving him a royalty too. "So I learned my lesson," he concluded, laughing, "which was, 'Dan, keep your big fat mouth shut when Beyoncé and her group are writing their songs.'"

With *The Writing's on the Wall*, the public would be able to experience the development of the distinctive style Beyoncé had started to toy with on the first Destiny's Child record. On the new "Bills, Bills, Bills," for instance, the syncopation she came up with for the chorus was very unusual. In fact, there had never been anything in pop or R&B that sounded quite like it. It had to do with the rhythm of the song and the way she was able to work around and inside the downbeat in a way that was completely unique. "With 'Bills, Bills, Bills,' that was the first time I had ever heard anyone do anything like that," recalled Dan Workman. "I remember thinking, 'That's so weird, so experimental. Can that be a hit record?' And son of a bitch if it wasn't."

With Beyoncé there was no frame of reference for what she had created stylistically. For instance, the late Michael Jackson was obviously very good at timing and swinging the beat in a traditional R&B way. He was incredibly knife-edged about it, razor sharp in fact. Some might argue, though, that his style was actually a refined derivative of what James Brown and maybe Otis Redding and Jackie Wilson had done before him. While Michael made it fresh and took it to places it had never gone before, there was at least some precursor to it. Beyoncé's style had no popular frame of reference whatsoever.

That said, Anthony Moore—Tony Mo.—wrote a song for Girls Tyme called "Blue Velvet," which featured many of these same kinds of staccato phrasings. This was the song Ashley Davis had trouble recording when Beyoncé was sent into the studio to relieve her—the defining moment in Beyoncé's career when everyone present suddenly realized what they had in her. Considering that an artist usually takes the totality of her experiences with her wherever she goes, there's little doubt that Beyoncé's distinctive style was influenced by her foundational work with Tony Mo. " 'Blue Velvet' was right in the pocket," he recalled, "and I would hear that same influence in a lot of her Destiny's Child performances."

The second DC album would also include, "Jumpin' Jumpin'," which would mark Beyoncé's first time receiving both writer and producer credits. She is credited with Chad Elliott and Rufus Moore on the writing and Elliott and Jovonn Alexander on the production.

At the time, Chad Elliott was an accomplished writer and producer with an extensive background working with, among many others, the Motown female group 702. One day he received a phone call from Teresa LaBarbera Whites telling him that she wanted him to meet "this great group in Houston." He flew to Texas from New York and met Mathew and Destiny's Child over a seafood dinner. This was back when they were working on the first album. Unfortunately, the timing was off, and Elliott wasn't able to contribute to that one. By the time they got to the second album, though, he was ready and eager.

For consideration, Elliott and his cowriter, Rufus Moore, and coproducer, Jovonn Alexander, sent Mathew a bunch of songs they'd been working on—musical tracks with no vocals. By mistake, the CD they submitted contained a song called "The Ambush Crew." Mathew loved the track and gave it to Beyoncé. She sat with it a few days and wrote the lyrics to what she would then call "Jumpin' Jumpin'."

"So I get this song back from Mathew one day with all of these new lyrics," Chad Elliott recalled. "I was freaking out because we never intended to send that song to Mathew. It was a total accident. It was a tune I was working on for a personal project. Then I heard the new lyrics, and I was blown away. I had intended it to be a rap record. When it came back to me, I was like, 'Whoa! What the heck is this? How did *this* happen?' Now it was a call for women to leave their significant others at home and go out clubbing. It was a female twist that took me by surprise: 'Ladies, leave your man at home, the club is full of ballers and their pockets full grown.' There was something democratic about it, too, because it was also telling men to do the same thing, without their women. I called Mathew right away and explained to him that the track had been submitted by accident."

"Well, what do you want to do, Chad?" Mathew asked. "Because you have to admit that what my daughter did with your track is pretty damn hot."

"Are you kidding me?" Chad said, laughing. "It's hotter than hot. Let me talk to my crew and get back to you."

Ultimately, Chad decided that the opportunity was too good to pass up. Thus it came to pass that "Jumpin' Jumpin'" would be the song with the distinction of being the very first one credited to Beyoncé as a cowriter and also coproducer.

Beyoncé's unique syncopated style of phrasing was also exemplified by "Jumpin' Jumpin'." "I think it was a whole new sound for a lot of people," she would recall. "The fans didn't even understand some of the lyrics. But that was the fun of it. They would have to play the song a million times just to get the lyrics straight, and in playing it over and over they got to love it even more. So it was sort of my way of getting them to give the song more than just a quick listen."

Also noteworthy on the second album would be the somber "Say My Name," the embittered calling-out of a man who insists he's in love with his girl but is suspiciously reluctant about expressing it when he's talking to her on the phone. It would become a classic Destiny's Child song, credited to all four girls in the group as songwriters, as well as Rodney Jerkins, Fred Jerkins III, and LaShawn Daniels. There was also the uptempo "Bug a Boo," a clever critique of a potential suitor who in the initial meeting is cool and collected, but once he gets a girl's phone number and e-mail address reveals himself to be a pest. Again, all four girls are credited as songwriters, as well as She'kspere and Kandi Burruss. Both songs are about subjects that love songs have covered since the beginning of time, but with a frankness that girl groups had rarely expressed in the past.

The Writing's on the Wall would debut at number six on the *Billboard* 200 on August 14, 1999, and spend an astonishing ninety-nine consecutive weeks on that chart. It would earn Destiny's Child six Grammy nominations. After "Say My Name" won two Grammys, the album did even more gangbusting business, ultimately selling almost ten million copies in the United States alone. Of its four singles, two—"Bills, Bills, Bills" and "Say My Name"—reached number one on *Billboard*'s Hot 100 singles chart. "At that point, I could see the press returning my calls a little sooner and with a little more enthusiasm," recalled Yvette Noel-Schure. "[They would say] 'I'm calling about *Destiny's Child*'! As opposed to, 'Yeah, well, I got that press package on that group...'"

Lydia Modelist-Aston, a member of the choir at St. John's United Methodist Church in Houston, recalled, "I remember Tina, Beyoncé, and Kelly coming to church one Sunday and sitting in the balcony, as they always did. Pastor Rudy [Rasmus] looked up to the balcony and said, 'Hey! Bey! I need to ask you a question. I just need to know one thing: *Can you pay my bills?*' Everybody fell out laughing, and then the band started playin' 'Bills, Bills, Bills.' Everyone was so proud of the girls, the congregation wanted to celebrate with them."

"I had a song on that second album, too," recalled Daryl Simmons, "which was ironic considering the trouble Mathew and I had in the past with the Elektra deal. But he called me and said, 'I'm looking for a ballad, something Beyoncé can really enjoy singing.' I said, 'Wow. I would be honored. Great!' So I wrote a very pretty song called 'Stay' just for her." With its solid verses, obvious hook, and strong bridge, "Stay," a love song about conflicted romance, seems almost traditional among all the hip-hop-influenced R&B on *The Writing's on the Wall*.

"Beyoncé came in with the girls, they were happy and successful, and it was such a great change from the last time I saw them, which was when they were crying their eyes out over getting dropped by Elektra," remembered Simmons. "We clowned in the studio, had a great time. When we were finished with the session, I said, 'Hey! Stay in touch with me,' and gave all the girls my phone number. They thanked me, Mathew thanked me, and we all hugged it out.

"Some time later, I ran into Destiny's Child at the Hartsfield-Jackson Atlanta airport. They were rushing somewhere and I was off to somewhere else. 'Where you headed?' I asked. 'We're fixin' to catch a plane,' they said, all out of breath. 'We're goin' to a show!' I said, 'Cool, well, look, call me sometime.' And, in unison, as they were racing by me, they all said, 'We *can't* call you! Mathew made us erase your number off our phones!' Then...'*See ya! Bye!*' And with that, they were gone. Well, that just cracked me up," Simmons concluded, laughing. "That was just so Mathew. Protecting his girls, as always. I thought, 'You know what? I ain't even mad at you, Mathew Knowles. I get it.'"

Lyndall's Nineteenth

On December 3, 1998, Lyndall Locke's nineteenth birthday, he was in his garage with five of his buddies, playing dominoes. His hair was a wild natural these days; he also had a stud just below the center of his lower lip, called a labret. Because he and his pals were all smoking pot, the atmosphere was so cloudy, they could barely see one another.

"Whatchy'all doin' in here?" came the voice from the other side of the garage door. When Lyndall went and opened it, he found Beyoncé standing there. She was seventeen now. He let her in and closed the door behind her. "Dang! It's sure thick in here," she said as she embraced him. He took her by the hand to the table. "Check it out. I'm winning," he told her. "Of course you are," she said, smiling. "It's your birthday!"

"Take a hit?" someone asked Beyoncé, handing her a joint.

"No, man. Beyoncé don't smoke," Lyndall said as he took the joint from her.

The girls had been on the road promoting *The Writing's on the Wall*, doing concerts and radio promotional appearances. They were just in town for a couple of days before having to head back out. Beyoncé said they'd been constantly rehearsing, Mathew pressuring them like always. "Good Lord, don't nobody need to have their *father* as their manager," she said, looking exhausted. When Lyndall said he actually liked "Big Mac," according to him, Beyoncé deadpanned, "That's 'cause *Big Mac* ain't *managing* you."

Lyndall then told the others present that he and his cousin Dallas Gillespie had earlier found the girls jogging on the nearby bayou. Laughing, Gillespie explained that Mathew had the girls jogging and singing at the same time in order to increase their breath control. "It was hilarious," he said.

"It ain't hilarious if you're the one doin' it," Beyoncé said. "I was freezing to death!"

"We rode our bikes all the way up there—it was, like, miles and miles until we found them!" exclaimed Lyndall. "Then we gave the girls some Gatorades. You appreciate that, baby?" he asked Beyoncé.

"Oh my God! Them Gatorades were so *good*," Beyoncé said as she wrapped her arms around Lyndall's waist.

194   BECOMING BEYONCÉ

As they all hung out together, the conversation turned to a magazine article that had just been published about Destiny's Child, one in which the writer mentioned that Beyoncé had a boyfriend. Lyndall's name was misspelled as "Lindell." Beyoncé frowned at the thought of it. She said that she wanted to telephone the writer and ask him to correct his article. Lyndall told her not to do it, though. He said he preferred the misspelling, that it helped to guarantee his anonymity. When Beyoncé asked why he didn't want to be known, he told her, "I'm thinking about your career, your *image*. Don't nobody need to find me back here smoking weed and then have it reflect back on you."

That night, there was an intimate gathering at Lyndall's home for his birthday. His mother, Lydia, baked a double-layer chocolate cake, his favorite, with red, white, and blue sprinkles. Of course, Beyoncé was at Lyndall's side. While everyone was casual in jeans and T-shirts, she looked more dressy in a short-sleeved floor-length silk dress, her brown hair pulled into a ponytail. Also present were Kelly Rowland, Angie Beyincé, and other friends and relatives, such as Lyndall's cousin Dallas. After Lyndall blew out the candles on his cake, Beyoncé presented him with his gift—a state-of-the-art PlayStation video game system.

"This is what you wanted, right?" she asked.

"Yeah," he said with a big smile, "and this, too," he added, pulling her in close for a birthday kiss.

Living the Dream

*M*y wife thought I was crazy," Mathew Knowles was telling Dan Workman over cheese-and-turkey sandwiches during a break in a recording session for the second Destiny Child's album. "I was this smart black guy working a six-figure job and I gave it all up to manage these girls," he said.

"Couldn't have been easy on your family," Dan said.

Mathew laughed. "You don't know the half of it. That's why the stakes are so high now." He noted that Destiny's Child had a hit debut album, but that in his view it should've done even better in the marketplace. He said that "a hell of a lot" was riding on the sophomore album, and that this was why he stayed in what he called "the approval loop. Nothing goes down without my approval."

"That probably makes you the bad guy in a lot of instances," Dan observed.

"Oh yeah. I'm the bad guy, all right," Mathew said with a chuckle. "But it's all good," he concluded. "I love my work. I *am* my work."

With the success of Destiny's Child's second album, Mathew had become power personified; it actually seemed to emanate from him. He may not have understood all of the fine details of the record business, but he was now a formidable presence in it just the same. He'd always been a confident, self-reliant man, which is one of the reasons he'd been so successful in the corporate arena. Now, flush with success in a new and maybe more competitive venue, he comported himself with even greater authority, his personality an intriguing combination of arrogance and likability. Already there were people in the record business who didn't care for him. That was fine with him. He wasn't out to make friends, he was out to make money. "I'm finally living my dream," he told Dan Workman. "This is it, right here and now. This is the dream."

Despite—and maybe because—of all he represented in her young life, Mathew's relationship with Beyoncé became more complex with the passing of the years. By the time she recorded the songs for *The Writing's on the Wall*, she was seventeen. When it came to her father, rebellion wasn't just a passing phase for Beyoncé, as it is for most girls her age. Once she decided to stand up to him—when she was about twelve—she would almost *always* stand up to him. She still listened to his advice, of course. However, she also often disagreed with him, and had no problem doing so. Therefore, father and daughter would be at loggerheads for many years to come. Both could attest to the fact that it was not easy navigating terrain where a business relationship intersected with a personal one. Beyoncé was headstrong, knew precisely what she wanted, and usually made sure she got it. Mathew, of course, was never easygoing either. If anything, the two were exactly alike.

In many ways, Beyoncé Knowles was like any other girl her age. Not only was her father often wrong in her mind, but so was her mother. She wasn't above talking back to Tina and disagreeing with her the same way she did with Mathew. The dynamic between mother and daughter was very different, though. Mathew had no choice; he had to listen to her opinion if it differed from his. She was, after all, as much client to him as she was daughter. Tina didn't have to put up with it, and she didn't.

One relative tells the story of being at a barbecue when Beyoncé suddenly announced that she was leaving to meet Lyndall. Tina reminded her that they were in the middle of a family night. She suggested that Beyoncé invite Lyndall over to the house, making it clear that she was not to leave. Beyoncé let out a heavy sigh as if she had the weight of the world on her shoulders. She then gave her mother a side-eyed glance of annoyance. The two had words, after which Beyoncé ran upstairs to her bedroom and slammed the door with all her might. Tina walked over to the staircase and hollered, "And you can stay up there for all I care." It was nothing if not a typical exchange between a mother and her teenage daughter.

"We did our fair share of sneaking around," Lyndall Locke recalled of him and Beyoncé. "If we wanted to be alone together, Beyoncé would ask her cousin Angie if we could hang out at her apartment. We'd go over there and hole up for hours. I'm sure that drove Tina crazy, Mathew too. Beyoncé was becoming a star, but she was also their little girl. I know they felt I was probably corrupting her," Lyndall concluded. "And they were right, I was," he concluded, laughing.

Beyoncé and Tina had their spats; there was nothing unusual about them. It was more unusual for a girl to disagree with her father over something like a recording session than it was having an argument with her mother about going out on a date.

For instance, around the time of the rehearsal for—not the actual recording of—one song for the second album, "Say My Name," Beyoncé and Mathew seemed to be in a disagreement about some aspect of a negotiation for the budget of Destiny's Child's third album, which was to be a Christmas album. It was a small budget; Beyoncé wished the label would give them more money. However, Mathew was doing the best he could; holiday albums are usually not big-budgeted projects. (In the end, Mathew was able to get not only what Beyoncé asked for this album, but more.)*

---

* Released at the end of October 2001, 8 Days of Christmas did respectable business for Destiny's Child, debuting at number thirty-five on the Billboard 200 LP chart. The album, buoyed by the title track as a single, ultimately went gold, selling half a million copies. Since its initial release, 8 Days of Christmas has been a perennial seller; by 2014 it had clocked more than two million copies and downloads worldwide.

During the rehearsal, Beyoncé thought her dad was being particularly recalcitrant. She didn't like the instrumental track for "Say My Name," thought it was too busy. Rodney Jerkins would remix it later, but at this time she was just trying to work with what she had in hand. She was impatient with it, though, and Mathew wasn't making it any easier with his own suggestions. "Daddy, I'm a grown woman," she finally told him. "Leave me be so I can rehearse this doggone thing." Of course, her bad mood had little to do with the rehearsal, and more to do with the budget of the holiday album.

"Oh, *hell no!*" Mathew exclaimed, jumping to his feet. "I *know* you ain't tryin' to talk back to me up in here!"

At that, Beyoncé very calmly rose and walked out of the room, her head held high, right past her father and out the door, effectively shutting down the rehearsal. She recognized her power; after all, without her there could be no rehearsal.

Mathew took a deep breath and exhaled heavily. When he asked Kelly if she thought Beyoncé would be returning, Kelly smiled sheepishly and said, "Not till you apologize."

Shaking his head and smiling with resignation, Mathew rose and left the room. Ten minutes later, he and Beyoncé returned, arm in arm, both seeming purely satisfied with whatever terms they'd come to that had quieted their tempers. "Now, let's get back to this song," he told her, kissing her on the cheek. "I think this thing is a hit, don't you?" Beaming at her dad, Beyoncé eagerly returned to the work at hand.

Vocal Lessons

*I*t was in 1998 that the respected vocal teacher Kim Wood Sandusky was contacted by Mathew Knowles to work with Destiny's Child. More specifically, Sandusky, an attractive blonde in her midthirties, was brought in to work with Beyoncé and Kelly. "It was an interview, actually," she recalled of that first meeting. "I showed up at Mathew's Music World Entertainment offices ready to work on a small electric piano with the girls. Immediately, I felt that the chemistry was there between Beyoncé and Kelly and myself as I took them through some vocal exercises. I knew they were observing me as much as I was them. Afterward, Tina took me aside. She was pleasant, but all business."

"What is it you think you can do for Beyoncé?" Tina asked the vocal coach.

"I think we need to build on her breathing stamina," Kim answered. "Some of her vocal muscles could also be strengthened for a richer, rounder sound. We also have to work on her air flow so that she has longevity." Kim added that Beyoncé was, in her estimation, "obviously a superstar." She said you could "hear it in her talent." Then she asked Tina, "She's in it for the long haul, isn't she?"

"We sure hope so," Tina answered, seeming pleased. She said that she'd love to have Kim work with both Beyoncé and Kelly and that the coach should talk to Mathew to work out the details.

In her subsequent conversation with Mathew, Kim realized he had a wide range of plans for Destiny's Child, from TV appearances to live concerts and recordings. "He sat on one side of his desk, I was on the other, and he laid out his ideas for the group, but more precisely for Beyoncé," Kim recalled of Mathew. "'I want to keep her voice in great shape,' he told me, 'because the demands on it for the next few years are going to be great. I like that you are concerned about longevity,' he told me, 'because that's my concern, too. Kelly, too. I have plans for her as well. Both girls need to be on point.'"

The next day, Beyoncé showed up at Kim's studio for her first lesson. "She pulled up in her Jag," Kim recalled, "and I remember thinking, 'How awesome is this? She's seventeen and has already attained such a great level of success.' 'Okay, so let's do it,' she said as soon as she walked in. And we began working. I first started working with her on 'Bills, Bills, Bills.' It was a mouthful of words! She and I worked not only on phrasing but on places to breathe so she could create onstage what she'd done in the studio. 'You can fix stuff in the studio, but live, it's all me,' she said, 'so I really need this to be right.' During that first lesson, I noticed her work ethic, her concentration and drive. I thought, 'I am really going to love working with this artist.' After about an hour and a half, the session was over. She got her things together, turned around, and said, 'Okay, see you tomorrow, Kim?' She had the biggest smile and sparkle in her eye. We hugged goodbye. Then, from that point on, we worked together for years."

The morning after Beyoncé's first lesson, Kelly showed up for hers. "Her voice was also great," Sandusky recalled. "I could see why Mathew wanted to build her too. There was a real quality there. When I evaluated it, I knew I needed to make her voice more powerful, and I also wanted to work on her breathing and stamina. Kelly had the same work ethic as Beyoncé. She was focused and had such joy about what she was doing."

Neither Mathew nor Tina ever talked to Kim about LaTavia or LeToya. It is arguable that neither was as much a consideration as they probably deserved to be, considering that they were half the group. In fact, both girls had talent.

Though LaTavia had started out as a rapper and not a singer, she'd grown into a capable vocalist. She had a deep and rich alto that rounded out the group's harmony and, when utilized to its best advantage, effectively held down its bottom. Some felt she sounded like Lisa "Left Eye" Lopes from TLC. Maybe LaTavia wasn't a lead singer, but not everyone can front a group. Though Beyoncé even slighted her by once claiming to Lola Ogunnaike for a *Vibe* magazine interview that she was "tone deaf," that wasn't really true. (Though she was quoted as having been talking about LeToya, clearly Beyoncé meant LaTavia, since Kelly clarified that they were referencing the "rapper" in the group.) In truth, LaTavia actually shared a lead with Beyoncé on one of the songs on *The Writing's on the Wall*, "Sweet Sixteen." She was also a great loyalist. She'd been with the group from the very beginning and wanted nothing more than to continue with it.

For her part, LeToya was a more than capable singer, a soprano who—again, when she was actually used—could really contribute to the upper reaches of the group's harmony. She could sing lead too, with no problems. Of course, Mathew—and many of the group's producers and engineers—didn't see it that way, because LeToya was no Beyoncé...but, again, who was? All LeToya wanted was the same thing the other girls wanted: to sing and to be appreciated for her talent. These days, she definitely wasn't getting that sense of fulfillment, though. "My self-esteem was very, very low," she would later confirm of this time in her life. "Beyoncé is very talented and I was thinking, 'I can't sound like that, so maybe I can't sing.'"

"In my opinion, LaTavia and LeToya weren't in the same vocal league as Beyoncé, and to a certain extent, neither was Kelly," said engineer Dan Workman. "But pop music isn't always just about the record. It's also about the presentation. LaTavia and LeToya looked great on TV, in the videos, and onstage. They did their thing, for sure, even if it wasn't always in the studio."

Their talent aside, it had gotten to the point where LaTavia's and

LeToya's presence in the recording studio sometimes wasn't even deemed necessary by several of their producers. Thus some songs credited to Destiny's Child were actually not group performances at all. Rather, they were just Beyoncé doing *all* the vocal parts herself. "I noticed, for instance, on 'Bills Bills Bills,' Kevin Briggs put Beyoncé in the booth and pretty much had her do the whole song, *all* the parts," recalled Workman. "Then, when he put the other girls in the studio for a bit, it felt to me like it was just out of courtesy. In some cases, their vocal takes weren't even mixed into the song, which they probably don't even realize to this day. By the time we got to 'Say My Name,' for instance, it was Beyoncé doing most of the heavy lifting with Kelly filling in some parts. I remember hearing a playback and asking, 'Is that LaTavia?' and Kevin would say, 'Nope. Beyoncé.' A little later, I would ask, 'LeToya?' and he would answer, 'Nope. Beyoncé.'"

Though Mathew's philosophy had always been that the other girls in the group weren't as important to its success as was Beyoncé, this present studio wizardry wasn't even his idea. It was all in the purview of producers who felt it was quicker and easier to just use Beyoncé for all the harmonies. When *The Writing's on the Wall* was released, it would definitely sound a lot more like a Beyoncé album than had the group's debut record.

For Beyoncé, this kind of attention had become a double-edged sword. On one hand, she was happy to do whatever she could to make the music sound the way the producers envisioned it. Of course, she also liked the attention. What artist wouldn't? She was doing what she loved to do, and she was being acknowledged for it. What she didn't much like were the stares from LaTavia and LeToya, who had become increasingly annoyed by the way they were being overlooked and disrespected. It was difficult for them not to blame Beyoncé. After all, it sometimes felt as if she was living not only her dream, but theirs as well.

Group Turmoil

On October 22, 1999, Destiny's Child kicked off a tour as opening act for another female group, TLC, an act the girls had long admired. After the first date in Toronto at the Air Canada Centre, they would stay on the road until December.

Destiny's Child ran a tight ship while on tour, even in those early days. As the tour accountant, Angie Beyincé always made sure the girls were properly paid. "I'd finish the show and go to the cash office with all the promoters and I'd count out the money," she told the writer Aaron Hicklin in 2014. "I'm a bad chick. I don't play. I went in there with all male promoters, and I'd count that money out. The first day I did that they were a dollar short. And I said, 'I'm missing a dollar.' They said, 'Oh no, baby girl,' to shrink me, to diminish me—'Oh no, sweetie pie, oh no, honey, no, no.' I just said, 'OK, I'll count again.' I shared a room with the choreographer at the time, and while she was sleeping I would stay up and count all the money, do the payroll, all the expenses. I only got maybe two or three hours of sleep each day. Then I'd be back at that cash office: *five* dollars short.' At the end of the tour, every single dollar was accounted for."

Though the shows were of the highest caliber and the backstage business was being admirably handled, it was while on the road with TLC that the girls in DC started to recognize what they believed were serious differences between them. The group had become divided, with Beyoncé and Kelly in one camp and LaTavia and LeToya in the other. LaTavia and LeToya had also begun to notice what they felt was more preferential treatment of Beyoncé than ever before by Mathew. "We started noticing Beyoncé was being focused on more in photo shoots and on television appearances," LaTavia Roberson said. "And there was just this attitude going on, not really from Beyoncé but from management [she was referring to Mathew] that the group was all about her and the rest of us, even Kelly, were sort of window dressing."

"I just became sick of it," LeToya stated. "Mathew's whole thing was, 'Look, Beyoncé is gonna be singing lead and that's the end of it. You don't like it? Go somewhere else and find a job singing, because this is *my* group and what I say goes.' He really believed that. I felt like, 'No, this is our group, not his group. When did *our* group become *his* group?' And then we started thinking the money was a little funny. I started thinking, 'Wait a second, I can't pay my bills. All these records we're selling and I can't pay my cell phone bill?'" Mathew later vigorously denied any suggestion that he had cheated the girls but in their minds at the time, as unhappy as they were with their general situation, it had become a niggle.

LeToya's brother, Gavin Luckett, put it this way: "LeToya was like, 'There's no reason why Beyoncé is driving a Jaguar right now and my momma is driving this old Mazda.'"

It certainly couldn't have helped when, at about this time, Beyoncé bought a champagne-colored Bentley to go along with her Jag, "an awesome little ride," as Lyndall Locke described it. (Since Beyoncé hated to drive, Lyndall did most of the driving in that relationship.) What is not known is whether or not the money for the car came from DC earnings or her parents paid for it as a gift. Whatever the case, Beyoncé now had not only double the luxury vehicles, but double the scrutiny from LeToya and her mother, Pamela. In sworn affidavits later given by mother and daughter, both would say they repeatedly asked Mathew not only for a full accounting of income but also the opportunity to inspect the group's records, but that these requests were always turned down. (Mathew denied owing LeToya money.)

"[The R&B group] Jagged Edge was appearing with Destiny's Child at the Cynthia Woods Mitchell Pavilion here in Houston, and backstage, they all started comparing notes," recalled Yvonne Boyd, LaTavia's aunt. "That's when the girls found out that Jagged Edge was making more money than they were making, and Jagged Edge was the opening act! They were afraid to ask Mathew about it, though. I told my niece, 'Look, Mathew works for you. You don't work for Mathew! You need to straighten this out!' When they finally did ask him, Mathew was enraged, I can tell you that much."

As questions about management became more prevalent, things between the girls continued to deteriorate. "The whole sisterhood thing was going right down the drain," was how Kelly later put it. It was true; there were days when Beyoncé and Kelly never even spoke to LaTavia and LeToya. "It was like being in a bad marriage when you have kids and you act like you're happy," said Beyoncé. "They lost focus," she added of LeToya and LaTavia. "They didn't want to do interviews, rehearse, or take voice lessons. Anybody who met us could see that me and Kelly were one group and they were another." (It should be noted that both LeToya and LaTavia insist that they never missed press interviews or rehearsals. Also, the voice teacher hired by Mathew, Kim Wood Sandusky, is clear that she was never asked to work with them.)

Beyoncé said that she believed LeToya and LaTavia had become distracted by the twins from Jagged Edge—Brian and Brandon Casey—who shared the bill with the girls on a few dates (not on the TLC tour but elsewhere during the year). "Boys got into their heads," Beyoncé concluded to writer Lola Ogunnaike. After one show with the band, Beyoncé told Kelly backstage, "Those greasy boys ain't going anywhere near my vagitis"—a slang word the girls used to use for vagina; LeToya actually coined the word. Also, because Jagged Edge's initials were JE, Beyoncé used to call the group "Juicy Earwax."

Apparently there was also some sort of fracas on the road with Jagged Edge when Mathew ejected LeToya's mom, Pamela, from the tour bus one night in Baton Rouge. In a sworn affidavit she would later give, Pamela Luckett claimed that Mathew called the police on her, forcing her off the bus. She said that the only reason she had been present was because LeToya had been suffering from asthma and needed her mother. But Mathew would later say that Pamela was not covered by the group's insurance policy and that this was the reason for her eviction. Jagged Edge's Brian Casey then went on record saying that he and his brother, Brandon, were so appalled that one of the mothers would be kicked off the tour bus that their group decided to vacate the bus as well. "We were just so disgusted," he said. "Not for one minute did those girls [Beyoncé and Kelly] put themselves in LeToya's shoes." (Following this incident, Mathew once again attempted to terminate LeToya. She was later reinstated.)

After Baton Rouge, LaToya's and LaTavia's discontentment was apparent to all. "I actually pulled Mathew aside," said the girls' makeup artist, Reggie Wells, "and said, 'I think you're going to have to pull those two out of the group. They seem not very thrilled to be doing this thing.' He looked at me and nodded as if this wasn't the first time he'd heard it."

"Then there was the problem of being on television and doing acceptance speeches," added LaTavia's aunt, Yvonne Boyd.

A recent highlight for DC had been the winning of their first major trophies at the Soul Train Lady of Soul Awards, where they won three honors, including Best R&B Soul Single for their first Columbia/Sony release, "No, No, No." During their acceptance speech, all four looked fetching in their gold-and-copper, Indian-inspired bare-midriff wardrobe. Beyoncé wore hot pants under a long sarong skirt that was cut on one side for maximum leg exposure, a strange but somehow captivating look. At the podium, she didn't take the center spot, though. She appeared content to allow LaTavia to control the acceptance speech. LeToya got in a few words, too, as Beyoncé simply smiled and nodded. "This award is dedicated to Miss Andretta Tillman," LaTavia announced to the cheering crowd. It was only when she and LeToya ran out of things to say, and the music began to swell, signaling the time for the girls to leave the stage, that Beyoncé demurely added, "We want to thank our fans."

"LaTavia usually did the speaking at those things because she was just a better speaker," said Yvonne. "She was a quicker study. Beyoncé took longer to get it together. But when LaTavia would take over, it upset Tina. 'Oh no,' she would say. '*Beyoncé* is the leader and *she* should be the one doing the talking, not LaTavia.' That showed me that behind the scenes, Tina was just as determined as Mathew to make sure Beyoncé shined. It wasn't a surprise, though. Of course, all the mothers wanted their daughters to shine. But it was becoming pretty clear that Beyoncé had an edge the other girls didn't have."

Sour Energy

November 2, 1999—Greenville, South Carolina

*T*he energy around here is *very* sour," Beyoncé stated.

"Not really…but…*whatever*," LeToya remarked as she shrugged her shoulders.

The girls were backstage following a performance at the Bi-Lo Center on the TLC tour. On this evening, their dressing room was full of people—musicians, stage crew, people coming and going. If Tina had been one of those present, there most certainly wouldn't have been a disagreement between the girls in front of witnesses, but she wasn't there. Tension between the group members had been building all day, from soundcheck through performance, and now, as they were packing up for the next stop.

If one were to delineate LaTavia and LeToya's grievances, it would come down to two. Rightly or wrongly (and Mathew has consistently denied any impropriety) they had questions about the money they were earning, and they felt they were not getting enough attention both on record and onstage. Unfortunately, these were subjects over which Beyoncé and Kelly had virtually no control. Or as Kelly put it in Greenville, "I ain't the manager. When I manage a group and you're in it, then we can talk. Look at your contracts. Does it say *Kelly Rowland—Manager*? No, it does not."

"You say you want to know what we're thinking," LeToya declared, "but every time me and LaTavia say what's on our hearts, you and Beyoncé jump down our throats."

"What is it you want me to do?" Beyoncé asked, raising her voice. She said that she'd already had many conversations with her father about the possibility of LaTavia and LeToya singing more leads. He simply wasn't open to the idea. She didn't see what else she could do. She suggested the girls speak up for themselves. Instead of coming to her, she said, they should set up a meeting with Mathew, especially LaTavia, who had known him since she was eight years old. However, LaTavia said Mathew made her feel disrespected. She said she'd tried to talk to him in the past, but felt that he was not interested in what she had to say. She felt she had "no voice" where he was concerned.

According to observers of the disagreement, Beyoncé then pointed out that she and her mother had recently watched an archival video of Diana Ross and the Supremes performing on a television program, and Miss Ross was wearing *two* sets of earrings on each ear to set her apart from the other girls, who just had one set per ear. Also, she said Ross was purposely blocking the camera from seeing the other two Supremes. "And I would never do that!" Beyoncé added. "I don't need to be a bitch," she concluded, "all I need is my talent."

One of the other girls pointed out that there was no reason for Beyoncé to try to separate herself. Cameramen already knew to follow her to the exclusion of the others because "*someone* tells them what to do, and I'm not sayin' who..."

As the girls disagreed, the observers in the room turned their heads from one to the other, as if at a tennis match. "I'm not gonna live my life this way, with everybody knowin' our business," Beyoncé finally said. With that, she stormed off.

When upset, Beyoncé would usually vacate the premises. She was good for confrontation only to a point, and then she could take no more. Either she would leave or she would shut down and conceal her feelings. "The silent treatment was her weapon of choice," Lyndall Locke would say. "She could tell you all she needed to tell you just being very quiet and staring you down. You didn't want to get the silent treatment from Beyoncé Knowles," he concluded, laughing, "and I should know, because I got it many times."

Kelly was more vocal. She'd been defending herself and her position in the group for many years. She would say what was on her mind, and be quite clear about it. "Y'all have issues with *Mathew Knowles*, not me and Beyoncé," she told them. "Stop throwing shade at me and Beyoncé when the truth is that you're pissed off at *Mathew Knowles*."

"But he doesn't care about us," LaTavia said.

"Well, make him care," Kelly told her. "Y'all are half of Destiny's Child, aren't you? *Make him care!*"

Disaffirmation

*I*t was December 15, 1999, when attorney Randy A. Bowman stepped off the elevator at Music World's headquarters in Houston, walked into Mathew Knowles's office, and handed him two certified letters. In separate but identical correspondence written on December 14, both LaTavia Roberson and LeToya Luckett proclaimed that they were "disaffirming" their personal management contracts with him, dated June 9, 1997. "This does not in any way impact my status as a member of Destiny's Child," said the letter. "I fully intend to continue as a member of Destiny's Child."

The girls further demanded that Mathew not transact any new business on their behalf either individually or as members of the group. "You do not have the authority to do so," the letter read. Mathew was instructed that all business should now be handled through attorney Bowman. Bowman had also dispatched a letter to Columbia/Sony attorney John Ingrassia indicating that his clients were now contemplating new management, though both fully expected to remain with Destiny's Child.

Kelly would later testify to a contentious chain of events that may have been the catalyst for LaTavia and LeToya's decision. A couple of weeks earlier, LaTavia didn't show up for a European promotional tour, "and in Destiny's Child we don't ever do anything like that," Kelly said. LaTavia insisted she was sick with a 104-degree fever. When Mathew got the call that she wasn't going to make it, he wasn't really very upset. He just sprang into action. They certainly weren't going to cancel the tour; he knew that much.

"Well, what are we gonna do?" LeToya asked him.

"We're going on," Mathew said. "Junella [Segura, the group's choreographer] can take LaTavia's place."

As always, Mathew was focused on pushing ahead, not allowing anything to get in the way of the group's forward momentum. Beyoncé agreed with him that it was a viable solution, as did Kelly. However, LeToya, often the lone dissenter, was not on board. "Uh-uh. This is our group member," she said. "You can't just replace a group member because she's sick." Though LeToya always spoke her mind, she was never much of a match for Mathew.

After he got the letters, Mathew summoned Beyoncé and Kelly. "I just got this from LeToya and LaTavia," he said when the girls walked into his office. Both girls were stunned when they read the correspondence. "But we were with them just yesterday, and they seemed fine," Beyoncé said. In fact, the group had just given a concert in Houston for KRBE at the Compaq Center, and it had gone well. "They want their own manager? Is that even possible?" she asked, bewildered.

"No way," Kelly emphatically stated, according to what she would later recall in a deposition. "You can't have two people managing the same group."

"But wait. That's not true," Beyoncé offered, again as per her own deposition. "We did it when Miss Ann was managing us with my dad."

"That was different," Mathew said.

"Not really," Beyoncé continued. "I'm just saying maybe we shouldn't discount it altogether. It's been done before."

Beyoncé noted that Mathew and Andretta Tillman had co-managed the group for a number of years, and she wondered if that prior situation was the foundation for LeToya and LaTavia's present request. However, Kelly observed that the only reason that previous arrangement worked—if in fact it could be said to have worked—was because "Mathew and Miss Ann were on the same page and doing things together." However, what LaTavia and LeToya were proposing, Kelly observed, was a scenario where two managers would likely be disagreeing on just about everything. In her mind, it wasn't even an option.

Beyoncé still wasn't convinced, and Mathew could read her ambivalence. He didn't think it would work, he said, but if she wanted him to, he would look into it further. However, he felt sure that their record company wasn't going to approve. "If you want to take that dog for a walk, fine," he told her, "but if it bites us on the ass, that's gonna be on us." Beyoncé felt she had to listen to her father's viewpoint. She opined that perhaps something better could have been worked out if they only had more time. However, LeToya and LaTavia had waited until just two weeks before filming of the video for "Say My Name," because, at least in Beyoncé's view, they thought that this was when the group would be at its most vulnerable. "But the more I think about it, the less surprised I am by it," she concluded. "Haven't we been expecting this from them for years?" She said that the only thing she found surprising about it "is that it took them this long to do it."

The more they talked about it, the more upset Beyoncé and Kelly became, until finally both were very emotional. "We told them to take up their grievances with you," Beyoncé told Mathew. "But I sure didn't think they'd do it this way."

The girls then did what they always did when they got upset: They called Tina. Tina told them to come straight home so they could all discuss it. They did as she suggested; Mathew stayed behind. "I'm the mother, so you know, it was more like crying spells, comforting them," Tina said as to what happened when the girls finally got home. "Nobody talked about business, because it was real painful for them."

That night at home, Mathew, Tina, Beyoncé, and Kelly tried to hash things out and achieve some clarity where this new problem was concerned. Mathew explained that since the girls had turned eighteen they could legally veto—or "disaffirm"—their management contract with him. In almost every state (including Texas), a minor can invalidate a contract upon reaching that age. This law, Mathew explained, is designed as a protection for minors who've entered into contracts they later feel are not in their best interests.

"So what do you girls want to do?" Tina asked.

"I just don't want to be a part of something this sketchy," Beyoncé said. "Maybe I should just go solo." Everyone looked at her with surprise. Of course, for years people had been telling Beyoncé she could be a single artist. However, she had always said the group was her priority. Perhaps now, though, given this dilemma, things had changed for her. She also realized that Destiny's Child was viewed by the record label as a group. Therefore, working as a duo with Kelly wasn't even a consideration.

There was some talk of maybe adding Solange to the act to round it out as a trio. In fact, Solange had shown great potential in recent years as a singer and songwriter. In the past, Mathew had been encouraging of her aspirations, while Tina was the one with reservations. Now both parents weren't so sure they wanted Solange in the business. It was a tough game, as they both well knew, and with so much of their focus always on Beyoncé, it was as if they hoped for their younger daughter to find another interest. While Beyoncé wasn't the only one in the family with talent, Solange would have a long way to go before being able to prove to her parents that she should be taken seriously. Maybe to placate her, Mathew agreed to let her go out on the road with Destiny's Child as one of its troupe of background dancers. But as for joining the group? That wasn't going to happen. Besides, she was only thirteen and her parents both felt she was too young.

"Maybe this is finally the end of Destiny's Child," Beyoncé said.

"Well, shoot, if you go solo then where does that leave me?" Kelly asked.

"You go solo, too, Kelly," Beyoncé answered. "You can do it. I know you can."

"I guess so," Kelly decided, seeming uncertain.

"Again, I want this to be your decision, girls," Mathew said. He hastened to add that his opinion was that they'd all worked too long and too hard to now throw away everything they'd achieved. He suggested that they think long and hard before making any final decisions about solo careers. Timing is everything, he warned them.

"What would you say about getting two *new* girls?" Tina offered.

"I'd be down with that," Beyoncé said quickly. Kelly agreed.

Tina then offered that if they did manage to somehow work the situation out with LeToya and LaTavia, one or both of them could still present a problem down the line, "and the group is going to just self-destruct." She said that LeToya suffered from asthma, and that LaTavia "is sort of sickly a lot, isn't she?" Tina felt they needed alternate members, two girls in the wings who could step in at a moment's notice and fill one or two spots in case of an emergency. She added, "Basically the other two girls don't sing anyway, they just dance. So we could have dancers in their costumes and it would still give the same visual effect." Though this idea sounded reasonable to everyone, it really wasn't true that LeToya and LaTavia *never* sang. Perhaps Tina was referring to lead vocals, most of which really were performed by Beyoncé and Kelly.

Depression

*T*he next morning, Beyoncé didn't emerge from her bedroom—and there she would remain for the next few weeks. "I became so depressed," she later said. "It was such a dark time for me. I felt sad, angry, and pissed off." Her publicist, Yvette Noel-Schure, recalled, "It was the first time I really saw her just sort of go into a shell." The girls' choreographer, Junella Segura, added, "I would be speaking to Tina and Tina would say, 'She didn't even get out of bed today.'"

While Beyoncé was sequestered in her room, Tina would check on her every few hours, if only to tell her how much she loved her. Sometimes she would climb into bed with her; mother and daughter would then softly pray. Or Beyoncé would put her head on Tina's shoulder and cry. They talked about old times: about "Miss Ann" and Girls Tyme, Debra and Denise, and everything that Mathew had done for Destiny's Child. After all, Beyoncé had been at the center of all of it. "You were there even before Kelly," Tina reminded her, according to what she later recalled. "Nobody has worked harder than you, and your fans know it!" Beyoncé said that the more she thought about it, the more certain she had become that the group's followers were going to blame her for its breakup since she was the lead singer. Tina told her that she couldn't worry about public opinion. If she made every move with an eye toward what the world would think of her, Tina warned, she would be paralyzed with fear for the rest of her career.

Since there were a couple of contracted engagements in the Texas area in the last two weeks of the year, Destiny's Child was forced to perform as a duet, just Beyoncé and Kelly. These were mediocre performances as a result of unfamiliar staging and vocals. There were also problems with sound and lighting cues. Everything seemed off with the absence of half the group. Beyoncé actually tripped and fell onstage. "We have no room to look sloppy right now," she complained after the first show, "so this is *not* good. It's not only about the missing girls, either," she added, "it's about connecting with the audience, and I can't do that when I bring all this drama onto the stage with me." After the Texas shows, she and Kelly did a telephone radio interview with WGCI in Chicago. Doing such things without LaTavia and LeToya was bad enough, but making it worse was that it officially put Columbia/Sony on notice that there was an internal problem.

On January 4, 2000, LeToya and LaTavia sent a letter to both Beyoncé and Kelly, chastising them for having appeared in public without them. They reminded Beyoncé and Kelly that they fully intended to remain in Destiny's Child, that their not wanting Mathew as their manager didn't mean they wanted out of the group. "What world are *they* livin' in?" Beyoncé asked when she read the letter. "Those girls have lost their minds!" Then she returned to her room, now more than ever uninterested in what was going on around her.

In the weeks after LaTavia and LeToya's disaffirmation letter, Beyoncé emerged from her room only to perform those couple of concerts and then attend church, as she always did, at St. John's Methodist. She would sit in the balcony, mostly unbothered by other churchgoers. Sometimes she would become so emotional hearing Pastor Rudy Rasmus speak, especially when it was about relationships, that she would break down into sobs, as reported by Lola Ogunnaike for *Vibe*. "Right now we're trusting you to fix our relationships, Lord," the pastor said one Sunday during the height of the conflict in Destiny's Child, "to put us back together like you intended us to be." Mathew and Tina were seated nearby, along with Solange. Kelly was a couple of rows away. "Thank you, Jesus," Beyoncé would repeat over and over again as if in a trance, while she rocked back and forth in the pew, her eyes closed, her head tilted upward. "Thank you, Jesus. Thank you, Jesus. Thank you, Jesus. Thank you, Jesus."

Beyoncé's Missive

No one fully understood her. Or if they did, they didn't want to ascribe feelings to her that they thought might be unattractive or make her seem self-involved. "LaTavia and LeToya were like sisters to her," people around her kept saying, "and that's why she's devastated by their leaving the group." That was the way everyone seemed to look at it. "Because they are so close," they kept repeating, "she is going to miss them so much." Either they didn't completely understand Beyoncé Knowles or, again, they were trying to protect what they thought was her image, because in truth, the emotions she felt were more complex than just feelings of longing for her defected singing partners.

Of course, on some level she would miss the girls. They'd been through a lot together, especially she and LaTavia. Some people, such as Taura Stinson—the writer who had penned Destiny's Child's first recording, "Killing Time"—felt that even though Kelly Rowland had an important place in Beyoncé's life, LaTavia was actually closer to her. Their relationship had been further cemented when LaTavia revealed a few years earlier the painful secret that she was being sexually molested. Beyoncé stood by her side and supported her throughout the ordeal. She did love her, and felt the same way about LeToya. In some respects, they were like sisters. But Beyoncé was also a practical young woman, a trait she shared with her mother and, to a certain extent, her father. By this time, she was accustomed to losing "sisters." After Ashley, Nina, and Nicki, she'd made up her mind that any of them could go at a moment's notice, and the show would have to go on. She had been ready to kiss LeToya goodbye some time before. In fact, she now felt that if they'd just fired LeToya back then, they might have been able to save LaTavia. But what was done was done. While she would miss both girls, she would get over it...just as she had the others.

Still, Beyoncé had a lot to get off her chest where LaTavia and LeToya were concerned, which is probably why she decided to memorialize her feelings in a letter to them. While it's not dated, it's known that it was received by the girls on January 5, 2000. She started off by saying, "I have shared some of the best moments of my life with the two of you by my side. I have also shared some of the worst." She then wrote that Destiny's Child had been her priority since the day they all met and "if anything, and I mean anything," ever got in the way of their success, it was not of her doing.

Beyoncé also reminded the girls of what Mathew had done for them, speculating that they had probably forgotten "the white house on Parkwood that you both spent many summers living in that we had to sell, the car we all piled into that we had to sell, the job that Mathew quit to dedicate countless hours to Destiny's Child. You were there when people called him crazy for dedicating his time and money to us," she wrote, adding, "It's very sad when people become successful that they forget how they got where they are and who helped them."

She noted that ever since she was nine years old, people had asked why she was in a group and not performing as a solo artist. She always explained that the reason for it was because she loved the girls and she didn't want to sing without them. However, when Destiny's Child had its first release, she received many offers to do "videos, soundtracks, albums and movies" as a solo artist. Still, she noted, she had turned them all down because she wanted to remain loyal to the group. She said she was sorry LaTavia and LeToya felt the offers she had received were merely because Mathew was her manager, and not because she was talented. Her "personal success," she wrote, was never as important as Destiny's Child's to her, which was why she'd turned down all of those opportunities. However, she hastened to add, "we all know that our contributions are not anywhere close to being equal, yet we all get paid equally." Beyoncé also noted that she never raised an objection to that financial distribution, though she said she certainly could have.

Additionally, she wrote, "I never asked for the best clothes or better treatment. In fact, I have settled for the worst on numerous occasions just to avoid a conflict and keep the peace. I also never complained when you didn't sing one note on numerous songs on the [presumably first] album. I've never complained when I was working my butt off in the studio as I did on the last album [the second, *The Writing's on the Wall*] when the two of you were both either sleeping or on your phones approximately eighty percent of the time. I never complained when the two of you were lip singing to *my* vocals on some of the videos and on stage." She said it was always her intention to convey to the public that their contributions were equal. In fact, she wrote, if one were to analyze the situation objectively, the only person who'd really been treated unfairly in the group was her.

What bothered her most, she wrote, was that LaTavia and LeToya had "made a business decision for the group without discussing it with myself or Kelly" concerning the disaffirmation of their contracts with Mathew. "Although we never would say it," she wrote, "we were no longer friends. I feel that the two of you did not enjoy my presence."

Beyoncé further noted that the last time "we had drama," both LaTavia and LeToya promised that there would be no further problems. She said she had warned them both that she could not continue to live her life with their constant upsets. "Approximately every three weeks (or less) there is drama caused by one or both of you," she wrote. She said it'd been that way for at least the last two years, "and I don't deserve this! So, don't think that this [presumably their no longer being in the group] is because of Mathew," she concluded, "it's just that I can't continue to live with the same drama that I have dealt with for so many years."

Quitting Destiny's Child?

$\mathcal{N}$o matter how depressed she was, Beyoncé definitely wasn't going to miss her next vocal lesson with Kim Wood Sandusky. Singing had always been her salvation; it could still lift her from the doldrums. In the midst of all this conflict in her life, she showed up at Kim's. "Are you okay?" Kim asked, concerned. The two sat next to each other on a wooden bench in front of a grand piano. "I'm just sad," Beyoncé confessed. "LaTavia and LeToya are leaving the group, and I don't know yet what I'm going to do." Kim put her arm around Beyoncé. "In a career like the one I know you're going to have," she told her, "you're going to have growing pains." She explained to her that this moment would probably not be the last time she'd feel such sadness or heartache, that it was all part of the process of growth in a tough industry. "Sometimes, change is good," she told her, pulling her in close. "Maybe it's good they left. Maybe this will open a new door for you."

"You may be right. Can we pray?" Beyoncé asked. The two women had often prayed at the start or conclusion of their lessons. "Of course," Kim said.

Years later, Kim Wood Sandusky recalled, "What I asked God to do for Beyoncé was to guide her through this storm and to raise her to heights that she'd never before known. I gave her some water as she collected herself. 'Okay, we have work to do,' I said. She pulled herself together and said, 'I'm ready, Kim.' And we got to it."

A big concern of Beyoncé's at this time had to do with Kelly's future. She felt a strong allegiance to her and realized that by going solo she was forcing her to do the same. Beyoncé understood Kelly well, though. Kelly was tough, maybe tougher than even herself. After all, Kelly never had it easy in any of the groups in which they'd sung together—how many times had her head been on the chopping block? Now that she'd finally made it, she wasn't about to let anyone snatch her success from her. No. She knew that Kelly would be just fine.

Then there was the matter of songs. Because Beyoncé had already begun writing for the next Destiny's Child album, she had a group sound in mind. Writing for solo performances was a very different task. Maybe going solo at this time was too soon, too rushed?

The next day, Beyoncé made her decision. First, she called the group's attorney Ken Hertz to give him the news. Then she faxed a formal letter to

Don Ienner, the president of her record label. Her decision? She was leaving Destiny's Child. She was sorry to see the group disband, but felt it was inevitable.

As soon as he received her letter, Ienner called Beyoncé and told her he fully supported her decision. He wanted her to be absolutely sure, though. Also, he wondered how Mathew felt about it. Beyoncé said that her father understood. She also said that as far as she was concerned, she wasn't leaving the group. Rather, the group had left her! After that call, Mathew telephoned the label's business affairs department to inform them of Beyoncé's decision. The reaction was not one of great surprise, given what they knew was going on. In the end, the label felt that Beyoncé would be a very successful solo artist and sell untold millions of records for them. Therefore, the plan was to give it a few more weeks and then make an official announcement to the press.

"Tomorrow, We Fight Back"

*A*fter about another week of Beyoncé's confusion and sadness, Tina Knowles had her fill of it. She went into her daughter's room, drew back the shades on all of the windows, and sat next to Beyoncé. "Do you want me to tell you the truth?" she asked her. "Because you know I always tell you the truth." Beyoncé nodded. "Okay. Fine. You need to dust yourself off and do what you have to do to continue your career," Tina said firmly. "We're gonna get through this thing together, you and me."

"But I don't know what to do," Beyoncé said. Even though she'd told the record company she wanted to go solo, obviously she was still conflicted.

"Then you need to get on your knees and pray," Tina told her, according to her later testimony. She added that it didn't really matter to her one way or the other what Beyoncé did, as long as she did *something*. All she really wanted was for Beyoncé to not let everything she'd worked so hard to attain "go down the tubes because of two girls." Beyoncé pointed out that the new video for "Say My Name" was about to be produced and that she didn't know how they would ever be able to do it with just herself and Kelly. "Well, we're sure not gonna figure it out laying up here in this bed, now are we?" Tina said. She added that she was giving Beyoncé the rest of the day to be sad. "But tomorrow? Tomorrow, we fight back," she declared.

What was Beyoncé's response to her mother's clarion call? "At that point," Tina would recall, "not much of anything. She didn't even have a reaction, she was so down."

More than anything, Tina hoped that Beyoncé would rally and get back to business. Since that didn't seem to be happening, she felt the time had come for her to take action. "As a mother, I had a responsibility to my child as well as to Kelly," she would later recall, "to try to help them through this period and to advise them to not just lay down and let somebody else be in control of their destinies. The video was coming up. Beyoncé and Kelly were saying, 'How are we gonna do a video with only two girls?' They were stressing out over it. So I made a decision. I followed my own advice, you could say."

Tina remembered a girl she'd heard about in Los Angeles named Tenitra Williams who had sung background for R&B singer Monica. Destiny's Child's choreographer, Junella Segura (who'd also worked for Monica), had mentioned to Tina that Tenitra was interested in either pursuing a solo career or maybe joining a group. When she asked Kelly about her, Kelly said she believed she and Beyoncé had met Tenitra somewhere along the way, but she wasn't sure—maybe in a hotel lobby in Atlanta. (Actually, the girls met her in July 1999 during the taping of a television special for Nickelodeon in Sacramento, California.)

For some inexplicable reason, Tina had an intuition about Tenitra; she knew she had to get in touch with her. So she made a few phone calls, and the next thing she knew, she was on the line with Tenitra, who lived in Rockford, Illinois. Tina told her they had an opening in Destiny's Child for what she called "an alternate," and asked if she would consider flying down to Houston for a meeting that very evening. "I made the arrangements for her trip personally," Tina later recalled. "And I also paid for her transportation out of my own pocket." She decided not to tell Mathew about it, however. She later testified, "I think he was still hoping things would work out with LaTavia and LeToya, and I didn't want to mess with that. If it could be worked out, fine. But I wasn't going to just sit around and wait to see what would happen next. That's not me. That's not how I do things. I wanted to do something. So I did. I found a new girl."

Later that afternoon, Beyoncé finally emerged from her bedroom. She looked rested, more relaxed. "So, what are we gonna do?" she asked, seeming a little more ready to take care of business.

"I already did it," Tina told her. "She'll be here tonight."

"Who?" Beyoncé said.

"Tenitra. The new girl."

A couple hours later, Tina and Solange picked up Tenitra at the airport and brought her back to the house. There they had a meeting—or, to be legally precise, as Tina later put it, "I had a *meeting* with nobody because I did not have the *authority* to have a meeting. I was just a mother trying to help out. Beyoncé and Kelly, *they* had a meeting with Tenitra. I just sat and watched. They talked and then heard her sing, and then they sang together. It worked! I could see the chemistry right away."

Tenitra Michelle Williams, nineteen, was born on July 23, 1980, in Rockford, one of four children. She was raised middle-class; her father worked as a car salesman, her mother as a nurse. She'd been singing since the age of seven and had been working behind Monica since around October 1999. She had a surprisingly strong voice, a clear tone that deserved to be spotlighted. It was no wonder she had been thinking of a solo career, but certainly joining a group as successful as Destiny's Child would be a major step toward broader recognition. At that first meeting, she made a big impression on everyone with her immediate willingness to be a team player. "What exactly is the problem?" she asked. "And what can I do to help?" After spending the night with the Knowleses, Tenitra flew back to Illinois to wait to hear. "I like her," Beyoncé told Kelly, "I really do." Kelly agreed, remarking, "She gives off a light, doesn't she?"

Meanwhile, Kelly recalled a girl she had met on the set of Destiny's Child's video shoot for "Bills, Bills, Bills." She was an eighteen-year-old extra named Farrah Franklin. Born on May 3, 1981, in Seattle, she was currently living in Los Angeles and a member of a singing group called Jane Doe, which was about to be disbanded. Tina flew Farrah to Los Angeles to meet with Beyoncé and Kelly. As had been the case with Michelle, they too hit it off. Farrah was an excellent dancer and a reasonably good vocalist. They actually weren't looking for great singers, though—they were looking for two girls who would fit the group's image for the "Say My Name" video. Whoever was selected would just be lip-syncing the song to LaTavia's and LeToya's voices.

Perhaps LaTavia and LeToya didn't fully grasp as much when they chose to disaffirm their contracts, but Mathew Knowles actually *owned* Destiny's

Child. When LeToya earlier wondered, "When did *our* group become *his* group?" the answer was: when he trademarked the name. Legally, he could put anyone in the act he wanted, replacing *all* the girls if that was his desire. Unfortunately, it seems that what LaTavia and LeToya may have lacked at this time was strong adult guidance. They were only eighteen. Though they were properly represented by lawyers and advisers, how could they be expected to fully grasp the gravity of the life-changing decisions they'd made? Some of the adults in their midst (including Pamela Lackett) tried to help, though. For instance, when they asked their original producer, Lonnie Jackson, for advice, he suggested they embark on a radio tour to fully air their grievances and garner the public's support. However, the girls didn't feel they had a voice. To them, it felt as if no one cared and, in a sense, maybe they were right. There being little room for sentimentality in show business, Mathew, Tina, Beyoncé, and Destiny's Child were more than ready to continue onward...without them.

Moving Forward with New Girls

*I*t was Friday, February 11, 2000, Kelly Rowland's nineteenth birthday. Mathew was sitting behind his desk at Music World headquarters in Houston, with Beyoncé and Kelly seated on the other side of it. He picked up the telephone and dialed Don Ienner, the president of Columbia/Sony. He then put him on speakerphone. "Donny, I have the ladies here," Mathew said. "We want to come to some kind of understanding as to how to proceed."

"Great. Hello, ladies," Don said.

"Hi, Donny!"

From this point on, according to her later testimony, Beyoncé did most of the talking. She was aware, she said, that she had previously informed the label of her plans to go solo, but now she wasn't so sure about it. "We've got two stand-ins for the ['Say My Name'] video next week," she said, "and if it goes well we're thinking maybe we might just add them to the group permanently."

"Well, that's a bit of a surprise," said Ienner.

"If not these two girls, maybe two others," Kelly chimed in.

"So, what do y'all think of that?" Mathew asked the record company executive.

"This is your call, Beyoncé," Don Ienner said. "And you too, Kelly." He added that if the girls wanted to continue as Destiny's Child, the label would support them. If they wanted to go solo, the company would sanction that decision as well. It was certainly gratifying for the girls to hear such unequivocal approval from the president of their label.

"Okay, now I'm fixin' to get excited," Beyoncé said after the call ended. She and Kelly leapt from their chairs and hugged each other while jumping up and down in the middle of the room. Meanwhile, Mathew sat behind his desk, grinning. It was good to see his daughter acting like her old self.

Now that the group had been rounded out, at least for the purpose of the video shoot, Beyoncé felt much better about things. "We taught the girls the routine [for the 'Say My Name' video] in one day," she recalled. "They had never danced in stilettos...it was crazy." After a few rehearsals, the choreography to the song looked so bad there was no way to use it on the video. "It looked terrible," Beyoncé recalled. "So we had an idea to just start posing on the beat. The director just started saying, bam, bam, *bam*—and on every bam we would strike a pose. And that became the whole video."

In spite of its minimal choreography, the video for "Say My Name" is stylishly shot, with a pop art feel. Each scene is filmed in a vivid color scheme and the girls' costumes match the surrounding furnishings perfectly, blending in seamlessly with their background. Makeup and hair are once again flawlessly done. Tenitra and Farrah definitely look like pop stars in orange costumes matching their surroundings. However, they are given little more to do than strike poses as Beyoncé sings. Oddly, Kelly appears in less than half of the video, leaving some to wonder about the reason for her exclusion.

The video shoot for "Say My Name," which was done in Los Angeles, had gone so well, it was quickly decided that, yes, Tenitra and Farrah would join Destiny's Child. They signed on the dotted line on February 18, 2000.

From the start, there were a few image concerns. For instance, Mathew sat down with Tenitra and told her that he felt it would be a good idea for her to start using her middle name, Michelle, as her stage name. He said the suits at Columbia/Sony viewed Tenitra as being "too ethnic" a name. If anything, this decision spoke to the label's determination to make sure Destiny's Child appealed to a white as well as a black audience—as if Caucasians would have been put off by the name Tenitra. Looking back on it all these years later, it's a little difficult to believe that the name business was even an issue, but apparently it was. Tenitra was fine with the alteration, though, saying she was very honored just to be in a group as successful as Destiny's Child. So from this moment on, Tenitra Williams would be known as Michelle Williams.

"You're kinda light, aren't you?" Tina told Farrah during a group meeting in which styling was the subject. Farrah agreed that, yes, she was light-skinned. "Would you mind spending some time in a tanning salon?" Tina asked. "Because you're replacing LaTavia, and she's more dark-skinned." Though Farrah was taken aback, she reluctantly agreed. "And also I think we need to dye your hair red, because LaTavia had a more reddish tone," Tina said. "Probably in six months you can wear your own color."

Of course, no one was trying to fool the public into believing that Farrah was LaTavia, but in terms of the group's branding it made sense to Tina to at least *try* not to make the transition be so jarring. Later, Farrah would complain to the media about having to make these changes, causing Beyoncé to have to defend it. "We needed one girl with red hair and one girl with black hair," she admitted, "because that's how the two girls who left looked. And that was also my mama's original vision for the group. She dyed each of our hair a different color. We figured this way every fan could relate to at least one of us, and each of us would have her own distinctive look. At the time, Farrah was fine with it. 'Okay,' she said, 'no big deal.'" Michelle later chimed in that Farrah's having made a big deal of those imaging issues was "very unnecessary bullcrap that's absolutely ridiculous."

"So, what do you think of the new girls?" Mathew asked vocal coach Kim Wood Sandusky after she finished working with Farrah and Michelle for the first time. It was an interesting turn of events that she was coaching the new girls since, by her own admission, she had never worked with LaTavia and LeToya. "Well, both are pretty good," Kim said, choosing her words carefully. "But Farrah... I just don't know about her."

"What do you mean?"

"She has a very pretty talent, don't get me wrong," Kim said, according to her memory. "But I'm not sure she has the... *personality*." She clarified that—at least on a first impression—she wasn't certain Farrah had the temperament to handle the kind of pressure that goes along with great fame. As far as her vocals were concerned, she said she—like all of them—could benefit from work on power, stamina, and breathing.

"And Michelle?"

"Oh, she's amazing," Kim said eagerly. She noted that not only did Michelle's voice have great character, but she also had a strong personality. "She's the real deal, that one," Kim said. "May I be candid with you?" she then asked.

"Of course."

"I think Michelle has the right chemistry to work with Beyoncé and Kelly. That's the perfect group right there: Beyoncé, Kelly, and Michelle. That's my gut." She said that not only did those three have a pleasing blend, but she felt that Michelle had the right frame of mind to be in a trio that was to be fronted by another girl. She allowed that she was more than happy to try to work Farrah into things, but that she had "a very strong feeling that we don't really need her."

"Well, that's interesting, because I was thinking along those same lines," Mathew said. He also noted that if there was one thing he'd learned from working with girls all these years it was that "these things have a way of working themselves out." For the time being, he suggested that Kim work with all four girls, "and let's see where that takes us."

Though Mathew may have had some reservations about Farrah, he was happy with her and Michelle's work on the video. His greater satisfaction, though, was in seeing Beyoncé not allow LaTavia and LeToya to lay ruin to her world. Now that he had time to process their actions, he was astonished by their naïveté. In the fickle record industry, it took no time at all to go from the top of the charts right down to the bottom simply because of one bad decision. He'd seen it happen repeatedly, simply as an observer of the business. "I remember him saying, 'Whatever it takes, I am going to protect what my daughter and I built together,'" said Chad Elliott, who had cowritten "Jumpin' Jumpin'" and was now vice president of A&R at Sony. "LaTavia and LeToya had also hurt his daughter, and to him that was personal. He now felt that Destiny's Child had to rebound quickly, that the sooner the former members were relegated to the past, the better off everyone would be."

If in fact Mathew felt LaTavia and LeToya had hurt his kid, hurt in return was what both girls would feel when they started hearing through the grapevine that Destiny's Child had filmed a video without them. They didn't believe—or didn't want to believe—it was true. They happened to be watching BET (Black Entertainment Television) a couple weeks later and heard the announcement that the new video for "Say My Name" was about to be broadcast. The two then watched in astonishment as the colorful and well-produced video aired for the first time, featuring two other singers alongside Beyoncé and Kelly. It was a crushing moment. LaTavia Roberson recalled, "We couldn't believe our eyes. There's not much more I can say about it. We simply just could not believe our eyes."

Given the circumstances, it was probably inevitable that LaTavia and LeToya would file a lawsuit against Mathew, Beyoncé, and Kelly. The suit, which was filed on March 21, 2000, accused Mathew of "greed, insistence of control, self-dealing and promotion of his daughter's interest at the expense of the plaintiffs." The suit also alleged that "in [Mathew's] mind, he was effectively the owner of Destiny's Child and complete master of the group." One colleague of Mathew's says he had a good chuckle at that particular stating of the obvious.

Roberson and Luckett also claimed that Mathew encouraged Beyoncé and Kelly to go on "a rampage to destroy" their careers. Moreover, they claimed, he had made untold dollars off their efforts as singers in the group, whereas they "made virtually none." Furthermore, the girls' attorney, Warren Fitzgerald, put forth the notion that his clients didn't quit Destiny's Child. If anything, it was Beyoncé who quit, which of course was true, even though she quickly reinstated herself.

After the suit was filed, LaTavia and LeToya told MTV that they had "nothing but love" for Beyoncé and Kelly and that their "issue was with management." When Kurt Loder of MTV passed their comments on to Beyoncé and Kelly during a taped interview, the two were incredulous. Kelly, never one to hold back, responded by saying, "Well, they slapped a nice lawsuit on us." With a sweet smile, Beyoncé added, "That's a lot of love," to which Kelly concluded, "That's some *hard* love, isn't it?"

Lyndall Lacks Purpose

*T*he litigation from disgruntled former Destiny Child members didn't put much of a damper on the group's upward trajectory, or on that of the Knowles family either. On June 28, 2000, with the phenomenal success of the group—who'd just appeared at the CFDA (Council of Fashion Designers of America) Fashion Awards two days earlier—the Knowleses were able to move into a new baronial-looking home on Missouri City's Lake

Olympia, just outside Houston, a gated property at 27 Swan Isle Boulevard. They paid anywhere from $300,000 to $400,000 (property records seem to have conflicting amounts) for the six-bedroom, nearly five-thousand-square-foot home. "It was definitely a step up," Lyndall Locke recalled. "Big rooms. Overlooked a lake. First time I walked into that place I was, like, 'Okay so *this* is how they gonna roll now?'"

While the new home was large, it was by no means a mansion. Still, there was an enormous entry and a living room filled with regal, oversized furniture. Mirrors on many of the walls made all of the rooms look even bigger than they actually were. The house was decorated by Tina in her larger-than-life, colorful style. Her huge kitchen was all white and always meticulously clean (with the assistance of a maid). The master bedroom suite was on the first floor, with a small closet holding Mathew's clothing, whereas Tina's were hung with care in a walk-in closet the size of a large bedroom. Upstairs were bedrooms for Beyoncé and Kelly, as well as for cousin Angie, who would stay with the Knowleses from time to time. Kelly's room was furnished in royal deep burgundy colors. Beyoncé's featured a genie-in-the-bottle theme, with colorful pillows of fuchsia, purple, and gold made (mostly by Tina) from the fabric of silk saris. Outside, the former garage was converted into a bedroom for Solange. In an upstairs den furnished in bright red were hung many of Destiny's Child's certificates and awards. Racks after rack of Destiny's Child costumes designed by Tina were carefully stored in a newly built garage.

As for the Knowleses' marriage, it would seem that there were still problems there. Billy Brasfield, Beyoncé's longtime makeup artist known as Billy B., recalled, "We were on tour, staying in New York at a hotel. It was very late, after hours. I was waiting for an elevator in the lobby when the doors opened and out walked Mathew with a young girl about Beyoncé's age. They weren't touching, or anything. But when the doors opened and they suddenly appeared in front of me, I instantly thought I knew what the deal was. There was this awkward moment when we were just staring at one another. I was like, Oh my God. What do I do? Then, they just continued walking together."

It was later rumored that Mathew and Tina had discussed divorce in 2000, possibly even talking about a division of assets. A divorce would not, however, occur that year. One likely reason was that Beyoncé's career was becoming bigger and greater with each passing day. Therefore, Mathew's work ethic would continue to deeply immerse him in her life, and thus also in his wife's. Still, remaining in a marriage that had not been serving them since almost day one could not have been easy. It was as if proverbial golden handcuffs were now keeping Tina tied to Mathew. She could not have been oblivious to the irony of it, either. After all, Tina's reasoning behind founding Headliners fifteen years earlier was so that she would not be at the whim of what she called "the adversity of a bad marriage."

The rewards were great, though—it's not as if there was only suffering. Being treated like stars everywhere they went was an exciting perk. If they went to a concert, for instance, they were treated with almost as much reverence as the starring act. Beyoncé was now so famous she could command backstage passes in an instant. Lyndall well remembers the time Janet Jackson performed at the Compaq Center in Houston. He and Beyoncé, along with the rest of Destiny's Child and Mathew and Tina, were all invited to the show. Afterward, the contingent went backstage for a meet-and-greet with the star. Though they had met her previously in Japan, it was still a big thrill to be in her presence; the girls had idolized Janet for years.

Perhaps because Lyndall was a little nervous, he jabbered on to Janet for a while. Finally she cut him off. "You remind me of one of my nephews," she said, referring to the guys in the Jackson family singing group 3T. "Well, your nephews must be pretty doggone *awesome*, then!" Lyndall joked. Though he was just being himself, jovial and disarming, the comment landed with a thud. As Mathew had warned him earlier, "You can't be actin' like no Arsenio Hall if you ain't no Arsenio Hall!" It was one thing to be "just folks" when they were all home alone eating Popeyes chicken, but not in front of Janet Jackson. (Or, as Beyoncé later told Taura Stinson, "Lyndall just says whatever he wants without thinking!") Seconds later, Angie walked over to Lyndall, put her arm around him, and asked him to follow her. She escorted him out of the dressing room. "That hurt," Lyndall would recall years later. "It cut deep."

Once he was out in the hallway, Tina exited Janet's dressing room to have a word with Lyndall. He couldn't help but notice how sleek and stylish she suddenly appeared to him. Her brown hair streaked with blonde highlights, she was wearing skintight black leather slacks with a matching tailored leather jacket and flouncy white silk blouse. A very large diamond ring glistened on each hand, as did a diamond bracelet on one wrist and matching watch on the other.

"No offense, Lyndall," she said, "but, goddamn! Do you always have to be so . . . *Lyndall?*"

"What do you mean?" he asked.

She sighed heavily. "Oh, I don't know," she said, shaking her head. "We just wish you could be . . . I don't know . . . *different*, I guess."

"But I am who I am," Lyndall said. He was feeling self-conscious but also a little defensive. "I mean, you know . . . I'm just me." He smiled boyishly at her. It usually worked with the opposite sex, but Tina was too experienced to be charmed by a self-possessed twenty-year-old.

Taking both of his hands into her own to lessen the blow, she advised that he just watch Beyoncé and emulate her behavior as much as possible. "You're a sweet boy, Lynnie," she concluded. "Just don't talk so much. Can you do that for me?"

"Okay," Lyndall said, feeling a little deflated. "I'll try."

Maybe it was understandable that Mathew and Tina were beginning to view Lyndall Locke as just a very sweet guy with no future. They must have wondered whether he would make their daughter happy in the long run but they also knew there were a lot of men after Beyoncé at this time who only wanted her because of who she was and who she was about to become in the entertainment industry. The Knowleses must have felt that Lyndall was a safer bet for her since he clearly had no ulterior motives. In fact, they would sometimes fly him to a city where Beyoncé was appearing if they felt she was lonely.

"Whatever state she was in, they would send Lyndall a ticket," recalled Lyndall's mother, Lydia. "Tina would say, 'Lyndall, please come.' I wanted to put an end to it. I said, 'Lyndall, look, this has to stop. I want you to make a life for yourself. That's Beyoncé's life, honey. That's not your life.' I didn't raise him to be available to somebody every time they snapped their fingers. I was afraid my baby was going to get his heart broken, if you really want to know the truth."

A few days after the Janet Jackson concert, Lyndall was at the Knowleses' home on Swan Isle; Mathew found him lounging on a chair near the pool while waiting for Beyoncé to get ready for a date. "*Yo!* What's up, Big Mac?" Lyndall asked, using his nickname for him. "Not much, Lyndall," Mathew answered.

Mathew seemed annoyed. At first, Lyndall didn't understand the reason. It hadn't occurred to him how he appeared under Mathew's scrutiny: a young man enjoying the fruits of Mathew's labors, whiling away the day by the pool with nary a care in the world. "Say, brother, why don't you and I go for a little walk?" Mathew asked. "Sure thing," Lyndall said as he rose. The two men walked toward the direction of the sparkling blue lake at the end of the Knowleses' expansive property.

"How old are you now, Lyndall?" Mathew asked as the two men meandered out onto one of the wooden piers.

"I'll be twenty-one at the end of the year," Lyndall said, all of this according to his distinct memory of the conversation.

Mathew nodded. He then noted that by the time he was twenty-one, "I had, probably, twenty-one different kinds of jobs."

Now it was becoming apparent what Mathew was getting at. "Then, you know, I quit my six-figure job to manage the girls. And now? Well, take a look around," he said, extending his arms out to the bucolic landscape. "Done pretty good for myself, right?" he asked.

"Yes, sir," Lyndall said, looking at him with admiration. "You're doin' it big, all right."

"I found my thing," Mathew added, "which is managing Beyoncé." He noted that he had "poured my whole heart and soul, everything that I am, into her." Now, he continued, he and Tina were wondering what it was Lyndall wanted to do with his life. Or, as he put it, "What is it that you want to pour *your* whole heart and soul into?"

Lyndall wasn't prepared for such a serious question. All he could manage was, "Not sure yet." He realized he should say more, but no words came to him.

Mathew stopped walking and faced Lyndall. "Well, look," he offered, his demeanor suddenly serious. "You gotta get it together, my brother." He said that he felt he should give Lyndall fair warning. "If you don't pull it together and find you a real career, she's gonna be long gone," he said. "You know how many men are after her now?"

"I know you're right, Big Mac."

"So what are you gonna do about it?" Mathew asked, pushing for an answer.

"All the men in my family are telling me to get a job, so I know I have to do that," Lyndall said weakly. "I'm working on it." His response sounded inadequate and he knew it. However, he was just starting to give thought as to what he would do with his future. He certainly hadn't been born with the burning ambition of a supremely focused Knowles family member. Up until very recently, he'd been satisfied with just letting life happen around him. If anything, he was maturing slowly and, it could be argued, normally for a young man his age.

"Well, you don't have time to waste," Mathew said, "because if you ask me, Beyoncé needs to be with someone who has it goin' on, and that sure ain't you. Now, I know you two been together for a lot of years," he continued, "but, *goddamn*, Lyndall! She's growin' now. And you ain't. Got it?"

"Got it, Big Mac," Lyndall said. "I hear you."

Mathew concluded by noting that Lyndall was a young black man in the United States of America in the year 2000, and as such, had opportunities most of the African Americans of his own generation never could have imagined. "So take advantage of them," he said. *"Do something with your life."* With that, Mathew Knowles turned and walked away from Lyndall Locke, leaving him out on the small pier, alone with his thoughts.

Beyoncé Makes a Decision about Farrah

*B*y the summer of 2000 when Destiny's Child toured England, the latest version of the group, with Farrah Franklin and Michelle Williams, seemed to have truly gelled. Though twelve-hour-a-day rehearsals were grueling, the girls got through them well and the results were definitely apparent in their excellent performances.

As the new recruits, Farrah and Michelle seemed content to defer to Beyoncé in press interviews. While each singer had her chance to talk, in the end there was no disputing the identity of the group's official spokeswoman. If Beyoncé began to answer a question, the others were sure to be quiet and let her finish. If there was any hesitation regarding a tough query, they looked to Beyoncé to handle it. For instance, in one television interview—now a popular YouTube clip—Kelly began speaking about LaTavia, saying she had recently seen her in a shopping mall. Before she had a chance to finish her thought, Beyoncé interrupted her. "Let's cut that over," she said, making it clear that she didn't want Kelly to finish (and obviously not realizing that the interview was live, not taped). Chastised, Kelly sheepishly glanced at Beyoncé, nodded, and said, "Yeah. You're right."

Whereas Michelle easily adapted to the status quo, Farrah began to express dissatisfaction about it after only three months. One issue for her was that it had become apparent that she wouldn't be singing leads anytime in the near future. While it may have been a goal of hers when she joined the group, it was unlikely to have been Mathew's intention. He actually wasn't even sure she could carry a tune. It didn't matter to him one way or the other, though. When the writer Lola Ogunnaike later asked why he allowed Farrah into the act if he was uncertain of her vocal ability, he answered, "Imaging. Plain and simple."

Though it had only been a short time since she joined Destiny's Child, Farrah could feel her confidence slipping away. "I felt I was losing my identity," she would later explain, "and I was not being treated like you would want someone treating your daughter." Apparently—at least to hear Beyoncé, Kelly, and Michelle tell it—Farrah couldn't let it go, especially when she realized Beyoncé was also getting all the best camera shots on television programs.

Farrah also had reservations about Solange's traveling with the act. She believed that payment for Solange's accommodations was coming out of her paycheck, that she was at least partially subsidizing the participation of Beyoncé's little sister on tour. It may technically have been true. Someone had to pay the dancers, and it would be normal for that expenditure to be part of the group's general overhead. However, Mathew wasn't open to discussing the specifics of this arrangement with Farrah.

If, on some level, the issues Farrah had with the group caused her to want out of Destiny's Child, she couldn't have orchestrated her departure more efficiently.

In the late spring of 2000, the group was scheduled to film an interview for MTV in Houston. However, the girls have said that Farrah, who still lived in Los Angeles, didn't want to fly to Houston. She felt the network should just shoot her part of the program at her home. After she and Mathew had words about it on the telephone, he demanded that she show up in Texas or face expulsion.

"She has lost her *damn mind*," Beyoncé exclaimed when told of Farrah's argument with her dad.

When Farrah finally arrived at the Knowleses' home, she was visibly upset. She explained that she'd been ill and had dragged herself from her sickbed to the airport because of Mathew's dictate. As soon as she walked into the Knowles home, she took one look at Mathew and reportedly refused to speak to him. Beyoncé was put off. She wasn't okay with Farrah walking into her home and ignoring her father. That, she felt, was way out of line and she told Farrah so. When Farrah tried to argue Beyoncé refused to back down. She was definitely in no mood to deal with Farrah. "I may be kind," she said, "but I'm not weak. None of the women raised in this house are weak." With that, she stormed from the room, muttering under her breath. Farrah then said something else, and Beyoncé—from the other room—shouted back that she was through talking.

For the next couple of months, things were tense. It began to feel to Farrah that the whole world was against her, mostly because the only people with whom she was in contact were in the Knowles camp, which she later told Lola Ogunnaike was "kinda like a cult. They don't have friends who aren't in the Destiny's Child clique."

In July 2000, Destiny's Child was scheduled to spend a busy weekend in Seattle, including radio interviews from as early as seven in the morning until late in the evening, and then more interviews the next day. It was a brief but punishing grind. During their stay in the city, they were also to be trailed by a camera crew from MTV to document their busy lives. After Seattle, they were scheduled to fly to Los Angeles to then catch a plane to Australia for yet more promotional work and a couple of concerts.

No sooner had the group gotten to Seattle than Farrah apparently decided to turn around and head back to Los Angeles. The three remaining girls told their interviewers that Farrah was "ill." During a break, Michelle telephoned Farrah back in Los Angeles. So far as she was concerned Farrah was saying that she would see the girls *after* Australia—in other words, she expected them to go abroad without her and she would catch up with them later in Houston. "No. You best meet us at LAX when we get there," Michelle warned her.

On July 14, the group left Seattle and landed in Los Angeles en route to Australia. When they didn't find Farrah at the gate, they began to panic. "Beyoncé called her using my cell phone," Michelle recalled, "and that's when the drama started."

"What do you mean you're not coming?" Beyoncé asked, according to her and Michelle's memory of events. She told her to get to the airport immediately because if she missed the plane she would not be able to make it to Australia in time. Farrah said she was at her apartment and wasn't leaving it. "She said she's not coming," Beyoncé, holding her hand over the receiver, told Kelly.

"*Oh no she didn't*," Kelly exclaimed.

By this time, Beyoncé had had enough of the new girl. Farrah may have been standing up for herself, but Beyoncé didn't see it that way. Her former partners, LeToya and LaTavia, had worked hard for many years and had earned their places in the group. Therefore they'd also earned the right to certain grievances, even if Beyoncé didn't agree with the way they'd aired them. But Farrah? After just five months? No. Beyoncé felt she simply had no right to be difficult. If anything, she should have been grateful. "But I believe there comes a point in your life when you are doing things that you wouldn't do normally and you're, you know, you're not who you are," Farrah would later say in explaining herself. "You realize that you're selling your soul for fame."

While on the telephone with Farrah, Beyoncé laid it on the line. "This is a business," she began. She then noted that the group had sold-out dates and thousands of fans expecting them. She added that Columbia had been planning the tour for months, since back when LeToya and LaTavia were part of the act. She told her that being in Destiny's Child was a job just like any other, and that the girls in the group couldn't decide not to show up just because they didn't feel like it. Farrah didn't seem to be budging. She was only eighteen; again, as in the cases of LaTavia and LeToya, one has to wonder if there was any truly strong leadership in her life. "Think like a *businesswoman*," Beyoncé said continuing to push. "Think *smart*."

Finally, Kelly had heard enough. "Please!" she exclaimed. She told Beyoncé to just tell Farrah to forget about it, to not go to the airport, to not even set foot in the car: "*Tell her to just stay her ass home*."

Beyoncé nodded. But before she had a chance to repeat Kelly's words, Farrah was gone. Now Beyoncé was fuming.

A few seconds later, Farrah called back. In this next—and last— conversation Beyoncé would ever have with her, Farrah said something about not wanting to continue on to Australia until she had a chance to "talk to management." Beyoncé knew what that meant; LaTavia and LeToya had always referred to Mathew as "management" when they were upset. "We don't have *time* for you to talk to management," she told her, raising her voice. "If you don't come on this trip," she told her, "there is no way that you can remain with this group."

It's not known how Farrah responded to Beyoncé's statement. All that's known are Beyoncé's parting lines to her. "Fine. I wish you the best," she concluded. "May God bless you. *Goodbye!*" And with that, she hung up the phone.

PART FOUR

Independent Women

Destiny's Three

$\mathcal{W}$ell, this is sure a fine time for Farrah to show her ass," Beyoncé told one of the crew on the way to Australia. About to change to go onstage, she was devouring a giant bag of Cheetos that she'd brought with her from the States. "What are we going to do?" the crew member asked. "We're gonna go on," Beyoncé said as she wiped yellow Cheetos dust onto the pants leg of her studded jeans. She was also wearing a pink-and-white-checked cashmere sweater along with a hot pink baseball cap. "We're not gonna let down our audiences." She said that "either you care in this business, or you don't." She cared, she added, Kelly did too, and she believed that Michelle did as well. What upset her most, she observed, was that she now had to be concerned about what the public and the press would say about yet another change in the group, and she thought she was done talking about this kind of thing. "But I guess I'm not," she concluded, "and I don't even know how to explain this thing with Farrah."

The girls had no choice: Destiny's Child had to go on to Australia without Farrah. By this point, Beyoncé was emotionally exhausted from the last couple of months of group madness. She was not at her best. "You could see a change in her mood," said one person close to her at the time. "She was definitely frazzled by the last few weeks of Destiny's Child psychodrama. You can't go through all of that chaos without it having some effect on you."

"There was a lot of eye-rolling going on at this time," was how one of Tina Knowles's friends put it. "As unique as she was as an artist, Beyoncé was also a typical teenager. Tina had been complaining about it before the girls even left for Australia, but not doing anything about it. She felt it was just because of all the pressure and anxiety. Given all that had happened with LaTavia and LeToya, Tina decided to let Beyoncé's bad mood ride awhile longer."

"Just do what I say," Beyoncé told the lighting director before one of the shows in Australia. "It's not so hard. It's simple. Make sure the audience can see us." Kelly looked at Beyoncé as if she was a person she'd never before met, while Michelle probably wondered what she'd gotten herself into. "Look, I've got a lot of songs to sing," Beyoncé told Kelly at one point. "The least you could do would be to work with Michelle on harmonies, don't you think?" Kelly just gave her a look. Then she and Michelle sequestered themselves in order to fine-tune their blend, as Beyoncé had suggested.

Despite whatever was going through Beyoncé's mind at this time, it turned out to be a blessing in disguise that Farrah was now out of the picture. It would be on the Australian tour that DC's magic three would be born—the grouping of Beyoncé, Kelly, and Michelle, the act that would go on to sell millions more records and redefine for the ages the musical genre of the female singing group.

After the girls spent a day or two restructuring the show and changing the choreography and harmonies to accommodate a trio—not to mention the sound, lights, and other technical elements that had already been set in stone but now had to be altered—they were as ready as they would ever be to perform in front of an audience on July 17. "Before we went out onto the stage, we joined hands as we always do before a show and prayed that this thing would work," Beyoncé later recalled. "And then we took a deep breath and just went out onto the stage.

"Once we were out there, it was as if there was a new kind of freedom," she continued. "We were so scared, but had called my dad before we went out and he said, 'Just do your thing, and don't worry about it. You'll figure it out once you get out there before an audience.' He was right. Once we were out there, it just worked."

"The best feeling in the world was when we first appeared as a trio," Kelly recalled. "I remember how intimidated I [once] felt when the others were around [presumably she was referring to girls who had left the group]. I felt insecure around them, like I wasn't talented when really I was. I felt uneasy. They made me feel shy. Whenever I would finally try to come out of my shell, something would happen, a fight or a look, and I would crawl right back in. Australia was the first time I did not have to hold back one bit because I knew there were two people on either side of me who loved me."

Without Farrah at her side, Michelle also had no choice but to give her all and hope her talent would speak for itself. It did. She revealed herself to be a dynamic singer and performer who could hold her own with her much more experienced group members. "I can only say that while I was onstage that night I felt a confidence I'd never felt before. When it came to singing the gospel medley a cappella, I knew I had to hold my own with Beyoncé and Kelly, and so I just let it out. I looked over at the girls and they were looking at me, like, 'Dang! We didn't know you had that in you!'"

After that first show, Beyoncé realized that her solo career had been indefinitely delayed. "I knew that we were a threesome now and that we wouldn't need to find a fourth girl," she recalled. She called Mathew from Australia to tell him the news. Beyoncé would later say she could hear the relief in his voice that they didn't have to break in yet another new girl. In fact, Mathew wasn't surprised by Beyoncé's call. After all, he had earlier predicted to Kim Wood Sandusky, when she said she felt that Farrah was probably not necessary, that the situation would work itself out.

The three girls then had a group meeting to celebrate the show's success, and also to contemplate their future. It just so happened that Mathew had recently committed Destiny's Child to a deal to sing a song and then film a video for the upcoming *Charlie's Angels* movie soundtrack. Beyoncé had gone into the studio alone—she did so often when recording demos for songs—and composed a song called "Independent Women." It said a lot about not only her identity, but her mother's, too, as well as many of the women she had known over the years.

When Mathew heard Beyoncé's composition, he was impressed, as were the suits at Columbia/Sony. Without even telling his daughter, Mathew sent the song to Sony Pictures for consideration on the upcoming soundtrack to the new *Charlie's Angels* film, which starred Cameron Diaz, Drew Barrymore, and Lucy Liu. It was accepted; Destiny's Child would be featured on the album with "Independent Women." The girls then went into the studio and recorded the song. (They had actually first recorded it with Farrah.)

"Independent Women" was released as the first single from the *Charlie's Angels* soundtrack in the fall of 2000 and would stay at number one on the *Billboard* Hot 100 for eleven consecutive weeks. The tune's staying power would be demonstrated fourteen years after its original release when a rendition of its catchy melody was used by retail giant Target in a 2014 back-to-school TV commercial.

On July 24, 2000, as the girls performed in Hershey, Pennsylvania, their record label announced that Farrah had left Destiny's Child after just five months. Billy B. recalled, "I remember an interview we did where Beyoncé said, 'We have a job to do, a responsibility to each other. We show up. If you don't show up, unfortunately you lose your job. It's that simple.' I remember thinking how tough it must be to, on one hand, befriend these girls but, on the other, be equipped to let them go if necessary."

Michelle was signed to an official contract just as a tour with Christina

Aguilera was finalized. It would kick off at the end of July and continue through mid-October with a punishing schedule of thirty-four dates across the country.

"All of the bad seeds are now *out* of Destiny's Child," Beyoncé said in a television interview at this time. Maybe it wasn't the most magnanimous way of putting things, but it was definitely how she felt.

With the applause of appreciative crowds still ringing in her ears after the Christina Aguilera tour, Beyoncé Knowles returned to Houston satisfied with herself and with her group. Maybe she was becoming a little too satisfied, though. Some of her actions of late did seem out of character. Perhaps it was only natural that she would be affected by her success, especially in that it came at a time in her adolescence when she was just beginning to define who she was as a young woman. She'd certainly been in her teenage-rebellion mode for some time now, often disagreeing with Mathew on important issues—par for the course between them—and sometimes even sassing her mother, which definitely wasn't acceptable to Tina.

One afternoon in November, Beyoncé, Tina, and Mathew were browsing in a record store when "No, No, No" began to play on the sound system. The Knowleses paused for a second to acknowledge the moment; it felt good. Tina then asked Beyoncé a question. However, Beyoncé found herself distracted by some cute guys who'd noticed her. "I was like, 'Oh yeah! I'm hot,'" she later recalled. She started singing along with her own voice, sexily moving her shoulders to the music and acting oblivious to the stares of the young men. When she didn't respond to her mother, Tina asked the question again. Still no response. "I'm *talking to you, Beyoncé*," Tina said, frustrated. Still no response. Beyoncé was just too involved with showing off for the opposite sex to care about her mom. Finally, Tina had enough. She hauled off and smacked Beyoncé hard, right across the face. Beyoncé was shocked, and her eyes went wide with alarm.

A startled Mathew ran over to his wife and daughter. "What in the world are you doing?" he demanded of Tina. This was unusual behavior. Mathew and Tina never physically disciplined the girls. "I just didn't get spankings growing up," Beyoncé later recounted. "They didn't believe in that."

"She thinks she's hot stuff," Tina said angrily. "Nobody cares about that record," she said, now facing Beyoncé, her eyes flashing. "You are *still* my child," she concluded.

Beyoncé was so stunned, she couldn't even speak.

"I brought you into this world," Tina said, still upset, "and I can take you right out of it. Now go sit in the car!"

"Tina had been seeing little signs of Beyoncé getting a big head," said one of her relatives, "and she didn't like it. She wanted to put an end to it in a dramatic way, and she certainly did just that. She didn't feel badly about it, either. 'It had to be done,' she said. Later she told both Beyoncé and Solange, 'I will set you straight when I see the need to do so, so don't y'all forget it. I mean business.' It never happened again, at least not to my knowledge."

"It was the best thing she could have ever done," Beyoncé would say many years later, "because for the first time I realized I was losing sight of what was important." When she talks about it today, she can't help but laugh. "She slapped the *crap* out of me," she told interviewer Steve Jones on television many years after the fact. "Well, I needed it," she said. "And guess what? When my child does it, I'm gonna do the same thing."

Why Ruin the Moment?

*I*n January 2001, Beyoncé Knowles and Lyndall Locke had been together for seven years. She was twelve when they met. Now she was nineteen and he was twenty-one.

A month earlier, Lyndall had joined Beyoncé on the West Coast on a business trip; the two stayed at the plush Beverly Wilshire hotel in Beverly Hills. "She told me that this was the hotel where Richard Gere and Julia Roberts shot *Pretty Woman*," he recalled. "She was excited about staying there. While she was working, I ran into [actor] Brian Dennehy in the elevator. I didn't know what to say, I was so tongue-tied. Then I found an old-school barbershop, got a nice shave and [hair]cut, and, on my way back to the hotel, ended up being harassed by a couple of cops. It was sort of ugly. They weren't used to seeing a young brother in that particular neck of the woods. So at that point I was definitely not feeling this new world of Beyoncé's."

A couple weeks later, on December 31, the Knowleses would be invited to NBA all-star Lakers player Shaquille O'Neal's New Year's Eve party in Los Angeles. The party was to take place at the recently opened Staples Center; Destiny's Child—who'd just received *Billboard*'s 2000 Artist of the Year award—was scheduled to perform. For safety reasons, it had been decided by Staples officials to stop serving liquor in the arena at 11:00 p.m. "But it was New Year's Eve and my whole thing was, 'Hell no. I want to drink,'" Lyndall recalls. "So I left the Staples Center and walked all the way back to the limousine that had taken us there—must have taken me thirty minutes. When I got there, I filled a big ol' Styrofoam cup with booze that was stocked in the vehicle, and then walked back to where we were all sitting." Upon his return, Mathew and Tina gave Lyndall a stern look of disapproval.

A few days later, Mathew had words with Lyndall. "Why are you *still* not representing yourself well?" he asked him. Returning to the limo for liquor was, as Mathew put it, "definitely not cool. How do you think that makes Beyoncé look?"

Filled with remorse, Lyndall could do nothing but agree. He had made a vow to be more concerned about Beyoncé's image, and now he had slipped up once again. "It's like I'm still down on the street corner in the 'hood, and you guys are way up there on the hill, ain't it?" he asked Mathew.

"*Then get your black ass up the hill,*" Mathew exclaimed. He said he couldn't help but wonder how many more times he was going to have to tell Lyndall to check himself. He then again asked: What was it going to take for Lyndall to be the kind of man with whom Beyoncé could be seen in public?

"Maybe I'm not that guy," Lyndall said sadly. "I know who I am, Big Mac. And maybe I'm just not that guy."

Mathew nodded, smiled, and shrugged his shoulders. "Okay," he said, patting Lyndall on the back. "I get it," he added, looking at him earnestly. "See you 'round, then, brother," he concluded as he walked away. To Lyndall, it felt as if in that moment Mathew Knowles had completely washed his hands of him.

The next day, Beyoncé took her turn with Lyndall. "You *so* didn't have to do that shit with the cup of booze," she told him. In fact, she disapproved of it anytime Lyndall drank alcohol. (Once, a writer for *Rolling Stone* wrote that she'd been drinking champagne at an after-party hosted by Wyclef Jean; she took umbrage. "I *don't* drink," she later told the magazine.)

Lyndall agreed with Beyoncé that the enormous cup of liquor had been a bad idea. However, he explained that he'd felt so uncomfortable and out of place at the event, he just needed some reinforcement. "All of those famous people high-fiving each other, slapping each other on the backs, and talking show business," he told her, "made me feel like I didn't belong." In fact, he said that he would have been a lot more comfortable sitting next to the chauffeur in the front seat of the limo and just having a nice quiet drink with him.

"Boy, stop your *trippin'*!" Beyoncé said, frowning. She then leaned her five-foot-seven frame into his own, which was just slightly taller. Giving her a lopsided, boyish grin, he pulled her in even closer, sliding his hands down her back. He loved her, he said, and didn't want to embarrass her. "But I gotta be honest with you, Beyoncé," he confessed, "I'm feeling like I'm getting in way over my head."

"You're *not*," she insisted. "But you really have to be more *conscious* of how things look," she said. "We talked about this before! I need to worry about..."

"I know... your *image*," Lyndall said, with an edge to his voice.

"I promise you," she said, "that one day I'll be such a big star, it won't matter what people say."

Before she could continue, he pulled her in and kissed her fully on the mouth. Years later, Lyndall Locke would say that he didn't believe for a second that a time would ever come when it wouldn't matter to Beyoncé what people said about her. But why ruin the moment?

A Man in Her Life. Not a Boy.

*I*t had been building for some time. By the beginning of 2001, it was obvious that Beyoncé's time with Lyndall was about to end. As often happens in troubled relationships, the two began to argue about subjects that weren't really at issue, since the ones that actually were crucial—such as what he was going to do with his life—seemed to have no easy resolution. For instance, they began to have petty disagreements about her hectic schedule.

Very often, Beyoncé would blow into town after having been on the road for a while and expect Lyndall to be completely available to her. It was understandable that she wanted to spend time with him. "I was in love," she would later say, "and it was so scary. Just the thought of completely letting go was dangerous."

Taura Stinson recalled, "My impression of the situation was that once Beyoncé started to see her dreams come true, she wanted to focus more on this love thing. So, she started to embrace the relationship with Lyndall even more, but she was also incredibly busy, which complicated things."

It was also understandable that Lyndall didn't want to feel controlled by Beyoncé and be ruled by her unpredictable itinerary. "We had this conversation multiple times," he recalled, "where I would tell her, 'Look, don't expect me to drop everything just because you come back home to Houston.' I was trying to act like I had a life. Who was I kidding? I didn't have no life. I just didn't want her to know it. I was dabbling with rapping at the time, like all of my friends, but I sure was no a rapper. I was a long way from being serious about it."

On February 8, 2001, Destiny's Child had a major concert in San Antonio at the Freeman Coliseum, then another brief performance five days later at the Hasbro corporate office in New York. At Hasbro, the girls were scheduled to do a few songs for the executives to celebrate the brand-new Destiny's Child dolls, which would hit the market in September. The original plan had been to go straight from Texas to New York. However, Beyoncé decided to pop into Houston on February 10 for two days, and then go on to New York from there. "Guess what, Lynnie?" she asked on the telephone with him. "I'm back! Let's hang out. It's Saturday night. Come on over!"

"No, Beyoncé," Lyndall said, already standing his ground. "I have plans. We talked about this! I told you, please don't surprise me, girl. I'm going to the studio with Joe and them, and I'll call you after."

"*Who the hell is Joe and them?*" Beyoncé demanded to know.

"Joe is one of my best friends and..." He stopped himself. "Wait a minute. Why the heck am I explaining this to you? I'll see you later, girl." And with that, he hung up the phone.

When he was finished with his friends, Lyndall dragged himself back to Mathew and Tina's home on Swan Isle Boulevard. He'd earlier smoked a couple of joints with "Joe and them," which was obvious by his demeanor. "You're high?" Beyoncé asked when he showed up at her door. "Are you kidding me?"

The two then had a raging argument about his not wanting to spend time with her. In the moment, Lyndall couldn't help but acknowledge to himself that the only reason she was able to have such a complete airing of her emotions was probably because she felt so comfortable with him.

Rather than continue to argue with her, Lyndall got up. "I'm outta here," he announced, heading for the door.

"Oh no," she said, "I don't *think* so."

"I know you're used to being treated like a star out on the road, but here, in this house? Here, you ain't no star, Beyoncé," he said. "Here, you're just the girl I love. Okay?"

"You don't have to tell me that," she said, insulted.

They parted company.

The next morning, as was their custom on Sundays when she was in town, Beyoncé and Lyndall attended St. John's Church together. Afterward, with Beyoncé driving her gray Jag—rare in that he was usually behind the wheel—the two drove over to Lyndall's mother's home for a moment so that he could change clothes and they could then spend the day together. Or at least that's what she expected to happen. However, Lyndall had already planned to spend the day watching the football play-offs with his father, Stephen. When he told Beyoncé of his plans, she said, "What are you talking about? You don't even *like* your dad! Since when do you spend time with *him?*"

"Yeah, but I'm working on that," Lyndall said defensively. "I already had this thing planned," he continued. "I *told* you not to expect me to drop everything just because you come home for a weekend! If you ain't down with that, you ain't down with me."

He then got out of the car. The two argued for about five more minutes while he was leaning into the passenger side of the vehicle. She explained she would be back in Houston for the annual Rodeo Houston show at the Reliant Astrodome in a week, but that there was no way she would be able to see him on that day because she'd be too busy with soundchecks with the crew, rehearsal with the girls, press interviews, and then the show itself. After that, the group had a full touring schedule that would keep them busy through the end of March. Then she would have to go to Los Angeles to put the finishing touches on her first movie, *Carmen: A Hip Hopera*, for MTV. In fact, she actually had no idea when she would be back in Houston, she said. If they wanted to spend time with each other, it had to be now. To Lyndall, it felt like an ultimatum. "You know what, Beyoncé?" he finally told her, frustrated. "Maybe we should just break up, then. I mean, if you don't have time for me."

She looked at him as if he had lost his mind. "What is the *matter* with you?" she demanded to know. "We are not breaking up over *this* bullshit."

"Well, maybe we are," he said.

"For real?" Beyoncé asked. "That's how it is?"

"Yeah," Lyndall shot back. "That's how it is."

Lyndall backed away from the Jag. Beyoncé put the vehicle in reverse, stepped on the gas, and peeled away without looking back.

She of Little Experience

Lyndall tried to smooth things over. He telephoned her constantly, hoping to reconcile with her. "Yo, Kelly! Tell Beyoncé to call me," he kept telling Kelly Rowland. "Boy, stop!" Kelly shot back. "She doesn't want to talk to you. So step off!"

"He has his nerve, throwing *you* shade," Solange said in front of some friends. "I'll go over there and show him what's what, if you want me to."

At fifteen, Solange was five years younger than Beyoncé, but in recent years she had also become her greatest champion. "If someone has a problem with my sister, that person has a problem with me," she liked to say. She was feisty, no one's pushover. As they got older, she and Beyoncé could not have been more different. Whereas Beyoncé often had trouble expressing her emotions, Solange was easily able to access her anger. Also, whereas Beyoncé had very few friends, Solange had an extremely busy social life. She had her own ideas about styling, too. Beyoncé was more than happy to adhere to Tina's advice when it came to the clothes she and the girls in her group wore and how they did their makeup, but not Solange. She had her own fashion sense—and usually it confounded Tina because it was so unusual. When Kelly broke her toe during the Christina Aguilera tour, Mathew finally let Solange into the group to replace her for a few shows. That's when Solange knew she didn't want to be in Destiny's Child, or in any other group, for that matter. She was more than satisfied to be one of the group's backup dancers, and even then she had a mind of her own.

In 2001, when Destiny's Child performed at an NBA Finals game in Philadelphia between that city's 76ers and the Los Angeles Lakers, Beyoncé, Michelle, and Kelly showed support for both teams by wearing a mixture of their colors and logos. However, Solange and another girl danced behind Destiny's Child in yellow tops and purple shorts, which are Lakers' colors. At the end of their performance of "Bootylicious," the whole ensemble was roundly booed. Piqued, Solange raised both hands to the audience and hollered something—it's not clear what—making it clear that she was annoyed. Later, she would report that she was taken to task for the small outburst. She didn't say by whom, but one would imagine it was by Mathew. "This is where I got in so much trouble for pop'n off," she said. "They boo'd us. At the end I put my hands up and was like, 'booooooo' *back* at ya'll." (Solange wasn't the only one who showed her displeasure in the moment. As the audience jeered, Beyoncé raised her mike above her head and appeared to surreptitiously give the crowd the middle finger!)

"She beats to a different drummer," is how Mathew put it in speaking of Solange, who, like Beyoncé, says, "I was fortunate to grow up in a mecca of incredible women." She later told writer Michael Hall, "I never defined myself by my sister. I have my own musical ideas, and marketing ideas, and imaging ideas. I have had arguments with my dad about the meaning of success. His meaning: at the end of the day, having something to show for how hard you worked—a wonderful home and wonderful family. My meaning: At the end of the day, I want to feel good about what I'm doing. No regrets. I want to *love* what I do."

In 2001, Solange sang the title song for the new animated television series *The Proud Family*, backed by Destiny's Child. It sounded exactly like a DC performance, though, and stylistically, Solange resembled her older sister. It would still be some time before she would find her own definition of herself.

"I could make him real sorry," Solange said of Lyndall, "that chump." Beyoncé asked her sister to please just stay out of it. Most people in their circle felt Lyndall was lucky Beyoncé didn't ask Solange to fight this particular battle for her.

After a few weeks, Lyndall finally stopped trying to reach Beyoncé. "All the while when we were fighting in the driveway, I was like, 'She ain't goin' nowhere. *I got this*,'" he would recall many years later. "I knew marriage was very important to her. Because we had always had this agreement that we'd end up married, I guess I was overconfident. But then when she was gone, she was really gone. I couldn't believe it."

"You don't need to be thinking about Lyndall anymore," Mathew told Beyoncé. "It's run its course. These things don't last forever," he told her. Of course, he knew Beyoncé was heartbroken, but the fact remained that she'd only had one boyfriend in her lifetime. Tina thought that maybe it was time for Beyoncé to play the field a little and see other fellows, and Mathew had to agree. "But not too many, because we've got a lot of work to do," he warned her. He definitely did not want her distracted by romance at this time in her life.

"She wasn't boy crazy anyway," recalled Destiny Child's voice teacher, Kim Wood Sandusky, who spent a great deal of time on the road with Beyoncé. "The three of them, Kelly and Michelle included, were looking for a man that would be in for the long term, who would grow old with them, have children, a family. They weren't out to just play around.

"I remember we were in New Orleans, leaving on a bus for Houston, when we got into a deep spiritual conversation about their potential mates," Sandusky recalled. "They were Christian girls who believed they'd meet their mates in God's time. I didn't know what the status was between Beyoncé and Lyndall. I felt, though, that it was a probably a first-love situation that had run its course."

In years to come, Beyoncé would be linked with the rappers Nas, Marques Houston, and Sean Paul, and actor and hip-hop artist Mos Def. She was even linked to basketball player Kobe Bryant, as was Kelly Rowland before her. However, Beyoncé would never have any sort of significant relationship with any of those men, despite what some would like to believe. In many ways, she was sheltered and protected, but by her own choosing. "I've always been very, very specific and very choosy—*very choosy*—about what I do with my body," she said in December 2014 in a short film she made entitled *Yours and Mine*, "and who I want to share that with."

Consider this: Beyoncé was with Lyndall Locke and loyal to him from the age of twelve to about nineteen. She loved him, and there was no way she would ever cheat on him. As she got older, she remained as devout as ever in her Christian beliefs that simply would not allow her to be promiscuous—not that she had any desire to be, anyway. "She was overseas somewhere, and she thought, 'I need to go to church,'" recalled her godmother, Linda Thomas, when speaking of Beyoncé's religious devotion, "so she jumped on an airplane and came to Houston to go to [St. John's] church, which says a lot for the church and a lot for her." Buttressed by her faith, she was more than satisfied with one boyfriend and never questioned her monogamy to him, no matter how many eligible and maybe even more suitable men were after her, especially after she became famous.

Then, at pretty much the same time it was over with Lyndall, another man would come into Beyoncé's life and she would be with him exclusively—as she is to this day. There would be very little lag time between the two paramours. Or, as Lydia Locke put it, "There was nobody between my son and the next man in Beyoncé's life. She went from A to B . . . and that was it."

First Screen Kiss

*B*eyoncé wasn't happy, and it wasn't because of Lyndall Locke, either. At least not in this moment. Standing before director Robert Townsend in her cream-colored silk robe, her face free of makeup and her honey-blonde hair pulled back from her face, she appeared even younger than her twenty years. Townsend had been wondering why she hadn't been on the set of *Carmen: A Hip Hopera.* Usually she arrived before everyone else, eager and ready to work. Though she'd never acted before, she was more than game. No matter how demanding a scene—crying, arguing, rapping, and even dying—she persisted in it until it was as close to perfection as possible. Today's challenge, though, seemed insurmountable to her, as Townsend would learn after he found her brooding in her dressing room. "I've had this day on my calendar for a month," she told the director. "Today's the day I have to . . . *kiss him.*" She was referring to her love interest in the movie, the twenty-six-year-old, ruggedly handsome Mekhi Phifer. "I don't think I can do it," she said.

"But I believe you can," Robert told her, putting his hand on her slim shoulder. "I know this is your first kissing scene, but I can help you with it."

"Do I really kiss him, though?" Beyoncé asked. "I mean, does he have to put his lips on mine? And . . . um . . . do I have to put my tongue in . . . you know? . . . his *mouth?*"

"Well, yeah," Robert answered. "I mean, it's got to look *real*, Beyoncé.' "

He couldn't help but be a little astonished by her innocence, her naïveté. After all, like most people, Townsend had been enthralled by her music videos and television appearances in which she looked anything but chaste in tight leather miniskirts and low-cut silk blouses. Getting to know her for the last few weeks, however, Robert came to understand that her seductive video and stage performances were all the result of smoke and mirrors. The truth about her was that not only did she have no real acting experience, but she seemed painfully short on life experience too. True, she could project herself in a tantalizing way in a music video, but being filmed while actually kissing a man? That was a stretch. "But it's all part of acting," he told her, his tone reassuring. "You're a beautiful woman," he added, stating the obvious. "You're going to do a lot of love stories in your career. Try this: We use a term called substitution," he continued. "If you've had a boyfriend in the past, pretend Mekhi is that guy. Kiss him as you would your boyfriend."

From the expression on Beyoncé's face, Townsend recalled that her wheels seemed to be turning. Of course, she could use her most cherished memories as he had suggested. "How often do I have to do it?" she asked.

"If you give it to me really good, we may only have to go with three takes," Robert said. "But I need it to be right, Beyoncé," he warned her. "You can't just kiss him on the cheek. It has to be passionate."

"Okay," she decided. "I'll do it."

After two hours of hair and makeup, Beyoncé was on set with about forty technicians—cameramen, key grips, lighting people, and the rest— staring at her, not to mention the cast. The scene began. Trying to ignore everyone, she locked herself into a determined embrace with Mekhi Phifer. Then, as her hands began to caress his head, she went in for the kiss. It was tentative. "Cut!" Robert exclaimed. "One more take," he declared. "You're holding back with your tongue," he told her. "I need more tongue." Beyoncé cringed. "Oh my Lord," she muttered. But she also nodded, determined to see it through.

Take two was better. "Cut! Make it *juicier*," Robert said. "Take three." She went for it again, this time fully committing, wanting to please. As she caressed his head, she kissed Mekhi with more passion than she probably thought possible in front of a camera. "Cut!" Townsend said with a big smile. "Not bad," he added, seeming happy.

There would be two more takes—one just because her mane of hair got in the way of the shot. Then, finally, it happened with take six—the kiss everyone had been waiting for, the "money shot"—and it was definitely worth the wait. Beyoncé kissed Mekhi as if the two were truly in love. It was intense, it was genuine ... it was great. "Cut," Townsend said when the scene was over. "We have it now! Good job, Beyoncé! Amazing."

"Dude! Get her off me!" Mekhi Phifer exclaimed. Feigning panic, the actor extricated himself from Beyoncé's hold, causing everyone on the set to dissolve into laughter. "I'm out here trying to be a *professional*," Phifer, a real ham, continued to gripe, "and this girl, she's all over me. Somebody tell her we're supposed to be *acting* here! I mean…*doggone!*" By this time, Beyoncé was doubled over as well. "That wasn't so bad at all," she said, clearly relieved.

Carmen: A Hip Hopera

$\mathcal{T}$he vehicle chosen for Beyoncé's acting debut, the television movie *Carmen: A Hip Hopera*, was a made-for-cable movie based not only on Georges Bizet's famous 1875 opera, but also influenced by African-American adaptations of *Carmen* from 1943 (on Broadway, starring Muriel Smith and Muriel Rahn alternating in the lead) and 1954 (on film, starring Harry Belafonte, Dorothy Dandridge, and Pearl Bailey). The rest of the cast of this MTV version included the aforementioned Mekhi Phifer, Mos Def, and cameos from contemporary hip-hop stars such as Jermaine Dupri, Lil' Bow Wow, Wyclef Jean, and Da Brat.

In the movie, Beyoncé plays seductress Carmen Brown, a vixen who becomes romantically and tragically involved with a cop, Sergeant Derek Hill (Phifer). After a series of misadventures set against a decidedly urban backdrop, Carmen—a fledgling singer and actress—dies, the victim of gun violence.

Directed by Robert Townsend, the brilliant director (and star) of 1987's *Hollywood Shuffle* and 1991's *The Five Heartbeats*, the movie was the perfect setting for Beyoncé to expand her horizons. Because she sings and raps in so much of it, it felt like familiar terrain. However, the actual acting in it was completely new for her. When Townsend had suggested her to MTV, the executives were skeptical. They knew she was beautiful and talented, but they doubted that she could act. Maybe they should go for an accomplished actress? But Townsend felt it important to cast a singer in the role, otherwise they would have to teach an actress how to rap, and, as he later put it, "good luck with that."

Though he hadn't yet met Beyoncé, he had an intuition about her. He knew in his gut that she could pull it off just by virtue of the way she performed in her music videos. She had the right instincts. He believed she knew how to act even if she didn't know she was doing it. So he telephoned Mathew and asked if Beyoncé might consider auditioning. He was a little nervous about even asking. "She was a pretty big star, and I was worried that she'd be insulted to have to read for a role," Townsend recalled. "But the word back to me was, 'Yeah, of course, she would be more than happy to audition.'"

Weeks later, Beyoncé met Townsend in MTV's New York office, accompanied by an A&R woman from her label and her bodyguard. A major reason for Townsend's success as a director is his knack for extracting the best performances from his actors and actresses. Part of that talent has to do with his understanding of people; he knows how to read them. It seemed to him that, though she tried to hide it, Beyoncé was, as he later put it, "freaking out" about the audition. He wanted to find a way to calm her nerves so that she could not only get through the audition, but also deliver her best performance.

"We're going to do a little improv," Townsend told his three visitors. "You guys are gonna act, too," he told the A&R woman and the bodyguard.

"But I'm no actor, Mr. Townsend," the bodyguard said, genuinely frightened.

"Well, my friend, today you are," Townsend told him.

The conceit would be that the bodyguard was a rap superstar who'd just performed in concert, and the A&R woman and Beyoncé were backstage groupies. "Just roll with it," Townsend told them. "Whatever you think you'd say in this situation, say it. Create a scene. Play with it and have fun."

As it happened, the record company employee and guard were so out of their elements and anxious about it, they could barely get through the improvisation. "The more nervous they were, the more relaxed Beyoncé became," recalled Townsend. "When she realized that she was really in her own lane, she started to get into it. That's when I could really start seeing her chops, and guess what? She definitely had chops!

"Beyoncé and I then talked for thirty minutes about the script," he continued. "'I can't wait to do the death scene,' she told me. So I said, 'Great. Let's do it. Let me see.' She must have done that death scene twenty different ways. She rolled around on the carpet in her stilettos. She crawled. I gave her direction like, 'You just got shot,' and she immediately reacted. Or, 'This time, you've over a rail in a theater and you look down and you feel your body leaving, leaving, leaving you . . . now,' and she acted it out. I thought to myself, 'Okay, cool, she gets it. She's not afraid to make a fool of herself. She's not afraid to fail, to look ugly, to make crazy expressions, to yell, to scream. Plus, she's also fearless.' And as an actress, if you're fearless, that's a major component to being great. Therefore, the next day I went back to the MTV brass and said, 'She can do it. This girl is an actress. Trust me. We need to cast her in this movie.' And we did.

"She was a gladiator throughout the entire production," he concluded. "When the dailies started coming in, the MTV guys said, 'She's never acted before? Are you sure? Because she's so damn good!'"

Carmen: A Hip Hopera was positioned by Beyoncé's creative team—led, of course, by Mathew—as an experiment to see just how well she might perform as an actress. The venture was a success. Besides her capable acting, Beyoncé looked great in the wardrobe—especially a crimson sequined dress that in her first few scenes shows off her legs to optimal effect. Numerous shots linger on her svelte curves.

Largely because of her prior work in music videos, Beyoncé seemed completely prepared to project herself in the best possible way in *Carmen: A Hip Hopera*. She intuitively knew her best angles; she understood not only how to make the most of each of her scenes, but also how to be generous to her fellow actors by allowing them to shine too. It helps a lot that the dialogue is punctuated by rap numbers (which essentially drive the storyline) and occasional singing; one song, "If Looks Could Kill (You Would Be Dead)," by Beyoncé and Mos Def, is a real standout. Today some critics feel that she is better in this, her acting debut, than in many of her subsequent movies.

Beyoncé explained of her role, "It's very risqué, and I wouldn't do any of the things she does in real life. I was concerned about my image," she admitted, "and how the kids—my audience—would take it.

"For instance, there's a seduction scene that I thought was a little too R-rated. There were moments I wanted to tone down. Robert was cool. He didn't want me to play anything that made me uncomfortable. Somehow, we made it work.

"I had my eyes wide open the whole time," she recalled. "Here I was, this kid from Houston with no acting experience telling this amazing director how I wanted to play the role. I felt like I had no business doing that. But in the end, I knew that it was going to be my image up there on the screen and I had to protect it. Destiny's Child is sexy, but don't get it twisted: We're not *bad* girls."

The filming of *Carmen* on a soundstage on Sunset Boulevard in Hollywood took Beyoncé miles away from her comfort zone of Houston family and friends, and catapulted her into a brand-new world. She was surrounded by a different set of people whose major passion wasn't music, it was acting. "My downtime during *Carmen* forced me to learn how to talk to people," she would say, "to let my guard down and be myself—all of that stuff that most girls probably learn how to do when they're thirteen."

Throughout the process of filming, Beyoncé forced herself to be open to new points of view—and sometimes even conflict—from wardrobe stylists, makeup artists, technicians, other actors, and, of course, director Townsend. "I found that there really are good people in the world," she recalled, "that maybe I didn't have to have my guard up all the time. I was always so scared, thinking people were out to get me. I don't want to say that's how I was raised, but definitely we closed ranks in my family."

Carmen: A Hip Hopera would air on MTV on May 8, 2001.

Enter Jay Z

*I*t was early January 2002. Beyoncé, now twenty, was putting the finishing touches on Destiny Child's third album before going to Los Angeles to work on the film *Austin Powers in Goldmember*, with Mike Myers. It would be her second acting role. Though she was nervous about it, she'd been somewhat boosted by her success in *Carmen: A Hip Hopera* and had confidence that she could pull it off. Tina would be joining her on the West Coast in a couple of weeks. She had to stay in Houston for a while and be available to sit for legal depositions concerning the lawsuits that had been filed by LaTavia and LeToya.

One evening before Beyoncé departed, she, Kelly, Tina, and two friends of theirs who lived in Houston went out for dinner at their favorite soul food restaurant, This Is It, in Houston. Beyoncé started the evening off by talking about the way it had ended with Lyndall. "Now I don't even know what's out there for me," she lamented.

"Well, what about Jay?" Kelly wanted to know, speaking of Jay Z. (Most people in his world call him Jay.) Beyoncé shrugged. "I'm still trying to get past Lyndall. I guess I have no choice but to try."

Beyoncé's makeup artist, Billy B., concluded, "Here's the truth. Lyndall had made it easy for Beyoncé. He let her off the hook, gave her a reason to move on, because all of us who knew her agreed that if Lyndall had pushed just a little harder, she might *still* be with him! He gave up too fast. She wasn't going to move on unless she had no choice, because that's just who she was at the time—loyal to Lyndall, or, maybe more to the point, loyal to the *idea* of Lyndall. She would have stayed with him 'till the cows came home. But at the end of the day, a major star like Beyoncé Knowles does not end up with a nice kid from the block named Lyndall Locke."

"I definitely believe that Lyndall intentionally pushed Beyoncé away," said his mother, Lydia. "I think he knew on some level that the only way both could truly grow into adulthood was separate and apart from one another. He did it for her as much as for himself."

Beyoncé had met Jay Z a few months earlier as a result of a song called "I Got It" by the rapper/singer Amil (Amil Kahala Whitehead). Mathew had cut a deal with Roc-A-Fella Records, Jay Z's label, for Beyoncé to appear on the recording as an experiment just to put her in the public eye as a solo act. This was back in early 2000, around the time of the LaTavia and LeToya disagreements, when Beyoncé was waffling about a career sans Destiny's Child.

When Beyoncé showed up in the studio to record her part of Amil's song, Amil wasn't present for the session. Beyoncé raced through her parts of the song quickly, leaving the studio feeling she'd done her best. A few days later, Jay called to tell her he admired her work and wanted to talk to her about a possible duet with him. She was intrigued, as was Mathew when she told him about it. There was no arguing that Jay Z was one of the most—if not *the* most—successful stars in the rap universe. What would it mean for Beyoncé's career to record a duet with him? Father and daughter agreed that it could be very interesting.

On October 20, 2001, Destiny's Child was on the bill with Jay Z and dozens of other acts at Madison Square Garden for the "Concert for New York City." This was a benefit show to honor not only the first responders from the New York Fire and Police departments to the tragedy of 9/11, but also those lost that tragic morning. There were dozens of stars on the bill, though Beyoncé didn't know most of them. That wasn't unusual. In fact, at about this time, MTV had asked her to work the red carpet for them, interviewing celebrities as they arrived for the MTV Movie Awards. The problem was that she didn't recognize any of the celebrities. Her makeup artist, Billy B., had to race up to her as each star approached and whisper the name in her ear: "That's Jim Carrey and his wife!" "That's Robert Downey!" He recalled, "She'd been working so hard for so long, she was completely out of touch with pop culture. We laughed our asses off that day, it was hysterical." Jay Z, though, was someone Beyoncé very much admired, so when she finally met him backstage at the Garden, she was impressed, as were Kelly and Michelle. When he casually asked for her number, she gave it to him. For the next couple of months, they talked on the telephone from time to time, getting to know one another.

A couple months later, Jay visited Beyoncé in Houston. "My sister Cheryl [LaTavia's mother] happened to be with Beyoncé when she saw Jay Z," recalled Yvonne Boyd. "She told me that while she was talking to Beyoncé, she was watching Jay Z out of the corner of her eye. He was talking to one of his friends and motioning toward Beyoncé. Cheryl thought she could read his lips and that he said, *'I'm gonna get her.'* "

Jay may have been self-assured, cocky even, as a result of his success, but apparently he did have certain self-esteem issues when he was a kid, at least according to his mentor, Jaz-O. "They talked about him bad when he was young, calling him 'Big-Lipped Shawn' and names like that," Jaz-O recalled. "But by the time he met Beyoncé, it wasn't about his looks anyway. It was, 'Okay, now, I got money. I got prestige. I got all street hustlers wanting to be me. I got rap artists wanting to spit like me. My stock is way up. So now I need a super prom queen.' Therefore, as a man growing into his own power, he would endeavor to pursue the most attractive girl out of the pack."

Before Beyoncé, Jay had gone from girl to girl. He was once involved with the singer Blu Cantrell; he also dated the late singer Aaliyah and the actress Rosario Dawson. It was also reported that a model named Shennelle Scott gave birth to a baby fathered by Jay. There are a couple of other reports like this one as well, other women who claim that Jay fathered their children before he was involved with Beyoncé. Jay Z has always denied they are true. "There were girls around," his friend Chenise Wilson told Jay's biographer Zack O'Malley, "but that wasn't his thing, being in girls' faces. He had his share, but he wasn't the kind of guy with a whole lot of girls. Jay is a very particular guy."

"He had his own way, know what I'm sayin'?" observed DeHaven Irby, a childhood friend of Jay Z's. "His own swag. He wasn't aggressive, he was smooth. Still, he was a player. I don't think Beyoncé could be described in the same way."

Another friend of Jay's reports, "He was a smooth talker, especially back then. He told Beyoncé, 'I've been with a lot of women, but I was always looking for you, girl.' It was a good line, but I'm not sure it landed the way Jay hoped."

Though Beyoncé and Jay were very different, Tina noted that lasting romance often grows from a good friendship and recalled that she "wasn't exactly crazy" about Mathew when she first started dating him, but that he later grew on her. She suggested that Beyoncé give Jay a chance, that she at least wait until she went out on a date with him before she made a decision about him. Though Beyoncé said she'd do as her mom suggested, she didn't seem very enthusiastic about it. Or as her uncle Larry Beyincé (Tina's brother and Angie's father) later put it, "He was after her and she wasn't interested. She told me she wasn't particularly fond of him. I heard rumors that they were together and she told me no. You know how women get that, like, '*Ewww.*' I guess she wasn't attracted to him."

If Jay did have his sights set on Beyoncé, he couldn't have selected a person more unlike himself. Certainly one of the aspects of his life that Beyoncé couldn't really relate to was his materialistic side. For him, everything was about money, and he would be the first to admit it. With his designer clothes, his platinum and gold jewelry, his private jets…everything about Jay spelled out success, in arguably the most crass, blatant terms. But that's the hip-hop world in a nutshell, really. The culture is all about materialistic excess. "Hell, yeah, for as long as I've known him, Jay has been motivated by money," observed Choke No Joke (whose real name is Arthur Alston); he worked as Damon Dash's videographer for Roc-A-Fella Records from 2000 to 2005. "Beyoncé is motivated by the challenge and the thrill of victory, not by money. You never hear her brag about money. I mean, she may name-drop some handbags, perfume, stuff like that in her lyrics, but her world does not revolve around materialism and riches, like Jay's. You couldn't even tell me what kind of car she drives."

In contrast to Jay Z, Beyoncé was, at this time of her life, in a "saving for a rainy day" phase. For instance, she and her good friend Taura Stinson visited the Galleria mall in Houston, shopping for new clothes. Beyoncé walked into the Christian Dior store and began admiring a floor-length tutu. Its cost was $2,200. "That is really cute," Taura told her. "You could wear it with a leather jacket! The contrast would be crazy!" Beyoncé studied the dress critically. "But can I afford this?" she asked. "I mean, two thousand dollars?" In fact, around this time she was in negotiations for a condominium in Miami—in a section called "Millionaire's Row"—and would also purchase two more condos there, including a studio apartment that was said to be merely a place for her and her guests to change their clothes after going to the beach.) "I mean, those doggone condos are going to wipe me out!" she exclaimed. "There's no way I can afford this dress," she decided as she carefully put it back on the rack." Taura laughed. "Girl, how many hit records have you had? Please! Of course you can afford that dress." Beyoncé's mind was made up, though. No dress. "I just have to be more sensible than that," concluded the woman who is today, thirteen years later, worth about a half billion dollars.

"Bootylicious"

*O*h, hell no," Mathew Knowles said. "*Hell no!*" He was on the telephone with Dan Workman, asking about a song Beyoncé had just finished recording at SugarHill Recording Studios for the third Destiny's Child album. When Dan told him that the tune was called "Bootylicious," Mathew exploded. " '*Bootylicious*'? What is *that* about?" he asked.

"Well, it's sort of a female empowerment song about being proud of… you know… your big… *butt*," Dan said. In that moment, he suddenly wasn't feeling very confident about the song.

"About *what*?" Mathew asked.

"Um… you know… about having a big butt, and… um… being… proud of it," Dan repeated, stammering. "I mean, she's saying something like, 'I don't think you're ready for this… um… *jelly*.' "

"*Oh, hell no*," Mathew repeated. "Beyoncé ain't sayin' no shit like that on no record."

"But you really ought to hear it first," Dan said. "I sent you a rough mix tape. Listen to it, Mathew."

"Look, my daughter ain't putting out no song about having no big butt," Mathew said. "You can count on that!" And with that, he hung up.

The next day, he called back. He had finally listened to the tape. "God-damn!" he exclaimed. "That *is* a hit, isn't it, Dan? I mean, that's a number one record!"

"Told you so," Dan Workman said, laughing. "Didn't I tell you?"

"By the time we got to the third album, it was really just Beyoncé doing the writing and producing," recalled Workman. As he remembered it, now there were no other producers in the room, at least not on the sessions he engineered. He recalled that Beyoncé would always come into the studio with a stack of CDs of tracks she'd been listening to at the time. She'd receive dozens of these tracks on a weekly basis, all submitted to her by various producers around the country who wanted to participate in a Destiny's Child project. After reviewing them, she'd select her favorites. She would write lyrics for the melodies she had chosen, and then enter the studio and put it all together—her lyrics with the tracks. Often she would add elements to the track herself, maybe go back in and make adjustments to what she'd been sent—which might require bringing musicians into the studio. In that case, she would end up with a producer's credit.

"One morning she came into the studio with this track she liked a lot because of a Stevie Nicks guitar riff at its beginning," Workman remembered. "It was from Nicks's song 'Edge of Seventeen,' from her [1981] solo album *Bella Donna*."

Beyoncé told Dan she'd first heard the track on a plane on the way to Japan, and thought it was interesting. The tape had been submitted to her by 8Bit—the former Rob Fusari. She and 8Bit had for the last couple of weeks been going back and forth on the telephone, composing lyrics for it. Though Fusari would be credited on the final product, he and Beyoncé would never actually be in the same room together while coming up with those lyrics, which was not unusual given her hectic schedule. These days a lot of songs were cowritten with people on the other end of a phone line. Now that much of it was done, Beyoncé sat with her legs crossed Indian-style on the wooden effects console behind Workman and began fine-tuning the lyrics, putting pencil to pad: "I don't think you're ready for this jelly / 'cause my body's too bootylicious." As she did so, Kelly Rowland passed the time by watching *Forrest Gump* on a portable DVD player. Michelle wasn't present. "We laughed when Kelly started calling me Lieutenant Dad, after the Gary Sinise character in the movie," Workman recalled.

"As I'm listening to Beyoncé go over and over the lyrics out loud, I was intrigued," he remembered. "When I asked her about the lyrics, she said, 'My whole thing is that it doesn't matter if you're a full-figured girl or what your body looks like, you should be proud of it.' She said she'd been at a radio station interview and one of the disc jockeys made a crack about her being a little thicker than the other girls. 'Young girls today get this message constantly from fashion magazines and TV commercials that you have to be a size two to be sexy,' she told me. 'What I want to say to women is, "No, you don't. You *can* be full-figured. You *can* have a little jelly. Just wear it proudly." *That's* what "Bootylicious" is about.'"

Dan Workman says he, Beyoncé, and Kelly spent about eleven hours in the studio on this one song. "Beyoncé spent ten of those hours writing lyrics and recording lead vocals. She would record three-part background harmony with just her own voice, and then double it—then you'd have six voices. She would stack it, and you would have layer upon layer of her voice. Then she'd listen to the playback of all those Beyoncé voices and say, 'You know, that one take, in the middle, that second one? I need to do that one over again. I made a mistake there. My inflection wasn't quite the same as the others, and my breath was a little different.' I would then isolate her voice on that one little bit and, sure enough, it would be just a tad different than the rest of the takes. However, in the totality of sound, no way could I have heard the discrepancy. Her ear was just so finely tuned, she could pick out a slightly different inflection in a whole sea of sounds. I've never before seen or heard of anybody have that degree of acuity and memory and, you know, savant type of control over what she was doing in the studio."

After Beyoncé pretty much had all of "Bootylicious" recorded with just her voice on all the parts, she sent Kelly into the studio. She stripped her lead vocal from most of the track and had Kelly record those sections herself. As she replaced her voice with Kelly's, she directed her friend every step of the way. Kelly by this time was her own kind of accomplished singer; she recorded the whole song in less than an hour. "She really knocked it out of the ballpark," recalled Dan Workman. "She ended up with most of the song, actually. Michelle came into the studio later and also recorded a small bit in the middle.

"But for the most part, it was just me, Beyoncé, and Kelly in the studio for 'Bootylicious,' a sort of crucible moment for us. I'll be forever grateful for the memory," he recalled. "Beyoncé included me in the process in so many ways: 'Is it too much?' 'Is the syncopation too complex?' 'Is it too weird?' 'Is it too outside the box?' So I admit I have ownership of my feelings about that session. I am fairly certain she did that for all of the producers and engineers she worked with. She knew how to get the best from people by allowing them to also be invested in the work. I had seen that method work so well with ZZ Top, and she did it even better because it was coming from a girl who wasn't even twenty-one! She was so talented she didn't need anything from me but to just shut up and push the levers up and down on the console. Yet when we left the studio that day, after eleven hours together, it felt like my victory too.

"Engineers often say they knew a record was a hit the moment they first heard it," Dan Workman concluded. "I've had that feeling before, but never as strong as that day. I drove home from the studio in my raggedy Toyota pickup truck thinking, 'You know what? This "Bootylicious" thing is going to turn out to be one of the biggest songs I've ever worked on.' I was right. Later, when I heard it on the radio, I was knocked out by it."

Before "Bootylicous" was released, there was some disagreement between 8Bit and Mathew about the distinctive Stevie Nicks sample (meaning a small but recognizable piece of music) that has since helped popularize the song. "I told him, 'Mathew, we need to take that sample out of there,'" said 8Bit. "'Give me a guitar and let me just redo it with a different twist, and I'm telling you, I'll have it feeling just the same if not better.'"

Actually, 8Bit had always intended to replace the Nicks sample anyway. The only reason it was even on the instrumental track he had submitted to Beyoncé was because he couldn't find his old cassette of Survivor's 1982 hit "Eye of the Tiger." He'd originally wanted to use the opening guitar riff from *that* song, but as just a placemark. He was always planning to eventually replace it with his own guitar work. "I'd learned after sampling Stevie Wonder's 'I Wish' for Will Smith's 'Wild Wild West' that I didn't want to lose 50 percent of the publishing for a very small sample," he explained. "Mathew wasn't having it, though. He felt strongly—and he was right, incidentally—that the Nicks sample was so unique and so identifiable, it would bring instant recognition to the song. Besides that, Beyoncé was completely wedded to it. There was no way she would agree to replacing it. So," he concluded, chuckling, "about 50 percent [of the publishing] got cut for that simple, repetitive, one-note Stevie Nicks sample."

When released on May 20, 2001, "Bootylicious"—the second single from Destiny Child's third album, *Survivor*—would go straight to number one on the *Billboard* Top 200. It would remain on the charts for twenty-eight weeks. The word "bootylicious" would become so popular, in fact, that it would be added to the *Oxford English Dictionary* in 2006: "(Of a woman) sexually attractive." (It should be noted, though, that the word was one that rapper Snoop Dogg first used in the 1993 Dr. Dre song "Fuck Wit Dre Day (And Everybody's Celebratin')." However, Snoop used the word to denote something as being weak not powerful, which is entirely different from Beyoncé's intent.)

There was even more controversy, though, after the song was released.

One night, 8Bit was watching Beyoncé being interviewed by Barbara Walters on television when she said she'd heard the Steve Nicks riff on an airplane and was thus inspired to write "Bootylicious." 8Bit thought that a more accurate explanation of what had occurred would have been that he had submitted to her a track he composed for her consideration, and that it included the Stevie Nicks sample...which *then* inspired her to *co*-write "Bootylicious." However, after years of doing television interviews, Beyoncé understood the merit of a good, economical sound bite. In show business, the truth often lies not in the facts but in the telling. The way she described the process was the simplest, easiest way to go about it. Still, 8Bit couldn't help but feel slighted. He reached out to Mathew, calling him on the telephone.

"Mathew, my phone is ringing off the hook," 8Bit said, "with people telling me they saw Beyoncé on TV last night saying how she got the idea for 'Bootylicious.' Now they think I've been bullshitting them this whole time I've been saying I was totally involved. I look like an idiot!"

"So, what's your point?" Mathew asked.

"Well, it would have been nice if she could have said she cowrote the song, or coproduced it."

Mathew laughed. "Are you kidding me?" he asked, "What business are *you* in? Nobody cares about Ron Fusari from Livingston, New Jersey," he said. "That's not what sells records. They want to believe it's all the artist. *That's* the person they're listening to. *That's* the person in front. It's not about you. What's the matter with you?"

Years later, 8-Bit recalls, "Obviously, I wasn't looking for Beyoncé to hold up a big banner that said, 'Hey, everyone! Guess what? "Bootylicious" was cowritten and coproduced by Rob Fusari!' That said, I was being totally naïve, immature, and wet behind the ears. I think I'd just been taken off guard by her interview. I'd been so excited to be producing alone [without his partner Vince Herbert] that I let my enthusiasm for it run wild. But Mathew was right. That's exactly how this business works. Looking back, it was a total mistake to call him about it," 8Bit concludes. "He and I were never quite the same after that."

Survivor

*D*an Workman couldn't help it; he didn't want to be a pest, but he was just always so fascinated by Beyoncé's process. "And where does *this* come from?" he asked her a few days after "Bootylicious" was recorded. At the time, she was in the studio putting the finishing touches on "Independent Women," whose message was that no man was needed to take care of her; she could do it herself: "If I wanted the watch you're wearing / I'll buy it / The house I live in / I bought it / The car I'm driving / I bought it / I depend on me."

"You're so young," Dan observed. "I'm just wondering…"

Beyoncé smiled bashfully. "Well, I have had at least *some* life experiences, Dan," she demurred. "The way I want to live, I don't want to ever be dependent on no man for anything. The women I have seen in my life have all been empowered," she explained. "I think that's a good message to pass on to young girls."

"It is," he agreed. "It's just that you're, what, twenty?" He said he found it astonishing that she would have this point of view already.

"I've been this way since I was a kid," she said. "That's just who I am, who my mom is. Solange and Kelly are the same way. Y'all men don't have to do anything for us. We'll do it ourselves."

There was more to it, of course. Certainly watching her mother navigate her difficult marriage while maintaining her sense of independence had to have influenced Beyoncé's thinking. In recent years, Tina had chosen to stay in the marriage for her own reasons, but financial security was no longer one of them. If she chose to leave, she could do so and still be wealthy. It was her decision not to abandon the marriage, and in that choice she found a certain power of her own, the kind that no doubt influenced her daughter's songwriting. That said, if one listens closely to "Independent Women," it's a statement of anger as much as it is of independence. The message in Beyoncé's lyrics is a complete *rejection* of victimization as much as it is a declaration of independence from it.

"What is it you really want to do with these lyrics?" Dan asked at the end of their conversation about "Independent Women." He already knew the answer, he just wanted to hear her say it.

"One word," she said with a smile. "Inspire."

With Destiny Child's third album, *Survivor* (most of which was recorded in the spring of 2000), not only would the group come into its own, but Beyoncé would clearly define who she now was as a performer and where she was headed as an artist. She would cowrite and coproduce almost every song. Unlike with previous albums, where all members of DC contributed lyrics, on *Survivor* Kelly and Michelle had only one writing credit, "Outro (DC-3) Thank You," at the album's climax, which amounted to little more than a recorded shout-out. The rest of the tracks were collaborations between Beyoncé and a production team that included D'Wayne Wiggins, Falonte Moore, Damon Elliott, Anthony Dent, Mark J. Feist, and Bill Lee, among others.

The only song on which Beyoncé is not credited as a writer is the group's cover of the Samantha Sang hit "Emotion," which was written by Barry and Robin Gibb. However, Beyoncé is credited as the song's producer, with Mark J. Feist and Mathew Knowles.

As executive producer of the album, Mathew had the huge responsibility of keeping a tight rein on song selection. He endeavored to make sure the album featured the best of the best. Or as Taura Stinson put it, "It started getting to the point where getting a song on an album of Beyoncé's was like winning the lottery."

"By this time, Mathew had started striking a real hard bargain," 8Bit recalled. "It was like, either you go his way and agree to his terms, or he was just going to pull your songs from the album. He told me he'd pulled some Rodney Jerkins tracks, he pulled a Timbaland track, and I think he even pulled a song written by his own nephew, all because those guys wouldn't agree to his terms relating to royalties and publishing. I was, like, 'Who is this guy?' But, hey, this was his daughter, and he was going to do what was best for her. And that's why I'm proud to say I have three really good songs on the album." (As Rob Fusari, he is credited with having cowritten and coproduced "Bootylicious," "Apple Pie à la Mode," and "Happy Face.")

When one considers the dustup Mathew caused when he began to single Beyoncé out from the other girls with whom she sang—going all the way back to Ashley Davis's departure from Girls Tyme—an excellent album like this one that was primarily crafted by his daughter was nothing if not sweet vindication. "The album is all Beyoncé inside and out," Mathew would later proudly admit. "It's not only the culmination of her vision of herself, it's the culmination of what I always saw for her, from the very beginning."

What's also fascinating about the *Survivor* album is that as much as it's a Beyoncé album in terms of writing and producing, it also reflects her democracy when it comes to her group members; it's the first album that features all of the girls singing lead on every song. That had always been Beyoncé's vision of the group anyway, and now it had finally come to pass. In a sense, she and Mathew both had their ways with this album—she was the greatest creative influence, but all three girls got to sing.

"When we did the 'Gospel Medley' on *Survivor*, it was cut live," recalled Dan Workman. "We literally had the three ladies set up in the studio behind a mike, and that's very difficult to do from a technical recording standpoint. Ordinarily, you'd record each girl individually and then mix the three vocal tracks together to make one sound. I honestly didn't know if Michelle was going to be able to hang with Kelly and Beyoncé. But she did, and it was effortless. 'She's the real deal,' I told Beyoncé. 'She's not just someone filling a spot.' Granted, they didn't use her a lot on the album. They'd drop her in for a few lines here and there, like icing on a cake. It was always good, and just enough to make you say, 'Okay. I get it. Very nice!'"

Beyoncé would say that she had radio criticism to thank for the inspiration behind the album's title track. While she was on tour with Christina Aguilera, she heard a drive-time disc jockey make a crack about Destiny's Child, comparing the group to the popular television show *Survivor*. He was wondering which girl would soon "get voted off the island." Beyoncé was annoyed. She wrote "Survivor" the following night on the plane to the next city. "I wrote it quickly because I was frustrated," she later recalled. "For me, it was all about what survival means for women, and how hard it is to be one when there are people out there who are trying to bring you down." (Anthony Dent actually wrote the music, and Beyoncé wrote the lyrics, the melody, and the vocal arrangement.)

In "Survivor," the chanting of "*what!*" in the chorus was actually Mathew's contribution to the song; thus he is credited as a cowriter. He said he just walked into the session while the girls were recording the song, had the idea, suggested it, and it worked. He explained that he'd wanted the chanting to suggest audience participation. While this may sound like an inconsequential contribution, in fact it propels the song forward.

With staggering first-week sales of almost seven hundred thousand copies—the highest first-week sales figures of any album in Columbia/Sony Records history—*Survivor* entered the *Billboard* albums chart at number one on May 19, 2001. It would be certified quadruple platinum in sales, and earn Destiny's Child three more Grammy nominations. It would go on to win a 2002 Grammy for Best R&B Performance by a Duo or Group with Vocals. It would also be a huge international success. By the end of 2001, it had sold almost ten million copies worldwide

"The *Survivor* album was the product of some of my favorite recording sessions with the girls," concluded Dan Workman of SugarHill Recording Studios. Workman recalled a day when Beyoncé had just finished a photo shoot and walked into the studio in full makeup with a wild tangle of hair extensions, looking for all the world like one of the world's great divas. The first thing she said when she showed up was, "Scuse me, y'all, I need to go wash this dang makeup off my face.' Then she borrowed a pair of scissors from my wife, Christi, and went into the ladies' room and cut off all of her hair extensions. She knew she had six hours of studio work ahead of her, and that there was no way she would ever get through it unless she was comfortable.

"She came out of the ladies' room looking pretty damn awesome," Workman recalled. "She was unconcerned about people taking her picture, or whatever. There was no 'Attention! Clear the hall! Beyoncé's fixin' to come out after cutting off all her hair!' She just didn't have that sort of pretense or concern. She was authentic, and that's what I think you get when you hear the *Survivor* album—her authenticity."

Lyndall Worries About Jay Z

*I*t wasn't surprising to people who knew them that after Beyoncé and Lyndall broke up, they eventually got back in touch and then continued as friends. They'd been a part of each other's lives for so many years, it was as if they were family. Of course, he also wanted her back as a lover and did his best to convince her. However, her mind was made up: Maybe one day, she told him, but not now. It wasn't as if she suddenly realized that a whole world of men was available to her, either. She'd just started to become interested in someone who had clearly been fascinated with her from the start. "She started mentioning this other guy to me a lot: Jay Z," Lyndall Locke recalled. "She began to casually drop his name into conversations, talking about 'Jay this' and 'Jay that.'"

"As I recall it, there was a lot of gray area at this time between my son and Beyoncé," said Lyndall's mother, Lydia. "It was understandable. When you've been with someone so long, the end is not so cut-and-dried. When Mathew and Tina sent for Lyndall to join Beyoncé on the road, like they had in the past, I heard Jay Z got all bent out of shape about it."

One afternoon, Beyoncé called from San Francisco while Lyndall wasn't home. He returned the call, and when she picked up, he learned that she was in her hotel room playing dice with Jay Z and the popular rapper and singer-songwriter Snoop Dogg. "What the hell are you doing alone in your room with *those* two?" he asked.

"Oh, please," Beyoncé exclaimed. "They're like my older brothers."

"Come on, Beyoncé," Lyndall told her, "you need to get real, girl. These guys are *not* your brothers! I'm a man and I know men. These old dudes are just biding their time while they figure out how to get into your drawers."

"But that's not true," Beyoncé said, sounding indignant. "And you don't own me, anyway," she added. "I'm *allowed* to have friends."

Years after that conversation, Lyndall would observe, "All I knew was that I didn't want her alone with rich and accomplished guys like Jay Z and Snoop Dogg. But she was living the fast life now with guys like that while I was still living at my mom's and looking for a job. Put it this way: It was starting to look not so good for me."

Andretta's Estate Sues

*E*ver since Destiny's Child became successful, the family and friends of the late Andretta Tillman had felt strongly that she'd not gotten proper recognition as both the act's original manager and later its co-manager with Mathew Knowles. The well-known and accepted story about Destiny's Child had somehow transmogrified into one about Mathew abandoning his six-figure job to manage the group and make a reality his daughter's dream, but usually with nary a word about Andretta. Likely, in terms of branding the group, it was thought to be a better and more concise tale than the more complex and accurate one that would have detailed "Miss Ann's" crucial role in cultivating the girls, from Girls Tyme through Somethin' Fresh, the Dolls, Destiny, and then Destiny's Child.

Destiny's Child did dedicate two songs to Andretta: "My Time Has Come (Dedicated to Andretta Tillman)" from the first album, which Tillman heard and enjoyed before her death, and "Outro (Amazing Grace—Dedicated to Andretta Tillman)" on the second, which is an a cappella rendition of the old spiritual. Also, the entire first album was dedicated to Andretta. Moreover, in individual acknowledgments written by each girl, each sent her love to Andretta. Arguably, it could be asked, what more could have been done?

The answer, as far as the Tillman estate was concerned, was plenty—and it had to do not only with fuller recognition for Andretta, but also a reasonable cut of the money the group had generated since her death, none of which had ever trickled down to the Tillman heirs. "They dedicated a couple of songs to my mother way back when, but the public had to ask, 'Who the hell is Andretta?'" observes her son Armon. "No one knew. They threw her name out there sort of like she was the Knowles family maid!"

"We even started hearing that Mathew was saying my mother didn't do anything for the group," Chris Tillman added. "We didn't understand it, and we wanted answers."

"Even if they had given Armon and Chris $500,000, that would have changed their lives," Pat Felton said. "After all, they were all but ruined when their mother died. It took years for them to recover. Considering all of the trials, tribulations, and tragedy that happened to Andretta as she worked to make Destiny's Child famous, for the boys to be left with nothing once the group was a success was a real shame."

By the beginning of 2002, Destiny's Child had sold roughly thirty million albums worldwide. Therefore, the stakes were high.

Mathew conceded what everyone knew, which was that in 1993 and 1994, he and Andretta had entered into management contracts with each individual member of the group that eventually went on to become Destiny's Child. The artists agreed to pay management fees equal to 20 percent of gross earnings and a 1 percent royalty, which he and Andretta would spilt.

But then in 1997—right around the time the girls signed with Columbia/Sony—according to Andretta's final contract with Mathew she was entitled to just 5 percent of the group's management income and Mathew was entitled to 15 percent. Both were also entitled to half of 1 percent of royalties. In exchange for this split favoring Mathew, he would pay all expenses.

The 1 percent royalty point was easy to calculate. In total, it came to $350,000. In fact, Columbia/Sony would later announce that it had been holding half of that amount in an account—meaning $175,000 for Tillman's heirs—$87,500 for each son.

But what about the management fee—Andretta's 5 percent? The amount the Tillman's heirs would be entitled to if *that* contract was still binding would take some time to calculate, but it could be many millions of dollars. In fact, the Tillman estate put it at about $30 million, which was more or less a ballpark guess. Mathew said, though, that he and Andretta had agreed to an *amendment* of their contract stipulating that she would abandon her management fee upon her death, and that her heirs would then only be entitled to that one-half percent royalty—the $175,000. Mathew was happy to give the Tillman heirs that much, but no more.

The problem, though, was that Mathew couldn't find the amendment document in which Andretta had abandoned her management commission. Under oath, he would say that "we're aggressively looking for it." One would have thought he would have kept such an important contract. However, it's probably not surprising that documents had gone missing. After all, Andretta had died without a will, which suggests that she really wasn't thinking in terms of preserving important papers either. Still, this scenario sounded very fishy to the Tillmans. How convenient it was for Mathew, they felt, that this particular amended contract had suddenly gone missing. They put forth the theory that if such an amended deal ever even existed, maybe this was the agreement they'd heard through the grapevine that Tina had Andretta sign at her deathbed. Remember, Pat Felton said she witnessed Tina having Andretta sign *something* the very morning of her death, though Tina later denied that was the case.

There were a lot of questions, and the Tillmans felt the only way to address them was to formally litigate. Therefore, in January 2002, the heirs of Andretta Tillman—Armon and Chris, her sons, and Effie Lee, her mother—sued Mathew, Beyoncé, and Kelly, claiming that they had been cheated out of more than $30 million.

"Denise [Seals] came to my house and said, 'They need documents and I know you're a pack rat. You must have *something* that will get them some money,'" recalled Deborah Laday. "She told me, 'Mathew's saying he brought Ann in, and you know that's a lie. We brought her in!' So a lawyer came to my house and I gave him copies of all of the contracts I had that pre-dated Mathew. I wanted to do anything I could to help Ann's boys get the money they deserved."

As well as questioning the money that should have trickled down to the Tillman heirs, the lawsuit also made quite a few eyebrow-raising allegations about Mathew. For instance, it alleged that he had "failed to inform Ms. Tillman that he had uncontrollable addictions to at least cocaine and extramarital activities." It further stated that he "failed to inform Ms. Tillman that his addictions to cocaine and extramarital sexual relations impaired his judgment relating to properly supervising minor Artists, impeded his ability to properly managing the finances of his business and/or the Artists." Also, it maintained that Mathew's personal challenges caused him to "squander money due and owing Ms. Tillman on drugs and extramarital sexual relations."

Attempting to expose Mathew's private life seemed to most observers to be a tactic designed to force a settlement. The Tillman attorneys had to know that including those personal allegations in the complaint would generate salacious reporting that might tend to embarrass the family, particularly Beyoncé. Indeed, explosive headlines appeared as expected, and the Knowleses would be duly humiliated.

Beyoncé chose to turn away from the allegations and simply not speak about them. One reporter in Houston ran into her in a restaurant while she was dining with friends and tried to get her to comment on the accusations. Looking up at him, she smiled sweetly and said, "I have nothing to say." However, when he continued to push, she rose from her chair at the table and left the premises.

If anything, this difficult situation served to provide Beyoncé with more of a reason to draw a line in the sand where the media's interest in her personal life was concerned. Slowly she was coming to the conclusion that the best thing she could do for herself and her family was simply not to comment about anything other than her professional career, and to do so across the board.

Obviously, Tina was upset about the suit and about the newspaper coverage. She had loved Armon and Chris since they were little boys. However, as was well known about her by this time, a war against her husband or any member of her family was a war against her. She was asked about it everywhere she went but knew better than to talk about it. Finally, tired of the inquiries, she told a reporter of Mathew, "He'd be dead if he spent $32 million on drugs and sex. My husband works sixteen hours a day. I don't know when he'd have the time for all this nonsense they're claiming. And Beyoncé knows in her heart her father hasn't done the terrible things he's accused of doing." Actually, the Tillmans were not claiming that Mathew had spent $32 million on drugs and sex, but rather that they were possibly owed that much from mismanagement conduct.

Realizing that his family would not be left alone until he made some sort of public statement, Mathew went on the offensive and gave a brief damage-control interview to *Star*, a popular tabloid. Some observers thought he was completely out of his mind to cooperate with a tabloid on such an explosive story, especially after it was published and they saw the headline: "Beyoncé's Dad Blows Millions on Drugs and Hookers—Mathew Knowles Interview: 'I Was a Sex Addict,' he tells Star." Actually, it was a clever way to tackle the scandal head-on before it had a chance to completely overwhelm them all. That Mathew chose to speak to the very market he knew would exploit the story and keep it going—the tabloid market—was a savvy way of handling what could have continued to be a prickly problem for the Knowleses. In the interview, he freely admitted that, yes, he had had personal problems with drugs and infidelity in the past. He suggested he had been in rehab twice, and mentioned sexual addiction as being one of his troubling issues.

After about a month, lurid tales about Mathew all but vanished as the audience that reads tabloids lost interest in the salacious details and—without comment from Beyoncé to keep them fully invested—moved on to the next, big celebrity scandal. What was done was done, though, and now it would be a matter of litigating the true facts of the matter—or whatever facts could be ascertained considering that Andretta Tillman was, sadly, gone and not able to testify on her own behalf.

Beyoncé's Deposition

*O*n November 20, 2001, Beyoncé showed up at the office of her attorney Dwight Jefferson, of Maloney, Jefferson & Dugas in Houston. It was 12:30 in the afternoon, and she was ready for business. Her face was scrubbed clean of most makeup, and she looked far younger than her twenty years. She was wearing a simple pink tank top with a black blazer and black trousers and matching heels. Her blondish hair was pulled into a ponytail, and she had on large gold hoop earrings. Her demeanor was intense and serious.

A couple of weeks earlier, the lawsuit LaTavia and LeToya had filed against Beyoncé and Kelly had been settled with a cash payout of $850,000 to the two former Destiny's Child singers. After legal fees and other costs, the girls likely ended up with about $225,000 each. When one considered the money they would have made in years to come as members of Destiny's Child, it seemed to most people as if they got a pretty raw deal. Clearly, at least in this case, standing up for their principles came with a steep cost. However one chose to look at it, though, one thing was certain: Beyoncé and Kelly were free and clear as far as that particular suit was concerned. Mathew was still on the hook for it, though.

In order to save time and money, a judge had decided that the two pending suits—the case filed by LaTavia and LeToya (against Mathew) and the one filed by Andretta Tillman's estate—would be joined into one umbrella litigation since so many of the issues were similar. Also, since Beyoncé and Kelly were still defendants in the Tillman suit (and witnesses in what remained of the LaTavia/LeToya suit against Mathew), they would still be forced to testify in both cases.

From November 2001 through March 2002, everyone named in these legal cases would be compelled to answer questions by attorneys under oath, in what are called depositions. This is often not an easy process; it can sometimes be combative. Sworn testimony gleaned from these sessions would then be used to formulate each side's case at the eventual trial. Since she had to go to Los Angeles to start work on her debut major motion picture, *Austin Powers in Goldmember*, Beyoncé was the first witness to be deposed, which was why she was at her lawyers' office on this November afternoon.

Beyoncé hasn't spoken publicly about her feelings regarding the Tillman case but it's the view of some of those who knew her then that she never wanted to be a party to any tactic that would minimize Andretta's role in her success. When she learned that Andretta's sons had received no money from the success of Destiny's Child, she was apparently surprised. However in a sworn affidavit she would later give, she said, that as far as she was concerned, when Andretta died, "it ended our relationship with her, contractual or otherwise" and that none of the Tillmans had ever indicated otherwise to her. In fact, she testified she ran into Armon Tillman at a party in December of 2000 who then told her that Pamela Luckett "had told him a bunch of crazy stuff about Destiny's Child. He asked what was going on with LaToya and LaTavia. I told him it was a long story. Our conservation was a good one and I had no inkling that he thought we owed him anything... certainly not millions of dollars." A week before the deposition, she had a conversation with her friend and former mentor Anthony Moore—Tony Mo.—during which she said, "To think that after everything we went through together it ends up in a courtroom is just unbelievable to me."

It seemed that the conundrum as Beyoncé saw it was that in giving Andretta her due, she didn't want to downplay Mathew's role in the success of the group. In many ways, things hadn't changed—it was still a battle between Andretta and Mathew, with Beyoncé squarely in the middle.

Beyoncé showed up with Tina and Kelly at her side for support. Much to their surprise, however, they found LeToya and LaTavia in the conference room waiting for them. The two were allowed to sit in on the deposition; it was their legal right as plaintiffs in the case. Of course, the two girls hadn't seen Beyoncé since the group's breakup. Polite greetings were exchanged before everyone was seated at a conference table.

One might imagine that having to answer questions about her feelings relating to LaTavia and LeToya as they sat at a conference table with her would have made Beyoncé feel uneasy. However, that doesn't seem to have been the case. "Does it make you uncomfortable to have your former singing partners here?" the Tillmans' attorney Benjamin Hall asked her. "No," she responded simply. When asked why, she answered, "Because, to be honest with you, I've got nothing to hide." When asked if she would be truthful in her answers, Beyoncé said, "Absolutely, yes. I'm always truthful." The deposition then began. Beyoncé had a stack of fashion magazines next to her at the ready, which she would casually thumb through during breaks.

During her deposition, Beyoncé was first asked to outline the reasons why LaTavia and LeToya had been replaced in the group. Hours were spent discussing the letter they sent disaffirming their management contract with Mathew, and Beyoncé's reaction to it and her subsequent depression and then anger, all of which she summarized as "a dark and depressing time in my life." She said, "I just wanted to get into my car and start driving and never look back." She also talked about the antagonistic letter she sent the girls, and said she didn't regret writing it. "I said what I needed to say and what I felt they needed to hear," she explained. When asked if she thought it had been harsh, she said, "I don't know. What can I say? Sometimes the truth hurts, doesn't it?" She then attempted to outline the history of the singing groups in which she'd participated prior to Destiny's Child, and Andretta's role in managing each incarnation. She demonstrated a great capacity for remembering details many had long forgotten. She also said she had "nothing but love for Miss Ann, but if you want to know the truth, she became very sick and my father had no choice but to step in. So," she said, choosing her words carefully, "it started out with Miss Ann doing all the work, yes, for sure, but then there was sort of a shift and my dad starting doing more."

At one point the questioning became tense when Sherry Chandler, representing the Tillman estate, began to interrogate Beyoncé as to exactly who paid for the girls' stage wardrobe, Andretta or Mathew. Beyoncé tried to make the point that at first it was Andretta, but then Mathew. However, Chandler kept cutting her off by claiming her answer to be "unresponsive." Finally, Beyoncé had had enough. "Look, I'm doing my best to remember things that happened when I was just a child and she's being unnecessarily aggressive toward me," she told her attorney Thomas Fulkerson. "I think she could have a little more respect, don't you? I'm not used to being talked to like this. It's not right." Fulkerson agreed and asked Chandler to tone down the rhetoric.

Beyoncé was then asked if she knew anything about her father's alleged drug habits. Her attorney objected and said she didn't have to answer the question. "But I *want* to answer it," she said. The lawyer then remarked, "The witness wishes to answer," to which Beyoncé firmly stated, "Absolutely not. I don't know anything about that, at all. My father has only cared about me and my career. I don't see how he would have time for drugs. It's a lie." The attorneys continued to push, but she was adamant. When then asked if she had ever heard of her father having extramarital affairs, her attorney again told her that she didn't have to respond. This time, she chose to take his advice. Instead, she just glared at the lawyer.

Beyoncé's deposition went on for more than eight long hours. It ended only because she began complaining of cramps in her arms and shoulders. "Please, y'all, I've had enough," she said. "I can come back some other day if you have more questions, but I'm definitely done for today." She was polite, but also firm and decisive. Tina backed her. "I think we can all agree that my daughter's been cooperative," she said. "But enough is enough. It's time for us to go home. Let's go, Beyoncé," she said as she started gathering her things. The two women smiled graciously at everyone around the table—LaTavia, LeToya, all of the lawyers representing both sides—and then they got up and took their leave.

Mathew's Deposition

 *M*athew Knowles's deposition would begin on January 29, again in the office of Dwight Jefferson.

Under oath, Mathew took full credit for Destiny Child's Columbia/ Sony record deal, though he conceded that the contract was signed during his co-partnership arrangement with Andretta. As the hours wore on, he seemed vague as to what Andretta's role had actually been with Destiny's Child. Seeming extremely frustrated, opposing counsel Benjamin Hall asked him in very precise terms, "At the time that she died, when God took her last breath away from her, at that moment just before that breath was taken, was she or was she not the co-manager of Destiny's Child?" Mathew answered simply, "Yes." He also testified that Andretta was a trustworthy person ("very much so") and that she never did anything he thought was contrary to the best interests of the group. "Ann and I never had a real argument," he testified. He also testified that he never threatened to pull Beyoncé from Girls Tyme if he could not co-manage the group. "I would never threaten Ann," he insisted. "I had a good relationship with her." When pushed though, Mathew admitted, "I don't recall saying that. I am not going to guarantee I never said that. I just don't recall saying it. I could have said it, but I don't recall saying it."

He testified that after Andretta's death he'd tried in vain to contact Armon and Chris "to see how they were doing. And I wanted to let them know that their mother and I had made an agreement that they would get 50 percent of that royalty point. Ann made it very, very clear she wanted to make sure that they got it because she had major concerns that her family would take the money from them, and they [the sons] would never get it."

Mathew also testified about the amended contract he had renegotiated with Andretta, the one that excluded the Tillman heirs from all but 1 percent of Destiny's Child's royalties—$175,000. He continued to insist that he and Tina had been looking for it but could not find it.

As far as LaTavia and LeToya (who were not present) were concerned,

Mathew said that their actions had "left Beyoncé feeling disappointment, sadness, betrayal, anger and fed up, if that's a feeling. I was sad for her. She was deeply depressed." He said that LaTavia and LeToya clearly had no idea of "the kinds of sacrifices that had to be made in order to be stars, and I don't blame them," he added. "Not everyone can do it. Some people just don't have what it takes. I mean, you can't expect everyone to be able to rise to the occasion like Beyoncé and Kelly."

When it came time to ask Mathew about his personal challenges and whether or not he had spent company money on them, the deposition turned particularly contentious. At his lawyer's advice, Mathew declined to answer all questions having to do with whether he spent partnership money on "chemical dependency," "illegal substances such as cocaine," "addictions, sexual or otherwise," or "counseling or medical treatment in a rehab center."

In an even more uncomfortable line of questioning, Mathew was also asked to identify by name certain strippers, lap dancers, and prostitutes whom opposing counsel had located and who they now claimed would testify against him in court. Again, acting on the advice of his attorney who felt that this line of questioning was "nothing more than a fishing expedition," he declined to cooperate. Benjamin Hall then produced receipts from bars and strip clubs that had allegedly been made out to Knowles, and asked for explanations. Mathew was instructed not to respond. Hall was told he would have to go back to the judge presiding over the case and ask her to compel Mathew to answer those questions at a future time.

Mathew's deposition took more than twelve long, arduous hours. By the time it was over, he was exhausted. "But you do what you have to do within the law," he concluded. "It's not like you have a lot of choice."

Tina's Deposition

*T*ina Knowles showed up at the offices of Maloney, Jefferson & Dugas at 12:30 p.m. sharp on March 22, looking as gorgeous as ever in black jeans with five-inch stiletto heels and a white wool sweater. Her dark hair fell to her shoulders, carefully parted in the middle. She wore long, dangling gold earrings, as well as a matching, glistening necklace. She seemed abundantly happy and at ease, eagerly answering in anecdotal fashion the first hour's questions from Warren Fitzgerald about the forming of Destiny's Child, as if telling folksy tales by a warm fireplace. Her southern charm and down-home graciousness was on full display. "I'm so bad with dates," she kept saying, apologizing for her occasional lack of specificity.

The climate changed dramatically, though, when the questioning became personal and Benjamin Hall tried to get Tina to admit that the Knowleses were "strapped" in 1996 and 1997. His point was that it was "inconceivable" that they could have contributed very much money to the eventual success of Destiny's Child, as they had claimed. He suggested that Andretta had contributed far more. Tina insisted, though, that "we were not strapped," despite the fact that, she conceded, they did have to sell their beloved home on Parkwood Drive in the Third Ward.

"But you couldn't even pay your Blockbuster bill!" Benjamin Hall exclaimed.

"Oh yes we could!" Tina insisted. "We were able to pay for movies from Blockbuster. Now, whether the movies were returned in our lifestyle with all those girls coming in and out and taking them home with them is another subject, but yes, I could pay a dollar for a rental. Please! I worked!"

The lawyer then began going over the Knowleses' list of creditors in painstaking detail, and, sure enough, Tina had long ago listed Blockbuster Video as a debt owed but not paid, for the amount of $344.25. "What about *that*?" he charged in what he may have perceived as a "gotcha" moment.

"I guess if it's on there," Tina said.

"Well, it's right here," he said, pointing to the entry.

"Uh-huh."

"The point is…" he began.

"What *is* the point?" she snapped.

"The point is that at the time of the 1993 bankruptcy filing," he pressed on, "your financial situation was such that you needed protection in the bankruptcy court from a $344 invoice from Blockbuster."

Left with no choice, Tina conceded as much, but she wasn't happy about having to do so.

She then talked in depth about Denise Seals and Deborah Laday, saying that she didn't feel comfortable with them, "because I wasn't sure they knew what they were doing. Their hearts were in the right place, but in this business that's usually not enough." She also recalled in great detail the day she met Andretta Tillman on Beyoncé's ninth birthday and how Andretta had intervened when Deborah—"who I felt was very controlling"—would not allow her access to the backstage area to greet her daughter. "I liked Ann right away," she said.

A great deal of time was then spent trying to determine if Tina had asked Andretta to sign a document relating to Destiny's Child on her deathbed. "Absolutely not," Tina said. The amended contract Andretta signed wasn't executed in a hospital at all, Tina testified. In fact, she said it was signed "seven months" prior to Andretta's death in the Knowleses' home. She confirmed that it was now lost. However, she specifically recalled the document as having stipulated that Andretta would abandon all of her management commissions at the time of her death, thereby preventing her sons, Armon and Chris, from ever inheriting them. The amended agreement called for the Tillman sons to get nothing more than their half-point royalty, she testified. She speculated that the document had somehow gotten lost when the Knowleses moved their files from their home office to the Music World headquarters. "We are looking high and low for it," she added. They'd even tried to find the person who notarized it, she said, but had no luck there either.

Finally, after six and a half hours, Tina's deposition ended at 7 p.m. By that time, she was emotionally and physically exhausted. Unfortunately, she was instructed to return in six days for more questioning.

When Tina returned for her second deposition on March 28, the day started with an intense interrogation about her husband's private issues. Had Mathew ever been treated for drug abuse? For sexual abuse? Tina's attorney instructed her not to answer either question. Was it true that Tina once told Cheryl Mitchell (LaTavia Roberson's mother) that Mathew was a drug addict? "Absolutely not," Tina said. When asked if she recalled writing a note to Mathew in front of Cheryl in which she criticized him for his drug use and for embarrassing her with his sexual improprieties, Tina insisted she would never have written such a note in front of another person. By this time, she was livid. However, she was also determined to not be intimidated. The attorney then brought forth three income tax statements in which Kelly Rowland was listed as "Kelly Knowles." How had that happened? The attorney asked if she and Mathew had been trying to suggest that Kelly was actually their secret biological daughter? And if not, were they looking for an illegal tax break? Tina chalked it all up to a clerical error. "I get the deduction anyway because she's living with me," she said with indignation. "So, please. Don't be ridiculous."

Following a couple more hours of heated interrogation, it was time for a much-needed break. Upon their return, Benjamin Hall started off by brusquely sliding a document before Tina and saying, "Page 15, ma'am."

"Be a gentleman," she chastised him. "Just show a little manners. I know that's hard for you."

After apologizing, the attorney tried to impeach Tina's oft-told story about how she came up with the name Destiny's Child. "I've looked for the word 'destiny' in the King James Version [of the Bible] and it just doesn't exist," he said. Tina explained that it might have been in one of the newer editions of the Bible. "Ma'am, do you have any *specific* biblical reference that you can cite as to where destiny comes from in Destiny's Child?" the attorney then asked impatiently.

"I can bring my NIV Bible up here and show you," Tina snapped back at him, "or the Women's Study Bible. That's the best I can do for you."

"Ma'am, did Ann Tillman have any participation in the selection of the name Destiny's Child?" the lawyer demanded to know, finally getting to his point.

"No."

"Have you heard that Ann Tillman had a niece that was born just one month before the group's name was changed to Destiny's Child, and that this niece was named . . . *Destiny?*"

The attorney was referring to the fact that in 1991, four years before the girls were rechristened Destiny's Child, Andretta Tillman's niece Kimberly Stewart gave birth to a daughter she named Destiny. Andretta's sister Jan Stewart-Langley says that she and Andretta were at the home of their sister Glenda in Tyler, Texas, when Andretta, who was admiring the baby, said, "Destiny! I'm gonna name my group after you. It's gonna be . . . *Destiny's Child.*" In other words, according to this account, it was *Andretta* who came up with the name. However, this was a full year after Denise Seals and Deborah Laday had already made use of it, so it was a moot point anyway.

"No," Tina answered. She seemed to have no idea what the attorney was talking about. Truly it would have been surprising if she had known anything at all about this particular Tillman family fact.

"Thank you, ma'am," Benjamin Hall then said in a very abrupt fashion. "I'm finished with you."

It wasn't over yet, though. Before the interrogation could end, Warren Fitzgerald—LeToya's and LaTavia's lawyer—had one more question for Tina: "Have you ever advised Kelly Rowland, who you claim is *not* your daughter," he clarified in a mocking tone, "to seek legal counsel?"

Just as Tina began to answer, Benjamin Hall cut her off and, addressing Warren Fitzgerald with equal sarcasm, said, "Hold on, now, Ben. You don't know that Kelly Rowland is not her daughter. After all, Mrs. Knowles has her all over her tax returns, doesn't she?"

By this time, Tina was fed up. "You know what?" she said, turning to her attorney, Dwight Jefferson. "Mr. Hall is really aggravating me right now with his cynical comments." Then addressing Hall, she demanded, "Keep them to yourself."

Once again chastised by Tina Knowles, Benjamin Hall said, "I will. I apologize, ma'am."

"Fine," Tina concluded. "Let's just be professional here now, shall we?"

Austin Powers in Goldmember

*I*n January 2002, while the ever-troubling lawsuits were being litigated against her family, Beyoncé Knowles flew to Los Angeles to complete work on her second acting job, in *Austin Powers in Goldmember*, starring Canadian comedic actor Mike Myers in the title role. She had actually started work on the movie in the fall of 2001, but now she was back on the West Coast for more filming.

While working on the film, Beyoncé found an elegant penthouse in Los Angeles in which to live with her cousin Angie Beyincé. This time, the freedom actually felt good to her. Whereas she'd been somewhat lonely while working on *Carmen: A Hip Hopera*, she'd now become friendly with many people in Los Angeles and had begun to relax into a new, more independent lifestyle She also took up painting at this time. She was particularly proud of an abstract work of art and enjoyed showing it to her friends. However, when Lonnie Jackson laid eyes on it, he asked, "Why does that woman have a beak on her neck?" It wasn't a beak, of course—even if it looked like one. Beyoncé, who took her painting almost as seriously as her music, was offended. "She kind of shut us down for a while after that," said Taura Stinson, who was married to Lonnie.

On her own in Los Angeles, Beyoncé could handle herself if need be. A telling story about her is that she was in a bar in West Hollywood enjoying a (nonalcoholic) drink with Angie when a handsome man caught their attention. The two cousins whispered in each other's ear, probably commenting on the man's appearance. Seeing this, his date began to eye Beyoncé suspiciously. For the rest of the evening, she didn't take her eyes off her. Finally, Beyoncé and Angie threw some money onto the bar, rose, and, in leaving, walked right past the woman. The stranger muttered under her breath, "*Heifers!*" Beyoncé is said to have stopped, stood before her, and, looking down at her, said, "Excuse me?" The woman rose to face her, nose to nose. Beyoncé sized her up, looked at her as if she'd lost her mind, and exclaimed, "*Honey, don't nobody want your man!*" They stared at each other for a moment, until finally the woman sat back down. Beyoncé and Angie walked out the door, heads held high. "The Houston girl comes out in me every now and then," Beyoncé would later say, laughing. "And you don't want to see her, that's all I'm sayin'."

The producer of *Austin Powers in Goldmember*, John Lyons, felt that Beyoncé was perfect for the role of the sassy Foxxy Cleopatra character when he saw her work in *Carmen: A Hip Hopera* on MTV. Foxxy was a coveted role—Liz Hurley and Heather Graham had played Myers's female foils in the two previous *Austin Powers* movies—and word had already been leaked that Jennifer Lopez was being considered. "I felt strongly that Beyoncé was our girl from the very beginning because she lit up every frame of *Carmen*, and that was just her first acting role," he recalled. "She has this Streisand-like quality, where you just know she can have this amazing career in both music and film, if she wants it." Director Jay Roach wasn't as sure as Lyons. He knew he wanted Beyoncé to sing the movie's theme song, but was holding out for a more accomplished actress to play opposite Myers.

Mike Myers called Beyoncé personally to ask if she would be interested in auditioning. She was bowled over. The timing was right, though. It just so happened that Destiny's Child had been scheduled to tour Europe—this was in the fall of 2001—but then the tragedy of 9/11 happened, and that itinerary was canceled. It was decided that a good way to fill Beyoncé's spare time might be with a movie. Her initial meeting with Myers and Jay Roach was nerve-racking, though. She found herself tongue-tied and bashful. "My heart was beating fast," she recalled, "my mouth was dry, my palms were clammy. I had to wipe my hands on my pants before I shook hands with Mike Myers." Thankfully, Tina was at her side. Actually, Tina was so personable, it was impossible for Myers and Roach not to be swept away by her. Roach was completely taken by her, as was Myers. In fact, Myers joked that maybe they should give *her* the role!

At the meeting, when asked if she'd like to do comedy, Beyoncé regretted her answer even as it was tumbling from her lips. "I don't think I'm very funny," she said, "so I'm not sure I can make people laugh. I'd like to try, though." She later said she realized in that moment that a better answer, one that might have instilled more confidence, would have been a simple "Yes." When the director looked at her with skepticism, she was sure she'd blown it. It was true, though: Beyoncé wasn't an inherently comedic person. Lyndall Locke recalled, "We used to laugh because she really could not tell a joke to save her life." That didn't mean she didn't have a sense of humor, though. She could certainly appreciate comedy. "But actually being funny?" Lyndall asked. "No, that wasn't Beyoncé's thing at all." (In all fairness to her, though, she can be pretty goofy when she wants to, crossing her eyes for friends, for instance; she can even cross them one at a time!)

The actual audition with Mike Myers went much better. In the interim, Beyoncé did some homework, including watching some of the movies on which the character Foxxy Cleopatra was based. The role was an homage to the tough but sexy female characters who had appeared in a string of 1970s "blaxploitation" films as portrayed by iconic actresses such as Pam Grier in *Foxy Brown*, Tamara Dobson in *Cleopatra Jones*, and Teresa Graves in the made-for-television movie and then cult series *Get Christie Love!* The genre began in 1970 and was pretty much over by 1979. Beyoncé and Tina watched quite a few of those movies in preparation for her audition.

A number of actresses had been brought in to read with Mike Myers and the other producers, who sat at a long table on one side of the room. The lighting was harsh, the climate tense. Though Beyoncé was extremely nervous, at least she looked the part in her 1970s-inspired catsuit and her teased-out hair. Mike Myers's easygoing attitude also went a long way toward relaxing her. The next day Beyoncé got the call from her agent that she'd been cast.

Panic

*T*he plot of *Austin Powers in Goldmember* couldn't have been more convoluted or—as might have been expected—ridiculous. It has to do with the time-traveling antics of Myer's character Sir Augustine Danger "Austin"

Powers, a womanizing British spy whose portrayal is heavily influenced by the colorful hippie culture of 1960s London, and his ongoing rivalry against his nemesis, Dr. Evil (also played by Myers). Beyoncé plays an FBI agent who goes undercover as a flashy disco entertainer. The wardrobe is heavily influenced by 1970s disco culture—and for Beyoncé that meant an oversized honey-brown Afro hairstyle along with lots of gold lamé and shiny leather.

On the first day of production, Beyoncé filmed the opening scene of the movie in her comfort zone, which was as a singer and dancer. She was featured in a major production number built around the song "Hey Goldmember," along with two other singers/dancers à la Destiny's Child. "I knew she had worked with other choreographers, so I didn't know how she was going to be with me," said Marguerite Derricks, who choreographed the number. "Though we had never worked together before, she came in and acted like she was my student. She didn't try to manipulate or control or ask me to change anything. She made everything work because she could make anything work."

Though things got off to a good start, they took a bit of a turn when it came time for Beyoncé to actually act. Singing and dancing came easy to her, of course. Acting was more of a challenge. One of the reasons things worked out so well for her in *Carmen: A Hip Hopera* was because of the care and nurturing of her director, Robert Townsend. On *Goldmember*, because there was such a huge cast, Beyoncé had to fend for herself. About a week into production, a rumor spread that she was having trouble remembering her lines and was thus holding up the movie. Everyone was said to be frustrated and supposedly wondered why the studio had ever decided to take a chance on her. Even if Beyoncé wasn't that quick to recall her script, she was certainly not holding up the production. Still, since she was always the perfectionist, it was going at a pace slower than she would have liked, and she couldn't help but be self-conscious about it. When the stories got back to her, she was deeply affected by them. "They said I looked pretty and was nice, but I basically wasn't doing the job," she later recalled. "I'd rather do an acceptable or exceptional job than just look pretty. I thought, 'Here I am, new to movies, and this mess is the first thing people are going to hear about me?'"

One critical magazine article hit her so hard, she read it repeatedly while trying to divine the writer's true intention because, surely, she thought, it couldn't have been just to hurt her. In the end her publicist advised her not to read it again.

"This will keep happening, so you have to accept it and move on," Tina told her one day on the set in front of witnesses. At the time, Beyoncé was getting her Afro wig styled, and as two beauticians worked feverishly on it, she looked miserable sitting in her studio fold-out chair. Meanwhile, an enthusiastic set photographer took pictures of her. "Smile, baby," Tina said under breath. "You don't want to be seen with that frown, now do you?"

"It's not fair," Beyoncé said, perusing the article again and ignoring her mother's advice. "Most of the stuff in here, nobody would ever have said about me. Or would they?"

"First of all, no, they wouldn't," Tina answered. She snatched the magazine from her daughter and handed it back to the publicist. More than anything, Tina just wanted Beyoncé to develop a thicker skin. "And second of all, you need to *stop*," she said. She told her daughter that one day someone would probably say far worse about her. In fact, she said she could guarantee it. "You know who you are, I know who you are, everyone here knows who you are, and God knows who you are," Tina said. "That's got to be enough." She said that if Beyoncé wanted more than that in terms of acceptance, she would be in for a lot of heartache.

Despite Beyoncé's best efforts, *Austin Powers in Goldmember* would be released in July 2002 to decidedly mixed reviews.

Solo Careers

No, Dad, that's not what I want," Beyoncé was saying. It was the spring of 2002, and she was in the Galleria shopping mall in Houston, walking with Lonnie Jackson and talking to Mathew about business. "We had a *plan* and I think y'all should stick to it," she continued, talking into her cell phone. Mathew usually acquiesced in these situations. However, it's fair to say that behind the scenes, his experience and business savvy always prevailed.

As Beyoncé and Lonnie walked along, Lonnie heard some girls talking loudly about Beyoncé. "Ooh, I *hate* her," one of them said. "*Look at her.* She thinks she's all *that!*" Beyoncé, still on the telephone, slowed her gait so that Lonnie could walk in front of her, acting as a shield. Though she noticeably tensed up, she had concerns other than those presented by a couple of troublemakers. "No, Daddy, do it *my* way," she said. "And then, when it's finished, I want you to *call me* and tell me it's done. Because *I mean it*, Daddy. Fine. Goodbye." Then, after a beat, "I love you, Daddy." There was a pause. She smiled and then clicked off. "Beyoncé would really smash on Mathew," Lonnie would recall years later, "and be aggressive with him. This was their dynamic together, though. Everyone knew that she wasn't intimidated by him."*

Once she was off the phone, Beyoncé and Lonnie quickened their pace as a crowd started to follow them. "We'd better get out of here, right quick," Beyoncé said with a grimace, "or I don't know what's gonna happen."

For the last few years, Beyoncé hadn't been able to leave the house without causing a scene of some kind. The escalation of Destiny Child's career with the *Survivor* album was swift, if not surprising. The combination of Beyoncé, Kelly, and Michelle had proved to be a winning one, first with the singles "Independent Women" (which went to number one), "Survivor" (thwarted from the top spot by Janet Jackson's "All for You"), and "Booty-licious" (also number one). The question on most people's minds these days, those who followed the girls' success as well as those who wrote about them in the media, was: When would Beyoncé strike out on her own? It seemed inevitable.

Beyoncé was already well on her way to a solo career because of *Carmen* and *Austin Powers in Goldmember.* As well as its title song, she also recorded a tune for the latter film, called "Work It Out," written with Pharrell Williams and Chad Hugo, that would be the lead single on the soundtrack album.

"Work It Out," when released in June 2002, would bear the distinction of becoming Beyoncé's first solo single release. Of course, it was no surprise that she would have a song on her own sans Destiny's Child. The surprise was that it would turn out to be a big flop. In fact, it wouldn't even crack the

---

* Lonnie Jackson recalled another very telling incident relating to Mathew which occurred at about this same time. The weekend Destiny's Child was scheduled to appear on "Saturday Night Live," Beyoncé invited Lonnie and Taura Stinson to the taping. When they got backstage, Mathew was standing guard. "Only one of you can go into the green room," he announced, referring to the backstage room where guests wait to go onstage. Since it happened to be Lonnie's birthday, the couple agreed that he should be the one to go back and greet Beyoncé. When Lonnie found her in the Green Room, Beyoncé immediately asked about Taura. Lonnie explained that Mathew wouldn't allow her backstage. "What? Screw that," Beyoncé exclaimed. "Mathew Knowles doesn't run the backstage area. Go get her!"

Billboard Hot 100! It also wouldn't appear on the R&B charts. How was this even possible? Certainly Destiny Child's entire career thus far had seemed to many observers to be nothing more than a launching pad for Beyoncé's eventual solo stardom. Now she'd finally taken the leap—and her record had failed?

At about this same time, Kelly Rowland and Michelle Williams had started talking about their own futures. In discussing it with the girls, Mathew came to an appreciation of what they hoped to do as solo artists. They had aspirations outside of Destiny's Child, and he realized it would be foolish to ignore them.

Two months before Beyoncé's record was released, Michelle became the first member of Destiny's Child to release a solo album—the contemporary gospel album *Heart to Yours*. Mathew had done an excellent job of presenting her as the first gospel artist of his Music World company, and with a surprisingly strong album. It peaked at number one on the *Billboard* Gospel Albums chart; it would go on to become 2002's biggest-selling gospel album. Michelle had been savvy enough to choose for her platform a genre completely different from Beyoncé's, and it worked to her advantage. Her success did beg the question, though, as to why Beyoncé's entree as a solo artist had failed.

Adding to the confusion, at the same time that "Work It Out" was released, a duet featuring Kelly was issued from the rapper Nelly's album *Nellyville*. Called "Dilemma," this was a perfectly constructed rhythm-and-blues song that sampled Patti LaBelle's classic 1983 song "Love, Need and Want You." It too was an instant hit, going to number one in ten countries, including the United States. It would also go on to win a Grammy for Best Rap/Sung Collaboration. Kelly had already finished her first solo album, which was to be called *Simply Deep* and would be released later in the year. The album would be an unqualified hit internationally, and is to date her biggest-selling record, with over two million copies sold. Its first single, "Stole," remains one of Kelly's most ambitious recordings with its message concerning teenage suicide. Listening to her adept vocal performance, it's difficult to believe she ever had so much trouble in Girls Tyme. Certainly her success was—is—hard-earned.

So what was one to make of the fact that the two "other" girls in Destiny's Child had solo hits while the group's leader, Beyoncé, floundered with her first release?

Much of the disappointment of the performance of "Work It Out" in the marketplace had to do with the song itself. With its retro, brass-infused feel, it sounded very much like something that might have been recorded by James Brown's backup band, the Famous Flames, back in the 1960s, maybe the early '70s. It was a funky sound, but maybe not commercial, not contemporary enough for a record-buying audience of 2002.

Also contributing to the song's failure was a definite sense of inflated confidence from her record label where Beyoncé's solo career was concerned. It was mistakenly thought that whatever they released would be a hit as long as her name was attached to it. However, the expectations from her public for a first release were so high, she really needed stronger product than "Work It Out" to satisfy. It was quickly decided that the best thing was for everyone to just forget all about the song.

Beyoncé's early stumble aside, when people wonder why the girls in DC have been able to remain close friends despite her subsequent towering presence, they need look no further than Mathew for the explanation. In what is considered a masterful strategy in the pop music world, Mathew would eventually do with Destiny's Child what Berry Gordy Jr. had never thought to do with the Supremes (or with any of his other groups, for that matter)—launch each member into a successful solo career. Because Mathew would allow each an outlet for her artistry, a reason to feel proud and accomplished, Beyoncé, Kelly, and Michelle would be able to avoid the kinds of petty jealousies and resentments that had been the ruination of many popular singing groups preceding them in the business.

Beyoncé Doesn't Forget

*I*t was the spring of 2002. Since her relationship with Lyndall ended, Beyoncé had made two movies, *Carmen: A Hip Hopera* and *Austin Powers in Goldmember*. Both experiences had been fulfilling, even if she had to admit to being lonely at times along the way. While singing with Destiny's Child, she'd also begun to recognize the conundrum experienced by so many superstars before her. Millions of people adored her and recognized her for her beauty and talent. In a sense she regularly made love to enormous audiences. Yet there wasn't that one special person in her life, a romantic interest with whom she could share the realization of her dreams. Of course men wanted to meet her. But she had to wonder, did they care about who she really was, or just her superstar status? That concern presented a hindrance to finding a real relationship. Kelly was more relaxed, telling her to enjoy this time while she could, because soon both would be married with children, "and then it's gonna be a whole different kind of drama."

Lyndall's situation was different. Finally getting his life together, he had enrolled in culinary school in Austin. It's likely that Mathew would have been proud of him. "You want to be a better man?" he used to ask him. "*Then be one!*" It took a while, but maybe Lyndall's mother, Lydia, put it best when she concluded: "My son proved that direction is sometimes more important than speed." What Lyndall really wanted, though, was for Beyoncé to look at him with new eyes, and miss being with him. Since the two were still on good terms, they would try to see each other in Houston whenever she was in town. Lyndall would take those opportunities to try to reconcile with her, but she wasn't having it.

"I was angry and feeling rejected," Lyndall Locke would admit many years later. "She could be stubborn when she wanted to be; she had dug her heels into the ground and wouldn't give me another chance. I did everything I could to get back with her and she was not budging. My whole thing was, 'I'm very sad and upset about the end of a romance that's been in my life for almost ten years, so why isn't she?'"

One muggy spring evening in 2002, Beyoncé and Lyndall were driving to her parents' Swan Isle home, Beyoncé behind the wheel of her Jag convertible, the top down, as usual. She never liked to drive, but toward the end of their relationship and especially now that they were broken up, she insisted on it. Maybe it was her way of feeling in control. She was home for just a few days before leaving for New Zealand, where on April 27 she and the girls would begin Destiny Child's world tour, the one that had to be rescheduled because of the September 11 tragedy. That she was about to embark on such an exciting adventure, yet had so little to say about it, made Lyndall feel even more disconnected from her.

"I remember looking into the side-view mirror of the car at my reflection and thinking, 'Dude, what are you gonna do? What *can* you do?'" Lyndall Locke recalled. "I turned and looked at her and she was so gorgeous, her long hair blowing in the wind, such a classic-looking beauty. I thought, 'Goddamn it, Lyndall, she used to be all yours. How'd you screw this thing up so bad?' She turned the steering wheel, and as we were hanging a left, the words came tumbling out of my mouth.

"Just so you know," Lyndall began, "after we got back together, a real long time ago? I cheated on you again."

Beyoncé didn't take her eyes off the road. "Exactly what do you mean by that?" she asked, her tone even.

"Well, I had sex with other women."

Though Beyoncé nodded, she didn't say a word. It wasn't the reaction he had expected. Because of the way her aviator sunglasses shielded her face, he had a hard time reading her expression. Like her mother, Beyoncé would never let a man see her true hurt feelings. "How many, Lyndall?" she asked.

"A few," he said, now not even wanting to look at her.

She took in the information and nodded thoughtfully. "All right," she said. "Thanks for being honest."

"I didn't know where that left us," Lyndall would recall. "I felt like crap. Her reaction told me that we were definitely over. I knew Beyoncé well," he concluded, "and I knew that she would never forget. Beyoncé doesn't forget. Beyoncé remembers."

World Tour 2002

*D*estiny's Child's world tour of 2002 was, not surprisingly, an unqualified success, with every date sold out—Australia, Japan, France, Germany, Holland, Sweden, Switzerland, England, Ireland—all a mad rush of countries, with no time for the girls to really see any of them. The schedule was packed not only with concert dates but also television and radio appearances, as well as photo sessions. There was no end to the technical challenges faced on the road, with lighting, sound, and other issues, not to mention the basic transportation of such a mammoth presentation from one country to the next. Mostly the girls tried to stay focused on their job—which was to perform. Beyoncé, though, couldn't help but want to know a little bit about everyone else's purpose; she was intrigued by—and very determined about—trying to influence as much of it as possible, especially the sound and the way it was mixed as it was being transmitted to her audience. Lighting cues were also an important concern of hers.

"As soon as we start to sing, the lights have to come up on cue," she said during technical check in Gothenburg, Sweden. "If you guys are even a second off, it'll completely ruin the moment." When the technician said he would do his best, Beyoncé frowned at him. That wasn't good enough. "You're not part of our crew, are you?" she asked skeptically. Of course, she knew he wasn't; she was familiar with all of those on the technical crew of their company. This particular person was just a freelancer brought in to assist. "Well, y'all need to check with each other," she said, "'cause if this doesn't work right, someone's gonna be really pissed off," she said, sounding stern. "I ain't kiddin', either."

"Yeah," Michelle agreed. "*Someone's* gonna be really pissed off," she repeated, motioning to Beyoncé.

"Not just me," Beyoncé said with a playful push at Michelle. "Your ass is gonna be in the pitch-black dark, too."

"Well, I don't need no light," Michelle said, teasing. "I'm my own light, that's how bright *I'm* gonna shine tonight."

"Okay, well good luck with that, then," Beyoncé said. "Me? I need a spotlight," she added, turning back to the technician. "So you best be sure I have one, and it better be big and bright, too."

The two girls then dissolved into laughter.

While on tour, Beyoncé had to make up her mind as to how she felt about Lyndall, especially in light of her growing interest in Jay. She actually couldn't get Lyndall off her mind. Even though he had let her down, in her mind he still must have seemed like family. It did seem as if she was able to see past his infidelity but still that kind of behavior wasn't what she wanted for her future. However, she didn't want to cut Lyndall out of her life. He was perhaps too much a part of her, especially in that he represented a time in her life before she was famous. "I feel like I need to hang on to him," she said at the time. "Maybe I'm just trying to hang on to who I was before all of . . . *this*," she added, referring to her fame. She didn't care, though. She wanted Lyndall in her life, and so he would remain in it—at least for the time being.

Maybe as a way of staying connected to Lyndall, she would often telephone his mother, Lydia Lockie, as she did when Destiny's Child visited Germany. "She would call me and say how much she missed my home cooking," Lydia Locke recalled. "I would say, 'Girl, shut your mouth! Do you realize that most people in this world don't get to travel like you do? So, enjoy it!' She would say, 'But I want some of your fried chicken and hot sauce, Mrs. Locke. I don't want no Wienerschnitzel!' We would laugh. 'When I come home,' she would say, 'Me and Lyndall are eatin' all your homemade pastries, and I don't care how fat I get, either!' I understood that she not only missed Lyndall, she missed me, too. After all, kids are raised by a village and I was certainly one of the villagers."

From time to time Beyoncé would also talk to Lyndall, of course. Meanwhile, though, she seemed to want to at least explore her options with Jay. The two would spend hours on the telephone, commiserating about life on the road, the loneliness of their profession, and anything else that was bothering her. Then, in the summer of 2002, they had the opportunity to vacation in the south of France. Though they wouldn't discuss publicly what, if anything, was going on between them, they didn't shy away from having their picture taken by paparazzi. At this early stage of their relationship, they were really just getting to know one another, though, taking it very slowly. "You have to understand," Jay told the writer Smokey Fontaine. "I don't even like for people to know what my girl looks like...and now I'm in a relationship with Michael Jackson!" Five years later, he would tell the same reporter, "We made a decision then to remain private about it. There are only a couple stories for the tabloids to write: 'They're a Couple!' 'They're Married!' 'They're Divorced!'"

One thing was certain: Jay knew how to show Beyoncé a good time. Being in Europe with him was a first-class experience in every way. She was dazzled not only by the sites—and certainly the south of France has little in common with Houston—but by his solicitous attitude toward her. With money being no object, it was only the best hotels, the best restaurants, the best nightclubs...the best of the best. It was difficult for a country girl not to get completely swept away by all of it. Jay felt Beyoncé deserved a good, relaxing, and even romantic experience. For someone who worked as hard as she did, having this downtime with Jay and being treated like a princess in a foreign country meant a lot.

"I remember at about this time my question to Beyoncé was: 'Why are you putting yourself out there with Jay Z?'" recalled Lonnie Jackson. "We got to talking about what people expect of her and how invested the public can become in what they hope is a big love affair. I suggested, 'Why don't we create a fantasy for people? You're becoming a sex symbol. People love you, so maybe let's give 'em a little fantasy.' She and I then wrote a song called 'Intimate Fantasy,' which was inspired by the public's growing interest in her and Jay Z. Ultimately the song was never finished, but I always felt it was the foundation for a lot of sexy, fantasy-like songs she would record in the future, like 'Baby Boy' and 'Naughty Girl.'"

While she was in the south of France with Jay, Beyoncé called Lyndall in Houston, very excited about what she viewed as a bit of a personal victory. "I just jumped off a yacht into the water," she exclaimed. "How cool is that? Jay didn't think I could do it, but I sure showed him."

"Wait up! You're hanging out with Jay Z again?" Lyndall asked. Apparently he didn't even know they were vacationing together. "What's up with you two?"

"Oh my God," Beyoncé exclaimed. "Not this again!"

All Lyndall knew for sure was that every time he heard her talk about Jay Z, it was like a knife in the heart.

Settlements

*I*n August 2002, the lawsuit against Mathew, Beyoncé, and Kelly filed by the Tillman estate was finally settled. By this time, most of those involved had given their depositions—the Tillman sons, Armon and Chris, as well as various business associates and friends and relatives, such as Andretta's mother, Effie Lee, who was the Executor of Andretta's estate. During the proceedings, there was no shortage of strange, awkward moments, such as when Beyoncé dropped in on Effie Lee's deposition. Beyoncé embraced the older woman—who she called "Granny"—and offered words of encouragement. Even though the Knowleses and the Tillmans were now on different sides of a bitter war, old familial ties still tugged at them.

As it would happen, Kelly Rowland's deposition was nothing less than devastating to the Tillmans' case. She went up against the lawyers several times. Always one to speak her mind, she actually accused LeToya Luckett and her mother, Pamela, of "probably tape recording our group meetings secretly because they were sneaky that way." She also said that LeToya had somehow stolen her and Beyoncé's Grammy tickets in 2001, thereby forcing the two of them to sit in "the peanut gallery even though we were all nominated for writing 'Say My Name.' Beyoncé and me, we had to sit up in the nosebleed section. I don't know where [the Luckett party] sat, but I'm sure it was somewhere on the floor." She was then asked to read out loud a letter she wrote to LaTavia and LeToya. "I refuse to be run over and receive punches from y'all," it said in part. "Y'all have taught me not to take crap from anyone and to always watch your own back."

When later asked how much money she made from sales of the *Survivor* album, Kelly was unhappy about being forced to answer. Finally, she snapped, "One million dollars, okay? Dang!"

In the end, whereas Beyoncé had been more than diplomatic, Kelly had been uncompromising. "Andretta never even spoke at the meetings," she testified, "unless there was some kind of disagreement with the parents, and then she was just the peacemaker." She said she was angry that the Tillman sons had filed a lawsuit and said they could have gotten money if they'd only just asked for it. "But suing our family? That's not cool," she said. Maybe her position wasn't so surprising, considering how much Mathew meant to her as a surrogate father. If the case had gone to trial, though, her testimony would have been deadly to the Tillmans' case.

The Tillmans had estimated their losses to be as much as $35 million. In the end, Armon and Chris received a total of just $1.25 million. Split between them, it came to $550,750 each. Gross attorneys' fees were $220,300, or 40 percent. After other miscellaneous expenses, each Tillman son received $232,127.21. Considering that the figure Mathew had in mind for them was $175,000 to be split between the two of them ($87,500 each), they made out better than they would have had they not sued. Still, the amount they ended up with does seem paltry, especially if Destiny's Child sold between twenty and thirty million albums, as widely reported, not to mention management fees that would have been generated by six years of touring (1997–2002), as well as lucrative merchandising of those tours. Today, the brothers feel they were pressured into the settlement. They say they were told that Destiny's Child owed Columbia/Sony about $9 million from unearned advances on their recordings and that if they went to trial they might not get any money at all!

It's difficult to say with any certainty who was told what in the context of the long-running and hard fought litigation. But if this is what the Tillman sons were told, it doesn't seem to make much sense based upon other available information. After all, Kelly testified that she received a check for $1 million for the third DC album. Record companies customarily don't give more money to artists who already owe them money. Rather, labels cross-collateralize against royalties due until the amount they owe is paid, and only then do the artists begin to make a profit. Who knows, maybe

Kelly's check was some sort of bonus or gift? Still, considering the records the group sold, it seems unlikely that Destiny's Child was in arrears to their label for $9 million, especially after that third, megahit of an album. However, as is generally the case, in signing the settlement deal the Tillmans released all future claims, meaning they would not be entitled to any proceeds from the upcoming fourth (or any other) DC album, or from any other tours.

To an outsider it seems that the biggest problem the Tillmans faced in the litigation was that Mathew and Tina insisted that Mathew's agreement with Andretta had been severely modified by joint consent to the Knowleses' advantage. Yet the Knowleses were unable to produce that new, amended contract. The Tillmans maintained that no such new amended deal existed. However, if it did exist, it was their opinion that this document must have been the one Andretta was said to have signed on her deathbed, suggesting (so far as they were concerned) that she was coerced into it. Of course, Tina and Mathew denied this, saying the document was signed much earlier. At a trial, according to legal experts, the agreements that actually *could* have been produced would have been considered valid, which may have favored the Tillmans. Given they settled the case before it could go to trial we'll never know what a judge would have decided.

Today, Armon Tillman is an entertainment manager in Houston; his company is called Tillman Management. Was the family satisfied with the settlement? "No. Absolutely not," he said. "On one hand, it wasn't about the money and we were all very clear about that. But if it did have to come down to a figure, if that was the only way to rectify things, then what we got wasn't enough. When you think of all the money Destiny's Child made? It wasn't enough. When you think of what my mom did, and what she gave up? It wasn't enough.

"To tell you the truth, some of the statements that were made in depositions and in settlement meetings made me feel worse than I had felt before the suit was filed," he added. "My mother lost her life. Give her her due, okay? I mean, damn! So am I, as her son, satisfied? No. I am not. But am I bitter? No. I am not. It is what it is. We fought. We did our best for our mother. That's what counts."

"A lot of people had said they loved my mom, but when it came time to show up for this thing [the case], man, did they run for cover!" exclaimed Chris Tillman. "Maybe they didn't want to take sides, I don't know. So I guess you could say it was a learning experience. It's just that sometimes in this life, you learn things you really don't want to know."

As for LaTavia and LeToya's suit against Mathew, that too was settled with an undisclosed monetary settlement. Many members of their families were also dissatisfied. "From the beginning, I told the girls, 'You do not settle with Mathew,'" recalled LaTavia's aunt Yvonne Boyd. "I said, 'Y'all need to take that dirty laundry and hang it out there on the line so *everyone* can see it.'" She felt that LaTavia would have received a bigger payout had they gone to court, one that in her opinion better reflected the many years her niece had put into the group since she was eight.

It would seem that no one who litigated against the Knowles family was very happy with the outcome. But now it was all over. Indeed, by the summer of 2002, Armon and Chris Tillman were relegated to the Knowleses' distant past. However, they would still have LaTavia and LeToya to contend with, because more trouble from them was right around the corner.

When the song "Survivor" was released, LaTavia and LeToya felt that Beyoncé had them in mind when she wrote it, especially given the line "You thought that I'd be stressed without you / But I'm chillin' / You thought that I wouldn't sell without you / Sold nine million." So they filed *another* lawsuit against her claiming that she had violated the settlement of the previous suit, which precluded either party from making "any public comment of a disparaging nature concerning one another." Not only was Kelly once again incorporated into the litigation as a defendant, but so was Michelle—and both girls did nothing more than just sing on the record!

Whereas some industry observers thought that LaTavia and LeToya's first suit against Mathew, Beyoncé, and Kelly had some merit, most thought this latest suit was pushing it. Was the song really about them? How could anyone but Beyoncé know for certain? Beyoncé, after the suit was filed, angrily observed, "No one knows what goes on in the head of a person who writes a song." Rather than fight it, though, she didn't want to spend another second on it and the litigation was duly settled.

"You wanna know what I think about them two girls?" Jay Z was overheard asking Beyoncé. The couple was in Houston, making their way through the busy airport getting ready to spend a few days with the Knowleses at the Missouri City home. "Forget about 'em," he said. "And just when you're fixin' to start thinkin' about 'em again? *Don't*," he said, putting his arm around her as they walked. "You feel me?" he asked.

The two were trailed by a phalanx of assistants and other functionaries, both his and hers. It was a very busy contingent. Some were on cell phones, talking very urgently. Others were conversing and taking notes as they were walking. One was especially annoying, trying to get Beyoncé's attention about a layout in *Vogue* she insisted that the pop star had to see "right now, it simply can't wait." Beyoncé shook her head and with a wave of her hand dismissed the idea of looking at the magazine in that very moment. "It can wait until I at least have a chance to sit down," she said. She was edgy; things had not been easy for some time. "Please!" she exclaimed. "Fashion can wait five minutes!"

In truth, Beyoncé hated the way things had gone down with her two former singing partners, especially with LaTavia, with whom she'd shared so much. It was difficult to reconcile that after working so hard and for so many years, their success—and the decisions each had made in light of it—was what finally laid ruin to their friendship. She had no choice but to accept what had happened and go forward with her life and career, figuring that LaTavia and LeToya were probably doing the same.

Actually, the next couple of years would be challenging ones for both LaTavia and LeToya. First, they started a new group with two other singers, called Angel. That didn't last long, however; no product was ever officially released. LaTavia in particular had a difficult time, and, as she put it, "I started to self-soothe with alcohol." She would eventually rally, pull herself together, and continue her career, mostly as an actress.

Today, LaTavia has her own hair/beauty line and is also an advocate for breast cancer awareness. (Her mom, Cheryl, is a survivor.) She still writes songs and owns her own music publishing company, and she is currently working on a memoir.

"When I look back on what happened with Destiny's Child, I wouldn't change a thing," LaTavia said in 2015. "I loved the girls. Any squabbles we had were because LeToya and I were so young and so frustrated with management. But even today, if I saw Mathew, I would give him a hug. The training I received from him has been invaluable in my life. Not only that, the Destiny's Child journey brought me to the place where I eventually had my daughter, Lyric, and I wouldn't trade her for the world."

As for LeToya Luckett, she eventually embarked on a successful music career of her own. Her first album, *LeToya*, went to number one on the *Billboard* charts in 2006, and a follow-up, *Lady Love*, made it to number twelve. She would also have a recurring role on HBO's Dwayne "the Rock" Johnson series *Ballers*, as well as appear on VH1's (and, more recently, Centric/

BET's) *Single Ladies* and HBO's *Treme*. In 2015, she was cast in an NBC drama pilot, *Love Is a Four Letter Word*.

In 2010, eight years after these various litigations were settled, Andretta, Tillman's son, Armon—now about 30—represented an artist who was up for a role in a movie. The audition was to take place, as fate would have it, at Mathew's Music World headquarters in Houston.

It had been years since Armon and Mathew last laid eyes on one another. Mathew passed by Armon twice in a hallway. Both times, he didn't seem to notice him.

A third time, though, he looked at Armon with a curious expression. After giving it a moment, Armon decided to walk down the hall and knock on Mathew's opened office door. By this time, Mathew was sitting behind his desk. "What can I do for you?" he asked as he gazed over his reading glasses at the visitor. With no small amount of hesitation, Armon said he realized that Mathew had seen him on the premises and was probably wondering who he was. "Well," he continued somewhat tremulously, "I'm... Andretta Tillman's son, Armon. How've you been, Mathew?"

Mathew's mouth dropped open. He fixed him with an earnest gaze for about fifteen, maybe twenty, seconds. The moment hung awkwardly. Finally, Mathew found his voice, again. "So... what can I do for you?" he repeated.

"Nothing," Armon said. "I just thought maybe you'd want to... I don't know... talk maybe?"

Even after everything that had happened, there was still a warm spot in Armon Tillman's heart for Mathew Knowles, a man who had, in many ways, been a father figure to him. However, any longing Armon felt for an emotional connection to Mathew was, at least judging by the older man's expression, not reciprocated. "Okay. Just leave your number with my secretary," Mathew suggested. So far as Armon could tell, he seemed somewhat confused and maybe just a little sad.

"No. On second thought, that's okay," Armon responded. "I just thought I'd say hello," he concluded with a small, amused smile. Then, as Mathew went back to his reading, Armon turned and walked away.

PART FIVE

Jay Z

Jay

$\mathcal{T}$his man has got such a sweet and kind heart," Beyoncé told Kim Wood Sandusky one night in a Manhattan hotel room. "He comes from a place of such compassion," she said. Years later, Sandusky recalled, "As I was listening to her talking about Jay Z, I sat there thinking, 'Okay, you know what? This man is going to be her husband.' I think he was opening up her heart in a way she didn't know was possible. Listening to the way she talked about him and seeing that sparkle in her eye, I knew something wonderful was unfolding in her life."

If the old axiom that opposites attract is true, perhaps that's one explanation as to how Beyoncé Knowles finally ended up with Shawn Carter, better known as Jay Z. Certainly they are from completely different worlds. She was raised middle-class in a relatively stable environment shielded from most problems by parents who—while they certainly had their own challenges—loved her and her sister unequivocally. By contrast, he was raised in a lower-income New York project called Marcy Houses (or Marcy Projects) in the Bedford-Stuyvesant neighborhood of New York by his mother, Gloria Carter. While Beyoncé spent her youth performing with Girls Tyme in the protective, safe environments of Andretta Tillman's home or that of her own parents, Shawn spent his childhood mixing in a tough neighborhood with gang members, drug addicts, and dangerous criminals. Beyoncé was raised Christian and is still religious. Jay has never claimed any sort of religious affiliation except for occasionally suggesting that he is a member of the Five-Percent Nation, a fringe organization founded in 1963 by Clarence 13X when he broke off from the Nation of Islam.

Shawn Corey Carter was the last of four children born to Gloria Carter and Adnis Reeves on December 4, 1969. Perhaps no one knows Jay like his childhood friend DeHaven Irby. "He lived across the hall from me in 5B," Irby remembered. "We met at around the age of nine. It was the projects, so everyone was close. Our mothers, sisters, brothers were all friends. It was one household, that's how we were raised. His mother, Gloria, was like my mother. Trust and loyalty stand out as to what kind of a person Jay was in my life. We played ball together, we did everything together. What I liked about him most was that you could depend on him."

In 1980, when Shawn was about eleven, his father abandoned the family. "Anger. At the whole situation," Jay Z told Oprah Winfrey when asked how he dealt with it. "Because when you're growing up, your dad is your superhero. Once you've let yourself fall that in love with someone, once you put him on such a high pedestal and he lets you down, you never want to experience that pain again. So I remember just being quiet and cold. Never wanting to let myself get close to someone like that again. I carried that feeling throughout my life."

When Shawn was about twelve, he experienced a defining moment in his life. He shot his older brother Eric in retaliation for stealing trinkets from him in order to support his crack cocaine addiction. The rapper Jaz-O—who would soon take Shawn under his wing—explained: "Shawn said it was an accident; he was trying to scare Eric. But things got out of hand. He shot him in the arm. Eric didn't press charges because he knew what he was doing, stealing from the family, was wrong. At the end of the day, they were still brothers. So, anyway...that was just a thing that happened. That ain't Shawn. Can't define Shawn by that shit."

Ultimately Eric forgave Jay and didn't press charges. Some in Jay's life have speculated, though, that it was then that his moral compass became twisted, making him believe he was somehow above the law. From that point onward, he went into a downward spiral and soon began selling drugs with his buddy DeHaven Irby. In his song lyrics, Jay Z claims to have been shot three times. His education was not a priority; he didn't graduate. "It was life during wartime," he recalled of the time he left home as a teen and began to turn a profit in the drug trade. "I lost people I loved, was betrayed by people I trusted, felt the breeze of bullets flying by my head," he said. "I saw crack addiction destroy families—it almost destroyed mine—but I sold it anyway."

Eventually, Jay began to pay attention to the sounds of the city around him, the rapping of those on street corners whose messages about their lives were similar to his own experiences. His incessant drumming on the kitchen table at all hours of the night was what caused his mother to finally recognize his innate sense of rhythm. She bought him a boom box as a birthday gift. It was then that he began coming up with his own rhymes and lyrics, freestyling about his life in the 'hood. His friends began to call him "Jazzy," a nickname that eventually evolved into "Jay-Z" (and, more recently, Jay Z, without the hyphen).

In the mid-1980s, Jay Z became a protégé of the rapper and record producer known as Jaz-O (Jonathan Burks) and began featuring on some of his earliest songs, such as "The Originators."

"When I met him, he had just turned fifteen, about 1984," Jaz-O recalled. "He was young, wet behind the ears. I was four years older and had just come back from two years of college. Everybody was sayin' this young guy in the neighborhood was the best MC in the projects. Mutual friends set up this sort of battle between us, him and me rhyming against one another. Different aspects of him reminded me of myself. He was so good, so *dope*...his cadence; he had stuff going for him that he didn't even know he had. He had raw talent. What I had was more polished. I also had knowledge of basic poetic license, metaphor, simile, onomatopoeia, so all of that is what I taught Jay when we started writing together."

When Jaz-O became the first rapper signed to the British EMI record label, he took Jay Z with him to the UK for a couple months as he recorded his debut album. "It was the first time Jay had been out of the country, the first time he experienced the record business," recalled Jaz-O. "He started to get a taste of the high life, too, with limousines and expensive dinners. He saw how much money could be made in the business. He started to get it that he didn't have to sell drugs for a living, that he had options."

Jay Z says he officially stopped selling drugs after he almost lost his life in a deal gone bad—"three shots, close range, never touched me—divine intervention," he has said. He added that "a fear of being nothing" made him reconsider his priorities; he didn't want to turn around and find himself in his thirties, still running the streets and looking to score his next big deal. "I started seeing people go to jail and get killed, and the light slowly came on," he recalled of his decision to leave the drug world behind at about the age of twenty. "I was like, this life has no good ending."

After a couple more appearances on songs by other popular rappers, Jay Z released his official debut single, "In My Lifetime," on the small label Payday in the summer of 1995. Once he started to become successful, he became less interested in maintaining a relationship with Jaz-O. "I couldn't get him on the phone anymore," said Jaz-O. "He began to surround himself with people who didn't want me around. I'm allergic to bullshit, and there was a lot of it around him. I heard him telling people, 'I came into the game on Jaz's back,' but at the same time he was hearing, 'Why the hell do you even have Jaz around? Get rid of him!' He did what he had to do. I get it. It's a business. He was done with me. But I got an ego, too. So I was done with him as well. It was too bad we never really had a good conversation about it."

Because of royalty issues with Payday, Jay Z started his own independent record label, Roc-A-Fella Records, with his friends Damon Dash and Kareem "Biggs" Burke. It has been said that no one believed in Jay like Damon; many people would go as far as to say that Damon actually "discovered" him (though, with all due respect, that honor should go to Jaz-O who Jay Z says actually tried unsuccessfully to sign with Rock-A-Fella). "Here was a guy with the same aspirations that I had," Dash recalled. "All we talked about was making money and how to spend it, what the best of everything was and how bad we wanted it."

In 1996, Jay Z released his first album, the critically acclaimed *Reasonable Doubt*, on the new label. The record went platinum and ushered in a new era not only for rap in general but for Shawn Carter as well, who had suddenly become a much-heralded voice for the genre.

A year later, Carter issued *In My Lifetime, Vol. 1*, in which he revealed controversial aspects of his childhood and upbringing. It became a huge record, going to number three on the *Billboard* Top 200. It was followed in 1998 by *Vol. 2 . . . Hard Knock Life*, another massively successful album, which sold over five million copies and won a Grammy. In 1999, he issued *Vol. 3 . . . Life and Times of S. Carter*, which sold another three million. Still, trouble seemed to follow him. In 1999, he was arrested for stabbing record executive Lance Rivera, who he believed had been bootlegging his music. He pled not guilty but later changed his plea to guilty of a misdemeanor. He was put on three years' probation.

A year later, the rapper released *The Dynasty: Roc La Familia*, doubtless his most accessible and soulful album, and another major hit. It was also at about this time that Jay became godfather to DaHaven Irby's firstborn, Christina. "It couldn't have been anybody else," Irby says, "that's how close we were." Jay took DeHaven to the hospital on a frigid Valentine's Day evening, the night Christina was born. The two men held her in their arms for the first time.

After his string of hits, however, DaHaven felt that Jay began to distance himself from him. "I actually don't know what happened," Irby said. "He started surrounding himself with people who made it impossible for those of us who had been close to him to get in touch. Now he's the godfather of Kanye [West]'s kid, and he acts like Christina isn't in his life, and I guess she's not because he's disappeared from both of us. The responsibility of being a godfather is that if something happens to me you make sure my daughter is taken care of. I have had to accept that if something happened to me, Jay would not be there for Christina. I don't know this Jay. I only know the one I grew up with, and it ain't this one. I miss the guy I knew, that's all I can say. I miss the guy I knew."

"Look, this is just what happens," observed Chad Elliott. Elliott, who would go on to cowrite and coproduce "Jumpin' Jumpin'" for Destiny's Child, happened to be a close friend of Jay's and Jaz-O's in these early days. At the time, he was a record executive who tried unsuccessfully to get Jay signed to Motown. "On his journey, Jay didn't always take the necessary steps to remember who was with him at the beginning, who really mattered, and I'm not talking about just the guy in the studio one night who told him how great he was, but the guys who were key in his life," he says. "But you have to understand, it's a fast-moving train, and when you're on it, it's not easy to stop and consider every aspect of the ride. You're just ridin' as fast as you can. So, yes, some of the passengers get lost along the way. That's just a fact, a consequence, if you will, of the road you have to travel to be successful in this business."

Obviously, there are people in his life who feel let down by Jay, which is not unusual—as Chad Elliott points out—in the lives of people who came from nothing, forged relationships with friends of similar circumstances, and then went on to great success. Jay Z was never one to look back. He is nothing if not a self-invented man; nobody ever gave him anything, his success is hard-earned. To become a phenomenon in the record business, he implemented much of the same skill set that made him a successful drug dealer, such as his ability to read people and intuit the next, best course of action. He has also been incredibly philanthropic; untold millions of his have gone toward his charitable efforts. Along with his drive and ambition, he is a master media strategist. Nothing is ever left to chance when it comes to his public image. "He is always thinking two steps ahead of everyone else," concluded Jaz-O. "If you think anything is ever an accident in terms of what you're seeing from Jay Z, you'd be wrong."

One night early in his career, Jay Z and Chad Elliott partied together in a nightclub in New Jersey. They left the club in the wee hours of the morning. Chad, the Motown executive, got into his Mercedes convertible, Jay, the rapper, in his white Lexus. The two pulled out onto a busy highway, and a short time later happened to end up stopped at a red light, side by side. They glanced at each other, took in each other's luxury vehicles, smiled, and nodded their approval.

"Lookin' good, my brother," Chad said to Jay.

Jay grinned at him. "Dude, I'm just tryin' to be like you," he told him.

"Don't worry about that, my brother," Chad said, "because you're gonna be so much bigger than me, it ain't even funny, Jay. *It ain't even funny!*"

With that, the light turned green, Jay Z stepped on the gas, pulled ahead of his friend . . . and was gone in a flash.

"'03 Bonnie & Clyde"

*I*n the spring of 2002, Jay Z called the rapper Kanye West to ask him to come up with an idea for a possible duet with Beyoncé. Coincidentally, West had already been toying with the notion of sampling the late rapper Tupac Shakur's song "Me and My Girlfriend" as the foundation for a new song on Jay's next album, *The Blueprint²: The Gift & the Curse*. He'd already composed an instrumental track for the song with musician E. Base and producer Just Blaze. When Kanye played it for Jay, Jay was so inspired by it that he had a video concept in mind for him and Beyoncé before he even had lyrics for the song. It didn't take long for him to come up with the rap, which is in part, "Let's lock this down like it's supposed to be / the '03 Bonnie and Clyde, Hov and B." ("Hov" and "Hova" are nicknames Jay Z took after proclaiming himself the "Jehovah of hip-hop"— the savior of the genre.) Beyoncé, on the hook, brings the song home with, "Down to ride to the very end, me and my boyfriend."

In August 2002, Jay and Beyoncé went into the studio to record the song. Released soon afterward, in October, it would end up being the lead single from *The Blueprint²: The Gift & the Curse* (which debuted at number one on the *Billboard* Top 200).

Considering that Beyoncé's first solo release four months earlier had been the disappointing "Work It Out," there was not only anticipation but also some apprehension for whatever she had in mind next. No one could have predicted a duet with the hottest rapper in the business.

Beyoncé—cool, aloof, and impossibly gorgeous in her bare-midriff outfits and a variety of ball caps—seems a very different character in the

"'03 Bonnie & Clyde" video from the young woman in the many Destiny's Child videos. As the two play criminals on the lam, her rapport with Jay is unmistakable. "We exchanged audiences," Jay would later recall to *Rolling Stone*. "Her records are huge Top 40 records, and she helped 'Bonnie and Clyde' go to number one. What I gave her was a street credibility, a different edge."

"What am I gonna do with this tattoo now?" Lyndall Locke asked Beyoncé after it was clear that she and Jay were now together. By this time, Lyndall had no choice; he had to accept it. Beyoncé had moved on, she was with Jay now, and there was no going back. Long ago he'd gotten a tattoo of the letters "B.G.K." on his upper thigh while on a high school senior trip to Mexico, for "Beyoncé Giselle Knowles." In helping him try to figure out what to do with the tat now, she suggested he have an "I" tattooed between the "B" and "G," and then have the "K" changed to an "L," thereby making it "B.I.G.L."—"for Big Lyndall," she said, laughing. "Problem solved!"

For Beyoncé, it would seem that the problem of Lyndall Locke really was on its way to being solved.

It seems unfair to point out the differences between Lyndall and Jay. After all, most men would pale when compared to Jay Z, an artist who used his talent, wit, and a language all his own to leave the ghetto behind and amass a veritable fortune. By the time he and Beyoncé began dating, he was on his seventh hit album and was said to have a net worth of $120 million. Though the two were still getting to know one another, Jay was proving himself as someone in whom Beyoncé could confide. Whereas she rarely had in-depth conversations with Lyndall about her career, with Jay such dialogue somehow seemed more natural. Since he was also in the business, he understood her and her lifestyle and some of the challenges she faced. He noticed, for instance, that she seemed not to be in touch with her anger. When she had a disagreement with her record label, she spent the week silently fuming over it. "You need to let that shit out," he told her. She said that her mother had taught her a more decorous way, which was, she said, "to count to ten." Jay suggested, "Count to three, you'll be better off."

He also noticed that she seemed suspicious by nature. Perhaps because of having been so protected for so long, Beyoncé didn't always trust people with whom she had to work who were not in her immediate circle. She knew it was true and had begun to work on it while on the sets of her movies. Jay was the same way, always had been. He too was working on it.

Conversely, when it came to her fans, Beyoncé had no discerning ability whatsoever. "At one point, Beyoncé thought *everybody* was her friend," recalled her bodyguard, Tony Brigham. "It took me and her dad to sit her down and talk to her, just for safety issues."

Beyoncé would vacillate back and forth as she worked to find a place where she could trust others yet also be protective, not only of her business affairs but also her personal safety. Jay did what he could to help. "Fact is, Bey, not everyone is out to get you," he would reportedly tell her, "though most people probably are," he would conclude with a chuckle.

Dangerously in Love

*T*hough there were a few songs on the first four Destiny's Child albums (including the Christmas album) that must have felt to Beyoncé like solo recordings, considering that she sang all of the parts, the truth was that she didn't have to bear full responsibility for those compositions. They were still released as Destiny's Child songs and as such were not branded with her name. Thus she was able to keep a certain distance from them. If the songs weren't successful in the marketplace, they wouldn't reflect poorly on her as much as they would on the group. Of course, most of those songs were wildly successful not only from a commercial standpoint but from an artistic one as well. Still, when the time came for Beyoncé to record a solo album, she felt intense pressure and anxiety about it. She had raised the bar so high for herself with Destiny's Child, she wondered how she would ever meet such standards. Adding to the pressure was that even with the support of a label that had always endorsed the idea of a solo career for her, it was now clear that success was not guaranteed in that venue. It was still a gamble, and she and everyone in her camp knew it.

Because Beyoncé felt that she needed a fresh approach to the album, she decided she didn't want to record it in Houston. Therefore, she and Mathew agreed that she should set herself up in a Miami hotel. "I wanted to be around the ocean," she told the *Washington Post*. "And I basically stayed at this hotel; downstairs was the studio, and that's what I did. I went from upstairs to downstairs to around the corner to work out, back to the hotel. With this album, I wanted to grow artistically as an artist and as a writer. It really was experimental," she said. "Everything I wanted to say, any chord

I wanted to play or sing, I did . . . any weird, strange minor harmony . . . every weird lyric that didn't make sense, I sang."

When word got out that Beyoncé was making a solo album, demos of songs came flooding in for her consideration. By now, producers and beat makers the world over knew that getting a song on a Destiny's Child album could make a new producer famous and rich, and an established one even richer; for them, the success of DC was at least an indicator as to what Beyoncé's own album might do in the marketplace. For Beyoncé's part, she wanted to create an album that reflected her growth and ambition as a singer, writer, and producer.

To find the best writers and producers to assist in her musical vision, Beyoncé spent two days personally interviewing potential collaborators from both coasts. She knew exactly what she wanted, too. After all, she practically grew up in the studio. Even before she knew the definition of a musical bridge or what an 808 was (the Roland TR-808, a popular programmable drum machine), she knew the function of both entities. Early on, she participated in the creation of her music and learned to deal with the egos of men who didn't always want to hear a woman tell them, "Play that again," "That hook doesn't work for me," or "We've tried it that way, now let's try it my way." She'd earned the respect of male collaborators for three reasons: First, she knew what she wanted; second, she wasn't afraid to say so; and third, her ideas consistently translated into hits.

Beyoncé wanted as many influences on the album as possible, so she selected some well-known artists as collaborators, including reggae star Sean Paul, Luther Vandross, OutKast's Big Boi, and Missy Elliott. A big influence, though, would be Jay Z, who would appear on two songs, "Crazy in Love" and "That's How You Like It." He would also cowrite two others.

"I worked with Jay Z on his album, so I asked him to do the same," Beyoncé recalled. "We work really well together in the studio. Hip-hop and R&B is always a great collaboration. There's a male point of view, and a female point of view. Men relate; women relate. He's one of the best rappers, I think." At this time, 2002, Beyoncé was adamant that she would not discuss her personal relationship with Jay, saying only, "We're just cool. We're just friends. We don't really know each other like that."

Jay may have been on her mind, but Lyndall Locke may have been too. He claimed she had written the title track of the album years earlier while with him. Lyndall recalls that Beyoncé wrote "Dangerously in Love" while the two of them were relaxing at her house in 1998. "She sang this song that she said was about us," he recalled. "It was crazy good. I said, 'You really gonna record that song and put it out into the world?' And she said, 'Yep, I sure am.' When I hear it today, it really hits me hard." (When the song was finally released, the public thought Beyoncé was referring to Jay with the lyric "I was in love with a Sagittarius / See the emotions he put me through," since Jay is a Sagittarius, born on December 4. However, so is Lyndall, who was born under that same sign, on December 3.)

The first song Beyoncé recorded for her album at Miami's South Beach Studios was "Naughty Girl," a sensual groove employing Donna Summer's 1975 hit "Love to Love You." She cowrote and coproduced the track with Scott Storch, with whom she'd collaborate on two other album tracks, the exotic "Baby Boy," featuring rapper Sean Paul, and "Me, Myself and I," a solid midtempo neo-soul track that Beyoncé would describe as "the celebration of a breakup."

Remarkably, when Beyoncé submitted the finished album, *Dangerously in Love*, to her record label, there was talk among the powers-that-be about not releasing it. In some respects, of course, this was a surprise, especially considering that the company had always suggested to Beyoncé that it supported her ambition to be a solo artist. However, with the stinging history of "Work It Out" still fresh on everyone's minds, an abundance of caution was now being exercised when it came to Beyoncé's music. Even the success of "'03 Bonnie & Clyde" wasn't enough to get rid of the bad taste left in the mouths of many by "Work It Out."

"They told me I didn't have one hit on the album," Beyoncé would later say. "I guess they were kinda right. *I had five.*" It was a joke in her act, but in truth Beyoncé would never forget Columbia/Sony's initial doubts about her. As she moved forward with both Destiny's Child and her solo projects, her subsequent actions—how she dealt with Columbia/Sony, her guarded faith in the label's belief in her, and her quest for control over how she was marketed and promoted—would reflect the label's original ambivalence about her debut album.

"Crazy in Love"

$\mathcal{B}$eyoncé was several tracks deep into the production of her first album when she began collaborating with the producer who would change pretty much everything for her in terms of her pop music career. Rich Harrison had worked on Kelly Rowland's successful 2002 solo album *Simply Deep*, contributing the track "Can't Nobody." He'd earlier cut his teeth with two Mary J. Blige projects. However, it was his writing and production of *All I Have*, the debut album of his protégée, singer Amerie, that really got Beyoncé's attention.

Most every successful songwriter, no matter how much in demand, has a song or two he is holding back for just the right act. For Harrison, that song was an idea he envisioned building around a sample he treasured from "Are You My Woman (Tell Me So)," a 1970 song by 1970s R&B vocal group the Chi-Lites. Written by Eugene Record, the group's lead singer and main songwriter, "Are You My Woman" wasn't even one of the Chi-Lites' most successful titles; the 1971 soul classics "Oh Girl" and "Have You Seen Her?" were the group's breakout hits. However, Harrison was taken with "Are You My Womans'" sensational horn riff. It was followed by a dramatic instrumental breakdown featuring an exciting cymbal riding over spirited percussion. Adopting that bit of the song, that sample, as one of his secret weapons, Harrison tucked it away to be unleashed at just the right time. "I hadn't really shopped it much," he said. "Sometimes you don't want to come out of the bag before it's right. If people don't really get it, you'll leave them with a foul taste in their mouth."

In December 2002, Harrison got the call to join the Beyoncé project, which Mathew had by then moved to Sony Music Studios in Manhattan. Elated, Harrison celebrated by going out on the town with friends. The next day, he arrived at the studio late and hungover. Overlooking his tardiness, Beyoncé asked him what music he had for her to hear. Harrison proudly played his prized horn sample, turning up the volume while standing back and waiting for the accolades. They weren't forthcoming. In fact, Beyoncé wasn't sure what to think; she was pretty sure she didn't like it. "I knew I was going to have to sell it a little bit," Harrison recalled, "because when [the song] comes on, it doesn't sound like anything that was being done at the time." Beyoncé actually thought the track sounded a little too old-school. "No one's using horn sounds today," she reasoned. Indeed, Beyoncé was reaching for what sounded current and hot in 2002, and in her opinion that didn't include horns.

However, after a couple more listens to Harrison's little sample, Beyoncé's reticence began to ebb. An explosive stage performer by nature, maybe she was seduced by the sheer excitement of the music: It was *big*, exhilarating, and action-packed. It felt like ... *showtime*. It was in Beyoncé's expression of concentration that Harrison found the hope he so desperately sought. "From her face," he said, "she was kinda like, 'I don't know, but I'mma ride with you anyway.'"

She may have been willing to "ride," but Beyoncé insisted that Harrison do all of the driving: Leaving the studio for a couple of hours, she told him to write an actual song around the sample while she was gone. The very idea of having to write for such a high-profile artist in such a short amount of time was frightening. If he didn't come up with something brilliant by the time Beyoncé returned, chances were good that she'd lose interest in the whole idea. However, Harrison definitely rose to the occasion; by Beyoncé's return two hours later, he'd written all the song's verses, leaving the lyrics on the bridge section for her to write herself. As the two discussed his work, Beyoncé happened to glance at herself in a mirror. Dressed casually with her hair not perfectly coiffed, she remarked out loud, to no one in particular, "Oh my God! I'm looking so *crazy* right now."

"Hey! That's the hook!" Harrison exclaimed.

Now Beyoncé was intrigued. After hearing the track repeatedly, she began singing the song's sassy "Uh-oh, uh-oh, uh-oh, no, no, no" hook, and the whole song came together from there. Ecstatic about its development, Beyoncé called Jay, who came to the studio at about three in the morning. Loving what he heard, he walked into the sound booth, put on headphones, and recorded his largely improvised rap verse in a matter of just minutes.

And thus was born "Crazy in Love," the song that blasted Beyoncé's solo possibilities wide open. It's the kind of hit every artist prays for, a smash that defines and/or redefines a whole career while catapulting it to the next level. Beyoncé confidently rides the driving rhythm as she sings with steely, soulful resolve of the delirious, *delicious* psychosis of love. For all his skills, Jay Z's rap interlude doesn't alter the fact that this song is really all about Beyoncé and her sexy association with its dynamic groove.

"Crazy in Love" was released on May 18, 2003. By the time *Dangerously in Love* was issued a month later—selling almost four hundred thousand copies in its first week—both the album and single were number one on

Billboard's respective charts. "Crazy in Love" would spend eight consecutive weeks at number one.

"Baby Boy," the next single from the album, did even better, reaching number one and staying there a week longer than its predecessor. "Me, Myself and I" and "Naughty Girl" were both Top Five singles.

Come awards season, *Dangerously in Love* pulled in trophies around the world, among them the 2004 Grammy for Best Contemporary R&B Album. Meanwhile, "Crazy in Love" also won Grammys for Best R&B Song and Best Rap/Sung Collaboration (with Jay Z), while the single "Dangerously in Love 2" won for Best Female R&B Vocal Performance.

Ultimately, *Dangerously in Love* would clock worldwide sales of more than twelve million copies and downloads. With this album, Beyoncé's career truly began to soar ... and there was no turning back.

The Birth of Sasha Fierce

*I*f the ability to be an icon is contingent on creating iconography, it involves the creation of a character that can be digestible to the world. That character is a version of the person who created it, but certainly not the true self. Most celebrities put forth an image that isn't really who they are in their private lives. Sometimes the image doesn't get in the way of the person's true identity because the two are so closely aligned. Madonna comes to mind. Her brazen stage persona is very closely connected to who she actually is in the real world. The same holds true for Cher, for instance. Sometimes, though, the iconography is in such opposition to the authentic nature of the celebrity that it causes genuine conflict. Michael Jackson, for example, created a tabloid image for himself in the 1980s with PR gimmicks that eventually backfired and then did serious damage to his reputation. Indeed, putting forth a false image for public consumption can be a dicey proposition, and it usually ends with the celebrity lamenting that the public doesn't really know or understand the true person behind the mask. In Beyoncé's life, "Sasha Fierce," whom she always described as her "alter ego," is the character she purposely created—an identity very much *not* in line with who she actually was as a person.

It could be said that with the creation of Sasha Fierce, Beyoncé was playing with fire and didn't even know it. She was too young and inexperienced to understand the potential consequence of creating a false sense of herself for the world. All she thought she was doing at the time was making a distinction between her more shy offstage personality and the self-possessed, sexy diva she became once she hit the stage.

How Sasha Fierce first manifested, she has said, was that one evening onstage, Beyoncé snatched off the expensive Lorraine Schwartz diamond earrings she was wearing on loan and, in a fit of showmanship, hurled them out into the audience. That's when her cousin Angie dubbed her "Sasha Fierce," suggesting a marked difference between the real Beyoncé and the one who would do such a thing. When the show was over and she'd gotten ahold of herself, Beyoncé told Angie, "Girl, you need to get out there and get me my earrings back, because I'm not payin' for them! They cost $250,000!" Angie actually found the person who'd caught the earrings, telling her, "Those are my cousin's!" and demanding their return.

The Sasha Fierce character was on full display in the "Crazy in Love" video that was shot in the late winter of 2003. Beyoncé conveys her sexuality through a series of intricate dance numbers and fashions mixing couture and street chic. One might speculate, at least based on this production, that the budding relationship with Jay had somehow freed her to explore her sensuous side.

In the video, we first encounter Beyoncé as she sashays down the middle of Mission Road in downtown Los Angeles with Jay racing in a car toward her. Her look is decidedly earthy: a plain white tank top, denim short shorts, and red pumps; her hair long, straight, and highlighted; her makeup minimal. After Jay declares "history in the making," Beyoncé drops to the sidewalk on all fours and starts singing: "I look and stare so deep in your eyes." A generation earlier, in 1984 at the MTV Music Awards, Madonna shocked and excited audiences by getting down on her hands and knees onstage and sensuously rolling around on the floor while singing "Like a Virgin." Beyoncé ups the ante by squatting to the ground and, in a series of fast cuts, manipulating her agile body into a series of erotically charged poses, her long legs working her red heels. During the routine she twists, gyrates, twerks, and lays her body flat out on the concrete.

Making the imagery even more impactful is that Beyoncé seems to have had breast augmentation surgery by this time; or in any event, she's much more voluptuous.

One aspect of the Sasha Fierce character is best described by Beyoncé's longtime makeup artist, Billy B. "From the time she was a child, Beyoncé could be intensely self-critical in an effort to make sure everything is just right onstage," he said. "By creating the Sasha Fierce character, she created an entity that could take the blame if something went wrong. After all, it wasn't her up there onstage, it was Sasha Fierce. Sasha Fierce was the brand, not Beyoncé. So, from my talking to her about it over the years, I think it was more than just 'Sasha is sexy and I'm not.' It was also a protective mechanism. The alter ego, Sasha Fierce, could make a mistake for which she, the real Beyoncé, didn't then have to suffer for. It was her way of separating the brand from the person. That's how I saw it, anyway."

Billy B. has a good point. Certainly, from the time she was a child, when most kids her age were building treehouses, Beyoncé was building an image, even if she didn't consciously know it—and the Sasha Fierce characterization was an early manifestation of it.

The problem with Sasha Fierce, which would become more evident with the passing of time, was that she became a psychological crutch for Beyoncé. She was one half of a split identity put forth by a young lady who might have been better served trying to merge all of the facets of who she was into one private personality. In the end, it wasn't just her sexy side that Beyoncé was trafficking with Sasha Fierce. It was her *anger*, and anyone could see as much by watching her performances. It was as if Sasha Fierce was a doppelgänger Beyoncé created to whom she attempted to transfer all of the protest she was feeling in her private life: about missing out on her childhood; about the way her father treated her mother; about the way she felt she'd been treated by Lyndall Locke; about the disloyalty of former singing partners; and maybe even about giving up her entire life for show business.

In a family that usually seemed out of touch with their emotions—or at the very least had gotten used to suppressing them—Sasha Fierce was an easy way out for Beyoncé Knowles, and one she was able to take with the approval of what probably felt to her like the entire world. It would be a few years before she would begin to understand the identity crisis—or maybe it's better viewed as an existential crisis, represented in her life by this untamed character.

Father Issues

*A*fter the success of "'03 Bonnie & Clyde," some music critics thought that Jay Z had introduced Beyoncé to a brand-new urban demographic. However, once "Crazy in Love" became a big hit, others began to feel that *she* was the one expanding *his* fan base. Later, she would record a song with Jay called "Upgrade You," in which she would expound on this popular notion, though mostly in terms of the two exposing one another to the better (read: materialistic) things in life: "How you gonna upgrade me?" Jay asks her in the song, "What's higher than number one?" In broader terms, though, speaking of his own core audience, there's little doubt that Beyoncé had a huge impact on it.

"Jay had his own unique demographic and it definitely wasn't a pop demo," recalled Choke No Joke. He was Damon Dash's videographer at Roc-A-Fella Records from 2000 to 2005. "He'd had a pop hit with 'Hard Knock Life' but he was still in the demo of the urban community," he recalled of Jay. "Aligning himself with Beyoncé, the cream of the crop of not just R&B but also the pop world, brought Jay Z into a whole other light with a whole new audience. When he got with Beyoncé, that's when you started seeing him wear suits, for instance, instead of baggy pants and base-ball caps. It started slowly, but it definitely built between 2003 and 2005. That's when Jay started presenting himself in an entirely different way.

"Call it fate, call it manipulation, whatever the case, Beyoncé came along at just the right time in his life," Choke No Joke continued. "In terms of his audience, Jay got more out of the bargain than she did. Anyone who questions that *she* upgraded *him* wasn't watching their careers from the beginning. There's no question that she helped him get more revenue by putting her brand next to his."

It's no coincidence that Jay Z became more fully involved with Beyoncé in 2003, the year his father died. By the time they returned to France in August 2003, they seemed to be on their way toward a full-blown rela-tionship. By his own admission, Jay would probably not have been able to sustain one with Beyoncé prior to this time because of deep-seated issues having to do with his father. He would say that his resentment of Adnis Reeves for having abandoned the family when he was eleven had been responsible for many of his bad decisions. It had also closed him off emotionally. Though Jay had vaguely discussed this problem with Beyoncé, he'd decided not to dwell on it with her. He liked her and didn't want to scare her away with too much information. He was already afraid his controversial background would be a burden for her to carry, not to mention one for her parents as well. So when it came to Adnis, he held back.

As it happened, Jay Z's mother understood that he would never be able to live a well-adjusted life until he once and for all settled matters with Adnis. "I remember very distinctly that I had a conversation with her in my kitchen," he said of his mother, Gloria. "I was saying, 'You know, Ma, I've really been trying to look inward, and maybe I'm just not meant to fall in love like other people do.' She just looked at me like, 'Hush up, boy.' She figured out what was wrong with me, and so she planned a meeting between me and my father. I was like, 'Ma, I'm a grown man. I don't need a dad now.'"

Of course, that meeting—in 2002, when Jay Z was thirty-three—wasn't easy for either father or son. "He showed up, and I gave him the real conversation," Jay Z recalled. "I told him how I felt the day he left. He was saying stuff like, 'Man, you knew where I was.' I'm like, '*I was a kid!* Do you realize how wrong you were? It was *your* responsibility to see *me*.' He finally accepted that."

Though Jay had long heard stories about it, Adnis finally explained the true reason he left home. He said that he'd become obsessed with finding the killer of his brother and that during his fruitless search—which began when Jay was just a boy—he became addicted to drugs. His life was a downward spiral from the point on. Jay understood. In fact, this heart-to-heart with Adnis completely set Jay straight, allowing him to release many years of anger and resentment. He then helped Adnis into a new apartment and even bought him furniture for it. However, by this time, Adnis was suffering from serious liver disease, the sad consequence of a life of heavy drinking.

On June 18, 2003, the night Jay Z and his partner Juan Perez opened their deluxe 40/40 sports bar and lounge in Manhattan, Adnis passed away. It was then that Jay began to understand that his mother likely knew that his dad was nearing the end of his life, and that there had been no time to waste in effecting reconciliation. Jay says that forgiving Adnis "absolutely" opened him up to the possibility of love in his life. It was after his father's death that he began to fully pursue with an open heart a relationship with Beyoncé. In a real sense, it was all about timing where Jay and Beyoncé were concerned. She came in at the tail end of his reconciliation with his father and was with him when Adnis died. Therefore, she understood a lot of what was going on with him as it unfolded, forging a bond with him that was undeniable, especially since she had her own father issues.

One of Beyoncé's relatives recalls a conversation between Beyoncé and Jay after Mathew and Beyoncé had a rather tense exchange relating to a business deal he was in the process of negotiating for her. She was concerned about the way the matter was being handled and had several suggestions. Mathew wasn't sure they were practical, though. After the success of "Crazy in Love," Beyoncé more than ever had her own ideas about video concepts, music selection, and especially her stage show. She seemed inclined to question much of what Mathew proposed.

Some thought Beyoncé would grow out of the phase in which she believed her father to be wrong about almost everything. For most teenagers, it was a natural part of going through adolescence. For Beyoncé, though, it was becoming more a way of life, especially by the time she turned twenty. Some couldn't help but wonder if she had conflicted feelings about Mathew, possibly because of the way he had conducted himself in his marriage to her mother. It did sometimes seem as if there was some underlying issue in her relationship with him other than just professional disagreement. It's difficult to know, though, since the family remained very private, especially when it came to Beyoncé's true feelings about Mathew now that she was famous. She may not have been candid with Jay about them either, not yet anyway. Even Kelly, in her deposition taken during the Tillman case, was clear that she and Beyoncé never discussed Mathew's infidelities. She said that she wasn't one to bring such matters up to Beyoncé because she knew it was something she just didn't want to discuss—and this was while they were living in the same house! While that seems a little hard to believe, it was Kelly's testimony just the same, and she was under oath when she gave it.

"I get your frustration about Mathew," Jay Z told Beyoncé, according to the witness to the conversation. "But look at how involved your father has been in your life. I *wish* I'd had a father like Mathew Knowles. Jesus Christ! Who knows how I would have turned out?"

Beyoncé saw Jay's point, but she offered her own that it was precisely *because* of the absence of Adnis in his life that Jay had been so motivated to make something of himself. Jay had to concede as much. Still, he had great respect for the way Mathew managed Beyoncé and for the sacrifices he'd made for her. It was clear to him that Mathew would do anything for his daughter. It was the little things that most impressed him.

When she got her first tattoo, for instance— a praying mantis on her left hip—Beyoncé was very unhappy with her decision. She simply didn't like it and was sorry she'd ever done it. Mathew told her not to beat herself up about it, though. In fact, he offered to get the exact same tattoo if it would make her feel better about things. Jay thought that little story said a lot about Mathew and never really forgot it. (Years later, Beyoncé would have the offending tattoo removed by laser.)

"For a man with no background in show business to have done what you did, it just blows my mind," Jay told Mathew. Mathew predicted that one day Jay would have a family of his own, and when that day happened he would know that "there are pretty much no limits to what a father will do for his kid."

There was no tension between Jay and Mathew when they first met, even though Beyoncé may have been nervous about how her parents were going to feel about Jay's past. She needn't have been concerned, though. "Jay is just such a gentleman," Tina said once she got to know him. "I'm so happy they got together. They're two smart people, and it's great for both of them. It's such a great match."

"Great match," maybe. But Jay was still no choirboy, and most people in the hip-hop world knew it.

Choke No Joke recalls what happened to him the night Damon Dash asked him to videotape Jay at a concert at Manhattan Center; this was around the time Jay first started dating Beyoncé. As the videographer shot footage of the performance, Jay seemed unclear as to whether or not he had the authority to do so. One of his handlers tried to get the tape from Choke. "Step off!" Choke warned him. But then suddenly a group of men jumped out of seemingly nowhere and swarmed the cameraman. During the ensuing fracas, someone tried to kick his camera from his hand, and when he did, his foot accidentally made contact with Choke's jaw, fracturing it. "When I got out of the Harlem hospital—face all swelled up lookin' like the dude from [the movie] *Mask*, my jaw all wired—I confronted Dame [Damon Dash]," Choke No Joke recalled. "He's like, 'Yo, Jay will take care of you, dawg.' So [Jay] offered me some paper [money]. I ain't saying how much. But if Jay denies it, I still got the check stub to prove it."

Brand Beyoncé

*I*s my daughter here?" Tina Knowles asked the receptionist at Music World's Houston headquarters. She stood before the employee with a sparkling, bugle-beaded black-and-white gown draped in her arms. It was carefully wrapped in plastic and probably worth many thousands of dollars. "I need her to try this on right quick," Tina said. "I think it's probably gonna be too long."

"She's in there with Mr. Knowles," the receptionist said, motioning to a closed door behind which was Mathew's office.

"How long have they been in there?" Tina wanted to know.

"At least two hours," answered the receptionist. "Should I interrupt?"

Tina mulled it over. "Probably not," she decided.

"Could be a while," said the receptionist.

"Tell me about it," Tina said with a laugh. "I'm just gonna leave this with you," she added as she handed her glittering creation to the receptionist. With that, she took her leave. She knew that once Mathew and Beyoncé sequestered themselves in his office, many more hours could pass before either would once again see the light of day.

By 2004, Beyoncé had entered the stage of her career where she wanted to know everything there was to know about the business behind it. Who better to teach her than her own father?

People have always looked for some sort of complex business plan when it came to the saturation of the Beyoncé brand, but it's not there. Mathew Knowles is an everyman sort of entrepreneur. While everything he did was of course structured and strategized, all of it sprang from his grassroots mentality as a salesman. It utilized the same philosophy that made him flourish in the many sales jobs he took on before Girls Tyme: Give the people what they want, give them plenty of it, and make sure the product is good so they keep coming back for me. By 2004, he'd made his daughter absolutely ubiquitous, bringing in untold amounts of money for everyone concerned: the product . . . the group . . . his family.

There seemed to be no end to the ways Mathew envisioned exposing Beyoncé to the masses, great ideas such as when he had her sing the national anthem before almost ninety million people at Super Bowl XXXVIII in Houston in February 2004. A week later, Mathew had her perform "Crazy in Love" during halftime at the NBA All-Star Game. By this time, she had replaced Britney Spears in television commercials for Pepsi. She was also linked to the Tommy Hilfiger brand as well as L'Oreal, representing products used by a cross-section of consumers, with nothing offensive or the least bit controversial. Later she would become a spokeswoman for Samsung and American Express. There was also a Wal-Mart commercial that showed the girls of Destiny's Child and the Knowleses exchanging Christmas gifts. There were countless foreign commercials, too, such as one in Egypt for Pepsi featuring Beyoncé with Jennifer Lopez as samurai sword–wielding martial artists. The group also partnered with many corporations for tour sponsorships, such as DC's "I'm Lovin' It" tour sponsored by McDonald's, which featured the girls in commercials.

Knowles told Michael Hall for *Texas Monthly*, "When you sell a product, you first have to design and build it, but also you have to figure out the needs of the customer. When we put the group together, we had a plan. We figured out our demographic, our customers, our imaging, what type of songs we're going to sing. It's not by accident that we write songs like 'Independent Women' and 'Survivor'—female-based empowerment songs. That's our customer base." Of course, those song ideas were Beyoncé's, not his, but as her manager Mathew wasn't above sometimes taking universal credit.

Despite the careful planning that went into Beyoncé's career, there would always be the occasional unfortunate misstep. Nothing was more incongruous, for instance, than seeing her pose with a box of Hamburger Helper. She became aligned with the product (in 2008) as part of Feed America's "Show Your Helping Hand" charity campaign. If anything, it served to put forth the impression that she would attach her name to anything if the price was right. (Not that she doesn't use the product in her private life, because she does. In fact, she jokingly calls herself "the *master* of Hamburger Helper.")

Certainly her film *The Fighting Temptations* (released in the fall of 2003) also falls into that category of miscalculations. Whereas *Carmen: A Hip Hopera* gave Beyoncé a meaty and multidimensional role, and *Austin Powers* had her playing off the campiness of her Foxxy Brown character, *The Fighting Temptations* gave her pretty much nothing; the character she played was just a pretty young woman who could sing. It's a full forty minutes into the ninety-minute film before she actually has a line!

That unfortunate dud aside, most everything else Mathew and Beyoncé touched at this time turned to gold. Thus Mathew was eager to share what he learned about branding and career management with Beyoncé, though it could be said that he wasn't always the most patient teacher. Laser-focused on and maybe even obsessive about whatever it was he was doing, of course he demanded her full attention. For instance, if he was in the middle of explaining the complex machinations of product licensing, the last thing he wanted to see was her pulling her BlackBerry from her purse to start texting Kelly. After a few false starts, Beyoncé soon began to devote herself completely to her pursuit of knowledge, taking copious notes during her time at Music World and reading as many books recommended by Mathew as possible.

Often Beyoncé's cousin Angie would sit in on these business meetings with Mathew. She was wise to the finer points of show business, having been on the road with Destiny's Child for years. She taught Beyoncé to be tough and ask questions, to not take anything for granted. "I don't want people to get the impression that I think they're lying," Beyoncé would say. "Well, guess what, girl? They probably *are*," Angie would tell her. Many people who were on the road with Destiny's Child have stories of the two cousins sequestered in one of their hotel rooms, reviewing accounting books and contracts. The two were known to have conference calls with promoters and with Mathew, and if there was any sort of discrepancy, most certainly Angie would find it.

One promoter with a long history in the concert business recalls having a discussion with Beyoncé during a Destiny's Child tour concerning the licensing of DC T-shirts being sold at the concession stand. The figures he was giving to her relating to the group's profits didn't make sense to her. "Hold up," she said. "Something's not right." She reached into her purse and whipped out a small calculator. She hit the keys quickly and came up with a number. "*This* is right," she said, holding up the calculator so he could see the computation. "Actually, that's not it at all," the promoter said. He took the calculator from her and did his own figures. "This right here, this is right," he said when he finished, handing the calculator back to her. Beyoncé still wasn't convinced. "I need to do some research on this and get back to you," she told him. As the story goes, the promoter's figures actually *were* accurate. The point of the anecdote, though, is that she was becoming the kind of entertainer who felt comfortable challenging even the most experienced person.

So how did Beyoncé square this abundant commercialization of her image with who she really was as a person—the icon versus the person? In 2004, she hadn't quite figured that out yet. She was still trying to create a balance between what she wanted the public to think of her and who she really was as a young woman. It's one of the reasons she never said much of a personal nature in interviews. It was fine with her if the public only knew of her what they saw in her endorsement deals. If all she was to her fans was a sexy girl in a poster, that was completely acceptable to her. She wasn't sure yet who she was separate and apart from the product known as "Beyoncé" anyway.

A cautious person by nature, Beyoncé had long before decided that rather than make the wrong statement about herself, she'd make none at all except those concerning her professional aspirations and a few platitudes now and again about how blessed she was to have her career. While she didn't appear to be very insightful, that was primarily because she was purposely vague, each response measured against its possible ramifications. In a sense it had to do with public relations, because she definitely had an image she was putting forth, but it also had to do with something else: fear of exposure.

Today, she still has critics who feel that she is disingenuous, or just plain "fake." If she comes across that way—and she sometimes does—it's really just a function of her being evasive by design. She'd rather be roundly criticized than completely exposed. Oprah Winfrey once told her that the one thing she regrets about her career is ever having discussed her boyfriend, Stedman Graham, in the media, that once she opened that door to her private life, there was never any closing it. She advised Beyoncé to keep it closed, and keep it locked. Though Beyoncé never forgot Oprah's words, she actually had been withholding parts of herself ever since she was a child, back when the other kids in school didn't even know she was a singer. She was raised to compartmentalize, to not share of herself, to protect her heart at all costs. "This business sucks every goddamn thing out of you," she once told Lyndall Locke. "I'm going to keep as much of myself for myself as I can. I'm sorry, but I'm just not going to give it all away. I don't care what people think about it, either."

Destiny Fulfilled

*B*eyoncé Knowles started the year 2004 on a bright note by purchasing a jaw-dropping new estate, a modern mansion set on about three acres, for which she paid a million and a half dollars. Built in 1973, it was almost ten thousand square feet, with five bedrooms, five full baths, and two partial baths. Floor-to-ceiling windows looked out at rolling, verdant hills and a lagoon-style swimming pool. The property was located in the gated community of tony Farnham Park in the prestigious Piney Point Village, west of downtown Houston.

Beyoncé never intended to live in the new home. She'd already spent about a million bucks on a condominium in Miami just north of South Beach, and would soon buy two more units adjacent to it. Thus in October 2004, while she was in Milan attending Fashion Week, she would sign the opulent Houston estate over to Tina as a gift. Tina would remain in residence there until 2013. (In 2005, Tina would also purchase a condominium in Manhattan for a couple million dollars. Beyoncé would purchase a condo in the same building on the next floor.)

Mathew and Tina had begun to live completely separate lives. Sometimes they would be together in the new lavish surroundings Beyoncé had gifted her mother, but sometimes they would not. Later, when Beyoncé and Jay moved in together, Tina would stay on one floor of the New York condo building and Mathew on the other. Though they'd arrive together in the lobby, they'd then retreat to their own floors.

Most of the rest of 2004 was devoted to finishing another studio album for Destiny's Child, their first since 2001, and completing another movie, *The Pink Panther* with Steve Martin.

Beyoncé had originally intended to follow up her first solo album, *Dangerously in Love*, with a CD of tracks that had not been utilized on that debut. However, when Mathew suggested another Destiny's Child album and tour, it felt like something she wanted to do. She missed Kelly and Michelle and wanted to reconnect with them. A true democracy was again shown, with all three sharing leads on songs that would be included on an album to be called *Destiny Fulfilled*. They would also share (along with a team of other songwriters) writing and producing credits, with the exception of "Bad Habit," on which Michelle was replaced by Solange in both categories. Beyoncé coproduced all of the songs.

It was during the recording of this album that the group realized it had reached the end of the line. In discussing their ambitions, they came to a fuller understanding of each other's solo aspirations and decided that trying to coordinate those individual goals around the always hectic DC tour schedule would be impossible. Therefore, they decided that the group would break up after this album and one more tour.

As owner of the Destiny's Child name as well as the act's manager, Mathew didn't really want to see the group end. It wasn't just business to him, either. He loved the idea of Destiny's Child and never lost his appreciation for what its success represented not only in his life but also in those of his family members. It was no surprise that he'd given the group's future a lot of thought. Back in 2003, according to some sources, his idea had been to add Solange to the act as a fourth member, then in 2005 to launch Beyoncé as a solo artist and continue DC as a trio—Solange, Kelly, and Michelle. Of course, all three girls would still tend to their solo careers.

Could the group continue without Beyoncé? Probably. After all, the Supremes continued with a Diana Ross replacement for a few years and didn't have nearly the kind of support Mathew promised Destiny's Child, nor did they have the label support DC had from Columbia/Sony. If Mathew did intend to add Solange the biggest stumbling block to his plan was that he was the only one interested in implementing it. Not only did Solange not want to join the group, but Kelly and Michelle didn't want to continue without Beyoncé. True to form, in 2003, Solange took the reins of her own career and released her first album on Columbia in association with Mathew's Music World, with the telling name *Solo Star*. It didn't do very well, though, peaking at just number forty-nine on the Hot 100 and disappearing after about a month. None of its singles even charted. (Today, *Solo Star* is a true collector's item; it can't even be purchased on iTunes!) Still, it was a start, and Solange was definitely more happy on her own than she ever would have been as a member of Destiny's Child.

Though there seemed to be no internal problems in the group, there was also a sense, admitted Kelly Rowland, that Destiny's Child should break up "while we are still friends." Her comment suggested that they were not so naïve as to think they were immune to the petty jealousies and insecurities that could contaminate their relationships with one another. They wanted to avoid those pitfalls as much as possible. The problem with their last album together—*Destiny Fulfilled*, which would be released in November 2004—was that because of Beyoncé's immense superstardom, it felt somehow superfluous. Still, it made it to number two on the *Billboard* 200, generating two major hit singles, "Lose My Breath" and "Soldier."

The three young women in Destiny's Child shared executive producer credit with Mathew on the album. According to observers, squaring what her cohorts wanted and what her father wanted—and how all of those ideas might coexist with her own—was extremely challenging for Beyoncé. As a growing artist, not being able to have complete freedom to realize *all* of her ideas would understandably be a frustration. But Mathew had ideas too. Not only was he very musical, but he understood what was viable in the marketplace, almost better than Beyoncé did. Beyoncé was esoteric and experimental in her taste. While many of her original ideas were good ones, Mathew didn't always feel they would result in the massive record sales. It seemed as if the fact that on some level Beyoncé still wanted her dad's approval made her capitulate more often than not.

In her acknowledgment to Mathew in the album's liner notes, Beyoncé couldn't help but allude to the tension everyone noticed during the recording of *Destiny Fulfilled*. She wrote, "Dad. We really went through it this time around. I know it gets hard for U being my father and my manager; I know it's hard to realize I'm a woman now. Know that U are my father first. My career means absolutely nothing to me without my family. I love U."

Schooling Each Other

*D*espite her growing chemistry with Jay, there was still a formidable challenge ahead for Beyoncé if she was ever to be in a committed relationship with him. In order for it to work, she would have to open up to him, be vulnerable to him, intimate with him, and not just in the physical sense. Of course, she had always been more comfortable compartmentalizing her life, as she had done with Lyndall. However, Jay demanded more of her. He wanted to know who she was on every level—the frivolous to the important, the personal to the professional. Simply put, he was fascinated by her. He wanted to delve into all of the inner workings of her family as well as her business affairs. Since the Knowleses had always been such intensely private people, all of this was new terrain for Beyoncé.

Making things all the more thorny was that Jay wasn't exactly the most forthcoming person either, at least when it came to his business concerns. It was something he, too, was working on at this time. He confessed to Beyoncé that he'd never allowed any woman to know everything about his career and that it was a stretch for him to imagine that such a thing was possible. Therefore, they definitely had in common their shared inability to communicate—and their having to work on it for each other.

It is also possible Beyoncé's father was not completely open to the idea of his daughter sharing details of her private business dealings with others. The business of Beyoncé's career had always been strictly a family affair, and if that was to now change it would likely have been a major adjustment for Mathew.

"No way was she as business-savvy as Jay," observed Jaz-O, "so you have to know that already Beyoncé was bouncing things off Jay, and he was advising her. Her father had done all of this in the past for her. With Mathew having been the *only* guy from the very beginning and now having to deal with the fact that suddenly there's this *other* guy ... and it's Jay Z? That had to be tough."

One of Beyoncé's intimates recalls her as having said that the relationship with Jay Z was "like the blind leading the blind." Something in her felt that it was necessary to see it through, though. Even Kelly Rowland said they should stick with it, that it would be in both of their best interests. "Sometimes I want to say, 'Jay, please just shut up,'" Beyoncé said privately at the time. "But I know I can't," she concluded, "and he knows he can't. So, yeah ... we're schooling each other, you might say."

At around this time—the summer of 2004—as Beyoncé considered the parameters of her relationship with Jay Z, he was in the process of ending his long-standing and pivotal relationship with Damon Dash and Roc-A-Fella Records. He'd been riding high with his hit "99 Problems," and was anxious to make some changes. "It was a money issue," recalled Choke No Joke, who still worked for Roc-A-Fella at the time. "Because they had another partner [Kareem 'Biggs' Burke], the profits had to be split three ways. They were spending a fortune on their first-class lifestyles, and Jay got to a point where he thought the expenditures were too high. For Jay to think that, you *know* they were high. There were other issues, too, having to do with their clothing line, Rocawear."

In 2004, Def Jam Records, which had owned a 50 percent stake in Roc-A-Fella, bought the label outright and named Jay as Def Jam's president. Most of Roc-A-Fella's artists followed Jay to the new label, including Kanye West. Then, in the fall of 2005, Jay bought Dame out of Rocawear, the hip-hop clothing line they'd owned together since 1995, which had generated millions for them. That transaction pretty much ended their relationship. The general consensus was that Jay stole Roc-A-Fella from Damon, then he stole Kanye, then he stole Rocawear. Actually, all of those were legitimate business dealings, but Damon later said he felt pressured into each of them. "[Jay] said, 'It's business,'" Dash recalled. "But we were always supposed to be about more than business, Jay especially. It's like if your brother leaves you."

With Damon Dash now decidedly out of the picture, Jay would continue to amass his fortune, all the while romancing America's sweetheart—as privately as possible, of course.

Choke No Joke recalls an incident that underscores the importance Jay and Beyoncé placed on their privacy in these early days. As Roc-A-Fella's videographer, Choke was once at the legendary Baseline recording studios in Manhattan documenting a session with one of the label's artists. Choke filmed the performer in the vocal booth, as Jay and Beyoncé watched from behind the console in the control room. The two spoke between themselves, commenting on the performance they were witnessing, easily relating to one another. They were obviously happy together, seeming more comfortable than ever with each other.

As the artist left the booth and walked through the control room, he nodded at Jay and Beyoncé as he walked past them on his way out of the studio. Continuing to tape him, Choke followed him into the hallway. Meanwhile, Jay watched, his eyes narrowing with suspicion. He rose and followed Choke in hot pursuit. "Hey! *You filmed us*," he charged, catching up to him. "Me and Beyoncé, you secretly got us on film!"

"What? *No, dawg*," Choke said. "I was just filming the artist coming out of the booth and then through the engineer room. I didn't film y'all."

"Yeah you *did*," Jay angrily insisted. "Let me see that camera." After Choke handed the camera to Jay, the rapper began to watch the video playback through the viewfinder. There was no footage of him and Beyoncé. "Oh, okay. Sorry," he said with a shrug. "My bad."

"There was a little paranoia goin' on", Choke No Joke would observe years later. "I understood it, though. Jay told me he didn't want what he had with Beyoncé to get ruined before it began. It was him and Beyoncé agreeing, 'Let's get to know one another before we tell the world and they start judging us, putting out crazy rumors before we even get a chance to know one another.' We'd be out in public and they'd orchestrate it so that Beyoncé's momma would sit between Beyoncé and Jay in order to prevent paparazzi from getting that one great shot they wanted so much, you know?"

"From my vantage point, the love between them was a very slow burn that grew out of her respect for him," said Beyoncé's makeup artist at the time, Billy B. "She had such great admiration for his talent and for his accomplishments. Also, in Jay Z she had met someone who was as smart—maybe smarter—than she was, and she was not only intrigued by that but turned on by it as well. She felt she could learn a lot from him. I remember thinking, My God! I think she's met the love of her life. I thought it was such a miracle for her, such a gift."

Choosing: Lyndall or Jay?

*W*hen considering her parents' marriage, Beyoncé was sorry they couldn't have been happier together. She thought they *deserved* a better marriage. However, their relationship was their own, only they could totally understand it, and she knew she had no choice but to accept it for what it was. She also knew that she wanted a different kind of relationship with Jay than what her mother had with Mathew.

Beyoncé had stayed in touch with Lyndall, even though she was incredibly busy. In March 2004 she went on the road with Alicia Keys and Missy Elliott for five weeks. After that, she began work on the *Destiny Fulfilled* album. In May, she began production on her next movie, *The Pink Panther*, in New York with Steve Martin. Though it would turn out to be a mediocre film when finally released in May 2006, it would consume her life for the next few months. In other words, she was as busy as ever. "We were still talking, though," Lyndall recalled, "but then at one point she said, 'I hate to tell you this, but Jay doesn't want me speaking to you.' I understood. What boyfriend wants his girl talking to her ex all the time?"

It came to a head in July 2004 around the planning of a July 27 baby shower for Solange, who was pregnant with her first child. Solange, who was eighteen, was now married to her high school sweetheart, Daniel Smith, a college football player. (The two had married in February; Daniel Julez J. Smith Jr.—better known to his family as just Julez—would be born on October 18.)

Solange still spoke to Lyndall from time to time and invited him to the shower. As a longtime friend of the family, she saw no reason why he shouldn't be present. Yes, she'd been angry with Lyndall when he and her sister broke up, but when Beyoncé got over it, Solange got over it too. However, when Solange told Beyoncé that she'd invited Lyndall to the event, Beyoncé wasn't sure how she felt about it. "Maybe you should ask Jay?" Solange suggested. Beyoncé agreed.

With the passing of time, it's likely Jay got tired of hearing Lyndall's name. He was against inviting Lyndall to the impending baby shower and pointed out to Beyoncé that it was a family affair. Beyoncé duly telephoned Lyndall to tell him that she didn't want him to come.

When he hung up from her, Lyndall erased Beyoncé's number from his cell phone's contact list. "I was mad in the moment, but after thinking about it, on some level, I knew that it had to be over between us," he explained. "For her sake as well as mine. Sometimes you need a clean break, and up until that time, Beyoncé and I never had one. It killed me, but I just had a feeling we needed to get off the merry-go-round, that neither of us would ever get to move on with our lives as long as we were in constant touch with each other, going round and round and round. But was it easy for me to do? Oh, no. Oh, hell no."

Beyoncé did the same. She couldn't allow Lyndall to remain an issue between her and Jay; Jay now meant too much to her. Therefore, after almost eleven years of ups and downs and highs and lows, she and Lyndall were finally, once and for all, finished. It was sad, but it had to happen.

Today, Lyndall Locke is a chef who owns his own catering business after having attended culinary school in 2002. He is successful and happy in life, having been in a stable relationship for many years. "After Beyoncé, I didn't have a relationship for a long time," he recalled. "I had some psychological issues about her to work out in my head before I could ever really try again with someone else."

Lyndall and his present girlfriend have a young son, Lyndall Eugene Locke II. "Now that I'm older, I can say that it all worked out beautifully for me," he said in 2015. "With Beyoncé, I learned a lot about what it meant to have a good woman, how to treat one, and also how *not* to treat one. I think in her life I represent this crazy guy from a much simpler, easier time. And for me, well, she's still the first girl I ever kissed at that Brian McKnight concert so long ago, when we were little kids. That stays with you. I know Beyoncé will never forget about me, and I won't ever forget her. I guess it's true what they say: You don't forget your first love."

PART SIX

Dreamgirl

The Problem with Dreamgirls

*W*hen Beyoncé Knowles was cast in *Dreamgirls*, it seemed obvious to most people that she would all but walk away with the entire movie. After all, by this time, late 2005, the twenty-four-year-old was a major recording artist, having sold millions of records not only with Destiny's Child but as a solo artist. Though she'd made a few films, they were not to much worldwide acclaim. So she definitely seemed on the verge of breaking out as a major star, provided that she could find the right vehicle.

"I'm not Diana Ross," Beyoncé always liked to say of herself, "and they are not the Supremes," she'd conclude of the other girls in Destiny's Child. It was ironic, then, that she thought a plum for her would be the Diana Ross character—"Deena Jones"—in the movie *Dreamgirls*. The Tony Award–winning Broadway show was loosely based on the iconic story of Ross's rapid ascension to stardom and the negative impact it had on the girls with whom she sang in the Supremes, Mary Wilson and Florence Ballard.

Back in December 1981, when *Dreamgirls* opened at the Imperial Theatre, the character of Deena Jones was tough and uncompromising. Though she had some regrets that her two singing partners in the Dreams so resented her climb to stardom, she did little to nothing to make them feel much better about it. In fact, she took full advantage of every opportunity afforded her by her boyfriend, Curtis Taylor Jr.—the Berry Gordy Jr. of the story—to become a major superstar. One casualty of her skyrocketing journey to fame was group member Effie White—the story's Florence Ballard—who was ousted from the act when she couldn't accept the attention being paid to Deena. In real life, Florence died at the age of thirty-two, still brokenhearted from her unhappy experience in the Supremes; a grieving Diana attended her funeral. However, *Dreamgirls* went for a glossy, happier ending; Effie was joyously reunited with Deena and the Dreams for a sentimental, all-is-forgiven farewell appearance.

The problem no one on Beyoncé's team apparently considered when it was decided that she should appear as Deena in *Dreamgirls* was that the show's two major numbers, "And I Am Telling You I'm Not Going" and "I Am Changing," are sung not by that character but by Effie White. Arguably, it's not even that the Effie role provides such a star turn for the actress playing it as it's that those two bombastic songs steal the show. It happened on Broadway when Jennifer Holliday played the part and sang them, it has happened in practically every non-Broadway production since then, and it was bound to happen in the movie.

It's worth noting that Whitney Houston understood the quandary of *Dreamgirls* when she considered starring in a film adaptation of it back in 1987. Producer David Geffen, one of the original backers of the theatrical presentation, paid a million dollars for the movie rights and then tried to mount a film version starring Houston as Deena Jones. Broadway lyricist and producer Howard Ashman (*Little Shop of Horrors*, *The Little Mermaid*) was set to adapt. It didn't escape Whitney, though, that the show's most famous and pivotal songs would not be performed by her. A few years earlier, she performed "I Am Changing" at a party hosted by her record label, Arista, and blew everyone away with it. She now wondered if it was possible to have the script of *Dreamgirls* rewritten so she could sing that song and "And I Am Telling You I'm Not Going" herself.

Whitney, just twenty-four and on her second album at the time, took what might be viewed as a diva's approach to dispensing with the problem. "Make it work," she said at the time. "Just rewrite the show. What's the big deal?" The big deal, of course, was that the production was too famous and well known to be dramatically retooled. Plus, Geffen would never have allowed it. He felt a responsibility to the show's original choreographer and director, Michael Bennett, who'd just passed away, to maintain its integrity. Therefore, Whitney made the right decision: She walked away from the movie. When she later included her own breathtaking rendition of "And I Am Telling You I'm Not Going" in her act, it always generated a standing ovation.

Now, almost twenty years later, it was back to the drawing board for *Dreamgirls*, this time with Beyoncé as Deena Jones.

The director of the film, Bill Condon—who wrote the screenplay for the film adaptation of the Broadway hit *Chicago*—says that when the idea was proposed to him to consider Beyoncé, he wasn't sure if she was right for the part. "I looked at everything she'd done on film—I got all the videos—and I still didn't have the answer to the question as to whether she could do it or not," he said. "The studio didn't want an imitation of the Deena Jones character by Beyoncé, but rather her own interpretation of it. But did she have the acting chops? I didn't know." Alicia Keys was also being discussed to play the role, but the problem with her was the same: Could she act?

To prepare for her audition, Beyoncé studied as many tapes of not just Motown artists but other 1960s stars as she could find. "I looked at every Cher video, Barbra Streisand, and, of course, Diana Ross and the Supremes," she recalled. In the end, her screen test was a success. According to producer Larry Mark, "It was thrilling to watch because she had absolutely done her homework. We never, ever auditioned or screen tested anyone else."

To fill the role of Effie White, the singer/actress Fantasia Barrino—who'd won the third season of *American Idol*—was at first considered. Ironically enough, it was ultimately decided to cast Jennifer Hudson, who'd only made it into the final top seven the same year that Fantasia won the popular talent contest. Though she hadn't won *Idol*, Jennifer was a fan favorite. A powerful singer, there was little doubt she could do the plum role justice.

As originally written, Deena would have been a juicy role for any actress as well. She was as manipulative and ambitious as she was beautiful and talented, yet also vastly insecure in her desire to please not only her mentor boyfriend but also her audience. However, since Beyoncé has never wanted to be associated with manipulation or ambition, the role would have to be substantially toned down for her. Another problem with *Dreamgirls* was that while it was a thinly veiled story about the Supremes, it could also be said to have been about Destiny's Child—with Deena Jones being Beyoncé and Curtis Taylor Jr. not her boyfriend but her father. In truth, it was probably all just a little too close for comfort. Beyoncé probably should have abandoned the idea, like Whitney—especially considering the conundrum presented by those two star-turn songs. Instead, she took on the challenge and then, to at least partly solve the song problem, agreed with the producers to include a number for her to sing, one she wrote with Henry Krieger, Scott Cutler, and Anne Preven, called "Listen."

Any potential problems with *Dreamgirls* were all but overlooked as everyone involved became swept away by the sheer excitement of it all. It was a terrific show onstage, and the opportunity to bring it to film was a thrilling proposition. One of the most intriguing aspects of prepping the film would be the close attention paid to accuracy when it came to the costumes. From period-style wigs to sequined frocks, costume designer Sharen Davis—with assistance from fashion designers Naeem Khan and Tina Knowles—faithfully re-created the dazzling image of the Supremes. "That's been the highlight of my career, thus far, dressing Beyoncé," said Sharen Davis.

Davis recalled meeting with Beyoncé and Tina very early in the production and reviewing all of the designs, obtaining their input, and coming to an understanding of their likes and dislikes. "I had racks of clothes for them to see," she remembered. "They were very interested in learning the process. Obviously, they have a lot of experience in fashion, but they didn't try to assert themselves. They were open to new ideas, and asked about my inspirations. While I did look to the Supremes, I didn't take as much from them as one might think. The Supremes were actually quite conservative in their wardrobe. I wanted a more provocative look. So I looked at 1970s-era Cher as my biggest inspiration. Her clothes were sexy yet classy, which is what I wanted for Beyoncé.

"She could wear pretty much anything," Davis continued. "Even a costume that wasn't very good, she had a way of making look terrific. There were a few designs the studio wasn't crazy about, but when Beyoncé put them on, they loved them, especially when she really becomes 'Diana Ross' in the last third of the movie. It has to do with her bearing, the way she handles herself, her walk ... her persona is so elegant." Beyoncé would later tell David Letterman that she kept Diana Ross's films *Lady Sings the Blues* and *Mahogany* playing constantly in her dressing room for inspiration.

Rehearsals for *Dreamgirls* began in early November 2005 and ended just before Christmas. Principal photography began in Los Angeles in January 2006, with second unit footage shot in New York City and Miami. The movie wrapped production by the beginning of April 2006. It would premiere in early December at the Ziegfeld Theatre in Manhattan and then be released nationally on Christmas Day 2006, to generally favorable reviews.

The cast had gotten along well during filming. It wasn't until the press junket that there was tension between Beyoncé, Jennifer Hudson, and the third girl in the Dreams, Anika Noni Rose (who played Lorrell Robinson). The girls couldn't help but be jealous of the wardrobe Beyoncé was wearing at these junkets. "You had a pop star, Beyoncé; a Tony Award winner, Anika [for the Broadway production of *Caroline, or Change*]; and a virtual newcomer, Jennifer, who was already making a lot of noise," recalled a source. "But throughout the whole press junket, Anika and Jennifer both wanted to be Beyoncé. Well, who doesn't?" The two apparently thought Beyoncé was given all the best wardrobe and, according to multiple sources, kept going to Sharen Davis and complaining about it.

When asked to confirm the anecdote, Davis said, "Yes, well, it's very true that Jennifer and Anika would see Beyoncé in an outfit and say,

'Damn! We want to look like her!' And I would have to say, 'You could never look like her!' She's Beyoncé! Just be *you*.' They were gorgeous, both of them! But, you know, when you have Beyoncé in the room she does tend to make a big impression."

The problem for Beyoncé was that she didn't make a bigger impression in the movie. Maybe it should have been expected. Considering Jennifer Hudson's talent as displayed on *American Idol*, it was a foregone conclusion that she would make a strong showing with Effie's "And I Am Telling You I'm Not Going" and "I Am Changing." What would have been impossible to calculate, though, was that Hudson would be so spellbinding in the rest of the movie. Who could have known? After all, she had virtually no acting experience, other than a few roles in community theater as a youngster. Still, she walked away with every scene in which she was featured. Suddenly with the release of this movie, Beyoncé, the accomplished pro, found herself in the shadow of a complete newcomer.

Most film critics praised the performances of Hudson, Eddie Murphy (also nominated for an Oscar in the Best Supporting Actor category), and Jamie Foxx without sending many accolades Beyoncé's way. The *New York Times* called her performance "static and detached. In her limited work in movies she has never seemed comfortable with acting, shying away from any emotional display that might compromise her steely, hieratic dignity," noted the critic A. O. Scott. "But when she sings, she is capable of warmth, vulnerability, even ferocity, all of which she demonstrates in 'Listen.'" It was certainly true that Beyoncé's performance of "Listen"—as Deena asserts herself and breaks free of the dominance of Curtis Taylor Jr.—is the best, most passionate moment she has in the film, but it doesn't come until an hour and forty-five minutes into it!

A little more daring would have gone a long way for Beyoncé with *Dreamgirls* because, as recalibrated, her characterization of Deena Jones turned out a little flat. While her singing moments are undeniably entertaining and she definitely lights up the stage when fronting the Dreams, she—and presumably the producers—pretty much sapped the part of any opportunities it might have had to showcase her depth as an actress. When Jennifer was nominated for and then won an Oscar, few people were surprised.

For Beyoncé, *Dreamgirls* may have proved to be a humbling experience. "This was tough goin' for her," said someone who knew her well at the time. "On one hand, she's this humble person, and no one disputes that about her. On the other, she has an ego like every other superstar in her position. So to have a blockbuster movie like this one ripped out from under her by a novice like Jennifer Hudson wasn't easy."

Beyoncé is a woman who calculates everything in her career with the greatest of precision. Thus it could be said that *Dreamgirls* provided a "teachable moment," the lesson being that sometimes the best-laid plans really do go awry. Of course, this conclusion was nothing new for her, not after so many years in a fickle business. However, it had been quite some time since she'd been reminded of it. To say she was very disturbed about *Dreamgirls* would probably be overstating things. Perhaps one of the saving graces about her career is that she's so relentlessly busy, she usually has little time to dwell on anything upsetting. It would be more accurate to say that she was thrown by it, surprised by it, dismayed by it … and anxious to forget about it.

The media wasn't about to let her do so, though. For months, she read press reports of Jennifer's surprising dominance in the film; she got to the point where she just stopped reading about *Dreamgirls* altogether. When reporters asked her about Jennifer during press interviews, Beyoncé would usually respond by paying her frozen-smiled compliments. However, this strategy made her seem a little disingenuous and fake, which was already an image problem for her. But what was the alternative? To one writer, she probably handled it best when, after being asked one too many times about *Dreamgirls*, she just rolled her eyes and said, "Next question, please."

From all accounts, as her manager, Mathew's position was that *Dreamgirls* didn't matter; his daughter was already a major star, had been for years, and everyone knew it. So what if she was being overlooked in a movie? He was ready to dismiss the whole experience, which wasn't surprising. After all, nothing ever really discouraged Mathew Knowles.

As for the music from the film, the soundtrack album, *Dreamgirls: Music from the Motion Picture*, quickly hit number one on the charts. "Listen" was the first single release. Though Chuck Taylor of *Billboard* magazine dubbed it "the performance of [Beyoncé's] career," true to form when it came to her songs culled from her movies, it didn't do very well on the charts, peaking at just number sixty-one on the *Billboard* Hot 100. It fared better overseas.

"Listen" was also nominated for a Golden Globe as well as an Academy Award. However, making the *Dreamgirls* experience all the more dismaying, Beyoncé wasn't nominated for an Oscar for her part in writing it because—as per Academy rules—only three cowriters can be acknowledged.

In 2000, LaTavia and LeToya attempted to disaffirm their management contracts with Mathew. To their extreme disappointment, they were replaced. Here's the new Destiny's Child—Michelle Williams, Beyoncé Knowles, Kelly Rowland, and Farrah Franklin at the CFDA American Fashion Awards on June 18, 2000. (REX/Araldo DiCrollalanza)

In the summer of 2000, when Farrah chose not to accompany the girls to Australia for a tour, she was axed from the act leaving just Beyoncé, Kelly and Michelle, posing here with Mathew Knowles. (Pam Francis/Getty Images)

An incredible father-daughter team, Mathew and Beyoncé at the premiere of Beyoncé's first major film, *Austin Powers in Goldmember*, at the Universal Amphitheater on July 22, 2002. *(Clinton Wallace/Globe Photos, Inc.)*

By 2002, Beyoncé and her longtime boyfriend, Lyndall Locke, had broken up and she was now dating Sean Carter—Jay Z. Here they are on MTV's "TRL" program, November 21, 2002. *(KMazur/WireImage)*

Mathew Knowles and Jay Z on February 7, 2004, at Clive Davis's pre-Grammy party in the Beverly Hills Hotel. (KMazur/WireImage)

Beyoncé and Jay Z on February 27, 2005, at the *Vanity Fair* party after the 2005 Academy Awards in Los Angeles. (REX/Richard Young)

As she thanked her parents during her speech at the "Billboard Woman of the Year" awards on October 2, 2009, only a few people knew of the family's turmoil behind the scenes. (Jemai Countess/Getty Images)

AlexSandra Wright and little Nixon, Mathew Knowles's only son. Alex's relationship with Mathew and subsequent pregnancy would be the catalyst for great change in the Knowles family. (© *AlexSandra Wright. Used by Permission.*)

Beyoncé performing the National Anthem at the Inauguration Ceremony of President Barack Obama in Washington, D.C., on January 21, 2013. *(REX)*

Beyoncé and Jay Z arrive at the Metropolitan Museum of Art in New York for the Costume Institute Gala Benefit celebrating Charles James: Beyond Fashion, on May 5, 2014. Never could they have imagined the scene that would take place later in an elevator between Jay and Beyoncé's sister, Solange. (*George Pimentel/WireImage*)

After the startling brawl in an elevator between Jay Z and Solange, the two emerge with Beyoncé—Jay holding his chin, apparently smarting from the fight. (© *Splash News/Corbis Rights Managed [RM]*)

On May 17, 2014, Tina Knowles arranged a family outing in New Orleans to clear the air. Here, Solange and Jay leave the gathering. (© *INFphoto.com/INFphoto.com/Corbis Rights Managed [RM]*)

When she was expecting, Beyoncé faced rumors that she was faking the pregnancy! Because she'd previously had a miscarriage, the false stories were all the more hurtful. Here she is arriving at the 2011 MTV Video Music Awards at the Nokia Theater in Los Angeles on August 28, 2011. *(Photo by Gregg DeGuire/FilmMagic)*

Jay Z, Beyoncé, and their daughter, Blue Ivy, onstage at the 2014 MTV Video Music Awards at the Forum on August 24, 2014, in Inglewood, California. *(Photo by Jason LaVeris/ FilmMagic)*

Though the road to becoming Beyoncé was paved with as much defeat as triumph, one would be hard-pressed to imagine a more exciting and accomplished life. *(Timothy A. Clary/AFP/Getty Images)*

Mother and daughter have been through a lot together, but they've emerged victorious. Here are Tina and Beyoncé at the House of Dereon launch at Selfridges in London on September 17, 2011. *(REX/Richard Young)*

Beyoncé and Jay Z onstage together in Pasadena during their successful "On The Run" tour, August 2, 2014. *(REX/Frank Micelotta)*

Beyoncé poses in the press room at the 56th Grammy Awards at the Staples Center on January 26, 2014, in Los Angeles. (*Photo by Jason LaVeris/FilmMagic*)

"Listen" had four, and it was decided by the committee that Beyoncé's contribution was the smallest.

Years later, in November 2008, Beyoncé would face an Internet backlash when it was reported on the MySpace page of a person identified as a friend of Jennifer Hudson's, known only as "Superstar James," that she did not reach out to Jennifer when Jennifer's mother, brother, and nephew were brutally murdered. Furthermore, because another media outlet reported that Beyoncé had been at the funeral service for all three, it was alleged by "Superstar James" that she was trying to stake claim to having attended the service to ingratiate herself with the public when in fact she hadn't. "Beyoncé did not come to the funeral nor did she call, text, send a card or, hell…send a damn email," wrote the source in his posting entitled "How Evil Can Someone Be?"

Though much of the public would like to think that when actresses make movies together they become close friends, that's usually not the case. While Beyoncé and Jennifer are friendly, they are not close. In fact, Beyoncé never claimed to have been at the funeral. The report that she'd been present was erroneous. Actually, she was attending the "Promote the Vote" block party in Philadelphia that day, and was widely photographed there. Of course, she could have canceled that appearance to attend the Hudson funeral, since she wasn't one of the official speakers—Jay spoke, as did P. Diddy and Mary J. Blige. For her own reasons, though, she decided not to do so.

It says a lot about the power of the Internet—and how it can shape public opinion—that still, to this day, some of the public holds it against Beyoncé that she never contacted Jennifer in her time of great grief, based entirely on that social media report. Certainly the perception that Beyoncé takes issue with Jennifer because of the way *Dreamgirls* turned out for her helps fuel rumors of bad blood between them. In fact, any communication between Beyoncé and Jennifer is unknown since neither woman has ever spoken about it. She definitely didn't attend the funeral, though. In terms of public relations, it probably would have been a very good idea for Beyoncé to make the effort—especially since she is well aware that the public believes that there's no love lost between her and Hudson. But how, then, would it have appeared to Jennifer's family members and true friends if Beyoncé made an appearance in order just to be photographed and thereby burnish her public image?

Beyoncé has actually been in Jennifer Hudson's company numerous times since 2008. For instance, Hudson attended Tina Knowles's sixtieth birthday party in January 2014 and seemed happy speaking to Beyoncé there. If there's bad blood between them, it's not apparent by the way they act in each other's presence.

When she looks back on *Dreamgirls*, Beyoncé still views it as a positive experience. "I loved it," she has said. "What a great opportunity it was!" Some would say, though, that this one really didn't work out well for her at all.

Beauty Is Pain

"Momma, hand me that masking tape," Beyoncé said, pointing to a roll of gray gaffer's tape on a table. Wearing a formfitting black catsuit, she was standing in front of a tall mirror while critically examining her reflection. "I don't like the way this looks," she said, examining her outfit. "The lines aren't sleek enough," she added. Beyoncé peeled the top of the outfit down past her waist.

"What in the world are you going to do?" Tina asked as she handed her daughter the roll of tape.

"I'm gonna fix it," Beyoncé said. She took the strong cloth tape—pressure-sensitive and most certainly never intended to be used on one's skin—and started wrapping it around her bare waist. "I'm gonna corset my waist with this tape," she concluded.

"Oh my God, Beyoncé," Tina exclaimed. "You can't do that! Do you know how that's gonna hurt when you take it off?"

"Momma, please!" Beyoncé said as she continued to wrap the tape round and round her waist, so tight she could barely breathe. She then pulled the top of her outfit over her shoulders and examined herself in the mirror. "There. That's looks pretty good," she said, satisfied. "Don't you think?" she asked, turning around and facing her mother.

There were actually two versions of videos for the song "Listen." One featured a performance of the song intercut with a fashion shoot and scenes from *Dreamgirls*. There was also one known as the "Director's Cut," which was a re-creation of a photo shoot. Directed by Matthew Rolston, it appears on the *Dreamgirls* DVD release.

In the "Director's Cut" storyline, Beyoncé, her face painted to look like a mannequin, appears as a fashion model at an important photography session. Behind the old-fashioned camera is a photographer who bears a striking resemblance to legendary fashion lensman Richard Avedon. There is also a prim-looking stylist, who brings to mind powerful *Vogue* magazine editor Anna Wintour, as well as attentive styling assistants. They all carefully watch as various elaborate looks are tried out on Beyoncé.

Although Beyoncé looks terrific in the wardrobe, no one at the session seems happy with the results. Though frustrated, she tries her best to get through it, but it's just not working. When an assistant attempts to liven things up by perching a ridiculously large parrot on her shoulder, Beyoncé has had enough. She storms off the set. Then, staring directly into the camera, she peels off her thick lashes.

"Ripping off her false eyelashes was the most iconic diva stunt ever," said makeup artist Billy B. of the video. "It's a statement of defiance and independence. The way I saw it as we were filming it, it was a direct message to her father. It was as if she was saying to him, 'Look at me. *Listen to me.* I'm my own woman and I always have been. I am not this commodity you think you created.'"

Shedding her manufactured self to reveal the person she is meant to be, Beyoncé then runs up the stairs to the rooftop wearing the simple black catsuit. It's designed to showcase her bodacious cleavage while her cinched midsection shows off her impossibly small waist. Only those aware of the backstory of what it took for her to get into the outfit realized that her tiny waist is a symbol of sacrifice, ingenuity, pain, and self-control—all of which Beyoncé has endured for years to achieve her ideal of herself.

As the song ends, Beyoncé is breathing heavily. She is drained. She stares at the viewer with a look of insubordination and self-satisfaction. The overall message: *Don't let them change you into something that you are not. Be yourself.*

"Because I was there, it takes my breath away when I see that video today," Billy B. added. "Every take was important to her. We were in a little studio, and she was singing full-out as if she was in a stadium in front of a hundred thousand people. With every take, she cried real tears. It was passionate, over the top, and meant everything to her. When it was over,

I cried. I would bet that if you talked to anyone at that shoot, they would agree that there was no way to be in that studio and not be affected by it."

Billy B.'s observation that Beyoncé's performance in the video seemed inspired by her relationship with her dad certainly seems true, even though Beyoncé didn't write many—if any—of the lyrics. She obviously saw a parallel. In her 2013 documentary, *Life Is but a Dream*, she positions a performance of "Listen" at the end of a compelling segment about her crumbling relationship with Mathew. Taking it a step further, the composition can also be said to state her true feelings about the experience of *all* of the outspoken women in her life who went up against Mathew over the years: Denise Seals, Deborah Laday, Andretta Tillman, and Tina Knowles— maybe even LaTavia Roberson and LeToya Luckett, especially given the lyric, "The time has come / For my dreams to be heard / They will not be pushed aside and turned / Into your own."

After the successful video shoot, Beyoncé was faced with having to remove the gaffer's tape from around her waist. "Oh my God, the screams!" exclaimed Billy B. "It was very, very painful. She was absolutely *wailing*, and Tina was trying to help her, saying, 'I'm sorry, Beyoncé, but I *told* you this was gonna happen!'"

Jay Z's "Affair" with Rihanna

*B*y 2006, Beyoncé—who would turn twenty-five in September—seemed truly exhausted by the demands of her career. Those around her noticed she often seemed depressed at this time, or maybe even sad. "She would just go into a corner and seem to disappear into herself," was how one person put it.

Many people in her life were uncertain as to exactly what was troubling Beyoncé. Was it her dad's management of her career? Her mother's ongoing sadness with Mathew? Maybe she was more upset about *Dreamgirls* than she'd let on? Or perhaps she was just pushing herself too hard. She wasn't returning her friends' telephone calls, which was unusual for her.

It would seem that Beyoncé's troubles in 2006 included her relationship with Jay and issues were rumored to have been plaguing the pair for about a year.

In 2005, the couple began having trouble coordinating their intensely busy and overscheduled lives. If it's true, as they say, that many couples have the same fight over and over again, with Jay and Beyoncé it would relate to work. He is said to have felt that she was too concerned and overwhelmed by it. She was definitely her father's daughter in that she could become completely consumed by work in a way that to outsiders may have sometimes appeared obsessive. The two were said to have broken up for a time during that year.

In 2006, Jay seemed to allude to the breakup in his song "Lost One," when he rapped, "I don't think it's meant to be / But she loves her work more than she does me." In his book *Decoded*, he would later explain that the lyric was "about how difficult it is to respect a lover as an autonomous human being, with separate needs and goals and timelines than yours. It's one of the hardest things about a real relationship. But it's worth it."

As it happened, a publicity stunt involving the up-and-coming Barbadian pop star Rihanna didn't help matters. Publicist Jonathan Hay recalled, "I was working for Vada Nobles, who wrote and produced 'Pon de Replay,' Rihanna's first single. Jay had just signed her to Def Jam. Well, it was my job to make sure she hit. However, when I pitched her to [the journalist] Jennifer Vineyard at MTV, she wanted a quote from Jay. I told her it should be no problem. But do you think I could get one? Hell no.

"I started sending him text messages saying, '*Dude!* Two sentences about Rihanna. That's all I need.' He'd write back: 'Hit me up later.' I would do so, but . . . still nothing. So, out of frustration and in an effort to generate some interest, I began to plant stories in the press that Jay and Rihanna were having a hot romance, and that Beyoncé was very jealous and pissed off about it."

The *National Enquirer* was the first to run Jonathan's sensational fabrication. From there, it erupted into a firestorm of media. The rumor of infidelity on Jay's part caused such a sensation, in fact, that it helped propel "Pon de Replay" to major hit status almost overnight, as the track went straight to number two on the U.S. *Billboard* Top 100 and then Top 10 all around the world. At first no one at Def Jam paid attention to the rumor; everyone was just glad that the record was a hit. But after Jay started asking questions about the campaign, he finally figured out that a rumor about him and Rihanna was at the center of it. He wasn't happy about it, including for a reason that hadn't crossed Jonathan's mind. "Jay called me and said, 'Dude! She's a *minor!*'" Hay recalled. "It was true; Rihanna was only seventeen; that hadn't even occurred to me!"

So, was Jay Z having a romantic relationship with Rihanna? "Absolutely not," says Jonathan Hay. "It was all a stunt. Am I proud of it? No. There was no integrity to it at all. Did it work? Hell yeah, it worked. It totally launched Rihanna's career."

According to well-placed sources, Beyoncé wasn't sure about the whole story. "It added a new twist to what was already a lot of drama between her and Jay," said a source.

Beyoncé and Jay were at Jay's 40/40 sports bar in New York one night with friends when they apparently got into it over Rihanna. Because it was a whispered argument over loud televised sportscasts, it was impossible to know for certain what they were saying. All that was said to have been heard over the din was Rihanna's name uttered several times, before Beyoncé stood up and left.

Though there are people in Beyoncé and Jay's circle who have long believed that the couple broke up over Rihanna, blaming any schism in their relationship on the Barbadian singer is probably overstating her influence on it. Like all couples there would have been other issues. Of course, without their direct testimony it's impossible to know what was going on behind closed doors. It's safer to conclude that the rumors about Rihanna probably didn't help. Surprisingly, Jay didn't blame Jonathan Hay for the imbroglio either. He chalked it up to a publicity gimmick gone bad and—as a man who fully understands the complexities of the record business and twists and turns of public relations—decided to just let it go. "It got ugly there for a minute between me and Jay, but it blew over," said Jonathan Hay. "I think if I hadn't made the song a big hit, he might not have gotten over it."

Not certain how to proceed with Jay, Beyoncé attended the 2005 Grammy Awards with a young and handsome R&B singer who goes by just his first name, Mario (Barrett). The two were photographed on the red carpet together—one of the rare times (maybe the only time) Beyoncé has ever been seen on a red carpet with a date other than Jay Z. Though Beyoncé looked stunning in a black gown with gold trim and a plummeting neckline, while posing with Mario she appeared uncomfortable. Of course, it has to be noted that Mathew accompanied his daughter and Mario that evening, which seemed odd to most observers. With her father present, it was as if Beyoncé wanted to be *seen* on a date with someone else . . . but not really *be* on a date with someone else.

It was clear to most people who knew her that Beyoncé needed more time to work through her feelings where Jay was concerned. However, he missed her. He wanted them to reconcile. "Jay is always going to be the alpha male, no matter the situation," said his childhood friend DeHaven Irby. "He's going to let the woman in his life only have so much room before he's going to want to have his way. A woman like Beyoncé who has been used to pleasing her father all her life is not going to have her independence very long with a guy like Jay. In other words, he's gonna have his way."

In the end, after she finished *Dreamgirls*, Beyoncé agreed to resume their relationship. It could be said that what she did not get as a result of this difficult time in her life was a full airing of her feelings. It was her choice, though. People close to her say that her frustration, and maybe even anger, only found its true voice in "Sasha Fierce." In fact, whenever Sasha was onstage during this time, she seemed angrier than ever. But Beyoncé? Not so much.

In an effort to smooth things, Beyoncé and Jay planned to take time off to be together and reconnect. But then in late March 2006, about a month into a planned vacation, she told Jay that she was itching to get back to work. Destiny's Child had just received their star on the Hollywood Walk of Fame, and after the ceremony, Beyoncé said she was thinking of recording a new album. He had to understand that she needed her work. She was too driven, too focused to just put it aside for long. If he wanted to be with her, he would have to make the necessary adjustments; singing and performing was always going to be a big part of the life and times of Beyoncé Knowles. As an artist himself, he could relate, and he loved her enough to work it all out in his head.

Beyoncé's 2006 hit "Ring the Alarm" seems to be about the rumored Jay Z/Rihanna affair. Though the couple had come to terms with the issue by this time, because she is an artist who writes from her own experience the subject was bound to come up in her lyrics. The lyrics to "Ring the Alarm" rage on about her refusal to let another woman end up with the perks—chinchilla coats, diamond rings, Rolls-Royce automobiles—she feels she deserves by virtue of the heartache she's suffered at the hands of her affluent boyfriend. "She's sold half a million gold / She don't love [you] that shit, I know," Beyoncé sings. It turns out that both of Rihanna's albums up to that time had been certified gold (half a million copies), falling short of

Beyoncé's multiplatinum status. Of course, Beyoncé later denied that the song was about Rihanna, and we may never know the truth as it's not as if she would ever publicly confirm such a thing.*

By the end of 2007, it definitely looked like Beyoncé and Jay had worked out any problems in their relationship. In December, she would toast their romance with friends and family at her side, proclaiming her love for him in an eloquent, honest, and emotional way. "I don't know where to start," she would say, gazing at him with loving eyes. Following a heartfelt speech she raised her glass of red wine toward him, and concluded, "Happy birthday. I thank God for you every day."

B'Day

*B*ecause of the pressures in her personal life, 2006 definitely wasn't the best of years for Beyoncé. However, when she found herself in the midst of emotional turmoil, she could always turn to music. Somehow her art was always able to guide her through any storm.

In May 2006, just before she left for the 59th Cannes Film Festival in France, Beyoncé called Columbia/Sony and asked the label's artist and repertoire department to book recording time at Manhattan's Sony Studios. She also provided a preliminary list of songwriters and producers with whom she wished to work, and asked the label to check on their availability. Moreover, she requested the utmost of discretion, which meant no mention to other label executives or to anyone else that she was going into the studio—and, surprisingly, this seems to have included Mathew. She would

---

* In July 2007, Beyoncé took a terrible fall onstage in Orlando while singing "Ring the Alarm." Wearing a long red coat, she toppled headfirst down a flight of stairs and hit her chin hard on the stage. Her stiletto heel had gotten caught in the hem of her coat. Amazingly, she got right back up and continued to perform. After the fall, she wagged her finger at the crowd and asked them to please not post it on YouTube. Of course, by the next morning it was all over the Internet. Beyoncé had to laugh. "Of course, that's what I expected," she later said. The fall was so dramatic and such big news, it was reported on CNN. In fact, Beyoncé has fallen so many times onstage, she's lost count. It's not surprising, though, considering the extreme athleticism of her performances. She still has a scar from that big tumble in Orlando, and says that it was so bad, if she hadn't gotten back to her feet immediately she would not have been able to finish the show.

later explain that the reason she didn't tell him of her plans was because she wasn't sure she was actually making a recording for release, that maybe she was just recording demos for future consideration, which she did all the time.

In fact, an album actually *was* contractually due from Beyoncé at this particular time. The original plan had been for her to release a follow-up to *Dangerously in Love* in 2004, but Destiny's Child's final album got in the way of it. After that, she became distracted by *Dreamgirls*. Still, a record was due.

With this pending project, Beyoncé sensed that she needed to make a move toward gaining some more independence from Mathew. As much as she craved his approval, something in her made her feel that with this album in particular, she had to make a statement not only to him, but to herself. It wasn't easy, though. As much as she wanted to spread her wings, there was still trepidation about it; he'd always been her safety net. However, when it came right down to it, Beyoncé would go deep within and somehow find the courage to do what she knew in her heart she needed to do, not only for her art but for her personal growth. It was clear to people in her life that indeed she was working on herself, taking small steps but steadily moving forward in her quest to becoming a more independent woman.

Of course, Mathew found out about it; he almost always knew what she was up to, even when she believed otherwise. However, there wasn't much he could do about his daughter's plans, except maybe wonder what it portended for the future.

For these recording sessions Beyoncé turned to a wide range of talented producers and songwriters, such as Rodney Jerkins; the Neptunes' Pharrell Williams and Chad Hugo; Rich Harrison; Kasseem "Swizz Beatz" Dean; Sean Garrett; the team of Stargate—Mikkel Storleer Eriksen and Tor Erik Hermansen; and Ne-Yo.

Working with a variety of producers and songwriters on one project was nothing new for Beyoncé; of course, that's how Destiny's Child records were made, as well as her debut solo album. However, for this record she decided to book every studio at the Sony facility in New York, and then have all of her producers and songwriters work on their respective tracks concurrently, while she went from room to room to work with them on different songs. She wanted the energy and excitement of that sort of mass creativity to be happening all at once.

"I came to the studio and saw the zone," Swizz Beatz recalled. "I said, 'Damn, everybody in here is *banging out*.' Rodney Jerkins had his session while Rich Harrison had his session going on. I was like, 'How am I going to compete with that? Okay, well...I'm just gonna do what I do, I guess.' I started banging out some tracks and I thought it might be too hard, but then Beyoncé would come in the room and be like, 'That's crazy good.'"

Actually, this way of multitask recording was a throwback to a bygone era. In the 1960s and '70s, black pop music labels such as Motown and Philadelphia International took such a "hit factory" approach, routinely putting together teams of staff songwriters and producers to work on a specific project. The approach created a competitive spirit that, theoretically, was good for getting results. The downside was that the process didn't always make for creating or sustaining goodwill among producers. When one producer knows that another one down the hall is trying to create music that will knock his out of the running, things can get a little uncomfortable. More significantly, a process with so many chefs in the kitchen doesn't always serve an artist's quest to create a singular signature sound for an album. The approach did, however, ensure that the work was done quickly. The songs that would end up on *B'Day*, released on September 4, 2006—Beyoncé's twenty-fifth birthday—were recorded in roughly two weeks.

What was exciting about *B'Day*—the spontaneity of its production— also proved to be its detriment. The project wasn't allotted the scrutiny of an objective overseeing ear. Indeed, by 2006, one of the misfortunes of Beyoncé's career was that it wasn't afforded the direction of a seasoned executive producer. Beyoncé and Mathew were the executive producers— as always—and by this time it was beginning to seem that the duo was maybe a little out of its depth. It's not known how much input Beyoncé let her father have on *B'Day*, but word in the street was: not much. Because Mathew was always known to have a more commercial ear than Beyoncé, she definitely could have used a little more of his input on the album.

Obviously, the pool of writers and producers from which Beyoncé selected her collaborators was talented. However, many of them were shortsighted in their ambitions, their skills not venturing beyond the realm of hip-hop and/or so-called neo-soul forms. By her second solo album, a music career the mammoth size of Beyoncé's was still sorely missing a signature song, an uptempo number or memorable ballad the whole world could sing. "Crazy in Love" was close, but some critics still didn't feel it would stand the test of time. Finding such a song is among the duties of an executive producer who is not the artist, an entity able to stand outside the project and know what it's missing. Had such a seasoned executive producer been on board for *B'Day*, no doubt he or she would have pushed Beyoncé and her collaborators to reach deeper than just "Déjà Vu," a punchy track later held up by her supporters as being a more organic sound for her. The truth about it, though, was that despite its heavy bass guitar and bold horn riffs, not even a cameo from Jay Z could save it from mediocrity.

"Irreplaceable," which Beyoncé cowrote and produced with the artist Ne-Yo and the team of Stargate, definitely redeems the album, though. It's a folksy hip-hop anthem about a woman who finds courage enough to end a long-term relationship with a man. Beyoncé's belittling lyric—"To the left, to the left / Everything you own in a box to the left"—immediately became a line of empowerment for women going through a breakup. If there was any song close to being *the* Beyoncé song on *B'Day*, it would have to be this one.

"Irreplaceable" would prove to be the collection's big hit single, going to number one on the *Billboard* Hot 100 chart, where it would remain for ten consecutive weeks. It went on to become the bestselling U.S. single of 2007, selling nearly five million copies and downloads, and helping *B'Day* ultimately sell more than eight million copies worldwide.

It didn't matter that upon *B'Day*'s release, national music critics were divided in their opinions; led by "Déjà vu," the first single release, followed by "Ring the Alarm," "Irreplaceable," "Get Me Bodied," and "Green Light," the album quickly went to number one in America. It would also go on to earn a 2007 Grammy Award for Best Contemporary R&B Album.

Alex

While Beyoncé seemed to be marginalizing Mathew in her career, he was about to embark on an unusual adventure of his own, and one that most definitely did not include her—or her mother.

Whatever secrets Mathew and Tina Knowles shared—whatever understanding they had come to and however they defined "husband and wife"— was something between the two of them alone. While the specific parameters of their marriage remained opaque to the outside world, what was clear to all was that the Knowleses were living successful, if not also largely separate, lives. When one considers the overwhelming financial struggles they endured during Girls Tyme's early days, it boggles the mind to take note of the rewards that came their way with the success of Destiny's Child and Beyoncé. By 2007, the couple was truly prosperous, with untold millions in the bank, along with their own thriving businesses—Mathew's in career management and Tina's in fashion design. Mathew had done very well for them both. He usually wasn't interested in risky asset allocation, always a puzzlement to attorneys and accountants who believed that the bigger the risk, the bigger the gain.

The main investment in Mathew's and Tina's life together, though, had most certainly been in the nurturing of Beyoncé, her brand and her career. She was a product of both of them in every sense of the word—and that truth would forever bind them. His life had been all about creating, producing, and promoting her. Now, in late middle age, he seemed to need time to explore his own identity, which may explain his relationship with Alex-Sandra Wright, known to her friends and family as Alex.

It started off as an exciting romance for Mathew. Maybe it was unorthodox, but as we have seen, Mathew and Tina never really had a conventional marriage. Women had always found him irresistible but by the end of 2007, he seemed to be looking for something more substantial. While he had known many women, likely none was as outspoken or independent as Alex. Of course, the irony was that for many years Mathew had butted heads with just this type of formidable woman—yet he was also strangely attracted to them.

Mathew met Alex in September 2007 when she was working for Microsoft. She was one of the company's brightest and most experienced staffers in its successful branding division. Knowles and an entourage of about ten people had flown from Houston to Microsoft headquarters in Seattle to meet with the firm about branding possibilities, not just for Beyoncé but for Solange too, whom Mathew was still also managing. Now signed to Polydor in conjunction to Mathew's Music World, Solange was preparing to release her sophomore album, *Sol-Angel and the Hadley St. Dreams*, a masterful throwback to the identifiable sounds of the 1960s and '70s. Mathew—who shared co–executive producer credit with Solange—had a number of carefully conceived marketing plans in mind for the album. In fact, it would be a bona fide hit when released, charting at number nine and selling a quarter of a million copies. Finally, it seemed that Solange was coming into her own as an artist of great depth and unexpected creativity.

As Mathew and his crew sat in one of the corporate offices listening to long-winded speeches touting the Microsoft brand, he couldn't take his eyes off Alex. At thirty-six, she was quite attractive, a shapely African-American beauty with long dark hair and penetrating, rich brown eyes. She was also on her laptop computer throughout the entire meeting, which visibly annoyed Mathew. He preferred that people not multitask, that they devote all of their attention to a single purpose. At one point, a song by Beyoncé began to play on the sound system, but clumsily rearranged as homogenized elevator music. It piqued Mathew's attention. "Who licensed that song?" he demanded to know as he bolted from his chair. No one was quite sure. His energy was so big, though, there was no way to ignore him. People went scrambling about, trying to find an answer to his question.

After the meeting, Mathew was scheduled to tour the Microsoft office. Looking down from his six-foot-six frame into her little work cubicle, he asked Alex to accompany him. She turned him down, explaining that she was busy, and then gave him her business card. He went on his way, but—true to his obsessive nature—began to bombard her with telephone calls, leaving copious messages on her voice mail. She was taken aback by his persistence, never having met anyone quite so determined. Finally, later that day, she returned his calls. They made plans to meet at the W Hotel that night in downtown Seattle. By this time, Alex had Googled Mathew in order to know exactly who it was with whom she was dealing.

"From a branding standpoint," she told him when she saw him again, "you really have your work cut out for you."

"What are you saying?" he asked. He seemed genuinely interested.

"Well, there's all of this stuff out there that says you're a real bully," she explained. "Do you really want to come across as a gangster? The Suge Knight of R&B? It's really not a good look for you, Mathew."

Alex Wright was born in Montreal in 1971 and raised in Alberta. She comes from an educated family; her parents were both doctors educated at McGill University. In fact, her mother was the first black woman ever to graduate from McGill. Her grandfather was the first black professor of pharmacology there. One brother, Chris, is a neurologist educated at Harvard, the other, Jonathan, an alumnus of Columbia Law School. Alex attended the University of Washington, majoring in communications. After moving to Los Angeles, she was an actress for a short time before beginning a successful career in marketing and branding. Her credits are wide-ranging; she has been associated with acts such as Run-D.M.C., Brian McKnight, Eddie Van Halen, Prince, Stevie Wonder, and Aretha Franklin. She was recruited by Microsoft in August 2007 to handle the PR and marketing of Microsoft's Zune product, its answer to Apple's iPod. Three months into her tenure at Microsoft, she was selected to deliver keynote addresses with Steve Ballmer on entertainment and technology, which she did with great success.

About an hour after they met in the lounge at the W Hotel, Mathew began to amp up his flirtation with Alex. Suddenly the earlier barrage of phone calls made more sense to her. Cocktails together ended with a very awkward kiss in the parking lot.

Mathew spent the next five days calling Alex until she finally agreed to see him again—but only if he submitted to having a dim sum dinner with her family and friends, a Sunday tradition for them. He agreed; his limousine dropped him off in front of the Chinese restaurant. No one present, other than Alex, knew that Mathew was Beyoncé's father when he walked into the eatery and joined the group. "Most people there wouldn't have even known Beyoncé's last name," said her brother Jonathan Wright, who was present. Still, Mathew completely captivated the crowd, winning them all over with his magnetic personality. It was then that Alex felt her heartstrings being tugged by him. "That's when I think I knew I was starting to fall for him," she said.

Over the next few weeks and then months, the relationship between Mathew and Alex intensified. They'd both happened upon someone who made them happy, and they just wanted to enjoy it. "When I got to know his story, I was more than intrigued," she recalled. "I so admire self-made men, and Mathew is nothing if not that. I saw that he's an innovator in every way."

"He became my sister's boyfriend and we considered him family right away," says Jonathan Wright. "I also looked at him as a mentor. I asked him how he got into the business and he told me this amazing story of how he got into managing Beyoncé, the way he went about self-educating so he could be among the best in the field. I didn't have access to a lot of successful older black men, so, yeah, I had great admiration for him."

Alex and the rest of her family were aware that Mathew was married. However, he made it clear to them that despite his marital status, he was a free man. Alex understood Mathew's marital predicament, though. She had no judgment about it. "I come from a family that does not get divorced," Alex said. "Money does not divorce. Also, coming from a successful black family, I understood that Mathew looked at divorce as a sign of weakness."

Very quickly, Mathew and Alex became a couple in pretty much every way other than in marriage. "I would see him just about every day," she concluded, "and it would be that way for the next two years of my life."

About to Blow?

$\mathcal{B}$y 2007, Beyoncé Knowles had been performing for at least the last twenty-two years, completely dedicated to being a vocalist of high standards and quality, always striving for unconditional perfection, never settling for anything less. Like her father, she had an obsessive temperament when it came to work; she simply couldn't relax. She always had so much to do, and she was determined to get it all done, no matter what it took. Her career was hard work, but that had always been true. It had definitely paid off for her. She'd never been surprised by her success, either. It had always felt somehow preordained. "How would you like me to describe you?" Australian television personality Liam Bartlett asked her in a March 2007 interview. "A legend in the making," she quickly answered. He was a little taken aback. "A legend?" he asked. She nodded and said, "Yeah." He smiled. "That's big," he remarked. "I *said,* 'in the making,'" she clarified. By 2007, all modesty aside, it did seem that the way she and Mathew had thus far masterminded her career was definitely one for the record books.

In April 2007, Beyoncé would embark on her third concert tour, The Beyoncé Experience, along with her all-female ten-piece band, the Suga Mamas. Together, Beyoncé and Mathew selected the musicians and singers from nationwide auditions. By making them all women, she was sending a purposeful and strong feminist statement. Most of these same ladies would accompany Beyoncé on her subsequent tours as well, including 2009–10's I Am…World Tour, 2013–14's Mrs. Carter Show World Tour, and 2014's On the Run Tour with Jay Z.

The rehearsals for The Beyoncé Experience began in March 2007, shortly after she wrapped up work on a new Samsung commercial in New York. A complicated show with numerous props and costume changes, in many ways it was a logistical nightmare. An entire volume could be written on the preparation and execution of this exciting multimedia presentation. Somehow, though, Beyoncé managed to pull it all together, as always. She'd always been an excellent leader, her positivity and decisiveness trickling down to everyone in her employ. "She's completely relentless in her pursuit of perfectionism," her creative director, Todd Tourso, would say in years to come. "It sounds cheesy, but that's why I'm willing to work so hard for her. When you have this type of leadership and muse and mentor, the sky's the limit."

"I had a friend attend a rehearsal, and afterwards, he said to me, 'Wow. She can be a real pain in the ass, can't she?'" said one member of her crew. "'She's so anal! How do you deal with it?' I said, 'Yeah, she can be tough, all right. But she's as tough on herself as she is on everyone else, tougher even.'"

"You're way too hard on yourself," Jay told Beyoncé one day at rehearsal in front of some of those working with her on The Beyoncé Experience. It wasn't going well that day, and he could see that she was suppressing her annoyance, maybe even her anger. "It's too much, Bey. Stop pretending like it's not," he told her. He suggested that she needed to try to release some of the tension that was interfering with her peace of mind, even her joy for the work. "Maybe you need to throw some shit around," he suggested.

She looked at him as if he'd lost his mind. "*Throw some shit around?*" Obviously, that had never been her style. It was Jay's, though, and it worked for him. If it took a temper tantrum to straighten things out at a rehearsal, so be it. In fact, Beyoncé had been watching Jay conduct his career for many years, and even though his show wasn't as complex in its execution as hers, he definitely seemed more relaxed while planning it. "Jay is so cool," she would say. "He can just stand onstage completely still, and the audience will go nuts," she told *Giant* magazine. "Me? I have to work it. I'm shaking it and throwing it and rolling around on the floor."

"I don't know what to do, Jay-Jay," Beyoncé said, using one of her pet names for him. "Just be *you*," he told her. "Stop trying so hard. Stop trying to please." Even though there were at least a hundred people present in the arena, for a few moments it looked to outsiders as if the two felt they were completely alone. Jay whispered in her ear as Beyoncé listened, smiled, and nodded. He comforted her and talked softly to her until he felt she was ready to continue with her rehearsal. Usually Beyoncé is unflappable; meltdowns are rare for her. No matter the stress, she has been in show business so long that she can usually handle it. Those who cared about her were happy to know that she had someone in her life she could turn to during those rare bad moments, especially since she seemed to be marginalizing Mathew these days. Not only did Jay truly care about her well-being and want her to be happy, but he seemed to take seriously the responsibility of helping her get through tough times. Eventually she was able to pull away from him and return to work, now seeming reenergized.

"I'm still trying to learn that I don't have to kill myself and be so hard on myself and be so critical and [that] I can smell the roses," she would later say. "I don't want to never be satisfied. I don't think that's a healthy way to live."

Always a people pleaser, she was still worried about how she was being perceived by others, even strangers. "In a way, she had way more heart than Jay," said Choke No Joke. "I've been with Beyoncé a lot of times where she would try to sign every goddamn autograph, and if she missed a few she'd have the limo driver circle the block and go back and finish. Jay? You ain't gettin' no autograph from him unless he's good and ready, and if he misses you, better luck next time. He ain't circling the block for no fan. In fact, it would annoy him that Beyoncé was so afraid some of her fans might not like her. 'Damn, girl!' he'd say. 'Don't you think you give 'em enough?'"

When Beyoncé would make certain changes in her behavior as suggested by Jay, he realized that a major motivation for her to do so was to please him. While he had always been the kind of man who wanted his own way, he was definitely changing, his own personal journey unfolding at the same time as Beyoncé's. In fact, from this time onward in his relationship with her, Jay would never cease to amaze people who expected him to be completely misogynistic because of his hip-hop background and reputation. It was as if his love for Beyoncé helped him understand that the bigger personal victory for her would be to make changes for the sake of her own growth, not just to make him happy.

Whereas many men in his position would have been happy to be with a woman who would only do his bidding, the more invested Jay became in Beyoncé, the more he was able to extract himself from the equation and want what was best for her own well-being. "He's basically nothing at all— and I mean *absolutely nothing*—like what you would expect him to be," said one of his close friends. "Sure, he has the swagger, he has the bad boy vibe, he has the dangerous gangster thing. But when it came to Beyoncé

Knowles, all of that shit had pretty much melted away by 2007. Everyone could see that she'd became his greatest concern."

Of course, Jay's best efforts aside, in many ways Beyoncé was still that same little girl trying her very best to please Dad. One of the major reasons she wanted The Beyoncé Experience to be a success was because she still wanted to make Mathew proud. She wanted to please her fans, too, of course, but that goal was so closely connected to satisfying her father, it had become difficult to separate the two.

Ironically, Beyoncé actually did have Mathew's approval. She just didn't know it. Rarely did he express it, or at least that has been her memory of things. However, the truth was that he was exceedingly proud of her, and always had been. Everyone in his life knew it, even if she didn't.

"My God, she was the light of his life," exclaimed Alex Wright. "He couldn't sing her praises enough. But when I would ask him, 'Does she know how you feel?' he would just shrug."

Alex says she felt that by 2007 the Knowleses were still a family that, maybe more than ever, held their feelings protectively close, unwilling—or maybe unable—to express to one another how they really felt for fear of what might happen, of what closely guarded truth might be revealed in the process.

"I came to believe it was a pathology that had been passed down through the years," Alex concluded, "and that there really wasn't anything any of them could do about it. I thought, 'My God, this has to be so painful for them.' I felt that the pressure had to be too much, that eventually something would have to give . . . that the whole thing was about to blow at any moment."

The Beyoncé Experience

*H*ow y'all doin'," Beyoncé shouted out to more than fifty thousand people at the Tokyo Dome on April 10, 2007, as she began her trademark strut down a massive stage to the exciting intro of "Crazy in Love." Accompanied by several female dancers, for the next two hours she would work nonstop, singing and dancing. By the time she'd finished her rip-roaring twenty-two-song set, which included a lengthy medley of her Destiny's

Child hits as well as a healthy selection of her most recent songs, she'd once again proved herself as one of contemporary pop music's greatest live performers. Longtime music journalist Steven Ivory put it this way: "If Tina Turner and Michael Jackson had a baby, that child would be Beyoncé." It's certainly true that her showmanship—her charisma, her vocal prowess and intuition; her sheer *athleticism*—recall the skills of both those great performers."

Like the great Tina Turner before her, with her troupe of dancers, the Ikettes, Beyoncé uses her own dancers to generate excitement and unified spectacle. However, the dancers bring attention *to* Beyoncé, who, while executing the same steps as her troupe, instinctively adds a subtle authority missing from the moves of the rest of the ensemble. Whereas back in the day Ike Turner had the last word on how his wife, Tina, and the Ikettes appeared and moved, no man is in control of what happens on Beyoncé's stage. Of course, for The Beyoncé Experience, as for all of her tours, she hires choreographers—but she runs her dance presentation from top to bottom herself.

For all her hip-hop swagger and preoccupation with producing videos and short films that are often modernist and surreal, Beyoncé's onstage sensibilities harken back to 1960s soul. When she paid tribute to Tina Turner in 2005 on the Kennedy Center Honors, with stunning rendering of Turner's "Proud Mary" (complete with three of Beyoncé's backup girls restyled to look exactly like the Ikettes), it was more clear than ever that Beyoncé is a performer in the oldest and most traditional style of R&B. Her outfits— sequin, leather, and lace creations—are sexy, but often in a conventional Vegasy style. Then again, it's her *traditional* approach to performing—the notion that the true entertainer is one who does onstage what few in the audience can do—that separates her from most of the stars of her generation. She understands that an audience wants to see a performer work hard.

The show in Tokyo was just the first of almost a hundred in Asia, Australia, North America, Europe, and Africa. Every night, Beyoncé gave the same level of exhausting energy.

Part of Beyoncé's process regarding total focus and concentration during tour dates has to do with picking and choosing with whom she socializes on the road. For instance, if a dancer who has been hired to perform on tour with her thinks that she is going to end up becoming close friends with the lady herself, she can forget it. It's not going to happen.

"Everybody thinks because we dance with her and are around her more than a lot of people, that we actually know everything that is happening, but we don't," said Tanesha Ksyn Cason, who under the stage name Miss Ksyn has danced with Beyoncé for many years. "Sometimes we don't even know for sure what the next leg of a tour will be. We usually find out through the fans. Like a fan will send us a flyer, 'Hey, you guys, we can't wait to see you here.' Then we go, 'Okay, cool, so I guess that's the next leg.' Later we might get an e-mail from our agents saying, 'I'm just letting you know, these are the next dates.'"

The dancers and musicians usually travel together and stay in one hotel, while the crew and other technical people travel separately and stay in another location, and Beyoncé and her personal staff in a third. Though she obviously knows where everyone else is staying, they don't know her exact whereabouts. The reasons are twofold. First, she wants her privacy. Second, she doesn't want to have to wonder if any of her touring personnel spilled the beans should the location of her hotel be leaked to the press. If no one knows where she's staying, they are all in the clear. "Truly, we'd just as soon not know where she is than have to worry about being under suspicion," said Miss Ksyn. "She's generous to us during rehearsals and performances, and then she likes her private time when we aren't working. No one has ever had a problem with that. You *want* to give it to her. You *want* her to have it. You feel she deserves it."

As much as she loved performing, by the time the tour ended in Taipei on November 12, Beyoncé was both emotionally and physically drained—a usual state of being for her in recent years. Still, there was work to do; another album was right around the corner.

I Am … Sasha Fierce

*I*n December 2007, as Beyoncé began work on her third solo album, it was as if she'd paid heed to the criticisms of her previous album, B'Day. Though B'Day had been a worldwide multiplatinum success, some commentators felt that it lacked focus and substance. Of course, in today's world of musical mediocrity, Beyoncé's tremendous talent, ambition, and relentless drive elevates whatever she records head and shoulders above her contemporaries, even if sometimes the tunes themselves are lacking, which many felt was the case with *B'Day*. "The *songs* are just not on *B'Day*," is how one critic succinctly put it. "In fact, I can't remember a single one of 'em." If there was an upside to such criticism, it was that it encouraged Beyoncé to ponder the notion of creating a record that would allow her to explore the memorable best of two musical genres—rhythmic songs people could remember, and ballads they would never forget.

Most observers agreed that the real problem with *B'Day* had been that Mathew hadn't been allowed to put his full imprint on it. In the process of settling that score, then, Beyoncé would give him much more latitude in the production of the next album. Apparently, whatever was going on in his personal life at this time had no bearing on his participation in her record, at least in Beyoncé's view—and she was the boss. Though grappling with conflicting emotions where Mathew was concerned, she was also adept, as we have seen, at finding ways to work around personal chaos when necessary. She knew she needed Mathew on this project. It was a wise move on her part. Mathew's influence as co–executive producer (with Beyoncé) would be to the great advantage on this album, which would be called *I Am ... Sasha Fierce*. In fact, this set would be the near-perfect amalgamation of father's and daughter's musical tastes and, as such, stand as a glorious testament to their many years of stellar work together.

Beyoncé's concept for *I Am ... Sasha Fierce* would take the form of a two-disc package: Disc One would be called *I Am ...* and would highlight the best of the midtempo songs at her disposal. Ultimately, she would decide on airy, introspective decidedly "pop" odes to love and relationships. These selections would call to mind the 1970s music business term "crossover," used back in the day when acts like Lionel Richie and Whitney Houston crafted mainstream pop designed to reach audiences beyond their black fan base.

Disc Two would be called *Sasha Fierce*. It would feature the kind of dance- and rap-influenced urban tracks with which Beyoncé had become synonymous, all under the auspices of the moniker she'd come up with for her aggressively sexy and angry alter ego.

To forge new ground for two discs worth of new music, Beyoncé would need new collaborators. Therefore, on board for this album would be some familiar names she'd worked with in the past—Rodney "Darkchild" Jerkins and Kenny "Babyface" Edmonds, among others. However, there would also be new blood, most notably Ryan Tedder, a multi-instrumentalist, songwriter, producer, and leader of the pop/rock band OneRepublic. Other names new to the Beyoncé camp would include songwriters Toby Gad and BC Jean, who contributed the *I Am* album opener, "If I Were a Boy," a poignant, introspective pop ballad about society's gender double standards (the only song on this collection that Beyoncé didn't write or cowrite).

"Beyoncé's whole trip is simple," said a close friend of hers. "She wants to inspire. That has always been her intention. If a song like 'Halo' comes along that she feels will do the job, she latches on for dear life and does what she can to make it the performance of a lifetime, a performance that would be considered inspirational. After she finished 'Halo,' she was very satisfied with it. 'It takes you to another place,' she told me. That's always her intention . . . to go to that other place and take her fans with her."

On Disc Two, *Sasha Fierce*, Beyoncé adeptly explored electronic pop with "Radio" and "Sweet Dreams." There was also the beat-laden "Video Phone" and "Diva," both personifying what Beyoncé viewed as the Sasha Fierce ethos. However, some fans questioned whether these songs were completely emblematic of the alter ego. After all, that dual identity wasn't put forth to exemplify a certain type of music as much as it was intended as a kind of performance art. Sasha was the angry Beyoncé, the iteration of Beyoncé who was fully able to access her true feelings—sexual or hostile—in dance and in attitude. Maybe this confusion was for the best, though. Maybe as the character aged in her life and Beyoncé began to lose her grip on what she really represented, such confusion might see Sasha Fierce finally slip away, or at the very least merge into the real Beyoncé. Maybe Sasha was actually becoming unnecessary?

While *I Am . . . Sasha Fierce* would produce a number of unforgettable songs, it was "Single Ladies (Put a Ring on It)" that would take Beyoncé's career to new heights. Producers/songwriters Christopher "Tricky" Stewart and Terius "The-Dream" Nash, along with Thaddis "Kuk" Harrell, are responsible for this spacey, ethereal, and ultimately exciting musical track. Nash's subject matter when he began the lyrics fit well with Beyoncé's ongoing musical narrative about women and empowerment. By the time she took it upon herself to finish it, the lyrics perfectly represented her outspoken, aggressively feminist image, making it the obvious choice for the first single from *I Am . . . Sasha Fierce* (released concurrently with "If I Were a Boy").

"Single Ladies (Put a Ring on It)" went beyond hit status to become nothing short of a cultural phenomenon, the Bob Fosse–inspired choreography of the video inspiring nothing short of a viral dance craze. "It's the cheapest video I've ever done," she told Welsh interviewer Steve Jones, "and it became the most iconic. I never thought I would have a body of work that would be such a huge part of pop culture." (Who could ever forget the Justin Timberlake takeoff of the video, performed with Beyoncé and Adam Samberg on *Saturday Night Live?*) Today, the song remains a theme and catchphrase (replete with the hand gesture featured in its stylized black-and-white music video) for the empowered woman. Beyoncé not only took the shame out of ditching a dead-end relationship, she actually made it cool and hip.

Not only would "Single Ladies (Put a Ring on It)" become one of Beyoncé's biggest songs—hitting number one on the *Billboard* Hot 100 on December 13, 2008, her fifth chart-topper—but it would push *I Am . . . Sasha Fierce* to the top of the charts as well. Eventually the album would sell more than eight million copies. Nominated eight times at the 52nd Annual Grammy Awards, Beyoncé would enjoy a record-setting six wins— at that time the most awards won by a female artist in one night.

Cadillac Records *and* Obsessed

$\mathcal{S}$he wanted to act. One couldn't blame her. Given the right role, she was very good at it. She also took it very seriously. However, because roles for African-American actresses have historically not been plentiful in Hollywood, Beyoncé didn't have a wide variety from which to choose. At the end of 2008, she starred in Sony Pictures' *Cadillac Records*, not at all a bad choice in terms of film opportunities.

When it was announced that Beyoncé would be playing R&B and blues singer Etta James in *Cadillac Records*, there was understandable skepticism in the media. Beyoncé had little in common with the ribald Etta, an abandoned child who battled racism and heroin addiction and whose performances of songs (such as her classic "I'd Rather Go Blind") spoke to a life of heartbreak and despair. In her obituary (January 20, 2012), *Time* noted that she'd "endured a life more wrenching than any of her songs." Beyoncé had certainly worked hard throughout her life, but, by her own admission, she hadn't really struggled, at least not the way Etta James had. Likely, if this film had been a biopic of James, the casting would have been met with much more derision. However, *Cadillac Records* purported to tell the story of the influence Chess Records of Chicago had on the birth of rock and roll in the 1950s with artists such as Chuck Berry (played by Mos Def, who had worked with Beyoncé in *Carmen: A Hip Hopera*), Willie Dixon (Cedric the Entertainer), Howlin' Wolf (Eammon Walker), and Muddy Waters (Jeffrey Wright in a true star turn). Since the earthy and profane James was to be just part of a large ensemble of characters, Beyoncé was able to take the role without much true criticism. Etta seeped into her very soul, so much so that she actually began to swear much more in her day-to-day after taking that challenging role . . . and she didn't mind it at all.

Darnell Martin, the movie's writer and director, says he wrote the part of Etta James in the movie specifically for Beyoncé. "She was the dream to play Etta," he told Smokey Fontaine for *Giant* magazine. The problem, though, was that Beyoncé was afraid of the part. She understood how much of a reach it would be for her, and the idea intimidated her. It was Tina who convinced her to take it.

"She'd been saying for a long time that she wanted to stretch out and do something that was totally different," Tina recalled. "Etta was down and dirty, she was tough. I felt like Beyoncé could kill it in that role. I knew she had it in her. She put up a little fight and said she didn't think she'd have the time to devote to it. I said, 'Well, it's up to you, but you're the one who has said you wanted to do something different. Here it is.'"

In her film career to date, Beyoncé has had two roles that truly showed her depth as an actress—her very first, as Carmen Brown in *Carmen: A Hip Hopera*, in which director Robert Townsend coaxed her into an impressive and wide-ranging debut, and her work as Etta James in *Cadillac Records*, for which Darnell Martin helped her mine golden moments that nuanced her performance and saved it from drifting into caricature. Of course, her performances on torch songs such as "At Last" and "I'd Rather Go Blind" are stellar; that comes as no surprise. While they don't exactly sound like Etta, they do evoke her pained sensibility as a vocalist. However, it's Beyoncé acting, which is gritty and sometimes startling in its profanity, that demonstrates an organic ability seldom explored in her movie roles. She would tell Oprah Winfrey that it was her "most fulfilling role."

At this same time, in 2008, Beyoncé gave one of her greatest performances in a tribute to Barbra Streisand at the Kennedy Center Honors when she sang "The Way We Were." The difference between Streisand and James is about as great a divide as one might find in our culture, yet

Beyoncé was able to deliver the Streisand tribute with just as much conviction, authority, and genuine heart as anything she did in *Cadillac Records*. There's no better demonstration of her amazing versatility than comparing these performances.

Cadillac Records was a triumph; not so her next movie—and her last, to date—*Obsessed*.

Filmed in the middle of 2008, mostly at Sony Pictures Studio in Culver City, California, *Obsessed* was likely better on paper in script form than it turned out onscreen. The plot concerns a happily married couple, Derek and Sharon Charles—played by Idris Elba and Beyoncé—who are forced to deal with an unstable and delusional stalker, Lisa, portrayed by Ali Larter.

Some might argue that the only reason to watch *Obsessed* (which was released in April 2009) is for the last ten minutes, during which Beyoncé's character discovers the stalker in her home and engages in a bloody fight with her that is both stunning in its brutality and comical in its over-the-top moments. The fight ends in the attic where Beyoncé is forced to balance herself on four-inch stiletto heels on wooden beams rather than risk falling through the insulation to the ground floor—which is exactly what the stalker does. Poor crazy Lisa ends up on the floor down below, and just as she appears to be getting up for what promises to be round two, a chandelier falls on top of her, killing her. This fight—which the *Washington Post* called "a demolition-derby catfight"—won an MTV Award for "Best Fight Scene."

Lance Gilbert, the stunt coordinator for the film, recalled, "Because Beyoncé comes from a live stage environment that involves the need to learn hundreds of moves in dance sequences, she was able to pull off the fight scene. She was accustomed to applying her memory and her skill set to the learning of techniques. She approached it as if it were a long dance sequence. We obviously used stunt doubles for the girls, but they were still required to do a lot of very complex movement. There was some boxing, there was some martial arts. It wasn't easy. When I taught her the headbutt, she was at first a little nervous about it. She read the script and was like, 'My gosh...I don't know'...But then she really wanted to take advantage of it. It's a dynamic move, and she made the best of it."

Beyoncé Marries Jay

*T*hough Tina Knowles had made some tough choices in her life, she was never one to complain about them. Yet she must have wanted more for both her daughters and for Kelly than to settle for a marriage that wasn't completely satisfying. Most mothers would want more for their children. She had no reservations about Jay Z as a potential son-in-law, though, that much was clear. Neither did Mathew. In fact, Mathew very much enjoyed his friendship with Jay and often boasted to friends about the expensive gifts, be it a watch or some other piece of fine jewelry, that Jay had given him. Jay is even said to have gifted Mathew with a pair of tennis shoes that cost $15,000. Mathew was proud of Jay's success, and happy that his daughter had found someone worthy of her love.

On April 4, 2008—about a week after Beyoncé finished work on *Cadillac Records*—ever so privately, true not only to her nature but to his, Beyoncé, now twenty-six, and Shawn Carter, thirty-eight, were married in New York City. The nuptials took place at Jay's high-ceilinged and light-filled 8,309-square-foot seventh-floor penthouse in Tribeca. (He'd purchased it back in September 2004 for almost $7 million. Beyoncé owns a couple of eye-popping condominiums in the city as well, including reportedly one at Richard Meier's glass-architecture On Prospect Park, but it was decided to hold the ceremony at Jay's.)

It was a small, lovely ceremony, with just forty guests, against an affluent Manhattan backdrop. Tina, along with Jay's grandmother, eighty-three-year-old Hattie, chose to prepare the meal themselves rather than have the event catered—there were Creole specialties like gumbo from Tina and soul foods such as oxtails and candied yams from Hattie. Among the guests, of course, were Mathew, Tina, and Solange; Jay's mother, Gloria; his grandmother, Hattie; Kelly Rowland and Michelle Williams; and the couple's friends Gwyneth Paltrow and her husband, Chris Martin (who collaborated with Jay on his 2006 album *Kingdom Come*). No cell phones were allowed; the guests were asked to leave them with the drivers hired to transport them to the wedding.

A large tent was set up on the building's roof and decorated in a royal theme. Certainly the flowers picked out by Jay were also of special note.

Four days earlier, on Monday, Amy Vongpitaka—owner of Amy's

Orchids in Non Nok Khai, a tiny town outside Sampran, Thailand—received a call at her Virginia warehouse from a top floral designer in Manhattan. She was told that there was a need for as many as one hundred thousand pure white dendrobium orchids for an important wedding. They had to be the whitest of the white, and there should be no stems, just blooms. Amy says she spent two hours on the phone with the designer and received via e-mail illustrations for exactly how the blooms should look—which, as described to her, were to be "fit for a palace." The designer also told her that it was Jay Z, not Beyoncé, who had met with her for more than an hour discussing these floral arrangements. Jay said that he wanted everything to be perfect for Beyoncé. Or as he put it to the designer, "I want the whole thing to be *dope*." He knew exactly how he wanted the blooms to look, and how they should be arranged.

Amy is used to producing orchids for big names from all over the world. Her clients have ranged from Snoop Dogg for his wedding to special orders for the queen of Thailand. Therefore this order was not unusual. However, because the turnaround time was especially tight, she was forced to employ extra people at her orchid farm in Thailand, fifty total, to pluck the delicate flowers. They were packed three boxes deep to protect their fragility. She won't say how much she charged for her services, but says she had to double her fee for each bloom because of the rush delivery. Online reports are that she charges $40 a bloom. If doubled for one hundred thousand orchids, this would total $8 million... *for flowers*! Amy Vongpitaka recalled, "Jay Z said, 'I want special. I want this, I want that. Expensive is no problem.'"

From the hundred thousand blooms, the wedding's floral designer finally chose between sixty thousand and seventy thousand of them, many of which hung as elegant eight-foot garlands from the ceiling.

Contrary to their often provocative public personas, Beyoncé and Jay chose a traditional marriage ceremony. Beyoncé wore a sleeveless floor-length white silk gown and long tulle veil and ruffled train. Her hair was pulled elegantly into a chignon. Jay sported a finely tailored black tux with black tie and white rose boutonniere. They were married by the Knowles's longtime family priest, Pastor Rudy Rasmus. All of the female guests were asked to wear white, and the men black suits, except for Mathew, who wore a silver jacket and black tie. Rather than throw rice at the newlyweds, the guests tossed what appear to have been white feathers.

Because of the secrecy surrounding the event, it is not known for certain whether or not Mathew walked Beyoncé down the aisle. According to

Alex Wright, whose relationship with Mathew was unfolding during this time, he did not. However, she didn't attend the wedding. She says that after Mathew returned to Los Angeles from the Manhattan ceremony, he told her that he didn't partake in that honor. That specific detail, though, is but one of the many that remain a mystery from this closely guarded affair.

Beyoncé's wedding band is a $5 million, eighteen-carat Lorraine Schwartz diamond ring. (She always takes it off before interviews because, truly, it's impossible for it to not become the topic of conversation, it's that dazzling.) "I can't think about how much it costs," she said privately. Still, after all of this time of affluent living, she marvels at her good fortune. "For any girl to wear something that costs this much...well...I can't even think about it or I'll get scared and put it in a box somewhere for safekeeping."

Since it would be at least six months before the couple would even confirm that they'd been married, some might say they were pathological about their privacy. However, they didn't care what others thought about the secrecy. When a couple months after the ceremony Jay obliquely referred to Beyoncé as a "friend" to a reporter for *Vibe*, the writer called him out on it. "You said your 'friend,' but this is your wife. Are you still not willing to confirm?" pressed the writer. "That's ridiculous for me to confirm," Jay said testily. "I don't have...I'm gonna say, I think that was a ridiculous question. I just think it's really a part of your life that you gotta keep to yourself. You have to, or you'll go insane in this type of business. You have to have something that's sacred to you and the people around you."

Obama

*B*eyoncé started the year 2009 off on a somewhat historical note by singing at the inaugural ball of President Barack Obama on January 20. She had only one day at home, at her and Jay's gated seven-bedroom, eight-bath Mediterranean estate in Miami (with its own boat dock on a barrier island described by *Forbes* as a "billionaire island fortress") before she had to prepare for her performance. For the president's first dance with First Lady Michelle Obama, Beyoncé sang Etta James's "At Last." It was a stunning performance.

Two days earlier, Beyoncé had closed the "We Are One: The Obama Inaugural Celebration at the Lincoln Memorial" with a beautiful rendition of "America the Beautiful." Of course, she and Jay had several opportunities to speak to the president and First Lady. Obama was so taken with the couple, he pulled from his vest a small card with his private cell phone number on it and handed it to Beyoncé. "Call me anytime," he told her. "I mean, anytime he will let you," he added, motioning to Jay and smiling. Beyoncé was so amazed, she immediately put the number on speed dial on her phone, though, to anyone's knowledge, anyway, she's never used it. In 2013, Jay mentioned on a radio show that he sometimes "had texts from Obama, of course," repeating a sentiment he'd made on his recording of "On to the Next One," where he rapped that he has Obama "on text." But two years later, in 2015, Obama appeared on *The Jimmy Kimmel Show* and said that he actually doesn't text—he only uses e-mail.

Certainly, to say that the Obamas and the Carters are friends would be exaggerating their relationship. They are friendly, but it's not as if they call each other every day. They live in different worlds. When or if the Obamas ever need them for something, a concert or fund-raiser or whatever, of course the Carters will be available to them. As Jay put it to one colleague, "We'd do it big for the Obamas, anytime."

In 2010, the Carters would tour the White House and take photos with the Obamas in the Situation Room. The Carters would later support Obama's reelection campaign, holding a $40,000-per-ticket fund-raiser for him. Three years later, in January 2013, it would be Beyoncé's great honor to perform the national anthem at the second inauguration of Obama as the fourty-fourth president of the United States. A controversy would erupt after the appearance when a Marine Band representative blabbed to reporters that Beyoncé had used a prerecorded vocal track. In fact, such a track is often used at big events such as the inauguration in order to avoid sound problems. However, these days the public and media are prickly about lip-syncing because it suggests that the vocalist can't really sing. Of course, in some cases that's true. But is there really any doubt that Beyoncé is a singer? Actually, on that important day, she was singing *along* with a prerecorded vocal and instrumental track. She would later explain that she didn't have time to rehearse with the orchestra and was therefore concerned about meeting her standards of perfection.

Beyoncé would decide to stay silent on the subject for a while before finally addressing it at a press conference to promote her upcoming Super

Bowl halftime performance. Before taking questions, she asked the reporters to please stand. She then sang the national anthem in full voice, loud and a cappella against a backdrop of a huge American flag. Of course, by the time she finished, the press corps were cheering. "Thank you guys so much," she said graciously. Then, with a sly smile, she asked, "Any questions?"

Trouble Brewing

*B*y October 2008, Mathew's romance with AlexSandra Wright had been going on for about a year. They were content, living their lives, doing their work. He had his business affairs relating to Beyoncé, Solange, and his Music World company, and she had hers in integrated branding.

Toward the end of the month, Mathew went to New York to meet with Solange. It didn't go well. Apparently, during a rehearsal for a showcase of her *Sol-Angel and the Hadley St. Dreams* album, father and daughter ended up in a very heated argument. They were both nothing if not strong-willed. "Solange is actually much more like her father than Beyoncé," observed one of Solange's friends. "Solange is candid, sometimes blunt. It may take some time, but eventually you will know where you stand with her, that's for sure."

"I've worked with her," says Choke No Joke of Solange. "I've produced shows for her. I've hung out with her. I've even tried to date her. She doesn't kiss ass, she doesn't toe the line. She has strong opinions and she lets record executives know about them whether they want to hear them or not."

In fact, at this same time, Solange released a telling song called "Fuck the Industry (Signed Sincerely)," which she wrote herself and which gave voice to her frustration over being compared to others in the record industry—including you-know-who. The first line is, "I'll never be picture-perfect Beyoncé." She also released a song on the *Hadley St. Dreams* album called "God Given Name," in which she sings, "I'm not her and never will be / Two girls going in different directions." She told one reporter, "I'm never going to be about sales and buzz, and I just wish people would get that about me, once and for all. I love my sister, but I am *not* my sister."

Perhaps making things even more complex for Solange is that she may be an unacknowledged writer on many of the songs recorded by

Beyoncé and Destiny's Child. For instance, Mathew told Houston newscaster Khambrel Marshall that Solange "wrote the number one songs on Beyoncé's first album." On that album, the number one songs were "Crazy in Love" and "Baby Boy." "Naughty Girl" and "Me, Myself and I" were also major Top Five hits. Solange is not credited on any of them.

Mathew has also said that Solange "wrote 50 percent" of Kelly's debut album, *Simply Deep*. In fact, she is credited with cowriting only two of the thirteen songs, "Simply Deep," a duet with Kelly, and "Beyond Imagination." Is Mathew overstating her contribution, or is it possible that she's not credited for at least five other songs? Keep in mind that the notion of songwriting credits is very nebulous in the record business. In fact, Beyoncé has often been accused of receiving credit for songs that she did not write; some of her critics in this regard say it would be more accurate to say she "tweaked" ideas that were the brainchild of other writers. (Many writers and producers who have worked with Beyoncé have vehemently disagreed with that assessment.) Given this terrain, one can't help but wonder how Solange might feel if in fact she is unaccredited as a songwriter on records that were major hits for Destiny's Child and Beyoncé. People often extend themselves for family, but as a woman who had long been trying to get people to accept her as an artist, one would think that if this is true of Solange, she might have her share of mixed emotions about it. One also has to wonder whether she is receiving royalties for these songs. Since she hasn't addressed the issue publicly, it's anybody's guess.

Only Mathew and Solange know the specifics of the disagreement they had in New York. Afterward, though, Alex says, "Mathew returned to Los Angeles and told me, 'I'm not going back to New York or Houston.' And he didn't."

Shortly after that incident, Tina and Beyoncé launched their latest House of Deréon collection, which was inspired by the wardrobe from *Cadillac Records*, at Bloomingdale's in New York. Then Beyoncé and Solange took off for Tokyo, where they were set to promote their new Samantha Thavasa handbag line. As always, the Knowles women appeared lovely and composed at their product launches, all three by now adept at concealing private sorrows when it came time to work.

Meanwhile, Mathew made the decision to move permanently to Los Angeles. First he and Alex settled into a suite in the Beverly Hilton. Then they leased a home in upscale Beverly Hills, with an option to buy. Alex says that Mathew told her that Tina, Beyoncé, and Solange were well aware of his new domestic situation. She had no reason not to believe him.

Whatever the feelings of the Knowles women regarding Mathew's move to the West Coast, everything seemed to be going well for him and Alex. She says she even began handling some of the integrated branding projects at his Music World. When he traveled she would pull as much as $3,300 a day from what she says was a joint bank account to handle their bills and other expenses.

"We could lock ourselves away from the world and just exist together," Alex recalled of her life with Mathew. "He was loving and attentive," she recalled. "When you're with him, you feel like you're the only person in his world. But it's because, whoever you are, you're his life raft in that moment, and as a result, you *are* the only person in his world. Still, he made me feel needed and I loved it," she recalled. "I could see that he was troubled by certain things, and I wanted to save him. It speaks to everything good and everything bad about me, as well as whatever it says about him."

Mathew may have been starting a new life with Alex, but he still had the old one, and it wasn't going to just go away. It was Beyoncé's idea to get the entire family together around the time of the 2008 Thanksgiving holiday. Everyone was flying into Houston for it, people from Tina's side of the family and from Mathew's. Also attending would be Jay's mother, Gloria Carter, and other relatives. However, Alex says that Mathew couldn't face it because he feared it might be nothing more than an excuse for everyone to pile on and challenge him.

"I remember it well," Alex said of the holiday. "Mathew was supposed to take a flight out to Houston the day before Thanksgiving. There were a lot of texts and e-mails flying back and forth between him and family members. He kept putting it off until the last minute. He kept changing his reservations, pushing the flight back . . . and then he just didn't go."

It's not known how Beyoncé felt about her father's absence at the reunion. What is known is that the event had taken a great deal of strategic planning because, as always, she was incredibly busy. Not only was she scheduled to perform on the *Today* show in New York in November, but she was committed to promoting *Cadillac Records* in Los Angeles with dozens of television and press interviews. She then had to attend the movie's premiere there with Tina. She'd also agreed to go to London to promote her single "If I Were a Boy" and album, *I Am . . . Sasha Fierce*. Then she was off to Monte Carlo to perform at the World Music Awards. Trying to pull together a family reunion in the midst of such orchestrated chaos could not have been easy; Mathew's not showing up for it had to have been upsetting. "I know they were angry," Alex said of the family. "Mathew told me that they were all upset."

After Thanksgiving, life continued for Mathew and Alex without much change. However, even when immersed in his private relationship with Alex, Mathew was still very much involved with the career of his famous firstborn.

In December 2008, Simon Cowell wanted Beyoncé to go to England to perform a duet with one of the two talented finalists of the television show *The X Factor*, Alexandra Burke. A few years earlier, though, Cowell had been quoted as making some rather unflattering comments about Beyoncé in *Esquire*. "I find the whole Beyoncé thing really mystifying," he said. "She's not sexy, she hasn't got a great body and she's not a great singer."

Though Beyoncé was obviously used to criticism, Cowell's commentary still hit her hard. It would have been one matter to criticize just one element of her persona, but all of it? It seemed wholly unfair. So when word got back to her and Mathew that Cowell wanted her to fly to the UK and appear on the show, their response was pure silence. It became clear that the only way she would consider the invitation would be if Cowell apologized—which is exactly what he did. Alex was in the room when Simon telephoned Mathew to say that he was very sorry.

"Mathew was quiet for most of that conversation," she recalled. "Simon did most of the talking. Then Mathew was like, 'Okay. Great. Thanks so much for calling.' He was nice to him. When they hung up, Mathew was elated. He said, 'He needs to bow down! Beyoncé's the queen. Beyoncé reigns supreme'...and on and on with that kind of talk. But that was just Mathew. He was enamored of his own daughter, awestruck by her. She was his golden princess, to the point where sometimes I wanted to say, 'Please, Mathew. Enough. Okay? Enough!'"

Satisfied with Cowell's apology to her dad, Beyoncé did end up traveling to the UK on December 13 to sing her song "Listen" as a stunning duet with Alexandra Burke. "It was still obviously in her head what I had said," Simon Cowell recalled, "though I apologized. I was wrong. [That night] she sang better than anyone I've ever heard in my whole life. Then, at one point, she looked over to me as if to say, 'Criticize *that!*' Her eyes. I'll never forget that look."

After Christmas 2008, Mathew and Alex went to Canada for two weeks

to visit Alex's family. Two months later, on February 17, 2009, Alex celebrated her thirty-eighth birthday. Mathew gave her some money she used
to host a lavish party. "This was a very happy time for both of us," she
remembered.

By the beginning of 2009, Beyoncé was twenty-eight and preparing to
embark on the I Am...World Tour. Mathew still trying to do his job for
her, taking charge as her ever-efficient, hands-on manager just as he'd been
doing since she was a child. However, there seemed to be great change in
the air.

In March, Mathew and Alex spent ten days at the Wynn in Las Vegas,
where Mathew negotiated a complex deal with Steve Wynn for a Beyoncé
video shoot, which was to take place there on August 2. Her live concert
would be filmed (and also recorded for CD release) at the Encore Theater
and later released as I Am . . . Yours: An Intimate Performance at Wynn Las
Vegas. It featured Beyoncé performing more than thirty songs, from her
Destiny's Child canon all the way through her solo career.

Despite Mathew's representing her in Vegas, Beyoncé was feeling a leaning toward making all pertinent decisions about her career. A year earlier,
she had even decided to start her own management company, called Parkwood Entertainment (named, of course, after the address of the Knowles'
former home in the Third Ward). Cadillac Records and Obsessed had both
been made as a result of coproduction movie deals through Parkwood.

"I started my own company when I decided to manage myself," she
would later say, even though she still technically was being managed by
Mathew when she started Parkwood. It would have been more accurate—
and fairer to her father, even—for her to say she was co-managing herself.
"It was important that I didn't go to some big management company," she
added. "I felt like I wanted to follow the footsteps of Madonna and be a
powerhouse and have my own empire," she further explained, "and show
other women when you get to this point in your career you don't have to go
sign with someone else and share your money and your success—you do it
yourself."

Alex and Mathew Expecting

*B*efore long, the distance between Beyoncé and Mathew became more profound; by the spring of 2009 it would seem they were speaking only intermittently, or maybe not at all. "For Beyoncé, it was business as usual," said one person who knew her at this time. "She was on tour so there were a million things going on. People would ask, 'Well, what does Mathew think?' Because that was protocol, getting Mathew to weigh in on everything. I mean, you wouldn't even think otherwise, ever. That's how it had always been! She would say, 'Don't worry about it. It's all good. I got it covered.' So no one knew what was going on where her father was concerned. She didn't seem upset or rattled about it, either. But, really, she never does. Sometimes it's when she's at her most casual that you suspect the worst."

"To be honest, I would have to say they weren't speaking at all," said Alex Wright of Beyoncé and Mathew. "I think by this time it was really fractured between them. All I know is that he told me they were not in communication."

While Mathew worked behind the scenes to solve the riddle of what might be going on with his daughter, Alex Wright says that the two of them discussed having children.

Considering the tumult of his life, if in fact Mathew really was contemplating having children with Alex as she claims, perhaps he thought a new family would give him something positive to anticipate. After all, he had spent years working hard for the women in his life—Tina, Beyoncé, and Solange—only to now find all three of them at loggerheads with him for one reason or another. Maybe he felt he deserved some peace in his life, a respite from the harsh judgment.

Alex became pregnant in May 2009. At around the same time, her mother, Enid, was diagnosed with cancer, making this a most challenging time for her family. The baby's due date was February 7, 2010, her mother's birthday.

In June, when she was certain of the pregnancy, Alex and Mathew took a trip to San Francisco to spend three days visiting her brother Jonathan. It was there, on June 2—while Beyoncé was in Belfast on her world tour—that Alex told Mathew and her brother about the pregnancy. According to her, Mathew was exuberant. "He hoped it would be a boy," she recalled. "His reaction was that it was a great thing," concurred Jonathan.

Mathew and Alex then flew to San Diego, where they had two beach houses, and celebrated with friends. However, while they were there, Mathew's cell phone began blowing up with texts and e-mails. "From what I could gather, everything seemed to be completely unraveling in New York with Beyoncé," Alex recalled. "It was getting bad."

After their time in San Diego, Mathew had their limousine driver pick them up for the ride back to Los Angeles. As Alex sat in the car with her feet on Mathew's lap, she decided to probe a little to find out exactly what was happening with Beyoncé. "I actually don't know what's up," Mathew said, sounding extremely worried.

"What do you think you should do?" Alex asked

He mulled it over. "I think I need to go to New York," he decided. "Like right now. This very second." Alex agreed. Mathew instructed his driver to take them straight to LAX. He hopped out of the car, suitcase in hand, and jumped on the next United flight to the East Coast. The driver then drove Alex back to the Beverly Hills residence. To her great surprise, Mathew returned the next day.

"Eventually, over the course of the next few weeks, we learned the shocking truth," Alex Wright continues, "which was that Beyoncé was having Mathew investigated. Apparently word had gotten back to her that there were some irregularities relating to money from the tour. She was about to have him audited."

Beyoncé's Audit of Mathew

She refused to believe it. When Beyoncé heard from the leading concert promoting firm Live Nation that Mathew might have been siphoning funds from her present "I Am . . . Tour," there was simply no way she would accept it. Of all of the people in her life, she trusted her father the most. She had just recently told a reporter that he was someone she knew in her heart "would ride and die for me." His relationship with Alex was obviously a sore spot for her. She loved her mother deeply and was loyal to her. Thus it had to have been difficult for her to reconcile that Mathew was living on the West Coast with another woman. Mathew had often told Beyoncé, "Business is business and family is family." However, it had become increasingly difficult for her to separate the two where he was concerned, though she continued to try. Now, in light of these alarming allegations, things were bound to become much more complicated between her and her dad.

Mathew would later explain that after Live Nation was unsuccessful in securing the rights to Beyoncé's next tour, executives from the company had told her that he had drawn funds generated from the present I Am . . . Tour. It's not known how much money was involved, but it had to have been a great deal, because that tour generated $119.5 million at the box office. In response to this stunning accusation, Beyoncé acted with great care. It would appear that she first confronted Mathew, who strenuously denied any wrongdoing. Mathew later said that he told Beyoncé, "The only way we will be able to understand this is through a court of law. That's the only way either one of us will be clear if someone in our camps did something that was incorrect."

Beyoncé decided that she just had to know the truth. She hired the law firm Reed Smith LLP to conduct a thorough audit. This was a bold move and she knew it. It was bound to affect everything between her and Mathew.

With the passing of time, as the audit was being conducted, things further deteriorated between Mathew and Beyoncé. "Even more business decisions were being made that excluded him," Alex Wright recalled. "Her staff by now had just made it a habit to not loop him in on everything. Their relationship seemed in even greater jeopardy. Yet so much of his identity still had to do with who she was in his life, and who he was in hers. We realized, though, what few people in the world knew: that what was now happening would gravely alter the texture and the forecast of the future for everyone."

At the end of July 2009, Beyoncé wrapped up the North American leg of her world tour. She was exhausted and ready for it to be over. It had been a tough emotional experience, especially given what was secretly going on in the background, the disintegrating relationship with her father.

Now that she would be back permanently, Mathew felt strongly that he again should go to New York to figure out once and for all the best course of action to take where his daughter was concerned. By this time, Alex was three months pregnant. While she hated to see him go, she knew he had no choice. "You have to figure this thing out," she told him. "I will miss you, but I'm not a stupid woman, Mathew. I get it. Go. Please. Handle your business with Beyoncé." Mathew would then leave the happy home he and Alex Wright shared in Beverly Hills, and return to Manhattan. "What I didn't count on," she says, "is that he would not be coming back."

Powder Keg

Once he was gone from her, Alex says Mathew broke off contact. No phone calls. No e-mail. No texts. The reasons for Mathew's decision to jettison her from his life were known only to him. Alex speculates, though, that when he returned to his "real" life—as opposed to the idyllic one he had created with her—he realized that it was in complete disarray. She could only assume it was as if he had enjoyed a lost weekend that lasted two years, and was then forced to return to the stark reality of his true existence. "I think he felt he had to step back into his family, live that life he had with them, and act as if nothing had happened," she says.

It felt to some as if Mathew also wished to go back in time and maybe reclaim some of the feeling of triumph and victory he'd felt with the success of Destiny's Child. Chad Elliott, who was vice president of A&R at Columbia, recalls visiting Mathew in Houston at around this time for a meeting. "Come with me," Mathew said, "I have something to show you." Elliott and two other record company executives, Kawan Prather and Guy Rouette, piled into Mathew's brand-new S-Class Mercedes-Benz and went for a drive. Mathew drove them to the Third Ward, to the home on Parkwood, the one he and Tina had to sell before it was repossessed by the bank. "You could see on his face how much this journey meant to him," recalled Elliott. "He said, 'This neighborhood is where it all began for me and Beyoncé. This was the beginning. All my savings were depleted,' he recalled, 'all my credit cards maxed.'"

While they were cruising down Parkwood, Mathew's car suddenly began to sputter just as it reached the house at number 3346. "Oh no!" he groaned. "You're not going to believe this," he said as the vehicle came to a halt right in front of his former home, "but we just ran out of gas." Mathew couldn't help but laugh at the irony. "Me being a show-off and *this* happens?" he noted with self-deprecating humor. One can't help but wonder whether or not he also recognized the symbolism of running out of gas at the site of where it all began, especially given that it now all seemed to be ending. If he did, he got over it quickly and proceeded to turn a potentially embarrassing scene into a memorable moment. The four men got out of the car and, in a muggy, 100-degree Houston day, trudged a mile and a half to a gas station for fuel, Mathew all the while chatting up former neighbors and friends from the block, reminiscing about the good old days, shaking hands and slapping shoulders as if running for office. "I saw then the sheer brilliance of this man as a public relations strategist," said Elliott. "He had this way of penetrating your soul when he looked at you, and the people we ran across that day adored him. It was amazing to watch, like bearing firsthand witness to his magical rags-to-riches story."

If only the magic could have lasted . . .

Predictably, because of Beyoncé's audit, the money Mathew had been spending on his lifestyle with Alex on the West Coast became an issue. The accountants wanted a fuller understanding of how he was financing it. In some ways, the situation was reminiscent of the Andretta Tillman estate legal battle years earlier when allegations were made accusing Mathew of having spent business money on a secret personal life. "That's when he cut me off financially," Alex claims. "I wasn't angry. It's what one does when one panics."

In August, Alex tracked Mathew down in Las Vegas. When she called him, she heard Beyoncé performing in the background; her show was in the process of being recorded at the Encore at Wynn for its DVD release, as per the lucrative deal Mathew had struck back in March. "I could hear the sheer excitement of it all, her amazing voice in the background, the audience's huge response to it," she said, "and I could also hear in Mathew's voice that he was high on the entire experience. That really set me off. As we spoke, he was completely dismissive of me. It felt to me like he was stepping back into his power, that he was now *Mathew Knowles* again, and that I and the baby were a thing of the past. That one phone call changed the trajectory of everything. Now I was angry."

The next time Alex saw Mathew, it was on television sitting next to Beyoncé at the MTV Music Awards broadcast on September 12, 2009, from Radio City Music Hall in New York. This public appearance was business as usual for Beyoncé. As always, she would push aside any turmoil and do what she had to do to present family solidarity for the sake of her career. "She was fine," said one member of her team. "Truly, if she was upset, you would never know it. She looked beautiful, she was in good spirits. I heard there was this big, high-stakes drama playing in the background between her and her father. But then I saw them together, smiling and happy, and I thought, 'Really?' They sure looked fine to me. I thought either everything was peachy-keen, or she's the greatest actress in the world. I also thought maybe she was just too busy to deal with it, especially that night." Jay was also very busy at this time. In fact, he was about to release what would be one of the biggest records of his career, "Empire State of Mind," with Alicia Keys, from his eleventh studio album, *The Blueprint 3*, which was presently at the top of the charts.

It was during the MTV Music Awards program that Kanye West—annoyed because Beyoncé hadn't won the award for Best Female Video for "Single Ladies (Put a Ring on It)"—famously interrupted Taylor Swift's acceptance speech. Swift had won for "You Belong with Me." "Yo, Taylor, I'm really happy for you and I'mma let you finish," Kanye said after grabbing the mike from her. "But Beyoncé had one of the best videos of all time!" The camera then shot over to a visibly mortified Beyoncé. Meanwhile, Taylor stood onstage stunned and speechless until the network finally went to a commercial break. Afterward, she burst into tears backstage. Later, when Beyoncé won for Best Video of the Year, she made her way to the stage and recalled her excitement at having won her first VMA when she was the seventeen-year-old lead singer of Destiny's Child. She then said, "I would like for Taylor to come out and have her moment." It was a classy move, much appreciated by the young pop star Swift.

What caught Alex's attention wasn't Beyoncé's magnanimous gesture, it was Mathew's contentment as he sat next to her in the audience. "I was no longer hearing from him, and it was becoming clear to me that he was trying to resume his former life without me," she recalled. "So...I hired a lawyer."

At the end of September 2009, Alex's legal team learned that Beyoncé was to be honored at a high-profile function hosted by *Billboard* in New York; she was set to be named the publication's Woman of the Year. Because this was such a prestigious honor, they suspected that Mathew would be present for it. They had been trying unsuccessfully to serve him with paternity papers for weeks, and it was decided to do so at the *Billboard* function on October 2. They even thought to use a female process server because they figured she would be more likely to get close to Mathew.

The deed was done; Mathew was served at the *Billboard* event without incident.

Though the Knowleses decided to try to remain calm, at least in public, things would reach a fever pitch in the public arena just the same. Because Mathew had been served at such a high-profile event, it was now known by the media that Beyoncé's dad had a mistress in Los Angeles who was pregnant. Someone from the popular website TMZ called Alex's attorney Neal Hersh to give him twenty minutes' warning before publishing a story about the scandal. Then, like a complete powder keg, it exploded at 9:15 p.m. Pacific coast time on the TMZ website.

Fractured Souls

On November 6, 2009, with his daughter now on tour in Egypt, Mathew Knowles returned to Los Angeles. "He showed up at our house unannounced at about 3:45 in the afternoon," Alex Wright recalled, "and I just remember him coming up the stairs very, very slowly. He has such bad knees, and they now seemed worse than ever. He seemed much older to me, worn down. He had on the exact same blue shirt and jeans he'd worn on the day I met him at Microsoft. I had to blink a couple of times, it was so surreal. I hadn't seen him since I served him at Beyoncé's function, and I didn't know what to expect."

Mathew walked into the home he had once shared with Alex, his eyes dark and haunted. "We spoke for a while and he seemed better," Alex says.

"I felt better, too. I then began to feel hopeful that we could get past this thing without it being even more of a circus. I felt that maybe we could move past it."

Alex's father, Virgil, and brother Jonathan quickly flew into town to help negotiate a peaceful accord. Everyone checked in to the Beverly Wilshire, which was to be command central for the negotiation of a treaty. At first it actually seemed as if the two had reached a compromise. But then things took a decidedly dark turn when, again according to Alex, Mathew asked that his name be removed from the birth certificate. "I said, 'No, Mathew!'" she recalled. "Why would I strip another human being of his identity? I would never give a child a false start in life.' I cussed him out in front of everybody. I've never been a shrinking violet, and he knew that.

"At one point, he even floated the idea of me handing the baby over to Beyoncé and Jay Z to adopt and then raise as their own. This, of course, was a big surprise. Of course I told him that it was out of the question. Looking back on it, I doubt that he even approached Beyoncé with the idea. I can't imagine that she and Jay Z would have ever agreed to raise a child born to her father and a woman who was not her mother." Mathew has never responded publicly to these claims.

"He showed up at my house after that meeting, upset," Alex recalled. "His whole thing was, 'I'm losing everything. You have to stop.' I felt badly for him. But I had *already* lost everything. Thanks to the press coverage, I had lost my credibility, my dignity, my reputation. The solution, in my mind, was for him to step up and support our child. But obviously by this time we were spinning out of control. We were fractured souls. There was no release of pain, just us holding on to it as tightly as possible."

Tina Files for Divorce

On November 11, 2009, Tina Knowles finally filed for divorce from Mathew Knowles. Her action came just a month after he was named in AlexSandra Wright's paternity suit. "When the family finally broke apart for real," Alex says, "it was devastating, across the board. It took my breath away. I didn't think it would ever happen. Mathew never thought they'd divorce. Despite all that had happened, family honor and loyalty was still everything to him. Besides that, Tina was the one good choice he'd made in his lifetime, and he definitely didn't want to let her go."

"One day, my world just exploded and I knew I had to get a divorce," Tina would recall years later in October 2014. After so many years of pain and unhappiness, she finally had to come to terms with the fact that the family she so treasured had been forever altered. Still, according to all accounts, it was impossible for her to truly hate Mathew for what had happened. She knew him well, and for years had been accepting of his faults. He would always be family to her. Of course, it would have been easy to blame him for everything, and obviously he was not without fault. However, Tina finally began to realize her own culpability in their codependent relationship. After all, it had been her choice to stay with him for more than thirty years; nobody forced her to remain in the marriage. In recent years, though, dealing with the ever-crumbling relationship had all but drained the joy from her days. Now painfully conscious of the emptiness in her life, she knew what she had to do. She would no longer live with the crushing oppression of a vacant marriage. She also knew she would have her daughters' support. In fact, she was counting on it. "We will now pull through and stick it out together," she reportedly told her girls, "because that's what family does."

From all accounts, Beyoncé, Solange, and also Kelly were pleased with Tina's decision, and proud of her for finding the courage to make it. Beyoncé was on tour in England on the day Tina filed, but mother and daughter had many long-distance telephone calls.

"It does something to your whole psyche, your whole self-esteem, because I had been married for thirty-three years," Tina later said, choking back tears. "I had never . . . I mean, I hadn't known anything else. I was very sad. My family is quite intertwined, so it was very difficult for me to detangle myself from it. But I knew that I didn't have a choice but to do that. I did it, but it was very hard."

The day after Tina moved to officially end her marriage, things also ended, and very badly, between Mathew and Alex. On the morning of November 12, there was to be one more settlement conference for the couple in the law offices of Neal Hersh and Judy Bogen. Though Alex thought they might be able to reach an accord, it wasn't meant to be.

"We *need* to finish this conversation, Mathew," Alex said as he prepared to bolt from the conference. "No. Actually we don't," Mathew concluded.

From that time on, Alex and Mathew would only communicate with each other through attorneys, and only see each other in court.

Nixon

𝒩ixon Alexander Knowles Wright was born on February 4, 2010. Because of the high-profile attention the pregnancy generated, Alex Wright was forced to use the pseudonym of "Kitty LaRoux" when she checked into Cedars-Sinai Medical Center in Los Angeles. Obviously, anyone who has any connection to Beyoncé, no matter how tenuous, becomes the subject of great paparazzi scrutiny when a scandal is breaking big. Luckily, the lady herself was able to hightail it out of New York after launching her new fragrance, Heat, at Macy's. Beyoncé was due to perform in Florianópolis, Brazil, the day Nixon was born, far away from U.S. media scrutiny.

A DNA test was conducted on March 4, which proved that Mathew truly was Nixon's biological father—not that there was any doubt about it. With four being an important number in Beyoncé's life—she was born on September 4, Jay on December 4, they were married on April 4, and she has the Roman numeral IV tattooed on her wedding finger—how ironic, then, is it that a child born on the fourth and then confirmed to be a Knowles on the fourth would end up being the catalyst for so much change in her family?

Despite all of the upset with Alex, Mathew eventually agreed to what would have to be considered a very substantial and generous financial package for her and Nixon: about $12,000 a month in child support, as well as a fund for many of Alex's legal and accounting fees and household expenses.

The Death of Sasha Fierce

𝒮he had been going strong for so many years that by 2010, twenty-eight-year-old Beyoncé Giselle Knowles was physically and emotionally drained, but not just by her record-breaking career, but by her personal life as well. "I was a bit numb and kinda lost," is how she put it. Certainly what had happened to her parents' marriage had been devastating to her and promised to alter the landscape not only of her personal life but her career as well. How could she now continue with Mathew as her manager, considering what had happened with AlexSandra Wright? And what of the audit presently being conducted? No matter its results, her professional rapport with Mathew would be negatively impacted as a result of her even having ordered it. Obviously, she had a lot of thinking to do. Thus Beyoncé would spend most of 2010 coming to terms with everything that had happened.

First, she went on the road with Jay, starting in Auckland, New Zealand. Then she spent five weeks relaxing in Australia, "taking in the sights of Melbourne, Brisbane, Perth, and my favorite Aussie city, Sydney. It was a carefree existence for me." After that, it was off to Japan, then on to London, and then Russia, where she took in the ballet *Swan Lake*. She whisked her nephew, Julez, to Paris. She also went to Croatia, where she says, "I floated on my back for close to an hour in the Mediterranean Sea. It was one of the best moments of my life." During her time off, Beyoncé had plenty of time not only to think about her parents, but also to take stock of her own life. What she came to realize was that she had been leading a somewhat inauthentic life for many years, at least since the age of sixteen. "There was a bit of emotion in me missing," she explained. "The world is so much bigger than people just screaming out your name, and that becomes a sort of fake world . . . it's not really who you are."

Beyoncé came to understand that the only way for her to truly come to terms with what was presently going on in her life was to once and for all strip away all of the artifice that she'd created around the brand "Beyoncé" and bring it into balance with the true Beyoncé Knowles. To one associate, she posed the question, "How can I handle everything going on in my life when I don't even know who I am yet? I need to get real." In other words, the time had come to at least consider trying to merge the icon and the woman.

The first step was to contemplate the fate of Sasha Fierce, the character she had created, which had come to embody the Beyoncé brand. Sasha was the doppelgänger in which Beyoncé's rage had been deposited for years. Things were now changing for her, though. She told friends that she was bored and even frustrated by the double identity, that she felt it was "false" and now wanted to start over again without it. She had begun to resent not being able to personally express her anger, her sexuality, and everything else that had been more easily articulated by the alter ego. That she only began to feel this way after her mother filed for divorce seems to be no accident. She was always influenced by Tina, and if Tina was finally finding her true voice, maybe it was time for Beyoncé to do the same.

Thus in 2010 the time came for her to finally kill off Sasha Fierce. It was time for Beyoncé to seek authenticity in *all* aspects of her life. "She knew that the only way she could deal with the confusion of her father's actions and her mother's sorrow was to come to a fuller understanding of herself," said one person close to her. "After all, how could she understand them if she couldn't understand herself? It wouldn't happen overnight, but the process had begun."

"My personal retreat gave me strength and a creative reawakening," Beyoncé said in recalling her time of contemplation and restoration, the break in her career in 2010. "I returned refreshed, renewed, and empowered to reevaluate my life and do things that will make a difference."

In retrospect, it could be argued that Beyoncé's great miscalculation at this time was in advertising to the media the death of Sasha Fierce, thereby turning her demise into a talking point in press interviews. "Sasha Fierce is done," she told a reporter for *Allure* magazine. "I killed her. I don't need her any more because I've grown, and I'm able to merge the two personas." To the Associated Press she said, "I'm a new person, a different woman. Beyoncé is more courageous, I think, than Sasha Fierce ever was, and maybe bolder." To United Press International she said, "'Sasha Fierce' is over. I'm different, now."

Killing off Sasha Fierce had been a proactive response from a person who'd spent her entire adult life as an icon and was finally feeling the vacancy of that existence. Beyoncé killed Sasha because she finally realized that the character wasn't a panacea for the existential crisis she'd been experiencing of late. But in advertising as much in the media, she risked turning the transformative experience into just another gimmick. As far as most of her public was concerned, the invention and then killing off of Sasha Fierce were both the same: performance art. Only Beyoncé would be privy to all of the important personal ramifications of finally abandoning her alter ego, which in the end was probably just as it should have been.

Mystery at Parkwood

It was February 2011 and Beyoncé had just returned to New York after attending the 53rd Annual Grammy Awards in Los Angeles. She had told her makeup artist, Billy B., "Tonight, I'm going as Mrs. Carter, not Beyoncé," meaning she wanted low-key makeup so as not to upstage Jay who would end up a multiple-winner, including two Grammys for "Empire State of Mind." Now back in Manhattan, she was anxious to get back to work.

As an artist, Beyoncé was almost always thinking of new concepts for songs, for video shoots, photo layouts, and concerts. However, there were other matters on the table at this time that needed to be resolved before she could continue with her career. Now she was sequestered with her attorneys and accountants in a conference room of her Parkwood Entertainment office. She'd been in constant communication with them for the last few weeks, suggesting to some observers that there might be great change in the air. True to her discreet nature, Beyoncé was not forthcoming about it. Even those closest to her—some of whom had been at Parkwood for years—weren't sure what was happening. A few thought there was a secret new album in the works, or possibly a forthcoming tour announcement. There was even a rumor that she and Jay were about to go on the road together.

In fact, Parkwood employees are often in the dark about what is going on with the boss. Beyoncé always keeps a tight rein on information, allowing only those with an urgent need to know the details of whatever secret project happens to be in the works. A constant refrain at Parkwood has people asking one another, "Do you have *any* idea?" Often, no one has a clue. When they eventually do find out what has been going on behind the scenes, it's often a big surprise and is viewed as yet another Parkwood adventure. No one holds Beyoncé's secretive nature against her. They all realize that it's in their best interest if they don't know exactly what's going on, especially if it's supposed to be a secret.

One thing was true, though, and everyone at Parkwood knew it. The weeks before this date, February 13, felt stressful. Beyoncé clearly hadn't been herself. She was sad, she was distracted, and she was short with people. At one point, some observers speculated that Beyoncé was pregnant.

At least that would explain her moodiness, which was strange and even off-putting. Expecting a baby wouldn't, however, explain the recent rash of meetings with attorneys and accountants, all of whom would arrive at Parkwood with solemn faces and then depart looking even more grim. With the passing of time, it was obvious that the joyous announcement of a pregnancy was not to be in the offing, especially when one day she slipped up in an elevator and told someone, "I'm protecting what it took me twenty years to build." It was a puzzling statement, upon which she did not elaborate.

On that same day, Tina came in to Parkwood to see her daughter. The two stayed in Beyoncé's office for two hours. When she emerged, Tina seemed just a little worse for wear. "This is a very strange time for the family," she told one of Beyoncé's inquiring colleagues in the lobby. "So much is about to change, it's hard to wrap my mind around it." When asked to elaborate, she shook her head and concluded, "No. I've already said too much." Though the Knowles women were short on detail and big on cryptic statements, it was abundantly clear that a seismic shift was about to occur in their lives.

The Hard Choice

*W*hat most people on Beyoncé's staff didn't know was that she'd been in the midst of an audit of her father, that its conclusions had come in, and that they didn't seem to be good. There was speculation that they suggested Mathew might have stolen money from her. Despite his vociferous denials, every decision Beyoncé would now make would have to be in light of these extreme circumstances, and also of course with an eye toward the authenticity she now sought in all aspects of her life.

So how did she really feel? What was the appropriate action to take? Not the people-pleasing move, but for *her* the *right* move?

In coming to these conclusions, Beyoncé would no doubt take her time and consider not only her present relationship with Mathew but also everything he had meant to her in the past, and even how he had informed her thinking as a woman. This reflective time must have forced her to grapple with issues concerning not only ambition and loyalty, but the rights of women to stand up for themselves in a male-dominated entertainment industry. Somehow, the long and storied history of how women in her life had crossed swords with Mathew over the years had suddenly become relevant.

As we have seen, throughout her life, Beyoncé had been able to consider Mathew her greatest advocate. However, other women in her life hadn't been so fortunate in their dealings with him, and Beyoncé now had to view him through that same lens. After all, how many strong, formidable women had she seen go up against him and seemingly lose? Denise Seals and Deborah Laday came to mind, as well as, of course, Andretta Tillman. The savvy Pamela Luckett had challenged Mathew on several occasions while campaigning for her daughter, LeToya, and also lost. Going back even further, the enterprising Carolyn Davis hadn't fared well either, when she and her daughter, Ashley, stood up to Mathew. These outspoken, independent women were all, in one way or another—some to a greater degree and some to a lesser—role models of Beyoncé's.

Then there were her former group members.

When she was younger, Beyoncé may well have viewed all of her fellow singers who disagreed with Mathew as just standing in the way of her own success. She might even have thought of them as naïve and maybe even foolish; they just didn't know how lucky they were, at least in her youthful opinion. It's not as if she fought hard for Ashley Davis or Nicki and Nina Taylor, LeToya Luckett, or even LaTavia Roberson. But now, so many years later in 2011, she couldn't help but reconsider their motives. Now, as an adult, Beyoncé had to wonder: Weren't these women just standing up for their own goals and desires against Mathew's different vision . . . and losing?

Making it even more complex was her experience of her father in relation to her mother. She'd spent most of her life watching Tina deal with years of marital discord, culminating with Mathew finally having a child with another woman. It had taken a heavy toll on Tina; Beyoncé was a firsthand witness to her suffering. In fact, many believed she would refer to these dark times in her 2014 song "Ring Off." In the lyrics, Beyoncé writes about years of crushing disappointment in a marriage and the way they whittled away at self-esteem: "In the mirror you would stare / And say a prayer / Like 'I wish he said I'm beautiful' . . . So tired of the lies and trying, fighting, crying." This pain may have been not only Tina's experience of Mathew but, as her mother's loyal daughter, Beyoncé's as well.

So now here she was at a true crossroads, faced with a crucial decision to make about her future with Mathew in light not only of present events but of past history. There was no going back anyway, was there? Even if it had not turned up any apparent wrongdoing, the audit had seriously compromised the professional trust between herself and her father. She could see no tenable future with Mathew as her manager. She had no choice and she knew it; she had to let him go. It would take courage, though. Did she have it?

Of course, Beyoncé knew that Mathew would be devastated by her decision to break off their professional relationship. She shared his grief. However, Tina had always told her that heartache was almost always temporary, and she hung on to that thought with everything in her. "If you're going through it, just know it's called 'going through it,'" Tina would say. "You're not gonna get stuck there. You're not gonna die. You're gonna survive."

When all was said and done, though, the basic question still remained: Did Beyoncé believe Mathew had stolen money from her?

Publicly, she hasn't said one way or the other—no surprise there. According to those who know her best, though, Beyoncé is much too critical a thinker—and has been around the complex machinations of tour accounting for too many years—to believe that a onetime audit could prove any incontrovertible truth about her father. After all, there was more than just DNA holding them together. Mathew would have to go a long way down a bad road before Beyoncé would ever believe the worst of him, and it doesn't have to do with facts or truth or evidence . . . it has to do with heart.

Still, she knew what she had to do, maybe not only for herself but for her family as well. They had taken care of her their entire lives. Now maybe it was time for her to take care of them. It was as if she recognized that the way so many troubling events had occurred, one after the other—the public revelation of Mathew's affair with Alex, the subsequent birth of Nixon, the audit results—presented the perfect opportunity for everyone to finally, once and for all, move on with their lives.

Mathew Fights Back

On March 28, 2011, in a statement from her management company, Parkwood Entertainment, Beyoncé Knowles made it official: "I've only parted ways with my father on a business level," she allowed. "He is my father for life, and I love my dad dearly. I am grateful for everything he has taught me. I grew up watching both he and my mother manage and own their own businesses," she wrote. "They were hard-working entrepreneurs and I will continue to follow in their footsteps."

Mathew Knowles followed suit the next day with his own prepared words: "The decision was mutual. We did great things together, and I know that she will continue to conquer new territories in music and entertainment. Business is business and family is family. I love my daughter and am very proud of who she is and all that she has achieved. I look forward to her great continued success."

Now that obligatory public statements had been made to put forth the image of solidarity, it was time for Mathew to unpack what had really happened. With so much on the line, he wanted—he *needed*—answers. "I don't step aside," he said. "*I step up*." He had spent the better part of his life doing everything he could think of to guarantee that Beyoncé was the best in her field, that she made pop music history. Now, after everything he had sacrificed for her success, it was supposed to be over—just like that? Not so fast. He was certain Live Nation was primarily responsible for ruining everything for him, and he wasn't going to just sit back and accept it. Instead, he hired the best lawyers he could find, and filed a legal action to investigate a potential federal claim he felt he might have against the concert promotion company.

"I have made numerous attempts to investigate whether Live Nation played a role in my termination," he told the court, "but I have been stonewalled at every turn. I believe that Live Nation was involved in the spreading of false rumors about me and that these false rumors contributed or caused the termination of the Personal Management Agreements between myself and Beyoncé."

In that filing, Mathew also stated that no sooner had Beyoncé fired him than she had signed with Live Nation to promote her next tour. He said he found that timing to be very suspicious. "This [Beyoncé's new deal with Live Nation] has resulted in a benefit to Live Nation of millions of dollars," he noted. He concluded that, based on the way Live Nation had recently been diversifying its interests, the company now stood in line not only to promote her next tour but maybe even to manage her. He wanted to depose anyone from that firm who might have had anything to do with her decision. He also demanded to see and review with his own accountants all of the results of Beyoncé's audit.

At the same time that Mathew was fired, Faisal Duranni, a top executive at Live Nation, took on the role of president of Beyoncé's management and production company, Parkwood Entertainment—which Mathew says he also found suspicious. Making things even more interesting, Faisal was still a top-level executive at Live Nation, and in fact was one of those responsible for that company's ongoing, multi-rights association with Jay Z's Roc Nation, worth more than $150 million. Mathew said that Duranni had been nosing around in his business and asking a lot of questions about the audit Beyoncé had conducted, and he wanted to know why. (Faisal's role with Beyoncé would be short-lived and in retrospect appears to have been just transitional as she took over her own management duties.) Moreover, Mathew wanted access to any and all communications Beyoncé may have had with Jay about his termination.

Also, there was the little matter of a $4 million payment made to Beyoncé by Live Nation right after she fired Mathew. Mathew wanted to know the purpose of that huge transaction. He suspected that maybe Live Nation had induced Beyoncé into some sort of side deal, something that would help her tie up loose ends with him by having them contribute money for just that purpose. In other words, if Beyoncé owed Mathew any money in their parting, Live Nation would pony it up for her. In order to figure out if this was the case, Mathew wanted any communications the company had with her relating to that payment.

Throughout it all, Mathew strongly and adamantly denied the allegations made against him. In an interview, he stated, "We absolutely have not taken any money from Beyoncé, and all dollars will be accounted for. In no way have we stolen money." He added, "The relationship with Beyoncé is extremely amicable. I want to make that clear. Where there's concern is the people that she's doing business with. I'm challenging all of these folks on integrity, professional integrity."

On October 4, 2011, Judge Sylvia A. Matthews of the District Court of Harris County, Texas, would rule against Mathew Knowles and in favor of Live Nation in his legal filing against the company. Thus Mathew would not be permitted to take any depositions of Live Nation executives unless he actually went the distance and filed a formal lawsuit against them. And that's where the legal paper trail seems to end. As of this writing, for whatever reason, Mathew Knowles has not proceeded with any sort of lawsuit against Live Nation Entertainment.

4

*B*eyoncé's album *4*, which would be released in June 2011, is well worth listening to in that it acts as a sort of creative bridge between her recording career with Mathew Knowles at the helm and the one she would have on her own without him. In fact, it's her first album on which Mathew is not co-credited with her as an executive producer. Some seventeen writers and producers worked on the project, which was recorded over a year's time.

Like its predecessor, *I Am . . . Sasha Fierce*, which was purposely designed to be accessible to the masses, *4* features the sorts of songs best produced by Beyoncé under Mathew's tutelage. They are represented on this collection by compositions like the jubilant, Motown-inspired "Love on Top," written by Beyoncé with Terius "The-Dream" Nash and Shea Taylor. With its repeated key changes showing off Beyoncé's soaring voice to its fullest advantage, it's one of the most exciting of her recordings. The song's allegiance to old-school R&B is driven home by its accompanying music video, which features Beyoncé and a male ensemble affectionately reenacting New Edition's clip for their 1988 hit "If It Isn't Love," where the group is in a loft rehearsing for a concert.

Certainly a standout on *4* is the Diane Warren ballad "I Was Here," one of those very rare anthems recorded by Beyoncé that was not written or cowritten by her. Inspired by the September 11 attacks, it's the perfect song for her in the way it reflects on her life and expresses her desire to leave behind some meaningful mark.

The album also showcases the kind of unusual, experimental material she would record in the future sans Mathew. In this respect, there's "Countdown," with its herky-jerky horns and odd, fragmented melody. Also in this same league is "Run the World (Girls)," an amalgamation of beats and chants. It's difficult to believe that Mathew would have approved of either of these compositions. He likely would have revolted against their overt lack of commerciality. In Beyoncé's defense, though, she was obviously serving up material that would satisfy her own urge to create at will without worrying about how it would be interpreted by others—an understandable impulse, especially at this time of such great discontentment and upheaval in her life.

Released in June 2011, 4—like the Beyoncé albums before it—debuted at number one. While it won its share of awards—among them R&B Album of the Year at the 2012 Billboard Music Awards—it sold "only" three million in sales internationally, a little more than a million of that in America. It was actually Beyoncé's weakest showing as a solo artist. Amazingly enough, the album's standout cut, "Love on Top," peaked only at number twenty in the United States. (It did win a Grammy for Best Traditional R&B Performance, though.) The album's final single, "End of Time," didn't even make the charts.

Some in Beyoncé's life suggest that the infrastructure at her Parkwood Entertainment wasn't yet completely stabilized and ready to fully function in support of 4. It seemed that at the very least, Beyoncé would have to get used to making promotional decisions once made by Mathew. She would have help, of course—especially from Jay—but she had wanted to be on her own, have the final authority over her career, and now that she had gotten her wish, she'd have to sink or swim.

There was also some confusion at this time as to what direction she should take; she even recorded twenty songs that were inspired by the Nigerian musician Fela Anikulapo Kuti, coproduced by Terius Nash (which is why his and Beyoncé's "End of Time" seems to draw from Kuti's sound). Beyoncé had said she wanted to do something "epic," but that's not unusual—it's pretty much her goal with every album. Some felt she missed the mark with 4, but it certainly wasn't for lack of trying. (It's worth noting that Beyoncé's Destiny's Child colleague, Michelle Williams, was one of the stars of a successful, touring production of the Tony Award-winning Broadway show Fela! about Kuti, who died in 1997 of AIDS. Jay Z was one of the show's producers.)

As well as choosing the right path to chart without Mathew, there were a great many other matters for her to start handling, such as budgets for videos, future recordings, photo shoots, and the planning of the next tour, always a huge undertaking. Also important was Parkwood's ongoing working relationship with Columbia/Sony, which seemed to not be at its most efficient with 4. All of these behind-the-scenes machinations were now under Beyoncé's purview, responsibilities some skeptics thought might crush her now that they were to fall on her slim shoulders. It was a frightening prospect. Could she do it all without her dad? She wasn't sure. She only knew she had to try.

Full Circle

*I*t was November 2011. By this time, Beyoncé and Jay were expecting their first child; she was about seven months along. She was also trying to give birth to something else that, while not as personal, still felt that way to her—she wanted to produce and codirect a documentary for HBO about herself, which she wished to title *Life Is But a Dream.*

In many ways Beyoncé Knowles has had—and certainly continues to have—a life that many people would consider well worth documenting. In fact, since 2005 she has had a "visual director" film of many of her waking hours. Like Michael Jackson, who also had what he called a "videographer" documenting his life and times, she believes that there is some value to be found in almost every moment. Certainly Jay understands; he has had his own videographers; Choke No Joke comes to mind. In a broader sense, it could be said that not only is Beyoncé hounded by paparazzi, but she has pretty much hired her own to trail her—with her permission. Thus all of the photos and video footage of her and Jay walking on the beach, or shopping, or eating at a restaurant, or just living their lives, makes one wonder: Do these people ever have a truly private moment? Almost everything they do is filmed and then carefully cataloged in what Beyoncé calls "my crazy archive" in her Manhattan office.

Untold man-hours go into making certain that footage of Beyoncé and her family can be located in a moment's notice, whether for her own enjoyment or perhaps for an authorized documentary or for use in her act, such as the family album montage shown at the end of Beyoncé and Jay's show during their 2014 On the Run Tour. Copies of almost every photo she has ever taken going all the way back to Girls Tyme can also be found in temperature-controlled archives. Moreover, most of Beyoncé's press interviews are also filmed; it's usually required that the journalist agree to this provision before sitting down with her. Amy Wallace of *GQ* wrote about showing up for an interview with Beyoncé only to find the star already seated in front of a camera, her framing carefully prearranged so much so that she couldn't even rise to say hello lest she ruin the shot. Jo Ellison told the same sort of tale about her cover story on Beyoncé in *Vogue*.

In late 2011, it was the star's decision to collect many of the iterations of Beyoncé, as it were, for what would become an autobiographical documentary for HBO. She wanted to draw from her extensive archives and, along with self-narration, memorialize her current state of mind. She felt she'd grown in many ways and had been able to find the strength to fire her father as her manager by reaching deep within herself to understand who she was as a woman, his influence on her life—good and bad—and then coming to a decision about him that would not be the people-pleasing choice she might have once made, but one that reflected her new sense of personal honesty.

A year earlier, she'd made a decision to live a more authentic life, and since that time, she'd endeavored to do just that. She'd quietly gone about the business of separating the parts of her life that felt true and organic from those that felt false and pretentious, and then moved forward committed to personal honesty and integrity. But how does one square this quest for authenticity with the strange employment of photographers to document every moment of it? The only way is to try to fathom the somewhat twisted reality of a world-famous celebrity, a person who has been famous since the age of sixteen. She's never going to live a life most people can truly understand, or make decisions that will be wholly comprehensible to anyone other than those who also find themselves famous. Basically, at this time in her life, Beyoncé was doing her best to make certain changes within the constraints of the life she had chosen for herself. For most people, that would have been mandate enough. However, for someone like Beyoncé, there was more to it: She now felt compelled to share the journey with the world.

The problem she faced right off was that, as it turned out, the archival footage she'd worked so hard to acquire only went back to 2005. Most of what she had prior to that year had been ruined as a result of poor storage. Since she wanted to use photos and videos of her years with Girls Tyme and its many incarnations, she telephoned her old friend Daryl Simmons for assistance. "Of course, it was great to hear from her," Simmons said. "It's like talking to my daughter every time we speak, that's how I feel about her.

" 'How's little DJ?' she wanted to know right off," Simmons recalled. "That's my son, who she used to babysit. 'Well, I guess little DJ is big DJ now,' I told her, 'because he's twenty-one!' After we laughed about that, she said, 'You know I'm managing myself now.' I told her I had heard. 'It's gonna be really hard, but I think I can do it,' she said. I told her, 'You'll be fine, Bey. You've got a good man, Jay, at your side. He's smart and he can help.' After she thanked me, we got down to business.

"She explained that she was doing a documentary and needed videos and pictures of the old days," Daryl continued. "I told her, 'You know what? I've been saving this stuff just for you. I have it right here in the same old brown Silent Partner box it's been sitting in for years.' She was amazed. 'Oh my gosh,' she said, 'can you bring it to New York? I'll send you a ticket.' 'Absolutely,' I told her. 'Of course!'

"I had my engineer take all the tapes and put them on a Zip drive for her so she could access it on a computer," he continued. "And I gathered up all the old pictures I had, stuff I forgot I even had. I put it all together and hopped on a plane for New York."

Once at Beyoncé's office at Parkwood Entertainment on Broadway, Daryl sat down with her in a conference room. She looked lovely. Her light brown hair was pulled into a ponytail. She had on black slacks, a white jacket, a white blouse, and sensible heels—she was in "Beyoncé: Business-woman" mode. "Can you believe there's a rumor out there that I'm not really pregnant?" Beyoncé asked Daryl as she tried to get comfortable in her chair. "Just when I thought I'd heard every dumb rumor there could ever be said about me, here comes this one—the most stupid one yet."

"But why would anyone think such a thing?" he asked.

"Oh, Lord, I gave up trying to figure people out a long time ago," she said with a laugh.

Daryl said he was proud of her and couldn't help but note how far she'd come "since we lost that damn Elektra deal."

She smiled. "Oh my God! I remember those conversations you used to have with us girls telling us to be careful what we wish for, we just might get it." She added that now that she had fame, she *wished* she could take her nephew—Solange's boy, Julez—to the beach. "And the lawsuits," she said, rolling her eyes. She noted that "some lady" was presently threatening to sue her for stealing a dance routine. "Like I can't come up with my own dance routines?" (Beyoncé may have been referring to Italian pop star Lorella Cuccarini, although she never specified a name. It's not known if Cuccarini actually accused Beyoncé of ripping her off, but her fans certainly did. Beyoncé finally admitted to being influenced, saying, "Thank

God for YouTube or I would have never been exposed to something so inspiring.")

"Bey, I knew you were gonna be big," Daryl said, "but I didn't know you were gonna be *this* big."

"Me neither," Beyoncé responded with a smile. She rested her hand on her stomach protectively. "It feels out of control sometimes," she added. "For instance, I can't do radio shows anymore."

Daryl asked her what she meant.

"Those morning drive-time shows," she explained. "They are the *worst.*" She said that she now refused to submit to them. "Would you believe that the last time I did a radio interview, the guy asked me on the air, 'Whose farts smell worse? Yours or Jay's?'"

Daryl burst out laughing, as did Beyoncé. "That was *it* for me," she said, shaking her head in dismay. "Sometimes I think about the old days with Miss Ann and you and the girls and I think, wow...that was such a simple, lovely time in my life. What happened, Daryl? With the Elektra deal, I mean. What really happened there?"

As Daryl gently explained the problems he and Sylvia Rhone both had with Mathew, Beyoncé listened carefully, her brow furrowed. "Well, I figured it was something like that," she finally observed, lowering her eyes. "But, my dad...for every mistake he may have made there were like a hundred things he did right," she concluded, "so, I can't fault him." Then with a chuckle, she added, "Him and his doggone boot camp training!"

Clearly, she was feeling sentimental. Daryl fanned the many pictures of her as a child in Girls Tyme, the Dolls, Somethin' Fresh, Destiny, and then early Destiny's Child on the conference table in front of them. "Nicki and Nina," she exclaimed while staring at one photograph. "Oh my gosh! Look how pretty they were! And Ashley! It feels like it was just yesterday."

Daryl then began to play some of the archival footage of the girls on his laptop. As he did so, Parkwood employees kept popping into the conference room to watch, none of whom had ever seen Beyoncé at that age. Daryl recalled that he had a big smile on his face as he watched the screen. "The girls rehearsing in my basement, sweatin' hard, dancing, working on their harmonies. 'This was the beginning of everything,' Beyoncé was telling people as they came in to watch. 'Can you believe that we were, like, ten? Look at us dance!' Before we knew it, the room was full of people amazed by what they were seeing. 'We were actually pretty damn good!' Beyoncé exclaimed. 'But we should have been! All we ever did was rehearse!'"

For the next four and a half hours, Beyoncé and Daryl watched video footage, reviewed photographs, and talked about the old days: Deborah and Denise...Andretta and her boys, Armon and Chris...To-to and Tony Mo....Lonnie Jackson and Arne Frager...Sha Sha Daniels...names she hadn't heard in years, none of which she could ever forget.

As the sun began to set, the time had come for the old friends to part company. "All of this stuff? It's yours," Daryl said, motioning to the memorabilia before them. "I just want you to have it all. This is your life right here. This is what you created, Bey."

Beyoncé looked as if she couldn't believe her ears. "Oh my God, Daryl. Thank you so much," she said, choked up. "You know, it's funny," she concluded, "but when you take the time to think about it and really analyze your life, you realize that all of the dots are connected and that all of it somehow makes perfect sense."

Life Is But a Dream

Of course, like most celebrities of her caliber, Beyoncé makes almost every move with an eye on image-making and protecting her brand. It's understandable, especially if one considers how many millions are at stake in licensing and advertising her image. She even has someone called a "brand manager" at her Parkwood Entertainment management company, Melissa Vargas. "Being her brand manager, I know what levels she is willing to expose and what she's not," says Vargas. "And she's a very, very private person."

Therein lies the problem she faced with the documentary *Life Is But a Dream*: Would it be possible to talk on camera about her life in an authentic, honest way, all the while picking and choosing which elements to reveal and how they should be explored? Doesn't the fact that the production is being shared with the public at all make it just another PR endeavor, another tool for careful branding? From all accounts, Beyoncé really wasn't considering these questions when she released *Life Is But a Dream* in February 2013, but perhaps she should have been. As its executive producer, codirector, and cowriter, she had just one intention with her documentary, though: She wanted it to be revealing and candid—to a point.

The film opened with footage and platitudes about the home Beyoncé and her family shared in the Third Ward of Houston. "I remember the moss on the trees," she said. "That house is my foundation." Of course, the most interesting aspect of the story behind this house isn't the moss on the trees that surround it, it's the fact that the family had to sell it rather than lose it at foreclosure since all of their money had been spent on furthering Beyoncé's career. With the absence of this subtext, it quickly became clear that she would not be putting forth the whole truth for public consumption, just parts of it.

She spoke about her father. "My dad knew that I needed his approval," she said. "And I think my father wouldn't give it to me. He kept pushing me and kept pushing me and kept pushing me." Quickly putting a positive spin on things, she added, "Every time he pushed me, I got better and I got stronger."

To her credit, she did speak about the complexity of her relationship with Mathew in a more candid way than ever before. "I'm feeling very empty because of my relationship with my dad," she said. "I'm so fragile at this point and I feel like my soul has been tarnished. Life is unpredictable but I felt like I had to move on and not work with my dad. And I don't care if I don't sell one record. It's bigger than the record. It's bigger than my career."

She continued by explaining some of the reasons behind her decision to let Mathew go. "I think one of the biggest reasons I decided it was time for me to manage myself was because at some point you need your support system and you need your family," she said. "When you're trying to have an everyday conversation with your parents and you have to talk about scheduling, and you have to talk about your album and performing and touring, it's just too stressful and it really affects your relationship. I needed boundaries, and I think my dad needed boundaries. It's really easy to get confused with this world that's your job that you live and breathe every day all day and then you don't know when to turn it off. You need a break. I needed a break. I needed my dad."

The off-camera interviewer then asked, "And did you get your dad back?"

Becoming emotional, she answered, "No. It was hard. I had to sacrifice my relationship with my dad. It was a stressful, sad, difficult time, but I had to let go."

All of what she had to say was true, but obviously there was so much more to the story, especially concerning the audit she had conducted of Mathew and how she truly felt about it. Also, what about her feelings on his relationship with AlexSandra Wright and the baby they had together, all of which played a part in her decision-making process where he was concerned? Obviously, she wanted to give of herself, but certainly not *all* of herself. Wasn't it, then, business as usual—picking and choosing what to share with the public, the only difference being that what she now shared was slightly more, though not totally, revealing?

Most reviewers dismissed the documentary as yet another attempt by Beyoncé to control her brand. "*Beyoncé: Life Is But a Dream* is as contrived as *Madonna: Truth or Dare*," wrote Alessandra Stanley for the *New York Times*, referring to Madonna's popular 1991 documentary, "but probably for good reason it is neither daring nor entirely truthful. It's an infomercial, not just about Beyoncé's talent onstage but her authenticity behind the scenes. She is a people-pleasing diva and she wants to keep it that way. This documentary doesn't really convey what life as a celebrity is like, but it does say a lot about how this celebrity would like to be seen."

The vast majority of critics agreed with the *Times*. Writing for the *New Yorker*, Judy Rosen observed, "*Life Is But a Dream* purports to offer a behind-the-scenes look at Beyoncé's life, but the nature of modern-pop mega stardom—the nature of Beyoncé herself—ensures that nothing will be exposed; the curtain is yanked back to reveal another curtain."

Beyoncé was said to be hurt and perplexed by the reviews, and to this day doesn't know what to make of them. Whereas she views almost everything as a learning experience, she still hasn't figured out what to glean from the experience of *Life Is But a Dream*. "I was really trying to do something genuine and was accused of doing just the opposite," she said privately.

Of course, her fans will always be less critical of these sorts of endeavors, and maybe that's what matters most. Beyoncé understands and appreciates her fan base and seems to know exactly what they want from her, what will satisfy them most. If there were any missteps with *Life Is But a Dream*, they didn't matter to her devoted (and extremely protective) fan base, which has in recent years become known as "the Beyhive." Indeed, as long as she can keep the "hive" satisfied, maybe she needn't worry about her critics.

PART SEVEN

Run the World

Blue Ivy

*T*hough some considered it a career misfire, going back and remembering her formative years with Girls Tyme for *Life Is But a Dream* had special meaning for Beyoncé Knowles, especially considering that she was now pregnant with her first child. Telling Jay they were expecting was a moment she has said she will never forget, and then sharing the news with her mother made the day all the more complete. Announcing it then to the world on the MTV Video Music Awards in 2011, after a stunning Motown-influenced performance of her old-school hit "Love on Top"—which had won the Grammy for Best Traditional R&B Performance—was something else she'd never forget. After she finished the song, she tossed the mike to the floor; it landed with a thud. Then she fluffed up her long blonde locks, unbuttoned her purple sequin Dolce & Gabbana tuxedo jacket to reveal just her white silk blouse, put her hands on the hips of her elastic-waisted pants, and stuck out her tummy, rubbing it with a glowing smile on her face. It was her way of confirming her pregnancy to the entire world. The place went wild. As people stood up and cheered all around Jay in the audience, Kanye West began jumping all over him in excitement. Twitter records indicate that 8,868 tweets went out per *second* from people sharing the news with one another.

On the whole, Beyoncé's actual pregnancy was not difficult for her. However, dealing with tabloid speculation about it was truly exhausting, especially coming to terms with the rumor she'd earlier mentioned to Daryl Simmons—that she wasn't really expecting at all.

This story took wing when Beyoncé appeared on the television program *Sunday Night* in Australia, interviewed by Molly Meldrum. As she sat down, it appeared that her stomach had collapsed under her. It wasn't much of a moment but it definitely gave rumormongers a lot to work with. The speculation was that she was wearing some sort of fake pregnancy apparatus because she and Jay had hired a surrogate to carry a child for them. Why? Supposedly so that the image-conscious Beyoncé wouldn't ruin her figure. No doubt, if AlexSandra Wright's assertion that Mathew had suggested she allow their child to be raised by Beyoncé had been made public, that revelation would have raised more than a few eyebrows during this time of rampant conjecture.

The story soon became major news; all of the networks in the United States carried it on their news broadcasts, even CNN. If the public wants to believe a rumor badly enough—and apparently many people wanted to believe this one—it will find many reasons, even if they are not logical, to confirm it. (There are still people who maintain that Beyoncé is a member of the Illuminati, for instance, with pretty much no evidence to support the claim. Incidentally, she is not.)

It was said that Beyoncé hadn't sat down on the Australia program the way a truly pregnant woman would "normally" do so. Then, as people closely examined photographs of her to determine how big (or small) her "baby bump" was, she was accused of giving conflicting reports as to when she was due—more supposed proof of a grand deception. And why, the conspiracists demanded to know, weren't there more clear pictures of her pregnant stomach?

If one examines the scandalous Aussie footage in question, it's clear that Beyoncé's red dress is merely folding under as she sits down. "It was a fabric that folded—does fabric not fold? Oh my gosh, so stupid," she observed.

What people didn't know, because she and Jay had kept it to themselves until she revealed it on her documentary, was that a couple years earlier Beyoncé had suffered a miscarriage. Therefore it felt particularly hurtful to her to know that there were people who believed she was faking a pregnancy. "To think that I would be that vain," she said. "I respect mothers and women so much, and to be able to experience bringing a child into this world—if you're lucky and fortunate enough to experience that—I would never ever take that for granted. I mean, it's the most powerful thing you can do in your life. And especially after losing a child, the pain and trauma from that just makes it mean so much more to get an opportunity to bring life into the world. It's something that you have to respect. There just seems like people should have boundaries. There's certain things that you don't play around with. And a child, you don't play around with that."

When it came to childbirth, Beyoncé couldn't help but be a little frightened. She'd always envied women who wanted multiple children, because she couldn't imagine having even one. She knew it would be painful, and she has a very low threshold for pain. Simple dental work can be a major ordeal for her. Plus, she'd been in the delivery room when Solange had her baby, and she admitted to being slightly "traumatized" by the experience. "I just had to remember that my body was made to do this," she recalled, "and that women have been doing it just fine for centuries, so why should I be any different?"

On January 7, 2012, with Jay at her side, Beyoncé gave birth to a baby girl, Blue Ivy Carter, at Lenox Hill Hospital in New York. For the birth, the Carters booked an entire wing of the hospital. Of course, when the press got wind of those accommodations it made her and Jay sound ridiculous and self-indulgent. In fact, Beyoncé can't just check into a hospital and have a baby like other women. A circus of media follows her wherever she goes. Plus, there's so much interest in her life, there's no way for her to have a private experience in a public place. Such special accommodations for celebrities are not at all unusual anyway. Cedars-Sinai Medical Center in Los Angeles, for instance, caters to many celebrity mothers and offers a "Deluxe Maternity Suite" for about $4,000 a night. Said a representative of Lenox Hill, "Our executive suites are available for any patient, including the food service and amenities provided to the Carter family." He added that the Carters were "billed the standard rate for those accommodations."

Still, it could be said that Beyoncé and Jay went overboard to guarantee their privacy. Lenox Hill Hospital allowed them to modify the private suite, and that *is* unusual. Did the Carters' teams really need to install a bulletproof door? That they did so speaks perhaps to the actions of a security team paid huge amounts of money to do *something*, so...why not that?

Making other patients very unhappy was that windows in the nearby neonatal ICU were blacked out so that nobody could see Beyoncé or her family when they were coming or going down the hallway to the Carters' suite, especially on the day she was to give birth. Also, the movement of new parents was severely restricted lest they accidentally run into Beyoncé or Jay Z. Many complaints were lodged about it to the press.

In Beyoncé's defense, it's a difficult situation, one not easily handled, when a woman who is a public figure would just as soon not be photographed while in labor and being pushed on a gurney from one room to another in a hospital. The fact remains that most people these days have smartphones and many would be quite open to the opportunity of taking photos of a superstar in labor and then selling them to an eager tabloid press. Given that stark reality, maybe it's easy to understand how a celebrity like Beyoncé might become somewhat overreactive about security concerns, so much so that someone on her team asked hospital workers to cover the lenses of security cameras on her floor with black tape. One consequence of all of this caution is that not many people saw Beyoncé in the throes of labor, and those who did were certainly not talking about it, which only served to fuel those pesky rumors that she was never pregnant.

Beyoncé and Jay had the name Blue Ivy picked out long before the baby was born. There have been many reports that the color is Jay's favorite. "My favorite hue is Jay Z blue," he rapped in "Go Crazy" with Young Jeezy. He also released three critically acclaimed *Blueprint* albums in 2001, 2002, and 2009. "Ivy is for the Roman numeral number IV," explained Larry Beyincé. He also cited the numeral 4 as being significant in her life.

After she had the baby—whom the Carters and most people in their circle refer to as simply "Blue"—Beyoncé was eager to lose the fifty-seven pounds she'd gained during the pregnancy. It was really just pressure of her own making; she's used to looking a certain way and couldn't wait to see that reflection in the mirror again. She also didn't want to allow herself to become comfortable with the weight she'd gained. She even booked a concert three months after the birth, as if to give herself a deadline. Then she went strict and she went hard, not only with her dieting but with her workout regimen. She did reach her goal, but looking back on it now she feels that her anxiety about it was totally unnecessary. If she has another baby, she's decided, she will take it easy afterward. "I'll give myself more time," she said, "because it was just not necessary to do it that fast."

Though Beyoncé and Jay have a team of functionaries who work for them at their homes in New York and Miami, Beyoncé made up her mind early on that she would not allow Blue Ivy to be raised by anyone but her parents. Of course, during the day, when the Carters are out and about doing business, their little girl is often home with her nannies—she has had as many as three at a time.

Where Blue Ivy is concerned, Beyoncé has vowed to take a similar approach to parenting as Mathew and Tina, no matter what field her daughter sees fit to enter. "Whatever makes her happy, I'm there," she has said, echoing her own parents' sentiments when it came to raising her. When Blue has the occasional childish temper tantrum, Beyoncé often lets her rip. She has told relatives that she wants her daughter to cry when she feels the need to do so, and to be free with her emotions.

One aspect of her life that she hopes to replicate with her daughter is the influence of strong, independent women. She will never forget all of the assertive women who helped guide her in the early days of her career, and those who influenced her to become the woman she is today. She wants the same for Blue Ivy, which is why she makes sure that Tina is an integral part of her life, and other women, too, such as her sister, Solange, her cousin Angie, and her close friend Kelly.

Going Forward

$\mathcal{A}$s Mathew Knowles held Blue Ivy closely, the infant sucked on a green pacifier and stared up at him with wondrous eyes. He ran his hands through her tangle of thick black hair. With tears in his eyes, he bounced her in his arms. While the touching scene was dutifully recorded for Beyoncé's documentary, *Life Is But a Dream*, he sang softly to her. Only he would know what was going through his head in those precious moments. It must have seemed not so long ago, though, that he had held Beyoncé Giselle in his arms in very much the same way.*

"It would be a lie if I did not say it had been difficult," he admitted of the breach with Beyoncé. "It was hard for me to let her go—it was hard for both of us to let each other go. And let's be clear on that. She didn't let me go, we both let each other go. That's a big difference."

Obviously this had been a challenging time in Mathew's life. He'd made mistakes, if not in his handling of Beyoncé's finances then certainly in his handling of his marriage to her mother. However, those who still loved him knew him well, and those who knew him well still loved him. Or, as Taura Stinson put it, "If you know Mathew as I know Mathew, you love him, flaws and all. You just do."

No doubt compounding Mathew's disappointment at this time was that he'd recently also lost Kelly Rowland and Michelle Williams as clients— Kelly first, back in January 2009, and then Michelle a year later in January 2010. Both women decided that they wanted different management, though they never publicly disparaged Mathew. Solange also decided to end her working relationship with her father at about this time.

Kelly, whose career continued unabated, happily married her manager, Tim Weatherspoon, in May 2014, and gave birth to a son in November,

---

* In 2014, Mathew won a six-figure settlement from a London tabloid after it erroneously reported that Beyoncé had refused to allow him to meet his granddaughter Blue Ivy.

Titan Jewell. Sadly, her mother, Doris Rowland Garrison, passed away that year after an extended illness. In the spring of 2015, Kelly signed a deal with the BET network to appear on a competition series called "Chasing Destiny," dedicated to finding the next major female singing group. Michelle has also continued as a singer, actress, and even reality star with the 2014–15 program *Fix My Choir*. She remains single and has become an advocate for the understanding of depression in the black community. She, herself, has battled the disease since about the age of fifteen.

In 2014, Kelly and Beyoncé joined Michelle for a dynamic, reggae-inspired re-working of the Nigerian gospel song, "When Jesus Says Yes," now titled "Say Yes," on Michelle's album *Journey to Freedom*. It brought a smile to hear the ladies back together again, and to see them performing in the song's video.

With the release of any song featuring the Destiny's Child women comes the always persistent rumor that the group might one day reunite. When they got back together for a brief segment during Beyoncé's performance on the Super Bowl halftime show in February 2013 in New Orleans, it made national news. All three, clad in sexy leather with knee-high boots, not only looked stunning, but were still in fine voice. After just a few minutes, Kelly and Michelle were excused from the stage, though, leaving it once again to the star of the show. Of course, fans of the two girls wanted a lot more. They were treated to a bit more when, two years later in April of 2015, the three women appeared together at the 30th Annual Stellar Gospel Music Awards in Las Vegas, performing a medley of the worship song, "Alpha & Omega" with "Say Yes."

Is another more protracted reunion possible? Mathew has said it's likely. It could be wishful thinking on his part, though. In fact, he still owns the Destiny's Child brand. If he wanted to, he could hire any three girls and call them Destiny's Child and, though the public might not be accepting of it, he would be perfectly within his legal rights. So if there's to be any sort of reunion, Beyoncé, Kelly, and Michelle would have to work with Mathew once again. Can that occur after everything that has happened? (It should be noted that the ladies were not introduced as Destiny's Child during either of the televised reunions but, rather, by their individual names.) While it seems like a long shot, if there's enough money in it, who knows? According to Billboard, the ladies' last tour together, "Destiny Fulfilled" in 2005, generated over $70 million in the United States, alone. In fact, Beyoncé, Kelly, and Michelle have discussed the idea of touring together once again but have stopped just short of figuring out how Mathew would work into their equation—or, maybe more aptly put, how *they* might work into *his*.

Only Mathew can speak to whatever feelings he may have over the way things worked out with Destiny's Child. What is known, though, is that after the break with Beyoncé, he did what he did many years before in a time of crisis, back when the Knowleses were suffering financial difficulties and he reinvented himself as Girls Tyme's manager. He self-invented again, this time as an educator. He teaches entertainment-related classes at Fisk University and Texas Southern University, and also gives seminars about how to make it in the competitive entertainment business at Houston Community College—the same campus where he took courses when he first started managing Girls Tyme.

After Blue Ivy came into the world, Mathew and Beyoncé seemed to make a concerted effort to speak to each other more often. Now that she too was a parent, she seemed to have a new understanding of and a deeper sense of empathy for her father. "I asked Mathew if he had seen Beyoncé [in 2014], and he said, 'Yes, of course,'" said Taura Stinson. "Maybe a year and a half ago, one of Tina's brothers passed, and of course, the whole family was at the funeral. Beyoncé, Mathew, and Tina went off on their own and spent time with the baby. I've seen pictures of Mathew holding Blue Ivy on Mathew's phone. So I know they are all trying..."

Just as she now recognized that Blue Ivy was the best thing that had ever happened to her, Beyoncé knew Mathew had long felt the same way about her. Finding their way back to one another would not be easy, though. "My understanding of it is that Jay Z was the one who talked her into mending fences with her Dad," said Lydia Locke, mother of Beyoncé's ex-boyfriend, Lyndall. She's correct, at least according to those in the couple's inner circle. Jay always felt that Beyoncé was lucky to have a father present in her life and, apparently, believes that the bond she shares with Mathew should never under any circumstances be broken. "Jay has made a lot of mistakes in his own life," said one of his friends. "So, he understands Mathew. He pushed hard to make sure that any divide between Beyoncé and Mathew never became too great."

To say that today Beyoncé and Mathew are extremely close would probably be overstating things. It's not going to happen overnight. However, they continue to try.

Mathew Today

On June 30, 2013, Mathew Knowles—now sixty-one—remarried after an eighteen-month engagement. His new bride was Gena Charmaine Avery, forty-eight. The ceremony took place in Houston. It was widely reported in the press that both Beyoncé and Solange snubbed the ceremony. Actually, Beyoncé was scheduled to appear at the Staples Center in Los Angeles on June 28, then in Las Vegas on June 29, and back again in Los Angeles on July 1. Meanwhile, Solange was in England on June 30, performing at Glastonbury Festival. Since Beyoncé had the day off—June 30—perhaps she could have made it to Mathew's wedding, but it would have been cutting it close. Certainly, though, considering the length of Mathew and Gena's engagement, one would imagine that schedules could have been better coordinated if attending the wedding was a priority. While Mathew made a statement explaining their absence, neither daughter made any announcement congratulating him on his new marriage.

Likely it wasn't easy for Beyoncé and Solange to see their father remarry, though without their testimony, one can't be sure. Most certainly it wasn't easy for Tina, who had been his wife for thirty-three years. "This is my family," she said. "My ex-husband is my family. You know, I don't want to get back into that at all [into a relationship with him], that's not what I want, but it still hurts. It's still a blow to your ego."

As Mathew navigated his new life with Gena, his former one with Alex still had its repercussions. He had agreed to a very substantial monthly payment to Alex of about $12,000 in child support for his only son, Nixon. Unfortunately, that agreement later became untenable for him, due to, he explained during a court hearing in January 2014, his having lost "my number one client."

More than anything, Mathew's testimony on the stand that day spoke to the diabolical nature of the music industry and how quickly and dramatically a participant in it can experience a reversal of fortunes. Mathew said that when he made the original child support deal, he was earning $3 million a year as Beyoncé's manager. He testified that his annual income derived solely from being a teacher had plummeted to just $100,000. He also added that after he lost Beyoncé as a client, his Music World Entertainment was foreclosed upon by the IRS.

For a man who had once dreamed of power, success, and doing something great with his life, Mathew's crisis seemed like a cruel turn of events. His predicament, at least as outlined by him in these proceedings, also seemed to suggest his innocence in the allegations leveled at him by Live Nation. If he had stolen millions from Beyoncé and was being truthful now, one had to wonder what happened to all the money.

He did concede that he'd recently received more than $400,000 as a result of an audit into Destiny's Child's income at Columbia/Sony, and another $250,000 from the proceeds of selling to Beyoncé his part of a condominium the two jointly owned. In the end, the judge ruled that Mathew's debt far exceeded any income, thereby justifying a major adjustment to his monthly child support payment, to $2,485 per month.

Since Nixon's birth, Alex has founded Motivating Other Mothers, a website dedicated to assisting mothers in handling a wide range of life-changing challenges, such as divorce and job loss. She has also returned to her previous career in branding. Today, she is raising Nixon with her present partner, Harvey Walden, with whom she has been with since the child was a year old.

Mathew has still not met Nixon. Neither has Beyoncé nor any other member of the Knowles family.

In July 2014, a year after his marriage to Gena, Mathew's past would catch up to him again when it was revealed that yet another woman—thirty-year-old TaQoya Branscomb—was demanding a DNA test to prove he was the father of a daughter named Koi who was born to her in 2010. The test came back with a 99.9 percent probability that Mathew was Koi's father.

Given that according to Alex and TaQoya, Beyoncé has not met their children or reached out to them, it would seem that her position on Koi is the same as it is with Nixon. These children are not her responsibility. Both have to do with Mathew's personal life choices, not her own.

Today, Mathew seems happy and content with Gena. "Recent years have not been easy for him," says someone who knows him well. "He's a man who has worked hard all of his life. It seems grossly unfair that he can't now just relax in his senior years. But, that said, he does somehow seem more at peace." One can't help but wonder if Mathew Knowles, always a restless soul, can ever be truly settled, or if that's even the kind of life he wants for himself. "All I can say is that there will always be another proposition for Mat," concluded his friend. "In other words, the man's not done yet. Knowing him, I can guarantee it."

A New Life for Tina

$\mathcal{T}$ina Knowles admitted that she still "hadn't had closure" where Mathew was concerned in the spring of 2013 when she learned that he was to remarry. It speaks to the depth of her love for him and his place in her family that despite so many revelations of late, she still felt bonded to him. Coincidentally, at the same time, Tina was the wedding planner for a very good friend of hers. This uneasy confluence of marital events was hard on her. She was unhappy, feeling insecure and desperately worried about her own future. True to her nature, though, it didn't take long for her to rebound.

"I let myself feel sorry for myself for a minute, but then my fight came back," she recalled in October 2014. "I thought, 'I'm so blessed. I have so many opportunities.' So I made a plan. I said, 'What do you want, Tina?' Well, I want some time off. So I took the time off. I started reading art books; I love art. I started traveling. I would travel with my daughter, but not to work. I had forgotten how to live. I realize now that it was low self-esteem, that it was being fifty-eight and having to start all over again. The other part was just that I had lost myself. I told my kids, 'You know what? You can call me and I'll come if it's something really important, but otherwise I'm taking care of Tina. This is my selfish moment.' Before I knew it, I started liking me again."

After Mathew's wedding, it was Jay Z's suggestion to her that Tina begin dating younger men. He just wanted her to have more fun in her life. However, Tina began seeing the handsome—and seven years her senior – actor Richard Lawson, who was also an acting teacher and motivational speaker. (He's probably best known for his role in 1982's *Poltergeist*.) Two years later, on April 12, 2015, the couple married on a 140-foot yacht in Newport Beach, California. Of course, Beyoncé and Jay attended the ceremony, as did Solange and her husband, Alan Ferguson. Tina's grandchildren, Blue Ivy and Julez, acted as flower girl and ring bearer. Kelly Rowland and Michelle Williams were also present. "It couldn't have been more perfect," Tina—who wore a diaphanous, white gown designed by Romona Keveza— said of her wedding day. She now identifies as "Tina Knowles Lawson." She continued, "To walk down the aisle and see all my friends and family and to see my handsome man standing there, and to know that at 61 you can still find love and have a magical day like that ... it was really beautiful.

"It's just been a great journey," Tina concluded of her life. "Most of the times in my life when things have been the toughest and the worst and I thought I would die and not get through them, they turned out to be the *best* times. My daughter wrote a song called 'Survivor,' and it's my favorite song because it says, when times get bad, I'm gonna work harder, and I'm gonna keep pushing and I'm gonna be positive and make it happen because I'm a survivor. That's been the story of my life."

Beyoncé: *The Secret Album*

*F*or a woman who spends most of her life under heavy public scrutiny, Beyoncé's solitary moments in the recording studio are much needed and appreciated. It's where she finds her greatest sense of serenity. Far away from the pressing crowds of her life, the small, confined space of a recording booth in front of a single microphone is where she's truly free to be herself, to concentrate fully on what she most loves to do, be exasperated by its many maddening flaws, and finally exhilarated by its carefully crafted perfection. All of it is a process privately conducted at a remove from prying and critical eyes. As an artist, she has always reveled in the creation of her music and has even admitted that she often finds the process more liberating and satisfying than the actual delivery of the product to the world for its final judgment. Obviously such solitary moments in the studio are also primarily responsible for her phenomenal success. After all, where would Beyoncé Knowles Carter be without her songs?

Beyoncé spends untold hours in the studio recording music she'd been working on for days, months, and even years, tinkering with the lyrics, the melody, the orchestration, trying to shape it in an effort to see if it's even worth sharing with her public. Her friend and coproducer The-Dream said it best when he summarized, "There's multiple albums being made. Most of the time, we're just being creative, period. We're talking about Bey, somebody who sings all day long and somebody who writes all day long. There's probably a hundred records just sitting around." Indeed, it's safe to say that many thousands of dollars are spent every year producing songs that will never find their way into the marketplace, tunes that didn't rise to the high standards Beyoncé has set for herself over the years. For the Carters, going into the studio together is one of their favorite pastimes. Over the years, Jay has produced many dozens of songs for Beyoncé that the public has never heard. Not only is their time together in the studio a creative outlet for them, but it's also a way for them to wind down and relax.*

For her next album, Beyoncé realized that she couldn't simply release another collection of well-produced but typical songs into the marketplace and then hope for the best. She would have to do something that would raise eyebrows, cause a sensation, and, maybe if she was lucky, even break a few barriers. Now more than ever, she needed to make a real statement about herself and her artistry. The stakes were high, and she knew it. "I have a lot to prove with this one, not to just everyone else but to myself," she said privately at this time. "I'm not blind to it. I know it, and I know what I have to do."

Since firing Mathew, for the last couple of years Beyoncé had been pondering the idea of an album that would be experimental in its creation and marketing. The standard way it unfolds in the music business—the way it happened for virtually all of her Destiny's Child and solo albums—was that the artist hands the music over to the label, which then decides when to schedule its release, leaking a song here or there to whet the public's appetite weeks, sometimes months, in advance. Then, when the album is finally issued, the label sends the artist out on a promotional tour to promote it. Finally, one video is produced for each single release over a period of months, and then that video is doled out to the public with its corresponding song. That's how it has been done for at least a generation. However, Beyoncé wondered what it would be like if that *wasn't* how it was done. She dreamed of using present-day Internet technology to simply put the music in the hands and ears of her fans when *she* was ready for them to hear it . . . and the way she wanted them to hear it.

When Beyoncé shared her idea with associates, they advised her that it couldn't be done. "Perhaps if you were a new, independent artist just

---

* In April 2015, it was reported by the popular personality DJ Skee that the Carters would release their duet album exclusively on TIDAL, the music subscription service Jay Z had recently bought for $56 million. Some media observers speculated that the release might spike interest in the music platform, which had been met with ambivalence from much of the public. Also in April, and without much acclamation, Beyoncé released an exclusive video on the service, her playing the piano and singing a new song, "Die With You."

starting out," reasoned one well-meaning member of her coterie. "But you're a machine; you can't even go to the bathroom without your label participating and without the press hearing about it." Beyoncé knew that wasn't completely true, though. After all, she had begun work on *B'Day* without Mathew knowing she was in the studio until it was too late for him to weigh in about it. To Beyoncé, *can't* pretty much always means *can*.

Her innovative idea was fascinating on another level because it showed an "old school" mentality that was probably, ironically enough considering the circumstances of her recent life, influenced by Mathew. She would note that back in the 1980s (and certainly before), an artist was judged by its audience based on an *entire* album, not just a few songs. But today, thanks to the Internet age of downloading music, fans don't have the opportunity to listen to a comprehensive work in total. As the listener points and clicks his way through the music, he's missing out on the chance to have a song actually grow on him, or to discover something about it he may have missed in the first few listenings.

"I feel like, right now, people experience music differently," she said. "I miss that immersive experience," she said. "Now people only listen to a few seconds of songs on the iPods and they don't really invest in a whole album. It's all about the single and the hype. So much gets between the music and the art and the fans. I felt like, I don't want anybody to give the message when my record is coming out. I just want this to come out when it's ready and from me to my fans. I told my team I want to shoot a video for every song and put them out at the same time. Everyone thought I was crazy."

Maybe she was "crazy," but she was also the boss, and so during the summer of 2012, Beyoncé's eccentric plan went into full-blown execution mode. The first thing that happened was that she and Jay rented a large home in the Hamptons on Long Island. She had a studio set up there, and then she invited about a dozen songwriters and musicians to come stay with her and Jay to write and record on whim. The idea was that she could kick back with her husband and their new child, and at the same time knock around musical ideas—"a working vacation." A house staff and chef were hired so that guests would be free to do whatever they liked—swim, play games, or simply relax—as long as they were also making music. In some ways, it was how she had recorded *B'Day*, with everyone working together at the same time at the Sony studio in New York, except now everyone had his own bedroom and private bath in a five-star setting.

Since everyone had careers to tend to and couldn't spend weeks on end at the Hamptons house, recording there eventually folded, and later in 2013 moved to Jungle City Studios in Manhattan. The project gained momentum when Jay introduced Beyoncé to Jordy "BOOTS" Asher, a young songwriter, singer, and multi-instrumentalist who had fronted and/or worked with several indie rock bands. Meanwhile, Beyoncé continued working with other songwriters and musicians, names she'd collaborated with before such as Ryan Tedder and Pharrell Williams, as well as names that were new to a Beyoncé production, such as Dwane "Key Wane" Weir, who would coproduce for the *Beyoncé* project the provocative "Partition," and Chauncey "Hit-Boy" Hollis, who collaborated with Beyoncé and others to create "Jealous," "XO," and "Flawless."

After the songs were recorded, videos had to be produced for *all* of them, again under the same cloak of secrecy. The dancers who appeared in the videos didn't even know exactly what they were filming, or why. All of the work was done while Beyoncé was on the road, and so as the dancers traveled by bus from one destination to the other, they talked among themselves, wondering exactly what was going on, but also knowing not to ask any questions to anyone in charge.

"It was actually thrilling," says Tenesha Ksyn Cason, a.k.a. Miss Ksyn. "We knew the song titles, but we didn't know how or when or even in what form the videos would be coming out. It was a tough schedule, too. I remember we were performing in Mexico during the South American leg of the Mrs. Carter tour. We flew from Mexico to Houston to shoot the beginning of the 'Blow' and 'Cherry' videos. We then flew back to Mexico the next day to do a show. Then back to Houston the day after that to finish shooting the two videos. Then we flew to Puerto Rico to perform the last show of the South American leg. You can imagine how organized all of this has to be to pull it off. Plus you're learning lots of new choreography at the same time.

"I remember being very nervous about using a hashtag I often use when doing makeup tutorials on social media: #Flawless," she recalled. "I thought, 'Oh no, I can't use that hashtag right now because that's the name of one of the secret songs! They're gonna think I'm hashtagging a song from the album.'"

Then, finally—like a thief in the night without prior announcement or promotion, in the early morning of December 13, 2013—it came: a fourteen-track collection of all-new songs simply titled *Beyoncé*. Issued exclusively through the iTunes Store, the initial release of *Beyoncé* featured no physical copy. Stunning in its musical eccentricity and its bold, in-your-face sexuality, the music was accompanied by seventeen short films that illuminated the album's lyrical content.

Immediately, two of the songs took off: "Blow," produced by Pharrell Williams, and "Drunk in Love," produced primarily by Timbaland. "XO," produced primarily by Ryan Tedder, also garnered immediate acceptance. Many stations, though, just played the entire album, which is unheard of these days.

With this record, Beyoncé had revolutionized the release of popular music in the twenty-first century. With no promotion or marketing platform, she'd put out an album available exclusively as a download in long form only that sold 1.3 million copies in seventeen days—seven days before physical copies were distributed to retailers. By the end of 2014, the album would go on to sell more than five million copies worldwide. Though none of the singles reached number one on the *Billboard* Hot 100—"Drunk in Love" peaked at number two on that chart—it didn't matter at all; the album sold close to a million copies in the first week alone, the fastest-selling album in the history of iTunes.

Beyoncé debuted at number one on the *Billboard* 200, making it her fifth consecutive number one album in America. She had completely changed the game; suddenly, singles and chart positions became nothing more than an archaic frivolity.

Professionally, the release of *Beyoncé* was obviously a huge achievement. As she stood in a conference room shortly after its phenomenal success and thanked the many members of her staff at Parkwood, only she, her family members, and her close friends recognized the true gravity of the accomplishment. After all, she'd done what she'd set out to do: She'd proved that she could hold her own without her father. It would never be the same without Mathew at the forefront of her career, and she had to accept as much. That didn't mean it wouldn't be worthwhile, though, and maybe even in some ways more rewarding. While the past was in the past, she now knew more than ever that the future held great promise.

Prologue to a Scandal

*T*hough it was just a few minutes of grainy black-and-white surveillance footage, it would become the subject of great fascination around the world. It would be examined frame by frame and discussed on the Internet and on major news outlets—ABC, NBC, CBS, CNN—as if of great national importance. It would also make for screaming newspaper and tabloid headlines. Many people would have an opinion about it, even though no one other than the actual participants in the event would know for certain what had occurred.

In fact, the footage—which was first revealed by the gossip site TMZ—was actually quite astonishing: Solange Knowles was seen kicking and punching Jay Z with all the skill of a novice mixed martial artist while a frustrated but ultimately useless bodyguard did what he could to hold her back. Meanwhile, Beyoncé stood by placidly watching, not making much of an effort to interfere, not looking stunned or surprised, just appearing completely disengaged. If it had been a scene concerning any other major celebrities, it probably would have made news. However, because it involved Beyoncé and Jay, both of whom had gone to such pains for more than ten years to protect their privacy, it took on special significance, as if it was a sneak peak into the shocking reality of their private lives.

Of course, there are many rumors about what had occurred to cause the dispute, which happened as the trio was leaving the Met Gala, an annual fund-raiser for the Metropolitan Museum of Arts Costume Institute in Manhattan. In order to understand what happened, it helps to have a little more insight into the kind of woman Solange Piaget Knowles has become with the passing of the years. "Fact is, she's more badass than ever," is how one of Solange's friends put it in 2014.

As we have seen, Solange has always been fiercely protective of Beyoncé. Back when Lyndall Locke broke up with Beyoncé, it was Solange who wanted to have it out with him. At that time, Beyoncé asked her to please leave the poor guy alone. Years later, Solange would tweet about once plotting to murder her sister's ex-boyfriend. She didn't name him, but Beyoncé has only had one other than Jay, and that's Lyndall. "I had a great plan, too," she tweeted, along with a happy face; obviously, she was being facetious, but even Lyndall today says he's glad she didn't follow up on her "plan," whatever it was. In more recent times when it comes to Jay, it's rumored that whenever Solange has felt that he has slighted Beyoncé in some way, she has stepped in to try to set him straight. No doubt she feels that it's her duty as her sister.

Beyoncé and Jay must have discussed their boundaries when it comes to cheating back in 2006 when the rumor went around that he was having an affair with Rihanna. Since then it has been widely rumored, especially in 2014, that Jay has cheated on Beyoncé. However, despite all the speculation and innuendo—and a mountain of gossipy tabloid stories—there's simply no credible evidence to support it. One thing is certain though, at least according to people who know them best: If Solange feels that Jay or anyone else has disrespected her sister, she will not let it pass.

Solange and Jay have been in each other's lives for almost fifteen years. Their relationship is said to be complex. They certainly have no animus for each other. They're more like siblings who have their explosive emotional moments and then get over them quickly and move past them. When Solange is angry with Jay, she makes sure he—and everyone else—knows it. It has been the backstory of their relationship almost from the beginning.

The Elevator

*I*t all started on May 5, 2014, when Beyoncé, Jay, and Solange attended the Met Gala. Swarmed annually by celebrities from around the world, the soiree is considered a major public relations and news event. All three were dressed appropriately for the occasion.

Beyoncé looked stunning as ever in a dramatic sheer black Givenchy evening gown covered in sparkling black-and-gold beads, crystals, and studs. The low neckline, cut almost to her navel, showed off a lot of skin, but she was tantalizingly covered in all the right places. Her makeup showed off a dramatic lip, achieved with deep wine lipstick. It was a classic noir vintage look, especially with her hair styled in a slick side-part chignon and her eyes covered by a veil, reminiscent of Marlene Dietrich's iconic look. Solange looked glamorous in a sleeveless pink V-neck Phillip Lim dress, with yards of tufted silk fabric and a bubble hem. She wore her hair in a short, choppy pixie cut. Meanwhile, Jay was dapper in his perfectly fitted white tux jacket with matching silk shirt, black slacks, and black bow tie.

Because of the attention the incident generated, one can't be blamed for hoping that the reasons behind it were explosive enough to merit such attention. It seems they really weren't. In fact, it appears to have been just a simple disagreement between family members, one that obviously got out of hand.

In talking to people who know Beyoncé and Jay and Solange, everyone has a version of the story. Of course, the only three people who know for certain what happened are the three principal players, and the bodyguard in the elevator with them. Here, though, is the most agreed-upon, credible account of what happened in that elevator. Naturally, none of the participants has verified this account, but according to people who know them best, this is what happened.

The chain of events is said to have begun when Jay said he wanted to attend an after-party hosted by Rihanna. It would overstate things to say that Beyoncé is jealous of Rihanna, but because of what happened almost seven years earlier relating to her, she may justifiably remain a little sensitive where she is concerned. Perhaps it was a business decision on Jay's part to want to attend the Rihanna party, since she'd just signed a new deal to record with his Roc Nation Records. Whatever his reasoning, he and Beyoncé had words about it—a "whispered argument" according to one source close to the situation—and that was the end of it. Jay was *not* going to be attending that party. Had it not been witnessed by Solange, it probably would have been over and done with. However, because Solange knew that Rihanna was a sore spot for her sister, she pulled Jay aside and had angry words with him. In response, Jay apparently told her to mind her own business, and then walked away from her. "Everyone knows little sister can be volatile," said Jaz-O. "You want to talk about a powerful woman not allowing herself to be shut down by a man? Well, that's Solange."

As soon as the three of them were alone in an elevator, along with Jay's bodyguard, we all saw what happened: Solange let Jay have it with a barrage of wild punches and kicks, all as the bodyguard tried to get between them. Beyoncé, for the most part, stood by passively, registering nothing on her face—she was just blank. At one point she bent down just to save the long train of her gown from the fray. It was as if she couldn't connect to the gravity of what was going on, or maybe a better way to put it is that, at long last, she had finally come face-to-face with the real "Sasha Fierce"—her own sister—and didn't quite know how to deal with it.

What is arguably more fascinating than what happened to cause the fracas in the elevator was watching the two Knowles women play out their roles, their true and authentic identities revealed to the world. In one corner, there was Beyoncé, a person who seems to have long had trouble grappling with complex emotions and now seemed unable to connect to the reality of her husband being attacked by her sister. In the other, we had Solange, who from all accounts has lived her life out loud without pretense, now accessing her rage as only she could, and not caring how anyone in her midst felt about it. She likely wouldn't have done so if she'd known cameras were filming, but she's capable of it—and we now know that for certain. After a few minutes, just when it seemed that Solange had finally calmed down, she went after Jay again, throwing in a few more kicks and punches for good measure before the elevator reached their floor. Perhaps luckily for the principal players, there was no audio.

"Solange's whole thing was, Look, I'm gonna check your ass real quick in this here elevator," observed Choke No Joke. "I'm not putting up with you and neither is my sister. Then, I'm gonna get off this elevator and play like nothin' ever happened. So, if you think about it, Solange can be a little political too, because she wasn't about to put him on blast in front of the masses, only behind closed doors."

Once the elevator doors opened, out stepped Beyoncé, Jay, and Solange, looking as if nothing the least bit unusual had occurred—Beyoncé with a faint and mysterious smile, Solange looking tense and maybe even a little out of breath, both sashaying their way toward their vehicle as if on a runway while flashbulbs popped all around them. The only telltale sign of anything untoward having occurred was poor Jay rubbing the side of his face, as if he'd caught a nasty right hook.

Matriarch in Charge

I don't know how we do this, but we do it as a family."

According to numerous well-placed sources, those were Tina Knowles's words when faced with the challenge of how to address what happened in

New York between her daughter and her son-in-law. The overriding principle upon which she had based her life since the birth of her children had always been that family came first and mattered most. Now that Mathew was no longer her husband, she and her daughters had reorganized with Jay Z and Blue Ivy at the core of their nuclear family. It's not that Mathew was no longer a part of them. He would always be Tina's first love and the father of her children. Life being complex, though, it would be easier, at least for now, for him to live his life with his own new family, his wife and her relatives. Meanwhile, Tina; Beyoncé; Jay; Blue Ivy; Jay's mother, Gloria; Solange and her son, Julez; and eventually her second husband, Alan Ferguson, and all of their extended relatives, such as Angie Beyincé, would continue on as a family.

Predictably, Beyoncé, Jay, and Solange were said to be embarrassed by the attention generated by the elevator incident. The best way to describe Beyoncé's reaction would be to say that she was mortified. When someone in her organization told her that the entire escapade was on tape, she was said to be stunned. It never occurred to her that the fight was being recorded. For a woman who has been building an image for herself since about the age of sixteen "Elevator Gate" was definitely not something for which Beyoncé was prepared, even all of these years later.

Certainly one aspect of the incident that worked in Jay's favor is that he didn't return Solange's fire. Imagine if he had struck her! "He showed real class by the way he handled himself," Mathew Knowles observed, saying, "He handled himself with respect."

Tina didn't even need the details of whatever happened to cause the fight. As Beyoncé, Jay, and Solange tried to explain them to her, she didn't want to know. The specifics didn't matter. Families have their troubles, and she had always known that hers was not exempt. It's just that their trouble had, more often than not, played out behind closed doors. What had never changed was Tina's belief that when her family is in crisis, they put their differences aside and come together. In the end, it wouldn't be up to Beyoncé's or Jay's publicists to fashion and then finalize a statement to address the fracas; that duty would fall on the family's matriarch. When her daughter and son-in-law had her review what their representative sought to put forth, Tina made subtle but important changes to it. She wanted it to be honest but, of course, without explicit detail. The important thing, as far as she was concerned, wasn't what had happened, it was how they dealt with it. "I will do what I have always done," she said when asked how she would handle the onslaught of publicity. "I will take care of my family." In doing so, she helped to shape and then gave her final approval of the following statement:

"As a result of the public release of the elevator security footage from Monday, May 5th, there has been a great deal of speculation about what triggered the unfortunate incident. But the most important thing is that our family has worked through it. Jay and Solange each assume their share of responsibility for what has occurred. They both acknowledge their role in this private matter that has played out in the public. They both have apologized to each other and we have moved forward as a united family. The reports of Solange being intoxicated or displaying erratic behavior throughout that evening are simply false. At the end of the day, families have problems and we're no different. We love each other and above all we are family. We've put this behind us and hope everyone else will do the same."*

A few months later, Beyoncé would include a reference to the elevator event in the remix of her song "Flawless" with Nicki Minaj, during which she rapped, "Of course, sometimes shit goes down when there's a billion dollars on an elevator." (Actually, as it happened, there was slightly more than "a billion dollars" on that elevator. According to multiple sources, Jay was worth $560 million at the time, Beyoncé $450 million, and Solange $5 million.)

Tina's statement, honest and direct, stood in stark contrast to what Mathew would say about the fracas. Mathew said he believed the controversy had probably been staged. Implementing old-school PR tactics, he called it a "Jedi Mind Trick," and suggested it had been a hoax concocted by the players not only to sell tickets for Beyoncé and Jay's upcoming tour, but to increase sales of Solange's recordings at a time when she was also starting her own record label, Saint Records. "Don't think it's just a coincidence that they were getting ready to go on tour and this happened," he said. "I happen to know that ticket sales increased after that episode, as did sales for Solange's album, which went up 200 percent. Oldest trick in the book."

---

* After the elevator incident, rumors spread that Solange may have been under the influence. She and her family insist that this was not the case. In fact, Solange has been diagnosed as having ADHD—attention-deficit/hyperactivity disorder. "People think I'm high even when I'm sober," she has explained. "I was diagnosed with ADHD twice. I didn't believe the first doctor who told me and I had a whole theory that ADHD was just something they invented to make you pay for medicine, but then the second doctor told me I had it."

Mathew handled the imbroglio like the great showman. Tina handled it like the great mother—two different sides of a coin, both playing out their true natures consistent with their personalities.

Two days later, Tina called a family summit in New Orleans. She and her daughters and granddaughter and Jay, along with Solange's fiancé, Alan Ferguson, and her son, Julez, shared a long meal at Café Amelie in New Orleans's French Quarter. They spent hours catching up and dining on Creole fare. When they exited the courtyard, they seemed united and happy as they posed for photographs. Of course, some thought there was a lot of media manipulation at play when these pictures surfaced in the press. That's to be expected. As far as Tina was concerned, if their critics thought the photos were contrived, so be it. She knew the truth. Even though they still had their problems, she knew they were united in their ongoing battle to find themselves... as a family.

"Alone Together in a Crowd"

*B*eyoncé bent down and adjusted three-year-old Blue Ivy Carter's collar on her little pink wool coat. The tot was also wearing a white ballerina's tutu, matching colored leggings, and red UGGs. It was a midwinter day in Los Angeles in early 2015. Beyoncé, Jay Z, and their little girl were standing in the basement level of a high-rise office building waiting for a car to meet them and whisk them away. They'd just finished a business meeting on a top floor and were now trying to avoid the crowd of people that had congregated in front of the building. Thus the wait in the basement. It was not only damp, it was dark. Faulty fluorescent lightbulbs flashed off and on while making weird buzzing noises. Beyoncé turned to her husband. "Come on, Jay," she said impatiently, "can we *please* get out of here?"

On their way down to the lower level, the Carters, along with two employees from the firm with whom they had met, made a quick pit stop in the main lobby. While there, Beyoncé took a peek around a corner at the growing throng. "It's just fans," she exclaimed to Jay. "No paparazzi." He seemed surprised; his dark eyes widened. "Great! Maybe we ain't famous no more," he quipped.

For some reason, Los Angeles was always easier for the Carters to navigate. Whereas most celebrities of their status are hotly pursued by photographers in the Hollywood area, not so Beyoncé and Jay. Perhaps it's because they're not expected to be found here. New York is considered their home base, at least as far as most of the stalking paparazzi are concerned. Today they didn't even have bodyguards with them, just the two associates from the office upstairs. Surprisingly, considering the intensity of their fame, they often moved about the West Coast metropolis without formal protection.

"Jay, I'm not waiting down here much longer," Beyoncé said. At that, he pulled his cell phone from his jacket and made a call. "Blue was fidgety, and so was her mother," said one witness to the scene. "'Why are we waiting down here hiding from our fans?' she asked me while Jay Z was on the phone. 'After all these years, Jay and I and Blue are used to being alone together in a crowd,' she told me. 'So it's really no big deal to me.'" Indeed, in recent years Beyoncé had less patience for the art of what Jay liked to call "the great escape"—stealthily moving in and out of buildings without being detected. The more famous they've become, the less interested she seems to be in hiding.

During the previous year, 2014, Beyoncé had definitely been at the top of her game. She'd doubled her earnings, generating $115 million, up from the previous year's $53 million. The increase was in large part thanks to two major tours, her Mrs. Carter and the couple's joint On the Run. Also generating money were her ongoing endorsement deals, not to mention her successful perfume line—"Heat," "Rise," "Pulse" (and variations of each scent that have generated more than $400 million in the last three years). Of course, the successful launch of her surprise album and video package substantially added to her wealth. Thanks in large part to that new music, she placed at number one on *Forbes*'s prestigious "Top Earning Women in Music 2014" list. In the spring of 2015, she signed new artists to her Parkwood Entertainment, young girls she plans to record and manage in much the same way she was once mentored in her own youth.

Earlier, during their meeting upstairs, the Carters had chatted easily with secretaries and other staffers. "Even though we were specifically told by our bosses not to speak to them—someone even told me, 'Please avoid making eye contact with Beyoncé and Jay Z in the hallways'—they were accessible to everyone," recalled one witness. With her hair a mass of blondish waves, parted in the middle and cascading to her shoulders, Beyoncé was wearing worn cutoff jeans and a tailored bright orange jacket over a simple white blouse. Beige, strappy stilettos completed the chic-casual look.

Someone produced a photograph and asked Beyoncé to sign it. It was a picture of her at about the age of eight, surrounded by towering gold and silver trophies, similar to one featured in her "Pretty Hurts" video. This one, though, had Mathew posing proudly at her side. A look of nostalgia crossed Beyoncé's face as she stared hard at the picture. "Do you remember that day?" she was asked. She nodded her head. A faint smile touched her lips.

Now, a half hour later, the Carters were still in the office building's basement, waiting for their car. "After Jay Z made a call, he learned that there'd been some confusion and that the Carters' driver was parked in front of the office building," recalled the witness. "Because of the restrictions of one-way street traffic, it would take him at least twenty minutes to circle the block and make his way down to the building's bottom level. Beyoncé wasn't having it. 'No way,' she said. 'We're going back up and out through the lobby.' Jay seemed taken aback. 'You sure?' he asked. She nodded. She said that Blue was cranky and wanted to leave. Besides, she added, 'They're *fans*, Jay! Why are we hiding down here from *fans*?' Jay said, 'I ain't goin' out there, Bey. I forgot my sunglasses!' Beyoncé looked at me and chuckled. 'He thinks when he puts his sunglasses on, people don't know who he is,' she said, rolling her eyes."

Today it's difficult to believe that a time ever existed when Beyoncé went out of her way to not be seen or photographed with Jay, or did everything she could to make sure Blue Ivy's face was not viewed by the public. These days she is known to post copious photos of family outings and vacations on social media. Rarely does a day go by when she doesn't post some picture of either a major event in her family's life or a simple moment of familial contentment. Of course, it could be said that the taking and posting of intimate family photos is just another marketing strategy—another version of herself put forth for public consumption, this time cast as a happy wife and mother. (Giving credence to this theory is the fact that she has often been accused of airbrushing the photos to glossy perfection.)

Such constant memorializing of a life calls to mind an interesting story: In 2013, while Beyoncé was performing "Irreplaceable" in Atlanta, she walked out onto a ramp into the audience and had audience members sing the chorus with her. When she got to one fan, he was busily recording her with his smartphone. "See, you can't even sing because you're too busy taping," she said, chastising him. "I'm right in your face, baby. You gotta seize this moment! Put that damn camera down!" Some cynics might be inclined to offer her the same advice, especially in April of 2015 when she posted copious pictures of her and Jay's vacation in Hawaii, commemorating their seventh wedding anniversary.

Maybe a more charitable way to look at it is to suggest that somewhere along the line, Beyoncé reconciled herself to her stardom and decided to relax into it. Whether altered or not, the photographs she posts do seem to suggest that she is at peace, as if she has finally merged the icon with the woman. Of course, it should be noted that, being a celebrity, she can't help but take advantage of the public relations angle to social media. If there is a rumor about discord in her family, she immediately posts photographs that could be seen to contradict the story. This doesn't necessarily mean the rumor is false as much as it suggests adept and continued protection of her image and that of her family. It's a practice that resulted in her being named as one of *Time*'s "30 Most Influential People on the Internet" in 2015.

With everyone in agreement, including Jay, they took an elevator back up to the lobby. As the two company employees flanked the Carters, they walked out of the building and met the scene head-on: a bevy of admirers shouting at them, some actually shrieking with delight, others taking pictures with smartphones, many thrusting forth publicity photos and asking for autographs. While Jay looked a little grim, Blue took it all in with wide, staring eyes. She was in her daddy's arms even though she was definitely getting too big to carry. Jay held on to her tightly, pressing her head into his shoulder while shielding her little face from the bright sun. Beyoncé, a veteran of such bedlam, was completely at ease. This was nothing for her compared to the aggressive crowds of fans and paparazzi through which she and Jay are used to navigating on an almost daily basis. A small group or major mob, it's all the same to her. She feels a unique camaraderie with her public, one that springs from the many experiences she has shared with them over the years. Whether rendered helpless by indecision, immobilized by uncertainty, or ready and eager to perform and light up a stage, she has always known she could count on her fans to be there for her through it all.

According to one person in the crowd, when someone thrust a vinyl copy of the first Destiny's Child album at Beyoncé with a pen for a signature, she stopped for a moment and quickly autographed it. "Do you ever see LaTavia and LeToya?" the breathless fan asked. "*Nope*," she stated. "Never." Her response was so abrupt, it took some by surprise. Then, after a beat, she added, "I mean, look, I ain't gonna lie." Her remark caused everyone within earshot to laugh.

Finally, after less than a minute, the Carters boarded their waiting black Escalade. "Thanks so much," Beyoncé shouted out just as the car door slammed behind her. Soon after the automobile lurched forward, one of its windows rolled down. As the vehicle merged into busy downtown Los Angeles, two delicate hands emerged from it. Using both index fingers and thumbs to form what looked like a heart, Beyoncé flashed the signal of appreciation back to the crowd of fans. She and her husband and daughter then disappeared into the chaos of the big city, their destination unknown but one that was sure to find them, once again, "alone together in a crowd."

ACKNOWLEDGMENTS

As an indicator of just how far Beyoncé Knowles has come in her career in little more than fifteen years, consider this: In 1999, I interviewed the original members of Destiny's Child—Beyoncé, Kelly Rowland, LaTavia Roberson, and LeToya Luckett—during a soundcheck break for the Lady of Soul Awards in Los Angeles. At the time, I was freelancing for a number of black entertainment publications. Considering that the girls had enjoyed a couple of hits by this time and that I had been riding the crest of a decent writing career, I thought I would have little trouble selling the article I wrote based on the interview. However, much to my surprise there were no takers; I couldn't sell the story! There was no interest.

About two years later, the American edition of my European bestselling biography of Madonna was published. While in New York on my press tour for the book, I appeared on a Fox News television program. "Who do you think is the heir apparent to Madonna?" I was asked. It didn't take long for me to come up with an answer. "Beyoncé Knowles," I said. The response? "Who?" asked the commentator. "I've never heard of her. And how do you say that name again?" I shared a smile with my publicist, Jonathan Hahn, who was standing in the wings. He knew how I (and a growing number of fans) felt about Beyoncé: She was a success just waiting to happen.

I went on with my writing career, penning biographies about a wide range of subjects, from Elizabeth Taylor to Marilyn Monroe to the Kennedys to the Hiltons. Of course, Beyoncé Knowles went on with her career, too, and as a result of her record-breaking achievements, today there aren't many people on the planet who don't know how to pronounce her name.

A couple of years ago, I was working on a book about a powerful political family dynasty when the idea to write about Beyoncé came to my mind. The family dynasty book wasn't gelling for me. I won't reveal the nature of it because, who knows?—I may still tackle it one day. When I told my publisher I wanted to ditch it for a biography about Beyoncé, I was worried about the response. I thought it was a good idea since there hadn't been a full-fledged, authoritative book about her. However, never before in my career had I ever stopped work on a book to switch to another topic. My publisher, though, was completely supportive (as always), and we agreed to a dramatic change in direction. Since I had written a Diana Ross biography, *Call Her Miss Ross* (my first *New York Times* bestseller), the idea of a Beyoncé biography somehow seemed like the perfect marriage of author and subject. Of course, Beyoncé and Diana have little in common in terms of temperament and personality, but they do have the same work ethic, the same drive . . . the same kind of awe-inspiring talent.

When I was given the green light, I couldn't wait to jump into a life history that, as it happened, turned out to be full of surprising twists and turns. I don't think I've ever enjoyed writing a book more than this one, a story full of strong, wonderful characters, with the lady herself at the center of such a memorable family drama. Of course, like all of my books, this one was a collaborative effort. Therefore, I would like to now acknowledge those who assisted me in this endeavor.

I am very fortunate to have been associated with the same private investigator and chief researcher for more than twenty years, and that is Cathy Griffin. For this book, Cathy really outdid herself. She found people who have never talked about Beyoncé in the past—scores of them, in fact—and conducted many interviews with each of them, going back to them repeatedly for the sake of detail and accuracy. Over the course of this project, she forged personal relationships with many of our important sources, not surprising considering her contagious personality. In fact, it's safe to say that most of the people who cooperated with this endeavor continue to maintain relationships with Cathy because they so much enjoyed being interviewed by her. Though I have expressed as much to her many times over the years, I just want to once again go on record as saying that not only is Cathy the ultimate professional in every way, but she is also a close and valuable friend. Long after we are gone from this earth, the work she has done on all of my books since 1990 will stand as testimony to how much she cares not only about me and my work, but also about the very people who trust us to tell their stories. In all of the years I have been publishing books, I have never had a disgruntled source, and that's largely due to the respect Cathy shows each and every one of them. So, again, I thank her.

It has been such an honor for the last seventeen years to call Grand Central Publishing my home. An author could not ask for a more nurturing environment. I am indebted to my publisher, Jamie Raab, for shepherding my work all of these years. I would like to also thank Jamie's very capable assistant, Deb Withey.

This is my third book with the amazing Gretchen Young as my editor. I would like to thank her for the many hours she invested in this project. We have such a great rapport, and I trust her implicitly. Thanks also to Gretchen's assistant, Katherine Stopa, for all of her help. I would also like to thank the ever-capable Marlene Plasencia.

As always, I would like to thank managing editor Bob Castillo for his invaluable contributions. Thanks also to our production editor, Yasmin Mathew. Special acknowledgment to Anne Twomey for her excellent cover design. Special thanks to my extraordinary book publicist, Linda Duggins. I would also like to thank Claire Brown in art, Sara Weiss in editorial, and Tom Whatley and Melissa Mathlin in production. A special thanks to my copy editor, Roland Ottewell.

I would like to thank John Pelosi and the staff of Pelosi Wolf Effron & Spates, LLC for their legal review of this work, which, as always, was thorough and much appreciated.

I would like to acknowledge my domestic agent, Mitch Douglas, for seventeen years of excellent representation. Mitch is a good friend as well as my agent, and I am eternally grateful to him.

I would also like to acknowledge my foreign agent, Dorie Simmonds of the Dorie Simmonds Agency in London, who has been a trusted friend for more than twenty years.

I am deeply indebted to Charles Casillo for his editorial work on *Becoming Beyoncé*. He had such a great understanding of these characters and helped me shape the way they are portrayed in this book. I am very appreciative.

Also, I would like to thank Steven Ivory, a good friend of mine for many decades. We started out at about the same time, writing for a black entertainment publication called *Soul*. He's a terrific writer, and I am happy to have been able to consult with him on the musical aspects of this work.

Lastly, I would like to thank my very good friend, Andy Hirsch, for the title of this book. We had countless conversations about this project, and during one of them, the words "Becoming Beyoncé" came tumbling forth from his mouth as his best way of describing what I was trying to convey with this story. It's a title that says it all, and I thank him for it.

THOSE WHO WERE FIRST IN BEYONCÉ'S LIFE...

With every book I write, new people come into my life, sources who become invaluable to my research. Rarely, though, has a book afforded me the opportunity to be exposed to so many truly inspirational people. When one considers the road traveled by Beyoncé on her way to becoming the superstar she is today, it's easy to understand her success given the kinds of people she met and worked with along the way. If, as they say, it takes a village to raise a child, the same certainly holds true when it comes to raising a superstar. In researching this book, I learned that many people who had been deeply involved in Beyoncé's career had never been properly credited for their participation. Part of my intention with this book, then, was to finally rectify that situation. Indeed, in the sense that this is a book of "firsts" in Beyoncé's life, these are the people who first groomed and nurtured her as an artist, and I would like to acknowledge their assistance to me.

Andretta Tillman was Beyoncé's first official manager. Sadly, she passed away in 1997, but her legacy lives on in her devoted sons, Armon and Christopher. I would like to thank them both for the many interviews they gave for this work in our effort to bring their mother to life on these pages. For too many years, Andretta has been overlooked, her contribution to Beyoncé's life and career all but forgotten with the passing of time, unintentionally or by design. It is my hope that with this book, Andretta gets the credit she has long deserved for her role in the success of Beyoncé Knowles, Destiny's Child, and all of its early incarnations. I want to thank Armon and Christopher for their assistance in this regard.

I also want to thank Andretta's brother Lornanda—To-to—for the many interviews he shared with us, as well as the photographs he provided from the Tillman estate. He's a real gentleman and someone I admire very much.

My thanks also to Andretta's sister Jann Stewart-Langley for the interview she gave us. Moreover, Andretta's nephew Belfrey Brown—who helped finance Beyoncé's early career—was very helpful to me. I appreciated his memories, as well as those of his and Andretta's very good friend Dawn "Sha Sha" Daniels.

Andretta's best friend, Pat Felton, was also extremely helpful in providing many memories over the course of many hours of interviews. I was struck by her steadfast devotion to Andretta, and I thank her for her trust. Also, I would like to thank Andretta's longtime friend, Bonnie Lee, for her wonderful recollections.

I must give special acknowledgment to Brian Kenneth (Kenny) Moore. If you would like to know more about Andretta Tillman, please allow me to point you to Kenny's book, *The Making of a Child of Destiny: The Andretta Tillman Story*. It's a terrific volume written by the man who was Andretta's businessman and close friend. Kenny helped us in more ways that I can enumerate here; I can't adequately express the depth of my appreciation. I highly recommend his book to any reader who would like to know more about Andretta's life and times. It can be purchased at http://www.theandrettatillmanstory.com.

Denise Seals and Deborah Laday were Beyoncé's managers before Andretta Tillman; they are responsible for discovering Beyoncé and then recruiting her for Girls Tyme. Both have never been acknowledged for their important role in Beyoncé's life. I want to thank them so much for their participation in this book. Who knows, without them Beyoncé might have become a star anyway; she's that special. But let the record show that it was these two women who found an eight-year-old girl at a talent show and first pushed her forward onto the road to stardom. It's also worth noting that Denise Seals was Beyoncé's first vocal coach.

Of course, Beyoncé is widely recognized for her dancing skills. If one wants to know how that all started, look no further than her first choreographer, Harlon "Keith" Bell. I thank him for his memories of those early days with Andretta Tillman, his group Tayste, and working with Girls Tyme.

An entertainer can only have one first producer and first writer, and in the case of Beyoncé those honors go to Alonzo (Lonnie) Jackson and Anthony (Tony Mo.) Moore. I want to thank them for the many hours of their time they devoted to this project. They were at the forefront of shaping Beyoncé's style, and it's my great honor to now credit them for their early work with an icon. They deserve to be properly acknowledged.

I would also like to recognize one of Beyoncé's first engineers, Arne Farger, who worked the board for those early Girls Tyme sessions in Sausalito. He has never been appropriately credited either. I thank him for his cooperation.

I would like to thank some of the first girls who ever sang with Beyoncé

Knowles, starting with LaTavia Roberson. LaTavia was just nine when she and Beyoncé joined Girls Tyme in 1990. Not only did she sing with Beyoncé, but she was one of her best friends all the way through Destiny's Child. As a fan of Destiny's Child, I was never comfortable with the way she was replaced in the group in the year 2000. I understand the situation much better after researching this book. Therefore, I have admiration for LaTavia and the way she spoke her truth all of those many years ago, and the way she has since rebounded in her life. I wish her the best. I also thank her for her cooperation with this book, and I am eternally grateful for the many previously unseen photographs she shared with us of her friendship with Beyoncé and the other girls. I would also like to thank her manager, Corey S. Guevarra, for his assistance.

Moreover, I would like to send my heartfelt thanks to LaTavia's cousins Nicki and Nina Taylor, both of whom also worked with Beyoncé as original members of Girls Tyme. Though I know it seems a lifetime ago to both of them, they were there at the start of it all just the same, and I want to thank them for sharing their memories. I would also like to thank their mom, Cholotte Taylor Ingram, for her time. Thanks also to Yvonne Boyd—aunt to LaTavia, Nicki, and Nina—for her memories.

Daryl Simmons is the man who first gave Beyoncé—along with her group, at the time the Dolls—the opportunity to record for a major label, Elektra Records. Though it didn't work out for them at that label, it certainly wasn't for lack of trying on Daryl's part. I'd like to thank him for reliving that frustrating time for us by sharing it for this book.

D'Wayne Wiggins is the producer who shepherded Beyoncé and the girls—Destiny at first, and then Destiny's Child—on their way to a label deal that saw the issuance of their first material, Columbia/Sony. Thank you, sir, for your memories.

Along with all of these firsts is Taura Stinson, who wrote the very first song Beyoncé and Destiny's Child released for Columbia/Sony—"Killing Time." Her contributions to this book are greatly appreciated.

The very accomplished Rob Fusari—now known as 8Bit—cowrote the first hit song Beyoncé and Destiny's Child released, "No, No, No." (He also cowrote "Bootylicious" with Beyoncé.) I appreciate his time very much.

Chad Elliott is the songwriter/producer with whom Beyoncé first collaborated, for their hit together, "Jumpin' Jumpin'." I thank him, as well, for his cooperation.

The esteemed director Robert Townsend was the first to direct Beyoncé on film, that being *Carmen: A Hip Hopera*. I thank him for his time and colorful memories.

On a list of firsts, certainly one's first love can never be forgotten. In Beyoncé's case, that would be Lyndall Locke. We actually lost count of how many hours Lyndall gave us for this work, all of his memories of being Beyoncé's boyfriend for almost ten years. I want to thank him sincerely for his trust. "For you, this is just another book," he told me, "but for me, this is my life. Please get it right." I hope he is satisfied with the results of his many hours of interviews. He's a real character, and I hope his uplifting personality comes through in these pages. Also, I would like to thank his mother, Lydia Locke, for her memories, and also for the lovely prom photos she contributed to this book. Thanks also to Lyndall's "Uncle" Jeff Harvey for his time.

ALSO, THANKS TO:

Those people with whom we were close to as children have a permanent place in our life's histories and are rarely forgotten. DeHaven Irby was Jay Z's closest childhood friend; the two got into plenty of trouble back in their outlaw days—and lived to tell the tale! I want to thank DeHaven for sharing his with me.

Jaz-O is the musician who gave Jay Z his first big break. I'm not sure he has been given the credit he deserves, and I hope his representation here in this work sets that record straight. I thank him for his help.

I want to acknowledge Christopher Lovett, Kelly Rowland's father. Though Kelly was all but raised by Mathew Knowles, she's Christopher's biological daughter and he has a side of a story that has never been told until now. He's a humble man who, I have come to believe, loves his daughter very much. I want to thank him for sharing his story here for the first time.

There are so many others who gave of their time for this book that it would be impossible to thank each individually, but their names can be found in the source notes. I would like them all to know how much I appreciate their cooperation. Here, though, I would like to give special acknowledgment to just a few more people: Florence Bowers, Tina Knowles's sister; Jonathan Hay, Jay Z's former publicist; Amy Vingpitaka, florist for the Carters' wedding; Reggie Wells and Billy Brasfield (Billy B.), both makeup artists for Destiny's Child and Beyoncé; Choke No Joke (Arthur Alston), videographer for Jay Z; Dan Workman, producer and engineer for Destiny's Child; Darryl Dunn, Mathew's college friend; Lisa Amosu, My Trendy Place proprietor; Kim Wood Sandusky, Destiny's Child vocal coach; Lance Gilbert, Beyoncé's stunt coordinator; Marguerite, choreographer for *Austin Powers in Goldmember*; Sharen Davis, costume designer for *Dreamgirls*; Tenesha Ksyn Cason, dancer in Beyoncé's show.

I'd also like to thank AlexSandra Wright for the hours she devoted to telling her full story for the first time. It's never easy opening up to a writer about the most personal of details, especially if they have been previously exaggerated or even falsified in the media. Whatever the circumstances, Alex and her son, Nixon Knowles Wright, have their rightful place in Knowles family history. I am very grateful to Alex for allowing me to tell her story in these pages. I would also like to acknowledge her brother Jonathan, her partner, Harvey Walden, and her attorney, David Ingram, for their interviews.

It was Mathew Knowles's decision not to cooperate with this book, though he did have a lengthy and very lively conversation with my researcher Cathy Griffin about the possibility on June 27, 2014. I have a great deal of respect for Mr. Knowles, as I hope is evidenced on these pages. It was also an honor to meet with his business associate, the critically acclaimed music and television producer Spencer Proffer, a man I admire very much.

Beyoncé, Tina, and Solange Knowles also did not wish to cooperate with us on this book. That's to be expected. This is my telling of their story, the way I see it based on all of my research. I understand that they will one day want to tell their stories their way, and I certainly wish mother and daughters the best with it.

GENERAL RESEARCH

I would like to extend my appreciation to the following very helpful people: Nolan Davis; Millicent Laday; Angela Taylor; Kevin Graves; Ron Reaves; Carol Kehlenbrink; Stephanie Bradford; Cindy George; Mari Tamburo; JR Jones; Teresa Whitmore; Lisa Amosu; Kevin Alred; Caroline Graham; Paul S. Howell; Howard Decker; John L. Moore; Unique PR; Katrina Dalton; Paul Francis; Dylan Howard; Becca Nelson; Jayne DiGregorio;

Steve Gaeto; Tyler Baxter; Sandra Marsh; Lydia Nicole; Christopher Howard; Anthony Hicks; Jason Bernard; Bryan Ashulman; David L. Ingram; Kellie Woldman; Fran Tolstonog and Jonathan Wright.

I would also like to acknowledge the following institutions: *Gadsden Times* (Alabama); Holy Family Catholic School (Galveston); Sisters of the Holy Family—Texas; Sisters of the Holy Family—Louisiana; Roman Catholic Archdiocese of Galveston-Houston; Gadsden City High School; Gadsden Public Library; Genealogy Department of Gadsden Public Library; *Galveston Daily News* (Texas); Etowah County Library; Litchfield Middle School (Alabama); Parker Elementary School; St. Mary's Elementary School; Houston Independent School District; *Houston Chronicle*; *Houstonia* magazine; *Texas Monthly* magazine; Newspaper Archives.com; Silent Partner Productions; HCP Servers; Ball High School; Central High School; Old Central Cultural Center; My Trendy Place; Rosenberg Library; Galveston County District Court; Galveston History and Texas Center; SugarHill Recording Studios; Harris County District Court; Harris County Appraisal District; Harris County Clerk's Office; Yale Baptist Church; Brentwood Baptist Church; Rutgers University; *Clayton News Daily* (Georgia).

I also want to express my gratitude to Pat Busch of the Harris County Appraisal District and Charles Clark, supervisor of the Harris County Clerk's Office, for their assistance.

Thank you to the following institutions: American Academy of Dramatic Arts; American Film Institute Library; Associated Press Office (New York); Lincoln Center, New York; Beverly Hills Library; University of California, Los Angeles; Corbis-Gamma/Liason; Glendale Central Public Library; Hedda Hopper Collection in the Margaret Herrick Collection of the Academy of Motion Picture Arts and Sciences, Beverly Hills; Lincoln Center Library of the Performing Arts; Kobal Collection; *Los Angeles Times*; Los Angeles Public Library; Museum of Broadcasting, New York; the former Metro-Goldwyn-Mayer studio archives, now part of the Turner Entertainment Group, Los Angeles; Museum of the Film; National Archives and Library of Congress; New York City Municipal Archives; New York University Library; *New York Daily News*; *New York Post*; *New York Times*; Philadelphia Public Library; Time-Life archives and Library, New York; Tribune Photo Archives, Overland Park, Kansas; Universal Collection at the University of Southern California; University of Southern California; and, finally, Rex Features.

Special thanks to the Museum of Broadcasting in New York and the Paley Center for Media in California for making so many archival television programs available to historians such as myself.

SOURCE NOTES

It is impossible to write accurately about anyone's life without many reliable witnesses to provide a range of different viewpoints. A biography of this kind stands or falls on the frankness of those involved in the story. A great number of other people went out of their way to assist me with *Becoming Beyoncé*. Friends, relatives, journalists, socialites, lawyers, celebrities, and business associates of the Knowles family were contacted in preparation for this book. I and my research team also carefully reviewed, as secondary sources, books about Beyoncé and her family members, as well as hundreds of newspaper and magazine articles written about them. I'm not going to list all of them here, though I will list those that I believe deserve special acknowledgment.

Also, in writing about a family as private as the Knowleses, a biographer such as myself will encounter many sources who would like to speak, but not for attribution. I have learned over the years that sometimes anonymity is important. Though I would prefer that all of my sources be acknowledged by name, it's not a reasonable or practical expectation. Therefore, when a source of mine or of one of my researchers asks for anonymity, I always grant the request.

The following source acknowledgments and extraneous notes are by no means meant to be comprehensive. Rather, they are only intended to give the reader a *general overview* of the kind of research that went into the writing of this book.

Prologue

Interviews: AlexSandra Wright (November 20, 2014); Harvey Walden (December 1, 2014); David L. Ingram (December 11, 2014).

Legal: "Summons and Notice of Hearing in Paternity Proceedings, re: *AlexSandra Wright, Petitioner v. Mathew Knowles, Respondent*," October 2, 2009; "Petition & Complaint," October 2, 2009; "Proof of Service"—*Wright v. Knowles*, LASC Case No. BF 037735; "Mathew Knowles, Called as a Witness on His Own Behalf…," *Wright v. Knowles*, LASC Case No. BF 037735, January 14, 2014.

Articles: "Beyoncé's Dad Slapped with Paternity Suit," TMZ.com, October 2, 2009; "Mathew Knowles Scandal: Beyoncé Daddy Is Baby Daddy to 'Scrubs' Guest AlexSandra Wright, Says Suit," by Sammy Saltsman, CBS News, October 5, 2009; "Paternity Test Confirms Beyoncé's Dad a Dad Again," by Blane Bachelor, *People*, March 25, 2010; "Beyoncé Accepts Billboard's Woman of the Year Award," *Billboard*, October 5, 2009; "Beyoncé Keeps Smiling Despite Her Father's Paternity Suit" (no byline), Popsugar.com; "Beyoncé: The Billboard Cover Story," by Gail Mitchell, *Billboard*, October 1, 2009; "Beyoncé Is Billboard's Woman of the Year," by Mariel Concepcion, *Billboard*, August 25, 2009; "Beyoncé's Dad Has a Love Child," *Indian Express*, March 25, 2010; "Mathew Knowles' Ex-Mistress Apologizes to Beyoncé, Tina and Solange," by Jasmine Denise Rogers, *Madame Noire*, March 2014.

Media: Beyoncé's speech at the *Billboard* Women in Music event, October 2, 2009; Q&A with Beyoncé at *Billboard* awards presentation, October 2, 2009.

Part One: Tina & Mathew

Interviews: Darryl Dunn, July 3, 2014; Bea Thomas, July 8, 2014; AlexSandra Wright, December 10, 2014; Chester Maddox, July 1, 2014; Denise Watkins, November 12, 2014; Deborah Laday, August 15, 2014; Denise Seals, September 13, 2014; Nina Taylor Hawkins, September 25, 2014; Nicki Taylor Lane, October 2, 2014; Brian "Kenny" Moore, July 13, July 26, August 2, August 10, August 15, 2014; Pat Felton, September 15, September 26, October 5, 2014; LaTavia Roberson, January 18, 2015; Lornanda "To-to" Brown, July 30, August 1, September 15, 2014; Belfrey Brown, July 26, 2015; Harlon "Keith" Bell, July 30, 2014; Alonzo "Lonnie" Jackson, July 14, July 16, July 22, July 23, August 29, September 6, 2014; Cindy Pack, June 16, 2014; Steven White, June 1, July 3, July 20, 2014; Thomas Eric Edmond, December 4, 2014, December 5, 2014, December 6, 2014; Kerry Knowles, June 15, 2014; Scherrie Wright, May 1, June 5, September 3, 2014; Anthony "Tony Mo." Moore, July 17, November 9, November 12, 2014; Armon Tillman, September 9, September 23, 2014; Arne Frager, July 7, 2014; Christopher Lovett, September 5, September 10, 2014; Florence Bowers, June 13, 2014.

Legal: "Affidavit of Beyoncé G. Knowles," July 3, 2001; "Affidavit of Beyoncé G. Knowles," September 5, 2001; "Affidavit of Beyoncé G. Knowles," February 1, 2002; "Affidavit of Beyoncé G. Knowles," March 28, 2002; "Deposition of Beyoncé Giselle Knowles," November 20, 2001; "Deposition of Mathew Knowles," January 29, 2002; "Deposition of Christopher Tillman," March 21, 2002; "Deposition of Celestine Knowles," March 22, March 28, 2002; "Deposition of Alonzo Jackson," April 21, 2002; "Deposition of Taura Stinson," April 24, 2002; "Deposition of Kelendria Rowland," December 18, 2001; "Deposition of Armon Tillman," March 20, 2002; "Deposition of Christopher Tillman," March 21, 2002; "Beyoncé Giselle Knowles—Answers to Interrogatories," November 1, 2001; "Mathew Knowles—Answers to Interrogatories," November 12, 2001; "Celestine Knowles—Answers to Interrogatories," November 15, 2001; "Kelendria Rowland—Answers to Interrogatories," November 1, 2001; "LaTavia Roberson—Answers to Interrogatories," November 15, 2001; "LeToya Luckett—Answers to Interrogatories," November 1, 2001; "Beyoncé Giselle Knowles—Answers to Second Set of Interrogatories," November 18, 2001; "Beyoncé Giselle Knowles—Answers to Interrogatories," November 1, 2001; "Armon Tillman—Answers to Interrogatories," December 10, 2001; "Christopher Tillman—Answers to Interrogatories," December 10, 2001.

Media: "Mathew Knowles on Fatherhood and Beyoncé," interview with Tony Cox, National Public Radio, November 27, 2006; Tina Knowles, Keynote Speech, Women &

Money Leadership Luncheon, October 2, 2014; Tina Knowles, interview on *Good Day New York*, May 8, 2012; Beyoncé Knowles performing at the Sammy Awards, 1988; "Pretty Hurts," Beyoncé music video, 2014; interview with Beyoncé (to promote *Beyoncé* CD), YouTube, December 2014; *Driven: Beyoncé*, VH1; *Before They Were Stars: Destiny's Child*, VH1; Tina Knowles Oral History, Living Archives, University of Houston, October 3, 2011; Girls Tyme's performance on *Star Search*, February 1992; "Just for Me—Pro-Line Hair Products," LaTavia Roberson commercial; LaTavia Roberson interview, Arise Entertainment 360, May 2014; LaTavia Roberson interview, *Madame Noire*, May 2014.

Volumes: *The Making of a Child of Destiny: The Andretta Tillman Story*, by Brian Kenneth Moore; *Destiny's Style*, by Tina Knowles; *Soul Survivors*, by Beyoncé Knowles, Kelly Rowland, and Michelle Williams with James Patrick Herman.

Articles: "Big Boy Always There," by George Butler, *Gadsden Times*, December 31, 1972; "Yes and No," *Gadsden Times*, September 7, 2001; Gadsden High School Yearbook, 1970; "The Untold Story of How Tina and Mathew Knowles Created the Destiny's Child Goldmine," by Lynn Norment, *Ebony*, September 2001; "Mathew Knowles Sister 2 Sister Interview," by Jamie Foster Brown, *Sister 2 Sister*, October 14, 2010; "Music Mogul Mathew Knowles Visits His Hometown," by Matthew Martin, *Gadsden Times*, August 22, 2010; "Tina Knowles Talks About Life, Love at Women's Luncheon," by Joy Sewing, *Houston Chronicle*, October 3, 2014; "Mother Mastermind: 5 Lessons on Career and Leadership from Tina Knowles," by Courtney Connley, *Black Enterprise*, October 8, 2014; "Tina Knowles Opens Up About Dating and Life After Mathew Knowles," *Huffington Post*, Black Voices, October 7, 2014; "Beyoncé: A Woman Possessed," by Touré, *Rolling Stone*, March 4, 2004; "Meet the People Behind Beyoncé," Out.com, April 8, 2014; "Miss Millennium: Beyoncé," by Amy Wallace, *GQ*, February 2013; "Beyoncé's Dad Blows Millions on Drugs and Hookers—Charges Lawsuit; Mathew Knowles Interview: 'I Was a Sex Addict' he tells, *Star*," *Star*, February 12, 2002; "It's a Family Affair," by Michael Hall, *Texas Monthly*, April 2004; "Our View: Getting Back to His Roots" (no byline), *Gadsden Times*, August 23, 2010; "Q & A: Mathew Knowles," SoulTrain.com, July 18, 2014; "How Would Kelly Rowland Fare on 'X-Factor'?," by Paulette Cohn, American Profile.com, October 29, 2013; "Beyoncé Instagrams Photographs of her Grandparents," by Hannah Ongley, Styleite.com, October 3, 2013; obituary of Albert Lumus Beyincé, *Galveston County Daily News*, August 12, 1982; obituary of Father Gerard R. Joubert, *Holy Rosary Catholic Church Newsletter*; obituary of Agnez Buyincé, *Galveston County Daily News* (no date); "LaTavia Roberson: I Want to Make a Musical Comeback," *Brown Sista*, July 17, 2006; "Manifest Destiny," by Cheryl Lu-Lien, *Baltimore Sun*, September 19, 2000; "Prairie View Today," by Frederick V. Roberts, Esq., YourHoustonNews.com, November 21, 2010.

Part Two: One Step Forward, Two Steps Back

Interviews: Dawn "Sha Sha" Daniels, July 7, 2014; Anthony "Tony Mo." Moore, July 17, November 9, November 12, 2014; Nicki Taylor Lane, October 2, 2014; Nina Taylor Hawkins, September 26, 2014; Daryl Simmons, July 29, 2014; Lyndall Locke, June 21, June 24, June 25, August 4, August 22, September 8, October 5, 2014; Belfrey Brown, July 26, 2014; Cholotte Taylor Ingram, September 27, 2014; Pat Felton, September 15, September 26, October 5, 2014; Lydia Locke, June 24, 2014; Tony Scott, August 3, December 4, 2014; Smokey Thomas, June 3, August 4, December 11, 2014; Delores DeHaven, May 5, June 1, July 3, 2014; Brian "Kenny" Moore, July 13, July 26, August 2, August 10, August 15, 2014; Bonnie Lee, October 22, 2014; D'Wayne Wiggins, July 23, 2014; LaTavia Roberson,

January 18, 2015; Lornanda "To-to" Brown, July 30, August 1, September 15, 2014; Christopher Tillman, October 2, October 9, 2014; Kerry Knowles, June 15, 2014; Scherrie Wright, May 1, June 5, September 3, 2014.

Legal: Public records showing tax liens on the Knowles property, 1990, 1992, 1993, 1994, 1995; correspondence from Mathew Knowles to Warren Fitzgerald, October 4, October 7, 1993; miscellaneous documents relating to Andretta Tillman's bankruptcy filing, June 3, 1994; miscellaneous documents relating to Mathew and Tina Knowles's bankruptcy, June 7, 1994; deed to Knowles property at 3346 Parkwood Drive, Houston; tax lien assessed against the Knowleses, March 30, 1995; public records ownership history of 3346 Parkwood Drive, Houston; public records relating to the purchase of property at 27 Swan Isle Boulevard, Missouri City, by Mathew and Tina Knowles; public records relating to all owners of 8207 Braes Meadow Drive, Houston; "Beyoncé Giselle Knowles—Answers to Interrogatories," November 1, 2001; "Beyoncé Giselle Knowles—Answers to Second Set of Interrogatories," November 18, 2001; "AFFIDAVIT of Pamela Luckett," November 25, 1998; "AFFIDAVIT of LeToya Luckett," November 25, 1998.

Contracts: Agreement between Andretta Tillman and Mathew Knowles pertaining to Ashley Tamar Davis stipulating that the two will share equally any monies derived by any management contract Andretta may enter into with Ashley, and that "Mathew Knowles agrees to total confidentiality of this agreement," January 3, 1993; "Agreement" between Silent Partner Productions and Beyoncé Knowles, LaTavia Roberson, Kelendria Rowland, and LeToya Luckett (collectively known as Somethin' Fresh), June 11, 1993; four separate "Personal Management Contracts" between Andretta Tillman and Mathew Knowles with Beyoncé Knowles, Kelendria Rowland, and LaTavia Roberson, each one dated January 3, 1993; "Personal Management Contract" between Andretta Tillman and Mathew Knowles and LeToya Nicole Luckett, February 11, 1993; "Addendum to Personal Management Contract" between Andretta Tillman and Mathew Knowles with Beyoncé Knowles, LaTavia Roberson, Kelendria Rowland, and LeToya Luckett (Professionally Known as the Dolls), June 1994; "Addendum" to personal management contract dated January 3, 1994; "Personal Management Agreement" between Andretta Tillman and Mathew Knowles with Beyoncé Knowles, LaTavia Robertson [sic], Kelendria Rowland, and LeToya Luckett (collectively known as Destiny), January 23, 1995; "Personal Management Agreement" between Mathew Knowles and Beyoncé Knowles, LaTavia Roberson, Kelendria Rowland, and LeToya Luckett (collectively known as Destiny's Child), June 9, 1997; "Personal Management Agreement" between Mathew Knowles and Beyoncé Knowles, Kelendria Rowland, Farrah Franklin, and Tenitra Michelle Williams (collectively known as Destiny's Child), February 13, 2000.

Correspondence: Between Warren Fitzgerald and Mathew Knowles relating to LeToya Luckett, October 5, October 6 ("We simply will not run our organization in fear," Knowles wrote relating to his and Andretta Tillman's ongoing negotiations with Pamela and LeToya Luckett, "nor will exceptions be made regarding our management contract. Three of the members of this group have given up a combined seven years of youth, one member a national TV commercial [presumably LaTavia] and the other a solo singing career [presumably Beyoncé] for the group Somethin' Fresh, which is based on teamwork"), October 10, October 15, and November 5, 1993; correspondence between Andretta Tillman and Arne Frager, September 12, October 19, November 8, and December 5, 1992.

Media: *Driven: Beyoncé Knowles*, VH1; *Before They Were Stars: Destiny's Child*; Tina Knowles, Keynote Speech, Women & Money Leadership Luncheon, October 2, 2014; *Boulevard of Broken Dreams: Destiny's Child*, E!, 2007.

Volumes: *The Making of a Child of Destiny: The Andretta Tillman Story*, by Brian Kenneth Moore; *Destiny's Style*, by Tina Knowles; *Soul Survivors*, by Beyoncé Knowles, Kelly Rowland, and Michelle Williams with James Patrick Herman.

Articles: "Mathew Knowles Sister 2 Sister Interview," by Jamie Foster Brown, *Sister 2 Sister*, October 14, 2010; "Tina Knowles Makes Fashion Choices," by Samantha Critchell, Associated Press, November 9, 2002; "Success Story—Destiny's Child," *Hit Quarters*, February 2, 2002; "Beyoncé's Dad Used to Make Kelly Rowland Cry," Mirror .co.uk, October 2, 2011; "Destiny's Child(ren)—Where Are They Now?," by Tracy Scott, *Houston Chronicle*, September 7, 2011; "Beyoncé: The Billboard Cover Story," by Gail Mitchell, *Billboard*, October 1, 2009.

Part Three: Destiny's Child

Interviews: Jan Stewart-Langley, October 21, 2014; Taura Stinson, October 15, October 18, November 21, 2014; D'Wayne Wiggins, July 23, 2014; Lyndall Locke, June 20, June 21, June 22, June 24, 2014; Rob "8Bit" Fusari, September 18, 2014; Anthony "Tony Mo." Moore, July 17, 2014; Pat Felton, September 15, September 26, October 5, 2014; LaTavia Roberson, January 18, 2015; Lornanda "To-to" Brown, July 30, August 1, September 15, 2014; Nicki Taylor Lane, October 2, 2014; Nina Taylor Hawkins, September 25, September 26, 2014; Christopher Tillman, October 2, October 9, 2014; Bea Thomas, July 8, August 15, October 15, 2015; Armon Tillman, September 9, September 23, 2014; Alonzo Jackson, July 14, July 16, July 22, July 23, August 29, 2014; Jeff Harvey, June 26, 2014; Mavis Miller-Gunther, July 2, 2014; Tony Scott, August 3, December 4, 2014; Smokey Thomas, June 3, August 4, December 11, 2014; Delores DeHaven, May 5, June 1, July 3, 2014; Reggie Wells, December 7, 2014; Chad Elliott, December 21, 2014; Kim Wood Sandusky, September 11, 2014; Dan Workman, August 27, 2014; Daryl Simmons, July 29, 2014; Yvonne Boyd, November 12, 2014.

Legal: Various deal memos relating to Destiny's Child contract with Columbia/Sony; Destiny's Child (individual group member) contracts with Columbia/Sony dated December 5, 1995; income tax statements from Mathew and Celestine Knowles included as exhibits in *Tillman v. Beyoncé et al.*; "Seizure of Savings Account Notice," March 1998; public records relating to the purchase by Celestine Knowles of property at 8207 Braes Meadow Drive, December 5, 1997; "Affidavit of Beyoncé G. Knowles," July 3, 2001; "Affidavit of Beyoncé G. Knowles," September 5, 2001; "Affidavit of Beyoncé G. Knowles," February 1, 2002; "Affidavit of Beyoncé G. Knowles," March 28, 2002; "Deposition of Beyoncé Giselle Knowles," November 20, 2001; "Deposition of Mathew Knowles," January 29, 2002; "Deposition of Christopher Tillman," March 21, 2002; "Deposition of Celestine Knowles," March 22, 2002, March 28, 2002; "Deposition of Alonzo Jackson," April 21, 2002; "Deposition of Taura Stinson," April 24, 2002; "Deposition of Kelendria Rowland," December 18, 2001; "Deposition of Armon Tillman," March 20, 2002; "Deposition of Christopher Tillman," March 21, 2002; individual contracts for Tenitra Williams and Farrah Franklin with Music World, February 18, 2000; *LaTavia Roberson and LeToya Luckett v. Mathew Knowles et al.* March 21, 2000; "Kelendria Rowland—Answers to Interrogatories," November 1, 2001; "LaTavia Roberson—Answers to Interrogatories," November 15, 2001; "LeToya Luckett—Answers to Interrogatories." November 15. 2001.

Correspondence: From Beyoncé to LeToya Luckett and LaTavia Roberson (undated); from Beyoncé to Don Ienner relating to her leaving Destiny's Child, January 7, 2000;

between Pamela Luckett and Mathew Knowles relating to LeToya Luckett, February 23, 1997; between Pamela Luckett and Mathew Knowles, February 21, 1997.

Note: We also referenced Music World's accounting of monies spent on Destiny's Child during the Farrah Franklin months, including, as noted in the document, twenty-four vocal lessons for both Farrah and Michelle at $75 each and twelve "group therapy" sessions at $250 each. Considering that Farrah was only in the group for about twenty months, it would seem that they were seeing a "therapist" every other week.

Media: *Driven: Beyoncé Knowles*, VH1; *Before They Were Stars: Destiny's Child*," clip of Destiny's Child winning Soul Train Award, 1998; *Life is But a Dream*; ; Destiny's Child on *Cribs*, 2001; Tina Knowles interview, *The Monique Show*, December 14, 2010; Tina Knowles, Keynote Speech, Women & Money Leadership Luncheon, October 2, 2014; *Boulevard of Broken Dreams, Destiny's Child*, E!, 2007; "Former Destiny's Child LaTavia Roberson: 'Beyoncé and I Were Almost a Vocal Duo,'" by Chris Witherspoon, *The Grio* May 7, 2014; "Former Destiny's Child Member Says She Was Molested at 7-Years-Old," by Chris Witherspoon, *The Grio*, May 17, 2014; LaTavia Roberson interview, *Wendy: The Wendy Williams Show*, May 5, 2014; *The Unauthorized Biography of Beyoncé: Baby and Beyond* (documentary); *Beyoncé: Fierce and Fabulous* (documentary); *Live at Roseland: Elements of 4* (concert film, 2011).

Volumes: *The Making of a Child of Destiny: The Andretta Tillman Story*, by Brian Kenneth Moore; *Destiny's Style*, by Tina Knowles; *Soul Survivors*, by Beyoncé Knowles, Kelly Rowland, and Michelle Williams with James Patrick Herman.

Articles: "Destined for Greatness," by Michael D. Clark, *Houston Chronicle*, February 11, 2001; "Divas Live!" by Lola Ogunnaike, Vibe, February, 2001; "Meet the People Behind Beyoncé," Out.com, April 8, 2014; "Destiny's Child," *Launch*, May 2002; "Destiny's Child," *World Pop*, July 2001; "Destiny's Child—Reunited and It Feels So Good," VH1 (no date); "Beyoncé Unwrapped," *Teen Hollywood*, August 10, 2003; "Beyoncé's Publicist Talks Destiny's Child's Early Days," by Shenequa A. Golding, *Vibe*, September 25, 2014; "Wyclef Jean," by Sarah Benzuly, *Mix*, August 1, 2003; "Fashion: Beyoncé Knowles' Mom Brings Creativity to Costumes and Glamour to Destiny Child's Image," by Linda Gillan Griffin, *Houston Chronicle*, June 24, 2001; "Ex-Destiny's Child Members Say Their Name Is Angel," by Teri Vanhorn, MTV News, March 5, 2001; "Destiny's Child in Hot Water over 'Survivor,'" Associated Press, March 2002; "Miss Millennium: Beyoncé," by Amy Wallace, GQ, February 2013; "Beyoncé's Heartbreak Single, 'Ring Off,'" by Kirthana Ramisetti, *New York Daily News*, November 20, 2014; "The Business of Beyoncé," by Christina Pazzanese, *Harvard Gazette*, September 24, 2014; "Sexy, Seductive Beyoncé Goes Lovey-Dovey Maternal," by Sara Taylor, *Fishwrapper*, November 21, 2014; "Stream Beyoncé's Newly-Leaked Singles," by Brennan Carley, *Spin*, November 20, 2014; "The Top-Earning Women in Music 2014," by Zack O'Malley, *Forbes*, November 24, 2014; "Reuniting Beyoncé and Kelly on 'Say Yes' Was Always the Plan, Michelle Williams Says," by Nadeska Alexis, MTV.com, June 24, 2014.

Part Four: Independent Women

Interviews: Billy Brasfield, October 2, 2014; Lyndall Locke, June 21, June 24, June 25, August 22, September 8, September 20, October 5, October 20, November 11, 2014; Robert Townsend, September 11, 2014; Yvonne Boyd, November 12, 2014; Jonathan "Jaz-O" Burks, October 20, 2014; Arthur "Choke No Joke" Alston, October 18, 2014; Taura Stinson, October 15, October 18, November 21, 2014; DeHaven Irby, October 27, 2014; Dan Workman,

August 27, 2014; Tony LaPierre, August 5, 2014; Dawn McClintock, June 5, 2014; Rob "8Bit" Fusari, September 18, 2014; Christopher Tillman, October 2, October 9, 2014; Armon Tillman, September 9, September 23, 2014; Hazel O'Connell, July 5, 2014; Maryann Baker, June 5, July 3, 2014; Marilyn Thomas-Baker, July 5, September 5, 2014; Jane Maxwell, September 15, 2014; Sam Elliott, October 5, 2015; Louise Adams, October 11, 2014; Ed Lovitz, June 11, 2014; Anthony "Tony Mo." Moore, July 17, November 9, November 12, 2014; Marguerite Derricks, September 10, 2014; Alonzo Jackson, July 14, July 16, 2014.

Legal: More than three thousand documents were referenced relating to the LeToya Luckett/LaTavia Roberson litigation (*LeToya N. Luckett, LaTavia M. Roberson v. Mathew Knowles, Individually and d/b/a/ Music World Management; Beyoncé G. Knowles; Kelendria T. Rowland; Farrah Franklin and Michelle Williams*, filed on March 15, 2000) and the Andretta Tillman Estate litigation (*Lornonda N. Brown, Armon Tillman, Christopher Tillman and Effie Brown v. Beyoncé G Knowles, et al.*, filed on January 4, 2002); "Affidavit of Beyoncé G. Knowles," July 3, 2001; "Affidavit of Beyoncé G. Knowles," September 5, 2001; "Affidavit of Beyoncé G. Knowles," February 1, 2002; "Affidavit of Beyoncé G. Knowles," March 28, 2002; "Affidavit of Kelendria Rowland," June 3, 2001; "Affidavit of Kelendria Rowland," August 4, 2001; "Affidavit of Kelendria Rowland," March 21, 2002; "Affidavit of Kelendria Rowland," April 15, 2002; "Affidavit of Mathew Knowles," April 1, 2001; "Affidavit of Mathew Knowles," September 2, 2001; "Affidavit of Mathew Knowles," March 20, 2002; "Affidavit of Tina Knowles," April 2, 2001; "Affidavit of Armon Roshaud Tillman," April 19, 2002; "Affidavit of Armon Roshaud Tillman," March 25, 2002; "Affidavit of Christopher Raynard Tillman," April 2, 2002; "Affidavit of Effie Lee Brown," April 10, 2002; "Affidavit of Lornanda Brown," April 16, 2002; "Affidavit of Linda Ragland [general manager of Music World Management]," January 25, 2002; "Deposition of Beyoncé Giselle Knowles," November 20, 2001; "Deposition of Pamela Luckett," December 13, 2001; "Deposition of Kelendria Rowland," December 18, 2001; "Deposition of Tenitra Michelle Williams," December 19, 2001; "Deposition of LeToya Luckett," December 17, 2001; "Deposition of LaTavia Roberson," December 19, 2001; "Deposition of Mathew Knowles," January 29, 2002; "Deposition of Effie Brown," February 19, 2002; "Deposition of Armon Tillman," March 20, 2002; "Deposition of Christopher Tillman," March 21, 2002; "Deposition of Celestine Knowles," March 22, 2002, March 28, 2002; "Deposition of Jonathan Cooks," March 26, 2002; "Deposition of Angela Phea," March 28, 2002; "Deposition of Alonzo Jackson," April 21, 2002; "Deposition of Taura Stinson," April 24, 2002; "Beyoncé Giselle Knowles—Answers to Interrogatories," November 1, 2001; "Mathew Knowles—Answers to Interrogatories," November 12, 2001; "Celestine Knowles—Answers to Interrogatories," November 15, 2001; "Kelendria Rowland—Answers to Interrogatories," November 1, 2001; "LaTavia Roberson—Answers to Interrogatories," November 15, 2001; "LeToya Luckett—Answers to Interrogatories," November 1, 2001; "Beyoncé Giselle Knowles—Answers to Second Set of Interrogatories," November 18, 2001; "Beyoncé Giselle Knowles—Answers to Interrogatories," November 1, 2001.

Correspondence: From LeToya Luckett disaffirming management agreement with Mathew Knowles, December 14, 1999; from LaTavia Roberson disaffirming management agreement with Mathew Knowles, December 14, 1999; from Gerald A. Margolis to Ron Wilcox, Senior Vice President, Sony Business Affairs, February 11, 2000 (outlining grievances of LaTavia Roberson and LeToya Luckett relating to Destiny's Child, Mathew Knowles, and Beyoncé Knowles); from Beyoncé G. Knowles to LaTavia Roberson and LeToya Luckett (undated); from Kelly Rowland to LaTavia Roberson and LeToya Luckett (undated); from Randy Bowman, Esq., to Mathew Knowles, December 21, 1999 (demanding that Knowles cease booking Destiny's Child in concert without the services of Roberson and Luckett); from Randy Bowman, Esq., to John Ingrasia, Esq., December 22, 1999 (outlining in timeline form all of Roberson's and Luckett's grievances against Mathew and Beyoncé Knowles and Kelly Rowland, prior to formal litigation against them); from Thomas M. Fulkerson, Esq., to Ben Hall, Esq., and Sherry Chandler, Esq., February 21, 2002 (attempting to disaffirm Beyoncé's and Kelly's management contracts with Andretta Tillman because "the contracts were entered into when they were between eleven and thirteen years of age"); "Release and Settlement Agreement Among Plaintiffs and Defendants Beyoncé G. Knowles. Kelendria Rowland etc...." (settlement of the Roberson/ Luckett case), December 21, 2000; "Hearing on Motions to Quash...for Protection...to Compel...to Appoint Auditor...for Contempt," January 25, 2002; "Transcript of Hearing Before Honorable Jane Bland," January 25, 2002; Columbia Records press release, "Destiny's Child Welcome Two New Members to Group," February 17, 2000.

Note: The content of Mathew Knowles's interview with *Star* ("Beyoncé's Dad Blows Millions on Drugs and Hookers—Charges Lawsuit; Mathew Knowles Interview: 'I Was a Sex Addict' he tells, Star," February 12, 2002, was confirmed with its writer, Bob Michaels, by attorney Benjamin L. Hall (see "Plaintiff's Response and Special Exceptions to Defendant's Motion for Sanctions," January 4, 2002, in the case of *Lornanda N. Brown et al. v. Beyoncé G. Knowles et al.*). Hall testified, "The contents of the Mathew Knowles interview will be published in the next publication of *Star* magazine. Plaintiff's counsel interviewed Bob Michaels, article writer for *Star* magazine, who confirmed Knowles' admissions." When researcher Cathy Griffin contacted Bob Michaels on July 24, 2014, he had nothing further to offer about the Mathew Knowles interview.

Media: *Driven: Beyoncé Knowles*, VH1 documentary; *Before They Were Stars: Destiny's Child*; "Beyoncé Answers Random Questions," Channel 4.com (*B'Day* promotion), 2006; Tina Knowles, Keynote Speech, Women & Money Leadership Luncheon, October 2, 2014; *Boulevard of Broken Dreams: Destiny's Child*, E!, 2007; "Mike Meyers on Michael Caine and Beyoncé," CBS News, May 31, 2014.

Volumes: *The Making of a Child of Destiny: The Andretta Tillman Story*, by Brian Kenneth Moore; *Destiny's Style*, by Tina Knowles; *Soul Survivors*, by Beyoncé Knowles, Kelly Rowland, and Michelle Williams with James Patrick Herman; *That's the Joint! The Hip-Hop Studies Reader*, by Murray Forman and Mark Anthony Neal; *Hip-Hop and Philosophy: Rhyme 2 Reason*, by Derrick Darby and Tommie Shelby; *Check It While I Wreck It: Black Womanhood, Hip-Hop Culture, and the Public Sphere*, by Gwendolyn D. Pough; *Empire State of Mind: How Jay-Z Went from Street Corner to Corner Office*, by Zack O'Malley Greenburg; *Can't Stop Won't Stop: A History of the Hip-Hop Generation*, by Jeff Chang; *Hip-Hop America*, by Nelson George; *Hip-Hop Revolution: The Culture and Politics of Rap*, by Jeffrey O. G. Ogbar.

Articles: "Meet the People Behind Beyoncé," Out.com, April 8, 2014; "Divas Live!" by Lola Ogunnaike, *Vibe*, February 2001; "Destiny's Child Battling Lawsuit from Former Manager's Family" (no byline), Associated Press, January 2002; "Suit over Destiny's Child Royalties Turns Nasty," by Jo Ann Zuniga, *Houston Chronicle*, January 12, 2002; "A Parent Who Knows Destiny," by Ashante Infantry, *Toronto Star*, March 20, 2005; "Michelle Williams' Depression," by Mark Kennedy, *Black Voices*, January 7, 2013; "Beyoncé," by Carissa Rosenberg, *Seventeen*, January 2009; "Beyoncé's Destiny," by Nina Malkin, *Seventeen*, June 2003; "Hiding in Plain Sight," by Shanel Odum, *Spin*, June 2007; "Beyoncé Strips Down" (no byline), *Spin*, June 2007; "Hip Hop Happens," by Steven Daly, *Vanity Fair*, November 2005; "Destiny's Child," by Lorraine Bracco, *Interview*, August 1, 2001;

"Destiny's Child—The Growing Pains of Fame," by Lynn Norment, *Ebony*, September 2001; "A Date with Destiny," by Jancee Dunn, *Rolling Stone*, May 24, 2001; "Bewitched, Bothered, Beyoncé," by Vanessa Jones, *Boston Globe*, August 5, 2007; "Fun, Fearless Female of the Year," by Lesley Rotchford, *Cosmopolitan*, February, 2006; "What Beyoncé Wants," by Allison Samuels, *Newsweek*, July 29, 2002; "A Child Destiny," by Alona Wartofsky, *Washington Post*, September 23, 2003; "Beyoncé a Fashion Designer?," by Booth Moore, *Los Angeles Times*, September 9, 2005; "Beyoncé's Mother Crazy in Love with Fashion," by Joy Sewing, *Houston Chronicle*, February 19, 2004; "Beyoncé's Mom, Tina Knowles, Helps Kelly Rowland Love Her Skin Tone, Singer Opens Up About Loving Her 'Chocolate-ness,'" by Mereb Gebremariam, *MStars News*, March 8, 2013; "Suit over Destiny's Child Royalties Turns Nasty," by JoAnn Zuniga, *Houston Chronicle*, January 12, 2002; "Destiny's Child Superstar Heads to a Golden Big Screen Debut," by Paul Fischer, FilmMonthly. com, July 17, 2002; "Afro-Licious," by Rock Fulton, *Daily Record*, July 21, 2002; "Independent Woman," by David Kent, *Herald*, July 13, 2002; "Jay Roach Discusses Beyoncé," by Stephen Schaefer, *Boston Herald*, July 22, 2002; "Beyoncé Knowles—The Austin Powers Interview," by Kam Williams, *Washington Informer*; "Producer Upset over Beyoncé Writing Snub," Express.co.uk, February 25, 2010; "A 20-Minute Conversation with Beyoncé's Uncle Larry," by Andrea Simpson, *Celebuzz*, Spring 2013; "Beyoncé Continues to Work Hard...," by Gail Mitchell, *Entertainment News Wire*, October 20, 2009; "Above and Beyoncé," by Lisa Robinson, *Vanity Fair*, November 2005; "Beyoncé Knowles: The Queen B," by Jason Guy, *Vogue*, February 11, 2013.

Part Five: Jay Z

Interviews: Kim Wood Sandusky, September 11, 2014; Jonathan "Jaz-O" Burks, October 20, 2014; DeHaven Irby, October 27, 2014; Arthur "Choke No Joke" Alston, October 18, 2014; Chad Elliott, December 21, 2014; Smokey Thomas, June 3, August 4, December 11, 2014; Delores DeHaven, May 5, June 1, July 3, 2014; Steven White, June 1, July 3, July 20, 2014; Thomas Eric Edmond, December 4, December 5, December 6, 2014; Kerry Knowles, June 15, 2014; Scherrie Wright, May 1, June 5, September 3, 2014; Hazel O'Connell, July 5, 2014; Maryann Baker, June 5, July 3, 2014; Marilyn Thomas-Baker, July 5, September 5, 2014; Jane Maxwell, September 15, 2014; Sam Elliott, October 5, 2015; Louise Adams, October 11, 2014; Ed Lovitz, June 11, 2014; Lyndall Locke, June 21, June 24, August 4, 2014; Eugene Record (with J. Randy Taraborrelli for *The Entertainers* radio program), July 4, 2003; Billy Brasfield, October 2, 2014.

Legal: "Affidavit of Beyoncé G. Knowles," July 3, 2001; "Affidavit of Beyoncé G. Knowles," September 5, 2001; "Affidavit of Beyoncé G. Knowles," February 1, 2002; "Affidavit of Beyoncé G. Knowles," March 28, 2002; "Deposition of Beyoncé Giselle Knowles," November 20, 2001.

Media: *Beyoncé: Ring the Alarm* (preparing and rehearsal for VMAs), 2006; Jay-Z interviewed by Zane Lowe (four-part interview), BBC Radio 1, July 2013; *Fade to Black*, Roc-A-Fella Films (documentary), 2004, *The Making of Collision Course* (DVD), 2004; *Backstage* (documentary), 2000; Tina Knowles, Keynote Speech, Women & Money Leadership Luncheon, October 2, 2014; CNN special, "Beyoncé Finding Her Way," February 9, 2013; Beyoncé interview, *60 Minutes*, CBS-TV, January 2010; *The Unauthorized Biography of Beyoncé: Baby and Beyond* (documentary); *Beyoncé: Fierce and Fabulous* (documentary); "Houston Newsmakers with Khambrel Marshall," interview with Mathew Knowles, August 17, 2014.

Volumes: *Motown: Hot Wax, City Cool, Solid Gold*, by J. Randy Taraborrelli; *Jay-Z: The King of America*, by Mark Beaumont; *Empire State of Mind: How Jay-Z Went from Street Corner to Corner Office*, by Zack O'Malley Greenburg; *It's Bigger Than Hip-Hop: The Rise of the Post-Hip-Hop Generation*, by M. K. Asante Jr.; *Hip-Hop Files: Photographs, 1979–1984*, by Martha Cooper; *Hip-Hop Decoded*, by The Black Dot; *The Hip-Hop Manifesto*, by Hozeh; *A Hip-Hop Story*, by Heru Ptah; *Pharrell: Places and Spaces I've Been*, by Pharrell Williams; *Jay-Z: The Playboy Interview*, by Playboy and Jay-Z.

Articles: "Meet the People Behind Beyoncé," Out.com, April 8, 2014; "Beyoncé Talks Fashion," by Lynn Hirschberg, *W*, July 2010: "Beyoncé: Fun, Fearless Female of the Year 2006," by Lesley Rotchford, Cosmopolitan.com, November 1, 2006; "Beyoncé Takes Credit for 'Writing' Songs," by Roger Friedman, Showbiz411.com, October 18, 2005; "The Wonderful, Wonderful Ride ...," by Richard Benson, *Telegraph Magazine*, 2003; "It's a Family Affair," by Michael Hall, *Texas Monthly*, April 2004; "Beyoncé and Boyfriend Jay-Z Go Public," by Maeve Quigly, *Sunday Mirror*, August 31, 2003; "A Comprehensive History of Jay Z and Beyoncé's Relationship," by Ana Silman, *Vulture*, September 9, 2014; "Beyoncé—Virgin until Age 23 (ish)," WaitingTillMarriage.org, October 23, 2011; "Beyoncé & Jay-Z's Love Story," by Dimas Sanfiorenzo, Globalgrind.com, April 3, 2013; "Jay-Z Gets Three Years Probation for 'Un' Rivera Stabbing," by Joe D'Angelo, MTV.com, December 6, 2001; "Jay-Z Hit on Assault," by Mitchell Fink, *New York Daily News*, December 3, 1999; "Oprah Interview with Jay Z," *O*, October 2009; "Jay-Z: The Boy from the Hood Who Turned Out Good," by Simon Hattenstone, *Guardian*, February 19, 2010; "Jay-Z Discusses Shooting His Brother..." by Simon Vozick-Levinson, *Entertainment Weekly*, November 22, 2010; "Jay-Z Speaks Out About Shooting His Drug-Addict Brother at Age 12 in New Memoir 'Decoded,'" by Bill Hutchinson, *New York Daily News*, November 22, 2010; "Why We're Always Going to Be Wrong About Beyoncé–Jay-Z Divorce Rumors," by Alex Abad-Santos, *Vox*, July 25, 2014; "Beyoncé—The Metamorphosis," by Mimi Valdes, *Vibe*, October 2002; "Destiny's Child," *Vibe*, 2001; "Above and Beyoncé," by Lisa Robinson, *Vanity Fair*, 2005; "Cuba Gooding, Jr., and Beyoncé Knowles," (no byline) *Jet*, September 22, 2003; "The World's Biggest Rap Star Reveals All," by Adam Park, *Clash*, September 8, 2009; "Jay-Z Camp Refutes Tupac-Biting Claims," MTV.com, October 9, 2002; "Jay-Z, R. Kelly Part Ways as *Best of Both Worlds* Tour Collapses," by Shaheem Reid, MTV.com. October 20, 2004; "Jay-Z, Kingdom Come," by Karl Wilkinson, *Observer*, November 12, 2006; "The Cat Who Got the Cream," by Chris Salmon, *Guardian*, November 9, 2007; "Deja Feud," MTV.com, October 8, 2002; "Jay-Z: The Life," by Dream Hampton, *Vibe*, December, 1998; "The Big Razz Interview: Beyoncé," by Adam Stones, *Daily Record*, September 10, 2004; "Beyoncé: The Billboard Cover Story," by Gail Mitchell, *Billboard*, October 1, 2009; "Beyoncé Learned a Lot from Her Parents' Marriage," Associated Press, November 25, 2008; "How to Run the World: The Story of How Beyoncé Seized It All," by Will Anderson, *Bard Free Press*, February 2013.

Parts Six and Seven: Dreamgirl and Run The World

Interviews: Sharen Davis, October 3, 2014; Billy Brasfield, October 2, 2014; Jonathan Hay, July 16, October 22, 2014; AlexSandra Wright, November 20, November 28, December 2, December 5, December 10, 2014; David L. Ingram, December 11, 2014; Jonathan Wright, December 5, 2014; Arthur "Choke No Joke" Alston, October 18, 2014; Robert DeLeon, August 3, 2014; Mavis Miller-Gunther, July 2, 2014; Tony Scott, August 3, December 4, 2014; Delores DeHaven, May 5, June 1, July 3, 2014; Smokey Thomas, June 3,

August 4, December 11, 2014; Thomas Eric Edmond, December 4, December 5, December 6, 2014; Steven White, June 1, July 3, July 20, 2014; Tenesha Ksyn Cason, November 23, 2014; Lance Gilbert, December 3, 2014; Amy Vongpitaka, December 1, December 7, 2014; Alonzo Jackson, July 23, August 29, 2014; Chad Elliott, December 21, 2014; Taura Stinson, October 15, November 21, 2014; Daryl Simmons, July 29, 2014.

Legal: *Knowles, Celestine B. v. Knowles, Mathew*, November 11, 2009; "Mathew Knowles, Called as a Witness on His Own Behalf...," *Wright V. Knowles*, LASC Case No. BF 037735, January 14, 2014; "Mathew Knowles' Petition for Pre-Suit Oral Deposition," July 2, 2011; "Petitioner Mathew Knowles' Verified Petition to Take Deposition Before Suit," July 11, 2011 (Knowles's original complaint against Live Nation); "Affidavit of Mathew Knowles," July 11, 2011; "Live Nation Entertainment Inc.'s Opposition to Petitioner Mathew Knowles' Verified Petition to Take Deposition Before Suit," August 17, 2011; "Transcript of Friday, August 19, 2011, Hearing, at 11:00 a.m. in the 281st Judicial District Court"; "Petitioner's Reply to Live Nation's Opposition to Petition to Take Deposition Before Suit," August 26, 2011; "Mathew Knowles' First Amended Verified Petition" (no date); "Mathew Knowles Reply in Support of Petition," August 26, 2011; correspondence from M. Rozales to Hon. Sylvia A. Matthews, August 26, 2011; "Live Nation Entertainment's, Inc., Surreply in Opposition to Petition to Take Deposition Before Suit," August 29, 2002 (the most comprehensive account of Live Nation's rebuttal of Knowles's allegations); "Compendium of Unpublished Case Cited in Live Nation's Surreply," August 29, 2011; "Sworn Affidavit of Mathew Knowles," September 1, 2011 (in which he best outlines his possible case against Live Nation); "Petitioner Mathew Knowles' First Amended Verified Petition to Take Deposition Before Suit," September 2, 2011 (the most comprehensive telling of facts from Mathew's side of the story relating to his dismissal as Beyoncé's manager); "Live Nation Entertainment, Inc.'s Motion to Strike," September 13, 2011; "Mathew Knowles Press Release Relating to Parting of Ways with Beyoncé" March 2011; "Affidavit of Danny David," September 13, 2011; "Petitioner's Response to Live Nation's Motion to Strike and Opposition to First Amended Petition to Take Deposition Before Suit," September 19, 2001; correspondence from Danny Davis, Esq. to The Honorable Sylvia A. Mathews, September 22, 2011; "Sworn Affidavit of Mathew Knowles," October 1, 2011; "Order Denying Rule 202 Petition," Sylvia A. Mathews, Judge Presiding, October 4, 2011; "Final Judgment Signed for Non-Adversary (Non-Jury)," October 4, 2011; "Mathew Knowles Call Decision to Stop Managing Beyoncé 'Mutual,' Billboard.biz" (Exhibit 4); "Texas Rules of Civil Procedure 202 ('Rule 202')"; "Mathew Knowles—Interrogatories," September 2, 2011; "Mathew Knowles—Answers to Interrogatories," September 10, 2011; "Live Nation—Interrogatories," October 1, 2011; "Live Nation—Answers to Interrogatories," October 30, 2011.

Media: Beyoncé appearances on *The View*, April 23, 2009, and July 28, 2011; *Today*, April 23, 2009; *Oprah*, February 2013; "Mathew Knowles on Fatherhood and Beyoncé," NPR, November 27, 2006; Mathew Knowles on *The Madd Hatta Morning Show*, September 11, 2014; AlexSandra Wright interview with Jim Moret, *Inside Edition*, February 2014; "Tina Knowles Life Story Added to 'Living Archives' at University of Houston," by Mommy Brown, Mommybrown.com, October 10, 2011; Tina Knowles appearance on *The Early Show*, November, 2009; Tina Knowles appearance on *Good Day New York*, May 8, 2012; Tina Knowles, Keynote Speech, Women & Money Leadership Luncheon, October 2, 2014; "CNN Special: Beyoncé Finding Her Way," February 9, 2013; *Life Is but a Dream* (Beyoncé documentary), 2014; Beyoncé interview on *60 Minutes*, CBS-TV, January 2010; *Yours and Mine* video by Beyoncé (YouTube), December 12, 2014; *Beyoncé: The Beyoncé*

Experience Live; *The Unauthorized Biography of Beyoncé: Baby and Beyond* (documentary); *Beyoncé: Fierce and Fabulous* (documentary); "Jay Z Physically Attacked by Beyoncé's Sister," TMZ, May 12, 2014; "Jay Z's Bodyguard Sucks; He Failed in the Elevator," TMZ, May 13, 2014; Mathew Knowles interview, *The Roula and Ryan Show*, August 2014; Mathew Knowles interview, "Houston Newsmakers with Khambrel Marshall," August 17, 2014.

Volumes: *Empire State of Mind: How Jay-Z Went from Street Corner to Corner Office*, by Zack O'Malley Greenburg; *Decoded*, by Jay-Z; *Jay Z: The King of America*, by Mark Beaumont; *From Jim Crow to Jay Z: Race, Rap, and the Performance of Masculinity*, by Miles White.

Articles: "Meet the People Behind Beyoncé," Out.com, April 8, 2014; "American Booty," by Jane Gordon, *Daily Mail*, August 14, 2010; "Jay-Z and Beyoncé: Marriage or Merger?," by Zack O'Malley Greenburg, *Forbes*, June 7, 2011; "Beyoncé Opens Up…," *Daily Mail*, February 14, 2003; "A Conversation with Beyoncé…" (no byline), *Cincinnati Post*, July 26, 2007; "Dreamgirls Costumes Re-create Motown Ambiance of the '60s," by Joy Sewing, *Houston Chronicle*, December 21, 2006; "Beyoncé Screen Test Left 'Dreamgirls' Producers Spellbound" (no byline), *Asian News International*, December 25, 2006; "Beyoncé Enjoyed Working on Dreamgirls," *AP Online*, November 28, 2006; "Beyoncé—Behind the B'Day Videos," by Jennifer Vineyard, MTV News, 2007; "Destiny's Wild" (no byline), *Washington Post*, April 25, 2009; "From Bootylicious Babe to BadAss" (no byline), *Sunday Life*, May 24, 2009; "An Open Letter, Mathew Knowles," by AlexSandra Wright, CNN, August 30, 2013; "Beyoncé Fired Dad Amid Accusations of Theft, Legal Documents Show," *Hollywood Reporter*, July 12, 2011; "Me, Jay-Z and I," by Caroline Prosser, *Daily Mail*, February 1, 2014; "Beyoncé, Mathew Knowles, Live Nation: How Much Is at Stake," by Zack O'Malley Greenburg, Forbes.com, July 7, 2011; "Beyoncé's Step Brother Nixon and His Mom Move into Trailer Park," by Dee Apphiaana, Stargist.com, April 24, 2014; "Beyoncé's Dad—DNA Test Shows…You're the Daddy," TMZ.com, September 18, 2014; "Beyoncé's Dad: I Didn't Steal from My Daughter," TMZ.com, July 11, 2011; "Beyoncé's Dad Sings the Blues About Houston's Entertainment Scene," *Houston Business Journal*, July 18, 2014; "Beyoncé's Dad Off the Hook for Now on Child Support," TMZ.com, April 24, 2014; "Did Live Nation Push Mathew Knowles Out as Beyoncé's Manager?," by Amos Barshad, *Vulture*, July 14, 2011; "The Untold Story of How Tina and Mathew Knowles Created the Destiny's Child Gold Mine," by Lynn Norment, *Ebony*, September 2001; "Beyoncé's Dad Hit with Second Paternity Suit," by Joel Anderson, BuzzFeed.com, July 7, 2014; "Famed R&B Singer's Father Sues Murdoch-Owned Publication for Defamation," by John Suayan, *Southeast Texas Record*, June 26, 2013; "Historic Downtown Site Faces New Musical Destiny," by Nancy Sarnoff, *Houston Business Journal*, June 1, 2001; "Behind the Music—The Business Empire of Mathew Knowles," by Cheryl Alexander, *Houston Lifestyle & Homes*, March 1, 2013; "It's a Family Affair," by Michael Hall, *Texas Monthly*, April 2004; "Beyoncé; Fired Father Mathew Knowles After Live Nation Accused him of Theft," by Gerrik Kennedy, *L.A. Times Blogs*, July 12, 2011; "Beyoncé Severs Management Ties with Father," by Gerrick Kennedy, *L.A. Times Blogs*, March 28, 2011; "Legal Documents Relating to Beyoncé, Mathew Knowles May Shed Light on Singer's New Management, Touring Deals," Billboard.com, July 13, 2011; "Mathew Knowles Talks Beyoncé Split: 'It Would Be a Lie If I Did Not Say It Has Been Difficult,'" by Cavan Sieczkowski, *Huffington Post*, March 25, 2013; "Mathew Knowles: I Did Not Steal from Beyoncé," by Nekesa Mumbi Moody, *Huffpost Celebrity*, July 15, 2011; "Mathew Knowles: 'We Absolutely Have Not Taken Any Money from Beyoncé," by Nekesa Mumbi Moody, Billboard.com, July 15, 2011; "Mathew Knowles Baby Mama and Son Evicted," by Jonathan Hailey, *Urban Daily*, April 11, 2014; "Beyoncé and Jay-Z Marry," by Michelle Tauber, *People*, April 21, 2008; "Beyoncé

Finally Opens Up About Secret Wedding," by Marisa Lausadio, *Essence*, October 2008; "At Last! Beyoncé Finally Gives Fans a Glimpse of Her Lavish Gown from Jay-Z Wedding," by Jade Watkins, *Daily Mail*, November 19, 2011; "Beyoncé Becoming More Fierce" (no byline), *Telegraph-Herald*, November 30, 2008; "Her Belfast Backstage Demands are Revealed" (no byline), *Sunday Life*, May 24, 2009; "Beyoncé in Big Trouble If New Album Flops as Predicted," by Roger Friedman, *Showbiz 411*, June 23, 2011; "Beyoncé's Parents Mathew and Tina Knowles Divorce After 31 Years of Marriage," by Emily Sheridan, *Daily Mail*, December 20, 2011; "Surprise! More Details on Beyoncé and Tina Knowles' University of Houston Campus Visit," by Clifford Pugh, *Culture Map Houston*, October 3, 2011; "Pop Star's Mom Sews Some Diva-licious Threads" (no byline), Htexas.com, September 1, 2007; "Beyoncé's Father Wanted Singer to Raise Half-Brother as Her Own, Claims Mother of Love Child," by Amelia Proud, *Daily Mail*, October 21, 2011; "Tina Knowles' Handbag," by Kristie Ramirez, *Texas Monthly*, September 2009; "Where Are They Now? Find Out What Happened to the Other Members of Destiny's Child," by Brittany Lewis, *Global Grind*, January 11, 2013; "Meet the People Behind Beyoncé," Out.com, April 8, 2014; "Beyoncé—Dreamgirl," by Tom Horan, *Telegraph*, November 8, 2008, "Beyoncé: I'm Proof You Don't Have to Be a Diva to Win," by Anna Pukas, *Express*, December 16, 2008; "Beyoncé Says She Killed Sasha Fierce," by Hillary Crosley, MTV News, February 26, 2010; "Above and Beyoncé," by Lisa Robinson, *Vanity Fair*, November 2005; "Beyoncé Knowles: The Queen B," by Jason Guy, *Vogue*, February 11, 2013; "The Video of Solange Attacking Jay Z Is Deeply Upsetting and Also Fantastic," by Kevin Fallon, *Daily Beast*, May 12, 2014; "Mrs. Carter Uncut," by Jo Ellison, *Vogue*, May 2013; "The Year That Changed My Life," by Beyoncé Knowles, *Essence*, July 2011; "Solange—Pastel Pop," by Britini Danielle, *Essence*, May 2014; "Beyoncé—She's the Boss," by Sheryl Sandberg, *Time* (cover of the 100 Most Influential People), May 12, 2014; "Beyoncé and Tina Turner" (no byline), *Ebony*, June 2014; "Jay Z," by Lisa Robinson, *Vanity Fair*, November 2013; "Beyoncé Liberated," by Aaron Hickland, *Out*, April 2014; "Beyoncé Buys $5.9 Million Houston Mansion for Mom," by Zondra Hughes, Rollingout.com; January 22, 2013; "Beyoncé Buys Home for Mom," by Graham Wood; *AOL Real Estate*, January 25, 2013; "Beyoncé's Momma Doin' It Again in Manhattan," by Mark David, *Variety.com*, November 21, 2011; "Tina Knowles Parties at Coachella," by Justin Ravitz, *Us Weekly*, April 15, 2014; "Tina Knowles Talks About Life, Love at Women's Luncheon," by Joy Sewing, October 3, 2014, *Houston Chronicle*; "Tina Knowles Reveals Battle with Low Self-Esteem After Divorce," by Iyana Robertson, *Vibe*, October 6, 2014; "Tina Knowles, Beyoncé Mother Dating New Boyfriend Richard Lawson: Ex-Husband Matthew [*sic*] Knowles Look-Alike?," by Crystal Henderson, Enstarz.com, October 31, 2013; "Meet the People Behind Beyoncé," Out.com, April 8, 2014; "Gender Equality Is a Myth," by Beyoncé Knowles-Carter, *Shriver Report*, January 12, 2014; "Above and Beyoncé," by Lisa Robinson, *Vanity Fair*, November 2005; "Beyoncé and Jay Z Reveal Footage of Blue Ivy's Birth During 'On the Run,'" by Lauren Cox, *Hollywood Life*, June 26, 2014; "'It's a Jedi Mind Trick': Beyoncé's Father Mathew Knowles Makes Shocking Claim Singer and Jay Z Used Divorce Rumours to 'Ignite' Tour Sales," by Iona Kirby, *Mail Online*, August 27, 2014; "Mathew Knowles Says Beyoncé and Jay Z Used Drama to Sell Tickets," by Victoria Uwumarogie, *Madame Noire*, August 27, 2014; "Solange Attacked Jay Z 'over Rihanna Party Invitation,'" CNN, May 14, 2014; "Mathew Knowles Weighs In on Jay Z/Solange Elevator Gate," by Sam, *The Grape Juice*, August 27, 2014; "Solange Knowles, Jay Z Fight Sparked After Rapper Made Plans to Attend Rihanna's Met Gala After-Party," by Marianne Garvey, Brian Niemietz, and Rich Shapiro, *New York Daily News*, May 13, 2014; "Could This Be the End of Beyoncé and Jay

Z?," by Stacy Brown, *New York Post*, July 19, 2014; "Beyoncé Sounds Like She's Calling Jay Z Out for Cheating," TMZ.com, July 2, 2014; "Jay Z Physically Attacked by Beyoncé's Sister," TMZ.com, May 12, 2014; "Review: 15 Thoughts on the Carters' 'On the Run Tour' and Their Evolving PDA," by Clover Hope, Vibe.com, July 12, 2014; "The $84M Reason to Stay Together," by Stephanie Smith, *New York Post*, July 29, 2014; "The Mythologizing of Jay Z, or Why the World Decided to Stop Worrying and Love the Rap God," by Marlow Stern, *The Daily Beast*, May 13, 2014.

PERSONAL ACKNOWLEDGMENTS

My thanks to Jonathan Hahn, a brilliant writer, my personal publicist, and good friend.

Thanks also to all of those from "Team JRT": attorney James M. Leonard; CPA Michael Horowitz of Horowitz, McMahon & Zarem in Southern California, Inc.; and also Felinda deYoung of Horowitz et al.

Thanks to: Andy Steinlen, George Solomon, Jeff Hare, Andy Hirsch, Samuel Munoz, Bruce Rheins, Dawn Westlake, Jeff Cook, Brandon Schmook, Richard Tyler Jordan, John Passantino, Linda DiStefano, Hazel and Rob Kragulac, Andy Skurow, Brian Newman, Scherrie Payne, Freda Payne, Susaye Greene, Barbara Ormsby, David Spiro, Billy Masters, Marlene Morris, Kac Young, Yvette Jarecki, Robin Roth, Mary Downey, Felipe Echeri, Alexandra Wescourt, Laura Fagin, Corey Sheppard, Rita Bosico, Deb Armstrong, Susan Kaya, Sal Pinto, Barb Mueller, David Gunther, Eric Edmonds, Chris Saunders, and Jillian DeVaney.

I also want to acknowledge my television producing partners and colleagues: Keri Selig, Jonathan Koch, Steve Michaels, Cari Davine, Joan Harrison, Steve Kronish, Eva Miller, Michael Prupus, Stanley Hubbard, Sherryl Clark, Tia Maggini, Arturo Interian, and Tanya Lopez.

I have always been so blessed to have a family as supportive as mine. My thanks and love go out to: Roslyn and Bill Barnett and Jessica and Zachary, Rocco and Rosemaria Taraborrelli and Rocco and Vincent, and Arnold Taraborrelli. Special thanks to my father, Rocco. A big smile, also, for Spencer Douglas.

All of my books are written with my mother, Rose Marie, in mind. We miss her very much.

Finally, I must also acknowledge those readers of mine who have followed my career over the years. I am indebted to each and every reader who has stuck by me over the course of my career. I am eternally grateful to anyone who takes the time to pick up one of my books and read it.

Thank you so much.

J. Randy Taraborrelli
Summer 2015

INDEX

extracts reading groups
competitions books new
discounts extracts
competitions
books new events
events books
extracts
new reading groups
interviews
events extracts
discounts
new books events
events new
discounts extracts discounts
www.panmacmillan.com
extracts events reading groups
competitions books extracts new